# Praise for *States of the Union*

"Drawing on readily available sources, David Kaiser provides a superb and concise political history of the United States. *States of the Union* provides the concise yet magisterial political history of the United States that today's college students desperately need but increasingly cannot find."

—James McAllister, Professor of Political Science, Williams College

"*States of the Union* is an unusual book. It looks at American political history as an experiment—as a continuing effort to keep what Washington called the 'sacred fire of liberty' alive in the world. Kaiser uses U.S. presidents' own words as a kind of lens through which to view this whole extraordinary story. And that approach is very effective. It puts the reader in direct contact with the relatively small group of people—the forty-six presidents—most deeply involved with managing the American project. It allows the reader, that is, to hear their voices and thus get a deeper sense for what they were doing and for how the experiment was going. The result is a wonderful book, one that anyone interested in American history will very much enjoy reading."

—Marc Trachtenberg, Professor emeritus, University of California at Los Angeles

"In this exceptional study of the speeches of American presidents, David Kaiser explores the way every chief executive—from Washington to Biden—has addressed public events, explained his policies and stated the nation's first principles. Filled with essential facts and written in lucid prose, Kaiser's book makes innovative use of State of the Union, Inaugural, and other official addresses as a record of the country's historic challenges and opportunities, international and domestic. At stake, the presidents realized, were the twin commitments of democracy itself: individual equality before the law and a government elected by the people. Kaiser finds no inflexible model of public address dictated by literary custom or party bias. Rather, most presidents met good and bad news alike with a sense of the responsibilities of their office, an awareness of precedent, and an estimate of citizens' needs. *States of the Union* truly brings to life both the leaders' personalities and the country's long history, making it a remarkable chronicle of the nation's political experience."

 —Anne Rose, Distinguished Professor of History and
  Religious Studies, Penn State University

"*States of the Union* surveys how presidential rhetoric has highlighted each president's policies and politics. Ably summarizing key elements of State-of-the-Union addresses and other major presidential speeches, historian David Kaiser analyzes how well they addressed major domestic and foreign policy issues of each era. Kaiser finds Lincoln's brief second inaugural as his masterpiece—and this book reprints it in full. The author judges Franklin Roosevelt as the president with the clearest vision and the greatest ability to translate it into practical reality, enabling him to have a unique impact on the history of the modern world. Kaiser also offers trenchant, up-to-date assessments of Obama, Trump, and Biden. Compact, well-written presidential history."

 —Richard Breitman, Professor Emeritus,
  American University

# STATES OF THE UNION

A HISTORY OF THE UNITED STATES
THROUGH PRESIDENTIAL ADDRESSES
1789–2023

## DAVID KAISER

## Books by David Kaiser

*Economic Diplomacy and the Origins of the Second World War* (1980)
*Postmortem: New Evidence in the Case of Sacco and Vanzetti*
(co-author William Young) (1985)
*Politics and War: European Conflict from Philip II to Hitler* (1990)
*Epic Season: The 1948 American League Pennant Race* (1998)
*American Tragedy: Kennedy, Johnson, and the Origins of the Vietnam War* (2000)
*The Road to Dallas: The Assassination of John F. Kennedy* (2008)
*No End Save Victory: How FDR Led the Nation into War* (2014)
*Baseball Greatness: The Best Players and Teams According to Wins Above Average* (2018)
*A Life in History* (2019)
*NFL 1965: The Most Exciting Season* (2021)

Published 2023 by Mount Greylock Books, LLC

Copyright © 2023 by David Kaiser

All rights reserved. No part of this book may be reproduced, stored, or transmitted by any means—whether auditory, graphic, mechanical, or electronic—without written permission of the publisher except in the case of brief excerpts used in critical articles and reviews.
For more information contact: kaiserd2@gmail.com

Library of Congress Control Number: 2023924540

ISBN: 978-1-7328745-3-4 (Paperback)
ISBN: 978-1-7328745-2-7 (Ebook)

Cover illustration by Michael Rohani.
Book design by DesignForBooks.com

Printed in the U.S.A.

# Dedication

To the people of the United States, living and dead.

*"For myself, looking back now from the extreme end of my task . . . I am full of fears and hopes. I see great dangers which may be warded off and mighty evils which may be avoided or kept in check; and I am ever increasingly confirmed in my belief that for democratic nations to be virtuous and prosperous, it is enough if they will to be so. . . .*

*"The nations of our day cannot prevent conditions of equality from spreading in their midst. But it depends upon themselves whether equality is to lead to servitude or freedom, knowledge or barbarism, prosperity or wretchedness."*

ALEXIS DE TOCQUEVILLE, *DEMOCRACY IN AMERICA*

# CONTENTS

|      |                                                                                  |     |
|-----:|----------------------------------------------------------------------------------|----:|
|    I. | A Great Experiment                                                              |   1 |
|   II. | George Washington                                                               |   7 |
|  III. | John Adams and Thomas Jefferson                                                 |  15 |
|   IV. | James Madison and James Monroe                                                  |  24 |
|    V. | John Quincy Adams and Andrew Jackson                                            |  40 |
|   VI. | Martin Van Buren, William Henry Harrison, John Tyler and James K. Polk          |  61 |
|  VII. | Zachary Taylor, Millard Fillmore, Franklin Pierce, and James Buchanan           |  85 |
| VIII. | Abraham Lincoln                                                                 | 108 |
|  XIX. | Andrew Johnson and Ulysses S. Grant                                             | 127 |
|    X. | Rutherford B. Hayes, James Garfield, and Chester A. Arthur                      | 149 |
|   XI. | Grover Cleveland and Benjamin Harrison                                          | 160 |
|  XII. | William McKinley and Theodore Roosevelt                                         | 182 |
| XIII. | William Howard Taft and Woodrow Wilson                                          | 202 |
|  XIV. | Warren Harding Calvin Coolidge and Herbert Hoover                               | 228 |
|   XV. | Franklin D. Roosevelt                                                           | 249 |

|       |                                               |     |
|-------|-----------------------------------------------|-----|
| XVI.  | Harry S. Truman and Dwight Eisenhower         | 287 |
| XVII. | John F. Kennedy and Lyndon Johnson            | 318 |
| XVIII.| Richard Nixon Gerald Ford, and Jimmy Carter   | 341 |
| XIX.  | Ronald Reagan and George H. W. Bush           | 372 |
| XX.   | Bill Clinton and George W. Bush               | 398 |
| XXI.  | Barack Obama, Donald Trump, and Joseph Biden  | 427 |
| XXII. | The American Experiment, 1789–2023            | 465 |
| Index |                                               | 471 |

# I

# A Great Experiment

*"The President . . . shall from time to time give to the Congress Information of the State of the Union, and recommend to their Consideration such Measures as he shall judge necessary and expedient."*

The Constitution of the United States, Article I, Section 3

Sitting in Philadelphia in the summer of 1787, the delegates of the thirteen states defined the powers of a strong chief executive under a new Constitution. Without much debate, they gave the president the obligation to report to Congress on the state of the new nation and to recommend necessary new laws. They presumably had in mind the example of the British King's Speech on the occasion of the annual opening of Parliament, in which the monarch customarily reminded the assembled Commons and Lords of their duties and discussed the immediate problems then facing the British nation—such as the rebellion in the American colonies from 1775 through 1783. That tradition has also survived into the twenty-first century, although for a long time now the monarch has effectively delivered the speech on behalf of the prime minister, who has actually written the address. The president, meanwhile, has remained the head of the United States government as well as its chief of state. By 1900 he had become the single most powerful political leader in the world.

This book uses annual state of the union addresses, inaugural addresses and other presidential messages as the sources for a concise political history of the United States.[1] Presidents, of course, have received various degrees of help preparing their addresses, but we are looking at them as records of events and administration policies, not as tests of literary skill. From the time of Washington onward, the annual address has customarily taken note of any unusual occurrences, surveyed the foreign relations of the United States, and given basic figures on the state of the federal budget. In more troubled times the president has had to discuss the progress of actual armed conflicts, breakdowns in public order, and fundamental political struggles. Given the extraordinary growth of the United States over the last 232 years, that alone makes the presidential addresses a record of astonishing historical change. During that time the population of Great Britain has increased from 9 million to 67 million, France has grown from about 25 million to 65 million, and the United States from 4 million to 330 million. Its area has grown from 865,000 square miles to 3.536 million, and it surpassed every other nation on earth in agricultural and industrial production by the twentieth century.

Yet the greatest drama that unfolds in these addresses was laid out by George Washington in his first inaugural address. Having cast off royal authority and the society of orders that went with it, the American people had begun a fateful experiment. "The preservation of the sacred fire of liberty and the destiny of the republican model of government," he said, "are justly considered, perhaps, as deeply, as finally, staked on the experiment entrusted to the hands of the American people." "The situation in which I now stand for the last time, in the midst of the representatives of the people of the United States," he said in his last annual message in 1797, "naturally recalls the period when the administration of the present form of government commenced, and I cannot omit the occasion to congratulate you and my country on the success of the experiment, nor to repeat my fervent supplications to the Supreme Ruler of the

---

[1] All presidential papers are now available on the web at www.presidency.ucsb.edu. Every specific document referred to in this book can easily be found there using the search engine, either searching within the appropriate month for "Annual Address" or "Budget Message"—December of the given year from 1789 through 1932, and January and February after that—or for searching for the exact date, which I have always given, for other messages. When quoting I have retained original punctuation and capitalization throughout.

Universe and Sovereign Arbiter of Nations that His providential care may still be extended to the United States, that the virtue and happiness of the people may be preserved, and that the Government which they have instituted for the protection of their liberties may be perpetual." The annual message has remained a kind of progress report on the nature and success of American democracy ever since, and the most effective presidents have done the best job of placing the events of the day in a broader historical context and convincing the nation that it is traveling on the right path.

Thus, Thomas Jefferson, in his inaugural in 1801, discounted the argument that republican governments must inevitably be too weak. "I believe this, on the contrary," he said, "the strongest Government on earth. I believe it the only one where every man, at the call of the law, would fly to the standard of the law, and would meet invasions of the public order as his own personal concern. Sometimes it is said that man cannot be trusted with the government of himself. Can he, then, be trusted with the government of others? Or have we found angels in the forms of kings to govern him? Let history answer this question." Twenty-one years later, in a special message to Congress on April 4, 1822, James Monroe mused about new internal threats. As the nation became vaster, it offered opportunities to ambitious generals or demagogues who might play on sectional interests to institute a new form of government. Ten years later, in July 1832, Andrew Jackson raised the question of the impact of economic inequality upon democracy. The Bank of the United States, he argued, allowed the rich and powerful to bend the government to its own purposes.

Taking office after a number of southern states had already seceded from the union, Abraham Lincoln argued from the beginning that the survival of free government—government elected by the people—depended upon the suppression of the rebellion, since a government whose citizens could freely renounce its authority was no government at all. After trying and failing to induce the rebellious slave states to accept compensation for gradual abolition and return to the union, he used the presidential war power to emancipate their slaves. Lincoln's death and the accession of white southerner Andrew Johnson led to a tremendous battle with Congress over the rights of the freed slaves, and to a very real transfer of power from the president to the legislature. Sharp, very even partisan divisions kept the presidency in check until the dawn of the twentieth century. Then two new issues took over.

Faced in 1897 with a bloody insurrection against Spanish rule in Cuba, William McKinley argued, first, that the Cuban people had some right to govern themselves, and secondly, that the United States had an obligation to civilization to bring the conflict to a close. His intervention in 1898 also allowed the US to seize another Spanish possession, the Philippine Islands. McKinley and his successor Theodore Roosevelt declared that the United States also had a duty to prepare the Philippine people for self-government—even though they decided to suppress a three-year insurrection against US rule first. Roosevelt frankly embraced imperialism on the European model, and also began preparing the United States for a possible intercontinental war. Woodrow Wilson was president when world war broke out in 1914, and he initially argued that the United States must remain an island of sanity in a war-torn world in order to make peace. Then, after 1917, he proclaimed a new world role for the nation, arguing that it must go to war with Germany to defend principles of international law and help create a new world organization to keep the peace. The United States helped win the First World War over Germany, but the Congress refused to agree to Wilson's plans.

Meanwhile, Theodore Roosevelt also gingerly introduced the other great issue of the twentieth century: the impact of concentrated economic power in a modern industrial society, and the role of government in moderating its effects. Both he and Wilson took some steps toward breaking up monopolies and recognizing the rights of organized labor, but these had not gone very far before a reaction brought three successive pro-business administrations into power from 1921 (Harding and Coolidge) through 1932 (Hoover). The Depression under Hoover assumed catastrophic proportions by 1932, and Franklin Roosevelt took office in 1933 with a huge majority in Congress. Then began the most fateful twelve years of American history.

Franklin Roosevelt used his annual messages, his broadcast fireside chats to the American people, and other messages to Congress to narrate two continuing, world-historical struggles. The first, which dominated his first seven years in office, aimed at both recovering from the depression and creating a more just economic order that would redistribute income and purchasing power to farmers and workers while restraining irresponsible speculation. His vision, which he implemented to a remarkable degree, also included the Social Security Act, new guarantees of workers' rights, and legislation to establish minimum wages and maximum hours. Because his measures did substantially (though not completely) reduce unemployment and misery, his congressional majorities increased in 1934 and again in 1936. Hitler and the Nazis had taken power in Germany in 1933 and the Japanese had begun expanding into China in 1931, but until 1937, Roosevelt said almost nothing to the American people about foreign threats, except to contrast his domestic path with dictatorship in other nations. Then, however, he began to argue that war overseas posed a real threat to the western hemisphere.

The fall of France and the threatened fall of Great Britain in the spring of 1940 definitely exposed the country to a possible attack, and Roosevelt explicitly began preparing the defense of the western hemisphere against German and Japanese threats. During the next eighteen months he undertook an active defense of the western Atlantic, announced huge new armaments programs, and in August 1941 committed the US—still at peace—to the defeat of Nazi Germany. He explicitly linked his domestic policies to the impending war, arguing that the US had to fight to defend political and economic democracy. After Pearl Harbor, he initially focused on the need for total mobilization of all resources, while explaining that it would take years to go on the offensive against Germany, Italy and Japan. By 1944 he was combining optimistic battlefield assessments with plans for a postwar world of full employment at home and peace abroad, ensured by a new international organization. Only these goals, he insisted, could justify American sacrifices. He evidently sold the American people on these goals, and because subsequent presidents essentially supported them all, his presidency shaped American society and America's role in the world at least until the 1980s. The American experiment—adapted to the industrial age—had now become a model for much of the world.

The postwar struggle for influence and military supremacy with the Soviet Union added another dimension to presidential action and rhetoric under Truman, Eisenhower, Kennedy and Johnson. Those presidents also faced a growing civil rights movement, which Kennedy and Johnson, in particular, eventually embraced. The anti-Communist struggle led Johnson into the Vietnam War, and he and his successor Richard Nixon spent many hours trying to explain it to the American people. Nixon also proposed a new model for world peace, involving better relations with the two leading Communist powers. At home, meanwhile, the New Deal coalition was cracking, paving the way for huge rhetorical and policy changes beginning in 1981.

Ronald Reagan explicitly repudiated the whole philosophy behind the New Deal, arguing in his inaugural that government was the problem, not the solution, and moving to reduce taxes and government regulation. That philosophy survived not only into the administration of his successor, George H. W. Bush, but into that of William Jefferson Clinton, who in 1996 declared that the era of big government was over and largely substituted a concern for crime for a concern for civil rights. Meanwhile, Bush had the honor of announcing victory in the Cold War, as the USSR collapsed. In 2001 George W. Bush proclaimed new international objectives for the US in the wake of 9/11, including the democratization of the Middle East and wars to prevent unfriendly nations from acquiring weapons of mass destruction. Economic deregulation led in 2008 to the first real financial panic since 1929, but Bush's successor Barack Obama responded very differently from Franklin Roosevelt. Then, in his 2017 inaugural, Donald Trump essentially declared war on most of the institutions and policies that had dominated the last seventy years of American life. Three years later, he had to try to find both words and actions to cope with the COVID pandemic.

President Joseph Biden has completed only two years of his term. Meanwhile, the country is surely more divided than at any time since 1861 over principles, policies and the proper role of the federal government. This book will show how well presidential messages have managed to lay out the principal issues of every era, how well or badly various presidents have solved them, and how the American people have registered their approval or disapproval at the polls. Once again, in turbulent times, a president must find a way to explain where we are and where he wants us to go effectively enough to bring the nation with him—as the best presidents have in the past.

# II

# George Washington

## 1789–97

George Washington had led the armies that had won independence in the Revolution and presided over the Constitutional Convention in 1787. Elected unanimously as president in 1788 and reelected in the same fashion in 1792, in 1796 he established the precedent that chief executives of the new republic would serve for only two terms. On April 30, 1789, he created the American tradition of the inaugural address, beginning by lamenting his abandonment of a much-desired retirement and professing his inadequacy to perform the task for which his countrymen had chosen him. He promised to obey the provision of the Constitution that instructed the president "to recommend to your consideration such measures as he shall judge necessary and expedient," but left it to the new Congress to devise for themselves the measures that they might prefer. He then referred, as he did so many times in the future, to the moral and intellectual qualities he found necessary for statesmanship: "There is no truth more thoroughly established than that there exists in the economy and course of nature an indissoluble union between virtue and happiness; between duty and advantage; between the genuine maxims of an honest and magnanimous policy and the solid rewards of public prosperity and felicity." And much was at stake: "The preservation of the sacred fire of liberty and the destiny of the republican model of government are justly considered, perhaps, as deeply, as finally, staked on the experiment entrusted to the hands of the American people." Washington specifically left it to the Congress to decide what amendments might be found necessary to the Constitution in light of the ratification process, a reference to the debate that would shortly propose the

Bill of Rights. He then renounced any salary during his term such as the Constitution had promised. Washington evidently felt that these words would serve for his whole eight years in office, because in 1793, after he had been unanimously reelected, he spoke just a couple of perfunctory paragraphs at this second inauguration.

Eight months after the inaugural, on January 8, 1790, Washington delivered his first annual message to the Congress, then sitting in New York City. Twelve states had now ratified the Constitution, and Washington referred to North Carolina's recent accession to the Union, while saying nothing about Rhode Island, which still lay outside it. Later that year the first US census counted 3.9 million persons within the United States, including 694,000 slaves—the highest percentage of slaves ever recorded in a census. Washington's home state of Virginia had about 748,000 inhabitants, followed by Pennsylvania (434,000), North Carolina (394,000), Massachusetts (379,000), and New York (340,000). He took very seriously the great enterprise of making the new American government work, and throughout his tenure, he spoke optimistically about the great enterprise upon which his fellow citizens had embarked. "I embrace with great satisfaction," he began, "the opportunity which now presents itself of congratulating you on the present favorable prospects of our public affairs. The recent accession of the important state of North Carolina to the Constitution of the United States (of which official information has been received), the rising credit and respectability of our country, the general and increasing good will toward the government of the Union, and the concord, peace, and plenty with which we are blessed are circumstances auspicious in an eminent degree to our national prosperity." He then touched one by one on issues and tasks that he would return to again and again in seven subsequent messages.

No problem was more important than making the nation's way in a dangerous larger world. Washington called repeatedly in his annual messages for new measures to improve the new state's capacity for self-defense. A free people, he said in January 1790, needed both arms and discipline to defend itself, and he asked the Congress more than once for laws or amendments to laws relating to the organization of the militia, which he had the right to mobilize in time of war. The issue of self-defense became more than theoretical in 1793, when Britain and France began the world war that lasted, with two brief interruptions, until 1815. "The United States," he said in December of that year, "ought not to indulge a persuasion that, contrary to the order of human events, they will forever keep at a distance those painful appeals to arms with which the history of every other nation abounds. . . . If we desire to avoid insult, we must be able to repel it; if we desire to secure peace, one of the most powerful instruments of our rising prosperity, it must be known that we are at all times ready for war." In the next three years Washington took advantage of the European war to negotiate the Jay Treaty with the British. It settled some outstanding issues unsolved since the Peace of Paris in 1783, including a British withdrawal from various forts within US territory on the northern and western frontiers, and made a plan to settle the boundary between Massachusetts (later Maine) and Canada. He also referred in his December 1795 address to new agreements with the Kingdom of Spain about the border with Florida, and with various North African rulers, designed to secure American trade and the release of certain US citizens then held in captivity. Diplomacy, he suggested in that same address, should allow the nation to continue to grow and prosper in peace. "If by prudence and moderation on every side the extinguishment of all the causes of external discord which have heretofore menaced our tranquility, on terms compatible with our national rights and honor, shall be the happy result, how firm and how precious a foundation will have been laid for accelerating, maturing, and establishing the prosperity of our country." In his last annual message, however, in December 1796, he also called for a stronger navy. The European powers were now fighting a world war, and such a navy might compel them to respect American neutrality or deter them from going to war with the United States.

Washington struck a similar balance between force and justice regarding relations with Indian tribes both within and outside the states of the US, which were already regulated by numerous treaties. He consistently combined the readiness to resort to force when necessary with a willingness to settle any disputes fairly. In December 1790, reporting on an expedition north of the Ohio River to deal with unnamed tribes that had made violent attacks upon American citizens, he said that the aggressors "should be made sensible that the Government of the Union is not less capable of punishing their crimes than it is disposed to respect their rights and reward their attachments." Ten months later, when the campaign was continuing, he hoped that coercion might give way to "an intimate intercourse" that would benefit both sides. This in turn would require "an impartial dispensation of justice," the careful regulation of "the mode of alienating [Indians'] lands," and the punishment of anyone who violated their rights. The superiority of American civilization in which Washington obviously believed carried with it certain obligations. "A system corresponding with the mild principles of religion and philanthropy toward an unenlightened race of men," he said, "whose happiness materially depends on the conduct of the United States, would be as honorable to the national character as conformable to the dictates of sound policy." In December 1793 Washington had once again to report that the Ohio campaign was continuing, and that troubles had developed with the Creek and Cherokee tribes in the South. Once again he carefully referred to offenses on both sides, to the need to enforce justice on all those who disturbed the peace, and to the need for fair and friendly relations with the tribes. In December 1795 he reported the conclusion of a treaty in Ohio, and blamed the continuing trouble with the Creeks in Georgia on American crimes. On several occasions he also referred tentatively to the possibility of extending "civilization" to Indian tribes. That many of Washington's hopes would in the long run fail to materialize does not mean that he did not hold them sincerely.

At home, the federal Constitution had laid out the framework of the national government, but had also left much of the work of actually creating it to the Congress. Washington repeatedly called for new measures in various fields. The Judiciary Act created the federal court system in 1789, and Washington called for unspecified, necessary changes to it in 1790 and 1792. In 1791 he referred to the agreement to establish the national capital in the new District of Columbia. He repeatedly called for improvements to the postal service, and stressed the need to make newspapers readily and cheaply available throughout the nation so as to inform the public on topics of national interest. He called for, and then reported on, the establishment of a mint to deal with a serious shortage of small change. He also proposed some educational measures. "Knowledge is in every country the surest basis of public happiness," he said in his first annual message, and it would contribute to "the security of a free constitution . . . in various ways: . . . by teaching the people themselves to know and to value their own rights; to discern and provide against invasions of them; to distinguish between oppression and the necessary exercise of lawful authority; between burdens proceeding from a disregard to their convenience and those resulting from the inevitable exigencies of society; to discriminate the spirit of liberty from that of licentiousness—cherishing the first, avoiding the last—and uniting a speedy but temperate vigilance against encroachments, with an inviolable respect to the laws." Only an educated people, he seemed to think, could make representative institutions work, and he therefore suggested that the Congress consider establishing a national university. He also called more than once for a military academy, a proposal that a future administration eventually adopted.

Washington never referred in his annual messages to some of the major measures undertaken by his Secretary of the Treasury Alexander Hamilton to establish the public credit, but he reported on the successful floating of several large loans in Holland and the successful capitalization of the first Bank of the United States. "Your own observations in your respective situations," he told the Congress in October 1791, "will have satisfied you of the progressive state of agriculture, manufactures, commerce, and navigation. In tracing their causes you will have remarked with particular pleasure the happy effects of that revival of confidence, public as well as private, to which the Constitution and laws of the United States have so eminently contributed; and you will have observed with no less interest new and decisive proofs of the increasing reputation and credit of the nation." By the end of his second term he began calling for a plan to retire the national debt.

The great domestic crisis of Washington's tenure, the Whiskey Rebellion in western Pennsylvania in 1794, became the subject of his longest annual message in November of that year. He described the revolt as a test both of the fundamental powers of the national government and of their proper exercise, much as Abraham Lincoln would do in a greater but parallel crisis sixty-seven years later. "When we call to mind the gracious indulgence of Heaven by which the American people became a nation," he began, "when we survey the general prosperity of our country, and look forward to the riches, power, and happiness to which it seems destined, with the deepest regret do I announce to you that during your recess some of the citizens of the United States have been found capable of insurrection. It is due, however, to the character of our Government and to its stability, which cannot be shaken by the enemies of order, freely to unfold the course of this event." The nation, he continued, had generally accepted the excise tax on whiskey leveled upon distillers by the Congress four years earlier, but in the four western counties of Pennsylvania, "a prejudice, fostered and embittered by the artifice of men who labored for an ascendency over the will of others by the guidance of their passions, produced symptoms of riot and violence." Passion and prejudice evidently struck Washington as the enemies of reason, enlightenment, and sound government, and the nation's leadership could not give way before them.

Although the Congress had attempted to meet some of the objections to the act, Washington continued, that had only emboldened its opponents, who began threatening the revenue officers. In response, the federal government ordered the US marshal to act. Armed men arrested him and attacked the home of the tax inspector, and both of them fled to the capital at Philadelphia. A Supreme Court justice informed Washington that the ordinary powers of government could not suppress this revolt. "[T]o yield to the treasonable fury of so small a portion of the United States," Washington commented, "would be to violate the fundamental principle of our Constitution, which enjoins that the will of the majority shall prevail," but he did not immediately order a military expedition against the rebellion, hoping that the threat alone might suffice, and sent commissioners authorized to pardon the rebels on the spot if they would submit in August 1794. They refused, and on September 25, 1794, he had told the militia to go ahead. The expedition included 15,000 men from Virginia, Maryland, Pennsylvania, and New Jersey, and after some hesitation, Washington decided to delegate his power as commander in chief and remain in the capital. The defiant citizens offered no resistance to the troops when they arrived, and the troops arrested some ringleaders and brought them to Philadelphia for trial. The episode, Washington now told Congress, had illustrated the devotion of all citizens, "the most and the least wealthy" of them side by side in the militia, to the Constitution and its principles. Washington had laid down the principle that animated Lincoln, as we shall see, in 1861: that an elected government, no less than any other, had to resort to force if necessary to preserve its authority against insurrection.

A year later Washington addressed the first Congress ever elected along party lines. The opposition Democratic-Republicans led by Thomas Jefferson had won a bare 54–51 majority over the pro-Washington Federalists in the House of Representatives, while the Federalists led 19–10 in the Senate. The president did not refer to the contest as he reported on putting the insurrection behind the nation. "The misled have abandoned their errors," he said in December 1795, "and pay the respect to our Constitution and laws which is due from good citizens to the public authorities of the society. These circumstances have induced me to pardon generally the offenders here referred to, and to extend forgiveness to those who had been adjudged to capital punishment. For though I shall always think it a sacred duty to exercise with firmness and energy the constitutional powers with which I am vested, yet it appears to me no less consistent with the public good than it is with my personal feelings to mingle in the operations of Government every degree of moderation and tenderness which the national justice, dignity, and safety may permit."

From time to time in these messages, Washington put the story of the new nation within a broader historical context, and explicitly referred to his trust in an unidentified supreme being. "Let us unite, therefore," he said in November 1794, "in imploring the Supreme Ruler of Nations to spread his holy protection over these United States; to turn the machinations of the wicked to the confirming of our Constitution; to enable us at all times to root out internal sedition and put invasion to flight; to perpetuate to our country that prosperity which his goodness has already conferred, and to verify the anticipations of this Government being a safeguard of human rights." In December 1795 he explicitly compared the state of the United States to the older and richer nations of war-torn Europe. "While many of the nations of Europe, with their American dependencies, have been involved in a contest unusually bloody, exhausting, and calamitous," he said, "in which the evils of foreign war have been aggravated by domestic convulsion and insurrection; in which many of the arts most useful to society have been exposed to discouragement and decay; in which scarcity of subsistence has embittered other sufferings; while even the anticipations of a return of the blessings of peace and repose are alloyed by the sense of heavy and accumulating burthens, which press upon all the departments of industry and threaten to clog the future springs of government, our favored country, happy in a striking contrast, has enjoyed tranquility—a tranquility the more satisfactory, because maintained at the expense of no duty."

The farewell address that Washington published on September 17, 1796, announcing his retirement from office, prophetically listed the dangers that he counted on his countrymen to meet. He warned at length of dangerous threats to the authority of the federal government, coming either from different regions of the nation or from opposing political factions. "The name of American, which belongs to you in your national capacity, must always exalt the just pride of patriotism more than any appellation derived from local discriminations," he said. He discussed the complementary aspects of the economies of the North, South, East and West, and insisted that only national unity prevented military contests among the states, which would burden them all with military establishments. "In this sense it is that your union ought to be considered as a main prop of your liberty, and that the love of the one ought to endear to you the preservation of the other." "The very idea of the power and the right of the people to establish government presupposes the duty of every individual to obey the established government," he continued. And while the spirit of party must always be present, the nation must carefully control it. The party spirit, he said, "serves always to distract the public councils and enfeeble the public administration. It agitates the community with ill-founded jealousies and false alarms; kindles the animosity of one part against another; foments occasionally riot and insurrection." "Religion and morality," he continued, were "indispensable supports" of political prosperity, necessary in particular to "popular government." He also warned against "permanent, inveterate antipathies against particular nations and passionate attachments for others," which might lead the government to "adopt through passion what reason would reject." Two hundred and twenty-seven years later these warnings echo loudly, and US history delimits the periods in which Washington's countrymen have been more or less successful in paying them heed.

# III

# JOHN ADAMS AND THOMAS JEFFERSON

### 1797–1801 • 1801–9

Having served as Washington's vice president for two terms, John Adams emerged in 1796 as the leader of the new Federalist Party in opposition to Thomas Jefferson's Republicans, and won the first contested election in US history by the narrowest of margins, 71 electoral votes to 68. Under the original second article of the Constitution, Jefferson became his vice president. The Federalists emerged with 20–10 and 57–49 majorities in the Senate and the House.[1] Adams, a Massachusetts attorney, had emerged as a revolutionary leader in the Second Continental Congress, and had helped Jefferson draft the Declaration of Independence. He had crossed the Atlantic during the Revolutionary War to serve as US minister to Holland, and had then become the first minister to Great Britain after the signature of peace in 1783, before returning to become vice president. In his inaugural address he surveyed the whole history of the new nation since the Revolution, sometimes from a rather personal point of view, and echoed Washington's warnings of the danger of faction, particularly if factions secured the support of foreign powers. The Federalists and Republicans sympathized respectively with the English and French in the world war that was entering its fourth year, and partisan conflict only got worse during Adams's single term in office.

---

1  All election statistics within this book come from the excellent Wikipedia pages devoted to particular presidential, senatorial and congressional elections.

Beginning in 1797, the world war and the US response took up most of the space in Adams's four annual messages to Congress. The French were seizing American ships trading with the British, and Adams reported in November 1797 that three American envoys had reached Paris to discuss the situation. Their journey led to the XYZ affair, in which three French negotiators demanded large bribes, and did not produce an agreement. By the time of his next annual message a year later, the United States had embarked upon its first major undeclared war with France, in which its small navy engaged French warships. Adams on December 8, 1798 avoided any specific reference to war or armed conflict, but praised "the spirit which has arisen in our country against the menaces and aggression of a foreign nation," the "manly sense of national honor, dignity and independence" that could "become the sure foundation of national prosperity and glory." Negotiations, he reported, had failed, and the French were posing unacceptable conditions for their resumption. He called therefore for more measures to strengthen the navy. The electorate evidently was not displeased, and the Federalists maintained majorities of 60–46 in the House and 23–9 in the Senate in the midterm elections of 1789–90.[2] Twice more, in December 1799 and November 1800, he reported that talks had failed to reach agreement, although they did very shortly thereafter in the last months of his term, allowing his successor to give up the conflict.

Unlike either his predecessor or his successor, Adams failed to use his annual messages to give the country the sense of an ongoing journey toward worthy goals. His addresses also referred to continuing border negotiations with the Spaniards and further talks growing out of the Jay Treaty with the British, and he reported in 1799 on a new rebellion in eastern Pennsylvania against a federal tax, this time a levy on land to pay for naval and military preparations. He never discussed an intense, ongoing battle for his own authority with Alexander Hamilton, who had become the real leader of the Federalist Party, or the Alien and Sedition Acts, which had sought to put some of his Republican opponents beyond the protection of the law, and which Kentucky and Virginia had attempted to

---

2 Until the passage of the Seventeenth Amendment in 1912 decreeing the popular election of senators, midterm elections for senators took place early the next year, after a new state legislature had been chosen.

nullify. Nor did he refer in November 1800 to the election in progress, which led to the first constitutional crisis in US history. The Republican ticket of Jefferson and Aaron Burr defeated Adams and Charles C. Pinckney by 73 electoral votes to 65, but when the electors met, the Republicans neglected to cast a few votes for someone other than Burr, leaving him in a tie with Jefferson. That threw the election into the House of Representatives, where state delegations could vote for either Jefferson or Burr. After 36 ballots, Hamilton swung the election for Jefferson, who took office in heated times indeed. The Democratic-Republicans meanwhile won a great victory in the elections to the House of Representatives, emerging with a 68–38 majority, and narrowed the Federalist majority in the Senate to 17–14. Jefferson became the first American president to speak directly to the political divisions within the new nation.

Jefferson began a characteristically verbose inaugural address on March 4, 1801 with a confession of his own inadequacy adequately to fulfill the great office to which he had been elected, balanced by the confidence that among his listeners and "in the other high authorities provided by our Constitution I shall find resources of wisdom of virtue, and of zeal on which to rely under all difficulties." He then turned directly to the heated political climate, counting on his countrymen now to "unite in common efforts for the common good." Having banished religious intolerance from the land, he continued, the nation "will bear in mind this sacred principle, that though the will of the majority is in all cases to prevail, that will to be rightful must be reasonable; that the minority possess their equal rights, which equal law must protect, and to violate would be oppression." The bitter conflict in Europe, he acknowledged, had echoed in the United States. "But every difference of opinion is not a difference of principle. . . . We are all Republicans, we are all Federalists." That remained the first and only explicit reference to any political party in an inaugural or presidential annual message until 1913. Then, in words that Lincoln echoed sixty years later, he put the American experiment and its new principle of government in a world-historical context. Some might fear that a republican government could not be strong, but "I believe this, on the contrary, the strongest Government on earth. I believe it the only one where every man, at the call of the law, would fly to the standard of the law, and would meet invasions of the public order as his own personal concern. Sometimes it is said that man cannot be trusted with the government of himself. Can he, then, be trusted with the government of others? Or have we found angels in the forms of kings to govern him? Let history answer this question."

Then Jefferson listed his "essential principles of our government." They included "equal and exact justice to all men," "peace, commerce, and friendship with all nations, entangling alliances with none"; a proper balance between federal and state authorities; "the jealous care of the right of election by the people"; "absolute acquiescence in the decisions of the majority, the vital principle of republics"; "economy in the public expense" and the principles of the now-ratified new Bill of Rights. Jefferson's insistence on the supremacy of the majority, echoing Washington's, corrects the view, now popular in some circles, that the founders saw a republic and a democracy as two different things. Even though nearly all the states still required property qualifications for voting, neither man recognized any association between wealth and political power, just as Jefferson, in referring to equal justice for all men, made no exception for the 19 percent of the population that the 1800 census had found to be slaves. The free population had in fact increased far more rapidly than the slave during the previous ten years. He concluded his address with the prophetic remark that "it will rarely fall to the lot of imperfect man to retire from this station with the reputation and favor which bring him into it," and declared his trust in "that Infinite Power which rules the destiny of the universe."

For the eight years of his tenure, Jefferson pursued remarkably consistent objectives in both domestic and foreign affairs. At home he successfully reversed the growth of the federal government and the public debt under the Federalists by securing the repeal of their relatively intrusive direct taxes, cutting the size of the federal workforce, and relying for revenue on the ample proceeds of duties on foreign imports. For the whole of his tenure he reported annually that the federal debt had been reduced by several million dollars a year. The debt fell from $83 million in January 1801 to $57 million eight years later. By his second term the reduction of the debt was not absorbing all the government's surplus revenue, and several times Jefferson asked Congress to consider whether some of it might be spent on "the improvements of roads, canals, rivers, education, and other great foundations of prosperity and union under the powers which Congress may already possess or such amendment to the Constitution as may be approved by the States." He evidently had no objection in principle to such "internal improvements" although he had doubts about their constitutionality, and he also called for a national university more than once. On another front, Jefferson in December 1806 referred in careful but striking language to the constitutional provision that allowed for the outlawing of the foreign slave trade in the following year. "I congratulate you, fellow citizens, on the approach of the period at which you may interpose your authority constitutionally to withdraw the citizens of the United States from all further participation in those violations of human rights which have been so long continued on the unoffending inhabitants of Africa, and which the morality, the reputation, and the best of our country have long been eager to proscribe." Like the founders in the Constitution, he did not challenge slavery where it already existed or assert the rights of Africans' descendants already in the country, but he made his feelings about the slave trade clear, while avoiding—as they had—the use of the word "slave" or "slavery." Like Washington, Jefferson did not in any annual message refer to the two constitutional amendments passed and ratified during this administration, apparently because the original document gave the president no role whatever in the process of amendment, leaving it to Congress and the states.

Jefferson referred in almost every annual message to relations with the Indians, who agreed during his tenure to sell more land in the Northwest Territories that became Ohio, Indiana and Illinois, and also in Georgia and Tennessee. Again and again he called for fair and friendly relations with the tribes and claimed approvingly that they were turning more and more toward agriculture and "domestic arts." In his last years he also reported on the establishment of relations with several tribes west of the Mississippi, some of whom had handed over members accused of murdering American citizens. The Indians, he claimed in December 1806, were "increasingly disposed" to place themselves under the patronage of the US. The reality was undoubtedly more complicated.

Regarding foreign affairs, Jefferson in his first annual message in December 1801 reported in great detail on a naval expedition against Tripoli and the Barbary pirates, and he frequently told the Congress in subsequent years that American warships had managed to protect American trade and American citizens in the region quite effectively. That, however, turned out to be a relatively minor preoccupation. The Anglo-French world war resumed in 1803 and continued through Jefferson's tenure and beyond. It led indirectly to the most remarkable achievement of his presidency, the purchase of the Louisiana Territory—nearly the whole western portion of the watershed of the Mississippi River—from France in 1803. After Spain (which was still administering Louisiana until almost the eve of the transaction) had closed US navigation through the mouth of the Mississippi, Jefferson had sent Robert Livingston to Paris to try to buy New Orleans and some surrounding territory. The envoy found Napoleon, needing ready cash, willing to offer the whole of Louisiana. "The fertility of the country, its climate and extent, promise in due season important aids to our Treasury, an ample provision for our posterity, and a wide spread for the blessings of freedom and equal laws," he told the Congress in a special session in October 1803. Three years later he congratulated Lewis and Clark and their men, as well as two shorter expeditions farther south, for having surveyed key parts of the new territory, although he did not mention any possible significance of Lewis and Clark having reached the Pacific Ocean. He reported the creation of a territorial government around New Orleans.

Like Washington and Adams, Jefferson in December 1807 had to report upon a new threat to federal authority. Aaron Burr, who had served as Jefferson's first vice president, had schemed after leaving that office to break off some southwestern states and set up a separate country. His conspiracy came to light, and he was tried for treason before Chief Justice Marshall in 1807. The framers had wisely drawn the definition of treason very narrowly, requiring two witnesses to an overt act of levying war against the United States, and the facts of the case certainly cast doubt on whether Burr's own conduct met that standard. The chief justice concluded that it did not. Commenting briefly on the now-decided case in his message of October 1807, Jefferson left it to the Congress to determine whether the laws against treason needed to be strengthened. They took no action.

The war between Britain and France resumed in the second half of 1803, and its naval aspects rapidly became the consuming issue of Jefferson's presidency, the source of his greatest frustrations, and the reason that his popularity—confirmed in a landslide reelection victory over Federalist Thomas Pinckney in 1804—had sunk to a low ebb when he left office. Like Woodrow Wilson 110 years later, Jefferson spoke repeatedly on behalf of the trading rights of neutrals in wartime, but neither London nor Paris had any intention of respecting them. Both tried to obstruct US trade with their enemy in any possible way, and both eventually tried to impose conditions on such trade that Jefferson would not accept. In his first message after the war had begun again in October 1803, he called upon his countrymen not to abandon the nation's peaceful path and take sides. Two years later, in December 1805, he called upon the Congress to assess the dangerous foreign situation and try to agree on appropriate measures. Both sides were preying on American commerce and trying to prevent American ships from trading with their rival or their rivals' American colonies, and "reason" demanded that the US oppose their claims. Spain was also threatening US frontiers with Florida and Mexico (which included what is now Texas.). War could happen, and he called for more fortifications in US ports, and due attention to the militia. The border situation remained perilous a year later, and he praised five hundred volunteer cavalrymen provided by "Orleans" and Mississippi to defend it. By the time Jefferson called a special session of Congress in October 1807, however, things had taken a new and more dangerous turn.

Earlier in that year, US negotiators led by James Monroe, dispatched to London to try to force the British government to respect American neutral rights and give up its habit of impressing American seamen whom they claimed to be deserters, had concluded an agreement contrary to their instructions, which had not secured Jefferson's objectives. When it reached Washington for approval, he had repudiated it. Then, in June, the British warship *Leopard* attacked and forced the surrender of the US warship *Chesapeake* on the pretext that its crew included British deserters. The negotiations over neutral rights had resumed in London and Jefferson now demanded reparations for the attack on the *Chesapeake* as well.

During the next year, as Jefferson reported in his last annual message in November 1808, he tried to find an alternative to war. The Congress passed an Embargo Act stopping all trade with belligerents, unless they agreed to allow neutral trade with anyone. Both sides refused to do that, and the embargo wreaked considerable economic hardship on American trading interests, although not enough, as he reported in the same annual message, to have decreased federal revenues significantly or stopped the steady retirement of the national debt. The unpopularity of the act showed in the congressional elections of 1808, when the Democrats' majority fell from 116–26 to 94–48 in the House. Jefferson nonetheless expressed satisfaction that the embargo on foreign goods had increased manufacturing in the United States itself, creating enterprises that he expected to continue whether foreign trade resumed or not. With only three months left in office, he left it to the Congress to decide what to do. It repealed the embargo, leaving it his successor, Secretary of State James Madison, to try to find a new solution to the problem of American neutrality.

In his second inaugural address in March 1804, Jefferson had congratulated himself on fulfilling his plans to reduce the size of the government and the national debt. He knew, he said, that some disapproved of the acquisition of Louisiana on the grounds that the addition of such large territories might endanger the union—"but who can limit the extent to which the federative principle may operate effectively? The larger our association the less will it be shaken by local passions; and in any view is it not better that the opposite bank of the Mississippi should be settled by our own brethren and children than by strangers of another family? With which should we be most likely to live in harmony and friendly intercourse?" Having just been reelected with the votes of nearly every state, he talked for several paragraphs about the unfortunate licentiousness of elements of the press. While counting on state laws against "falsehood and defamation," he also took comfort that his fellow citizens had remained "cool and collected," and that they had in the election "pronounced their verdict, honorable to those who had served them and consolatory to the friend of man who believes that he may be trusted with the control of his own affairs." This experiment, he thought, had proven that "since truth and reason have maintained their ground against false opinions in league with false facts, the press, confined to truth, needs no other legal restraint; the public judgment will correct false reasoning and opinions on a full hearing of all parties; and no other definite line can be drawn between the inestimable liberty of the press and its demoralizing licentiousness." That conclusion remained to be tested anew in various periods of American history, not least our own.

Jefferson's Democratic-Republican Party, now known as the Republicans, established its hegemony in Congress in the midterm election of 1802, emerging with majorities over the Federalists of 114–28 in the House and 27–7 in the Senate. Its dominance continued almost unchecked until the extinction of the Federalists in 1824, and only three times during the 1802–24 period did its majorities in the House and Senate fall below a 3–1 margin. No majority party has ever enjoyed anywhere near such prolonged dominance since.

In December 1808 he ended his last annual message on another note of optimism, thanking both Congress and the people for the confidence they had shown him—even though that confidence had now fallen to a low point indeed. "Looking forward with anxiety to future destinies, I trust that in their steady character, unshaken by difficulties, in their love of liberty, obedience to law, and support of the public authorities, I see a sure guaranty of the permanence of our Republic; and, retiring from the charge of their affairs, I carry with me the consolation of a firm persuasion that Heaven has in store for our beloved country long ages to come of prosperity and happiness." The growth of liberty and democracy, he continued to believe until his death, represented human progress, made possible in turn by some invisible higher power.

# IV

## JAMES MADISON AND JAMES MONROE

### 1809–17 • 1817–25

In late 1808, James Madison, for eight years Jefferson's secretary of state, defeated the Federalist Charles C. Pinckney by a popular majority of 2–1 and by 122 electoral votes to 47. The Federalists had become a regional party and all but two of Pinckney's electoral votes came from New England. Madison had served as a key member of the Constitutional Convention of 1787 and of the very first Congress, and he had more experience in the new government, clearly, than any of his predecessors. He inherited a most difficult foreign situation, which swallowed up most of his attention and led him into the independent nation's first major war in 1812. The nation escaped from that conflict intact early in 1815, but Madison did not leave a distinguished record behind as president.

Focusing on the foreign scene in his first inaugural address, Madison introduced a moral, legalistic approach to foreign policy that has frequently characterized the approach of US presidents in times of conflict. The difficulties that had come across the nation, he said—a reference to the economic hardship that resulted from Jefferson's embargo—did not reflect "any unwarrantable views. . . . nor, I trust, any involuntary errors in the public councils." The blameless United States faced "the injustice and violence of the belligerent powers," and he could not know when they would revoke "their arbitrary edicts." Then followed a long list of sound principles in foreign and domestic affairs, a brief tribute to his predecessor, and a declaration of trust in the rest of the government and the citizenry. In sharp contrast to Jefferson eight years earlier, he did not indicate any policies that he wanted to pursue.

Because Britain, still in the midst of its world war with Napoleon's empire, now ruled the seas, it alone could enforce its will upon American shipping, and for four years, Madison discussed futile efforts to persuade the British to respect American rights as he saw them. He reported in his first annual message in November 1809 that a British envoy had reached a tentative agreement in Washington but that his government had subsequently repudiated it. The French had also refused to compensate Americans for previous losses. A year later in December 1810 he reported that the French had repealed some of their decrees closing off the European continent to foreign trade, but the British had not. In November 1811 he told Congress that Britain refused to lift its Orders in Council, which required all neutral trade with Europe to pass through Britain, because London claimed that the French decrees remained in force. Neither nation had agreed to compensate the US for previous losses. Relations with Russia, Sweden and Denmark, he said, were good, and he warned the Congress to be ready for war with Britain.

When in fact Madison finally asked Congress for a declaration of war on June 1, 1812, he began by protesting the British practice of impressing US seamen (on the grounds that they were really British subjects, whom they did not recognize an US right to naturalize), and insisted that the nation had expressed its willingness to meet any genuine grievance. Blockading British warships, he said, had "added the most lawless proceedings in our very harbors, and have wantonly spilt American blood within the sanctuary of our territorial jurisdiction." The British blockade, he claimed, was a "pretended" one under international law, since the British lacked the ships to make it fully effective. Although France had now opened its trade to the US, the British refused to allow such trade until the French opened Europe to British products as well. Neither the successive bans on US trade with the British, nor offers to repeal them and even join Britain in the war with France if France persisted in acts against US trade, had persuaded the British cabinet to change course. Taking a very legalistic approach, Madison repeatedly accused the British of violating their own principles. Madison added that Indian tribes on the Canadian frontier, encouraged by the British, had perpetrated outrages on American settlers. Congress, he said, must now decide whether "to commit a just cause into the hands of the Almighty Disposer of Events," while remaining open to any honorable settlement. After several weeks of debate, a declaration of war passed the House 79–49 and the Senate 19–13.

By the time of Madison's annual message on November 4, word had reached the United States that the British cabinet—fearing yet another war at one of the lowest points in the struggle against Napoleon—had repealed the Orders in Council that were one of the main pretexts of the war. Madison told Congress that the United States had made a peace offer, but that offer insisted that the British repudiate the principle on which those orders had been based as well as the orders themselves, and accept the American position on impressment. Once again, foreshadowing the line that other presidents would take in future wars, he contrasted the pure motives and tactics of the United States with the perfidy of their enemies, and specifically the atrocities that allied Indian tribes had committed on behalf of the British. He had also to note that an invasion of Canada from Detroit had terminated with the surrender of the whole American force, while boasting of some small victories at sea. General William Henry Harrison was putting together a large force in Kentucky, Ohio, Pennsylvania and Michigan to deal with hostile Indians, and Madison called for more and better-organized militia. Yet in a portent of more serious developments to come, he also noted that Maine and Connecticut had refused to provide troops to defend the frontiers, suggesting that the United States "are not of one nation for the purpose most of all requiring it."[1]

In the election then in progress, Madison won over DeWitt Clinton of New York, but with a much reduced margin of 128–89 in the Electoral College, and the barest of majorities in the popular vote—by far the closest election yet held under the Twelfth Amendment. Nearly all New England, New York, and New Jersey voted for Clinton, and the Republicans' majority in an enlarged House fell from 107–36 to 114–68. In his inaugural on March 4 Madison insisted that the war "is stamped with that justice which invites the smiles of Heaven on the means of conducting it to a successful termination," and that the nation had declared it to save

---

1 Although Maine remained simply part of Massachusetts until 1820, it was often referred to separately.

its spirit and its rank among nations. The country was now fighting for its "national sovereignty on the high seas and the security of an important class of citizens," its sailors. "Already have the gallant exploits of our naval heroes proved to the world our inherent capacity to maintain our rights on one element." On December 7, 1813, he had better news to report: thanks to Oliver Hazard Peary, the United States now controlled Lake Erie and was doing well on Lake Ontario as well. Generals Coffee and Andrew Jackson were mounting an expedition against the Creek Indians—another British ally—and General Harrison had won his victory at Tippecanoe. The British, however, still refused to recognize American naturalizations and had refused an offer of mediation from the emperor of Russia, now an important British ally. The northern border was secure. "In fine, the war, with all its vicissitudes," he said, "is illustrating the capacity and the destiny of the United States to be a great, a flourishing, and a powerful nation, worthy of the friendship which it is disposed to cultivate with all others, and authorized by its own example to require from all an observance of the laws of justice and reciprocity."

Madison sent his next annual message on September 20, 1814, when a wartime financial crisis had forced him to call Congress into session more than two months early. From 1810 through 1812 he had continued Jefferson's practice of retiring several million dollars of the national debt annually, but in December 1813 he had had to report that $24 million of $37.5 million in total revenue had come from loans. The government had borrowed another $11 million in the first half of 1814, and he warned of new loans ahead. The war in Europe now seemed to be over and the powers were making peace, but the British still rejected the Russian mediation offer, and he worried out loud that they might turn their full force against the United States. Madison had to refer to the British raid that had taken and burned much of Washington, DC and Alexandria, Virginia, although he added that the British had had to retreat and that their attack on Baltimore had failed. American troops had won victories in Plattsburg and across the Niagara River, General Jackson had made peace with the Creeks, and privateers had captured many British ships. Still, the British were using barbaric means to threaten both American prosperity and American national existence, and the nation had to fight on. Within a month, the British offered to open peace talks in Ghent, and soon agreed to settle the war by returning to the prewar status quo.

We have seen that Washington (in the Whiskey Rebellion), Adams (in a tax rebellion in Pennsylvania), and Jefferson (with the Burr conspiracy) had all dealt with challenges to the authority of the federal government. In the last stages of the war Madison faced by far the most serious challenge yet, as several governors in New England—where the war had never been popular—essentially refused to take any part of it. Madison however chose not to mention this crisis in his annual message, and the New England states met in Hartford in December and January 1814–15 to discuss potentially drastic action. Andrew Jackson's victory over the British at New Orleans, followed by the news of the Treaty of Ghent that had already been agreed to, saved the country from its most serious constitutional crisis yet. In his last two messages, in December 1815 and 1816, Madison reported that the nation was generally at peace, although trouble with the southern Indians was brewing again. In the first of those two he thanked "a superintending Providence" that while war continued elsewhere, "the United States are in the tranquil enjoyment of prosperous and honorable peace." He had to report however that the national debt had risen from $39 million to $120 million, and that the country now needed a uniform national currency based on precious metals, which the issuance of paper money had driven out of circulation. A year later he could report a surplus of $9 million in the revenue and new debt reductions, which, he said, a new Bank of the United States might help. Having allowed the bank's charter to expire in 1811, the second Republican president had now gone over to the views of the Federalist Alexander Hamilton. Congress agreed to recharter the bank in 1816.

In several messages Madison praised the growth of American industry in response to the British blockades, and in his last message he hoped that the nation would never depend so much on foreign manufactures again. In December 1814 he had called for protective measures for industry, particularly for branches related to defense. The long conflict with Britain and the war put other state-building measures on the back burner. Madison called repeatedly for the reorganization of the militia to make it more useful, and for additional military academies and, once again, for a national university, which might create a truly national intellectual and political elite. He also reiterated Jefferson's call for roads and canals, if necessary via constitutional amendment. None of these projects bore fruit.

The 1810 census (which Madison never mentioned in an annual address) had found that the nation's population had increased by 36 percent, to 7.2 million, in the last ten years. New York had now passed Virginia as the most populous state, and only 17 percent of the nation's inhabitants were now slaves. By the end of Madison's tenure, Tennessee, Louisiana, Ohio and Indiana had become states. In his very last message he congratulated the nation on the fortieth anniversary of independence and implied that the barely successful outcome of the war, as well as the expansion of the nation, vindicated the nation's principles and its new form of government. Despite more than two difficult years of war, the new nation marched bravely ahead.

James Monroe became the fourth Virginian to occupy the White House in 1817. A combat veteran of the Revolutionary War, he won office in Virginia politics and as a US senator before serving Jefferson as an envoy in Europe and Madison as secretary of state and secretary of war. His party caucus chose him to succeed Madison in 1816 over William Crawford of Tennessee, and he carried every state but three, all in New England, against Rufus King, and won a popular majority of more than two to one. The Federalists almost completely disappeared during his first term while Republicans began to break into factions, and in the 1820 election Monroe came within one electoral vote of unanimity. During his eight years in office Monroe devoted very close attention to the problems of an expanding nation.

Like his overwhelming election, Monroe's 1817 inaugural address illustrated the enthusiastic consensus that now prevailed among the political class of the United States and the citizens who voted them into office. He found nothing but a triumphal record in the forty years since independence and twenty-eight since the adoption of the Constitution. The country had enlarged its territory and prospered. The balance between federal and state power had worked well, and individuals had thrived. "On whom has oppression fallen in any quarter of our Union?" he asked, ignoring, of course, the slave population. "Who has been deprived of any right of person or property? Who restrained from offering his vows in the mode which he prefers to the Divine Author of his being? It is well known that all these blessings have been enjoyed in their fullest extent; and I add with peculiar satisfaction that there has been no example of a capital punishment being inflicted on anyone for the crime of high treason."

What dangers, he asked, might threaten the country? Throughout the nation's history, he said, "the government has been in the hands of the people." Their intelligence, their independence and their virtue had given it its success, and if the population "retains its present sound and healthful state everything will be safe." "It is only when the people become ignorant and corrupt, when they degenerate into a populace, that they are incapable of exercising the sovereignty," leading to "usurpation," and the people "become the willing instruments of their own debasement and ruin." Thus, by wise and constitutional measures, the nation should "promote intelligence among the people as the best means of preserving our liberties." Striking an even more commonplace note about foreign dangers, he argued for stronger fortifications and naval forces, and for measures to make the militia more effective (without mentioning the specific problems of the recent war). He called for internal improvements to draw the nation closer together, and measures to encourage domestic industries. Some Republicans, by this time, had evidently become Hamiltonians on these points. He promised to work for further economies in government.

The founders' hope that the United States would mark a new stage of civilization had now become, for Monroe, a certainty. "Never did a government commence under auspices so favorable, nor ever was success so complete," he declared. A "high destiny" further awaited the nation, and he closed with the routine profession of faith in "the Almighty." Monroe enjoyed eight years of peaceful administration, and during that time, he set the nation on some very important paths. In foreign affairs he took the first steps toward creating a more equal and open environment for international commerce, and he eventually introduced the idea of the United States as an inspiration and support for liberty in other nations. At home he expounded and implemented some new ideas about internal improvements, and sketched out the nation's future course of expansion to the Pacific coast. He also foresaw the end of the tribal presence of Indians east of the Mississippi River.

No one knew, of course, that a full century would elapse before the European powers would embark upon a new world war that would once again involve the United States. Monroe evidently expected another such conflict relatively soon, and he put through a wide-ranging program of fortifications designed to keep foreign ships away from the nation's ports. In his second inaugural he reported the expert view that those fortifications could hold as many as 20,000 foreign troops offshore until the militia had assembled enough men to deal with them, as Maryland and Virginia had failed to do in 1814 when the British burned Washington. He also continued building up the navy—which continued to patrol for pirates in the Mediterranean, the Gulf of Mexico, and the Pacific—and reorganized the army, giving it a headquarters in Washington. Beginning in 1818 he referred repeatedly and proudly to the use of navy ships to suppress the African slave trade, and in 1822 he reported having asked the European powers to treat slave traders from any nation as pirates, thereby depriving them and their cargo of any legal protection. A treaty to that effect with the British was awaiting ratification when he delivered his last annual message in December 1824.

In foreign affairs, Monroe negotiated patiently and at length to resolve long-standing questions with the major European powers. Different teams of negotiators settled some residual issues from the Treaty of Ghent with the British, and the US still sought compensation for maritime losses at the hands of the French, now ruled by a restored Bourbon monarchy. On the nation's southern border, Florida posed a continuing problem. The authority of Spain did not go much further than its garrisons at St. Augustine on the Atlantic and Pensacola on the Gulf of Mexico, and Monroe claimed that the territory included too many adventurers, slave traders, fugitive slaves from the US, and hostile, ferocious Indian tribes. He explained in November 1818 that he had sent a force under General Andrew Jackson, a hero of the War of 1812, over the border in self-defense. By December 1819 he had concluded a treaty with Spain that dropped old American maritime claims in exchange for the cession of Florida, while also fixing the southwestern boundaries of the country along the Sabine, Red, and Arkansas Rivers. It took years for both sides to ratify the treaty, partly because of revolution in Spain, but meanwhile, the Congress established a Florida territorial government. During the same years, Monroe's government—led by Secretary of State John Quincy Adams—negotiated new agreements with both France and Britain that marked a significant move away from the mercantilist tradition toward modern free trade. The treaties dropped the customary practice of charging heavier duties on goods brought into a nation in foreign ships than on those carried by one's own, and the US unsuccessfully sought access for its ships to trade with the British West Indies. By December 1823, Monroe could also report negotiations with both the Russians and the British about the three nations' different rights on the north Pacific coast of North America.

Meanwhile, the Spanish settlers in South America were waging long wars of independence against Spain. The conservative powers of Europe—the Holy Alliance of Austria, Russia, Prussia, and its former enemy France as well—periodically threatened to intervene against them. Monroe in November 1818 welcomed their decision at the Congress of Aix-la-Chappelle to do nothing but try to mediate. In November 1820 he noted that peace talks between the Spaniards and South Americans had begun. By December 1822 liberal revolts had broken out among the nobility in both Spain and Portugal, and the Greek people had begun a revolt against the Ottoman Turks who had ruled them for centuries. For the first of many occasions, an American president tried to combine partisanship and legal neutrality in such a situation. The great sympathy for Greece among the American people, Monroe said, reflected the example that ancient Greece had provided the world of "public and personal liberty," and he noted "a strong hope . . . that these people will recover their independence and resume their equal station among the nations of the earth." He also praised the great but moderate effort in Spain and Portugal "to improve the condition of the people," while affirming a belief "that the destiny of every independent nation in what relates to such improvements of right belongs and ought to be left exclusively to themselves." In the midst of this troubled situation, he continued, "the United States owe to the world a great example, and, by means thereof, to the cause of liberty and humanity a generous support. They have so far succeeded to the satisfaction of the virtuous and enlightened of every country." Monroe had declared the US the leader of a worldwide political movement.

With a possible war once again threatening, Monroe, like Madison before him and Lincoln forty years hence, proclaimed his faith in the ability of American institutions to handle a great crisis. "It has been often charged against free governments," he said, "that they have neither the foresight nor the virtue to provide at the proper season for great emergencies; that their course is improvident and expensive; that war will always find them unprepared, and, whatever may be its calamities, that its terrible warnings will be disregarded and forgotten as soon as peace returns. I have full confidence that this charge so far as relates to the United States will be shown to be utterly destitute of truth."

A year later, in his annual message on December 2, 1823, Monroe redefined the relations between the two hemispheres in the doctrine that bears his name. "The occasion has been judged proper for asserting," he said, "as a principle in which the rights and interests of the United States are involved, that the American continents, by the free and independent condition which they have assumed and maintain, are henceforth not to be considered as subjects for future colonization by any European powers. . . . The citizens of the United States cherish sentiments the most friendly in favor of the liberty and happiness of their fellow men on that side of the Atlantic. In the wars of the European powers in matters relating to themselves we have never taken any part, nor does it comport with our policy so to do." The political systems of the Europeans and Americans differed, and the United States were devoted to their own.[2] "We owe it, therefore, to candor and to the amicable relations existing between the United States and those powers to declare that we should consider any attempt on their part to extend their system to any portion of this hemisphere as dangerous to our peace and safety. With the existing colonies or dependencies of any European power we have not interfered and shall not interfere, but with the Governments who have declared their independence and maintained it, and whose independence we have, on great consideration and on just principles, acknowledged, we could not view any

---

2 US citizens customarily referred to "the United States" in the plural until after the Civil War.

interposition for the purpose of oppressing them, or controlling in any other manner their destiny, by any European power in any other light than as the manifestation of an unfriendly disposition toward the United States."

The European powers, he noted, had intervened in the internal affairs of both Spain and Portugal, and every nation must take an interest in their use of such measures. "Our policy in regard to Europe, which was adopted at an early stage of the wars which have so long agitated that quarter of the globe, nevertheless remains the same, which is, not to interfere in the internal concerns of any of its powers; to consider the government de facto as the legitimate government for us; to cultivate friendly relations with it, and to preserve those relations by a frank, firm, and manly policy, meeting in all instances the just claims of every power, submitting to injuries from none.

"But in regard to those continents [the Americas] circumstances are eminently and conspicuously different. It is impossible that the allied powers should extend their political system to any portion of either continent without endangering our peace and happiness; nor can anyone believe that our southern brethren, if left to themselves, would adopt it of their own accord. It is equally impossible, therefore, that we should behold such interposition in any form with indifference. If we look to the comparative strength and resources of Spain and those new Governments, and their distance from each other, it must be obvious that she can never subdue them. It is still the true policy of the United States to leave the parties to themselves, in the hope that other powers will pursue the same course." While leaving no doubt where the United States stood in the emerging contest between monarchy and democracy, Monroe forswore any active intervention in others' affairs, but defended the right of western hemisphere nations to rule themselves. A year later, Monroe noted that in the continuing wars in Greece and South America, "the cause of independence, of liberty and humanity, continues to prevail." The new Latin American states had established governments "similar to our own," a course in which "we ardently wish them to persevere," while acknowledging their right "to institute for themselves the government which, in their judgment, may suit them best." Although the fledgling Federalist and Republican Parties had taken opposing positions toward the French Revolution in the 1790s, Monroe became the first US president to take sides even rhetorically in political struggles abroad. He would not be the last.

Monroe was also the first president to refer explicitly to what we now call a recession, after an economic contraction in postwar Europe and an attempt to restore US currency after its expansion during the recent war led to a credit crunch and the Panic of 1819. In November 1820 he noted that purchasers owed $23 million for public lands which many could not pay, and suggested some debt relief for them—an actual federal response to economic crisis. He repeatedly noted the growth of American industry and suggested raising some tariffs on industrial products to support it. Even though he recommended and secured the repeal of some war taxes, the revenue continued to grow and to allow for ample retirement of the federal debt. As his first term drew to a close in November 1820, Monroe reported that the debt had fallen from $158 million in October 1815 to just $67 million then. The panic forced the government to borrow a few million the next year, but in December 1823, Monroe suggested that the debt might be almost entirely retired by 1835.

On April 4, 1822, Monroe sent Congress a special message on the question of internal improvements—perhaps the longest state paper that any U.S. president had generated so far. Roads and canals, he made clear, were critical to the future of the nation, but what role could the federal government play in building them? Addressing the question of the extent of federal powers, he declared, not for the first time, that both the state and federal governments had "a common origin or sovereign, the people," and that they were "amenable to the power which created it." Because the people, not the states, had created the federal government, it rested on a compact to which the states were not parties and executed "its own powers independent of them"—an interesting commentary on the theoretical possibility of secession, which he evidently rejected. But did the federal government enjoy the power of seizing land for roads and canals and the power to police them after they came into operation? After a very detailed look at the Constitution, he argued that it did not. On the other hand, he argued provocatively, the federal taxing power and the corresponding power to spend money were so broad that it lay with the people, acting as voters, to approve or disapprove their application and to remove any abuses of it, and he specifically rejected the idea that the Supreme Court could disallow an appropriation. Congress could therefore in his view appropriate money to finance roads and canals, but the states would have to acquire the necessary property and supervise the necessary construction and maintenance. He specifically called for money to repair the Cumberland (later National) Road which crossed the Alleghenies. Given the enormous economic and political benefits that a much larger system of roads and canals might provide, however—including a tighter union among the states—he recommended a constitutional amendment to allow the federal government to undertake "a great national network"—a precursor, really, of the interstate highway system.

"The only danger to which our system is exposed," Monroe said, "arises from its expansion over a vast territory. Our union is not held together by standing armies or by any ties other than the positive interests and powerful attractions of its parts toward each other. Ambitious men may hereafter grow up among us who may promise to themselves advancement from a change, and by practicing upon the sectional interests, feelings, and prejudices endeavor under various pretexts to promote it. The history of the world is replete with examples of this kind-f military commanders and demagogues becoming usurpers and tyrants, and of their fellow-citizens becoming their instruments and slaves." How far should the nation expand? This he declined to say, limiting his vision to "a range of states on the western side of the Mississippi"—but new considerations might lead the nation to go farther. In conclusion, he asked for funds to make a general survey of a series of possible roads and canals in different parts of the country, including canals to link the Chesapeake Bay to the Ohio River and the Ohio River to the Great Lakes. Congress agreed to that survey, and those canals were eventually completed. "The establishment of our institutions," he concluded, "forms the most important epoch that history hath recorded. They extend unexampled felicity to the whole body of our fellow-citizens, and are the admiration of other nations. To preserve and hand them down in their utmost purity to the remotest ages will require the existence and practice of virtues and talents equal to those which were displayed in acquiring them." And in his last annual message, he proposed establishing a fort at the mouth of the Columbia River—another portent of things to come.

The 1820 census counted 9.6 million American inhabitants, a full 33 percent increase in ten years. The slave population of 1.5 million represented a new percentage low. Monroe also spoke repeatedly, and in unusually blunt, and sometimes chilling, terms, about the status and future of the Indian tribes. In December 1817 he reported that the United States had bought nearly all the Indian land in Ohio and much of it in Michigan and Indiana on terms favorable to the United States "and, it is presumed, not less so to the tribes themselves." They had also bought a Georgia tract from the Cherokees and arranged to buy most of their land east of the Mississippi in exchange for new land west of that river. This, he argued, was simply the inevitable direction of history. "In this progress, which the rights of nature demand and nothing can prevent, marking a growth rapid and gigantic, it is our duty to make new efforts for the preservation, improvement, and civilization of the native inhabitants. The hunter state can exist only in the vast uncultivated desert. It yields to the more dense and compact form and greater force of civilized population; and of right it ought to yield, for the earth was given to mankind to support the greatest number of which it is capable, and no tribe or people have a right to withhold from the wants of others more than is necessary for their own support and comfort." The treaties with the Lake Erie tribes encouraged individual ownership and cultivation and provided a stipend, and the government should continue our "humane and liberal policy" and try to promote "their improvement in the arts of civilized life." He spoke similarly in November 1820, referring to money Congress had passed to help some tribes become more agricultural. "In their original state," he said, "game is their sustenance and war their occupation, and if they find no employment from civilized powers they destroy each other. Left to themselves their extirpation is inevitable." In his last annual message he repeated that the expansion of settlements threatened the Indians with "extinction" if they could not undergo "civilization"—not because of physical threats, evidently, but because hunter-gatherer societies could not survive next to agricultural ones. To remove them forcibly from the territory they now occupied, however, "would be revolting to humanity and utterly unjustifiable," and he hoped to persuade them to settle between the Mississippi and the Rockies. Today, some find nothing but tragedy or crime in the expansion of European settlements at the Indians' expense, but history has proven out Monroe's claim that hunter-gatherer societies must give way to agricultural ones on every continent.

Throughout his tenure, in short, Monroe promoted and celebrated the expansion of the United States, its economy, and its means of transportation. He was doing what he could to create a more open international trading environment and suppress the slave trade, and with Britain's critical help, he kept the European powers from intervening against the new Latin American Republicans. He believed that the nation represented a new form of government by the people, and he saw its ideals making gains elsewhere in the world. In the midst of this hopeful picture, he did not once refer at any length to the great controversy that threatened to disrupt the Union in 1819–20, the debate over the admission of Missouri as a state and the legality of slavery within it. For the first time the House and Senate debated not merely the question of whether slavery would exist in a new state, but the broader question of whether slavery represented a positive good with roots in the ancient world and the Old Testament, as some southerners argued for the first time, or an evil incompatible with the principles upon which the republic was founded. After a lengthy and bitter debate, Missouri won admission with slavery along with the admission of Maine, until then a district of Massachusetts, as a separate state as well, leaving an equal balance in the Senate between free and slave states, and with the additional provision that all other territory north of latitude 36' 30"—Missouri's southern boundary—would be "forever free."[3]

The debate and its outcome convinced the aged Thomas Jefferson, among others, that the slavery question must someday destroy the Union, and the sectional divide it revealed might well have been one of the dangers that Monroe hoped a new system of roads and canals might head off. Yet the president, while signing the Missouri Compromise into law, said nothing about the broader issues involved in any message to Congress. Missouri and Maine were the fifth and sixth new states to join the union during Monroe's presidency, after Indiana, Mississippi, Illinois and Alabama. The cotton gin had now made slave-based southern agriculture far more

---

3 For a detailed account of the debate see George Dangerfield, *The Era of Good Feelings* (London, 1953), pp. 217–45.

profitable and a new plantation system was spreading through the Deep South, while northern abolitionism was becoming somewhat more militant. Future presidents would have to say far more on the subject than Monroe, who preferred, like most of his founding generation, to say as little about the anomaly of American slavery as possible.

# V

# JOHN QUINCY ADAMS AND ANDREW JACKSON

## 1825–29 • 1829–37

Having reigned without effective opposition for most of James Monroe's two terms in office, the Republican Party disintegrated into factions when the time came to choose his successor in 1824. John Quincy Adams, who as secretary of state appeared to be the heir apparent like Madison and Monroe before him, faced opposition from Secretary of the Treasury William Crawford of Georgia; Henry Clay of Kentucky, the Speaker of the House, who favored tariffs and internal improvements; and Andrew Jackson of Tennessee, who had distinguished himself in the wars against the British and the Creek Indians in Florida, and established a reputation as a man of the people despite his status as a southern planter. Crawford had some support within the party caucus of officeholders in Washington, but the other candidates decided to boycott it and face him in the election after various state legislatures or conventions endorsed one or another of them. Eighteen of the twenty-four states now chose their presidential electors by popular vote, but the other six included some of the largest, such as New York. Jackson finished first in the balloting with 99 electoral votes, 33 short of a majority. Then came Adams with 84, Crawford (who was now seriously ill) with 41, and Clay with 37. Jackson won the popular vote in those states that cast it by a comfortable plurality, with Adams second. Under the Constitution, the choice of the president now went to the House of Representatives, voting by state delegations for one of the top three candidates. Clay, thus excluded, became a key figure in the drama. Adams won on the first ballot with Clay's support, secured in some private conversations that neither man ever described in any detail. An obscure congressman then publicly accused Clay of having sold his support in return for a promised appointment as secretary of state. No one could prove the charge—and Adams went ahead and made the appointment. Jackson and his supporters, furious, claimed that a "corrupt bargain" had thwarted the people's will. Adams became the first president of doubtful legitimacy to take office, and really never recovered from the circumstances of his choice.

Adams began his one and only inaugural by noting that the first generation of national leaders had now passed away. While the first five presidents had all taken part in the Revolution, he and his rival Jackson had both been born in 1767, making them just twenty-one when Washington was first elected. He quickly reviewed the remarkable expansion of the nation since 1776, all under the cheapest government in the world. "From evil—physical, moral, and political—it is not our claim to be exempt. We have suffered sometimes by the visitation of Heaven through disease; often by the wrongs and injustice of other nations, even to the extremities of war; and, lastly, by dissensions among ourselves—dissensions perhaps inseparable from the enjoyment of freedom, but which have more than once appeared to threaten the dissolution of the Union, and with it the overthrow of all the enjoyments of our present lot and all our earthly hopes of the future." Party strife, he continued, had grown out of the great European war and faded after it was over. He pronounced himself firmly in favor of internal improvements. Referring in closing to "the peculiar circumstances of the recent election," he asked for the Congress's help in continuing down Monroe's path. The election, however, had finally split the Republican Party into two factions named after the popular hero who had lost it. The Jacksonians, as they were called, now controlled the Senate, 25–20, while Adams's supporters, the Anti-Jacksonians, narrowly controlled the House, 109–104.

Adams stuck to his principles for four years without any major new initiatives in either foreign or domestic affairs. Year after year his reports on foreign affairs touched on the same topics. The country negotiated more reciprocal trade treaties with the old nations of Europe and some of the new ones of South America, but the British government by 1826 had completely shut off US trade with its West Indian possessions once again, and he eventually asked the Congress to consider some retaliatory steps. Three years into his term he reported that London had at length consented to settle a long-standing issue arising out of the Treaty of Ghent, an indemnity for slaves the British had carried away at the end of the War of 1812. By 1827 he reported happily that Spanish forces had finally left Central and South America, but he also regretted some ongoing disputes over neutral rights with the new Empire of Brazil, and the failure to hold a great Latin American peace conference. The US agreed on new tariff reductions with France, but old claims for maritime losses remained unsettled. In December 1826 Adams paid a special tribute to the late Tsar Alexander I of Russia—whom he had known personally when he was the American minister to St. Petersburg late in the Napoleonic Wars—and described him as "a long tried, steady, and faithful friend" who had understood that "frank and friendly intercourse" with the new republic would help himself and his people. Two years later he noted that another war had broken out between Russia, our traditional friend, and the Ottoman Empire, from which the US was divided by distance, religion, and maxims of government. He hoped that the other powers would stay out of the war and that it would result in the independence of Greece, as indeed it did. He reported repeatedly on the progress of fortifications and the growth of the navy designed to make the nation secure against invasion. In 1825, in a characteristically American burst of optimism, he reported "that peace and prosperity prevail to a degree seldom experienced over the whole habitable globe, presenting, though as yet with painful exceptions, a foretaste of that blessed period of promise when the lion shall lie down with the lamb and wars shall be no more."

At home the nation continued to retire its debt at a pretty steady pace. Adams in December 1825 gave the first detailed breakdown of annual federal expenditures of $24 million: $7 million for the expenses of the various federal departments; $1.5 million for Revolutionary War pensions; another $2 million for fortifications, ordnance, and the navy; $1 million for internal improvements; half a million for land purchases from the Indians and annuities for them; and $8 million in principal and $4 million in interest on the national debt. He also referred to extensive forgiveness of debts owed the government for the sale of public lands at what had turned out to be inflated prices. The next year he had to report another slump, owing to the "severe shock" to "the commercial and manufacturing interests in Great Britain." That, for reasons he did not explain, had reduced imports into the US, and thus revenue, most of which still came from tariffs. He referred explicitly to the "depression" of 1819–22 and the revival that had lasted until early 1826. In December 1827 he reported that the revenue had continued to fall during the first two quarters of that year, but was reviving. A year later, he went in some detail into the impact of British trade policies, which were shutting out American foodstuffs and timber despite food shortages in Britain, while admitting cotton almost duty-free to benefit British manufacturers at the expense of North American competitors. He implored the Congress to pass retaliatory tariffs to make sure that the various parts of the US economy might be treated more equally, but tariffs had already become a sectional issue, since the southern states wanted to keep their increasing cotton exports flowing. Was the Congress "impotent to restore the balance in favor of native industry destroyed by the statutes of another realm?" He even worried out loud that certain state legislatures might try to pass laws obstructing the execution of federal statutes, as had happened in the past. This problem he bequeathed to his successor.

On another domestic front, the surveys Monroe had initiated for various road and canal projects throughout the west and south of the nation continued to produce reports. They now envisioned extending the National Road (which eventually became US 40) to Missouri, and building various canals, including one across the Florida peninsula. In December 1826 he reported proudly on the growth of the Post Office, and also referred movingly to the deaths of the second and third presidents (the second, of course, his own father) on the fiftieth anniversary of the signing of the Declaration of Independence. In December 1828, he once again reviewed the history of policy toward the Indians and hinted at a new departure. The nation had initially decided to treat the Indians as independent nations, while also regarding them as savages "whom it was our policy and our duty to use our influence in converting to Christianity and in bringing within the pale of civilization." "We have been far more successful in the acquisition of their lands than in imparting to them the principles or inspiring them with the spirit of civilization," he continued, and even relatively civilized tribes had claimed sovereignty within states. "This state of things requires that a remedy should be provided—a remedy which, while it shall do justice to those unfortunate children of nature, may secure to the members of our confederation their rights of sovereignty and of soil." He referred Congress to a report of the secretary of war, which described attempts to persuade the Creeks of Alabama and the Cherokees of Georgia to move to territories west of the Mississippi. It also laid out the strategy of bringing tribal leaders from the Northwest to Washington, "and letting them see for themselves how comparatively feeble they are," rather than "leave them in ignorance, or to be enlightened by the only remaining alternative of marching forces into their country, and scourging them into submission and peace." Both mercy and economy recommended the first alternative.[1] The country had appropriated $50,000 to compensate the Cherokees for "removing," and $15,000 to pay for parties of Choctaw, Creek, Cherokee and Chickasaw Indians who were exploring possible new homes west of the Mississippi. Secretary of War Thomas L. McKenney described the possibilities open to the Indians as he saw them in no uncertain terms. While they must perish, he argued, if left among "a population whose anxiety and efforts to get rid of them are not less restless and persevering than is that law of nature immutable," they might yet be placed "in a situation, where by the adoption of a suitable system for their security, preservation, and improvement."

John Quincy Adams had already served the nation well as minister to Russia and as secretary of state and principal author of the Monroe Doctrine before his presidency. He subsequently had the most consequential political career of any ex-president, serving in the House of Representatives from 1830 until his death in 1848. There he became the leading congressional abolitionist, eventually overcame southern opposition to congressional debate on the institution of slavery, and conceived how a president might emancipate the slaves under his war powers in the event of secession and civil war. Yet his presidency was doomed almost before it had begun, and in 1828, Andrew Jackson resoundingly defeated him with 178

---

1 Report of November 1, 1828, http://digicoll.library.wisc.edu/cgi-bin/History/History-idx?type=article&did=History.AnnRep2639.i0004&id=History.AnnRep2639&isize=M.

electoral votes to 83, and nearly 56 percent of the popular vote. The Jacksonian Party, which had already won a majority in the House as well as the Senate in 1826, now enjoyed majorities of 113–100 in the House and 27–20 in the Senate. Thus began a new era of American politics in tone and substance, as Jackson's annual messages clearly showed.

Although Jackson was exactly the age of John Quincy Adams and came into office with no experience in the national government, he struck a more mature and confident tone in his major addresses than any of his predecessors. Most of the population no longer remembered the era before Washington's presidency, and Jackson spoke as the leader of a well-established and increasingly strong nation, determined to take steps that would place it on an even sounder footing and avoid the pitfalls that had doomed republics in the past. In his first inaugural he promised to seek economy in government to "counteract that tendency to public and private profligacy which a profuse expenditure of money by the Government is but too apt to engender," and looked forward to the payoff of the national debt, "the unnecessary duration of which is incompatible with real independence." Eight years later the country had accomplished that remarkable feat. Together with a slim majority in Congress, he adopted the policy of removing the remaining Indian tribes in the Midwest and South to a new Indian territory west of the Mississippi in what is now Oklahoma. In 1832, at the end of his first term, he emerged as the first president to take an interest in the *distribution* of wealth within American society, and used executive power to destroy the Bank of the United States on the grounds that it favored the rich against the interests of the common people, and had used its own wealth to corrupt American politics. While he never convinced Congress to act on another of his most cherished projects, the abolition of the Electoral College and the direct popular election of the president and vice president, he used his office to address national issues more vigorously than any of his predecessors, or any of his successors until Abraham Lincoln.

Jackson's very lengthy annual messages generally began with a survey of the nation's foreign relations, beginning with individual European states and moving to the tumultuous scene to the south, where Central and South America were forming new states and new governments. In the first, in December 1829, he expressed satisfaction to find the nation at peace and a hope to see "our brethren of the human race secured in the blessings enjoyed by ourselves, and advancing in knowledge, in freedom, and in social happiness." The government must settle all differences with other nations on strict principles of right and wrong. Himself the victor against the British in the Battle of New Orleans in 1815, he looked forward to "the most cordial relations" between the two states. As it turned out, he was still lamenting the failure to resolve one outstanding issue—the boundary between Maine and Canada—a full seven years later, but new agreements soon allowed US ships to trade with the British West Indies and even to take West Indian produce elsewhere. In December 1830, in the wake of the new French revolution that had replaced the restored Bourbon dynasty with the somewhat more liberal Louis Philippe, he lauded "the important modifications of their Government, effected with much courage and wisdom by the people of France," which had "naturally elicited from the kindred feelings of this nation that spontaneous and universal burst of applause in which you have participated." He paid tribute to Lafayette, the personal link between that revolution and America's own, and to the moderation of this French upheaval. Long negotiations eventually settled in principle the US maritime claims against France dating back to the wars of 1792–1815, but things went wrong when the French legislature refused to appropriate the money to pay them and Jackson threatened to seize French property in return. The controversy was still pending when he left office. Jackson annually reported on parallel negotiations with various other European powers, referring several times to domestic disturbances in Spain and Portugal which had complicated them.

Reflecting in December 1832 on the turmoil in many of the new Latin American states, Jackson stated a general policy toward such situations. "Our best wishes on all occasions, our good offices when required, will be afforded to promote the domestic tranquility and foreign peace of all nations with whom we have any intercourse," he said. "Any intervention in their affairs further than this, even by the expression of an official opinion, is contrary to our principles of international policy, and will always be avoided." A year later he welcomed Spain's decision finally to abandon its opposition to Latin American independence. In December 1834 he reported that the government was trying to carry on new boundary talks with Mexico, also in the throes of domestic conflict. "Unfortunately," he said a year later, "many of the nations of this hemisphere are still self-tormented by domestic dissensions," and he specifically asked the US attorneys on the Mexican border (that is, the border with what is now Texas) to prevent American citizens from taking part in a Mexican civil war. A year later, the Texan revolt against Mexico threatened war with that nation. Acknowledging that the American people sympathized with one side, he warned of "the great error of suffering public policy to be regulated by partiality or prejudice." The US must "neither anticipate events nor attempt to control them. . . . The known desire of the Texans to become a part of our system, although its gratification depends upon the reconcilement of various and conflicting interests, necessarily a work of time and uncertain in itself, is calculated to expose our conduct to misconstruction in the eyes of the world. There are already those who, indifferent to principle themselves and prone to suspect the want of it in others, charge us with ambitious designs and insidious policy." He also referred to, and partially disavowed, an American general's decision to take troops from Arkansas across the Mexican border to forestall an Indian attack. The United States, he said, was already in relations with the new government of Texas—which he did not mention was composed of US citizens. Not for a decade did Texas become part of the union on the eve of the Mexican War.

On the domestic front, Jackson's initial messages focused on the related issues of tariffs and internal improvements. Tariffs remained the source of most of the government's revenue, with the sale of public lands in second place. Internal improvements, which both Monroe and John Quincy Adams had favored to varying degrees, offered the most obvious chance to spend it. Jackson had other ideas. In his second message in December 1830 Jackson rejected legislation to finance lighthouses and a Kentucky canal company (the home state, of course, of his great rival Henry Clay). He did not believe, he explained, that the government should own stock in private companies, and the tranquility of the federal union depended on a very equal distribution of any federal money for internal improvements, which so far had not taken place. The country needed some compromise on this issue. "Every state," he said, "cannot expect to shape the measures of the General Government to suit its own particular interests," making compromises necessary. "Acquiescence in the constitutionally expressed will of the majority, and the exercise of that will in a spirit of moderation, justice, and brotherly kindness, will constitute a cement which would forever preserve our Union." Two years later he called for a constitutional amendment defining and limiting the federal role in internal improvements. In the same message of 1830 he spoke similarly about tariffs. The country had entered a mild slump marked by a fall in prices, and he rejected sectional attempts to blame it on tariffs, ascribing it instead to a shortage of gold and silver, and warning against making tariffs a sectional issue. That in fact had already occurred, and in the 1830 midterm elections, four House candidates from South Carolina were elected on a new Nullifier ticket, claiming the right to invalidate federal laws within their state.

In his very first message, in December 1829, Jackson raised the issue that as much as any other would define his presidency. The First Bank of the United States, founded thanks largely to Alexander Hamilton, had lasted from 1791 until 1811, when Congress refused to reauthorize it in a close vote. President Madison had not mentioned that issue in any annual message. Madison and the Congress chartered the Second Bank five years later, near the end of his term, and it was the closest thing the US then had to today's Federal Reserve. Jackson noted that its charter would expire in 1836 and suggested that it should not continue in its present form. "Both the constitutionality and the expediency of the law creating the bank are well questioned by a large portion of our fellow citizens," he remarked. It had not established "a uniform and sound currency," and he thought a new national bank, "founded upon the credit of the Government and its revenues," might be better. The next year he again proposed a new institution as part of the Treasury, one that would sell bills of exchange but have no stockholders and make no loans. State banks would issue paper currency, and the new US Bank would accept it as long as it was redeemable in specie.

Jackson's great political rival Henry Clay of Kentucky—the leader of the Anti-Jacksonians, whom he always blamed for his loss of the 1824 election in Congress—convinced Congress to throw down the gauntlet on behalf of the Bank in the late spring of 1832, passing a law to reauthorize its charter four years early. Jackson replied on July 10 with his veto message, taking the side of the common man against great economic interests in a way that no previous president had ever done. He had already spoken on behalf of the common people on several issues, asking for gentler laws of bankruptcy that would turn failed men into productive citizens again, and trying to make public lands readily available for sale. Now, he attacked both the Bank and the kind of capitalism it stood for as "unauthorized by the Constitution, subversive of the rights of the States, and dangerous to the liberties of the people."

The Bank, said Jackson, enjoyed the exclusive stamp of the authority of the federal government, and thus "a monopoly of the foreign and domestic exchange." This had increased the value of its stock and made a great deal of money for its stockholders, and a rechartering would probably increase its value by $7 million more, much of which would go to foreign stockholders. The public would receive only a fraction of the gain in compensation. The government, Jackson suggested, should sell this banking monopoly on the open market, where it might receive much better terms. The new act put state banks on a better footing than individuals in their dealings with the Bank of the US, he said, and this "does not measure out equal justice to the high and the low, the rich and the poor." Because most of the Bank's stockholders lived in the Northeast or in Europe, it tended to redistribute money from the West and South to those areas. More stock transfers might put the Bank under the control of a foreign nation with whom the United States might find itself at war. And Jackson disputed a Supreme Court opinion affirming the constitutionality of the act, arguing that "the Congress, the Executive, and the Court must each for itself be guided by its own opinion of the Constitution. Each public officer who takes an oath to support the Constitution swears that he will support it as he understands it, and not as it is understood by others." The Bank enjoyed many privileges that the "necessary and proper" clause of the Constitution could not justify. And then, after a lengthy discussion, Jackson put the question in the broadest political and economic terms.

"It is to be regretted that the rich and powerful too often bend the acts of government to their selfish purposes. Distinctions in society will always exist under every just government. Equality of talents, of education, or of wealth cannot be produced by human institutions. In the full enjoyment of the gifts of Heaven and the fruits of superior industry, economy, and virtue, every man is equally entitled to protection by law; but when the laws undertake to add to these natural and just advantages artificial distinctions, to grant titles, gratuities, and exclusive privileges, to make the rich richer and the potent more powerful, the humble members of society—the farmers, mechanics, and laborers—who have neither the time nor the means of securing like favors to themselves, have a right to complain of the injustice of their Government. There are no necessary evils in government. Its evils exist only in its abuses. If it would confine itself to equal protection, and, as Heaven does its rains, shower its favors alike on the high and the low, the rich and the poor, it would be an unqualified blessing. In the act before me there seems to be a wide and unnecessary departure from these just principles." The bank charter and other laws had created new interests and classes, which had led to sectional conflict and threatened the future of the union. "It is time to pause in our career to review our principles, and if possible revive that devoted patriotism and spirit of compromise which distinguished the sages of the Revolution and the founders of our Union."

"I have now done my duty to my country," Jackson concluded. "If sustained by my fellow-citizens, I shall be grateful and happy; if not, I shall find in the motives which impel me ample grounds for contentment and peace." His fellow citizens did not disappoint him. Congress sustained the veto. The first Democratic National Convention had already blessed his reelection, and he defeated Henry Clay of the "National Republican Party"—shortly to be called the Whigs—by 219 electoral votes to Clay's 49 (with 18 others cast for minor candidates). He won about 54 percent of the popular vote to Clay's 37 percent. His party—now known as the Democrats—emerged with a House majority of 143–63, but narrowly trailed Clay's in the Senate.

In that same year of 1832 the tariff question posed the first serious threat to federal authority and the Union since 1814. The Congress revised the tariff somewhat over the violent objections of representatives from South Carolina, in particular. In November 1832, a South Carolina state convention declared the tariff laws of both 1828 and 1832 void within that state as of February 1, 1833. In his annual message on December 12 Jackson faced the issue of federal authority head-on. "It is my painful duty to state that in one quarter of the United States opposition to the revenue laws has arisen to a height which threatens to thwart their execution, if not to endanger the integrity of the Union. Whatever obstructions may be thrown in the way of the judicial authorities of the General Government, it is hoped they will be able peaceably to overcome them by the prudence of their own officers and the patriotism of the people. But should this reasonable reliance on the moderation and good sense of all portions of our fellow citizens be disappointed, it is believed that the laws themselves are fully adequate to the suppression of such attempts as may be immediately made." In the very same message, he asked for lowering the tariff to levels sufficient to counteract the regulations of foreign nations and to protect the manufacture of articles essential in time of war.

Later that month Congress did revise the tariff downward somewhat, but South Carolina did not back down. In an extraordinary special message on January 16, 1833, Jackson reported that a state convention in South Carolina had declared all tariff laws null and void, called upon federal officials in South Carolina to take an oath to that effect, and promised secession from the Union if the federal government used force against the state. The governor had endorsed the resolutions and the legislature had followed with acts to block the tariff law's execution. They would take effect just two weeks later on February 1, and the state was making military preparations to resist the federal government. This, he said, constituted aggression against the federal government, which was "nevertheless determined that the supremacy of the laws shall be maintained.... If these measures cannot be defeated and overcome by the power conferred by the Constitution on the Federal Government, the Constitution must be considered as incompetent to its own defense, the supremacy of the laws is at an end, and the rights and liberties of the citizens can no longer receive protection from the Government of the Union." "The right of the people of a single State to absolve themselves at will and without the consent of the other States from their most solemn obligations," he continued, "and hazard the liberties and happiness of the millions composing this Union, cannot be acknowledged. Such authority is believed to be utterly repugnant both to the principles upon which the General Government is constituted and to the objects which it is expressly formed to attain."

Jackson recognized an individual (though not a state) right to resist "long and intolerable oppression," as asserted in the Declaration of Independence, but this could only come into play when legal remedies such as a suit in the Supreme Court or an attempt to amend the Constitution had been exhausted. Having no choice but to recommend action to ensure that the laws were faithfully executed, Jackson asked the Congress to revive the law of 1795 that had allowed Washington to suppress the Whiskey Rebellion. "After a successful experiment of forty-four years," he continued, "at a moment when the Government and the Union are the objects of the hopes of the friends of civil liberty throughout the world, and in the midst of public and individual prosperity unexampled in history, we are called to decide whether these laws possess any force and that Union the means of self-preservation. The decision of this question by an enlightened and patriotic people cannot be doubtful." Congress now began debating a new Force Bill to allow troops to enforce the tariff—which passed the Senate, but not the House—and a new compromise tariff bill sponsored by Henry Clay. When the latter bill passed, the South Carolina nullification convention met once again and rescinded its ordinance. Jackson became the fifth president, after Washington, Adams, Jefferson and Madison, successfully to resist an attempt to disrupt the Union. Twenty-eight years later, after South Carolina in different circumstances had carried out its threat to secede, Abraham Lincoln, as we shall see, also defined the issue as the preservation not only of the Union but of the whole democratic experiment for which it stood.

All through Jackson's first term, government revenues had consistently outpaced expenditures by as much as $15 million a year, and in his annual message of December 1833 he announced that the public debt had now fallen to $4.8 million and would be paid off within another year. He also reported on further, decisive battles in his war with the Bank. In August, he said, he had received a report from the Bank's government-appointed directors "establishing beyond question that this great and powerful institution had been actively engaged in attempting to influence the elections of the public officers by means of its money, and that, in violation of the express provisions of its charter, it had by a formal resolution placed its funds at the disposition of its president to be employed in sustaining the political power of the bank." Would the people govern through their representatives, or would the secret influence of money and power control their decisions? He had ordered the secretary of the treasury to withdraw the government's deposits from the Bank—he did not mention that he had had to appoint not just one, but two new secretaries before finding one who would do his bidding—and defied a resolution of the House of Representatives to keep them there. A year later he argued that the Bank had subsequently refused loans to put pressure on Congress to save it, causing real distress in the country, but congratulated Congress and the country for "the virtue and firmness to bear the infliction," and that the country found "relief from this wanton tyranny in vast importations of the precious metals from almost every part of the globe." By withdrawing its deposits and placing them in state banks, the executive had severed all connection with the Bank, and the nation had learned "that the mischiefs and dangers which flow from a national bank far over-balance all its advantages."

Jackson had now embraced a different monetary theory in support of his policy, and in December 1835 he noted the continuing increase in gold and silver coinage. These could become the medium of "the ordinary transactions connected with the labor of the country," while state banks might be forbidden from issuing notes of less than $20. "The great desideratum in modern times," he said, "is an efficient check upon the power of banks, preventing that excessive issue of paper whence arise those fluctuations in the standard of value which render uncertain the rewards of labor. . . . The attainment of such a result will form an era in the history of our country which will be dwelt upon with delight by every true friend of its liberty and independence. It will lighten the great tax which our paper system has so long collected from the earnings of labor, and do more to revive and perpetuate those habits of economy and simplicity which are so congenial to the character of republicans than all the legislation which has yet been attempted." Privileges and monopolies that concentrated wealth, he repeated, posed the greatest danger to American democratic institutions. During 1836, he signed a new law requiring the federal government to withdraw deposits from any state bank that suspended the redemption of its notes in specie.

A relatively primitive capitalism already dominated the western world when the United States created itself in the late eighteenth century. Capitalism's emphasis on individual rights under the law accorded with the personal liberty the new state was meant to enshrine. But Jackson, we now know, was right: unchecked, capitalism operating through sophisticated financial institutions has an irresistible tendency to promote greater and greater inequality of fortunes, with inevitable political results. He and Franklin Roosevelt remain the only two presidents in US history to argue explicitly for the restraint of this tendency and to take what steps they could to oppose it. In both cases the setbacks they administered to the growth of inequality turned out to be temporary, but Jackson deserves to be remembered for that, nearly two whole centuries later, every bit as much as he does to be remembered for his role in the American Indian tribes' loss of their title to land east of the Mississippi, and their removal to the Indian Territory that eventually became Oklahoma, to which we now turn.

In 1829, agricultural societies had been encroaching upon the lands of hunter-gatherer societies like those of the American Indians for thousands of years. The arrival of Europeans on the American continent had accelerated that process, and epidemics of European diseases had wiped out large portions of many Indian tribes in what is now New England and elsewhere. Wars had also contributed. Although the new federal government had signed treaties with a number of tribes in the Midwest and South giving them sovereignty over specified territory, they were increasingly surrounded by new white settlements that took away the habitat of the game on which they depended. We have seen that new treaties had purchased a great deal of land from the tribes, and that both Monroe and John Quincy Adams had endorsed the idea that the tribes might survive only if they were removed to a new home west of the Mississippi. Jackson, who had had many dealings with Indian tribes in both peace and war, endorsed this policy, secured congressional support for it, and implemented it during his two terms. He also discussed it at length in every single one of his annual messages.

"Our ancestors found [the Indians] the uncontrolled possessors of these vast regions," Jackson said in December 1829. "By persuasion and force they have been made to retire from river to river and from mountain to mountain, until some of the tribes have become extinct and others have left but remnants to preserve for a while their once terrible names. Surrounded by the whites with their arts of civilization, which by destroying the resources of the savage doom him to weakness and decay, the fate of the Mohegan, the Narragansett, and the Delaware is fast over-taking the Choctaw, the Cherokee, and the Creek. That this fate surely awaits them if they remain within the limits of the States does not admit of a doubt. Humanity and national honor demand that every effort should be made to avert so great a calamity." He proposed to designate a territory west of the Mississippi, outside the boundaries of any state or territory, for their use, with separate districts for each tribe. Those who preferred to stay within the boundaries of the states must submit to all their laws.

Jackson's policy became the subject of a long, fascinating and highly contentious debate in Congress. Its opponents pointed out quite correctly that the president was in effect siding with several states, led by Georgia, in violation of treaties contracted between such tribes as the Cherokees and the federal government. Having guaranteed Cherokee lands within Georgia in 1802, the federal government had also promised the Georgia government to try to acquire them through further negotiations. The federal government as we have seen had managed to do so in both the South and what then counted as the West, but the Cherokees had refused to yield further. The Georgia government had now claimed that the Cherokees had never been anything but tenants at will, first of the British crown and then of Georgia and the US government, and that the federal government had forfeited its rights by failing to arrange for the transfer of the Cherokees' property. Jackson's message, opponents pointed out, effectively sided with the Georgia government and unilaterally invalidated binding treaties.

The Congress eventually approved this policy by very narrow votes, and designated some of the territory of present-day Oklahoma as Indian Territory. It also appropriated funds to finance the movement of the tribes. Unfortunately, because the US censuses at this time did not even attempt to count Indians who were not citizens, we do not know how many tribal Indians still resided within the nation's borders. One congressman estimated it at about 60,000 people; another, 76,000.[2]

Jackson reported in December 1830 that the new policy would remove most Indians from the new states of Alabama and

---

2 Register of Debates, House of Representatives, 21st Congress, 1st Session, pp. 994, 1092 (May 15, 1830).

Mississippi. The Choctaw and Chickasaw tribes had already agreed to it. These measures, he said, would "enable them to pursue happiness in their own way and under their own rude institutions" and "retard the progress of decay, which is lessening their numbers." "Toward the aborigines of the country," he continued, "no one can indulge a more friendly feeling than myself, or would go further in attempting to reclaim them from their wandering habits and make them a happy, prosperous people." No previous measure had managed to stop their disappearance. Nor, he added accurately if chillingly, was there anything new about this process. "In the monuments and fortifications of an unknown people," he said, "spread over the extensive regions of the West, we behold the memorials of a once powerful race"—the Mound Builders as they have come to be called—"which was exterminated or has disappeared to make room for the existing savage tribes. Nor is there anything in this which, upon a comprehensive view of the general interests of the human race, is to be regretted. . . . What good man would prefer a country covered with forests and ranged by a few thousand savages to our extensive Republic?" He even compared the Indians' forced migration to the migration from Europe to North America and to the further migration of white citizens into the interior.

In December 1831 Jackson mentioned that Congress had appropriated $500,000 for the voluntary removal of the Indians, and that the Chickasaws, Choctaws, and perhaps half the Cherokees had agreed to go. He expected similar results in Ohio and Indiana and insisted again that these changes benefited the states, the harmony of the Union, and the Indians themselves. "What the native savages become when surrounded by a dense population and by mixing with the whites," he wrote in response to criticism from the Northeast, "may be seen in the miserable remnants of a few Eastern tribes, deprived of political and civil rights, forbidden to make contracts, and subjected to guardians, dragging out a wretched existence, without excitement, without hope, and almost without thought." In December 1832 he had to report that the government had not managed to make a settlement with the Cherokees of Georgia. After another year had passed he still had to express the hope that "portions of two of the southern Tribes"—the Cherokees and the Creeks, whom he did not name—"had still failed to recognize the necessity of emigration. . . . That those tribes cannot exist surrounded by our settlements and in continual contact with our citizens is certain. They have neither the intelligence, the industry, the moral habits, nor the desire of improvement which are essential to any favorable change in their condition. Established in the midst of another and a superior race, and without appreciating the causes of their inferiority or seeking to control them, they must necessarily yield to the force of circumstances and ere long disappear." Only removal to new territory could save them. Some northern congressmen had violently and effectively disputed this during the 1830 debate, citing impressive statistics of the Cherokees' agricultural progress. Jackson on the contrary praised the resettlement in the West. "The experiment which has been recently made has so far proved successful. The emigrants generally are represented to be prosperous and contented, the country suitable to their wants and habits, and the essential articles of subsistence easily procured."

In December 1834 Jackson said that arrangements to remove the Creeks were underway, that they would soon be completed with the Seminoles, but that the Cherokees still resisted. A year later he said that only those Cherokees and two bands of Indians in Ohio and Indiana, each numbering in the hundreds, had not agreed to move. He defended the policy in the strongest terms. "To these districts the Indians are removed at the expense of the United States, and with certain supplies of clothing, arms, ammunition, and other indispensable articles; they are also furnished gratuitously with provisions for the period of a year after their arrival at their new homes." There they could take up agriculture or hunt buffalo. The United States was building schools and mills for them and providing tools, and annuities sometimes over $30 for each individual. In December 1836, in his last message, he reported that a treaty with the Cherokees had at last been concluded.

The scrupulous historian must report the words of the past as they were uttered and the events as they took place. Jackson certainly exaggerated the cooperation his government received from the tribes, and several critical treaties were only signed after coups d'état that replaced a hostile tribal leadership with a compliant one. And in 1835, in *Worcester v. Georgia*, Chief Justice Marshall and the Supreme Court ruled that the Cherokee nation within Georgia was sovereign and not subject to the laws of the state. That ruling did not in the least invalidate any treaty that the Jackson administration could reach with tribal leadership, but it could have been used to try to prevent states from encroaching upon lands granted to Indian tribes in previous treaties, and thus, in theory at least, have made it unnecessary to remove the Indians to save them from state-sponsored encroachments and ruin. Jackson however had made clear that he did not think anything could be done about such state action and predicted, correctly as it turned out, that Georgia would not obey the decision. Meanwhile 15,000 Cherokees left for Indian Territory on the "Trail of Tears," where 4,000 are estimated to have died. In due course, we shall see how presidents not yet born came to announce that Indian Territory, more than sixty years later, had become the territory of Oklahoma, and was itself opened to white settlement. Jackson's Indian policy—which as we have seen was neither unique to him nor without serious opposition—remains a chapter in the spread of a modified European civilization, and European immigrants and their descendants, over the North American continent.

While Jackson's Indian policies have become offensive in the twenty-first century, another favorite proposal of his now enjoys considerable support in public opinion. That was nothing less than the abolition of the Electoral College and the direct popular election of the president and vice president, preferably for a single term of either four or six years. Here Jackson obviously spoke from bitter experience. He never forgave the House of Representatives for selecting John Quincy Adams over himself in 1824, even though he had won a substantial plurality of popular votes cast, and he always believed that Henry Clay, who had been eliminated from the voting in the House because he had finished fourth in the initial electoral count, had corruptly swung the House vote to Adams in return for becoming secretary of state. "In this as in all other matters of public concern," he argued in his first annual message, "policy requires that as few impediments as possible should exist to the free operation of the public will. Let us, then, endeavor so to amend our system that the office of Chief Magistrate may not be conferred upon any citizen but in pursuance of a fair expression of the will of the majority." He recommended "an amendment of the Constitution as may remove all intermediate agency in the election of the President and Vice-President. The mode may be so regulated as to preserve to each State its present relative weight in the election, and a failure in the first attempt may be provided for by confining the second to a choice between the two highest candidates."

Jackson repeated this proposal more briefly in every one of his next seven annual messages. It is not altogether clear from his words exactly what he had in mind. A simple count of the popular vote would not "preserve to each State its present relative weight in the election," since that weight, then measured in electoral votes, included extra electors in the slave states awarded according to the three-fifths clause of the Constitution. Did he mean artificially to inflate the vote totals in those states before adding them to the others, or was he simply suggesting that the current number of electoral votes be awarded, state by state, according to the popular vote in that state? Or was this simply a *pro forma* bow to states who might be worried about losing their clout? In any case he understood—as many contemporary advocates of abolishing the Electoral College seem to ignore—that the country would need a second round of voting to anoint a real winner in cases where no one had won a majority the first time around.[3] The proposal appears not to have generated any support in Congress, which never debated it, and I have not been able to find any evidence clarifying the details of how it would have worked. Yet it confirms that Jackson of all our early presidents believed most strongly in direct democracy.

Jackson touched on many other matters. He called in December 1833 for legislation in response to the increasing number of fatal accidents on steamboats, and he complained two years later that railroads, an even newer form of transportation, were using monopoly power to charge the Post Office exorbitant rates for carrying mail. He repeatedly and unsuccessfully asked Congress to create new federal judicial circuits for the increasing number of new states, who still lacked that layer of judges, and he also asked them to provide uniform laws for the two halves of the District of Columbia, which at that time was still a square extending into northern Virginia, and whose residents lived separately under the laws they had inherited. And his December 1835 message included the first hint of the emerging national controversy over slavery. He complained specifically that the Post Office was subject to "attempts to circulate

---

3 This of course is the system used today by foreign nations such as France that elect their chief of state by popular vote.

through the mails inflammatory appeals addressed to the passions of the slaves, in prints and in various sorts of publications, calculated to stimulate them to insurrection and to produce all the horrors of a servile war." No respectable portion of the country, he said, could approve "conduct so destructive of the harmony and peace of the country, and so repugnant to the principles of our national compact and to the dictates of humanity and religion," and to the compromises of the Constitution. Most citizens of the "nonslaveholding states" disapproved of these activities, he said. The states must discourage such activity, and Congress should try to ensure that the Post Office did not assist in this "wicked" agitation. In the North William Lloyd Garrison had started his paper, *The Liberator*, a few years earlier, and John Quincy Adams, now in the House of Representatives, had begun a long and ultimately successful battle to allow for discussions of slavery on the floor of Congress.

During Jackson's first term, the 1830 census found that the nation's population had increased by another 33.5 percent in the previous decade, to 12.8 million. In the last year of his presidency Arkansas and Michigan became the first states admitted to the Union since Maine and Missouri in 1820–21. Jackson, by far the most influential president of his generation and his era, remains a powerful symbol of the many contradictions of the new republic, and shall therefore remain, as he was in life, one of our most controversial presidents as well.

# VI

## Martin Van Buren, William Henry Harrison, John Tyler, and James K. Polk

### 1837–49

Martin Van Buren handily defeated several regional Whig candidates in 1837, and the Democrats retained a reduced 128–100 majority in the House and a 34–17 edge in the Senate. Van Buren's election marked several milestones in US history. Van Buren had been born in 1782, after the Battle of Yorktown, and only a year before Britain officially recognized American independence. John Adams and Thomas Jefferson had been elected vice president under the original Constitution, which awarded that office to the runner-up in the electoral vote for president, but Van Buren was the first man to succeed to the presidency after being elected vice president on a party ticket, as he had been in 1832. Van Buren had been the fourth vice president to hail from New York, which was to remain the most populous state until the 1970 census, but he was the first New Yorker to reach the White House. His tenure also confirmed a well-established rule of early American politics. Every southern president from Washington through Jackson served two terms, but the two Adamses and Van Buren all lost their bids for a second one.

Following in his predecessors' footsteps, Van Buren in his inaugural celebrated the success of the American experiment. The government, he said, "quietly but efficiently performs the sole legitimate end of political institutions . . . doing the greatest good to the greatest number." The Englishman Jeremy Bentham's utilitarian creed had apparently become mainstream US thinking. He also expressed the hope "that America will present to every friend of mankind the cheering proof that a popular government, wisely formed, is wanting in no element of endurance or strength." He mentioned only one specific issue: the growing abolitionist agitation against slavery. "The last, perhaps the greatest, of the prominent sources of discord and disaster supposed to lurk in our political condition," he said, was the institution of domestic slavery. "Our forefathers were deeply impressed with the delicacy of this subject, and they treated it with a forbearance so evidently wise that in spite of every sinister foreboding it never until the present period disturbed the tranquility of our common country." He pledged specifically to veto any, proposal to abolish slavery within the District of Columbia and to oppose any attempt to interfere with it "in the States where it exists." He returned to the subject in December 1839 and again a year later, but only to condemn in the strongest terms the continuing illegal slave trade and to propose new measures against it. He specifically proposed that the Congress outlaw any trade at all between American ships and the "slave factories" on the coast of West Africa, "giving an example to all nations in this respect which if fairly followed cannot fail to produce the most effective results in breaking up those dens of iniquity."

Like Jackson, Van Buren customarily began his annual messages with a survey of the nation's foreign relations, which remained relatively stable during his term. One issue remained intractable. In December 1837 he mentioned new attempts to settle the Maine-Canada boundary, and four years later he expressed the hope that agreement was near. In December 1838 he condemned an armed, unauthorized invasion of Canada by American private citizens who apparently were trying to assist Canadian revolutionaries. While Americans had every right to express their sympathy for foreigners struggling for their liberty, only Congress had the right to authorize armed intervention. In the same message, he mentioned that the new Republic of Texas had withdrawn an application to join the Union "for reasons known to you"—evidently the opposition of Texans who favored continued independence. Talks also continued with Mexico over losses of American property. Van Buren also reported in December 1838 that Russia did not want to renew the 1824 treaty that allowed both US and Russian ships to trade anywhere on the north Pacific coast. The Russians wanted to stop American traders from selling liquor and weapons to natives in what is now Alaska.

Economic crises and controversies dominated Van Buren's term of office, and he responded to them by implementing more and more of Jackson's views on banking and hard money. Well over a century later, an American economic historian argued persuasively that the panics of 1837 and 1839 grew out of economic changes across the ocean, not the crimes or Jackson-inflicted wounds of the banking community, but Van Buren treated them as a symptom of threats to democracy and an opportunity to propose a lasting cure.[1] He was the first president who sought actively to use public policy to counter an economic downturn.

The panic that struck the nation's banks and crippled the economy led Van Buren on September 4, 1837, to call Congress into a special session. He laid out his views in a lengthy restatement of the Jacksonian creed. In the spring, nearly every bank in the nation had suspended specie payments, which under the law of 1836 would have required the government to withdraw its funds from all of them. In addition, commerce and federal revenues had fallen so far that the government would soon not be able to meet its obligations—especially since another recent law had required that the government do so only in specie or convertible notes! Noting discreetly that the crash had generated a violent partisan controversy over its causes, Van Buren gave his own view. He documented an enormous expansion of credit of all kinds, which had inflated the prices of public lands and real estate, financed unprofitable internal improvements, fueled imports that the nation could not afford, and spread "luxurious habits founded too often on merely fancied wealth, and detrimental alike to the industry, the resources, and the morals of our people." Nor was the problem merely national: Great Britain had also greatly expanded credit with disastrous results. Acknowledging that a strong minority still favored a new national bank, Van Buren rejected it on the grounds that the people had voted it down in the last two presidential elections. He now advocated separating government revenue and expenditure from the

---

1 Peter Temin, *The Jacksonian Economy* (New York, 1969).

banking system altogether. To deposit its revenue in banks left the government at the mercy of private interests, and allowed them to profit from sums belonging to the whole nation. They inevitably pushed speculation too far, and "the ruin to which it leads falls most severely on the great laboring classes, who are thrown suddenly out of employment."

Defending his scheme against accusations that it was designed to increase government patronage, he pleaded with the Congress to consider it dispassionately before taking the action it deemed appropriate. And, noting that the suspension of specie payments by the banks had, *pace* Gresham's law, driven gold and silver almost completely out of circulation, he insisted that the government should continue to require it in payment of its obligations to fight that unfortunate trend. In the short term, he asked Congress to authorize the issuance of several millions of Treasury notes, rather than to deposit accumulating revenue in state banks again. And he rejected calls for direct assistance to private interests. "It is not [government's] legitimate object to make men rich or to repair by direct grants of money or legislation in favor of particular pursuits losses not incurred in the public service. This would be substantially to use the property of some for the benefit of others." The crisis was, in any case, temporary, and should not tempt the government to go beyond its legitimate powers. "It is under such circumstances," he concluded, "a high gratification to know by long experience that we act for a people to whom the truth, however unpromising, can always be spoken with safety; for the trial of whose patriotism no emergency is too severe, and who are sure never to desert a public functionary honestly laboring for the public good." Not until 1933 would a president discuss an economic crisis and possible remedies for it in such detail again.

The deeply divided Congress failed to act, and Van Buren repeated his proposals more concisely in his first annual message in December 1837. A year later—in the midst of congressional elections in which the Whigs reduced Democratic margins to 126–116 in the House and 28–20 in the Senate—he reported on a very difficult twelve months. The balance in the Treasury now stood at about $2.7 million, with about $8 million in Treasury notes outstanding. Owing in part to expenditures on the movement of Indian tribes and the war against the Seminoles in Florida, the government would probably spend about $40 million in the coming year. It had reduced the tariff, as well. Despite withdrawals of foreign capital, he argued, business was now recovering. The banks had resumed specie payments, encouraged by the government's refusal to deposit money in them otherwise. He renewed his call for the independent treasury.

While economic radicalism grew within the Democratic Party, another round of bank failures occurred early in 1839. In December of that year Van Buren noted that a combination of lower tariffs and lower imports owing to economic depression had reduced federal receipts by several millions a year, and called upon the Congress to restrict appropriations. He estimated expenditures had been reduced from $32 million in 1838 to $26 million this year and he hoped for another $5 million cut in 1840. He again blamed the new economic crisis on the banks, who had simply extended too much credit too quickly, leading to an inevitable collapse. The Philadelphia and New York banks, he explained, were so powerful that their own suspension of specie payments quickly spread elsewhere, and they were also in thrall to London finance, which made the United States vulnerable to a bad harvest in Britain. For these reasons the government should not deposit its revenues in these banks, but rather collect it in specie and hold it in an independent treasury. Banks would always be necessary, but the state and federal governments must "check, so far as may be practicable, by prudent legislation those temptations of interest and those opportunities for their dangerous indulgence which beset them on every side" by keeping public money out of them. Cycles of expansion and contraction, he said, had caused depressions in 1817–18, 1823, 1831 and 1834, as well as 1837 and 1839. The framers had never intended such an expansion of paper currency. "By ceasing to run in debt and applying the surplus of our crops and incomes to the discharge of existing obligations," he continued, "buying less and selling more, and managing all affairs, public and private, with strict economy and frugality, we shall see our country soon recover from a temporary depression, arising not from natural and permanent causes, but from those I have enumerated, and advance with renewed vigor in her career of prosperity." The nation had fought a difficult struggle against privilege but this had not, as in other countries, required a revolution. Jackson and Van Buren had for the first time used the presidency to call for active national measures that might militate against what we now recognize to be the natural tendency of unregulated capitalism: an increase in economic and political inequality and a tendency toward booms and busts. Not until the next century would the Congress hear such language from a president again.

By the time Van Buren gave his last annual message in December 1840, he had lost his bid for reelection to William Henry Harrison and the Whigs, who had waged a "man of the people" campaign that combined widespread popular support with the backing of the business community. Van Buren did not refer to his defeat at the polls in his message and took the opportunity once more to defend his performance in office and restate the Jacksonian creed. Despite the recurrent economic crises and reductions in revenue, the government had financed the removal of the Cherokees to the tune of $5 million and spent $14 million on the Seminole war, and only $4.5 million in Treasury notes remained outstanding. Fortunately, he said, the government had not created a new public debt, which would inevitably have found its way into foreign hands. Already the nation spent $12 million a year servicing private foreign loans. National debts also favored bankers, who always wanted to see them increase. During the previous year Congress had in fact passed the sub-treasury scheme, and he called for new attempts to reduce expenditures. Higher debts would lead to higher taxes, the "prostitution of political power" for the benefit of particular classes, and the impoverishment of the people. The defunct Bank of the United States had been an unconstitutional threat to the republic. "Have we not a right to expect," he concluded a bit pathetically, "that a policy the object of which has been to sustain the public service independently of either of these fruitful sources of discord will receive the final sanction of a people whose unbiased and fairly elicited judgment upon public affairs is never ultimately wrong?" That expectation had not come true.

Van Buren also reported annually on the progress of the policy of removing the Indians beyond the Mississippi. In December 1837 he traced it all the way back to Thomas Jefferson, and argued that only about a dozen tribes, all in the North, had so far declined to move. A year later he reported proudly on the removal of the Cherokees beyond the Mississippi: "their removal has been principally under the conduct of their own chiefs, and they have emigrated without any apparent reluctance." "That a mixed occupancy of the same territory by the white and red man is incompatible with the safety or happiness of either is a position in respect to which there has long since ceased to be room for a difference of opinion," he said. The government, he said, had now purchased 116 million acres from Indian tribes for $72.6 million. The tribes were now "highly prosperous" in Indian Territory, he claimed, and would benefit from "the acquisition of individual wealth and the pursuits of agriculture." The Seminoles in Florida however remained recalcitrant and had begun a new war by murdering some settler families and the sailors and passengers on some wrecked ships. Two years later he reported that they were largely subdued, but had not submitted.

A strong reaction against twelve years of Jacksonian democracy swept the Whigs and William Henry Harrison into power in 1840. Harrison carried 19 of 26 states, with 234 electoral votes to 60 and nearly 53 percent of the popular vote. The Whigs also took control of the House and Senate by majorities of 142–98 and 27–22. In a long inaugural address on March 4, 1841, Harrison departed from all precedents and explicitly repudiated many of the controversial acts of his last two predecessors. Showing a wide knowledge of history, he suggested that the United States had nearly succumbed to diseases that had killed democracies of the past. While he echoed Van Buren's dictum that the aim of government was "to produce the greatest good to the greatest number," he argued that recent developments had borne out the fears of some framers that the executive was too powerful and might become a monarchy. (The Whig Party had in fact named itself after British parliamentary parties resisting monarchical claims.) He specifically recommended against more than one presidential term on the grounds that too much time in power tended to corrupt, and renounced a second term of his own. He attacked attempts by presidents (clearly Jackson was meant) to become legislators by overusing the veto power, and he worried aloud about the president's excessive control of public finances, enforced by removals of successive secretaries of the treasury. He opposed a purely metallic currency—on the grounds that it would be certain to promote inequality! Referring to anti-slavery agitation without mentioning its name, he said that citizens of some states should not try to interfere in the affairs of others. They might express their opinion, but "organized associations of citizens requiring compliance with their wishes too much resemble the 'recommendations' of Athens to her allies, supported by an armed and powerful fleet"—a reference to the Delian League at the time of the Peloponnesian War that suggested he was well acquainted with Thucydides. He even implied that Jackson had followed in the footsteps of Julius Caesar, Oliver Cromwell, and Simon Bolivar, usurping the power of the government in the name of democracy. He also warned of the excessive influence of parties and invoked the warning of the fall of the Roman Republic, and promised, "All the influence that I possess shall be exerted to prevent the formation at least of an Executive party in the halls of the legislative body."

Harrison had no chance to make good on any of these promises. He apparently became ill on inauguration day, and died just a month later. Then, for the first but not the last time, the nation learned about perhaps the greatest weakness of its amended Constitution—the possibility opened up by the Twelfth Amendment of the accession of an almost random politician via the vice presidency.

Harrison had won the Whig nomination in 1840 over Henry Clay, the acknowledged leader of the Whigs in Washington, because party managers in several key states thought that he would be a much stronger candidate. Clay had expected to be a leading voice in the administration and he was even more confident of this when the almost unknown Virginian John Tyler took over. It did not work out that way. Although Congress quickly abolished the Independent Treasury, Tyler vetoed a bill providing for a charter for a new Bank of the United States. By the time he gave his first annual message in December 1841, most of Harrison's cabinet had resigned and most of the Whig Party leadership opposed him.

Tyler in that message did not refer to the manner of his accession to the presidency. He began, as was now customary, with a survey of foreign affairs, dwelling in great detail of the acquittal of an Englishman, Alexander McLeod, for murder arising out of the destruction of the steamboat *Caroline* in 1837 near the Canadian border, where the British authorities in Canada thought it was assisting a rebellion. Then Tyler angrily asked for restitution for American ships seized off the coast of Africa by British warships, on the grounds that they were trading in slaves.

A year later, Tyler reported on perhaps the greatest triumph of his presidency. Fifty-nine years after the Treaty of Paris had secured the independence of the United States, Secretary of State Daniel Webster had negotiated a treaty finally settling the boundary between New England and Canada. The treaty also pledged both nations to patrol the African coast to try to stop the slave trade, while the British gave up their claimed right to visit and inspect American ships in the area. Finding however that they could not yet agree on the Oregon boundary in the northwest, the two governments had left that question open. Tyler boasted that US relations with the other European powers were most amicable, and that the nation wanted nothing but peace for all the world, secured through equal and impartial justice. "Our great desire," he said, "should be to enter only into that rivalry which looks to the general good in the cultivation of the sciences, the enlargement of the field for the exercise of the mechanical arts, and the spread of commerce—that great civilizer—to every land and sea." Revolutions in many of the new Latin American states, he said, had "obstructed" their relations with the United States. A year later, in December 1843, he reported that the United States was claiming all the territory from latitude 49' (the boundary with Canada east of the Rockies) to 54' 40" in talks with Britain. US citizens, he reported, were already settling in Oregon in significant numbers, and he asked for a second time for the construction of a chain of fortified posts along the way. The US minister to Prussia was trying to negotiate a trade treaty with the Zollverein, the Prussian-led customs union that a number of German states had joined, to lower duties on cotton and tobacco in exchange for easier entry of certain manufactured goods. A year later, in his last message, Tyler had to note that the Senate had declined to ratify the treaty that had been signed. The 1843 message, however, also foreshadowed the greatest war that the new nation had ever undertaken.

Although a number of foreign states had recognized the independence of Texas, Tyler noted in December 1843, Mexico had refused to do so, and had continued its war against Texas in low key for eight years. Bluntly taking the Texans' side, Tyler attacked the war, which might give other nations cause to intervene. "Considering that Texas is separated from the United States by a mere geographical line; that her territory, in the opinion of many, down to a late period formed a portion of the territory of the United States; that it is homogeneous in its population and pursuits with adjoining States, makes contributions to the commerce of the world in the same articles with them, and that most of her inhabitants have been citizens of the United States, speak the same language, and live under similar political institutions with ourselves," he said, "this Government is bound by every consideration of interest as well as of sympathy to see that she shall be left free to act, especially in regard to her domestic affairs, unawed by force and unrestrained by the policy or views of other countries. In full view of all these considerations, the Executive has not hesitated to express to the Government of Mexico how deeply it deprecated a continuance of the war and how anxiously it desired to witness its termination." The Mexican government had also threatened war if the United States annexed Texas, and Tyler called on Congress not to be deterred from discussing the question. Clearly he stood firmly for expansion. He did not mention the issue that made annexation controversial: that southerners had already introduced slavery into Texas, and that its annexation would add a new slave state to the Union.

A year later, in December 1844—after Tyler had failed to win either party's nomination for president, and James K. Polk had defeated Martin Van Buren for the Democratic nomination and won the election against Henry Clay while calling for the annexation of Texas—Tyler called for that again. Since Mexico had refused to stop its war with Texas, he said, no other alternative was left the executive but to invite Texas to conclude a treaty of annexation. Mexico was still threatening war. The Senate had refused to ratify Tyler's treaty of annexation, thus, he said, passing the question to the American people. "A controlling majority of the people and a large majority of the States have declared in favor of immediate annexation," he said—the most specific reference to the outcome of a presidential election yet made in a State of the Union address. Congress responded, ratified the treaty, and annexed Texas to the Union in the waning months of Tyler's presidency. Florida joined the Union at nearly the same moment, and war loomed as Polk took office.

Meanwhile, Tyler, like his two predecessors Jackson and Van Buren, had thrust himself right into the middle of the controversies over banking, currency, and the economy. Thanks in part to the continuing Seminole War, the government was running a deficit when he came into office, and Congress during 1841 had authorized a $12 million loan. Having already vetoed a new Bank of the United States,

Tyler expressed some Jacksonian skepticism about private paper money in his first annual message in December 1841. The value of different bank notes, he said, now varied so much that it might be better to force banks that suspended specie payments into bankruptcy (the practice that did become the law of the land later in the century with many fateful results from 1872 until 1933). "In view of the great advantages which are allowed the corporators [sic], not among the least of which is the authority contained in most of their charters to make loans to three times the amount of their capital, thereby often deriving three times as much interest on the same amount of money as any individual is permitted by law to receive," he said, "no sufficient apology can be urged for a long-continued suspension of specie payments." Now he proposed a new federal authority, insulated from presidential control, which might issue notes redeemable in gold and silver up to the value of 75 percent of the annual national revenue. A year later, as economic difficulties continued, Tyler gave the most thorough survey of money and credit problems yet offered by a president. The nation had essentially balanced revenue and expenditure at $34 million, he said, including $8 million in payments on the revived public debt. But the country was still suffering, he argued, from excessive "bank capital and bank issues" in the years 1833–38, leading to excessive money, higher prices, and a boom and bust. Thanks largely to European loans, the circulation of banknotes had grown from $61 million in 1830 to $149 million in 1837. He repeated and elaborated his proposal for a new authority that would issue a new currency that would replace circulating Treasury notes. "The choice in the present state of public sentiment," he said, "lies between an exclusive specie currency on the one hand and Government issues of some kind on the other." Because some states had borrowed beyond their means for internal improvements, the country faced a credit crunch and couldn't raise the money it needed in Europe. Once again, however, Congress rejected his plan, and the Democrats regained control of the House by a 146–72 margin—an extraordinary gain of 49 seats—in the midterm elections.[2]

A year later Tyler reported an interesting and long-lasting innovation: the nation's fiscal year would now begin every July 1 and

---

2  The size of the House had been reduced from 242 to 223 members since 1840.

end on June 30. Not for another 133 years was the start of the year extended yet another three months to October 1, where it remains today. The country was still borrowing about $5 million a year, partly because of reductions in the tariff under Jackson and Van Buren, but the surplus of paper money, Tyler now reported, had been happily succeeded by the substitution of the precious metals and paper promptly redeemable in specie; "and thus false values have disappeared and a sounder condition of things has been introduced." He renewed his own currency proposals, while noting that the recovery made them less urgent. In his very last message he noted an extraordinary improvement in revenue. Even after paying $7 million in interest and $5 million in principal on the public debt, the Treasury expected a surplus of $7 million at the end of the fiscal year. Government bonds now traded above par, the currency was perfectly sound, and the difference in currency values between regions had been reduced to a trivial level. Like some of his predecessors, he now warned against a permanent surplus and called upon Congress to keep taxes low.

Tyler meanwhile had reported in 1842 that the war against the Seminoles in Florida appeared to be almost over, and praised the success of the continuing Indian policy. The tone of his last message leaves little doubt that he felt he had earned a second term, but his extraordinary talent for alienating the other leaders of his supposed party and of the nation had made that impossible. The coming war with Mexico for which he had helped lay the foundation—and which he would gladly have undertaken himself—would move the nation into a new and turbulent era, during which the questions of slavery and disunion would come to the fore.

Born in 1795, James K. Polk at forty-nine was the youngest man yet to assume the presidency. He was the first president from the Transcendental generation—the generation that gave the nation its civil war—and he spoke in his inaugural with the confidence of a man who had spent his whole adult life within an expanding and generally prosperous state. A Tennessean and protégé of Andrew Jackson—who died just before Polk took office—Polk had defeated Henry Clay by 170 electoral votes to 105 in Clay's third and last bid for the presidency in 1844, while promising to serve only one term. The Democrats kept healthy majorities of 142–79 in the

House and 34–22 in the Senate. Polk won by strongly supporting the annexation of Texas, which Clay refused to advocate, and endorsing the claim to the whole Oregon territory all the way to latitude 54' 40"—the border of Russian America. He presided over four critical years of US history, during which the country achieved nearly the complete frontiers of what became the first forty-eight states. Nor was this in any sense a coincidence. Polk's inaugural and annual messages display a keen historical sense, and a remarkably acute vision of his country's future and its emerging place in the world.

"If the more aged and experienced men who have filled the office of President of the United States even in the infancy of the Republic distrusted their ability to discharge the duties of that exalted station," Polk began his inaugural, "what ought not to be the apprehensions of one so much younger and less endowed now that our domain extends from ocean to ocean, that our people have so greatly increased in numbers, and at a time when so great diversity of opinion prevails in regard to the principles and policy which should characterize the administration of our Government?" Like all his predecessors, he lauded the country's extraordinary achievements, but also referred to the danger of disunion, even to quoting the famous toast of his idol Jackson, "Our Federal Union—it must be preserved." Schemes and agitations designed to destroy "domestic institutions existing in other sections—institutions which existed at the adoption of the Constitution and were recognized and protected by it," he added, would lead to the dissolution of the Union. He opposed any new national bank and called for the repayment of the public debt. Polk praised Congress's passage of the law that offered statehood to Texas, and declared in defiance of Mexican threats of war that the question of annexation concerned Texas and the United States alone. He also promised to "assert and maintain by all constitutional means the right of the United States to that portion of our territory which lies beyond the Rocky Mountains," including Oregon, to which he claimed "clear and unquestionable" title, ratified the presence of settlers.

The annexation of Texas and the subsequent war with Mexico dominated Polk's administration. In his first annual message in December 1845, he reported that both the government and people of Texas had accepted the terms of the Joint Resolution that John Tyler had sent them in the last days of his administration, and had written a state constitution. It remained only for the new Congress to pass a law incorporating Texas before next March 3, when its current government would cease to exist. This "bloodless achievement," whose territorial extent was bound to have a deep influence upon America, was without parallel, he said, in the history of the world. It had succeeded "despite . . . the diplomatic interference of European monarchies," including Great Britain and France. Unfortunately, he continued, no sooner had Congress passed the Joint Resolution than the Mexican government had broken off diplomatic relations and begun threatening and preparing for war. Texas had asked for help, and the United States had sent troops into the somewhat disputed territory between the Nueces River and the Rio Grande and a squadron of warships to the Mexican coast.[3] Mexico now threatened to attack unless Texas would renounce annexation to the US. Then Polk began laying the foundation for a war of tremendous expansion.

Earlier presidents, as we have seen, had routinely referred to American citizens' monetary claims against Mexico for loss of property, and regretted their inability as yet to settle them. Polk now recounted their history in much more detailed and angrier terms. Treaties of 1830 and 1843 had not led to any payments. Because Mexico was a fellow American Republic, he said, the US had indulged it in ways that it would not have done for a European power. Mexico, he concluded, had now offered to resume diplomatic relations, and he had dispatched a distinguished Louisianan to conduct them. The claims upon Mexico would soon provide a pretext not only for war, but also for the annexation of enormous territories.

Turning from one possible major war to another, Polk reviewed in similar detail the history of the Oregon question. Long negotiations had led to the conventions of 1816 and 1827, which had allowed citizens of both the US and Great Britain to settle anywhere in Oregon territory, the vast region bounded by the northern border of Mexican California in the south, the Pacific in the west, Russian America (later Alaska) at 54' 40" on the north, and the Rocky Mountains in the east. In the negotiations under Tyler the US had offered to set the border at the 49th parallel (already the US-Canada border east of the Rockies), but the British had wanted to extend

---

3 Following contemporary usage, Polk frequently referred to the Rio Grande as the Del Norte River.

that border only as far as its intersection with the Columbia River, which would then become the boundary all the way to the Pacific. The British had refused the offer of the 49th parallel again after Polk came into office, and now, he said, the US had asked for title to "the whole Oregon territory." In chilling diplomatic language, he disclaimed responsibility for the consequences of failure to reach an agreement. He complained that the US had not yet given legal protection to its citizens within the territory, as the British had done, even though our settlers were multiplying rapidly and giving themselves free institutions. Forcing the issue, he asked Congress to terminate the convention of 1827. The nation's enormous growth and rising greatness, he continued, "are attracting the attention of the powers of Europe, and lately the doctrine has been broached in some of them of a 'balance of power' on this continent to check our advancement." Quoting the Monroe Doctrine, he declared that we could not permit their interference, or any application of that European principle in North America. Polk had turned 1846 into perhaps the most fateful year yet in the history of the new nation.

Five months later, on May 11, 1846, Polk asked Congress to declare war on Mexico. That nation, he reported, had refused to receive the new envoy, and instead had "invaded our territory and shed the blood of our fellow-citizens on our own soil." In his detailed account, Polk said that General Herrera, the Mexican ruler, had refused to receive envoy John Slidell because he was threatened with revolution at home. General Paredes had seized power on December 30 and become president. Texas had already declared that its border extended to the Rio Grande, which Mexico disputed, and Polk had sent troops across the Nueces, commanded by General Zachary Taylor. Mexican troops had crossed the Rio Grande and surrounded some US cavalrymen, who had surrendered. Asking for an authorization to raise volunteers, Polk said that a "large and overpowering force" would be the best means of bringing the war to a prompt and satisfactory end. He was ready, he said, to start negotiations at any time. Congress declared war.

Just one month later, Polk submitted a new British proposal on the Oregon boundary to Congress in a very brief message. The British now offered the 49th parallel as the boundary with Canada, and he was prepared to accept. He made no specific recommendation, but asked for the Senate's views before signing the treaty, as

Washington, he said, had done more than once. Giving up the 54' 40" line, the Senate rapidly agreed. No two-front war would occur.

By the time Polk gave his next annual message on December 8, 1846, the Mexican War had become extremely controversial, with a number of Whigs—including young first-term congressman Abraham Lincoln of Illinois—arguing that Texas and the US had no right to the territory between the Nueces and the Rio Grande where the war had broken out. More significantly, the war was evidently unpopular among the electorate, which had given the Whigs a narrow 116–110 majority in the House while the Senate remained Democratic. Polk came out swinging. The view of the war as "unjust and unnecessary and as one of aggression on our part upon a weak and injured enemy" would "encourage" Mexico and protract the war, giving the Mexicans "aid and comfort"—an obvious reference to the treason clause of the Constitution. Then he surveyed once again the origins of the war, laying the foundation for his war aims.

The wrongs the US had suffered since Mexican independence, he now claimed, were "without a parallel in the history of modern civilized nations," and the US might have avoided the war by acting more firmly sooner. Other presidents, as we have seen, had frequently referred to US claims against Mexico and many other nations in different parts of the world, but Polk abandoned their calm and unspecific language. "Our citizens engaged in lawful commerce were imprisoned, their vessels seized, and our flag insulted in her ports. If money was wanted, the lawless seizure and confiscation of our merchant vessels and their cargoes was a ready resource, and if to accomplish their purposes it became necessary to imprison the owners, captains, and crews, it was done. Rulers superseded rulers in Mexico in rapid succession, but still there was no change in this system of depredation." Jackson had implied in 1837 that war might be justified, but the US had felt too much sympathy for the sister republic on its borders. Even after a new agreement failed to end outrages, we had let them begin hostilities.

Texas, Polk explained, had originally gone to the US in 1803 as part of the Louisiana Purchase, but had been ceded to Spain in 1819 as part of the Florida treaty. Mexico had claimed it in its 1824 constitution. It had encouraged US citizens to emigrate and they had lived happily under Mexican rule until a dictatorship established in 1835 abolished the state constitution. Texas's successful rebellion had followed, and the United States and other countries had recognized its independence. The Rio Grande had been the recognized border in 1803 when the US first acquired Texas, he said, and General Santa Anna had recognized it as the Texas border in the treaty that he signed as a prisoner in 1836. After the US finally decided on annexation, General Paredes had seized power on a war platform. Polk accused him of hoping to bring a European power into Mexico and admitted that the US had decided to try to remove him from power and had helped the exiled general Santa Anna to return from Cuba. Paredes had indeed fallen in August.

Polk turned to the course of the war. American warships had blockaded both Mexican coasts and American troops had won a series of victories in northern Mexico. That was not all. "By rapid movements, the province of New Mexico [comprising most of present-day New Mexico and Arizona], with Santa Fe, its capital, has been captured without bloodshed. . . . Our squadron in the Pacific, with the cooperation of a gallant officer of the Army and a small force hastily collected in that distant country, has acquired bloodless possession of the Californias [both upper and lower], and the American flag has been raised at every important point in that Province." Polk then hinted at a claim to these vast new territories, bigger than the entire original thirteen states. "The war has not been waged with a view to conquest," he claimed, but the US had prosecuted it vigorously "to obtain an honorable peace, and thereby secure ample indemnity for the expenses of the war" and "the previous injuries to our citizens." The US had also exercised the right and duty of conquerors to govern these occupied territories pending a peace, establishing temporary governments and "assimilating them as far as practicable to the free institutions of our own country." Little if any resistance was "apprehended," he said, from their inhabitants. So far Mexico had refused to make peace.

The situation remained unresolved when Polk delivered his next message to the divided Congress in December 1847. No nation, he claimed, had ever won so many glorious victories in so short a time, but the Mexicans still refused to make peace. Talks had opened in May as US troops advanced upon Mexico City, and the government had asked for large cessions of territory as an indemnity. The US had no choice, Polk argued—Mexico had no money to make good our claims, and the US would forfeit them if we signed a peace treaty without securing them. Congress, he said, would never have declared war and appropriated $10 million for it had they not expected an indemnity and they knew it could only consist of territory. "The doctrine of no territory is the doctrine of no indemnity," he said, and such a policy would mean that the war was wrong! Our negotiators had demanded the Rio Grande boundary to 32 degrees latitude and the provinces of New Mexico and the Californias—but they would be willing to do without Lower California. Mexico, he added, would never be able to hold on to these two provinces anyway, and some European power would inevitably try to secure them. This the United States could not permit. Polk bluntly laid out the enormous advantages offered by these provinces. "If brought under the government of our laws their resources—mineral, agricultural, manufacturing and commercial—would soon be developed." The California harbors would open to us the commerce of the Far East. The provinces contained only "an inconsiderable portion of the Mexican people." (The 1850 census would count 62,000 New Mexicans and 92,000 Californians, the latter figure much swollen by the gold rush.) Polk asked for the immediate establishment of territorial governments in both provinces. Meanwhile, the nation must continue its occupation of most of Mexico and levy heavy military contributions to try to force the Mexican government to agree to peace. He was willing to help the Mexicans reestablish free republican institutions, but a simple withdrawal would lead to endless guerrilla warfare and European intervention.

After lengthy and difficult negotiations during which Polk's commissioner, N. P. Trist, sometimes exceeded his instructions, Polk submitted a treaty with the Mexican government securing his territorial objectives on February 22, 1848. He recommended its ratification, with the exception of one article, and the Senate agreed to it after a long debate in early July. Polk did not stand for reelection, keeping an 1844 promise to serve only one term, and General Zachary Taylor had now been elected to succeed him from the Whig Party, confirming how controversial the war had been.

Polk's last annual address was an enormous survey of matters both foreign and domestic—the longest annual message yet delivered by a president. Since the treaty's conclusion, he said, relations with Mexico had been "of the most friendly character." The war, he said, had impressed both Americans and foreigners alike with its evidence of US military strength, based upon "a volunteer army of citizen soldiers," raised "without drafts or conscriptions." Men of every profession had volunteered for the army. In contrast to the War of 1812, this one had proven beyond all doubt "that a popular representative government is equal to any emergency which is likely to arise in the affairs of a nation." Then he reviewed the extraordinary transformation of the United States during the previous four years.

Oregon to the 49th parallel, he noted, was "all that was insisted on by any of my predecessors"—albeit far short of what his party had demanded in 1844. With the addition of Texas, New Mexico, and Upper California, "the United States are now estimated to be nearly as large as the whole of Europe." Texas, including major tributaries of the Mississippi, would have remained a danger outside the United States, New Mexico had "much fertile land" and "rich mines of the precious metals," and California, he said prophetically, could be compared in significance to the Louisiana Territory in 1803. One could not yet estimate its wealth, and it would "command" the rich commerce with Asia, the Pacific islands, and the whole Pacific coast of the Americas. "A great emporium will doubtless speedily arise on the Californian coast"—probably on San Francisco Bay—"which may be destined to rival in importance New Orleans itself." The discovery of gold in California, he noted, had created an enormous labor shortage there, as the whole male population, including deserting soldiers and sailors, went inland to try their luck. Polk had to note, however, that the Congress in its recent session had failed to establish much-needed territorial governments in California or New Mexico because of a huge controversy over slavery in those territories. We must not, he said, allow controversies of "a domestic question which is coeval with the existence of our Government itself" to stand in the way of this step. He saw clearly that the future of the Union was at stake, and its failure would delight those who would perpetuate "thrones and monarchical or aristocratical [sic] principles." The army had numbered men "from slaveholding and nonslaveholding states," and the two sections, he declared, must compromise on this issue. Although Polk obviously would have preferred to leave the issue alone, he now became the first president to take a stand on the critical issue of the next dozen years, the extension of slavery into new territories.

Climate and other factors, he argued, made it quite unlikely that slavery would ever thrive in New Mexico or California. Still, he argued, Congress did not need to legislate on this question, and some argued that it had no power to do so. He favored leaving the issue to the people of these territories acting in convention. "Noninterference," he thought, was the true doctrine of the Constitution on this question, but "upon a great emergency, and under menacing dangers to the Union, the Missouri compromise in respect to slavery was adopted," drawing the line of 36' 30" between slave and free states. That line had been extended farther west when Texas joined the Union, and Polk suggested extending it to the Pacific. In any case, territorial government in California and New Mexico could not wait. If the US took full advantage of its new territory, he predicted, "the present generation" might live to see New York replace London and other European capitals as the center of the commercial and monetary power of the world. Meanwhile, in each of his annual messages, Polk reported on new treaties that had secured more Indian land within the United States and moved more Indians west of the Mississippi, where they were progressing, he said, in both education and agriculture. The slavery question—and more specifically, whether Congress could in fact forbid slavery in any new territory—had also stopped the creation of a territorial government for the vast Oregon Territory in 1847, and in this last message in 1848, Polk complained that this failure—now recently corrected—had led to the outbreak of an Indian war, one that such a government would have been able to prevent by making a treaty with the Indian tribes.[4]

Polk in this final message also applauded the dramatic events taking place in Europe, where a revolution in France in February 1848 had rapidly spread into Germany, Italy, and various provinces of the Austrian empire. "The Government and people of the United States hailed with enthusiasm and delight the establishment of the French Republic," he said, "as we now hail the efforts in progress to unite the States of Germany in a confederation similar in many respects to our own Federal Union. If the great and enlightened German States, occupying, as they do, a central and commanding

---

4 Oregon at that time included the future states of Oregon, Washington, and much of Idaho and Montana.

position in Europe, shall succeed in establishing such a confederated government, securing at the same time to the citizens of each State local governments adapted to the peculiar condition of each, with unrestricted trade and intercourse with each other, it will be an important era in the history of human events. Whilst it will consolidate and strengthen the power of Germany, it must essentially promote the cause of peace, commerce, civilization, and constitutional liberty throughout the world." Britain had also made a fateful change in policy in 1846, eliminating its duties on imported grain, and leading to dramatic increases in American exports. Alas, within another year, the election of Louis Napoleon Bonaparte as French president, foreshadowing the return of the French Empire, had dashed such hopes in France, and a resurgent Prussian government had crushed the German revolutionary movement as well. In the long run, however, Polk's hopes for the spread of democracy in Europe were destined to come true. The settlers in Texas had brought about the war that expanded the nation to its new limits, but Polk saw more clearly than any earlier president the coming of the American century.

This was not all. Polk's administration also won the last great triumphs for Jacksonian economic theories at home, including lower tariffs and a new independent treasury.

In his first annual message of December 1845, Polk gave figures for gross and net US imports ($102 million net) and exports ($99 million net) during the fiscal year that had ended in June, the first president to do so. The Treasury had taken in $29.8 million and spent $30 million, and held a balance of $7.7 million, with a public debt of $17.1 million. Calling in good Jacksonian fashion for the earliest possible liquidation of the debt, he explained that the money had remained in the Treasury because of the Mexican emergency. Then he made two sweeping proposals.

Without using the modern economic term "diminishing returns," Polk argued that the existing tariff—passed in 1842 by the narrowest of congressional margins—held down both trade and revenue, since some duties were so high that they shut out imports altogether. The tariff must be limited to the rate necessary for revenue, he argued, and there should be no or very low duties on articles of mass consumption. Some rates now favored the rich against the poor, and the whole system burdened everyone except "the capitalist who has made his investments in manufactures." He proposed the abolition of all fixed duties in favor of a uniform *ad valorem* tariff—a fixed percentage of the value of the imported goods.

Polk then took a long historical look at the issues of banking and public finance. Echoing Van Buren—whose Subtreasury had been abolished under Harrison—he called for a new Independent Treasury, the kind of institution which, he thought, the founders had foreseen, which would keep federal moneys in public hands, rather than putting them in banks. Banks had proven "faithless" in earlier crises, he said, and the government had faced a crisis under Van Buren when the banks stopped meeting their obligations. Polk's new treasury would not issue paper or make loans, and it would receive payments only in specie. The people and their government, he argued, must keep their money in their own hands in order to govern themselves. Polk also proposed reductions in the price of public lands that had not attracted buyers at the current price, and measures to prevent financial institutions from buying land that settlers had already occupied.

A year later, in December 1846, Polk reported that reduced tariff rates agreed upon in the last session had now gone into effect, and celebrated their impact. Some of the previous rates, he repeated, favored only "the comparatively few who had invested their capital in manufactures." Previous rates were too low on luxuries and too high on necessities, and the rich were now paying "a just proportion of taxes" necessary for the support of the government. Britain, he reported, had taken a similar step by repealing its Corn Laws and lowering other duties. "After ages of experience the statesmen of that country have been constrained by a stern necessity and by a public opinion having its deep foundation in the sufferings and wants of impoverished millions to abandon a system the effect of which was to build up immense fortunes in the hands of the few and to reduce the laboring millions to pauperism and misery." Their protected classes, like our own, had given up only after a long struggle. This was probably the most specific comment on the domestic politics of another nation yet uttered by a president. Our farmers, "a large majority of our population," had benefited the most, but everyone prospered when they did. They could now supply "not only the home demand, but the deficiencies of food required by the whole world." He also noted that Congress had created his Independent Treasury.

In December 1847 Polk proudly reported that net imports had risen to $138.5 million and net exports to $150.6 million, a 50 percent increase in just two years. Customs revenue was also on pace to increase from $23 million to $31.5 million despite lower rates. Driven by the ongoing war, expenditures had totaled $59.5 million in the last fiscal year, with revenues just $26.3 million, and the public debt had reached $45.7 million, with $18.5 million in new loans anticipated in the next eighteen months. The new Independent Treasury accepted nothing but specie, and it had handled the increased receipts and expenditures perfectly well. Thanks largely to exports to Britain, the nation had imported $22.3 million in specie in the past year, and much of it had been coined by the mint and circulated instead of finding its way into bank vaults. He continued to argue for easier terms on public lands, as well. With its increased commerce, the US might soon have the world's largest merchant marine. Polk had emerged as a prophet of economic growth through trade—the first presidential proponent of what came to be called globalization.

Delivering his last message in December 1848 after the Whig victory in the election, Polk combined another proud survey of his term with a veritable jeremiad against any new deviation from the Jacksonian path. Both net imports and net exports had increased again, to $133.8 million and $132.9 million, and Treasury receipts totaled $57 million, including $20.7 from loans and Treasury notes. The new "constitutional treasury" was still working well, he claimed, and for the first time—according to Polk—a severe economic crisis in Europe had not spread to the US, because the vast imported specie in the previous year had not gone into bank vaults and fueled a new round of reckless expansion of paper currency.[5] The public debt had reached $65.8 million but he thought it might rapidly be paid off. He also warned in heated terms of the dangers of returning to the policies of the Madison and Monroe administrations after the War of 1812—the "unconstitutional" enlargement of federal powers under

---

[5] Polk's analysis of the workings of his Independent Treasury was confirmed decades later by David Kinley, *The History, Organization and Influence of the Independent Treasury of the United States* (New York, 1893).

the "American system," including a national bank. "The authors of the system drew their ideas of political economy from what they had witnessed in Europe, and particularly in Great Britain. They had viewed the enormous wealth concentrated in few hands and had seen the splendor of the overgrown establishments of an aristocracy which was upheld by the restrictive policy. They forgot to look down upon the poorer classes of the English population, upon whose daily and yearly labor the great establishments they so much admired were sustained and supported." They too had wanted to create an aristocracy of wealth with the help of a national bank, a high protective tariff, and a large national debt. The Constitution clearly outlawed all this, he argued, and it was only after great hesitation, and under the pressure of national financial embarrassment, that Washington in 1791 had agreed to the first Bank of the United States, and that Madison in 1816 had agreed to a new one. The banks had made the rich richer and the poor poorer—"an organized money power, which resisted the popular will and sought to shape and control the public policy." Now the nation had learned "that banks, national or State, are not necessary as fiscal agents to the Government." Internal improvements—a centerpiece of Whig policies for which he had vetoed two bills—remained dangerous, a lever that could open the way to the return to the whole American system. He then made a long defense of the veto power as such, designed, he said, as a check on popular passion, and a means of protecting the smaller states.

"During the period I have administered the executive department of the Government great and important questions of public policy, foreign and domestic, have arisen, upon which it was my duty to act," he concluded. "It may, indeed, be truly said that my Administration has fallen upon eventful times. I have felt most sensibly the weight of the high responsibilities devolved upon me." Polk died of cholera just a few months after leaving office. Two years later, the 1850 census counted 23 million inhabitants of the country, compared to 17 million in 1840—a 35.9 percent increase—and 13 million in 1830. Polk had rightly predicted that the United States would become the world's leading nation. But the acquisitions of California and New Mexico—whose future status he had not been able to resolve—set off the controversy over slavery that would shortly plunge the country into disunion and civil war.

# VII

## ZACHARY TAYLOR, MILLARD FILLMORE, FRANKLIN PIERCE, AND JAMES BUCHANAN

### 1849–61

Having won their first presidential election in 1840 behind military hero William Henry Harrison and lost in 1832 and 1844 behind their greatest statesman, Henry Clay, the Whigs in 1848 had won again with Mexican War hero General Zachary Taylor, a Kentuckian. Even though much of his Whig Party had opposed the Mexican War, Taylor and his vice president, the obscure New Yorker Millard Fillmore, defeated Democrat Lewis Cass of Michigan by 163 electoral votes to 127 and a 5 percent margin in the popular vote. The Democrats won a 113–106 plurality in the House, where minor parties held 13 seats, and elected the new Speaker only after 63 ballots, while retaining a 33–22 margin in the Senate. Taylor represented a generational step backward, being a full eleven years older than Polk. The first career professional soldier to reach the White House, he entered office in the midst of a deepening crisis over the related issues of the future of California and New Mexico, the power of Congress over slavery, and the preservation of the Union. His inaugural, however—the shortest ever delivered to date—gave not a single clue as to his policy preferences on any major issue.

Taylor's one annual message in December 1849 began with some comments on the confused European situation. The United States had reached a new agreement with Britain promising completely equal treatment of each other's ships in all their ports. Taylor had stopped the construction of a warship which the new would-be German Empire, headquartered in Frankfurt, had hoped to use against Denmark in a conflict over the duchies of Schleswig and Holstein, because it would violate US neutrality. More recently, as the Kingdom of Prussia and other German states moved to crush the revolution that had created the new regime in Frankfurt, he had closed the new Frankfurt legation and sent US diplomats to Prussia instead. Recognizing his countrymen's sympathy for the Magyars or ethnic Hungarians, he had sent a representative to Europe with instructions to open relations with an independent Hungary if its fight for independence from Austria succeeded, but instead, Russian intervention had crushed the revolt. The US's gentle attempts to encourage European democracy had failed.

Closer to home, Taylor reported negotiations with Nicaragua for a treaty that might lead to the construction of a canal between the Atlantic and the Pacific—one that the US, he said, could not allow any other power to control. The Mexican Isthmus of Tehuantepec, which the Mexican government had refused to sell, and Panama, were other possible canal sites, and a railroad across Panama was already under construction, a key link in communications with California. He also asserted the country's natural interest in the Sandwich (Hawaiian) Islands, and reported that some Americans were privately trying to "Christianize" the natives, and induce them "to adopt a system of government and laws suited to their capacity and wants." They too must be kept out of foreign hands. Taylor was pointing down a path that the government would intermittently follow to its end over the next half century.

The peace treaty with Mexico mandated large continuing payments to the Mexican government to "purchase" California and New Mexico, Taylor reported, and these would create federal budget deficits of $5–10 million in each of the next two years, which loans must cover. A good Whig, he asked for higher tariffs and unspecified revisions of the Subtreasury system. At length he turned to the most pressing issue. California had now called a convention and written a constitution and would soon apply for admission to the Union. Taylor recommended approval without mentioning that that constitution banned slavery from the state. He expected New Mexico to follow suit shortly, and he recommended allowing them both to write their own laws rather than worsening a national controversy over "those exciting topics of a sectional character which have hitherto produced painful apprehensions in the public mind." Looking ahead, he called for a new mint in California to coin the plentiful gold, and a survey for a possible transcontinental railroad. He concluded with a vigorous plea to preserve the Union.

During 1850 that task fell to Congress more than to the president, and the aging Whig statesman Henry Clay took the lead. The compromise bills he introduced admitted California as a free state; authorized the creation of a new territory of New Mexico without any restrictions on slavery; banned the slave trade (but not slaveholding) within the District of Columbia; and imposed heavy new obligations on the northern states to return fugitive slaves. Abolitionists from the North and fire-eaters from the South led by the dying John C. Calhoun opposed the compromise, preferring to let the slavery issue come to a head and face secession and war, and Taylor had not taken a stand on it when he died suddenly of cholera in July 1850. It fell to his successor Millard Fillmore to sign the bills when they passed later in the year, and he did.

Born in 1800, Fillmore had served in Congress from 1835 through 1843, rising in the Byzantine politics of the Empire State. He had hoped to become Henry Clay's running mate in 1844, but another New Yorker got the nod. He remained active in New York politics and won statewide office in 1847. He proved the right man in the right place at the Whig convention of 1848, in which Taylor had defeated the luckless Henry Clay. He was the fifth vice president from New York, the largest swing state.

Five fateful months after succeeding Taylor, in December 1850, Fillmore asked Congress to regard his first annual message as his inaugural address. He referred immediately to the great slavery controversy. "It was hardly to have been expected," he said, "that the series of measures passed at your last session with the view of healing the sectional differences which had sprung from the slavery and territorial questions should at once have realized their beneficent purpose." Compromise was "unwelcome to men of extreme opinions," but he endorsed these measures, "a final settlement of the dangerous and exciting subjects which they embraced," and exhorted his countrymen to accept them. In his three messages, Fillmore, the only Whig politician to become president, emerged as the only real White House spokesman that that party ever had.

In foreign affairs, Fillmore reported on several different attempts to expand the influence of his expanding nation in the world at large. In his first message, delivered in December 1850 as the monarchs of Europe finished crushing the revolutions that had convulsed much of the continent, he reaffirmed the right of every nation to manage its internal affairs according to its will, and renounced any attempts to maintain a balance of power, or to instigate revolutions. He did, however, secure the release of Hungarian revolutionary Louis Kossuth from detention in the Ottoman Empire and gave him asylum in the US. A year later, he referred to unspecified calls upon the now-powerful nation to abandon Washington's policy of staying out of European entanglements, partly because of the advent of steam navigation. "It is said that we ought to interfere between contending sovereigns and their subjects for the purpose of overthrowing the monarchies of Europe and establishing in their place republican institutions. . . . This is a most seductive but dangerous appeal to the generous sympathies of freemen." France, he noted, had come to grief at the time of its revolution because of its attempts to spread it. Revolutions did not always establish freedom, and the United States had had free institutions before its own.

Fillmore's second focus was the Caribbean, where the United States was pursuing intermittent talks with the government of Nicaragua, the Indians of the Mosquito Coast, and the Mexican government regarding various different railroads or canals across the Central American isthmus. In December 1851, he reported in great detail on an extraordinary incident in Cuba—an invasion by a private American force earlier in that year that eerily foreshadowed the Bay of Pigs landing 110 years later. Southern slaveholders had begun to covet Cuba as a possible addition to the US, and thought they could take advantage of a revolution against its Spanish rulers to secure it. Working in New Orleans, they sold "Cuban bonds" to finance their expedition, set sail, and landed near Havana. Like their 1961 counterparts, they found that reports of revolution were greatly exaggerated, and the authorities captured, tried and executed nearly all of them in short order. Although Fillmore was now trying to secure the release of a few remaining prisoners, he expressed no sympathy whatever for what they had done, declared that they had "forfeited the protection of their country," and asked Congress for new legislation against such outrages. Cuba remained an issue a year later, and in his last message Fillmore opposed adding it to the United States, a step that would add "a population of a different national stock, speaking a different language, and not likely to harmonize with the other members," while reviving the whole controversy over slavery. And in that same last message, he announced the dispatch of Commodore Perry's naval force on a mission to Japan, to ask its government to relax the "inhospitable and antisocial system" that it had maintained for two centuries, while insisting that the mission was friendly and peaceful.

Meanwhile, higher revenues allowed the government to run an annual surplus of $5 million or so with revenues and expenditures in the neighborhood of $50 million, and continued to reduce the public debt. Major debt items included multimillion-dollar payments to Mexico to complete the Treaty of Guadalupe Hidalgo, and to Texas, which had given up its claim to the Rio Grande as its western boundary and accepted the borders that it enjoys today in exchange for cash payments. Imports began to outrun exports, with specie, led by California gold, making up the difference. In fiscal year 1852, his last in office, imports reached $207 million worth of goods and exports $186 million—including $37.2 million of specie. Europe had recovered from its famines of the 1840s, and agricultural exports had fallen accordingly. In December 1851 Fillmore warned that the flood of gold was fueling inflation and speculation threatening disastrous consequences as in the past, but these turned out to be some years away. In December 1850 Fillmore also called in good Whig fashion for changes in the tariff to favor industry, and force foreign manufacturers to lower their prices to compete. He also wanted to move from *ad valorem* tariffs to specific duties, not least because the *ad valorem* rates had turned out to encourage fraudulent reports of value. He repeated that proposal the next year, but without result.

An estimated 124,000 Indians within the newly acquired territories of Texas, New Mexico and California worried Fillmore, and he called for more US cavalry to deal with them in his December 1850 message. The tribes of Texas and New Mexico were "a constant source of terror and annoyance," devastating farms, destroying crops, occasionally committing murders, and making transportation difficult. Two years later he complained that Congress had failed to ratify treaties with tribes in California and Oregon that would have confined them to specific territories. Texas, which claimed all the land inside its borders for white settlers, had also refused to do so. 8,000 soldiers of the 11,000-man army were now defending Texas and New Mexico against hostile tribes

In December 1851 Fillmore had to report that in one respect, at least, the Compromise of 1850 had failed to quiet the nation. In some northern locales, violent mobs had obstructed the execution of the new Fugitive Slave Act. Defending the act, Fillmore accused the opponents of trying to overturn the Constitution and "rend asunder this Union." He pleaded with his countrymen to respect that compromise until such time as changes in the settlement had proven to be necessary. The Whig Party did not apparently regard Fillmore as a candidate of national appeal, and at the 1852 convention they replaced him with yet another general, the aged Winfield Scott, who had first distinguished himself in the War of 1812 and shared the command with Taylor in the Mexican War. Scott lost to Democrat Franklin Pierce in a landslide, and both the slavery controversy and the role of the presidency itself soon entered into a new phase.

The Democratic Party, divided into many factions and hamstrung by the rule that required a two-thirds majority to nominate a candidate for president, had turned to Franklin Pierce, a former congressman and senator from New Hampshire, partly because so few people knew anything about him. He too had served in the Mexican War, and his relative youth—he was forty-seven—had trumped the appeal of the aged Winfield Scott, who carried only four states. The Democrats simultaneously increased their House majority to 150–68, with 27 seats held by splinter parties, and had an effective 35–21 majority in the Senate. Pierce's inaugural address had echoes of James K. Polk, whom he had known in the House of Representatives. He began it with nationalism, noting that many on both sides of the Atlantic were speculating about the growing power of the United States. Separating himself from the faction of his party that favored active intervention to promote democracy in Europe, he proposed "sympathy, encouragement and hopes" for others favoring "rational liberty," but advocated leadership by example. He called openly for the acquisition of unspecified possessions "not within our jurisdiction," not only for the protection of the US, but for the sake of world commerce— all for the sake of the distant future as well as the urgent present.

That formulation might have included both Cuba, which Pierce coveted, and the Hawaiian Islands. Meanwhile, he reaffirmed the Monroe Doctrine's rejection of any new foreign colonization within the hemisphere.

Reaffirming another Jacksonian principle, Pierce pledged economy in government, but surprisingly promised to keep politics out of appointments. He also promised to keep the federal government strictly within the limits of its powers, as a means to maintain concord "in regard to the questions which have most seriously disturbed public tranquility." Then he stated, as no other president had done, the southern position on slavery. He believed "that involuntary servitude, as it exists in different States of this Confederacy, is recognized by the Constitution. I believe that it stands like any other admitted right, and that the States where it exists are entitled to efficient remedies to enforce the constitutional provisions"—a clear reference to the Fugitive Slave Act, which should be "cheerfully" obeyed. Just a year later, however, the young Democratic senator Stephen Douglas of Illinois persuaded Pierce to help overturn the earlier Missouri Compromise, with fateful results.

Although Pierce failed to negotiate the acquisition of Cuba with Spain, he took a consistently strong nationalist line in foreign affairs. He sent William Gadsden, a South Carolina railroad magnate who wanted eventually to build a transcontinental railroad on a southern route, to Mexico to haggle over the unresolved boundary between New Mexico territory and Mexico proper. He negotiated the Gadsden Purchase, which gave the US a new strip of land in what is now southern New Mexico and Arizona that would be critical to such a railroad in exchange for $15 million. Pierce submitted the treaty to the Senate on February 10, 1854, and it ratified it later that year. The expansion into the West collided with new Indian tribes, and massacres led Pierce to ask in December 1854 for an expansion of the army. A year later, new regiments were in the field.

A dispute with Britain over US rights to Canadian fisheries had broken out in the last year of the Fillmore administration, and Pierce discussed it in his first annual message in December 1853, and reported that it had been settled a year later. The Crimean War between Britain and France on the one hand and Russia on the other had broken out during 1854, and gave the US another opportunity to press its view of neutral rights at sea, which would allow any neutral to carry any goods except military contraband within its own ships to any belligerent port. The British and French observed this principle during the current war but refused to recognize it as binding. Eventually European negotiations led to the Declaration of Paris in 1856, which adopted the US view of neutral rights but also insisted on the abolition of privateering. Pierce refused to agree to that, as he explained in his annual messages of December 1854 and December 1856, because the United States might need once again to resort to privateering against the much stronger British Navy. More trouble with Britain arose during 1855. Pierce accused the British of violating the 1850 agreement between the two powers on Central America, in which, he said, London had promised not to try to occupy or assume sovereignty over any part of the region. Now strengthening their positions in "Balize" (later British Honduras) and on the Mosquito Coast, the British argued that these were preexisting positions not covered by the treaty. They had also been actively recruiting American men to fight in the Crimean War, in violation of US law. A year later, in his last message, Pierce said that the enlistment question was settled and a satisfactory new treaty on Central America was on its way. Meanwhile, any progress on the Nicaraguan canal project had halted because that small nation now had two competing governments, and the government of New Granada (later Columbia) had imposed prohibitive duties on traffic on the new railway across Panama. A government-inspired mob had violently attacked the railroad company there, and the US had stationed warships in the harbors of Panama City and Aspinall to protect US interests. And at the other end of the world, Pierce reported in December 1854 that Perry's treaty had opened up two Japanese ports to American trade.

The budget surplus Pierce inherited from Fillmore continued to grow, and revenue set a new record of $73.9 million in fiscal 1856. Despite the $3 million annual payments to Mexico to complete the Gadsden Purchase and further payments to Texas, Pierce's administration reduced the public debt from $69.2 million to $31 million at the end of his term. In good Jacksonian fashion, Pierce proposed paying it off as soon as possible and called for lower tariffs that would provide for the normal expenditures of $48–50 million. The rapid growth and expansion of the nation now put another economic issue on the table, federal land grants for new railroads.

After favoring them in his first message and promising surveyors' reports on transcontinental railroad routes, Pierce in December 1854 declared that he had withdrawn 30 million acres previously reserved for that purpose. The United States now had 17,000 miles of railroads, many of which were operating so far below capacity as to be threatened by bankruptcy. Rather than encouraging new and extravagant hopes of expansion, he preferred to leave the issue to the states. This was the beginning of a very long story. He was equally skeptical about internal improvements generally.

In his first message, Pierce pointed out that the population of the United States had been doubling every twenty-five years or so, reaching 23.2 million in the 1850 census. With health improving and further immigration from Europe, Asia, and Latin America, the country might maintain that rate for fifty to one hundred years, and some of his adult listeners would live to see the population top 100 million. That turned out to be exaggerated: population reached just 76.1 million in 1900 because birth rates declined after the Civil War. "It is evident," he said, "that a confederation so vast and so varied, both in numbers and in territorial extent, in habits and in interests, could only be kept in national cohesion by the strictest fidelity to the principles of the Constitution as understood by those who have adhered to the most restricted construction of the powers granted by the people and the States," who must in turn "cultivate a fraternal and affectionate spirit, language and conduct in regard to other states." In that very same month, however, Pierce agreed to Democratic senator Stephen Douglas's plans for two new territories, Kansas and Nebraska—plans that rent the nation asunder over the slavery question as never before.

The Missouri Compromise of 1820, which allowed Missouri to enter as a slave state while outlawing slavery north of its southern boundary of latitude 36' 30", had been so divisive that President Monroe, who signed it, had never even referred to it in an annual message. Polk in his last annual message had suggested that the Missouri Compromise had been an emergency measure of dubious constitutionality, but had simultaneously suggested extending the line all the way to the Pacific to settle the controversy over California and New Mexico. Douglas and other Democrats, with Pierce's blessing, now proposed to organize two new territories, Kansas and Nebraska, and leave the question of slavery in those territories to their settlers, explicitly repealing the prohibition north of 36' 30". Their bill passed only after a lengthy and violent debate, and utterly transformed the political landscape, especially in the North. Douglas and Pierce apparently did not understand that northern voters opposed further extensions of slavery. In the 1854 midterms the Democrats shrank from 150 House members to 83. They faced 54 remaining Whigs, 51 anti-slavery members of the American or Know Nothing Party, 31 Anti-Nebraskans—former Democrats who opposed the new act—1 Free Soiler, and 13 members of the newly formed Republican Party, which also opposed extending slavery in the territories. The sole Free Soiler, Nathaniel Banks of Massachusetts, was elected Speaker of the new House by a mere plurality after a struggle lasting two months and 133 ballots. Pierce in response doubled down on the southern position.

By the time Pierce gave his third annual message on December 31, 1855, he had become the first presidential spokesman for the new militant southern view of slavery and the history of the young Republic. The American Revolution, he said, resulted in "the foundation of a Federal Republic of the free white men of the colonies, constituted, as they were, in distinct and reciprocally independent State governments. As for the subject races, whether Indian or African, the wise and brave statesmen of that day, being engaged in no extravagant scheme of social change, left them as they were, and thus preserved themselves and their posterity from the anarchy and the ever-recurring civil wars which have prevailed in other revolutionized European colonies of America." Never before had any president in such a message distinguished so bluntly among Americans of different races or asserted the superiority of his own. The "larger relative colored population" distinguished, more than anything else, the southern from the northern states, and while this population, "held in subjection," might cease to exist in some states—as indeed it had—it might increase in others. "The general safeguard of the Union against either invasion or domestic violence," he argued, included a promise to defend slavery, but now, attempts in some states to impose their views upon others had turned "friendly states" into "distracted, hostile ones." Although the northern states could not heal their own "social evils," they were trying to reform the institutions of others. He rejected northern claims of unequal treatment, arguing that the pre-constitutional Northwest

Ordinance of 1787, banning slavery from the territory between the Ohio and the Mississippi, had been pushed by Virginians—yet adding that its validity had lapsed when the Constitution was adopted! The nation had added Louisiana, Florida and Texas for the benefit of all, not merely the North or the South.

Pierce questioned the legality of the Missouri Compromise and defended the right to repeal it. The Compromise of 1850 had left the slavery question to the people of California, New Mexico, and recently organized Utah, and had also given the federal government a new role in the return of fugitive slaves. Congress had naturally treated the new territories of Kansas and Nebraska in the same way. The repeal of the Missouri Compromise confirmed that no part of the United States could use the federal government "to dictate the social institutions of any other portion," and no new state could be refused admission because some older ones disliked its institutions. He concluded with an attack on the abolitionists—without using that word—who "have so surrendered themselves to a fanatical devotion to the supposed interests of the relatively few Africans in the United States as totally to abandon and disregard the interests of the 25,000,000 Americans." "The unshaken rock of the Constitution" would surely stand firm against "all the wild and chimerical schemes of social change which are generated one after another in the unstable minds of visionary sophists and interested agitators." Although the Dred Scott case was slightly more than a year away from its decision, Justice Taney's reasoning had evidently already become the orthodoxy of the Democratic Party.

Pierce in this message did not discuss the actual situation in Kansas, where rival factions of pro- and anti-slavery settlers had already formed separate governments in separate capitals while drawing on various forms of support from outside the state. The pro-slavery forces had won several elections with the help of large numbers of voters temporarily imported from Missouri. In a lengthy message about a month later, however, on January 24, 1856, he blamed the trouble on the abolitionists' "extraordinary measure of propagandist colonization of the Territory of Kansas," which had provoked a contrary reaction in Missouri, and declared an anti-slavery government illegal and insurrectionary. Later in the year he dispatched federal troops to preserve order, but the future of Kansas remained very much unsettled when he left office.

By the time the Democratic Party convention met in the summer of 1856, the Whig Party was dead, and the Democrats knew they would be facing an opponent from the new Republican Party, formed to oppose any extension of slavery into new territories. Pierce became the first sitting president ever denied renomination by his own party, largely because the nation was frightened by the violence that his policies had unleashed in Kansas. The elderly James Buchanan, his minister to Great Britain and formerly secretary of state under James K. Polk, replaced him, and defeated the Republican candidate John C. Frémont, whose election would probably have led to the immediate secession of some southern states. Buchanan had won just 45.3 percent of the vote against the Republicans and the anti-slavery Know Nothing Party and its candidate former president Millard Fillmore, but the Democrats also regained control of the House with 132 seats against 90 Republicans and 14 Know Nothings. Pierce in his final annual message in December 1856 treated the election as a complete vindication. The people had "maintained the inviolability of the constitutional rights of the different sections of the Union" and "emphatically rejected . . . mere geographical parties." Some new associations—by which he clearly meant the Republican Party—pretended only to oppose the extension of slavery into the territories, but "are really inflamed with desire to change the domestic institutions of existing States." Their object—abolition—could only be accomplished at the cost of "burning cities, and ravaged fields, and slaughtered populations, and all there is most terrible in foreign complicated with civil and servile war." Many good citizens had fallen prey to passion, sectional prejudice, and reciprocal hatred. The voice of the people had pointedly rebuked "the attempt of a portion of the States, by a sectional organization and movement, to usurp the control of the Government of the United States." Many states had passed laws "forbidding their officers, under the severest penalties, to participate in the execution of any act of Congress whatever" in order to defeat the Fugitive Slave law. He repeated the entire review of the history of the slavery question that he had given a year earlier. Claiming (falsely as it turned out) that federal troops had quieted the situation in Kansas, he made clear that he hoped that the territory would continue to allow slavery. He concluded with the hope that the nation might now turn to this generation's task, "maintaining and extending the national power." It was not to be.

Since James K. Polk, the roster of presidents had alternated quite regularly between those born in the eighteenth century and those born in the nineteenth. Thus Taylor (from the eighteenth) had succeeded Polk (nineteenth), followed by Fillmore (nineteenth) and Pierce (nineteenth.) Buchanan, born in 1791, became the oldest man to take office as president in 1857, at sixty-six, and the first to turn seventy in office. A lawyer from Pennsylvania, he had served in the War of 1812 and switched from a Federalist to a Jacksonian Democrat. He had won seats in both the House and the Senate. Like the two Adamses and Thomas Jefferson, he had also spent several years in Europe representing the United States, first in St. Petersburg and then, under Pierce, as minister to the Court of St. James, the senior diplomat in Great Britain. As president, Buchanan presided over four highly contentious years dominated by crises in Kansas over slavery and increasing antagonism between the North and South, and historians have given low marks to his presidency. His annual messages, however, reveal him to be a thoughtful man of a powerful intellect, who had formed and shared strong and often acute opinions on almost every major subject, and who took, or proposed, vigorous actions on several fronts. Congress, paralyzed by partisanship, rarely responded.

After renouncing a second term at the outset of his inaugural address, Buchanan began exactly where Pierce had left off three months earlier, congratulating the nation for ending the controversy (as he saw it) over slavery in the territories by electing himself and Democratic majorities, and expressing the hope that the argument might die along with the "geographical parties" that it had spawned. "All agree that under the Constitution slavery in the States is beyond the reach of any human power except that of the respective States themselves wherein it exists," he declared inaccurately, and the twenty years of controversy over this question had been "the prolific source of great evils to the master, to the slave, and to the whole country." Moving on, he decried the large budget surplus and advocated appropriating it to "great national objects" with a clear constitutional warrant, such as the reduction of the debt, a larger navy to safeguard the land routes across Central America, and a "military road" across the country to California.

In December, nine months later, Buchanan faced a new and serious economic crisis, and gave a Jacksonian diagnosis and response. "In the midst of unsurpassed plenty in all the productions of agriculture and in all the elements of national wealth," he said, manufacturing was suspended, public works retarded, many enterprises abandoned, and "thousands of useful laborers" thrown out of employment. (Regretfully, there were no unemployment statistics in 1857 or for many decades after that.) Imports and government revenue had fallen too far to finance the large appropriations of the Congress in its last session, necessitating a loan. He blamed "our extravagant and vicious system of paper currency and bank credits," and the speculative gambling that it had unleashed. 1,400 separate banks controlled the amount of currency in circulation, answering only the interests of their stockholders. The banks, he said, must be required to convert their notes into gold and silver at all times. To do so they needed larger reserve requirements than the one-third maintained by the Bank of England, because their small size made them more vulnerable—yet a Treasury report had found that their specie reserves in January 1857 equaled just one-seventh of their combined deposits and note circulation, despite an influx of $400 million in California gold. Buchanan noted proudly that because of the independent treasury, the federal government had *not* had to suspend specie payment of its obligations, as it had in 1837. Buchanan rejected a new Bank of the United States, which would also look first to its stockholders' interests. The solution rested with the states, who must mandate a one-third reserve ratio, increase the minimum denomination of bank notes first to $20 and then to $50, and force banks that could not meet their obligations to liquidate. Congress might in fact pass a uniform bankruptcy law for all banks. None of these suggestions appears to have gone anywhere, but Buchanan's faith in "the buoyancy of youth, the energies of our population, and the spirit which never quails before difficulties" as agents of recovery bore fruit quite rapidly. A year later he noted the beginnings of recovery and repeated his proposals, but the Congress left the problems of credit expansion, booms and busts to future generations.

As it turned out, normal revenue fell from $73.9 million in fiscal 1856 to an estimated $57.6 million in fiscal 1858, and only Treasury notes and loans enabled the government to continue spending at the rate of about $75–80 million a year. By December 1858 the national debt was back up to about $35 million. Buchanan insisted, however, that normal revenues could meet the government's needs once the economic crisis was over, and repeatedly asked for lower tariffs based on specific duties per product, not ad valorem duties that encouraged fraud and had negative economic consequences. Congress did not respond.

Buchanan, as befitted his diplomatic background, pursued a very active foreign policy. In December 1857 he discussed further difficulties with Great Britain over the interpretation of the Clayton-Bulwer treaty and rights in Central America. Since independence, he noted trenchantly, the United States had continually concluded treaties with Britain, only to spend years or decades arguing over what they meant. London and Washington were still bickering over their most recent agreement of October 1856, and the British were negotiating directly with Honduras over their claims there. Two years later these claims remained unsettled, and Buchanan had to report a violent conflict with the British over the destiny of San Juan Island in Puget Sound, where the British disputed the rights of American settlers. He had sent a certain Col. George Pickett with a couple of hundred soldiers to protect them, and Lt. General Winfield Scott to supervise operations in Washington Territory, leading apparently to an easing of the crisis, even though sovereignty over the island remained in dispute. Finally, in his last message of December 1860, Buchanan reported that the British had accepted our version of the new treaty and had given up some of their pretensions around Honduras. They had also given up their claim to search US ships suspected of carrying slaves to Cuba.

In China, meanwhile, the British and French were involved in a new armed conflict with the government over trading rights around Canton, and Buchanan in December 1857 dispatched a new US minister to work with them, while maintaining a strict neutrality in the war. A year later he reported a satisfactory trade treaty with China, and the successful implementation of the new treaty with Japan. China had ratified that treaty, he said in December 1859, even though the American minister had refused to meet with the emperor so as not to have to bow to him in the customary humiliating manner. The biggest diplomatic problems concerned Latin America and the Caribbean.

Year after year, Buchanan complained that Spain had refused to settle US claims against Cuba—or, more importantly, to yield to his overtures to purchase that island, an idea he justified in December

1858 on humanitarian grounds. Cuba was now the only territory in the world that legally imported slaves from Africa, and that trade required the United States and Britain to maintain naval forces off the African coast solely to stop slaves from going there. "As long as this market shall remain open," he continued, "there can be no hope for the civilization of benighted Africa. Whilst the demand for slaves continues in Cuba wars will be waged among the petty and barbarous chiefs in Africa for the purpose of seizing subjects to supply this trade. In such a condition of affairs it is impossible that the light of civilization and religion can ever penetrate these dark abodes." He also referred specifically to the capture in August 1858 of a slave ship "with more than 300 African negroes [sic]" on board by the American navy off of Cuba, and asked Congress for money to send them to Liberia, the new country founded by Monroe where freed US slaves could settle, and to support them there. He evidently believed along with many of his white countrymen that while slaves in the United States lived under civilized conditions, the trade in Africans remained barbaric. To make the talks with Spain succeed, Buchanan asked for money to meet its claims regarding the slave ship *Amistad*, to which Congress evidently failed to agree. In his very last message, he reported progress on a settlement of the claims on Spain, but not on the purchase of Cuba, which he endorsed once again, repeating the same arguments.

Foreshadowing later presidents, Buchanan also proposed an expanded US role in the Caribbean to protect the three routes across the Central American isthmuses of Mexico, Nicaragua, and Panama. When he came into office, the United States was arguing with the government of New Granada—later Colombia, which included Panama in its territory until 1902—over the exorbitant duty that government had levied on goods transported on the new railroad across the Panama Isthmus. Pointing out that our 1846 treaty guaranteed the neutrality of Panama, Buchanan in December 1857 asked for a law making naval and land forces readily available to act should that neutrality be threatened. He repeated this proposal a year later, pointing out that Nicaragua had so far refused to ratify a treaty allowing us to keep the route across its territory open, and that an 1853 treaty with Mexico committed both nations not to obstruct the movement of goods across the Tehuantepec isthmus. Another year later he added a new mission, to protect the Central American countries against revolution, to his proposal, but Congress never acted on it. Partisanship now ruled that body as never before, and to judge from the fate of Buchanan's numerous proposals on different issues, the House and Senate were too bitterly divided on slavery to reach agreement on almost anything else.

Buchanan made an even more novel proposal regarding Mexico. That nation, he remarked in his December 1858 message, had known almost nothing but a series of military rulers since independence, and the latest of them, General Zuolaga, was now waging a civil war from Mexico City against constitutionalists in other parts of the country. Both sides were extorting money from foreign residents, and United States citizens now had $10 million in claims on the country, which no one would pay. Although Buchanan hoped that the constitutional forces led by Benito Juarez, the legitimate ruler, might settle these questions if victorious, he proposed seizing territory within the adjacent provinces of Chihuahua and Sonora, both to contain rampaging Indian tribes and the general anarchy that reigned there, and to establish military posts until Mexico was once again at peace under competent authority. Nothing had improved a year later, and many American citizens, including three physicians, had been murdered or robbed. Buchanan asked for the authority to use military force, both to protect the rights of US citizens and to "restore peace and order to Mexico itself," a goal in which US citizens "must necessarily feel a deep and earnest interest." The US also needed to prevent the intervention of a European power—which as it happened was indeed destined to occur. Mexico was now "a wreck upon the ocean. . . . As a good neighbor, shall we not extend to her a helping hand to save her?" He repeated his proposals for Chihuahua and Sonora, as well as a request for a new territorial government in Arizona. In his last message in December 1860 he noted that Congress had refused to adopt this proposal, but that the government had concluded a treaty with the Juarez government. This was the first of many presidential initiatives designed to pacify one or another part of Latin America, and Buchanan certainly ranks as a founder of US imperialism in the region.

At home, slavery and Kansas dominated Buchanan's first two years. The slavery controversy entered a new phase in the week of his inauguration, when Chief Justice Taney handed down the Dred

Scott decision arguing that Negroes could never be US citizens and that the Constitution protected slaveholders' rights throughout the territory of the United States.[1] In December 1857 Buchanan reported at length on developments in Kansas. The "revolutionary organization," he said, referring to the anti-slavery forces, had tried to discredit the election for a state constitutional convention by boycotting it. The convention had gone ahead with a pro-slavery constitution, and the legislature had declined to submit it to a vote of the whole people before submitting it to Congress for approval. Buchanan in his first month in office had insisted that such a vote take place. The convention had then reconvened in September 1857, and had agreed to submit the slavery question to a new vote—which had not yet occurred. Buchanan pledged to accept the result, but added that, *pace* the Dred Scott decision of the previous March, slaveholders already in Kansas would be able to keep their slaves there in any case.

Things looked quite differently a year later. New legislative elections in January 1858 had elected the anti-slavery forces. Buchanan had submitted the Lecompton Constitution—the pro-slavery one—to Congress for approval on the assumption that the electorate of Kansas would then cast a final vote on slavery, but Congress refused to accept it. Congress passed its own statehood proposal, which disallowed certain controversial land grants, and effectively gave Kansas an ultimatum: they could either accept it, or remain a territory until their population had reached 93,420, the size of an average congressional district. The territorial government had rejected the bill, and thus they would have to wait. Buchanan suggested writing this sensible principle—that a territory needed a population equivalent to a congressional district before joining the Union—into law. It would have kept Alaska, but not Hawaii, out of the Union in the late 1950s. The Kansas question, Buchanan complained, had occupied nearly all the attention of Congress for two full sessions, and the required delay would benefit everyone. He did not find it necessary to discuss Kansas at any length in either of his last two messages, and it did not become a state until after the outbreak of the Civil War. Meanwhile, the 1858 midterm elections

---

1 It should be noted that dissents by Justices McLean and Curtis made an overwhelming case that Taney was wrong as a matter of law and history.

revolutionized the country. Alarmed and sometimes incensed by *Dred Scott,* the electorate reduced the administration Democrats in the House from 113 to only 83. The new Republican Party elected the largest delegation with 113, while 19 southern Democrats ran as a new Opposition Party and 14 northern Democrats ran as antislavery independents. The Democrats however retained a 38–25 edge in the Senate.

Another new territory, Utah, provided nearly as much drama in 1858 and 1859. The Mormons had settled the Salt Lake Valley in 1847, and Congress had created a territorial government in the Compromise of 1850. President Fillmore had appointed Brigham Young, the Mormons' spiritual leader, as the territorial governor. Buchanan in December 1857 sounded an alarm. The settlers, he said, recognized Young as their ruler by divine right, and Young had forced other federal officials to withdraw for their own safety, leaving "no government in Utah but the despotism of Brigham Young." Facing the emergency with the fortitude of George Washington in Pennsylvania or Andrew Jackson in South Carolina, Buchanan had appointed a new governor and dispatched him to Utah with an escort of federal troops. "With the religious opinions of the Mormons, as long as they remained mere opinions, however deplorable in themselves and revolting to the moral and religious sentiments of all Christendom," he said, referring obviously to polygamy, "I had no right to interfere." Young however had been trying to keep any settlers out who would not obey him, while training troops and collecting arms to resist the United States. "This is the first rebellion which has existed in our Territories," Buchanan thundered, "and humanity itself requires that we should put it down in such a manner that it shall be the last. To trifle with it would be to encourage it and to render it formidable. We ought to go there with such an imposing force as to convince these deluded people that resistance would be vain, and thus spare the effusion of blood." He asked for, and got, four new army regiments to do the job. No president has ever talked about any other group of Americans the way Buchanan and several successors talked about the Mormons. Taking up the story again a year later in December 1858, Buchanan reported that Young had mobilized and declared martial law to meet the threat of federal forces, and burned a federal supply train. In March 1858 Buchanan sent two emissaries to Utah offering a full pardon to all if they would submit at once. This and the large force he had dispatched, he reported proudly, had done the job, and the new governor now ruled over the territory. Unfortunately he could not find similar courage to deal with a greater emergency a year later.

Buchanan made several other interesting proposals in his last years in office as well, but the deeply divided Congress failed to act on any of them. It refused to organize a new Arizona territory, and it did not respond to his calls for a transcontinental railroad along the new southern border of the country. He also complained repeatedly that Congress had developed a habit of waiting, in odd-numbered years, until just hours before it was required to adjourn on March 4 to submit important appropriations bills. Some of the states had not yet elected new senators and congressmen by that time, and thus the president had almost no choice but to sign the bills, since the government needed the money, and no full Congress had yet been elected that he could summon to pass new ones after he had vetoed them. He proposed a law requiring the states to elect their new representatives well in advance of March 4. He also reported annually on the growing deficit of the Post Office, which had reached $7 million—more than 10 percent of federal expenditures—in the previous year. And like many of his predecessors, he asked Congress to pay more attention to the needs of the District of Columbia, which the legislators, to judge from the frequency of this complaint from the White House, regarded with almost complete indifference.

Buchanan sent his final annual message to Congress on December 3, 1860. Pierce's and Buchanan's hope that the Kansas-Nebraska Act and the Dred Scott decision had put the slavery question behind the nation had proven false. A year earlier, Buchanan had declined to refer more than briefly to "the recent sad and bloody occurrences at Harpers Ferry"—John Brown's raid on the arsenal, the first step in a plan to set off a slave rebellion around the South. He had then repeated his hope that the settlers in the new territories might settle the issue at the ballot box, one by one, allowing "natural causes" to determine slavery's fate. Half a year later, the Republicans nominated Abraham Lincoln of Illinois on a platform of no more slavery in the territories, while the Democrats split in two between southerners who wanted an eternal and absolute right to bring slaves into any new territory and northerners led by Stephen Douglas who wanted to leave the question to the people. Each faction nominated its own candidate, and some old Whigs put together a fourth party, the Constitutional Union Party, which was strong in the border states. The Deep South made clear that Lincoln's election would lead immediately to secession. In November, an unprecedented turnout of 81 percent of eligible voters gave just under 40 percent of the popular vote to Lincoln, but that was enough to carry nearly the entire Northeast, Midwest and West Coast, good for 180 out of 302 electoral votes. Southern Democrat John Breckinridge won all the states south of Virginia and Tennessee; John Bell of the Constitutional Union Party took Tennessee, Kentucky, and Virginia; and Douglas won only Missouri and part of New Jersey. By the time Buchanan gave his last address, South Carolina, Georgia, Florida, Alabama and Mississippi had all called conventions to discuss secession from the Union, and South Carolina's was set to convene before the end of the month. Buchanan tried to rise to the occasion, while remaining faithful to the views he had repeatedly expressed before.

Buchanan once again blamed the abolitionists (without using that word) for the crisis. They had created the trouble over the territories and the Fugitive Slave Act, but worst of all, their three decades of agitation had made "southern matrons" fear to go to sleep at night. The North need only leave the southern states alone: "As sovereign States, they, and they alone, are responsible before God and the world for the slavery existing among them. For this the people of the North are not more responsible and have no more right to interfere than with similar institutions in Russia or in Brazil"—nearly the only other outposts of western civilization, he might have added, where slavery remained legal. Yet at the same time, he quickly added, Lincoln's election gave no just cause for dissolving the Union. Only a plurality had elected him, and the South should judge him by his acts. The Supreme Court still protected slaveholders' rights in the territories, and he counted upon it to overrule an abolitionist measure that the Kansas territorial legislature had passed earlier that year. One could not fairly blame the federal government for certain states' refusal to enforce the Fugitive Slave law, or assume that Lincoln would violate it. If however the northern legislatures would not repeal their acts of defiance, he thought the southern states could secede.

Buchanan seemed to waver on this point, acknowledging that the state ratification conventions in 1787–88 had not envisioned secession, and that Jackson had demolished the idea in his great anti-nullification message of January 16, 1833. He also quoted Madison to the effect that the ratification conventions had taken ultimate sovereignty away from their states and given it to the federal government, a point confirmed by many different provisions of the Constitution. The Union under the Constitution was designed for perpetuity, like that of the Articles of Confederation before it. The framers "never intended to implant in its bosom the seeds of its own destruction, nor were they at its creation guilty of the absurdity of providing for its own dissolution. . . . Secession is neither more nor less than revolution. It may or it may not be a justifiable revolution, but still it is revolution."

Yet having in these words anticipated the arguments of his successor, Buchanan disclaimed the authority to put them into action. The president's duty to enforce the laws in South Carolina had become impossible to perform, because all federal officials had already resigned. He denied a federal power to compel a state to remain in the Union by force of arms, because the Constitution did not provide for declaring war against a state. (It did, of course, provide for extraordinary measures to suppress "invasion or rebellion," and it gave the states no war powers of their own.) Congress, in any case, would have to design and approve any steps to keep states in the Union, and he did not think that force could succeed. "Suppose such a war should result in the conquest of a State; how are we to govern it afterwards?" he asked—anticipating, it must be said, the terrible problems the nation would face after 1865. "Shall we hold it as a province and govern it by despotic power? In the nature of things, we could not by physical force control the will of the people and compel them to elect Senators and Representatives to Congress and to perform all the other duties depending upon their own volition and required from the free citizens of a free State as a constituent member of the Confederacy." Such a war would in any case destroy the foundation of the nation, which rested upon public opinion, "and could never be cemented by the blood its citizens shed in civil war." To avert it, he suggested a constitutional amendment guaranteeing the right to hold slaves, the right to hold them within territories until such time as they were admitted as states as their own constitutions decided, and the obligation to return fugitive slaves.

Buchanan pled fervently for the preservation of the Union. "But may I be permitted solemnly to invoke my countrymen to pause and deliberate before they determine to destroy this the grandest temple which has ever been dedicated to human freedom since the world began? It has been consecrated by the blood of our fathers, by the glories of the past, and by the hopes of the future. The Union has already made us the most prosperous, and ere long will, if preserved, render us the most powerful, nation on the face of the earth. In every foreign region of the globe the title of American citizen is held in the highest respect, and when pronounced in a foreign land it causes the hearts of our countrymen to swell with honest pride. Surely when we reach the brink of the yawning abyss we shall recoil with horror from the last fatal plunge.

"By such a dread catastrophe," he continued, "the hopes of the friends of freedom throughout the world would be destroyed, and a long night of leaden despotism would enshroud the nations. Our example for more than eighty years would not only be lost, but it would be quoted as a conclusive proof that man is unfit for self-government." His successor shared this view, but drew very different conclusions from it.

Because the institution of slavery never commanded the assent of the whole American nation, and because it could not possibly be reconciled with much of the language of the Constitution and the Bill of Rights, early presidents had done their best to ignore it. The growth of the nation had made that impossible, and now, in late 1860, the issue began to split the Union. The impending drama within the eighty-four year-old nation would determine not only its own political future, but that of Western Europe, and eventually most of the world.

# VIII

## Abraham Lincoln

### 1861–65

Faced with a rebellion against federal authority, the government under Abraham Lincoln mobilized unprecedented resources, fought the longest and costliest war seen within the western world since the time of Napoleon, and transformed the United States. The issue of the maintenance of federal authority, which in different ways had troubled the administrations of Washington, Adams, Jefferson, Madison, Jackson, and all the presidents since Zachary Taylor now boiled over, and four years of war settled it decisively and abolished the institution of slavery. Lincoln, a Whig turned Republican, was a relatively obscure lawyer and politician from Illinois who had served just one term in Congress during the Mexican War, and lost a well-publicized campaign for the Senate against Democratic leader Stephen Douglas in 1858 in the Illinois legislature, even though he had defeated Douglas in the popular vote. The Republican convention of 1860 had chosen him over better-known figures such as William Seward of New York (who became his secretary of state) and Salmon P. Chase of Ohio (who became his secretary of the treasury and later chief justice of the Supreme Court) partly because he was much less known and therefore less controversial. By some miracle of history he turned to be exactly the man the nation needed.

Twenty-three years before taking office, at the age of twenty-nine in 1838, Lincoln had given an address in Springfield, Illinois, foreshadowing the civil war and identifying the fundamental rhythm of American history. What, he asked, would his own generation, born after the founding of the new nation, do with its inheritance? The founders had risked everything to demonstrate "the capability of a people to govern themselves," and the success of their experiment had won them enduring fame and esteem. Now however a new generation had grown up. "It is to deny, what the history of the world tells us is true, to suppose that men of ambition and talents will not continue to spring up amongst us. And, when they do, they will as naturally seek the gratification of their ruling passion, as others have so done before them. The question then, is, can that gratification be found in supporting and maintaining an edifice that has been erected by others? Most certainly it cannot. . . . Towering genius disdains a beaten path. . . . It thirsts and burns for distinction; and, if possible, it will have it, whether at the expense of emancipating slaves, or enslaving freemen."[1] Lincoln himself would fulfill this prophecy in due time, but when he delivered his inaugural address on March 4, 1861—after the secession of South Carolina, Mississippi, Florida, Alabama, Georgia, Louisiana, and Texas—he stressed the immediate task of restoring and preserving the Union.

The inaugural foreshadowed Lincoln's rhetorical and political strategy for the first two years of the impending conflict: leaving no doubt of his objective, yet leaving as much room as he could for a peaceful resolution of the crisis. Addressing the rebellious states, he denied that their peace and security was in danger, and quoted his campaign declaration that he had "no purpose, directly or indirectly, to interfere with the institution of slavery in the States where it exists," nor any right to do so. He repudiated armed invasions like John Brown's and reaffirmed the validity of the Fugitive Slave Act. He refused, however, to recognize secession. "A disruption of the Federal Union, heretofore only menaced, is now formidably attempted," but perpetuity remained the fundamental law of all national governments. The Articles of Confederation had explicitly declared it and the Constitution had established a "more perfect Union." Even if one believed that the Union was a contract among states, individual parties did not have the right to break it. Acts of secession, he said in an echo of Jackson, were legally void, and violence against the United States would be insurrectionary or revolutionary. "I trust this will not be regarded as a menace, but only

---

1 http://www.abrahamlincolnonline.org/lincoln/speeches/lyceum.htm.

as the declared purpose of the Union that it *will* constitutionally defend and maintain itself." Bloodshed would occur only if "forced upon the national authority." He would confine himself to securing federal property and collecting duties and imposts.

Lincoln believed somewhat optimistically that the rebellious states included many loyal citizens, and he addressed them directly, asking them what rights of theirs had truly been violated. Whether states or the federal government should enforce the Fugitive Slave Act, and whether Congress could prohibit slavery in the territories, he said, remained open questions. Supreme Court decisions, he said in an obvious reference to *Dred Scott*, settled individual cases, but should the court irrevocably rule on great matters of national policy, "the people will have ceased to be their own rulers." The minority must submit. If it could successfully secede, it would soon face further secession in its turn. "Plainly the central idea of secession is the essence of anarchy. A majority held in restraint by constitutional checks and limitations, and always changing easily with deliberate changes of popular opinions and sentiments, is the only true sovereign of a free people. Whoever rejects it does of necessity fly to anarchy or to despotism. Unanimity is impossible. The rule of a minority, as a permanent arrangement, is wholly inadmissible; so that, rejecting the majority principle, anarchy or despotism in some form is all that is left." If a constitutional amendment might solve the crisis, he urged state conventions to propose it.

"Why should there not be a patient confidence in the ultimate justice of the people?" he asked. "Is there any better or equal hope in the world? In our present differences, is either party without faith of being in the right? If the Almighty Ruler of Nations, with His eternal truth and justice, be on your side of the North, or on yours of the South, that truth and that justice will surely prevail by the judgment of this great tribunal of the American people. . . . Intelligence, patriotism, Christianity, and a firm reliance on Him who has never yet forsaken this favored land are still competent to adjust in the best way all our present difficulty." "The momentous issue of civil war" lay in "your hands, my dissatisfied fellow-countrymen, and not in mine. . . . We are not enemies, but friends. We must not be enemies. Though passion may have strained it must not break our bonds of affection. The mystic chords of memory, stretching from every battlefield and patriot grave to every living heart and hearthstone all over this broad land, will yet swell the chorus of the Union, when again touched, as surely they will be, by the better angels of our nature."

More than a month later, while secession conventions in both North Carolina and Virginia voted to stay in the Union, Lincoln decided to resupply the garrison in Fort Sumter, in the harbor of Charleston, South Carolina. By now the seceding states had formed the Confederacy, and on April 12 and 13 Confederate troops bombarded the fort and forced it to surrender. On April 15, Lincoln issued a proclamation asking for 75,000 militia men to suppress the insurrection in the seven seceded states, specifically by recapturing federal property, and calling the new Congress into session on July 4. On that day he greeted them with a long message amounting to an unscheduled report on the state of the Union, the steps he had taken, and his objectives in the war.

The attack on Fort Sumter, Lincoln said in a brief review of the last four months, had "forced upon the country the distinct issue, 'immediate dissolution or blood.'" Then he defined the issue before the nation in world-historical terms. "And this issue embraces more than the fate of these United States. It presents to the whole family of man the question whether a constitutional republic, or democracy—a government of the people by the same people—can or cannot maintain its territorial integrity against its own domestic foes. It presents the question whether discontented individuals, too few in numbers to control administration according to organic law in any case, can always, upon the pretenses made in this case, or on any other pretenses, or arbitrarily without any pretense, break up their government, and thus practically put an end to free government upon the earth. It forces us to ask, Is there in all republics this inherent and fatal weakness? Must a government of necessity be too strong for the liberties of its own people, or too weak to maintain its own existence?

"So viewing the issue, no choice was left but to call out the war power of the Government and so to resist force employed for its destruction by force for its preservation." Thus from the beginning did Lincoln define the struggle as a battle for democracy itself, not merely on behalf of the United States, but for the whole world.

The seceding states, he noted, had not responded to his call. Some border states, he continued, favored the Union, but in Virginia, North Carolina, Tennessee and Arkansas—which had all joined the Confederacy after Sumter—Union sentiment was "nearly repressed and silenced." The federal government would answer the call of loyal Virginians (in the northwest portion of the state) to protect them. Lincoln made further calls for militia and increases in the regular army and navy. Specifically, he wanted 400,000 men and a $400 million appropriation—many times the normal annual revenue of the country—to make the struggle "a short and decisive one."

Meanwhile, Lincoln reported, he had authorized the commanding general of the army to suspend the writ of habeas corpus, specifically in Maryland, where secessionists had seized Baltimore and temporarily blocked troops from getting from the North to Washington. The Constitution, he pointed out, allowed this measure "in time of invasion or rebellion," and although some thought the Congress must authorize it, he could not have taken the time to summon them and still save the situation. "Are all the laws but one to go unexecuted," he asked, "and the Government itself go to pieces lest that one be violated?" He left it to Congress to consider authorizing legislation, which eventually passed. The word "secession," he declared, was an ingenious sophism to make rebellion acceptable, claiming the right of any state to dissolve the Union. "The little disguise that the supposed right is to be exercised only for just cause, themselves to be the sole judge of its justice, is too thin to merit any notice. With rebellion thus sugar coated they have been drugging the public mind of their section for more than thirty years"—a clear reference to the nullification controversy. He rejected state "sovereignty." The Union, and not themselves separately, procured their independence and their liberty, and no government could allow secession and survive. He speculated optimistically that only in South Carolina was there an actual majority of legally qualified voters favoring disunion.

"It may be affirmed without extravagance," he continued, "that the free institutions we enjoy have developed the powers and improved the condition of our whole people beyond any example in the world." This, he said, was "essentially a people's contest." The Confederacy had dropped "We the people" from the preamble of its constitution, taking credit for it as "deputies of the sovereign and independent states." The war sought to preserve a government "whose leading object is to elevate the condition of men; to lift artificial weights from all shoulders; to clear the paths of laudable pursuit for all; to afford all an unfettered start and a fair chance in the race of life." The common people understood this, and although the army had lost a substantial portion of its officer corps to the other side, virtually no common soldiers had deserted. "This is the patriotic instinct of plain people. They understand without an argument that the destroying the government which was made by Washington means no good to them." The popular government must prove that bullets could not overturn the verdict of ballots. He promised in peace to be guided by the principles he had stated in his inaugural—the only reference in this message, and an implicit one at that, to the slavery question. "As a private citizen," he concluded, "the Executive could not have consented that these institutions shall perish; much less could he in betrayal of so vast and so sacred a trust as these free people had confided to him. He felt that he had no moral right to shrink, nor even to count the chances of his own life in what might follow," he said prophetically. Having done his duty, he asked the Congress to do theirs. "And having thus chosen our course, without guile and with pure purpose, let us renew our trust in God and go forward without fear and with manly hearts."

Five months later, on December 3, Lincoln delivered his first annual message. With no great military victories to boast of, Lincoln reviewed the political developments of the year. Not only had the "insurgents"—his favorite word for the rebelling southerners—failed to secure any support north of the Mason-Dixon line, but Delaware, south of it, had remained loyal, and Maryland had repaired all the rail lines and burnt bridges from its insurrection, supplied seven regiments to the government and none to the enemy, and cast a record-breaking vote for the Union. Kentucky and Missouri stood firmly in the Union camp, and Union loyalists controlled western Virginia. The young and popular General George McClellan had replaced the aged Winfield Scott.

And then, for the first time, Lincoln gingerly addressed the future of slavery. The Republican majority in Congress now contained a good many dedicated abolitionists, and an act of August 5, 1861 had declared all property used to support the rebel cause subject to confiscation and freed any slaves employed by the Confederate Army or navy. Lincoln suggested that several loyal states (as he hoped) might begin freeing slaves as well. Congress, he said, should provide some compensation to their owners—perhaps only in the form of partial tax relief. Lincoln before running for president had stated that the black population could never live on an equal footing with the white, and now he speculated that "the free colored people of the United States" might also be sent as colonizers, "so far as individuals may desire." He then replied elliptically to those pushing for abolition. "The war continues. In considering the policy to be adopted for suppressing the insurrection I have been anxious and careful that the inevitable conflict for this purpose shall not degenerate into a violent and remorseless revolutionary struggle. I have therefore in every case thought it proper to keep the integrity of the Union prominent as the primary object of the contest on our part, leaving all questions which are not of vital military importance to the more deliberate action of the Legislature." He would be glad to consider a new law relating to the confiscation of property, although "we should not be in haste to determine that radical and extreme measures, which may reach the loyal as well as the disloyal, are indispensable."

Then he turned once again to the political stakes of the war. "It continues to develop that the insurrection is largely, if not exclusively, a war upon the first principle of popular government—the rights of the people," he declared. The insurgents talked of restricting the suffrage, "with labored arguments to prove that large control of the people in government is the source of all political evil," and even hinted at a monarchy. And with a bow to Jacksonian democracy, this onetime Whig attacked "the effort to place capital on an equal footing with, if not above, labor in the structure of government.... Labor is prior to and independent of capital. Capital is only the fruit of labor, and could never have existed if labor had not first existed. Labor is the superior of capital, and deserves much the higher consideration." Many men—a majority indeed—belonged neither to labor nor to capital, since they worked for themselves, both in the North and in the South. And free laborers could acquire capital and become proprietors. "This is the just and generous and prosperous system which opens the way to all, gives hope to all, and consequent energy and progress and improvement of condition to all. No men living are more worthy to be trusted than those who toil up from poverty; none less inclined to take or touch aught which they have not honestly earned." They must not surrender their political rights.

In conclusion, Lincoln looked broadly upon the future of the United States. "From the first taking of our national census to the last are seventy years," he said, "we find our population at the end of the period eight times as great as it was at the beginning. The increase of those other things which men deem desirable has been even greater. We thus have at one view what the popular principle, applied to Government through the machinery, of the States and the Union, has produced in a given time, and also what if firmly maintained it promises for the future. There are already among us those who if the Union be preserved will live to see it contain 250,000,000. The struggle of today is not altogether for today; it is for a vast future also. With a reliance on Providence all the more firm and earnest, let us proceed in the great task which events have devolved upon us."

Although Lincoln and the Republicans entertained great military hopes for 1862 in general and McLellan's new Army of the Potomac in particular, he continued in the first half of the year to look for some way to induce the South to give up the rebellion. He also tried to start the emancipation ball rolling closer to home. In a special message just three months later on March 3, 1862, he declared that the "leaders of the existing insurrection" were counting on the eventual support of the border states. "To deprive them of this hope substantially ends the rebellion," he declared most optimistically, and the nation might do so by "initiating" emancipation. He proposed "gradual and not sudden emancipation" as "better for all," noting that the cost of the war would easily purchase all the slaves in any named state. While leaving the choice up to the loyal states, he repeated his December promise to employ "all indispensable means" to save the Union, including measures that could not yet be foreseen should the war continue. On April 6 he signed a law abolishing slavery in the District of Columbia with some compensation for the owners, and referred to possible colonization again. And on July 12, when Congress was about to adjourn, he addressed a message to all the representatives from the border states pressing his plan for gradual and compensated emancipation again, arguing that it was "one of the most potent and swift means of ending [the war.]" He warned them that "friction and abrasion" would end the institution in their states in any case if the war continued and proposed colonization somewhere in South America. Once a critical mass of freed slaves had settled there, "the freed people would not be so reluctant to go." No immediate response followed. Pressed by more radical Republicans to declare abolition at once, Lincoln wrote the editor Horace Greeley on August 22 that his objective remained the preservation of the Union, not the destruction of slavery, and that he would gladly save the Union without freeing any slaves, by freeing all the slaves, or by freeing some but not others. Meanwhile, McClellan's Peninsular Campaign had failed spectacularly in the spring, Lee had won further victories in the summer, and the Confederates had invaded both Maryland and Kentucky. Lincoln decided that the time to move into a whole new phase of the war had come.

On September 22, after McClellan had won a bloody, narrow victory over Lee's army at Antietam in Maryland and sent it back into Virginia, Lincoln issued the Emancipation Proclamation, to be effective if the war was still in progress on January 1. He repeated his pledges to aid any loyal state that would adopt "immediate or gradual abolishment of slavery within their respective limits," and to continue efforts to colonize "persons of African descent with their consent upon this continent or elsewhere." The hope that free black Americans might choose to settle elsewhere was proving as illusory as the hope that the Confederacy might willingly submit. Then he decreed freedom, assisted by US civil and military authorities, for all slaves held by disloyal citizens in the rebellious states as of January 1. Any state might avoid emancipation by submitting to federal authority and electing new representatives by that date, and Lincoln again offered compensation to loyal citizens. Lincoln relied specifically on his war powers as commander-in-chief, which customarily included the right to confiscate enemy property. The rebellious slave owners had effectively forfeited their right to their slaves, which he had acknowledged in his inaugural, by waging war upon the federal government. The measure did not, of course, extend to slaves in Missouri, Kentucky, Maryland and Delaware.

On December 1, Lincoln delivered his second annual message to a lame duck Congress, in the wake of elections in which the Democratic Party had made some gains. Without much good military news to discuss, Lincoln simply referred the Congress to the reports of the secretaries of war and of the navy for information on the course of the war. The rebellious states had not, of course, mended their ways in response to the threat of emancipation, and he took some time to discuss possibilities for the foreign colonization of freed black Americans. Only Liberia and Haiti—to which he had given diplomatic recognition at the beginning of his term—had agreed to accept any, but they were not popular destinations. Then he tried to rally the nation behind the war. He quoted his inaugural regarding the catastrophic consequences of disunion, saying that it would be impossible to draw a border to stop fugitive slaves. He also referred repeatedly to "the great interior region bounded east by the Alleghenies, north by the British dominions, west by the Rocky Mountains, and south by the line along which the culture of corn and cotton meets [sic]," including part of Virginia, part of Tennessee, and all of Kentucky—an area with ten million people, which might reach fifty million in fifty years. Any division of the country in two would cut off this area's essential access to the sea. To avoid this catastrophe, he proposed a constitutional amendment to provide for compensated emancipation within one generation. Any state agreeing to abolish slavery before the first of January 1900 would be compensated for the full market value of their slaves with 1 percent federal bonds. All slaves who had "enjoyed actual freedom by the chances of war" would keep it, with compensation for loyal owners, and Congress would provide the money for the colonization of "free colored persons with their own consent." "Among the friends of the Union there is great diversity of sentiment and of policy in regard to slavery and the African race amongst us. Some would perpetuate slavery; some would abolish it suddenly and without compensation; some would abolish it gradually and with compensation: some would remove the freed people from us, and some would retain them with us; and there are yet other minor diversities." The nation, he said, needed to compromise.

In the new Congress that might take over at any time after March 4, the Republicans would lose 25 seats while the Democrats gained 27, and would only enjoy a 112–72 majority with the help of 25 members of the new Unionist Party from the border states. Opposition to abolition had played a big role in the voting, and Lincoln obviously respected its importance. "The emancipation will be unsatisfactory to the advocates of perpetual slavery," he said, "but the length of time should greatly mitigate their dissatisfaction.... Another class will hail the prospect of emancipation, but will deprecate the length of time. They will feel that it gives too little to the now living slaves." Defending compensation, he even acknowledged that slaves were indeed property, and he justified payment on the grounds that the North, as well as the South, "use cotton and sugar and share the profits of dealing in them." Presenting a table of the population of the United States in every decennial census—the first table ever included in an annual message—he noted that the average increase of 34.6 percent every ten years would increase the population from 31 million in 1860 to 103 million people in 1900 and 252 million in 1930.[2] Such an increase would make the cost of emancipation relatively light, much cheaper than continuing the war. While once again endorsing colonization, he also described some of the opposition to free black people remaining as "largely imaginary, if not sometimes malicious." Denying that emancipation would lower the wages for white labor, he argued that a biracial nation was possible. "It is dreaded that the freed people will swarm forth and cover the whole land. Are they not already in the land? Will liberation make them any more numerous? Equally distributed among the whites of the whole country, and there would be but one colored to seven whites. Could the one in any way greatly disturb the seven? There are many communities now having more than one free colored persons to seven whites and this without any apparent consciousness of evil from it. The District of Columbia and the States of Maryland and Delaware are all in this condition." In any case, "cannot the North decide for itself whether to receive them?"

This lengthy, carefully argued appeal leaves no doubt that Lincoln meant it seriously, and that, had the rebellious states accepted it and returned to the Union, he would indeed have stayed the execution of the Emancipation Proclamation. His plan, he said, would shorten the war, reduce its cost, and restore and perpetuate national authority and national prosperity. Could any other means do the same? "In giving freedom to the slave we assure freedom to the free—honorable alike in what we give and what we preserve.

---

2 These figures like some earlier estimates, turned out to be much too high. No one foresaw a big drop in the birth rate in the decades after the Civil War.

We shall nobly save or meanly lose the last best hope of earth. Other means may succeed; this could not fail. The way is plain, peaceful, generous, just—a way which if followed the world will forever applaud and God must forever bless." But this appeal also fell flat, and on January 1, 1863, Lincoln formally put the Emancipation Proclamation into effect, while specifying that it applied only to the southern territories that federal troops did *not* yet occupy. He commanded all US authorities, civilian and military, to recognize the freedom of slaves within rebellious areas, while "enjoining" the slaves to "abstain from all violence, unless in necessary self-defense"—a response to many accusations of attempting to promote a violent slave rebellion. The two-year attempt to find a largely political solution to the war had failed, leaving the conflict to be decided on the battlefield.

In the meantime, Lincoln presided over an unprecedented mobilization and transformation of the US economy. The new scale of federal expenditure required by the war had become apparent by the time of Lincoln's first annual address in December 1861. Buchanan had proudly reduced federal expenditures to $55.4 million in fiscal 1860, but Lincoln reported that they had reached $84.6 million in fiscal 1861, ending July 1. More importantly, they had reached $98.2 million *in the first quarter of the fiscal 1862*. In December 1862 he reported that expenditures and revenues had kept pace for the rest of that year, reaching net figures of $487.8 million in revenue and $474.7 million in expenditure—including $394.4 million for the War Department, and $42.7 million for the Navy Department.[3] Loans had increased the government's total indebtedness by $433.6 million. The enormous expansion of credit had forced the nation's banks once again to suspend specie payments, and the Congress in early 1862 had passed the Legal Tender Act, which had created $100 million in Treasury-issued currency on the spot, redeemable not for specie, but for government bonds.[4] Lincoln now declared that this had been the most economical way

---

3 Lincoln himself carefully distinguished theses net figures from gross figures for both revenues and expenditures that included hundreds of millions of loans that simply reimbursed existing loans, and thus did not add to the national debt.

4 See Henry Adams, "The Legal Tender Act," *The Great Secession Winter and Other Essays, 1860–61*(New York, 1958), p. 137.

of paying the soldiers and meeting other demands, and that it had satisfied, "partially at least, and for the time, the long-felt want of an uniform circulating medium. . . . A return to specie payments, however, at the earliest period compatible with due regard to all interests concerned should ever be kept in view." As it turned out, three more presidents occupied the White House before keeping the promise to make the new "greenbacks" convertible. Lincoln also asked for new "banking associations," which might exchange government bonds for circulating notes that could replace private bank notes. This new system of national banks, the nation's first, went into effect, and in December 1863 Lincoln praised it for exceeding its supporters' expectations. Net revenues for fiscal 1862 had totaled $720 million, including $69.1 million in customs under the new Morrill Tariff, $37.6 million in "internal revenue"—an unprecedented income tax—and $595.7 million in new loans. Net revenues and expenditures for fiscal 1864 rose to $884.1 million and $865.2 million, with customs providing $102.3 million, internal revenue $109.7 million, and net new loans $623.4 million. At the time of Lincoln's last annual message in December 1864, the public debt had reached an astonishing $1.741 billion, more than twenty times what it had been when Buchanan left office. The loans now included $450 million worth of greenbacks, which were trading at a substantial discount. National banks now totaled 584, and Lincoln asked for new restrictions on note issues by state banks. We shall find that the financial measures of the Civil War burdened the nation for decades to come.

Meanwhile, Lincoln spoke repeatedly, if only broadly, about the dangers of a potentially critical foreign situation. The Confederacy counted upon recognition by the major European powers to help it win independence, and both the British and French governments, well aware of the potential global power of the growing US nation, would not have been unhappy to see them achieve it. To Lincoln's great disappointment, they recognized the Confederacy as a lawful belligerent, though not a legal government, exempting any warships that the Confederates might send out on the high seas of the charge of piracy, but going no further. In December 1861 Lincoln said that "the disloyal citizens of the United States . . . have received less patronage and encouragement than they probably expected" from this source, and that the Europeans were coming to realize that their commerce—the interest the Confederacy had counted on—would suffer more from disunion than Union. Still, he asked for money to strengthen fortifications on the coast and, significantly, on the Great Lakes, the maritime frontier with British North America. In December 1862 he regretted that the Europeans had apparently been ready to withdraw their partial recognition from the insurgents, but "the temporary reverses which afterwards befell the national arms, and which were exaggerated by our own disloyal citizens abroad, have hitherto delayed that act of simple justice." The blockade of southern ports had inevitably created controversies over the rights of neutral shipping, and he was taking care to treat the Europeans fairly. Lincoln also referred to the international political implications of the war, which Europeans of all political stripes increasingly viewed as a contest between northern democracy and southern aristocracy. The war, he said, had "excited political ambitions and apprehensions which have produced a profound agitation throughout the civilized world," but the US had refrained from any intervention in the affairs of foreign nations. This also referred implicitly to the French intervention in Mexico, where the Emperor Napoleon III of France had tried to establish the Hapsburg prince Maximilian as ruler in opposition to Juarez. In December 1864 Lincoln reported attempts to build an overland telegraph through Russian America (Alaska) and across the Bering Strait to link North America, Asia, and Europe.

Lincoln also found time to discuss other internal matters and the future growth of the nation. In December 1861 he noted that the Indian tribes south of Kansas in Indian Territory had "renounced their allegiance to the United States and entered into treaties with the insurgents," while driving the leaders of some loyal tribes, including the Cherokees, out of the territory. Meanwhile, the Sioux in Minnesota had attacked settlers, killing eight hundred and destroying substantial property. A year later he mentioned several new treaties that secured the removal of additional Indian tribes, which he hoped would secure peaceful relations with the remainder. The nation had a duty to attend to their material well-being, further their progress "in the arts of civilization," and increase the propagation of the Christian faith. On another front, Congress at length followed the recommendations of Lincoln and several predecessors and established the Department of Agriculture.

Lincoln in December 1861 mentioned the establishment of the new Colorado, Nevada and Dakota territories, and by 1864 he could add that Nevada had joined the Union and Idaho and Montana were moving toward organization as well. New discoveries of precious metals were drawing more and more settlers westward. According to a contemporary Republican authority, the addition of new states was designed to make the rebel states a smaller minority within Congress once the war was over and they had returned to the Union.[5] Remarkably enough, congressional Republicans did not allow the war to stand in the way of authorizing the construction of a transcontinental railroad from Sacramento to Omaha. "The great enterprise of connecting the Atlantic with the Pacific States by railways and telegraph lines has been entered upon with a vigor that gives assurance of success," Lincoln said in December 1864, "notwithstanding the embarrassments arising from the prevailing high prices of materials and labor." Last but not least, Lincoln in his last message reported that the operations of the Post Office, for the first time in many decades, were paying for themselves. An increase in traffic in the North, and the loss of unprofitable routes in the rebel states, was responsible.

By the time Lincoln sent his annual message of December 1863, events allowed him to report on a relatively favorable year. A year earlier, after twenty months of war and some gains, "the tone of public feeling and opinion, at home and abroad was not satisfactory. With other signs, the popular elections then just past indicated uneasiness among ourselves, while, amid much that was cold and menacing, the kindest words coming from Europe were uttered in accents of pity that we were too blind to surrender a hopeless cause." Armed vessels built in Europe had been wreaking havoc on northern commerce, and the European governments had refused to block them. The crisis had led to the Emancipation Proclamation, which had turned out to be a turning point. Eleven months later, the rebel borders had been pushed well back, and federal troops had completely opened the Mississippi and split the Confederacy in two. Tennessee and Arkansas were almost completely liberated

---

5 James G. Blaine, *Twenty Years in Congress, from Lincoln to Garfield*, vol. II (Norwich, Conn., 1886), pp.274–75. Andrew Johnson in 1867 vetoed the admission of Nebraska and Colorado (the former passed over the veto.)

and ready for emancipation, and loyal Missouri and Maryland were working toward that step. 100,000 former slaves now served in the military, and "so far as tested, it is difficult to say they are not as good soldiers as any." No servile insurrection had occurred, foreign opinion was more favorable, the British had stopped the construction of new rebel warships, and recent local elections had gone well. All this had enabled him to take up the question of the rebels' return to the Union, which he addressed in a separate proclamation on the very same day.

That proclamation drew on the president's pardon power to lay out a blueprint for peace. Lincoln offered to pardon all those treasonous citizens engaged in rebellion, and restore their property rights—except as to slaves—if they would take an oath of allegiance to the Constitution and pledge to support all acts of Congress and presidential proclamations with reference to slaves. Exceptions included diplomatic officers and agents "of the so-called Confederate Government," those who resigned judicial positions under the United States to join the rebellion, Confederate army and naval general officers, and anyone who had unlawfully treated "colored persons or white persons" held as prisoners. As soon as one-tenth of qualified voters in any state had taken that oath, they might elect a new government, although Congress retained the right to refuse to seat particular representatives. Referring to the proclamation in his annual message, he said that it was intended to rally those desirous of returning to the Union, and allowed for other possible means of achieving this goal. The Emancipation Proclamation, however, would stand.

In his last annual message in December 1864, Lincoln made a very rare reference to a military operation in progress, "General Sherman's attempted march of 300 miles directly through the insurgent region"—that is, from Atlanta to Savannah. The result was as yet unknown, but Sherman reached Savannah just weeks later. By now Lincoln had been reelected over Democrat George McClellan, whom he had relieved of command of the Army of the Potomac two years earlier, with 55 percent of the popular vote and every state but New Jersey, Delaware, and Kentucky. The Republicans had also made big gains in the House of Representatives, and Lincoln suggested that that House now pass the Thirteenth Amendment to the Constitution abolishing slavery before the new one came into session, as it had failed to do months before. The people, he said, had spoken, and in such a crisis, their leaders should obey them. Even though 90,000 soldiers had been unable to vote, he noted, the total vote in the loyal states had increased over 1860, indicating that the nation now had more men than before the war began, despite hundreds of thousands of deaths. The end of the war was near—Grant was now besieging Petersburg, just south of Richmond—but unfortunately, "the insurgent leader"—Jefferson Davis—seemed unwilling to negotiate for anything less than "severance of the Union," to which he could not agree. Lincoln did not quite live to see the war end four months later.

Despite the unprecedented scale of the task that he had almost accomplished, the total length of Lincoln's annual messages fell well short of those of many of his predecessors in their four-year terms. That reflected his relentless focus on the great issues of national unity, slavery, and the future, as well as his willingness to leave many details to others. During his four years in office, Lincoln had led the nation through the second great recurring crisis of its national life. The first such crisis, from 1774 through about 1794, had included the Revolutionary War, independence, the adoption of the Constitution, and the first tests of the new institutions under Washington. We have seen how the related issues of expansion and slavery, triggered in part by the successful war against Mexico, had led to the breakup of the Union and the Civil War. Lincoln himself, remarkably, had predicted in 1838 that the ambitious men of his own generation would never rest content in simply "supporting and maintaining an edifice that has been erected by others"—that is, the growing republic of Jefferson and Jackson—but would seek new accomplishments of their own, "whether at the expense of emancipating slaves, or enslaving freemen." It would take another decade or more to sort out the paradoxical results of the Civil War, but the crisis created both a new United States and a new political order, as we shall see—one that would last until the next great crisis began in 1929.[6] The simple yet inspiring language in which Lincoln from

---

6 The eighty-year cycle was identified by William Strauss and Neil Howe in two books, *Generations, the History of America's Future* (New York, 1991), and *The Fourth Turning, An American Prophecy* (New York, 1997). For Lincoln's speech at the Springfield Lyceum see http://www.abrahamlincolnonline.org/lincoln/speeches/lyceum.htm..

his inaugural forward had defined the enormous national and international stakes of the conflict and the way in which he turned war for the Union into a war to end slavery showed unparalleled leadership and political skill. Success in the war, he claimed, would not only make the United States the world's leading nation, but also help spread democratic government throughout the civilized world and help bring slavery, a feature of human society from earliest times, to an end. Events vindicated his judgment.

His greatest masterpiece remained to be delivered. His second inaugural—one of the briefest ever written—laid out, once again, the great issues of the struggle he had led, tried to put them in historical perspective, and even explored the motives of the higher power in whom Lincoln evidently believed. For all these reasons, it deserves the honor—unique within this book—of quotation in full.

"At this second appearing to take the oath of the Presidential office there is less occasion for an extended address than there was at the first. Then a statement somewhat in detail of a course to be pursued seemed fitting and proper. Now, at the expiration of four years, during which public declarations have been constantly called forth on every point and phase of the great contest which still absorbs the attention and engrosses the energies of the nation, little that is new could be presented. The progress of our arms, upon which all else chiefly depends, is as well known to the public as to myself, and it is, I trust, reasonably satisfactory and encouraging to all. With high hope for the future, no prediction in regard to it is ventured.

"On the occasion corresponding to this four years ago all thoughts were anxiously directed to an impending civil war. All dreaded it, all sought to avert it. While the inaugural address was being delivered from this place, devoted altogether to *saving* the Union without war, insurgent agents were in the city seeking to *destroy* it without war—seeking to dissolve the Union and divide effects by negotiation. Both parties deprecated war, but one of them would *make* war rather than let the nation survive, and the other would *accept* war rather than let it perish, and the war came.

"One-eighth of the whole population were colored slaves, not distributed generally over the Union, but localized in the southern part of it. These slaves constituted a peculiar and powerful interest. All knew that this interest was somehow the cause of the war. To strengthen, perpetuate, and extend this interest was the object for which the insurgents would rend the Union even by war, while the Government claimed no right to do more than to restrict the territorial enlargement of it. Neither party expected for the war the magnitude or the duration which it has already attained. Neither anticipated that the *cause* of the conflict might cease with or even before the conflict itself should cease. Each looked for an easier triumph, and a result less fundamental and astounding. Both read the same Bible and pray to the same God, and each invokes His aid against the other. It may seem strange that any men should dare to ask a just God's assistance in wringing their bread from the sweat of other men's faces, but let us judge not, that we be not judged. The prayers of both could not be answered. That of neither has been answered fully. The Almighty has His own purposes. 'Woe unto the world because of offenses; for it must needs be that offenses come, but woe to that man by whom the offense cometh.' If we shall suppose that American slavery is one of those offenses which, in the providence of God, must needs come, but which, having continued through His appointed time, He now wills to remove, and that He gives to both North and South this terrible war as the woe due to those by whom the offense came, shall we discern therein any departure from those divine attributes which the believers in a living God always ascribe to Him? Fondly do we hope, fervently do we pray, that this mighty scourge of war may speedily pass away. Yet, if God wills that it continue until all the wealth piled by the bondsman's two hundred and fifty years of unrequited toil shall be sunk, and until every drop of blood drawn with the lash shall be paid by another drawn with the sword, as was said three thousand years ago, so still it must be said 'the judgments of the Lord are true and righteous altogether.'

"With malice toward none, with charity for all, with firmness in the right as God gives us to see the right, let us strive on to finish the work we are in, to bind up the nation's wounds, to care for him who shall have borne the battle and for his widow and his orphan, to do all which may achieve and cherish a just and lasting peace among ourselves and with all nations."

Six weeks later, he was dead.

# IX

## ANDREW JOHNSON AND ULYSSES S. GRANT

### 1865–9 • 1869–1877

The stormy presidency of John Tyler had given the American nation the first glimpse of the hazards of the vice-presidency. William Henry Harrison's death had brought to power a nominal Whig whose views more closely resembled those of the opposition party, leading to endless struggles with Congress. Millard Fillmore's succession had a less destructive impact, but Andrew Johnson's accession to office after Lincoln's assassination led quickly to a new constitutional crisis. Faced with a crucial wartime election in 1864, the Republican Party had replaced Hannibal Hamlin of Maine with Johnson, a senator from East Tennessee who had never given up his seat in 1861 and emerged as a determined War Democrat over the next three years. The Reconstruction era that began on his watch has been one of the most controversial in American history, and Johnson's reputation has risen and fallen dramatically over the last 160 years. His opposition to Republican Reconstruction policies in general, and to equal political rights for black Americans in particular, probably did not change the course of history very much, but it created the most serious crisis yet, by far, in relations between the White House and Congress. Johnson, who survived impeachment in the last year of his term by the narrowest of margins and rarely had his way on important policy questions, emerges from his key addresses as a determined ideologue of a particular school and, in some ways, an acolyte of the old Jacksonian tradition.

On May 29, 1865—just six weeks after Lee surrendered at Appomattox—Johnson pardoned most "participants in the rebellion," provided that they had not held high civil or military leadership positions under either the US or the Confederacy, and that they took an oath to the Constitution and promised to support all new laws and proclamations relating to the emancipation of slaves. The Thirteenth Amendment had by then passed the Congress and the states ratified it by the end of the year. In his first annual message in December, Johnson argued that the southern states had never ceased to exist as legal entities, even as most of their citizens rebelled. He had appointed provisional governors, and the states had called conventions, written new constitutions, and held state and federal elections. These constitutions denied the vote to freed slaves, and new "Black Codes" restricted their rights in many other ways. Acknowledging that the House and Senate had the exclusive power to judge "the elections, returns, and qualifications of its members," Johnson asked that the new southern legislators be seated when their states had ratified the Thirteenth Amendment as a pledge of renewed loyalty. This the Republican-dominated Congress would refuse to do. He denied any executive power to extend the vote to freed slaves, denied that Lincoln had ever intended to do so, and said that the power to extend suffrage rested with the states, who would do so "if [the freed slaves] show patience and manly virtues." Meanwhile the nation must assure "the security of the freedmen in their liberty and their property, their right to labor, and their right to claim the just return of their labor." Johnson concluded his address with a long paean of praise for America's growth, wealth, power, and democratic institutions, but he did not believe, as he rapidly made clear, that the four million freed slaves could possibly become equal citizens in the near future.

The session of Congress that began in December 1865 confirmed the split between Johnson and its Republican majorities. On February 19 Johnson vetoed a bill establishing military authority over the ex-Confederate states, with police power to protect freedmen against whites. The Senate failed to override that veto by just two votes.[1] On March 27 Johnson vetoed a far more sweeping Civil Rights Bill. Anticipating some provisions of the Fourteenth Amendment, that bill granted full citizenship to all those born

---

1 *Chicago Tribune*, February 21, 1866, p. 1.

within the United States and assured all citizens equal rights under the law. This, Johnson argued, usurped rights belonging to the states. It also gave judicial powers to agents of the new Freedmen's Bureau and potentially to the army, and thus, Johnson argued, gave more to the colored race than to the white. Congress overrode this veto. And on May 15 Johnson vetoed the admission of Colorado to the Union—a step taken by the Republicans to try to increase their congressional majorities—on the quite defensible grounds that the territory numbered only 30,000 inhabitants, just one-quarter the size of a normal congressional district. In his second annual message in 1866, Johnson complained that only his own home state of Tennessee of all the former Confederacy had been allowed to seat representatives in Congress. By this time, an overwhelmingly Republican Congress had won election by a landslide in the recent congressional elections. The new Congress convened on March 4, 1867.

Six major vetoes followed in 1867. In January Johnson vetoed a bill for Negro suffrage[2] in the District of Columbia, which, he noted, white voters had overwhelmingly rejected in the previous year. (Congress had finally granted the District an elected government.) Later that month he vetoed new bills to admit Colorado and Nebraska as states because the bills required them to grant Negro suffrage. Congress overrode the DC suffrage and Nebraska vetoes. In early March, Congress also overrode Johnson's veto of the Tenure of Office Act, which reversed nearly eighty years of precedent and denied the president the right to remove appointed officials without the consent of the Senate. Later that month, Congress passed a sweeping new Reconstruction measure—and passed it over the president's veto as well.

The Republican majority wanted to find a way to establish friendly governments in the southern states, and since only Louisiana, Mississippi and South Carolina had actual majorities of black citizens, this required the disenfranchisement of significant numbers of whites as well as the enfranchisement of blacks. As Johnson pointed out in his veto message, the bill called for elections to new constitutional conventions open to all not "disenfranchise

---

2  As in previous works, I am using contemporary terminology here.

for participation in the rebellion." Federal registrars would supervise the registration, and perjurers would be subject to trial and conviction under martial law. The law also demanded Negro suffrage, even though, as Johnson pointed out, most northern states did not yet allow it. In July he vetoed yet another law establishing military government all over the South. Huge majorities overrode these vetoes as well. Johnson retaliated, in a sense, on September 7, extending his pardon of former Confederates to a much larger group and excepting only a very small group of Confederate civilian and military leaders.

Johnson launched a full-scale attack on the Reconstruction measures in his December 1867 annual message. The new laws, he said, had interrupted a peaceful Reconstruction process and destroyed the Union as the nation had understood it by temporarily depriving states of representation in Congress and trampling individual rights. He demanded their repeal and the withdrawal of the unconstitutional powers they had given the central government and the military, and appealed frankly to white supremacy. "It is manifestly and avowedly the object of these laws," he said with some accuracy, "to confer upon Negroes the privilege of voting and to disfranchise such a number of white citizens as will give the former a clear majority at all elections in the Southern States. . . . The subjugation of the States to Negro domination would be worse than the military despotism under which they are now suffering." While it was "the glory of white men" to have established and maintained free government, "in the progress of nations Negroes have shown less capacity for government than any other race of people." The ballot remains "a privilege and a trust. . . . The great difference between the two races in physical, mental, and moral characteristics will prevent an amalgamation or fusion of them together in one homogeneous mass. If the inferior obtains the ascendency over the other, it will govern with reference only to its own interests for it will recognize no common interest— and create such a tyranny as this continent has never yet witnessed." Democrats, who had uniformly opposed these measures, had won some victories in state elections, and Johnson claimed that public opinion stood behind him.

The Republican Congress, of course, ignored these pleas, and Johnson in June 1868 vetoed two more bills readmitting seven southern states to the Union, provided that they pledged to maintain the

Negro suffrage guaranteed by their new constitutions and required voters to swear an oath to the equality of all citizens. These acts also passed over his veto. Ironically, Johnson on July 7, 1868, announced the ratification of the Fourteenth Amendment. Delivering his last annual message in December 1868—a year in which he had barely survived an impeachment trial, and failed to receive the presidential nomination of either party—he stuck to his guns, declaring that the Reconstruction Acts had "substantially failed and proved pernicious in their results," and complaining that Virginia, Texas and Mississippi still lacked the right to seat representatives in Congress. He did not refer to the Fifteenth Amendment, which a lame duck Congress was now considering while U. S. Grant waited to take office.

Meanwhile, other national business went forward, much altered by the enormous impact of the war. In his first annual message Johnson took a Jacksonian line toward the related issues of the hugely expanded national debt—a full $2.74 *billion* as of October 1, 1865—and the currency. The nation, he said, must work to eliminate the national debt within about thirty years and insist upon "the greatest moderation and prudence" from the new national banks, which could issue notes backed by government bonds. Unsecured paper currency, or greenbacks, had increased all the way to $700 million, and he wanted to exchange them for government securities "that may be made redeemable at the pleasure of the government." Moreover, since the people had risked and sacrificed their lives for the Union, "the property and income of the country should bear their just proportion of the burden of taxation," while tariffs "should be so adjusted as to fall most heavily on articles of luxury leaving the necessaries of life as free from taxation as the absolute wants of the Government economically administered will justify." Although expenditures had exceeded revenues by $112.2 million during the last fiscal year, he predicted a surplus of $111.7 million for the fiscal year that would start in July 1866. "As we have amazed the world by the suppression of a civil war which was thought to be beyond the control of any government, so we shall equally show the superiority of our institutions by the prompt and faithful discharge of our national obligations." The government, springing from and made for the people, should "be strong in its power of resistance to the establishment of inequalities," and ought not to allow monopolies, perpetuities, and "class legislation."

The financial news continued good for the remainder of his administration, thanks largely to the high Morrill Tariff of 1862, which provided the government with ample revenue. In December 1866 he reported receipts of $558 million and expenditures of $521 million during the last fiscal year, and predicted $436 million in revenue and just $350 million of expenditures in the next one. Even though 126,722 military pensioners now cost the government $33 million a year, he cut his estimate for the elimination of the debt to twenty-five years. A year later Johnson had more to say about the $700 million in legal tender notes, which were now circulating at about half their professed value in gold and silver. Because they had been declared valid for all debts except the interest on government bonds, they had essentially driven large sums of specie off the market. Since 1849, Johnson noted, the country had mined $1.174 billion worth of specie, coined $874 million, and exported $741 million. Of the remaining $433 million, nearly $300 million was missing in action.[3] Johnson demanded a reduction in the circulation of the notes, but without suggesting how it might come about. He called once again for a revised tariff that would put more of the burden on luxury items. He also complained about corruption within the revenue system. The public knew that "enormous frauds have been perpetrated on the Treasury and that colossal fortunes have been made at the public expense. . . . Some of the taxes are so laid as to present an irresistible temptation to evade payment. There can be no doubt that the open disregard of constitutional obligations avowed by some of the highest and most influential men in the country has greatly weakened the moral sense of those who serve in subordinate places." Unfortunately, he said, the Tenure of Office Act passed over his veto made it impossible for him to remove corrupt officials.

Johnson's last annual message in December 1868 included a remarkable survey of the impact of the Civil War on the nation's finances. In 1790, with a population of four million, the government spent $4.2 million; now, with thirty-eight million people, it spent $372 million, a tenfold per capita increase. (Johnson did not make this calculation, but per capita economic growth of 3 percent

---

3 This figures do not seem to add up, but they are the ones he gave on December 3, 1867.

a year would have made this increase possible.) In 1861–65 the federal government had spent nearly twice as much money as it had spent from 1789 through the first half of 1861—$3.3 billion—and thanks to the cost of the army in Reconstruction and service on the debt, it had spent another $1.6 billion in the past four years. The national debt, meanwhile, had gone from $75 million in 1789 to $127 million in 1816, nothing on the eve of the Mexican War, $64 million in 1860, and $2.874 billion by mid-1865. The debt and the currency question presented two huge problems. First, foreigners held much of the debt, which might allow them to "enslave" forty million Americans. Secondly, banks could buy government bonds with greenbacks, earning them an effective 9 percent return on their investment instead of the official 6 percent, and then issue loans with 6 percent interest, free of state and federal taxation, and thus realize a net return of 17 percent on their original investment. He suggested applying that 6 percent interest to the payment of the principal on the national debt, still leaving the bondholders with a handsome profit. This was the last Jacksonian gasp heard from the White House for more than six decades.

Johnson retained Lincoln's ambitious and effective secretary of state, William Seward, and generally relegated his relatively brief remarks about foreign affairs to the latter parts of his annual addresses. In the first one, however, he laid out the very serious issue between Great Britain and the US that had arisen as a result of the war. "British ships, manned by British subjects and prepared for receiving British armaments," he said, "sallied from the ports of Great Britain to make war on American commerce under the shelter of a commission from the insurgent States. These ships, having once escaped from British ports, ever afterwards entered them in every part of the world to refit, and so to renew their depredations." These ships—led, although he did not say so, by the steam warship *Alabama*—had driven US commerce from the seas, and British commerce had replaced it. The administration had asked the British to submit the enormous US claims against them to arbitration, but the British had refused. Meanwhile, the French Empire of Napoleon III had taken advantage of the Civil War to send French troops to Mexico, where they set up the Hapsburg Maximilian as a monarch in opposition to the Republican government of Benito Juarez. Johnson did not refer directly to this, but noted that presidential statements had twice before headed off European invasions of the Americas, and seemed to threaten war against a European power that challenged "republicanism" in the Americas.

Two years later, in December 1867, Johnson proudly announced that the French had withdrawn, and that Mexico was trying to reestablish constitutional government. The *Alabama* claims, however, remained unsettled when he left office. Relations with various European powers also suffered from arguments over the military obligations of naturalized Americans who had returned to certain German or Italian states, who then tried to conscript them into their armies. "The annexation of many small German States to Prussia and the reorganization of that country under a new and liberal constitution," he said in December 1867 in reference to Chancellor Bismarck's new North German Confederation, had led him to reopen this question, and a year later he indicated that the government had reached agreement with many German states on it.

Within the western hemisphere, Seward and Johnson embarked upon ambitious plans for new expansion. While Americans generally date the emergence of modern American imperialism from 1898, the events of that year actually grew out of initiatives from at least three decades earlier. Seward in 1867 arranged for the purchase of Russian America—that is, Alaska—from the Russian Empire, but Johnson said almost nothing about it in his next annual address, or at any other time. In December 1867, however, he declared a need for a naval station in the Atlantic to keep "transatlantic enemies" away. "I agree with our early statesmen," he said, "that the West Indies naturally gravitate to, and may be expected ultimately to be absorbed by, the continental States, including our own." The government had concluded a treaty with the king of Denmark securing American sovereignty over St. Thomas and St. John in the Virgin Islands. The Senate never took it up. A year later he renewed the request for its ratification and provided a more general defense of imperialism. "The acquisition of Alaska was made with the view of extending national jurisdiction and republican principles in the American hemisphere," he said. The treaty with Denmark extended this policy, and more generally, "Comprehensive national policy would seem to sanction the acquisition and incorporation into our Federal Union of the several adjacent continental and insular communities as speedily as it can be done peacefully, lawfully, and without any violation of national justice, faith, or honor." Soon the United States would have to help solve the "political and social problems" of Haiti, the Dominican Republic, and Cuba. While some believed that our political system could not be spread beyond North America, he suggested that the principles of free government "as embraced by our Constitution" might eventually "comprehend within their sphere and influence the civilized nations of the world." He specifically proposed the annexation of Haiti and the Dominican Republic. Once again the Senate declined to act, in part at least because Senator Charles Sumner, the chairman of the Foreign Relations Committee, bitterly opposed Johnson's Reconstruction policy. More prophetically, Johnson in his last State of the Union address promoted a new commercial treaty with the Hawaiian Islands, whom he expected eventually to "voluntarily to apply for admission into the Union."

Johnson reported regularly on other new developments within the United States. The Central Pacific and the Union Pacific had begun building the transcontinental railway during the war, and he gave brief progress reports in each of his annual addresses. The nation granted title to millions of acres every year to new settlers under the Homestead Act, another wartime measure. In December 1867, he reported that the government was seeking new treaties with various Plains Indian tribes in order to move them farther away from the new railroad, "an object of national importance" that "should not be interrupted by hostile tribes." He also reported on the extremely rapid reductions in the army, which fell from one million men to about 50,000 within two years, and the navy, which fell from 530 active vessels in 1865 to 206 in 1868.

Early in 1868 Congress impeached and tried Johnson for violating the new Tenure of Office Act after he tried to remove another key Lincoln appointee, Secretary of War Edwin M. Stanton. Some Republicans regarded the impeachment as an unnecessary partisan attack in Johnson's last year in office, and the Senate acquitted him by a single vote, 35–19. By July 1868 the Democratic Party had nominated New York governor Horatio Seymour for president and the Republicans had selected General Ulysses S. Grant. Undaunted, Johnson on July 17 submitted a special message to Congress proposing several constitutional amendments, reflecting, as he saw it, some of the lessons of his tenure. Two proposed the direct popular election of senators—still chosen under the Constitution by state legislatures—and a limit on the tenure of federal justices. Another proposed to alter the presidential line of succession so that an official of the executive branch would succeed a former vice president like himself, should he die or be removed from office.[4] Last and most importantly, he revived and filled out Andrew Jackson's proposal for the direct election of the president. Johnson recommended that the people of each congressional district choose one presidential elector via the popular vote—a plan that would have fulfilled Andrew Jackson's 1833 objective of maintaining the current weight of each state within the process. If when these votes were opened in October no candidate received a majority, a second round between the two leaders would take place in December. Echoing Jackson once again, he proposed a single six-year presidential term. Four years of increasingly bitter conflict with the congressional leadership had evidently done nothing to shake Johnson's confidence in his own views. Congress took no action on any of these proposals. Johnson skipped his successor's inaugural.

The youngest man yet to take the oath of office at forty-six, Ulysses S. Grant had led successful campaigns against Fort Donelson, Vicksburg, Chattanooga and Richmond during the Civil War. His first inaugural address showed unusual confidence and breadth of vision. Nearly all his predecessors had expressed concern that they might prove unworthy to fill their predecessors' shoes, but he accepted his great responsibilities "without fear," determined to secure "the satisfaction of the people." Grant laid out a vision of a great future. Turning away from Johnson's and the Radical Republicans' bitter partisanship, he revived the tone of earlier presidents. The new questions arising from the rebellion "should be approached calmly, without prejudice, hate, or sectional pride, remembering that the greatest good to the greatest number is the object to be attained. This requires security of person, property, and free religious and political opinion in every part of our common country, without regard to local prejudice." The nation's increasing wealth should allow it to pay its great debt within another

---

4 Had Johnson been convicted in his impeachment trial he would have given way to Senator Ben Wade of Ohio, a Radical Republican and president pro tempore of the Senate.

twenty-five years. "The young men of the country—those who from their age must be its rulers twenty-five years hence—have a peculiar interest in maintaining the national honor," he continued. "A moment's reflection as to what will be our commanding influence among the nations of the earth in their day, if they are only true to themselves, should inspire them with national pride." He spoke for mutual respect in foreign affairs, Indian policies tending toward "their civilization and ultimate citizenship," and the ratification of the Fifteenth Amendment forbidding racial restrictions on voting. Grant in his eight years unfortunately found it hard to live up to this ideal vision of leadership, partly because the Congress had become accustomed to running the government under his predecessor and would not surrender its new role. With respect to the great domestic questions of public credit, the economy, and Reconstruction, the end of his first term marked a dividing line, and we shall look at those questions one term at a time.

The election of 1868 had confirmed that continued Republican rule depended in part on keeping much of the South Republican. Grant had won the popular vote over New York governor Horatio Seymour by just 52.7 percent to 47.3 percent, and Seymour had carried his home state, New Jersey, Maryland and Kentucky. In the South, Virginia, Mississippi and Texas cast no electoral votes because they had not yet formed governments acceptable to the Republican Congress, and the Republicans had carried the Carolinas, Tennessee, Arkansas, Alabama and Florida, while losing Louisiana and Georgia. Grant reported annually on the progress of Reconstruction. Seven southern states had been restored to the Union, he reported in December 1869, and Georgia would have joined them had not its legislature immediately expelled all its colored members while admitting ex-Confederates disbarred from office by the Fourteenth Amendment. He asked Congress to admit newly elected representatives from Virginia, while awaiting the results of elections in Texas and Mississippi. A year later he noted that Virginia, Mississippi and Texas now had representatives back in Congress and Georgia might soon as well, but "regretted" that "violence and intimidation" had denied voting rights to citizens "in exceptional cases in several of the states lately in rebellion." The Ku Klux Klan was now organizing in various parts of the South, and Congress in April 1871 passed an act authorizing the president to suspend habeas corpus wherever legal authority broke down. Grant in December of that year noted that he had done so in nine counties of South Carolina in October, after violence had struck "thousands of inoffensive and well-disposed citizens," including members of opposing political parties and freedmen trying to exercise their rights. On the other hand, Grant suggested that removing political disabilities from leading Confederates under the Fourteenth Amendment might also help pacify the South, since rebels who had not yet taken an oath to the Constitution were no more guilty than those who had. Congress implemented that recommendation in the spring of 1872.

In the same December 1871 address Grant spoke bitterly about conditions within a western territory. "In Utah there still remains a remnant of barbarism, repugnant to civilization, to decency, and to the laws of the United States," he said. "Territorial officers, however, have been found who are willing to perform their duty in a spirit of equity and with a due sense of the necessity of sustaining the majesty of the law. Neither polygamy nor any other violation of existing statutes will be permitted within the territory of the United States." Three years later, in December 1876, he complained that the Utah legislature was evading and defying the will of the US government and called for a stronger anti-polygamy law. This turned out to be only the next round of a struggle that extended through four administrations.

The payment of the debt and the restoration of the currency remained Grant's next priorities, after Reconstruction. With the help of his secretary of the treasury George S. Boutwell, Grant laid down a policy of preserving a substantial federal surplus for debt reduction while refunding portions of the debt with lower-interest, long-term bonds that saved the government as much as two percent per year. In December 1872 he reported that these policies had reduced the debt by $87.1 million, $117.6 million, $94 million, and about $86 million in each of the last four years, for a total of $363 million—about 14 percent of the total in 1868. In the preceding fiscal year the government had taken in $374.1 million in revenue, including $216.4 million from customs and $130.6 million in internal taxes. Of the expenditures of $377 million, a full $227.3 million went for principal and interest on the debt. Meanwhile, the price of $100 gold in legal tender notes fell from

$134 in 1869 to $115 in 1870. The pension bill climbed steadily, and by 1872 it had reached an annual $30.2 million, including 95,405 invalids; 113,518 widows, orphans and dependents;3,179 naval pensioners; and $2.3 million for surviving veterans of the War of 1812.

Grant referred to the goal of resuming the redemption of government notes in specie but never made any specific proposals about it. He also repeatedly called for help for American steamship lines that would reclaim more of our trade from foreign bottoms, and for more trade with the Far East. In December 1876 he revived the old Whig tradition of internal improvements and proposed new canals to link the southeastern ports with the Mississippi. Congress evidently remained deaf to most of his pleas.

Grant revived the tradition of discussing foreign affairs at the beginning of his annual addresses, and he and his secretary of state Hamilton Fish picked up where Seward had left off on several fronts. While he abandoned the treaty to acquire the Virgin Islands, he submitted a treaty in June 1869, and advocated it in December of that year, for the annexation of the Dominican Republic. Interests within that country were also pushing the treaty, and Grant argued that some European nation would establish its own port there if the United States did not annex it, and perhaps eventually make it a state. Grant pointed out that an adverse trade balance was eating up much of US production of gold and silver, and the country could save $100 million of it by getting coffee, tea and sugar from this new territory. (He could not, of course, anticipate that baseball players would eventually become the country's major export to the US.) The Dominican people, he said, wanted the free institutions that the US could provide, and prosperous free labor there would encourage the abolition of slavery in Cuba and Puerto Rico, where it survived under Spanish rule. The nation had only 120,000 inhabitants, but Grant argued prophetically that it might eventually support ten million.[5] Meanwhile the island would provide a critical naval base in the Caribbean. The Republican Party now enjoyed a Senate majority of 57–9, but Charles Sumner of Massachusetts, the chairman of the Foreign Relations Committee,

---

5 The Dominican Republic has about eleven million people today.

led the opposition to the measure partly on the grounds that he did not believe that the United States should annex territory inhabited by nonwhites. He brought along enough additional Republicans to block the treaty, and it died without a vote.

Simultaneously, a thirty-year crisis had begun in the neighboring island of Cuba, where an insurrection against Spanish rule broke out. Grant in December 1869 expressed sympathy for the insurgent cause and predicted that Spain's remaining Caribbean colonies would win independence, but argued that the insurgents were not strong enough to be recognized as belligerents. Three years later he reported that the two parties were still locked in a stalemate, and that a feeble Spanish step toward the abolition of slavery had gone nowhere. Grant in December 1871 had praised the onset of abolition in Brazil, then the only other outpost of slavery in the western hemisphere. Grant also asked, not for the last time, for a law to forbid Americans from owning slaves elsewhere. In 1873 Grant praised a new Spanish republican government for abolishing slavery in Puerto Rico and attempting to do the same in Cuba. Spanish warships were blockading the island to keep help away from the rebels, and in October 1873 a gunboat had stopped the US steamer *Virginius* and taken its fifty-three passengers and crew into a Cuban port where they were summarily executed. Grant had put the navy on a war footing because of an "outburst of indignation," but he now merely demanded the return of a few survivors, an indemnity, and punishment for the guilty parties. By 1875 the Spanish authorities were using more brutal tactics against the rebels, and pressure to intervene had evidently grown. Grant resisted it again in his December message, arguing at length that the insurgents still lacked "a substantial political organization, real, palpable, and manifest to the world," which would justify recognizing them as a belligerent. He still hoped that Spain would agree to peace, and hinted at a new policy if it did not. Four more presidents would struggle with the Cuban independence question. Elsewhere in Latin America, Grant eventually helped secure an armistice in a long war between Spain and the nations on the west coast of South America, and to negotiate an agreement with Columbia on a canal across the Panama Isthmus.

On the Atlantic front, Grant inherited, and immediately dismissed, a negotiated agreement with Britain on the *Alabama* claims that in his opinion granted the United States much too little. In

December 1871 he announced a breakthrough. "The year has been an eventful one in witnessing two great nations, speaking one language and having one lineage, settling by peaceful arbitration disputes of long standing and liable at any time to bring those nations into bloody and costly conflict. An example has thus been set which, if successful in its final issue, may be followed by other civilized nations, and finally be the means of returning to productive industry millions of men now maintained to settle the disputes of nations by the bayonet and the broadside." The British and the US had agreed to submit the *Alabama* claims to neutral arbitration and had agreed on new principles of wartime maritime law that they would submit to other sea powers as well. They had also settled a dispute over navigation on the Great Lakes and the St. Lawrence River, which had opened up in the previous year with "the colonial authority known as the Dominion of Canada," which Grant had called "a semi-independent and irresponsible agent" in December 1870. (The British North America Act had created the Canadian government in 1867.) In December 1872 he reported that the British had agreed to pay $15.5 million in gold to settle the *Alabama* claims. The emperor of Germany had also arbitrated the Anglo-American boundary dispute over the San Juan Islands in Puget Sound, and Grant proudly noted that for the first time in its history as an independent state, the United States had no outstanding boundary disputes with Great Britain. The settlement with Britain began a long-term US effort to find peaceful means of settling international disputes that continued at least into the aftermath of the First World War.

In other European developments, the Franco-Prussian War had broken out in mid-1870, and the US had assumed protection of German nationals living in France. In September a revolution overthrew Napoleon III as the French armies collapsed, and Grant in December 1870 congratulated the new republic. "While we make no effort to impose our institutions upon the inhabitants of other countries, and while we adhere to our traditional neutrality in civil contests elsewhere," he said, "we cannot be indifferent to the spread of American political ideas in a great and highly civilized country like France." He had had to decline a French request to help make peace, however, because the North German Confederation resisted it. The Union victory in the Civil War had impressed Europe as a victory for democracy over aristocracy, and Great Britain, Germany and Italy all took major steps toward more representative government as well in the late 1860s, vindicating Lincoln's view of the stakes in that conflict.

Grant showed a great interest in other workings of the federal government. Once again echoing his immediate predecessor, Grant raised the growing issue of civil service reform in his second annual message in December 1870. Custom now gave senators and representatives of the ruling party almost total control of appointments in their states, and the Senate in 1869 refused to repeal the Tenure of Office Act that gave it the power to keep men in office, even though the White House had returned to Republican hands. Grant now spoke generally of altering "the manner of making all appointments," but said nothing definite either then or in the next three years in similarly brief references to the issue. Meanwhile, he repeatedly praised the operation of the new Department of Agriculture and the Education Bureau within the Department of the Interior. He was delighted to announce in December 1873 that new District of Columbia authorities had paved the streets and were rapidly making the city "a capital of which the nation may well be proud," and to report the progress of the new State, War and Navy Building next to the White House—the edifice known today as the Executive Office Building. He also revived after nearly half a century the idea of a university within the District, but Congress again failed to act. The national Land Office continued to distribute millions of acres a year in homesteads, and additional millions to railroads. Grant began to suggest that the latter grants might have become excessive. The Post Office still ran an annual deficit, but it had fallen somewhat in his last year. In December 1875 Grant proposed a truly revolutionary constitutional amendment, one requiring all states to maintain free public schools for all children, while prohibiting any religious instruction within such schools or the spending on any public funds on religion. Designed both to guarantee education for all in the South—where antebellum governments had never provided it even to the whites—and fight the influence of the Catholic Church, this amendment got nowhere in Congress.

Although some scandals and the civil service reform issue had split the Republican Party by the end of Grant's first term, the incapacity of the Democrats saved him from any embarrassment at the polls. Dissident Independent Republicans bolted the party, held their own convention, and nominated distinguished Republican newspaper editor Horace Greeley as their presidential candidate. Lacking a strong candidate of their own, the Democrats decided to endorse Greeley, now a critic of Reconstruction. The elderly Greeley carried six states—Texas, Tennessee, Kentucky, Missouri, Georgia, Maryland and Delaware—in the election, but died before the Electoral College could meet, leading many Democratic electors to vote for other candidates. This remained the low point of Democratic Party fortunes for exactly a century

In his second inaugural address, Grant boasted that he had tried in his first term "to restore harmony, public credit, commerce, and all the arts of peace and progress. It is my firm conviction that the civilized world is tending toward republicanism, or government by the people through their chosen representatives, and that our own great Republic is destined to be the guiding star to all others." Then he stated bluntly that the former slave "is not possessed of the civil rights which citizenship should carry with it." He promised to do whatever the executive branch could to secure them, but added that "social equality is not to be legislated on." "The colored man" needed fair treatment and a fair chance to develop. "The states lately at war," he added, "are now happily rehabilitated." Just a few days earlier, on February 25, Grant in a special message to Congress described how he had had to intervene to try to resolve a post-election dispute in Louisiana between two competing slates of state officials, each of which claimed to have been elected.

Seven months later, and before he had a chance to deliver his next annual message, a panic on Wall Street plunged the nation into perhaps the worst economic crisis in its history to date. Like the housing market in 2007–8, the market for railroad bonds in the early 1870s was so inflated that it was bound to collapse. In October 1873 a major New York bank failure spread through the nation with catastrophic effects on farm income, industrial production and employment, and the crisis spread rapidly through the whole industrialized world. No major nation kept unemployment figures in those days, and economists attempting to model unemployment for this period have admitted that their results are very tentative, but the distress must have been comparable to that of 2008–10, if not

1929–33. "In the midst of great national prosperity," Grant began his December 1873 address, "a financial crisis has occurred that has brought low fortunes of gigantic proportions; political partisanship has almost ceased to exist, especially in the agricultural regions." Grant's proposed responses reflected conservative economic orthodoxy. The last fiscal year had finished with a $43.3 million surplus, but he now anticipated a deficit thanks to falling revenues, and proposed cutting back spending on public buildings, rivers and harbors, and even on claims for "losses incurred in suppressing the late rebellion." Although the currency had retained its value, Grant declared that the nation could not agree to redeem greenbacks in specie until "our exports, exclusive of gold, pay for our imports, interest due abroad, and other specie obligations." He blamed the panic on the banks' use of seasonally high deposits as call money in the stock market and proposed new restrictions on the national banks' handling of their deposits. Grant also came out firmly against inflation, which many farmers wanted to reduce their burden of debt. Five months later, on April 22, 1874, Grant vetoed a measure to increase the circulation of paper notes by $100 million and insisted that only a return to specie payments would cure the country's ills.

In December 1874 Grant opened his address referring to "a prostration in business and industries such as has not been witnessed with us for many years." He appeared to blame the crisis on "a spirit of speculation" begotten by the circulation of legal tender notes, rejected inflation again, and insisted on a sound currency as the only remedy. Grant reported a surplus of only $2.3 million for the previous fiscal year and anticipated just $9 million for the coming year. He complained that Congress might have reduced taxes too much and opened unfortunate loopholes in tariffs, and suggested increasing revenue with new taxes on coffee and tea and higher ones on whiskey. A year later he praised a new law that had set January 1, 1879, for the redemption of legal tender notes in specie, called for exchanging about $2 million monthly of these notes for government bonds, and renewed his tax proposals, which Congress had rejected. In his last, retrospective annual message of December 1876, Grant boasted that while taxes had fallen by $300 million over seven fiscal years, the debt had been reduced by $435 million, and refunding operations had reduced annual interest from $130 million to $100 million. Best of all, the balance of trade had shifted from a deficit of $130 million in 1869—paid for with specie—to a surplus of more than $120 million in 1876, indicating that the January 1, 1879 deadline for resuming specie payments would be kept.

Indian affairs entered a new and critical phase during Grant's presidency. The building of the transcontinental railway brought workers, soldiers and settlers into the last Indian hunting grounds on the Great Plains and in the foothills of the Rockies. Speaking frankly in his first annual message, Grant conceded that the conduct of the whites was responsible for much of the robbery, murder and war between whites and Indians, but said that the nation now had to deal with the situation as it was. "No matter what ought to be the relations between such settlements and the aborigines," he said, "the fact is they do not harmonize well, and one or the other has to give way in the end. A system which looks to the extinction of a race"—which some countrymen evidently were advocating—"is too horrible for a nation to adopt without entailing upon itself the wrath of all Christendom and engendering in the citizen a disregard for human life and the rights of others, dangerous to society." He saw no solution but to settle and protect the Indians on large reservations, encourage them to become individual landowners, and give them territorial government. A year later he had turned the oversight of some reservations over to the Society of Friends, who might "Christianize and civilize the Indian, and train him in the arts of peace." Three more annual reports later, in 1872, he declared the new policy an unqualified success for railroads, settlers, and Indians alike. More tribes were moving into Indian Territory, which needed a territorial government to protect them from white inroads. He said nothing specific about a number of punitive military actions taking place against recalcitrant tribes, some of them involving massacres of dozens of innocents, that were taking place on the Great Plains and elsewhere.[6]

Grant reported new disturbances in 1874, and announced a year later that an influx of miners into the Black Hills in the Dakotas was making it harder to maintain the Indians' rights, and that the government might have to withhold payments due the

---

6 These are covered very thoroughly in Peter Cozzens, *The Earth Is Weeping, The Epic Story of the Indian Wars for the American West* (New York, 2016).

Indians to get them to "relinquish" the new gold fields. On July 8, 1876, Grant discreetly sent Congress reports from several military authorities describing the disastrous defeat suffered by General George Armstrong Custer. He did not mention that catastrophe in his last annual message but confessed that he had not managed to remove the miners from Sioux lands in the Black Hills, because the vast reserves of gold would have induced troops to desert had they been sent for that purpose. Now a new treaty to give the key areas to the whites awaited congressional action.

Grant's second term witnessed a determined white southern counterattack on Reconstruction, which he attempted to forestall. In December 1873 he asked for a new law "to better secure the civil rights which freedom should secure, but has not effectually secured, to the enfranchised slave." In September 1874 Grant had to deliver another five-day ultimatum to white southerners in rebellion against the Reconstruction government of Louisiana. In his annual message three months later he explained that large, well-armed bands had spread terror and committed murders among large populations to deter them from voting. By the time Grant gave this address to a lame duck Congress, the combination of the economic crisis and numerous scandals involving officials of his administration had led to a remarkable Democratic sweep in the congressional elections of 1874, with the Democrats gaining 94 out of 293 seats and taking control of the House of Representatives, 180–103. 4,082 troops were still trying to enforce Reconstruction in twelve states, he reported—including Kentucky and Maryland—and while many complained about this, without it, "the whole scheme of colored enfranchisement" would become a mockery. Democrats in Arkansas had called a new convention, replaced the Reconstruction constitution, and elected a new government, and Grant left that situation in the hands of Congress, which was investigating it. Recognizing that "executive interference with the affairs of a state" was "repugnant to public opinion," he hoped to make it "unnecessary and obsolete." He consoled himself that "the better part" of the southern citizenry preferred to obey the law, and acknowledged that some states lived under "the most trying governments," whose "oppressive taxation" brought too few benefits. "Treat the Negro as a citizen and a voter, as he is and must remain, and soon parties will be divided, not on the color line, but on principle," he said optimistically. Later in that same month he issued a new proclamation designed to subdue an insurrection in Mississippi that the governor could not put down. On January 13, 1875, in a special message to the Senate, Grant detailed the many acts of violence with which Louisiana whites had sought to maintain their power against the Republicans of Louisiana, including the April 13, 1873 Colfax massacre of about sixty black people, including local government officials, "a butchery of citizens," Grant said, "which in bloodthirstiness and barbarity is hardly surpassed by any acts of savage warfare." He lamented that "no way can be found in this boasted land of civilization and Christianity to punish the perpetrators of this bloody and monstrous Crime," noted some other acts of political murder, and defended his decision to send federal troops back into Louisiana to enforce election results and keep the elected Republican governor in office in late 1874.[7]

In February 1875, the lame duck Republican Congress had passed a new Civil Rights Act in the wake of the death of Radical Charles Sumner, giving black citizens equal access to all public accommodations, and the right to sit on juries. Grant signed it, but the bill left it to black citizens themselves to seek enforcement in court. By 1876 only North Carolina, Florida, and Louisiana still had Republican governors, with South Carolina's state house in bitter dispute. Democrats had returned to power in all the other states of the old Confederacy, as well as in the border states of Maryland, West Virginia, Kentucky, and Missouri. The attempt to Republicanize the South was almost dead, and most white southerners did not want to treat freed slaves as equals.

Grant gave his last annual message on December 5, 1876. A dispute was building over the recent electoral contest between Rutherford B. Hayes, Republican, and Samuel Tilden, Democrat, in which Louisiana, South Carolina and Florida all eventually sent in two different sets of results. Saying nothing about the election, Grant tried to defend his overall record. He opined that since he had come into office without political training, errors of judgment had to be expected. Most of his mistakes, he argued, came from the appointment of the wrong men, "in nearly every case selected

---

7 Several of the Colfax murderers were eventually convicted in federal court, but the Supreme Court threw out those proceedings as a federal usurpation in 1876.

without a personal acquaintance with the appointee, but upon recommendations of the representatives chosen directly by the people." This was the closest he ever came to referring to many high-level scandals that had come to light in his last years in office. He had also come into office in the wake of a rebellion during which "a large percentage" of the North's population sympathized with the rebels, and after four years of controversy over the question of whether "control of the government should be thrown immediately into the hands of those who had so recently destroyed it." Then he proudly listed his greatest accomplishments with respect to the federal debt and foreign relations. He once again advocated the annexation of the Dominican Republic, which might have provided a refuge for some of "the emancipated race" of the South, where "whole communities," victims of "great oppression and cruelty," might have gone. He did not believe or propose that all of them should do so, but the option might have been a powerful bargaining counter. "It is not probable," he concluded, "that public affairs will ever again receive attention from me further than as a citizen of the Republic, always taking a deep interest in the honor, integrity, and prosperity of the whole land." That promise he did not quite manage to keep. While doing his best to secure the rights of freed slaves, Grant had taken several tentative steps pointing toward a new era in both foreign and domestic affairs, marked by imperialism, attempts to settle disputes peacefully, and a more professional civil service. He left behind a fractious and undisciplined Republican Party, increasingly divided between reformers and regulars, and a white South now ready to resume local political control by fair means or foul.

# X

# Rutherford B. Hayes, James A. Garfield, and Chester A. Arthur

## 1877–85

By 1876, having won control of the House of Representatives and most of the South and facing a scandal-plagued Grant administration, the Democratic Party was looking forward to returning to the White House at last. For the second time in three elections they nominated a Democratic governor of New York, Samuel J. Tilden, who had helped bring down the corrupt Tweed Ring in New York City. It took the Republicans seven ballots to nominate Governor Rutherford B. Hayes of Ohio—who committed himself to serve just one term—over the controversial James G. Blaine of Maine, who had recently had to admit interceding in Congress to help a railroad in which he had an interest, and Oliver Morton, the Republican machine candidate. Violence and intimidation marked the election in the critical southern states of Louisiana, South Carolina, and Florida, the only states still occupied by federal troops. On election night Tilden appeared to have carried all those states, as well as the rest of the South, all the border states, and Indiana, New Jersey, New York, and Connecticut, with a comfortable electoral majority. The House remained narrowly Democratic and the Senate narrowly Republican. Republican authorities in the three occupied southern states, however, sent in their own electoral votes to Congress, leaving the Congress to choose between two sets of electors. After weeks of controversy, the two parties agreed to a fifteen-member commission divided evenly among the House, the Senate and the Supreme Court, to decide which electors to certify.

Voting on party lines, the commission voted 8–7 to certify the Hayes electors from the three disputed states, giving him the election by one electoral vote. In exchange, Hayes agreed to remove the federal troops from those three states, all of which quickly returned to Democratic control thanks to the intimidation of their black populations, which in Louisiana and South Carolina constituted a majority. Democrats complained about the "stolen election" for at least eight more years.

Hayes began his inaugural with Reconstruction. "Many of the calamitous effects of the tremendous revolution which has passed over the Southern States still remain. The immeasurable benefits which will surely follow, sooner or later, the hearty and generous acceptance of the legitimate results of that revolution have not yet been realized." Once the impoverished southern states had "a government which guards the interests of both races carefully and equally," all "so-called party interests lose their apparent importance." The two races must work together. Education, he argued, would promote this, and he called for "liberal and permanent provision" for free schools by state governments—still a novelty in the South—supplemented by federal aid, a revolutionary idea. Allying with Republican reformers, Hayes then called for a "thorough, radical and complete reform" of the civil service, eliminating the practice of appointments for partisan service at the behest of congressmen and senators and providing secure tenure. Predicting a brighter economic future, he called for an early return to specie payments. He referred in conclusion to the work of the electoral commission, called the general acceptance of its decision a cause for "general rejoicing," and pleaded for unity. Hayes maintained the same high-minded, ambitious tone throughout his term, but made little headway against resurgent Democrats, who tried to use congressional power to strip away the last vestiges of Reconstruction, and machine Republicans who resented his civil service proposals.

Although Hayes ended the federal occupation of the former Confederacy, he kept Reconstruction issues in the foreground of all four of his annual addresses. Proclaiming the pacification of the country "the most important of all our national interests" in December 1877, he claimed that national harmony had demanded his controversial troop withdrawals, the measures "best adapted under the circumstances to attain the end in view." The South was reviving economically and lawless acts had diminished, he said, and he was determined to see that the former slaves' rights were respected. He also repeated Grant's call for federal money to improve education. But when commenting on recent elections, his messages of 1878 and 1880 complained that black citizens had been blocked from voting either by violence (especially in South Carolina and Louisiana) or by fraud. He never, however, threatened to impose local martial law to arrest members of the KKK, as Grant had done—although in July 1877, he did call out military forces to deal with a violent railroad strike in Maryland, West Virginia, and Pennsylvania, and boasted that December that the troops had put an end to "very serious riots" without actually having to use force. In 1879 and 1880 Hayes vetoed appropriations bills, threatening a government shutdown, because the Democratic House had attached riders ending the role of federal marshals in elections. He won those battles but the Republicans were slowly losing the war for equal suffrage in the South.

Hayes took a similarly strong, moralistic tone toward the emerging issue of civil service reform. Both parties and the "intelligent masses of the people," he said in December 1877, agreed on its need, and he endorsed an end to legislative influence on appointments and asked for more money for Grant's moribund Civil Service Commission. This Congress would not give, but two years later, Hayes daringly commended to the Congress a favorable report by the commission chairman on the effects of civil service reform in Great Britain—a most unusual use of a foreign example in a domestic argument. The British had ended parliamentary patronage and implemented a system of competitive examinations. He also asked for a law to prevent party assessments upon officials for campaign contributions. In December 1880, after the election of his successor, he returned once again to this battle, boasting of having instituted competitive examinations for positions in the largest customshouses and post offices, arguing for "a complete divorce between Congress and the Executive in the matter of appointments," and the repeal of the Tenure of Office Act. The Congress had still failed to act on the issue when he left office.

Hayes scored his biggest triumph over the related questions of public credit and the currency. Like Grant, he faced pressure to agree to coin more silver from agrarian interests who wanted to reduce the value of their debts, and when he vetoed a bill to do so in February 1878, Congress passed the bill over his veto. The demand for silver coins turned out to be much less than expected, however, since consumers apparently expected them to fall in value. Like Grant, Hayes insisted on the need to return to specie payments, and in December 1879, he congratulated the Congress on the successful execution of the resumption act that had passed under Grant. Nor was this all. The Treasury was successfully refunding large portions of the debt at lower rates of interest, and interest payments had fallen by $14 million annually since he had taken office. Best of all, a suddenly favorable trade balance, fueled largely by agricultural exports, was now increasing the nation's stock of specie. A year these trends had become even more favorable. His last annual message reported that the government had run a $66 million surplus during the previous fiscal year, spending $267.6 million, with $95.8 million in interest payments and $56.8 million for pensions accounting for more than half of it. The total national debt had fallen from $2.756 billion in 1865 to $1.886 billion. Silver dollars had fallen to 88.5 cents, reflecting the actual value of their silver, and he recommended coining larger ones to make them equal in value to gold. The world was rebounding from the depression of 1873 and Hayes boasted that the nation's economic health was not only better than that of any other country, but the best in the history of the world.

In December 1879, Hayes noted that the Supreme Court had rejected a Mormon argument that a seventeen-year old law against polygamy infringed upon their religious freedom, and called for better enforcement measures, which would allow Utah to become a state. In his last message a year later he argued that the nation must take away "the political power of the sect which encourages and sustains it [polygamy]," and which now controlled the entire territorial government. Mormon power was now expanding into other territories, and Hayes wanted a new territorial government with a governor and judges or commissioners appointed by the president and confirmed by the Senate, such as Ohio had enjoyed under the Northwest Ordinance of 1787. Alternatively Congress might deny polygamists the right to vote, hold office, or serve on juries. The US simply must restore "the sanctity of marriage and the family relation," maintain "religious liberty and the separation of church and state," and keep territories open to "virtuous immigrants of all creeds." Congress did not respond. Closer to home, Hayes called repeatedly for money to complete the half-finished Washington Monument, to create a new national museum within the Smithsonian Institution, to build a new fireproof Library of Congress, and to drain the swampland of Washington, which still included most of what is now the National Mall. He praised some important improvements in the appearance of the nation's capital, but the swamps remained wet as he left office. He also failed to convince Congress to provide a territorial government for Alaska.

In his first annual message, Hayes noted that the army had recently brought some long campaigns against Indian tribes to a close. "Many, if not most, of our Indian wars have had their origin in broken promises and acts of injustice upon our part," he said, "and the advance of the Indians in civilization has been slow because the treatment they received did not permit it to be faster and more general." He endorsed the policies of his secretary of the interior, the German immigrant Carl Schurz, which focused on encouraging Indian agriculture and education, and asked for laws allowing Indians to become homesteaders and citizens. Despite a few more small uprisings, Hayes continued to praise these policies in subsequent years, reporting on the education of some young Indians at the Hampton Institute in Virginia—the black college at which Booker T. Washington had been educated—and the founding of Indian schools at Carlisle, Pennsylvania, and Forest Grove, Oregon. Schurz's attempts to allow Indians to acquire individual title to lands would eventually allow the government to open reservations to settlement and advance the country "toward the solution of the Indian problem, in preparing for the gradual merging of our Indian population in the great body of American citizenship."

Hayes meanwhile had a remarkably quiet administration in foreign affairs. His messages generally took note of friendly relations and routine new agreements with various states. Spain had temporarily managed to subdue the Cuban insurrection, taking the question of intervention off the table. The Mexican border had been so turbulent that both the Mexican and US armies had been given the right to cross it in pursuit of hostile Indians, but Hayes in December 1880 reported that it had quieted down, and looked forward to the rapid construction of railroads linking the two countries. The US was trying to make peace between Chile on one side and Bolivia and Peru on the other, and in his last message, Hayes asked the Congress to approve an agreement with Colombia that would allow the US to construct a canal across Panama (still part of Colombia). The new Canadian government still lacked any diplomatic authority and a new fisheries dispute with Britain dragged on.

Even if Hayes had chosen to renounce his earlier pledge and seek a second term, he would have almost certainly failed to gain the Republican nomination. He had never won the confidence of the party bosses, and they had gotten behind ex-President Grant's campaign for a third term. Grant began the convention balloting leading the field with a plurality over James G. Blaine of Maine and John Sherman of Ohio, but could not get close to a majority. In the 36th ballot the opposition united behind a new candidate, the respected House member James A. Garfield of Ohio. The Democratic Party meanwhile tried something new, choosing Winfield Scott Hancock, a distinguished Union Army general in the Civil War, who had never before run for office. With the Democrats now fully back in control in the South, Garfield won another very close election by carrying the two critical swing states of New York and Indiana.

Garfield's inaugural began on a triumphant note. Looking forward to a celebration of the centennial of the Battle of Yorktown, he referred to the colonists' struggle "not only against the armies of a great nation, but against the settled opinions of mankind." Their Constitution had succeeded brilliantly, and after the Civil War, "the Union emerged from the blood and fire . . . purified and made stronger for all the beneficent purposes of good government." Despite "serious disturbance to our southern communities," he continued, the Negro race could not become a "permanent disenfranchised peasantry in the United States." The states would earn repose and safety only by keeping the ballot "free and pure." The federal government must also assist in the fight against illiteracy. Echoing Hayes about a strong currency, the need to end polygamy, and civil service reform, Garfield seemed likely to emerge as another foe of the Republican bosses, known as "Stalwarts," and he confirmed that by immediately fighting and winning a dramatic struggle with their leader, Senator Roscoe Conkling of New York, over the choice of the Collector of the Port of New York, the most important single patronage appointment in the country. On July 2, 1881, however, Garfield was shot in Washington by Charles Guiteau, a mentally ill Republican Party worker who had been seeking a job in the administration. After six weeks of debilitating illness during which he could not perform the duties of his office, Garfield died on September 18.

His vice president, as fate would have it, was a New York machine politician, Chester A. Arthur, who had held the office of Collector of the Port of New York himself from 1871 until 1878, when Hayes had managed to fire him after a long struggle with Congress. His accession shone an even brighter light upon the civil service reform issue, not only because a would-be officeholder had shot Garfield, but also because the assassin had actually declared to his arresting officers, "I am a stalwart and Arthur is president now!" Arthur, however, surprised the country by moving it toward a new era. His long, measured annual addresses took an entirely businesslike approach to government, generally free either of partisanship or of any crusading spirit. He was the first post—Civil War president to put the great issues of the war and Reconstruction completely behind him.

"An appalling calamity has befallen the American people," Arthur opened his first annual message in December 1881, before turning quickly to foreign affairs. No major issue ever threatened the peace during his administration, and he gradually reported on progress on several fronts. By December 1884, he could note that the war between Chile, Bolivia and Peru was coming to an end. His administration failed to reach an agreement with Colombia over the construction of a canal in Panama, but in December 1884 he reported on a new accord with Nicaragua to build one there. He repeatedly noted that the US had asked the Russian Empire to end its "proscription" of its "Hebrew" population, which had also affected Jewish Americans visiting Russia. The Mexican and American armies continued to cross back and forth over the border to control hostile Indians. In March of 1882, Arthur courageously vetoed a bill that would have banned the immigration of any more "Chinese laborers" into the United States for twenty years. A new treaty the previous year had allowed the US to "restrict" that immigration, but not to prohibit if for twenty years, as the bill did. These laborers, he said bluntly, had profited the United States, building parts of the transcontinental railroad and undertaking enterprises that Caucasians would not. Arthur however failed to stick to his guns: Congress passed a similar law shortly thereafter reducing the period of restriction from twenty years to ten, and he signed it.

Every year, Arthur gave detailed reviews of federal revenues and expenditures. In December 1881 he reported ordinary revenue in the last fiscal year of $360.8 million. $198.2 million came from customs receipts, and $138.1 million of them came from the port of New York—an index of the importance of the collectorship which he had held himself, and which Hayes and Garfield had struggled to control. Expenditures, led by $82.5 million in debt interest and $50.1 million for pensions, totaled just $260.7 million, and the entire $100.1 million surplus went to pay off government debt. Meanwhile, exports exceeded imports by $259.7 million. He called, not for the last time, for reducing taxes, but Congress took little action. The revenue rose in fiscal 1882 but then began to fall, and Arthur reported revenues of $398.3 million—$214 million from customs—in his last message in December 1884. Congress had by then reduced internal taxation by about $55 million, but the surplus had reached $132.9 million, most of which again went to reduce debt. He pointed out that the progressive retirement of government bonds threatened a crisis in the banking system, because since the Civil War the national banks used those bonds to fulfill their reserve requirements. He suggested that the government cut taxes on the banks and ease those requirements. Although he did not say so, the federal budget surplus under his administration must have reached an all-time high.

Arthur went into similar detail about various other federal activities. In December 1881 he reviewed the pension situation, citing 193,000 pending claims, which at current rates would take six years to adjudicate—while others piled up. In 1882, he courageously vetoed the annual Rivers and Harbors bill on grounds of extravagance. The total appropriation, he noted, had grown from $4 million in 1870 to $11.5 million in fiscal 1882, and this bill asked for $18.7 million. Even though it did include money to drain the swamps south of the White House—as he and his predecessors had often demanded—it had too many projects of purely local importance for him to sign it. Congress overrode the veto, but the next December Arthur said that $4.7 million remained to be spent and recommended against another such measure in 1883. He echoed Hayes's calls for stricter measures against polygamy in Utah—including a change in the law to allow wives to testify against husbands in these cases—for unspecified federal aid for education, and for money to help build up an American merchant marine. In December 1881 he reported a new threat to public order, a band of "armed desperadoes known as 'Cowboys'" who had been committing lawless acts of brutality in the territory of Arizona. These were the gang that was tangling with US marshal Wyatt Earp in Tombstone, where the gunfight at the O.K. Corral had taken place in October, and Arthur eventually suggested that the army might be allowed to help territorial governments keep public order—something recently outlawed under the Posse Comitatus act. Arthur also took a keen interest in the navy, calling for its "thorough rehabilitation" in his first annual message, and two years later he reported that three modern cruisers and some new double-turreted monitors were now under construction—the first step, he said, toward a navy that could cope with the great powers of the world.

In his first annual message Arthur definitely called for an end to the policy of allowing the Indians to continue a "savage life" on reservations. The problem was no nearer a solution than half a century before—referring to the time of Andrew Jackson—and he favored giving them more education, encouraging agriculture, and bringing reservations under state law. He continued to repeat these proposals, while noting that only the Southwest now faced an Indian uprising.

Last but not least, Arthur's administration took real steps forward on civil service reform. His first message included a long discussion of the English system. While offering to sign a bill implementing it if Congress passed it, he expressed reservations about limiting entry into the system to those under twenty-five and about life tenure for officials, and suggested "pass examinations" instead of competitive ones, that is, tests that would simply certify the competence of a preferred candidate. Local elections during 1882 showed growing support for some measure, and after losing control of the House of Representatives, the Republicans decided to pass legislation—the

Pendleton Act—in the lame duck session of December 1882, which Arthur opened with a call for action. That act instituted competitive examinations for positions in Washington and in all customshouses with at least fifty employees, limited entry to the lowest grades, but left open a loophole, permitting "voluntary" contributions to campaigns by officials.[1] Arthur praised the new system in his last two messages to Congress.

Citing the problems occasioned by his predecessor's two-month fatal illness, Arthur called repeatedly for a new law to provide for presidential disability. Not for more than eighty years did Congress act to solve this problem. He also suggested changes in the law of presidential succession, a line-item veto that would have allowed him to reject specific parts of the Rivers and Harbors bill, and a law on the resolution of disputed presidential elections—all without result. Arthur referred only once in annual messages to issues arising from Reconstruction, in December 1883, after the Supreme Court, by an 8–1 margin, had struck down the Civil Rights Act of 1875, guaranteeing equal access to public accommodations for all. "Any legislation whereby Congress may lawfully supplement the guarantees which the Constitution affords for the equal enjoyment by all the citizens of the United States of every right, privilege, and immunity of citizenship," he said, "will receive my unhesitating approval." The new, overwhelmingly Democratic Congress took no action.

The presidential election of 1884 confirmed that the Reconstruction era was over. Arthur was seriously ill by then, but still stood for renomination. He lost on the fourth ballot to the charismatic, controversial James G. Blaine, a party favorite who had narrowly lost bids for the nomination in 1876 and 1880. The Democrats nominated their third governor of New York in five elections, Grover Cleveland of Buffalo, a reformer who had been elected just two years earlier. Neither candidate had served in the Union Army. Because he had been caught red-handed taking money in exchange for getting a railroad bill approved in Congress in 1876, Blaine symbolized corrupt Republicanism for many voters, and some independent Republicans, known as Mugwumps, defected to Cleveland. Cleveland meanwhile had to deal with a revelation early

---

1 Ari Hogeboom, *Outlawing the Spoils. A History of the Civil Service Reform Movement, 1865–1883* (Urbana, IL, 1961), pp. 236–52.

in the campaign that he, a bachelor, had acknowledged fathering an illegitimate child. In one of the dirtiest and most heated campaigns in American history, Cleveland emerged the winner by the narrowest of margins, thanks to a margin of 1,149 votes in his home state. He also won Connecticut, New Jersey, Indiana, and every one of the former slave states. The Democratic Party—until now so closely associated with the losing side in the Civil War—had returned to power. Arthur commented on the result a month later in his last annual message. "When it is remembered that at no period in the country's history has the long political contest which customarily precedes the day of the national election been waged with greater fervor and intensity," he said, "it is a subject of general congratulation that after the controversy at the polls was over, and while the slight preponderance by which the issue had been determined was as yet unascertained, the public peace suffered no disturbance, but the people everywhere patiently and quietly awaited the result." The 1880 census meanwhile counted fifty million US inhabitants, another 30.2 percent increase from the thirty-nine million figure from 1870, and more than the leading western European nations of Great Britain, the new German Empire, and France.

# XI

# Grover Cleveland and Benjamin Harrison

### 1885–89, 1893–97 • 1889–93

To Grover Cleveland fell the task of redefining the Democratic Party in a new era. His two terms and the single term Republican Benjamin Harrison served between them turned into a fascinating era of party struggle over economic questions in general and the tariff and the federal budget in particular. "Amid the din of party strife the people's choice was made," he began his first inaugural, "but its attendant circumstances have demonstrated anew the strength and safety of a government by the people. . . . At this hour the animosities of political strife, the bitterness of partisan defeat, and the exultation of partisan triumph should be supplanted by an ungrudging acquiescence in the popular will and a sober, conscientious concern for the general weal." Echoing Van Buren, William Henry Harrison, and Grant, he pledged himself to "the greatest good to the greatest number," counting on a Democratic House and a Republican Senate to put partisanship aside. He promised a foreign policy based upon independence, peace and neutrality, fair and honest treatment for the Indians on a path to eventual citizenship, and the repression of polygamy in the territories. There should be "no pretext for anxiety," he added, "touching the protection of the freedmen in their rights or their security in the enjoyment of their privileges under the Constitution and its amendments." Any questions as to their fitness for citizenship should deal only with the need "for their improvement." Not for nearly three years did he find the defining issue of his first administration.

Cleveland's foreign policy combined a new degree of interest in certain distant lands with a determination not to embark upon any imperialist adventures. In his first annual message in December 1885, he reported having withdrawn Arthur's treaty with Nicaragua calling for the construction of an interoceanic canal, because it also pledged the United States to the unilateral defense of the canal, a feature "inconsistent with . . . dedication to universal and neutral use," and implying excessive obligations. He did not reject a Nicaraguan canal but proposed a "ship railway"—a railroad that could load and carry small ships—across Mexico's Tehuantepec isthmus.[1] He also reported that the United States had signed the European agreement creating the Belgian King Leopold's Congo Free State and had opened diplomatic relations with Korea. In subsequent messages he talked about progress toward an international copyright convention, and thanked Congress for increasing the pay of US diplomats abroad. He also had to detail new fisheries controversies with Canada, where the new Canadian authorities were trying to restrict the activities of US fishermen. On February 20, 1888 he sent a treaty recently concluded with the British that he claimed removed long-standing ambiguity about the rights of American fishermen to the Senate. With the election looming, the Republicans in the Senate refused to allow Cleveland this triumph, and the treaty failed to obtain a two-thirds majority in August. Trying to regain control of the situation, Cleveland on September 12 declared in a special message that he was "by no means disposed to abandon the interests and the rights of our people" and asked for a law authorizing him to suspend Canada's right to receive British goods shipped through US ports without paying any tariffs on them if restrictions on American fishermen resumed. The Senate blocked that measure as well. Meanwhile, Cleveland followed up eagerly upon Arthur's start at building a new navy. That task, he said in December 1885, was critical, since the nation lacked "a single vessel of war that could keep the seas against a first-class vessel of any important power." He also called for new coast artillery, and reported in December 1888 that work on it had begun.

Closer to home, Cleveland in his December 1885 message surveyed the Indian problem in frank and sometimes chilling language.

---

1 Ship railways were a popular concept in the late nineteenth century, but none seems ever to have been completed.

"It is useless to dilate upon the wrongs of the Indians," he said, "and as useless to indulge in the heartless belief that because their wrongs are revenged in their own atrocious manner, therefore they should be exterminated. They are within the care of our Government, and their rights are, or should be, protected from invasion by the most solemn obligations." He saw "general concurrence" that the nation should work for their "civilization and citizenship," and that they could "readily assimilate with the mass of our population." Their numbers were now estimated at 260,000—which suggests that in the following 135 years they have increased faster than the rest of the population. While some were "lazy, vicious and stupid," others were "industrious, peaceful, and intelligent," and had advanced far down the road to civilization, with laws, elected officers, and schools. He asked for six commissioners to investigate the widely differing conditions on various reservations and make recommendations for each. A year later he noted that the Apache chief Geronimo, after rising up and killing some white settlers, had surrendered to the army, and that his band was now imprisoned, but not tried for murder. The Indians could no longer subsist "by the chase and the spontaneous productions of the earth," he said; "barbarism and civilization cannot live together." He recommended more education and more division of Indian land into individual plots. In December 1887 he repeated these proposals and reported that one-third of Indian children were now in schools. Europe was now spreading the values of western civilization over much of the rest of the world, and successive presidents had made clear that assimilation was in their opinion the only real option for the Indian population.

Cleveland as mayor of Buffalo and governor of New York had participated in the growing effort to make government more efficient and scientific and extend its reach somewhat, and he continued to do so as president. In his first term he called repeatedly for replacing individual fees for federal prosecutors and other judicial officials with salaries, and recommended the construction of a first federal penitentiary. Congress, quite evenly divided and still jealous of its independence, did not respond. He fervently defended civil service reform, whose critics, he argued, spoke only from partisanship. "The civil-service law does not prevent the discharge of the indolent or incompetent clerk," he said in December 1885, "but it does prevent supplying his place with the unfit party worker. Thus in both these phases is seen benefit to the public service." Cleveland continually issued executive orders updating the new civil service regulations and putting more officials under them. In that same address he delivered the most scathing attack yet upon polygamy, contrasting "the cheerless, crushed and unwomanly mothers of polygamy" and their husbands with the exemplary couples of the rest of the nation, and calling for a ban on the entry of Mormons into the US from overseas. In December 1888 he reported proudly that a new 1887 law on polygamy had led to nearly six hundred convictions in Utah and Idaho territories and declared optimistically that the practice was nearly at an end.

The related issues of the federal budget and the tariff loomed larger and larger as Cleveland's term went on. 1884 had seen another panic and recession, and Cleveland in December 1885 noted that revenues, expenditures, and the federal surplus had all fallen significantly during fiscal 1885, to $322.7 million, $260.2 million, and $63.5 million. The country continued to run a large trade surplus with $784.4 million in exports and $622.8 million in imports. Cleveland argued for the first time that the budget surplus was excessive and that tariffs on necessities should be reduced. A firm believer in the gold standard and sound currency, Cleveland also attacked the 1878 Silver Purchase Act, which in seven years had forced the government to purchase silver to coin $215.8 million silver dollars, whose value was pegged at that of gold even though their silver content was worth less on the open market. Citing (though not attributing) Gresham's law that bad money drives out good, Cleveland claimed that people had started to hoard gold and that a flood of depreciated currency would eventually inflate prices, hurting the poor and workingmen. "Labor lacks employment and suffering and distress are visited upon a portion of our fellow-citizens especially entitled to the careful consideration of those charged with the duties of legislation. No interest appeals to us so strongly for a safe and stable currency as the vast army of the unemployed"—the first use of "unemployed" in its modern sense in a presidential address. He called for a halt to silver coinage.

Cleveland decided to make a name for himself on another fiscal issue during the spring and summer of 1886. Although the Civil War had ended twenty-one years earlier, thousands of veterans were still making new disability claims every year. The Pension Bureau seemed to be granting them on a relatively generous basis, and when it failed to do so, claimants frequently persuaded their congressmen to introduce a private bill granting them a pension by name. Both congressmen and senators seemed willing if not eager to pass these bills on behalf of their colleagues' constituents as well as their own. Cleveland had other ideas. During the session of Congress that began in 1885 and sat well into the summer of 1886, he vetoed 103 private pension bills. His short, succinct messages frequently illustrated the almost ludicrous nature of some of the claims, such as the man who said he had fallen from his horse and permanently injured himself on the way to the enlistment office. Since Union veterans tended to be Republicans, these vetoes may well have energized the opposition party, but he regarded them as one aspect of his drive for cheap and honest government.

In the next fiscal year, Cleveland reported in December 1886, the administration managed to cut expenditures while revenues rose and the surplus increased to $94 million, more than one-quarter of total revenues of $336.4 million and nearly half of collected tariffs. The Democratic majority in the House had just shrunk somewhat in the congressional elections, and Cleveland was evidently looking toward his reelection campaign in two years. He not only pointed out that the government would soon run out of easily redeemable debt, but also raised the specter of economic injustice. Laboring men who effectively paid the tariff on necessities like sugar into the Treasury were asking if they were receiving their fair share of advantages. "There is also a suspicion abroad that the surplus of our revenues indicates abnormal and exceptional business profits, which, under the system which produces such surplus, increase without corresponding benefit to the people at large the vast accumulations of a few among our citizens, whose fortunes, rivaling the wealth of the most favored in antidemocratic nations, are not the natural growth of a steady, plain, and industrious republic." The impact of industrialization upon economic equality was becoming an issue for the first time, and Cleveland was hinting at a revival of the Jacksonian tradition to combat it.

In December 1887, with the election looming, Cleveland took an unprecedented step. After weeks of intense work—he prided himself on writing all his messages himself—he devoted his entire annual address on December 6, 1887 to the related questions of the surplus and the tariff. The collection of a surplus, he said, constituted an "indefensible extortion and a culpable betrayal of American fairness and justice." The surplus withdrew money from circulation, "thus crippling our national energies, suspending our country's development, preventing investment in productive enterprise, threatening financial disturbance, and inviting schemes of public plunder." The surplus had reached $55.6 million in the last fiscal year. The government had redeemed every bond that it could redeem on demand, and had paid significant premiums on additional bonds that it retired. He anticipated $113 million in surplus this year, more money withdrawn from the economy. Echoing Jackson and Van Buren and Polk, he argued that depositing that money in the nation's banks would create too close a relationship between government and business. Rejecting new and unnecessary expenditures, he demanded that Congress reduce the revenue, and specifically the tariff.

American consumers, Cleveland argued, effectively paid the tariff on imported goods, since their prices included a premium at least equal to it. While industry and labor might need some protection, he attacked "a condition which, without regard to the public welfare or a national exigency, must always insure the realization of immense profits instead of moderately profitable returns." So strongly had interested parties resisted any change that many suspected "an organized combination all along the line to maintain their advantage." Ticking off statistics for the various components of the labor force, he claimed that only 2.6 million out of 17.4 million working people were making goods subject to the tariff, and they too were paying higher prices for many goods because of it. Then Cleveland fired the first presidential shot in a long and consequential battle. Domestic competition "is too often strangled by combinations quite prevalent at this time, and frequently called trusts, which have for their object the regulation of the supply and price of commodities made and sold by members of the combination." Warning of revolution, he argued that without timely and reasonable relief, the people might "insist upon a radical and sweeping rectification of their wrongs." Duties on raw materials and necessities should fall.

The message was a political gamble—one that failed. A tariff reduction measure eventually passed the House of Representatives after a bitter debate in July 1888, but the Republican-controlled Senate took up an entirely different Republican bill and adjourned in October, in the midst of the presidential campaign, without taking action. James G. Blaine was now ill and disdained another run for president, and the Republicans turned to Benjamin Harrison of Indiana, the second most critical swing state after New York. Harrison favored protection, and business interests made an all-out effort to defeat Cleveland and tariff reform. Fate also took a hand. We have seen that the Republicans had also refused to ratify Cleveland's fisheries treaty with Britain, and were accusing him of subservience to London on this question and the tariff. Cleveland decided to reverse course in August, and asked Congress for a law retaliating against the treatment of US fishermen. A California Republican then wrote Sir Lionel Sackville-West, the British minister in Washington, professing friendly feelings toward Britain and asking him whom he should vote for. Sir Lionel foolishly replied that he expected Cleveland, if reelected, to pursue a conciliatory policy. Blaine, campaigning for Harrison, sprang the letter on the nation's voters late in October, and got some indirect revenge when Harrison defeated Cleveland 233–168 in the Electoral College, even though Cleveland narrowly won the national popular vote. For the third consecutive presidential election, New York alone decided the result, swinging its thirty-six electoral votes over to Harrison by about 25,000 votes. The Republicans also won back a majority in the House and kept their edge in the Senate.

Cleveland in his lame duck address in December 1888 asked again for retaliatory legislation against the British and reported that he had demanded the recall of the British minister because of his "unpardonable . . . interference by advice and counsel with the suffrages of American citizens in the very crisis of the presidential election then near at hand." When the British had refused, Cleveland had ceased to recognize him. He also mentioned signing a new bill to exclude Chinese laborers from the country, passed after a new agreement with the Chinese government. Then he renewed his call for lower tariffs and his attack on concentrated wealth and power. In the early days of the Republic, he said, "Combinations, monopolies, and aggregations of capital were either avoided or sternly regulated and restrained." Now, "our businessmen are madly striving in the race for riches, and immense aggregations of capital outrun the imagination in the magnitude of their undertakings . . . . We discover that the fortunes realized by our manufacturers are no longer solely the reward of sturdy industry and enlightened foresight, but that they result from the discriminating favor of the Government and are largely built upon undue exactions from the masses of our people. . . . As we view the achievements of aggregated capital, we discover the existence of trusts, combinations, and monopolies, while the citizen is struggling far in the rear or is trampled to death beneath an iron heel. Corporations, which should be the carefully restrained creatures of the law and the servants of the people, are fast becoming the people's masters." He predicted that farmers and workers—some showing increased signs of radicalism—would reject this. "Communism is a hateful thing and a menace to peace and organized government; but the communism of combined wealth and capital, the outgrowth of overweening cupidity and selfishness, which insidiously undermines the justice and integrity of free institutions, is not less dangerous than the communism of oppressed poverty and toil, which, exasperated by injustice and discontent, attacks with wild disorder the citadel of rule." A dozen years before Theodore Roosevelt, Cleveland had thrown down the gauntlet against concentrated economic power. He echoed Jackson's opposition to "powerful monopolies and aristocratic establishments."

Cleveland also boasted that his administration had reclaimed more than 80 million acres of public lands from "illegal usurpation, improvident grants, and fraudulent entries and claims." Monopolies, he added, should not be allowed to seize large tracts of desert or the water that could irrigate them. He also noted that 60,000 pensioners had been added to the roles, making their total 452,557, of which 12,000 and 21,000 respectively had been granted to soldiers or widows for service in the War of 1812 and the Mexican War. Pensions now cost $78.8 million, one-third of annual expenditures. The system needed reform. "The laxity of ideas prevailing among a large number of our people regarding pensions is becoming every day more marked. The principles upon which they should be granted are in danger of being altogether ignored, and already pensions are often claimed because the applicants are as much entitled as other successful applicants, rather than upon any disability reasonably attributable to military service."

The Republican Party had founded its sixteen years of postwar rule on high tariffs that subsidized industry, and, Republicans claimed, protected the salaries of American workers. The tariffs both allowed the government to retire much of the wartime debt and to pay pensions to the veterans of the Union Army who formed part of its loyal constituencies. The Silver Purchase Act had also sought to appeal to agrarian interests. Cleveland had attacked every element of this Republican strategy. The tariff, the surplus, pensions and silver purchase remained critical issues in his successor's administration, but they received very different treatment from Benjamin Harrison.

A former Union general, a successful lawyer, and a leader in Indiana politics, Harrison was the grandson of William Henry Harrison. He had actually lost more elections than he had won, serving just one term in the Senate from 1881 to 1887 before Democrats gerrymandered the state legislature, won back a majority, and voted him out of office. In his inaugural he referred to the upcoming celebration of the centennial of Washington's presidency and surveyed the enormous progress of the United States. In addition to the nation's territorial and population growth, he said, religion now had more influence, charity had increased, "the virtue of temperance is held in higher estimation," and "on the whole the opportunities offered to the individual to secure the comforts of life are better than are found elsewhere and largely better than they were here one hundred years ago." The reference to temperance was no accident. Liquor laws were becoming a local issue in many states, pitting largely Democratic and Catholic Irish and German immigrants against old-line WASP Republicans. He then praised protectionism, which he implied the recent election had vindicated. Referring to the increasing industrialization of the South, he speculated that it might unite the sections and solve the race problem. "Is it not quite possible that the farmers and the promoters of the great mining and manufacturing enterprises which have recently been established in the South may yet find that the free ballot of the workingman, without distinction of race, is needed for their defense as well as for his own?" he asked. Calling upon great corporations to "more scrupulously observe their legal obligations and duties," he warned, echoing Cleveland, that if the rich disregarded the law, the poor would follow suit. Introducing another new issue, he said the nation must identify and exclude unfit immigrants of all races. He conceded that the surplus was too large, and endorsed civil service reform. Lastly, reviving the key issue of Reconstruction, he asked for a new federal election law to protect the vote. "If in any of the States the public security is thought to be threatened by ignorance among the electors," he said, "the obvious remedy is education."

In his December 1889 message to the new Republican Congress Harrison proposed a new tariff bill, despite "the wide divergence of opinion as to the objects that may properly be promoted by such legislation." He endorsed "the protective principle," while calling for reduced duties on tobacco and spirits. Congressman William McKinley of Ohio pushed through the tariff that bore his name, raising the average tariff duty from 38 percent to 49.5 percent. The increases and resulting price increases drew howls of protest from Democrats and the emerging Populist Party that was growing in strength in the South and West. Yet as Harrison proudly pointed out in his second annual message in December 1890, the bill had also eliminated duties temporarily on coffee, tea, hides, "and the lower grades of sugar and molasses." In a breakthrough in trade policy and executive power, the law authorized the president to negotiate new trade agreements with exporters of those commodities that would lower their duties on American products in return for keeping their commodities duty free in the US. The tariff law itself relieved the executive of the need to submit them to the Senate as a treaty requiring a two-thirds vote. Commenting on the bill in December 1890, Harrison predicted "the quickening and enlargement of our manufacturing industries, larger and better markets for our breadstuffs and provisions both at home and abroad, more constant employment and better wages for our working people, and an increased supply of a safe currency for the transaction of business." And a year later, in December 1891, he proudly reported that his administration had indeed concluded new trade agreements along these lines, with Brazil, Santo Domingo (the Dominican Republic), and Spain, the latter covering trade with Cuba and Puerto Rico. A year later he reported further such agreements with seven more nations. Harrison had discussed a conference of North and South American nations in Washington in 1889–90 in his first two annual addresses, and now, in 1891, he boasted that our exports had risen 20 percent to many American nations, that these were the only countries from which our imports were increasing, and that the US might acquire one-third of the total trade of Central and South America provided that the government strengthened its merchant marine—a request that he made annually without result.

Cleveland, as we have seen, had argued that high tariffs were creating monopolies with excessive economic power, and Harrison echoed his words in December 1889. "Earnest attention should be given by Congress to a consideration of the question how far the restraint of those combinations of capital commonly called 'trusts' is a matter of Federal jurisdiction," he said. "When organized, as they often are, to crush out all healthy competition and to monopolize the production or sale of an article of commerce and general necessity, they are dangerous conspiracies against the public good, and should be made the subject of prohibitory and even penal legislation." Seventeen states, in fact, had already passed some kind of antimonopoly legislation between 1867 and 1889—twelve of them in the latter year.[2] After a lengthy progress through Congress, both houses passed what is known as the Sherman Anti-Trust Act late in the 1890 session. The new law broadly and very vaguely banned any "conspiracy in restraint of trade." The Republicans evidently wanted to make some gesture against monopolies to balance the pro-monopoly impact of the more important new tariff.[3] Although nothing came of the bill in the short run, it became a crucial piece of legislation in the twentieth century.

By the time of his second annual message in December 1889, Harrison and the Republicans had also conceived an alternative approach to the pension question. The existing law provided pensions for veterans with disabilities incurred in service. Claimants often had trouble proving the origins of their disability, he said, but "that very many of those who endured the hardships of our most bloody and arduous campaigns are now disabled from diseases that had a real but not traceable origin in the service I do not doubt." To solve the problem he proposed pensions for any veteran who

---

2 George J. Stigler, "The Origin of the Sherman Act," *Journal of Legal Studies*, vol. 14. No 1 (January 1985), p. 6.

3 Peter R. Dickson and Philippa K. Wells, "The Dubious Origins of the Sherman Antitrust Act: The Mouse That Roared," *Journal of Public Policy & Marketing*, Vol. 20, No. 1(Spring 2001), pp. 3–14.

had now "been overcome by disease or disability," and the Congress agreed—a step toward some kind of social security system.

In a third important measure in the 1890 session, Congress passed a new Silver Purchase Act, increasing the monthly amount of silver that the Treasury was obligated to buy with notes. That bill pleased the western states, whose number was rapidly increasing, and agrarian interests who wanted higher prices to reduce their burden of debt, and apparently won some of their representatives over to the McKinley Tariff. Harrison in December 1890 had to report, however, that the price of silver had unfortunately fallen since the act passed. A credit crunch and a mild panic had intervened thanks to the near-failure of Barings Bank in Britain, which had invested unwisely in Argentina, and both American and foreign interests were exchanging newly coined silver for gold at a profit. The silver issue would return with a vengeance later in the decade.

The nation suffered a relatively mild panic in late 1890, brought on in part by the financial crisis in Europe. Anti-Catholic and anti-immigrant measures by Republican administrations in some Midwestern states alienated many voters, and some citizens disliked the higher tariff and the pension bonanza. The Democrats in November 1890 won a stunning victory in the congressional elections, gaining 86 seats and emerging with a majority of 238–86. Cleveland had agreed to add six new states to the Union: the Dakotas, Montana, Idaho, Washington and Wyoming—and Republican victories in those states preserved a 43–39 edge in the Senate. That meant that the Democrats could not undo either the McKinley Tariff or the pension bill. A year later in December 1891, Harrison reported that the Pension Bureau had added 102,000 new pensioners under the 1890 law, that annual pension expenditures had reached $118.5 million during the last fiscal year, and that they might reach $145 million during the current fiscal year. Despite that increase, the surplus of revenues over expenditures had reached $105 million out of receipts of $387.1 million in fiscal 1889, and remained at $105.3 million in fiscal 1890 when revenue reached $464 million.[4] Revenue remained quite stable during fiscal 1891

---

4 Harrison reported total federal revenues of $464 million in fiscal 1891 but that figure, he said, included the revenues of the Post Office, the first time that Post Office revenues and expenditures had been included in the overall figures.

at $458.5 million, but pensions helped raise expenditures all the way to $421.3 million, cutting the surplus by nearly two-thirds to $37.2 million. In his last annual message in December 1892, Harrison reported revenues of $429.9 million and expenditures of $416 million in the last fiscal year. Customs receipts had fallen $42.1 million, partly because of the elimination of the sugar duty. Meanwhile, pensions, which had averaged $28.3 million a year under Cleveland, had risen to $108.2 million a year now. "The parade on the 20th of September last upon the streets of this capital of 60,000 of the surviving Union veterans of the War of the Rebellion," he added, "was a most touching and thrilling episode." The new Silver Purchase Act in 1890 had increased silver purchases to $51.1 million in the last fiscal year.

The race question still divided the parties. While Cleveland had said very little about it after his inaugural address, Harrison renewed Grant's and Hayes's call for federal aid to help educate "the emancipated slave and his descendants." The "colored people," he said in his December 1889 address, brought to America against their will, "have from a standpoint of ignorance and poverty—which was our shame, not theirs—made remarkable advances in education and in the acquisition of property.... But notwithstanding all this, in many parts of our country where the colored population is large the people of that race are by various devices deprived of any effective exercise of their political rights and of many of their civil rights." Addressing the lame duck Republican Congress a year later, he asked Congress to strengthen the 1872 law that had given federal officials a role in the registration of voters and the supervision of elections and allowed them to certify the results. "Equality of representation and the parity of the electors must be maintained," he said, "or everything that is valuable in our system of government is lost." Disregarding claims that such legislation will "revive race animosities," he insisted that he must "secure to the citizen his constitutional rights." The Congress immediately took up the bill, but after a Senate debate, nine Republican senators from the West joined all the Democrats and voted it down. In December 1891 Harrison raised the issue again, and added a request for a federal law to outlaw the gerrymandering of congressional districts. "If I were called upon to declare wherein our chief national danger lies," he said, "I should say without hesitation in the overthrow of majority control by the suppression or perversion of the popular suffrage." This too got nowhere. The gerrymandering issue resurfaced 120 years later in another era of extreme partisanship. He repeated this request a year later, and also demanded "the strongest repressive legislation" against "the frequent lynching of colored people accused of crime," which had begun to increase. The Democratic Congress did nothing.

Harrison evidently wanted to go further than Congress in expanding the regulatory role of the government. His annual messages called for national bankruptcy legislation, strict control of water rights in desert areas, and laws to require better brake systems and couplings on trains, whose accidents killed several thousand workmen and injured about 20,000 every year. He called repeatedly for subsidies for the merchant marine to match those provided by the British and other governments to theirs. And in his last message he became the first president to propose new limits on immigration from Europe. A year earlier he had protested that anti-Semitic legislation in Russia might drive as many as one million "Hebrew" immigrants to the United States. While paying tribute to the industry and self-reliance of "the Hebrew race," he declared that the "sudden transfer of such a multitude . . . is neither good for them nor for us." Now in December 1892 he spoke more broadly of "a duty to our own people, and especially to our working people, not only to keep out the vicious, the ignorant, the civil disturber, the pauper, and the contract laborer, but to check the too great flow of immigration now coming by further limitations." Congress did not act. And on January 4, 1893, Harrison declared victory in the long war against polygamy. Citing requests from Mormons and non-Mormons in Utah and an anti-polygamy manifesto of the Mormon Church, he issued a general pardon for polygamy to all those who had given it up since November 1, 1890. The Bureau of Indian Affairs, meanwhile, negotiated reductions in the size of Indian reservations totaling twenty-three million acres, much of which was immediately opened to white settlement. Like its predecessors, his administration encouraged education, land ownership and citizenship for the Indians.

In foreign policy Harrison took small steps toward a broader world role. He not only championed closer commercial relations with Hawaii, but also argued repeatedly for "improving the harbor of Pearl River and equipping it as a naval station"—a fateful measure indeed. He praised progress toward a Nicaraguan interoceanic canal, and reported the conclusion of an agreement with Great Britain and Germany to support a particular government in Samoa, where all three nations had a private presence. The new Canadian authorities continued to make transportation through their territory difficult, and Harrison in December 1890 suggested building a new canal east of the Niagara River to avoid the Welland Canal, and "the opening of ship communication between the Great Lakes and one of our own seaports" to avoid the St. Lawrence River. In his last annual message he boasted that the navy would soon have nineteen modern steel ships, compared to three when he took office, with improved armor plate, torpedoes, and ammunition—some of it better than any other in the world.

Harrison was a lame duck by the time he delivered that message. The negative political fallout from the tariff law had not dispersed, and farm prices had recently fallen. Cleveland became the first modern party candidate to stand for election three times running,[5] and avenged his narrow 1888 defeat with a very solid victory, with 277 electoral votes to 145 for Harrison and 22 for the Populist James Field, who carried five western states. The Democrats also maintained a 238–124 edge in the House, and by December 1893 they had a 42–38 majority in the Senate. In the same last message, Harrison presented a series of statistics on US economic growth. The "national wealth"—a statistic developed well before gross national product—had increased from $16.2 billion in 1860 to $62.6 billion in 1890, while railroads grew from 30,000 to 168,000 miles. The production of cotton fabric, iron and steel was growing very rapidly, and imports and exports had reached record highs of $829 million and $1.03 billion in 1892. He did not mention that the nation's population had grown from thirty-one million in 1860 to sixty-three million in 1890. "There never has been a time in our history," he said, "when work was so abundant or when wages were as high, whether measured by the currency in which they are paid or by their power to supply the necessaries and comforts of life." Harrison predicted that "the prevailing party" would now try to lower the tariff, and speculated that this would in fact

---

5 Jackson had also run in three consecutive elections but he had not been a party candidate in the first two.

depress wages. As it turned out, both parties had become hostages to the ups and downs of a powerful but unstable economic system.

Few presidents have stuck so determinedly to their principles as Grover Cleveland, and he restated two of them in his second inaugural. Nothing was more vital, he said, than "a sound and stable currency," and the nation could not "defy with impunity the inexorable laws of finance and trade." With these words he declared war on the Free Silver movement, which wanted to coin more silver to inflate prices and relieve agrarian distress, and on the 1890 Silver Purchase Act. He reaffirmed his opposition to "protection for protection's sake," complained of "wild and reckless pension expenditure," and attacked "immense aggregations of kindred enterprises and combinations of business interests," which federal power should restrain. Lowering tariffs was "a necessary incident of our return to right and justice." Before the new Congress could meet, however, the worst panic since 1873 struck the nation in May 1893. Cleveland on August 8, 1893 delivered the first emergency economic message of any president, calling the Congress into immediate session to save the currency.

Cleveland explained the problem succinctly. Despite abundant agricultural and industrial production, a credit crunch was bringing economic activity to a halt—because, he said, of the Silver Purchase Act. From 1890 through July 1893 the act had forced the Treasury to purchase $147 million worth of silver with notes redeemable either in silver or gold. In practice the government had to redeem them for gold to maintain the value of silver, and both US and foreign interests were draining the Treasury gold reserve rapidly—about $49 million since May 1892. Should this continue, US currency would soon be backed by "depreciated silver" and the country would cease to be "a nation of the first class." He had planned, he said, on a special session to consider tariff reform, but now repeal of the act must come first.

Congress had repealed the act by the time Cleveland delivered the first annual message of his new term in December 1893—albeit with more opposition from agrarian Democrats than from Republicans. Yet Cleveland had to report more bad economic news. More than two hundred banks had either failed or suspended redemptions of their notes in the year ending October 31, and only half of them were expected to return to operation. Gold exports had set a record of $108.7 million in the last fiscal year, and exports had fallen $182 million to $847.7 million, while imports totaled $866 million. (Like all major panics, this one had struck Europe as well.) He expected the silver purchase repeal to help the economy rapidly. In the same message he noted that Congress was already hard at work on the tariff reform for which the country had spoken. He recommended an end to tariffs on raw materials to reverse unemployment, and also mentioned that Congress was contemplating a tax on investment to make up for lost revenue, since the surplus had shrunk under the pressure of pensions and falling revenue to just $2.3 million.

A year later the situation was much worse. Cleveland in December 1894 reported that ordinary expenditures had fallen by $16 million while revenue had fallen by $88 million to $372.8 million, creating a record peacetime deficit of $68.8 million. Congress had passed a tariff reform bill, but Democratic protectionists had worked with Republicans in the closely divided Senate to make its reductions marginal rather than fundamental. A disgusted Cleveland let it become law without his signature and asked for new changes in his annual address. It had included the new income tax on investment income, but the Supreme Court ruled that tax unconstitutional by a 5–4 vote in the spring of 1895—the first limitation on the taxing power that it had ever imposed. Customs revenues had in fact fallen by $73.5 million in fiscal 1894, but mostly because imports had fallen by $64.7 million. The Treasury had had to float two bond issues for gold to restore its gold reserves. Cleveland proposed a series of steps to ease credit from national and state banks, and even suggested "a safety fund for the immediate redemption of the circulating notes of failed banks"—a forerunner of the Federal Deposit Insurance Corporation. By this time, however, the congressional elections had transformed the political situation. In the revenge of 1890, the Republicans gained 110 seats in the House and emerged with a 253–93 margin, as the Democrats lost a full 9.7 percent of the popular vote. When the state legislatures had finished their work they had gained two seats in the Senate while the Democrats lost four, and three Populists and a Silverite now held the balance of power there.

In December 1895 Cleveland returned to currency questions again, proposing in effect to undo all of the changes wrought by Civil War finance. Under an 1878 law affecting the planned redemption of greenbacks with specie that began in 1879, the Treasury could not retire the greenbacks, but had to put them back into circulation, making them in effect the nation's first permanent paper currency. The Treasury had consistently sought to maintain a $100 million gold reserve. The Silver Purchase Act had put another $150 million of redeemable certificates in circulation, raising total Treasury liabilities to $500 million. The combination of the McKinley Tariff, which reduced exports, and free silver agitation, which encouraged the hoarding of gold, Cleveland argued, had led to constant drains on the Treasury gold reserves, which fell to $65.4 million in early 1894. The Treasury had had to replenish them with a series of bond sales totaling $162 million in 1894–95, but the gold run had continued and the reserve had fallen to below $80 million again. To stop the continual exchanges of greenbacks and silver purchase notes for gold, Cleveland proposed to retire them, offering low-interest long-term bonds in return. He proposed other steps to encourage the national banks to issue more notes to make up for the $478 million of retired government notes. While revenue was adequate, almost none of it now came in gold. With the new election eleven months away, Cleveland also blasted the advocates of unrestricted silver coinage—increasingly strong within his own party—which he said would debase US currency and destroy purchasing power and credit. Describing the problem as critical, he said he would accept any solution proposed by Congress.

They did not act, and in December 1896, in his last annual message, Cleveland had to report a deficit of $25.2 million in the federal budget and a loss of another $79 million in gold. Once again he expressed his regret that the legal tender notes or greenbacks, an artifact of Civil War finance, still circulated, and pleaded for a means to take them out of circulation. Financial peace and safety, he said, would return only when the government got "out of the banking business and the accumulation of funds" and simply collected what it needed to spend. He also renewed his attack on trusts, whose "tendency is to crush out individual independence and to hinder or prevent the free use of human faculties and the full development of human character. Through them the farmer, the artisan, and the small trader is in danger of dislodgment from the proud position of being his own master." The current laws against them, he said, did not work, but he questioned whether further federal laws would be constitutional.

Although no president had seen fit to say so, the US was now larger in population, as well as territory, than any western European nation. Cleveland in December 1895 mentioned that his administration had implemented a law passed in the last days of the Harrison administration and upgraded its representatives and missions in Britain, France, Italy and Germany from ministers and legations to ambassadors and embassies, with Russia soon to follow. He was also implementing an 1890 congressional resolution to conclude arbitration treaties with every possible nation. In foreign policy, Cleveland meanwhile took a recognizably anti-imperialist line. In December 1893 he mentioned that a pro-American revolt had removed the Hawaiian queen and concluded an annexation treaty with the Harrison administration, but he withdrew it and sent a new envoy who denied the legitimacy of the new government and tried to restore the monarch. A rebellion had also broken out in Samoa. The tripartite agreement, he said in December 1894, "has utterly failed to correct, if indeed it has not aggravated, the very evils it was intended to prevent. . . . Our participation in its establishment against the wishes of the natives was in plain defiance of the conservative teachings and warnings of the wise and patriotic men who laid the foundations of our free institutions." Japan had attacked China in 1894, and Cleveland noted in December of that year that the US had assumed the duty of protecting Chinese and Japanese nationals in each other's countries—as Grant had for the French and Germans in 1870–71—and offered to mediate a settlement if the parties desired. In December 1895 he reported that a new and larger insurrection had broken out in Cuba, and that the United States was maintaining its neutrality again. He gave a sophisticated analysis of that conflict a year later, noting that while Spain ruled all the major towns, the insurgents roamed at will over most of the countryside. Both sides were destroying property and the Spaniards had "concentrated" much of the rural population. While some vehemently demanded that the US recognize the rebel government or even go to war, Cleveland declared the country "a peaceful nation without dreams of conquest" and expressed the hope that Spain might end the conflict by granting "genuine autonomy." The US had offered to guarantee such an agreement. "Higher obligations," he warned on behalf of his successor, might draw the US into the conflict if it continued.

Cleveland took a more forthright stance in a dispute between Britain and Venezuela over that nation's border with British Guiana. In December 1894 he explained that diplomatic relations between the two nations had broken down, and that the United States was trying to get them restored and to secure arbitration, "which Great Britain so conspicuously favors in principle and respects in practice," and which her "weaker adversary" fervently sought. The issue escalated in July 1895. Cleveland recounted in December of that year that the US, remaining opposed "to a forcible increase by any European power of its territorial possessions on this continent," protested British attempts to expand British Guiana and demanded again that the British submit to arbitration without preconditions. A few days afterwards the British government rejected the contemporary relevance of the Monroe Doctrine and refused the demand. On December 16 Cleveland submitted another message to Congress restating the American position and asking for money to create a commission to study the boundary question and declare the opinion of the United States, and thenceforth to "resist by every means in its power" any attempt by Britain to extend its territory further as "willful aggression." The British government turned more conciliatory, and Cleveland in December 1896 could report not only that they were submitting the boundary dispute to arbitration by British and American commissioners, but also that they were willing to conclude a general arbitration treaty with the United States—a big victory for the new American approach to international conflict. Meanwhile, Cleveland reported in successive addresses on the reorganization and consolidation into larger posts of the army, the continuing growth and better equipment of the navy, and the construction of more modern coastal defenses. In December 1895 he mentioned that the navy was stationing more ships in trouble spots such as the Far East (where the Sino-Japanese War was in progress) and the Argentinian coast (in the midst of a dispute that the US eventually arbitrated between Argentina and Brazil).

Cleveland struggled with other domestic issues with varying degrees of success. In December 1896 he expressed satisfaction that Congress had at last agreed to compensate federal legal officers with salaries rather than fees, and that Fort Leavenworth had finally become the first US federal prison in response to his many pleas for one. Although he boasted of uncovering numerous frauds within the pension system, he could not stop the extraordinary effects of the 1890 law. In December 1894 he reported that of 959,544 total pensioners—937,505 dating from the "late Civil War"—469,344 had been added under that legislation. The total reached 970,675 by the end of his term, and he complained in December 1896 that abuses in the system had done "incalculable harm in demoralizing our people and undermining good citizenship." In that message he also broke down the total immigration of 340,484 in the last year into numbers of immigrants over fourteen from each country and the percentage of illiterates among them, with Italy, Austria-Hungary and Russia leading in both categories. While he made no recommendation, some bias could obviously be inferred. He also reminded Congress that the Union Pacific and Central Pacific railroads would not be able to pay off tens of millions of bonds coming due in the next few years that had paid for the transcontinental railroad, and raised the possibility of foreclosing on them.

And in July 1894, in the midst of the economic crisis and the struggle in Congress over the tariff, Cleveland faced the biggest, most disruptive labor dispute in American history to date. A Chicago strike against the Pullman manufacturers of railroad cars—which had been cutting wages—spread to the American Railway Union led by socialist Eugene V. Debs, and paralyzed rail traffic in much of the Midwest and Far West. Prodded by his attorney general Richard Olney, Cleveland agreed to ask for an injunction to end the strike, and, when the strikers failed to obey, issued a proclamation on July 8 entitled "Law and Order in the State of Illinois, especially in Chicago."[6] It dispatched the military to restore order and warned all against joining "unlawful obstructions, combinations and assemblages." A similar proclamation relating to railroads all through the Northwest and in California and Utah and New Mexico territories followed the next day. Cleveland got nonpartisan support from nearly all the nation's press, and the strike collapsed. Cleveland, who had also claimed to be ensuring the delivery of

---

6 For an account of the strike see Allen Nevins, *Grover Cleveland, A Study in Courage* (New York, 1938), pp. 611–28.

the mails, made only the briefest reference to this episode in his December 1894 annual address, and never said anything about the underlying labor–management issues or the rights of labor. Other presidents would soon have to say more.

The industrial and agricultural economic crisis dominated Cleveland's second term. He pressed his own solutions courageously and vigorously, but they were not effective. He also lost control of his own party. He declined to run yet again, and watched in horror as thirty-six-year old William Jennings Bryan of Nebraska secured the Democratic nomination to succeed him on a Free Silver platform. He essentially remained neutral in the campaign, while Republican candidate William McKinley—he of the tariff—ran on a strict gold standard platform. Free Silver had come to play within the Democratic Party the role that the Vietnam War did in the same party after 1968, and Bryan's candidacy, like George McGovern's in 1972, lacked the support of many party leaders. Bryan did much better than McGovern, but his support was confined to the South and West. In one of the most sectional elections in American history, McKinley amassed 271 electoral votes to 176 for Bryan, adding California and Oregon to a solid block of states north of the Ohio and east of the Missouri. Within two years, McKinley had moved American history into an entirely new era.

# XII

# WILLIAM MCKINLEY
# AND THEODORE ROOSEVELT

1879–1901 • 1901–1909

William McKinley began his first inaugural address on March 4, 1897, on an unusually religious note. "Our faith teaches that there is no safer reliance than upon the God of our fathers," he said, "who has so singularly favored the American people in every national trial, and who will not forsake us so long as we obey His commandments and walk humbly in His footsteps." He identified the continuing federal deficit as the nation's biggest problem, and promised to call the newly elected Congress into session later in the month to pass a higher tariff that would protect American labor and raise the necessary revenue. He spoke of the continuing economic depression but made no other specific suggestions. Congress did as he had asked, but the tariff had very disappointing results. In December 1898 McKinley had to report that both imports and customs revenue had *fallen* in the last fiscal year, and the government had run a deficit of about $38 million despite extraordinary receipts of $64.8 million from the sale of the bankrupt Pacific railroads, which the government had foreclosed on. For the second time, he echoed Cleveland's proposal to retire the Civil War–era greenbacks. Thanks in part to war, the deficit grew to $89 million in fiscal 1899, but the president boasted in December of that year that "conditions of confidence" now prevailed throughout the country, that industrial exports had reached new highs, and that gold was now flowing into the nation. He predicted a $40 million surplus for the current fiscal year. The economy grew at a remarkable pace, and in December 1900 McKinley boasted of a surplus of $81.2 million. Exports had grown from

$512 million to $1.394 billion in just four years. By then, however, a new set of imperial issues had taken over center stage.

In December 1897 McKinley began his discussion of foreign affairs with a long review of the renewed insurrection in Cuba, now more than two years old. Endorsing the Cuban people's "inalienable right" of a "measure of self-control," he attacked Spain's "cruel policy of concentration"—herding thousands of peasants into concentration camps, a term coined at that time, to deny support to rebels. Spain had rejected Cleveland's 1896 offer to mediate the dispute, and McKinley in October 1897 had asked the Spanish government to reach a settlement and warned that the United States would not wait indefinitely for one. A new Spanish government had acknowledged the US's concerns, pledged reforms, and promised to carry out military operations more humanely. Listing three possible alternatives—the recognition of the rebels as belligerents, a neutral intervention to impose a "rational compromise," or taking the sides of the rebels—he expressed no preference, while definitely rejecting annexation.

Five months later, on April 11, 1898, he asked for a declaration of war on Spain. Knowing that the United States had never actively intervened in such a conflict, he began by promising to reconcile his recommendations with "the precepts laid down by the founders of the Republic and religiously observed by succeeding Administrations to the present day." The Spanish government had refused another offer to try to settle the conflict, and McKinley attacked the "concentration"—that is, forcible resettlement—of perhaps 300,000 Cubans in four provinces, half of whom might have died as a result. Citing a precedent established by Andrew Jackson when Texas rebelled against Mexico, he refused to recognize the rebels until they had won a clear victory—which he said seemed beyond the capacity of either side. "The forcible intervention of the United States as a neutral to stop the war," he said, was "justifiable on rational grounds," and the nation had a responsibility to stop barbarities on its doorstep. Lastly, he referred to the recent explosion of the battleship *Maine* in Havana harbor, in which 260 men had died, and the conclusion of a commission that an underwater mine had caused it.[1] He asked Congress for the authority to "use

---

1 This has never been definitely established.

the military and naval forces of the United States" to establish a stable government in Cuba. Congress rapidly agreed.

Following the example of certain British and French interventions overseas, McKinley had in effect claimed a right and a duty to act to restore order and preserve civilized values in another land. Thanks in part to young assistant secretary of the navy Theodore Roosevelt, the war with Spain immediately escalated. Roosevelt had sent the navy's Pacific squadron to the vicinity of the Philippines on the eve of the war. Just six days after Congress declared war on April 25, 1898, Admiral Dewey's squadron smashed the Spanish fleet at Manilla Bay. On May 19, well before US troops had landed in Cuba, McKinley issued an executive order announcing the dispatch of "an army of occupation to the Philippines for the twofold purpose of completing the reduction of the Spanish power in that quarter and of giving order and security to the islands while in the possession of the United States." McKinley's annual address in December recapitulated the origins of the war and gave a detailed account of operations in the Philippines, in Cuba, and in Puerto Rico, which the US had also occupied, leaving Spain without possessions in the western hemisphere. American forces had prevailed everywhere with very few casualties, and Spain had asked for peace on July 26. The peace treaty, he explained, confirmed that Cuba would become independent and that the United States would annex Puerto Rico and retain the Philippines, but did not define their future status. McKinley on December 21 issued an executive order establishing a military government throughout the Philippines, but astonishingly, although the Senate only ratified the peace treaty with Spain by the narrowest of margins—a bare two-thirds majority—on February 6, 1898, McKinley never made a public address explaining why the United States wanted to annex the Philippines and what the government planned to do with them until after the treaty was ratified.

McKinley had already begun expanding US territory into the Pacific even before the Spanish–American War. In his December 1897 annual message he had asked Congress to ratify the treaty his administration had concluded with a pro-American government in Hawaii providing for its annexation—the step Cleveland had rejected. This, he said, was the logical result of our seventy-five-year quest to keep Hawaii out of the hands of any other power. The Senate ratified the treaty. By December 1899 McKinley was ready to discuss the future of the Philippines with Congress. Noting that the US had paid $20 million to Spain for their cession, he declared, "I had every reason to believe, and I still believe that this transfer of sovereignty was in accordance with the wishes and the aspirations of the great mass of the Filipino people." He had however declined to jointly occupy the territory along with native insurgent forces that were fighting the Spaniards, and demanded instead that all Filipinos submit to US rule. He denied the claim of Emiliano Aguinaldo, the insurgent leader—whom he did not deign to name—that the US had promised immediate independence, and submitted a report from commissioners on the scene detailing the insurrection against the US forces that had now broken out. "Our obligations to other nations and to the friendly Filipinos and to ourselves and our flag," they said, "demanded that force should be met by force. Whatever the future of the Philippines may be, there is no course open to us now except the prosecution of the war until the insurgents are reduced to submission." McKinley insisted that the people of the islands "will enjoy a prosperity and a freedom which they have never known before" as soon as the rebellion was suppressed, and insisted that the islands "cannot be abandoned . . . at once to anarchy and finally to barbarism." Nor could we leave the mass of the people at the mercy of "the minority of armed insurgents." Congress must prescribe the final form of their government after the rebellion was suppressed. The United States had joined the European effort to impose "civilization" on poorer tropical lands. In the same address McKinley asked for a new territorial government for Hawaii and a better one for Alaska, now the scene of a gold rush.

By December 1900 he could report the formation of a new American commission that would assume civil authority as soon as the revolt was definitely suppressed, including authority over taxes, government spending, an educational system and a new civil service. The US must teach the Filipinos the essential principles of liberty and law, including many provisions from the Bill of Rights. It should treat the "uncivilized tribes" of the islands in the same way that the nation had treated the Indians, allowing them to maintain their tribal governments, "surrounded by a civilization to which they are unable or unwilling to conform." In the same address he reported that Cuba had elected a convention to write a constitution. He did not mention the Platt Amendment—just passed by the Senate—that asserted a US right to intervene in Cuba if necessary to preserve a friendly and effective government there. McKinley had in effect founded a new form of specifically American imperialism, promising to train the Philippine population and encourage the Cubans in self-government along US lines—something no European colonial power was yet doing in the vast European colonial domains. Bolstered by victory abroad and economic recovery at home, McKinley in 1900 defeated Bryan by a larger 292–155 margin in the Electoral College, as the Democrats carried just four western states in addition to the southern and border states. In a brief second inaugural, he had to acknowledge that the insurrection was still going on. "We are not waging war against the inhabitants of the Philippine Islands," he said. "A portion of them are making war against the United States. By far the greater part of the inhabitants recognize American sovereignty and welcome it as a guaranty of order and of security for life, property, liberty, freedom of conscience, and the pursuit of happiness. To them full protection will be given." The recent war "imposed upon us obligations from which we cannot escape and from which it would be dishonorable to seek escape." Bryan had run on an anti-imperialist platform, and the American people, McKinley said, "reject as mistaken and unworthy the doctrine that we lose our own liberties by securing the enduring foundations of liberty to others."

American troops went even farther afield in 1899–1900. In December 1899 McKinley reported that some had had to land in China to protect American citizens from violence in Peking.[2] A year later he gave a long and detailed report on the Boxer Rebellion against a growing western presence. "The telegraph and the railway spreading over their land, the steamers plying on their waterways, the merchant and the missionary penetrating year by year farther to the interior," he said without irony, "became to the Chinese mind types of an alien invasion, changing the course of their national life and fraught with vague forebodings of disaster to their beliefs and their self-control." He had circulated proposals among the great powers to strengthen the Chinese government and ensure equal treatment for foreigners, but they had failed to act. Parts of the Chinese Army had joined the Boxers and they had taken control of

---

2 As it was then known—now Beijing.

a good deal of northern China, attacking foreigners and murdering converts to Christianity. The US had sent 5,000 troops from the Philippines as part of an international relief expedition to relieve the siege of the foreign legations at Peking, he said, obtain redress for wrongs already suffered, protect American life and property, and prevent the spread of disorders. He demanded "exemplary and deterrent punishment of the responsible authors and abettors of the criminal acts" that had inflicted "grievous injury," and "adequate guarantees of the liberty of faith" for Chinese and foreigners alike. His successor had to give another update a year later. Convinced of the technological and political superiority of their civilization, the western powers had begun imposing their will and some of their values all over the world, and the United States under McKinley had become a full participant in this process.

McKinley also pushed the expansion of the American military to meet its new responsibilities. He continued the expansion and modernization of the navy, asked for a 100,000-man army (to include a 65,000-man force in the Philippines) in December 1899, and reported that that force remained necessary a year later. At home, McKinley pushed for some small but important advances in the role of the federal government. Noting a yellow fever epidemic in December 1898, he asked for a commission to study the causes of the disease—which had not yet been linked to mosquitoes—and he repeated that proposal a year later. And in December 1899, McKinley acknowledged the evil of "combinations" that controlled the market for some necessities and stamped out competition, and recommended that Congress study possible future legislation to control their power further. He did not however make any specific recommendations or try to make use of the Sherman Act. And like every president since Grant, McKinley pleaded fruitlessly for government intervention to strengthen the US merchant marine, which had never recovered from the Civil War and carried only a tiny fraction of the nation's mushrooming foreign trade. He said less about race questions than any previous Republican president. He spoke out against lynchings in his first inaugural, but the lynchings he complained of in his December 1899 address had taken the lives of Italian nationals in Louisiana, creating a serious international incident. A year later he recommended that Congress make the lynching of foreign nationals a federal crime, but said nothing about the lynching of American citizens. Lynchings averaged 126 a year, the vast majority against black Americans, during his term.[3]

On other foreign fronts, McKinley in December 1897 and 1898 reported on further preliminary work on a Nicaraguan interoceanic canal, but in 1899 he had to report that the Nicaraguan government had declared that the existing agreement with the American canal company had lapsed after ten years. Colombia, however, had allowed a US Panama Canal Commission to make a survey in its territory as well. In 1899 he noted that Britain and Venezuela had settled their boundary dispute through arbitration. Predecessors including Grant in 1873 and Arthur in 1881 had promoted American participation in great international industrial expositions in Europe, and McKinley in December 1899 proclaimed the enormous significance of an imminent Paris exposition. "In this age of keen rivalry among nations for mastery in commerce," he said, "the doctrine of evolution and the rule of the survival of the fittest must be as inexorable in their operation as they are positive in the results they bring about. The place won in the struggle by an industrial people can only be held by unrelaxed endeavor and constant advance in achievement." The United States' "astounding increase" in world market shares reflected their "national character," as the Paris exhibition would show. And in that same address, he announced a coming Pan-American exposition to take place in 1901, in Buffalo.

That event cost him his life. McKinley in two different annual addresses had expressed the nation's sympathy for the peoples of Italy and Austria-Hungary after their king and empress, respectively, had been assassinated by anarchists. In September 1901, as McKinley shook hands with a long line of Americans at the Buffalo exhibition, another anarchist named Leon Czolgosz—an immigrant—concealed a pistol inside a bandage and fatally shot him. Theodore Roosevelt, the former assistant secretary of the navy who had become a national hero leading an army regiment in Cuba in 1898, won the governorship of New York later that year, and become vice president in 1901, now took over at just forty-two years old, the youngest president in US history. An activist, a moralist, and a visionary, Roosevelt stepped eagerly into McKinley's shoes,

---

3  http://law2.umkc.edu/faculty/projects/ftrials/shipp/lynchingyear.html.

laying out bold new courses of action for the nation both abroad and at home that anticipated all the great issues of the new century.

Theodore Roosevelt was the most prolific writer ever to occupy the White House. Beginning with the two-volume work *The Naval War of 1812*, which he began as a Harvard undergraduate, he had published twenty-two books in nineteen years from 1882 through 1900, including four volumes entitled *The Winning of the West*, several more on hunting, and three biographies of statesmen. He had begun his career as a reform Republican in the New York State Assembly in the early 1880s but had forsaken the Mugwumps and stuck with James G. Blaine in 1884. His eight annual addresses had relatively little in common with those of his predecessors. Running to as many as 25,000 words—that is, more than one-third of the length of this book so far—and filled with unusually emotional language, they read more like sermons on the greatest issues of the new century: the United States' new role as a world power on the one hand, and the problem of concentrated economic power in the industrial age on the other. In the world at large he exhorted his countrymen to seek peace while preparing for war, while at home, he repeatedly identified great economic evils that must be solved with moderate means, in opposition to extremists of all kinds. He evidently regarded the details of the federal budget as someone else's business, and almost never included a simple accounting of the government's revenues and expenditures, in contrast to every single one of his predecessors. Nor was he particularly successful in getting Congress and the country to adopt the specific measures he advocated, even though he was elected by a landslide in his own right in 1904 and the Republican Party had solid control of Congress throughout his presidency. Yet Roosevelt spoke for the educated elite of his own and the next-youngest generation, and he stated and restated the principles that guided their leadership through the critical first half of the twentieth century.

McKinley had been dead for less than three months when Roosevelt gave his first annual address in December 1901. He began it with a 2000-word commentary on McKinley, his death, and the political implications of his assassination—an order of magnitude more attention to his dead predecessor than John Tyler, Millard Fillmore, Chester Arthur or even Andrew Johnson had given to theirs. Of the three presidential assassinations, he said, this one was by far the most dangerous, since the killer was "an utterly depraved criminal belonging to that body of criminals who object to all governments, good and bad alike, who are against any form of popular liberty if it is guaranteed by even the most just and liberal laws, and who are as hostile to the upright exponent of a free people's sober will as to the tyrannical and irresponsible despot." Nor was this simply an isolated act. "This criminal was a professed anarchist, inflamed by the teachings of professed anarchists, and probably also by the reckless utterances of those who, on the stump and in the public press, appeal to the dark and evil spirits of malice and greed, envy and sullen hatred." Such men deserved no protection. "No man or body of men preaching anarchistic doctrines should be allowed at large any more than if preaching the murder of some specified private individual. Anarchistic speeches, writings, and meetings are essentially seditious and treasonable." Congress should ban anarchists from entering the country and find ways to punish those who remained. As it turned out, Congress debated such bills over the next six months, but never passed any.[4]

In the same message, Roosevelt defined his approach to the concentration of wealth. Complex and accelerating industrial development had faced the country "with very serious social problems," and the nation needed new laws to regulate "the accumulation and distribution of wealth." He was no revolutionary. The poor, he said, had gained as well, "captains of industry" had done much for the nation, and "on the whole, and in the long run, we shall go up or down together," since "disaster to great business enterprises" must affect us all. "Many of those who have made it their vocation to denounce the great industrial combinations which are popularly, although with technical inaccuracy, known as 'trusts,'" he said, "appeal especially to hatred and fear. These are precisely the two emotions, particularly when combined with ignorance, which unfit men for the exercise of cool and steady judgment. . . . Combination and concentration should be, not prohibited, but supervised and within reasonable limits controlled." He called for a Department of Commerce and Labor to gather information on great business enterprises, and Congress agreed to it. A year later he listed

---

4 "Record of This Congress," *New York Times*, June 29, 1902, p. 1.

"monopolies, unjust discriminations, which prevent or cripple competition, fraudulent overcapitalization, and other evils in trust organizations and practices" as fit targets for federal regulation. His appeal to "cool and steady judgment" echoed the founding fathers.

By December 1903 Roosevelt's Justice Department had tried to put these views into practice. The great Northern Securities antitrust case was pending in the Supreme Court, after a lower court had ruled against a critical railroad merger in the Midwest and Northwest. "The corporation which is honestly and fairly organized, whose managers in the conduct of its business recognize their obligation to deal squarely with their stockholders, their competitors, and the public, has nothing to fear from such supervision," he said. The antitrust laws were "a common-sense and successful effort" to make corporations serve the public good. A few months later the Supreme Court narrowly upheld the Northern Securities verdict. He repeated in December 1906 that the American people wanted to stop particular corporate evils, but "without hostility to wealth, either individual or corporate." The great railroads emerged as a particular focus of his interests, and in 1906 Congress passed the Hepburn Act, allowing the Interstate Commerce Commission to set maximum railroad rates in response to unreasonable increases. In a special message on January 31, 1908—when he had already ruled out another term—Roosevelt called for the authority of the Interstate Commerce Commission to extend further over freight rates and the issuance of railroad stocks and bonds. In a slightly more radical tone, he called such measures "part of the campaign to make the class of great property holders realize that property has its duties no less than its rights," in order to prevent a revolution that might take their rights away. Meanwhile, he adhered faithfully to Republican tariff policies.

Roosevelt became the first president to pay sustained attention to organized labor, and his recommendations for labor paralleled those he made for big business. In December 1902 he endorsed "associations or unions of wage workers," provided that they respected the rights of others. He wanted to protect women and children from night work or excessive hours in all industries working for the federal government, and he called, as he did almost every year, for a "factory law" regulating working conditions in the District of Columbia that could serve as a model for the nation.

Congress did eventually ban child labor in the District, but went no further. Significantly, Roosevelt did not endorse the view of some Republican progressives that the commerce clause allowed the federal government to ban the interstate sale of any goods made by children. Meanwhile, he argued that with labor rights went labor responsibilities. Roosevelt in December 1904 endorsed federal interference in labor disputes that interfered with the mails or interstate commerce or in response to appeals from the state. If labor used unspecified "improper means," "all honorable public servants" must expose such wrongdoing as resolutely as they would that of a great corporation. He repeatedly rejected calls to abolish federal court injunctions against strikes, while acknowledging that some injunctions might have gone too far. In December 1906 he warned against "the infinite harm done by preachers of mere discontent . . . the honest man has as much to fear from the demagogue as from the evil rich." Yet he also advocated an eight-hour day for all railroad employees, declared it to be a proper national goal, and called child labor in factories "a blot on our civilization." In 1902, Roosevelt had made history when he convinced mine owners and coal miners to return to work before the nation froze all winter and accept arbitration of their dispute, but not until December 1906 did he suggest that this episode might be a model for settling future strikes. In December 1907 he praised the Congress for passing an employer liability law guaranteeing workers compensation for accidents, but the Supreme Court overruled it a few weeks later. He returned to all these themes in his very last annual message in December 1908, repeatedly warning of the equally serious dangers posed by predatory capitalists on one hand and socialists on the other. "'Class consciousness,'" he said, "where it is merely another name for the odious vice of class selfishness, is equally noxious whether in an employer's association or in a workingman's association." He also pointed out—as no other president had ever done—that the US was well behind the major European industrial countries in establishing employer liability for accidents. Congress passed such a law limited in its application to interstate railroads.

Roosevelt took the same stern but moderate approach toward the related issues of North–South relations and race. In October 1901, the new president provoked a vehement outburst of southern bigotry when the news leaked that he had invited the Negro leader

Booker T. Washington to dinner at the White House. He never referred to that incident publicly himself. "We are now indeed one Nation," he said in December 1901, "one in fact as well as in name; we are united in our devotion to the flag which is the symbol of national greatness and unity; and the very completeness of our union enables us all, in every part of the country, to glory in the valor shown alike by the sons of the North and the sons of the South in the times that tried men's souls." On February 13, 1905, Roosevelt at a Lincoln Day dinner in New York discussed the race question in typically tentative and evenhanded terms, showing ample regard for the views of white southerners. "The ideal of elemental justice meted out to every man is the ideal we should keep ever before us," he said. "It will be many a long day before we attain to it, and unless we show not only devotion to it, but also wisdom and self-restraint in the exhibition of that devotion, we shall defer the time for its realization still further." The fate of "the colored man" must depend far more upon his own effort than upon the efforts of any outside friend. "Every vicious, venal, or ignorant colored man is an even greater foe to his own race than to the community as a whole . . . the prime requisite of the race is moral and industrial uplifting. . . . If the standards of private morality and industrial efficiency can be raised high enough among the black race, then its future on this continent is secure." Quoting and paraphrasing a North Carolina bishop, he said that men must "keep in mind the fact that there must be no confusing of civil privileges with social intercourse. Civil law cannot regulate social practices . . . . The suffrage should be based on character and intelligence for white and black alike." Opposition to "social equality" was the early twentieth-century code word for continuing, or increasing, segregation of the races, and southern states now used educational requirements to disenfranchise black and some white voters.

Lynchings fell to less than one hundred a year during his term, but still occurred more than once a week. Roosevelt discussed them at length in his 1906 annual address. An "epidemic of lynching and mob violence," he said, sprang up in various parts of the country—"peculiarly frequent in respect of black men," largely because of "the perpetration, especially by black men, of the hideous crime of rape," a more abominable crime even than murder. Yet he quickly added that two-thirds of lynchings did not involve rape, and that many victims were "innocent of all crimes." Typically, he quoted two southern governors and a bishop attacking lynchings—but also blamed "Negroes" for failing to turn in criminals among them. "There is no question of 'social equality' or 'negro domination' involved"—referring to white southern buzzwords—"only the question of relentlessly punishing bad men, and of securing to the good man the right to his life, his liberty, and the pursuit of his happiness as his own qualities of heart, head, and hand enable him to achieve it." He then called upon the white man not to allow "the Negroes in a mass to grow to manhood and womanhood without education," and attacked demagogues who incited lynching out of "greed for office." The southern states had however completed the disenfranchisement of most of their black populations during the 1890s with the help of poll taxes and especially literacy tests, and the South was more Democratic than ever. During his first term, Roosevelt also continued to preach the assimilation of the Indians and their conversion to modern ways of life, but he dropped them from his annual addresses in his second term. Oklahoma meanwhile was admitted to the union as a state, with its Indian lands much reduced.

Good character, Roosevelt continually argued, made good businessmen, good labor leaders, good nations, and good men and women. He attempted without much success to apply the same rule to the increasingly controversial subject of immigration. The depression of the mid-1890s had reduced immigration into the US to about 229,000 in 1898, but it rose about fivefold in the next decade, reaching 1.285 million in 1907.[5] The population meanwhile had risen to seventy-six million in 1900, a somewhat slower 21 percent increase since 1890. "We cannot have too much immigration of the right kind, and we should have none at all of the wrong kind," he said in December 1903. "The need is to devise some system by which undesirable immigrants shall be kept out entirely, while desirable immigrants are properly distributed throughout the country." "We should not admit masses of men whose standards of living and whose personal customs and habits are such that they tend to lower the level of the American wage-worker," he said a year

---

5  https://www.migrationpolicy.org/programs/data-hub/charts/annual-number-of-us-legal-permanent-residents.

later; "and above all we should not admit any man of an unworthy type, any man concerning whom we can say that he will himself be a bad citizen, or that his children and grandchildren will detract from instead of adding to the sum of the good citizenship of the country." In December 1905 he referred to a recent report of the Commissioner General of Immigration arguing that undesirable immigrants had frequently been recruited by "agents of the great transportation companies." "We cannot afford to consider whether [an immigrant] is Catholic or Protestant, Jew or Gentile; whether he is Englishman or Irishman, Frenchman or German, Japanese, Italian, Scandinavian, Slav, or Magyar," he said, but "every man of Anarchistic tendencies, all violent and disorderly people, all people of bad character, the incompetent, the lazy, the vicious, the physically unfit, defective, or degenerate should be kept out. The stocks out of which American citizenship is to be built should be strong and healthy, sound in body, mind, and character." And while he supported the exclusion of all Chinese laborers who, he said, would depress wages and the standard of living, he welcomed "Chinese students, business and professional men of all kinds," not least to improve relations with China itself. He never mentioned the 1907 Gentlemen's Agreement with Japan, in which the Tokyo government agreed to stop Japanese immigration into the United States.

Roosevelt in his second term raised other issues that remain alive to this day. Beginning in December 1905, he called for legislation to regulate commerce in "misbranded and adulterated foods, drinks and drugs," and Congress responded with the 1906 Pure Food and Drug Act. In December 1906 he called for the federal financing of federal election campaigns to stop the corruption of elections. In December 1907 he trumpeted the need to preserve the nation's forests, irrigate arid lands, build dams, and improve the nation's waterways, and protested the fencing off of large portions of public lands for grazing. In December 1905 he called for Yosemite, a California redwood grove, the Grand Canyon and Niagara Falls to become national parks, and he suggested using such parks to preserve the elk and other western animals. His ecological concerns extended into the Bering Sea, where Grover Cleveland in his second term had first tried to reach agreements with the British, Russians and Japanese to stop the excessive slaughter of seals. In December 1906 he reviewed this controversy in far greater detail than either Cleveland or McKinley, noting that the

Pribilof Island seal herds had fallen from an estimated 4.7 million seals in 1874 to about 180,000 then.

In early 1907, a failed attempt to corner the copper market led to a serious Wall Street panic, and only the determined intervention of J. P. Morgan—now the owner of U.S. Steel—managed to prevent another 1894-style collapse. The panic led to another significant recession in the last two years of his term, but the relentlessly upbeat president never referred to it in an annual address. Roosevelt in December 1907 and 1908 called for unspecified measures to restrain dangerous speculation, but Congress, where Republicans maintained a large majority despite losing 28 House seats in 1906, did not respond. And in 1906, 1907 and 1908, he called for progressive inheritance taxes to reduce inequality of wealth, and some new form of income tax that the Supreme Court might find constitutional. These were matters of principle rather than financial necessity for him. In his very last annual address in December 1908 he finally mentioned for the first time that his administrations had run four surpluses and four deficits in eight years, with a net surplus of $99.2 million. Still, he left a significant deficit to his successor.

Meanwhile, Roosevelt introduced a new perspective on world affairs to the White House. He embraced the status of a world power in his second annual message in December 1902. "The events of the last four years have definitely decided that, for woe or for weal, our place must be great among the nations," he said. "We may either fall greatly or succeed greatly; but we cannot avoid the endeavor from which either great failure or great success must come." This sense of mission defined his foreign and defense policies, and his idea of the nation's new imperial role. Roosevelt also identified some of the great international problems that would preoccupy the twentieth and twenty-first centuries. "Over the entire world, of recent years," he said in his first annual address, "wars between the great civilized powers have become less and less frequent. Wars with barbarous or semi-barbarous peoples come in an entirely different category, being merely a most regrettable but necessary international police duty which must be performed for the sake of the welfare of mankind." In December 1903 he observed "a real growth among the civilized nations of a sentiment which will permit a gradual substitution of other methods than the method of war in the settlement of disputes." Arbitration could not settle everything, but prudence, firmness and wisdom might "do away with much of the provocation and excuse for war, and at least in many cases to substitute some other and more rational method for the settlement of disputes." Two years later, he suggested that outrages against humanity might justify intervention overseas. While within the United States, he claimed, even the worst crimes, such as lynching, were "never more than sporadic" and menaced only individuals, not classes, "in their fundamental rights," a nation like the US inevitably wanted to express its horrors at "the massacre of the Jews in Kishenef [sic]"—a reference to a recent Russian pogrom—or the "cruelty and oppression" of Armenians in Turkey, also subject to frequent massacres.

By December 1904 the Russo-Japanese War was raging in the Far East, but Roosevelt never discussed it at any length or, astonishingly, ever referred to his own role in bringing the parties together to negotiate peace in Portsmouth, New Hampshire, in 1905, for which he became the first US citizen to win the Nobel Peace Prize. In December 1905 he welcomed the convening of a second Hague Conference to promote international peace. He scorned pacifism. "Our aim is righteousness," he claimed, and that would sometimes lead us to war. He attacked "the sentimentalist who dreads oppression less than physical suffering, who would prefer a shameful peace to the pain and toil sometimes lamentably necessary in order to secure a righteous peace." But he pushed the search for alternative means to settle at least some international disputes. In December 1907 he reported that the second Hague Conference had created a permanent court of arbitration and agreed not to use force to collect international debts unless the debtor had refused arbitration. It had however rejected a long-standing American demand for the protection of neutral private property at sea during wartime.

Meanwhile, Roosevelt paid unprecedented attention to the state of the nation's military and naval forces. Year after year, he laid out his goals for the weaponry, size, organization, and training of the army and navy in detail that no other president has ever come close to matching. He was content to leave the army at 60,000 men after the end of the Philippine insurrection, but he insisted that it should conduct annual large-scale maneuvers and that the nation should prepare to expand it rapidly in time of war. In December 1907 he called for a larger medical corps and higher army pay, and stressed the importance of company first sergeants and sergeant majors. He successfully advocated for the creation of an army general staff and a parallel body for the navy. The construction of the navy since the Arthur administration, he declared in his first annual address, had made the victory over Spain possible, and by the end of his term he was calling for eight battleships of the most modern type—double the current strength—along with many other auxiliary craft, all listed by him in detail. He frequently advocated more gunnery practice for the navy, and in his December 1907 address, echoing his friend the naval theorist Alfred Thayer Mahan, he insisted that the navy not be divided into widely separate detachments that might be defeated one by one in a new war. He complained repeatedly about promotion practices in the two services, which he said should never value seniority over ability, and made specific recommendations for the curriculums of the service academies. He left no doubt, in short, that he wanted the nation to be ready to participate in a large-scale war among great powers.

Roosevelt also welcomed and expanded the imperial mission that had begun with the war with Spain. His instinct for the middle ground governed his attitude toward the Philippines. He immediately embraced the task of giving the Philippines self-government in his first annual address, while warning that their various tribes stood at different stages of civilization and that many were more than "thirty generations" behind "our ancestors" in their political development. Some thought we had gone too far, others not far enough, but the task required "patience and strength." He repeated in December 1904 that the Philippines were "utterly incapable" of independence "or of building up a civilization. . . . There are points of resemblance in our work to the work which is being done by the British in India and Egypt, by the French in Algiers, by the Dutch in Java, by the Russians in Turkestan, by the Japanese in Formosa," but the United States was making more of an effort to give the natives more responsibility than those nations. Relations with Cuba did not go smoothly. A year into his term in December 1902 he reported that the nation had in fact given Cuba its independence, while adding that the congressional Platt Amendment laid down "that Cuba must hereafter have closer political relations with us than with any other power." Four years later, he reported that in August 1906 an insurrection had broken out in Cuba and the government had collapsed after asking the US to intervene. We did so, he said, to prevent European intervention, sending the navy, the army, the secretary of war, and an assistant secretary of state, and establishing a provisional government. New elections and a new government would follow the restoration of tranquility. Roosevelt expressed the hope that the Cuban people "will realize the imperative need of preserving justice and keeping order in the Island. . . . If the elections become a farce, and if the insurrectionary habit becomes confirmed in the Island, it is absolutely out of the question that the Island should continue independent; and the United States, which has assumed the sponsorship before the civilized world for Cuba's career as a nation, would again have to intervene and to see that the government was managed in such orderly fashion as to secure the safety of life and property." In December 1908 he noted that new elections had taken place and that the United States troops would be gone in a few months. Meanwhile, he called without success for Congress to extend US citizenship to the people of Puerto Rico.

Cuba was merely one theater in a much broader imperialist offensive around the Caribbean. Its centerpiece was the Panama Canal. In December 1903 Roosevelt narrated a turbulent year on the isthmus. Authorized by the Senate in June 1902, he had negotiated a treaty with Colombia allowing the US to build a canal across the isthmus and control a strip of land around it in perpetuity, but the Colombian government refused to ratify it. "When it became evident that the treaty was hopelessly lost," he continued, "the people of Panama rose literally as one man . . . with astonishing unanimity the new Republic was started," and the United States recognized it at once. As a matter of fact, Roosevelt had favored provoking the secession of Panama from Colombia as soon as the Bogota government had rejected some of the terms of the treaty, and Americans had been deeply involved in starting the revolt.[6] Colombia, the president continued, had proven over half a century that it could not keep order on the isthmus, and the United States had had to land troops there six times, taking advantage of special rights granted by the 1850 treaty with Colombia that had led to the building of the railroad. To fail to act under these circumstances, he said, would have shown "folly and weakness" amounting

---

6 See David McCullough, *The Path Between the Seas* (New York, 1977), pp 329–86.

to "a crime against the nation." He submitted a treaty just concluded with the new Panamanian government, which the Senate approved. In November 1906, Roosevelt visited the Canal Zone to see the construction of the canal, the first president to travel outside the US while in office. "I chose the month of November for my visit," he told the Congress in a December 17 report, "partly because it is the rainiest month of the year, the month in which the work goes forward at the greatest disadvantage, and one of the two months which the medical department of the French Canal Company found most unhealthy." The report, about half the size of one of his massive annual addresses, described living conditions, the labor force, the machinery employed, and the progress of the Culebra Cut—the huge excavation of the mountain the canal had to traverse—and the efforts to eradicate the mosquitoes which had now been shown to carry yellow fever. While problems, he said, were of course inevitable in such a large and unprecedented task, he expressed "contempt and indignation" for American "slanderers" who were "trying to interfere with, and hamper the execution of, the greatest work of the kind ever attempted, and are seeking to bring to naught the efforts of their countrymen to put to the credit of America one of the giant feats of the ages." The canal was still nearly six years away from completion when he left office.

This, however, was not all. Roosevelt also assumed in the Caribbean the role that Britain and France, in particular, were playing in North Africa and elsewhere: the western power that would usurp sovereign functions of independent, less developed states that could not meet their international obligations. He claimed the authority to do so under the Monroe Doctrine, which obliged the US, he said, to play this role to keep any European powers from trying to play it within the western hemisphere. In December 1903 he described how Great Britain, Germany and Italy had jointly blockaded the ports of Venezuela to compel the payment of its debts. The United States had stepped in and reached an agreement with Venezuela to set aside revenues to pay those debts and those of eight other powers, including the United States. When the three blockaders demanded precedence, Roosevelt convinced them to submit the dispute for arbitration to the new court at The Hague. The Dominican Republic was the next target of this policy. In December 1905 Roosevelt explained that turmoil and unpaid foreign debts had impelled a new leader to ask for US help a year earlier. Stepping in just in time to prevent European intervention, he said, the US had signed a treaty allowing American officials to take over the collection of Dominican customs, reserving 55 percent of the proceeds to pay foreign debts. Already, he boasted, the Dominican government's 45 percent was more than its own corrupt administration had provided previously. The Monroe Doctrine, he said, included an obligation to keep order among the peoples of the Caribbean. It did not aim at their sovereignty: "No just and orderly government has anything to fear from us."

By 1907 Roosevelt's endless activity on all fronts and relentless moral exhortation had captured the imagination of much of the American people, although his moderation on economic questions had alienated some of the more progressive members of his own party. Still only forty-eight years old, he nonetheless declared in June 1907 that he would not seek another elected term, even though many Republicans were clamoring for him to do so. By late that year he was actively promoting the candidacy of his secretary of war, William Howard Taft of Ohio, to head off a draft. Taft, who had also served as governor of the Philippines but who had never before run for elective office, won the nomination. The Democrats, who had lost to Roosevelt in a landslide in 1904 behind conservative New Yorker Alton B. Parker, turned to William Jennings Bryan for the third time. Taft won very comfortably with 51.6 percent of the popular vote to Bryan's 43.1 percent, and a 321–162 margin in the Electoral College, appearing to confirm that the Republicans now enjoyed a permanent majority.[7] During the next forty years, the economic and social forces that Roosevelt had identified at home and the growth of great-power competition abroad transformed both the nation and the world beyond all recognition.

---

7 Minor parties led by the Socialist Party divided the rest of the popular vote.

# XIII

## WILLIAM HOWARD TAFT AND WOODROW WILSON

### 1909–13 • 1913–1921

Having reached the presidency as Theodore Roosevelt's hand-picked successor, William Howard Taft began his inaugural address by pledging to maintain and enforce the laws intended to suppress "the lawlessness and abuses of power" of great combinations in railroads and industries. Then, in a dramatic break with Roosevelt, he announced that he would call the new Congress into immediate session to revise the tariff—and perhaps to pass a graduated inheritance tax—to make up a current budget deficit of $100 million. He also called for cuts in expenditures, while pledging to continue the construction of the Panama Canal and advocating improvements in the Mississippi and Ohio Rivers. Later in the address he discussed at some length, for the first time since the Benjamin Harrison administration, the voting rights situation in the South. With black Americans now effectively disenfranchised throughout the region, the Democrats controlled it entirely, and some Republicans in 1908 had called for enforcing the provision of the Fourteenth Amendment providing for a reduction in congressional representation for states that denied large portions of their adult male population the vote. Dismissing this proposal as a "secondary consideration," Taft discussed the "progress and present condition of the Negro race." The Thirteenth and Fourteenth Amendments, he said, had been "generally enforced"—a statement that must have stunned black southerners denied equal protection of the laws—and Taft effectively blessed the new white southern approach to suffrage. "While the fifteenth amendment has not been generally observed in the past, it ought to be observed, and the tendency of Southern legislation today is toward the enactment of electoral qualifications which shall square with that amendment . . . the domination of an ignorant, irresponsible element can be prevented by constitutional laws which shall exclude from voting both negroes and whites not having education or other qualifications thought to be necessary for a proper electorate." He endorsed appointing black citizens to federal office, but not where "the race feeling is so widespread and acute" as to interfere with the performance of their duties. Denying any race prejudice of his own, he echoed black spokesman Booker T. Washington, looking forward to better feeling in the South, encouragement of "the industrial and intellectual progress of the Negro," and the exercise of the franchise by those who deserved it.

The special session of Congress eventually passed the Payne-Aldrich Tariff in the late summer of 1909. The House bill had lowered tariffs, but the Senate managed to get some of them raised. An intense, bitter campaign by Republican progressives to create a powerful independent tariff commission to investigate rates failed, and tariff receipts and domestic prices increased during the subsequent fiscal year. That alienated both Republican and Democratic progressives and got Taft's presidency off to a rocky start. In March 1910, progressive Republican congressman George Norris of Nebraska staged a coup against conservative Republican Speaker Joe Cannon and broke his power over the House with Democratic support. The progressive spirit was winning more and more adherents around the nation, and in the November 1910 elections the Democrats won 55 new House seats and emerged with a 227–161 majority, while the Republicans kept the Senate. That Congress proceeded to pass two critical constitutional amendments authorizing federal income taxes and requiring the direct election of senators by the voters, not state legislatures—which Taft never mentioned. Both won ratification in early 1913. In 1912 the new Congress passed bills lowering certain tariff rates, but Taft vetoed them.

In a special message to Congress in January 1910 Taft took moderate positions on the related questions of trusts and railroad regulation. The 1906 Hepburn Act, which had given the ICC some power over railroad rates, was not working, because railroads could challenge its decisions in federal court, and he proposed ways of making their recommendations take immediate effect. Regarding trusts, he refused to condemn monopoly in and of itself. Firms might legally become monopolies by using economies of scale to cut prices, but they must not legally cut them to artificially low rates—as Standard Oil, most famously, had done—or force their customers into exclusive agreements. Rejecting laws that tried to distinguish good from bad trusts, he called instead for a federal corporation charter law. Congress failed to act on such a law, fearing that it would serve business interests.[1] Taft made no further recommendations for ICC or antitrust reform in his December 1910 address, after the Republicans had lost control of Congress. A year later, he essentially handed the antitrust issue off to the Supreme Court, which had broken up Standard Oil and the American Tobacco trust in two "epoch-making" decisions, spurring conservative calls for the repeal of the Sherman Act. In the last three or four years, he said, "the heavy hand of the law been laid upon the great illegal combinations that have exercised such an absolute dominion over many of our industries. . . . The anti-trust act is the expression of the effort of a freedom-loving people to preserve equality of opportunity. It is the result of the confident determination of such a people to maintain their future growth by preserving uncontrolled and unrestricted the enterprise of the individual, his industry, his ingenuity, his intelligence, and his independent courage." Taft hardly referred to organized labor in his annual addresses at all, although he called for new legislation on injunctions against strikes. A workmen's compensation law was pending in Congress when he gave his last annual message in December 1912. On his last day in office he signed a new bill separating the Department of Commerce and Labor into two independent departments.

Meanwhile, Taft ran a fiscally stringent administration. His cabinet worked zealously to cut federal employment and expenditures, and in December 1909 Taft estimated the deficit for fiscal 1910 at $34.1 million, plus $38 million more for the Panama Canal, now scheduled for completion on the first day of 1915. Departmental cuts totaling $42.8 million for fiscal 1911, he said, should eliminate

---

1 "Fear Stetson Bill Will Be Put Aside," *New York Times*, December 1, 1910, p. 8.

the deficit for that year. Two years later, in December 1911, he noted that the government had indeed run a surplus of $47.2 million, not counting additional spending on the Panama Canal, with revenues of $701.3 million and expenditures of $654.1 million. The Post Office had run a small surplus, the first one since 1884. The Treasury Department, Taft boasted, had eliminated 542 employees in Washington and 1,259 around the country. In his last annual address in December 1912—which he divided into three separate parts—Taft predicted a relatively small surplus for the current fiscal year as well, with essentially unchanged expenditures. In a portentous development, Taft in that address also endorsed the report of the Monetary Commission that had been formed after the panic of 1907, and which had appeared early in 1912. It had recommended the formation of a National Reserve Association, a corporation that "was, in certain of its faculties and functions, a bank," with its stock divided among state and local banks, for whom it could function as a lender of last resort. The new Democratic Congress had declined to act on the proposal, bequeathing it to Taft's successor.

Taft in 1910 endorsed the admission of Arizona and New Mexico to the Union as the forty-seventh and forty-eighth states, and Congress obliged in 1912, rounding out the territory of the "lower forty-eight." In his last annual message in December of that year he noted that a bill to grant citizenship to the residents of Puerto Rico had passed the House and awaited Senate action. It did not pass. Taft on the other hand opposed another pending bill to grant independence to the Philippines in eight years, calling it "absolutely without justification." "Disregarding even their racial heterogeneity and the lack of ability to think as a nation," he said, "it is sufficient to point out that under liberal franchise privileges only about 3 percent of the Filipinos vote and only 5 percent of the people are said to read the public press. To confer independence upon the Filipinos now is, therefore, to subject the great mass of their people to the dominance of an oligarchical and, probably, exploiting minority." Philippine independence now divided the imperialist Republicans from the mostly anti-imperialist Democrats. He also opposed an elected government for the District of Columbia. He repeatedly proposed staging a great exhibition in 1913 to commemorate the progress of "the Negro" in the fifty years since the Emancipation Proclamation, but Congress declined to act. Taft was also the first president in US history never to make any reference to the status and condition of the Indians in annual addresses.

Taft's addresses dealt with foreign policy in the older traditional way, as a series of specific controversies, without any of the metahistorical musings Roosevelt had favored. New talks with Britain created a new commission to settle fishery disputes with the Canadians, and an arbitrator resolved a new dispute over the boundary in Passamaquoddy Bay. Taft reported in December 1909 that the receivership of Dominican customs was working well, and the next year, he noted that US warships had helped force President Zelaya from power in Nicaragua, which was now negotiating a new agreement to pay its customs with the US. He submitted a treaty to that effect in 1911, and had to dispatch 2000 Marines to help put down a new Nicaraguan revolution in 1912. The government concluded similar treaties with Honduras, and also with Liberia. Mexico presented more serious problems. Taft explained in his December 1911 address that the American minister in Mexico expected a great rebellion against the Mexican dictator Porfirio Diaz to break out shortly, endangering Americans there. Taft had promptly mobilized an army division and two brigades on the border and sent naval squadrons to the Mexican Atlantic and Pacific coasts—to be ready, he explained, to intervene to protect American lives and property if Congress asked him to do so. Intervention had not proven necessary, Diaz had left the country in May, and Francisco Madero had been elected to replace him in October. In his last December 1912 message Taft reaffirmed his policy of "patient non-intervention."

In December 1911 Taft reported that the US had at last signed a "north Pacific sealing convention" with Britain, Japan and Russia, a "measure of great importance" that opened up the possibility of an international game law to protect all seaborne mammals. In the Far East Taft reported that the US was participating equally in sizable currency and railroad loans to China, and relations with Japan remained good despite the "gentleman's agreement" that had essentially banned Japanese immigration since 1907. He also noted Japan's annexation of Korea. In a portent of great events to come, Taft in December 1911 referred to the Second Moroccan crisis between Germany and France and the threat of war in the Balkans as "causes of uneasiness in European diplomacy," but denied any direct concern to the United States. He said nothing about the Balkans a year later, after the Balkan states had successfully occupied nearly all of Turkey's territory on the European continent.

As for defense, Taft cut both army and navy appropriations as part of his economy drive in his first two years, while pushing for fortifications on Corregidor in Manila Bay in the Philippines and at Pearl Harbor in Hawaii. By December 1912 he had reversed course, asking for more officers and men in the army, more cruisers and battle cruisers to match other leading navies, and a long-term program of two battleships a year until the navy had a total of forty. The Congress appropriated money for only one in 1911, and in December 1912 he asked them to authorize three for the coming year to make up for it. The United States wanted peace but had become a world power, and the defense of the Panama Canal, its trade, and its missionary presence around the world required "sufficient naval power to give force to our reasonable demands, and to give weight to our influence in those directions of progress that a powerful Christian nation should advocate." He also noted approvingly that the army had created a reserve of discharged soldiers and increased cooperation with the National Guard.

Taft had failed to respond to the progressive spirit that had been growing around the country. He had also alienated Theodore Roosevelt, who had spent his first year out of office traveling in Europe and Africa, and returned disappointed in Taft's turn away, as he saw it, from his policies. In February 1912, Roosevelt announced himself as a candidate for the Republican nomination, and he took advantage of a new institution—direct presidential primaries in twelve states—to roll up delegates. Taft did not back down, and won the nomination at a stormy Chicago convention, largely thanks to delegates from southern states—controlled in most cases by federal officeholders—whom the Roosevelt forces tried and failed to unseat. The established Republican leaders knew Taft was almost certain to lose but had come to hate Roosevelt. Roosevelt bolted and formed the Progressive or Bull Moose Party. An equally exciting Democratic convention in Baltimore nominated Woodrow Wilson, a native Virginian who had become a professor and president of Princeton before winning one term as governor of New Jersey in 1910. Wilson secured just 41.8 percent of the popular vote—slightly less than Bryan in 1908, and the second-lowest

Democratic percentage since 1872—but Roosevelt and Taft divided the Republican vote with 27.4 percent and 23.2 percent, respectively, and Wilson won 435 electoral votes to 88 for Roosevelt and just 8 for Taft. The Democrats also gained an astonishing 61 seats in the House—newly enlarged to 435 members—for a 291–134 majority, and won a narrow 47–45 majority in the Senate, their first in twenty years. Wilson had a great opportunity to leave a mark on domestic policy, and he was determined to take advantage of it. And in August 1914—just seventeen months after he took office—the first general war in a century broke out in Europe, leading him within three years to attempt to reshape world politics even more fundamentally than he tried to do for national politics.

Wilson remains the only professional academic ever to reach the White House. A graduate of the College of New Jersey—later Princeton—he had become a lawyer in his twenties, but abandoned the law and returned to academia, earning his doctorate in political science. After teaching at two small colleges, he had returned to his alma mater, which shortly thereafter renamed itself Princeton, in 1890. Named president of the university in 1902, he introduced reforms designed to make it academically more rigorous and socially more democratic—with mixed results. Meanwhile, he was nearly as prolific a writer as Theodore Roosevelt, with books including *Congressional Government*, *Constitutional Government in the United States*, and a five-volume *History of the United States*. He had immediately adopted a less academic speaking style, however, when he entered politics in 1910.

Wilson's first inaugural treated the recent election as an epoch-making event, referring specifically to the newly won control of the White House, House and Senate by the Democratic Party—the first mention of a party by name in an inaugural since Jefferson's ironic "We are all Federalists, we are all Republicans" in 1801. The nation, he said, wanted to use the Democratic Party "to interpret a change in its own plans and point of view." While life was "very great" in its material aspects, in the "moral force" displayed by men and women seeking to rectify wrong, and in "a great system of government," "evil has come with good." "We have been proud of our industrial achievements, but we have not hitherto stopped thoughtfully enough to count the human cost, the cost of lives snuffed out, of energies overtaxed and broken, the fearful physical and spiritual cost to the men and women and children upon whom the dead weight and burden of it all has fallen pitilessly the years through." "The great Government we loved has too often been made use of for private and selfish purposes, and those who used it had forgotten the people. . . . We have come now to the sober second thought. . . . Our work is a work of restoration." He attacked the tariff, the existing banking and currency system "perfectly adapted to concentrating cash and restricting credits," and the industrial system that "holds capital in leading strings" and "restricts the liberties and limits the opportunities of labor," and called for more efficient agriculture, more development of rivers, and better care of forests and industrial by-products. Justice demanded sanitary laws, pure food laws, and laws setting the conditions of labor. "The feelings with which we face this new age of right and opportunity sweep across our heartstrings like some air out of God's own presence, where justice and mercy are reconciled and the judge and the brother are one. . . . I summon all honest men, all patriotic, all forward-looking men, to my side. God helping me, I will not fail them, if they will but counsel and sustain me!" Not even Lincoln in the midst of the Civil War had used such messianic language. Building on the more reserved analyses of his great rival Theodore Roosevelt, Wilson anticipated the language twenty years later of Franklin Roosevelt—who coincidentally joined his administration as assistant secretary of the navy—and laid the rhetorical foundation for more than half a century of reforms. Yet his inaugural also highlighted his tragic flaw: his certainty that he spoke at all times for the American people and the people of the whole world, with God on his side as well.

Rather than wait until the following December, Wilson immediately called the new Democratic Congress into session on April 1, 1913. Addressing a joint session just a week later on the tariff question, he became the first president formally to present major legislation to that body, and he repeatedly addressed both houses during the next two years as they passed three major pieces of legislation. He confined himself entirely to general principles. The burden of tariffs must be lightened, he said, as "the whole country" understood. The nation should abandon the idea that industry was entitled to "the direct patronage of the government." Echoing Grover Cleveland twenty-five years earlier, he argued that tariffs had created monopoly, and lower ones could make producers "efficient, economical and enterprising." Congress got to work, and the House passed the bill on May 8 and sent it to the much more closely divided Senate. On May 26, Wilson issued a statement on "The Tariff Lobby." "Washington has seldom seen so numerous, so industrious, or so insidious a lobby," he said. It was spending "money without limit" on newspaper advertisements "to create an appearance of a pressure of opinion antagonistic to some of the chief items of the Tariff bill.... The Government in all its branches ought to be relieved from this intolerable burden and this constant interruption to the calm progress of debate."

The Underwood Tariff bill, named after the Democratic leader in the House, bogged down in the more closely divided Senate. On June 23, Wilson broadened the agenda of reform, delivering another message to a joint session to call also for banking and currency reform, which Congress had failed to pass for Taft during 1912. While the Washington summer heat inconvenienced all and threatened the health of some, he said, all must make personal sacrifices to do consequential work. The lower tariffs would set the producers of America free, but they needed banking and currency reform to use their freedom. "Our banking laws must mobilize reserves; must not permit the concentration anywhere in a few hands of the monetary resources of the country or their use for speculative purposes in such volume as to hinder or impede or stand in the way of other more legitimate, more fruitful uses. And the control of the system of banking and of issue which our new laws are to set up must be public, not private, must be vested in the Government itself." The responsible congressional committees had consulted him and were ready "to suggest action." He asked Congress to complete "this great enterprise of exigent reform." Shortly thereafter, Congress passed the Underwood Tariff, which also included the first income tax passed under the newly ratified Sixteenth Amendment to the Constitution—a one percent tax on the income of the richest three percent or so of the population.

Wilson broke another key precedent when he delivered his first annual address on December 2. Since Thomas Jefferson, as we have seen, presidents had submitted their reports on the state of the union in writing, and they had grown steadily along with the country, peaking under Theodore Roosevelt at nearly 25,000 words. Wilson delivered this address in person, and it ran to just 3,353 words. It lacked many of the address's customary parts, such as a quick summary of federal revenues and expenditures, or the finances of the Post Office, or the condition of the Indians, and the summary of foreign policy—which we shall look at in due course—was brief. The country, he said, "waits with impatience" for the passage of what was now called the Federal Reserve Act to "set credit free from arbitrary and artificial restrains," and passage followed a few weeks later. He asked for additional legislation to make more credit available to farmers. He also made the most remarkable proposal for the conduct of national elections since Andrew Jackson suggested eliminating the Electoral College. "I feel confident that I do not misinterpret the wishes or the expectations of the country," he said characteristically, "when I urge the prompt enactment of legislation which will provide for primary elections throughout the country at which the voters of the several parties may choose their nominees for the Presidency without the intervention of nominating conventions." Conventions composed of national officeholders and candidates would meet only to write platforms and ratify the people's choice. It took about sixty years for this plan to come into effect without federal legislation.

On January 20, 1914, Wilson put forth the third big item on his domestic economic reform agenda in another address to a joint session on trusts and monopolies. With the Federal Reserve System a reality, its time, he said, had come. Legislation, he said, must respond to opinion, and opinion toward monopolies had evolved over a whole generation. While some businessmen defended monopoly, "the average business man is convinced that the ways of liberty are also the ways of peace and the ways of success." With a touch of Roosevelt's evenhandedness, he declared that "the antagonism between business and government is over," and promised "as easy and simple business readjustments as possible in the circumstances." He asked specifically for legislation to ban interlocking directorates—men simultaneously serving on the boards of various corporations—which combined "those who borrow and those who lend" and "those who sell and those who buy." This measure would "bring new men, new energies, a new spirit of initiative, new blood, into the management of our great business enterprises. It will open the field of industrial development and origination to scores of men who have been obliged to serve when their abilities entitled them to direct." He wanted a new "interstate trade commission" to help make the antitrust laws clear to business, and individual penalties for those who violated public policy and sound business practices. Lengthy deliberations in Congress led to the passage of the Clayton Act in October, specifically making certain monopolistic practices such as price discrimination illegal, restricting mergers and acquisitions, and prohibiting interlocking directorates in directly competing firms. Congress also in that session created the Federal Trade Commission to help enforce the antitrust laws.

Not since Washington's time had a single peacetime Congress enacted so many dramatically new policies. Wilson's sweeping rhetoric implied that the country had entered a new era of free competition, but he undoubtedly exaggerated the extent of the changes he had wrought. The Underwood Tariff reduced total customs collections only slightly in its first year, whereupon imports and duties fell rapidly because of the European war.[2] The Federal Reserve System simply followed the recommendations of the independent commission that the Republicans had created after 1907, and as it turned out later, was not robust enough to prevent the greatest panic and economic collapse in US history in 1929–33. The Clayton Act did not revolutionize antitrust enforcement. The initially modest income tax became revolutionary when the United States entered the world war in 1917. None of these measures could do what Wilson promised for them: to create a "New Freedom"—the slogan of his campaign—by breaking up monopoly and opening up vast new fields of endeavor for individual enterprise. In practice they had more in common with Theodore Roosevelt's evenhanded, incremental proposals during his tenure than with Wilson's own revolutionary rhetoric.

Wilson in his first two years also showed an unusual ability publicly to ignore unpleasant subjects. A new generation of black political leaders had warmed to his candidacy and gave him their support in 1912. The Democratic victory also returned the white South to national power for the first time in many decades, and Wilson's cabinet, including southerners like William Gibbs McAdoo

---

2 Taussig, F. W., *Tariff History of the United States*, p. 528.

of Georgia and Josephus Daniels of North Carolina, imposed segregation in federal government offices for the first time in 1913. Wilson had a stormy private meeting with black leaders about this policy, in which he insisted that segregation benefited both races, but never said a word about it in public. We shall see that he also failed to mention certain less inspiring aspects of his foreign policy.

And secondly, while taking advantage of the opportunity offered by the collapse of the Republican Party in 1912, Wilson had not transformed American politics. In October 1914, in the midst of the congressional elections, Wilson published a message to House leader Oscar W. Underwood "Expressing Appreciation for Legislative Work." It was really a campaign manifesto. The passage of his "great program," he said, had served the people "as they have seldom if ever been served before." The program had "a single purpose, namely, to destroy private control and set business free." "Justice," he added, "has been done to the laborer," who for unspecified reasons would no longer be "an object of sale and barter." While "we"—the Democrats—"would have no dealings with monopoly, but reject it altogether," "our opponents" merely wanted to regulate it. "I look forward with confidence to the elections," he said. "The voters of the United States have never failed to reward real service." The Democratic Party, united, strong, and confident, was now "the only instrument ready to the country's hand by which anything can be accomplished," while the Republican Party, even before its split, had been "utterly unserviceable as an instrument of reform." "Every thoughtful man sees that a change of parties made just now would set the clock back, not forward. I have a very complete and very confident belief in the practical sagacity of the American people." Wilson misjudged his countrymen. In the Senate, where the voters rather than the legislature chose the winners for the first time, the Democrats gained three seats and increased their majority to 56–39, but the Republicans in the House gained a whopping 62 seats, won a slight plurality of the popular vote, and cut the Democratic majority to 230–196.

"The country, I am thankful to say, is at peace with all the world," Wilson announced in his December 1913 annual message, "and many happy manifestations multiply about us of a growing cordiality and sense of community of interest among the nations, foreshadowing an age of settled peace and good will." He proudly reported that the State Department had now negotiated thirty-one arbitration treaties with nations covering four-fifths of the world, promising to submit any disputes with them to an impartial tribunal and awaiting its report, while failing to credit his secretary of state, William Jennings Bryan, the chief author of this policy, by name. Then Wilson turned to Mexico, now in the midst of civil war, and introduced a new doctrine to US foreign policy: the idea that governments had to meet certain political standards to secure recognition by the United States. In February 1913 General Victoriano Huerta had overthrown the short-lived democratic Madero government. Although American ambassador Henry Wilson had supported Huerta's coup in the waning days of the Taft administration, Wilson had entirely repudiated Huerta by December 1913.[3] "There can be no certain prospect of peace in America until Gen. Huerta has surrendered his usurped authority in Mexico," he said; "until it is understood on all hands, indeed, that such pretended governments will not be countenanced or dealt with by the Government of the United States . . . Mexico has no Government, only a military despotism." He expressed confidence that Huerta's power was crumbling and that his regime had not long to live. Four months later, on April 20, 1914, Wilson in a special message to Congress complained that Huerta was taking unfair actions against Americans, and that this threatened to draw the US into war not with Mexico, but with Huerta himself. Mexico, he repeated, had no government, and he asked for and received authority to use the armed forces to secure from Huerta "the fullest recognition of the rights and dignity of the United States." Just days later he authorized the landing of American troops in the port of Vera Cruz, ostensibly to prevent the landing of a German ship carrying arms for Huerta, now locked in civil war with the Constitutionalist Venustiano Carranza. The troops stayed for several months, and Carranza eventually ousted Huerta.

In his annual message in December 1915 Wilson boasted that the US had left Mexico's fortunes in her own hands rather than take advantage of her distress, and had respected Mexico's right of revolution. Subsequent messages showed a remarkable ability

---

3 See the extraordinary book by Friedrich Katz, *The Secret War in Mexico* (Chicago, 1980), pp. 96–108.

to avoid unpleasant subjects. He made no statement when he sent American troops under General John J. Pershing to try to punish Mexican rebel Pancho Villa for a cross-border attack in 1916. Nor did he ever discuss armed intervention and prolonged occupation in both Haiti and the Dominican Republic, designed to restore order and allow for the payment of those nations' debts, like the earlier interventions under Roosevelt and Taft. He did in his first annual message suggest that Hawaii and Puerto Rico would permanently remain part of the United States—perhaps, it seemed, as new states—and he reversed Taft's stand and insisted that the US must prepare the Philippines for the soonest possible independence.

In the last days of July and the first few days of August 1914, the First World War broke out in Europe when Austria-Hungary attacked Serbia, Russia mobilized against Austria-Hungary, Germany declared war on Russia and France, and Britain went to war with Germany. In the first days of August, Wilson made a private, belated and futile offer of the good offices of the United States to the powers in an attempt to head off the war.[4] By August 19, when he issued a message on neutrality, he had chosen his new course. Every man who really loved America, he said, would speak in a true spirit of neutrality. To take sides would "seriously stand in the way of the proper performance of our duty as the one great nation at peace, the one people holding itself ready to play a part of impartial mediation and speak the counsels of peace and accommodation, not as a partisan, but as a friend." In his annual message in December he held out the hope that the US might help the warring nations make peace, but also called for preparedness measures that did not violate the traditional prohibition against a standing army, such as encouraging privately organized camps to provide military training to volunteers and a stronger national guard. He also raised again the hardiest perennial of post–Civil War annual messages, the increasingly urgent need to build up a merchant marine.

In the spring of 1915 Germany, struggling under an effective British blockade, unleashed unrestricted submarine warfare around the British Isles, and sank the liner *Lusitania* on May 7, killing 1,198

---

4 Luigi Albertini, *The Origins of the War of 1914* (Oxford, 1952), vol. III, pp 700–1.

people, including 128 Americans. Three days later, speaking to newly naturalized Americans in Philadelphia, Wilson ignored the sinking and implored his listeners to think first not only of America, but also of humanity, "for America was created to unite mankind by those passions which lift and not by the passions which separate and debase." Then he sent a series of diplomatic notes to Germany from May 11 through July 21, asserting neutral rights to travel on belligerent ships, denying any German right to sink them, and promising to hold the Germans to a "strict accountability" for any future outrages, and demanding reparation for lives lost. Bryan, who believed that any determined stance would lead to war, resigned. The German government did order submarine commanders to stop sinking merchant ships without warning, and Wilson in his December 1915 annual message did not refer to the submarine dispute and declared that no current controversy was likely to "lead to any serious breach of amicable relations." Instead, he bitterly attacked naturalized Americans who had in word and deed tried to weaken American authority and American industry—a reference mainly to acts of sabotage designed to help Germany. He asked for new laws to "crush out" "such creatures of passion, disloyalty and anarchy."

Wilson excelled at *defining*, if not *implementing*, sweeping, idealistic policies, and he developed his fateful approach to the world war from April 19, 1916, when he had to respond to new sinkings by German submarines, to April 16, 1917, when he addressed the nation after Congress had declared war on Germany. On the earlier date, he claimed that the United States had hitherto shown great patience, partly because of the friendship that the American people felt toward "the German nation," but that submarine warfare was "incompatible with the principles of humanity" and the rights of neutrals, and that the United States would have to break diplomatic relations with Germany if its government did not renounce this tactic—a clear prelude to war. Once again the German government decided to heed his warning, and such sinkings stopped. Now Wilson had to win reelection against a united Republican Party, which spurned Roosevelt's attempts to rejoin it and nominated Supreme Court justice Charles Evans Hughes of New York, who had taken no part in the great party split. Wilson campaigned as the man who had kept the nation out of war, and Hughes did not advocate a different policy.

As the campaign began in August 1916, a railroad labor dispute led to Wilson's last great domestic triumph. Railroad employees were demanding an eight-hour day with overtime for any additional hours, and the railroads had refused to grant it. The unions, representing 400,000 men, refused to submit the dispute to arbitration, and Wilson on August 29 warned the Congress that a devastating strike paralyzing the economy would now begin on September 4. "It seemed to me," he told the Congress, "in considering the subject-matter of the controversy, that the whole spirit of the time and the preponderant evidence of recent economic experience spoke for the eight-hour day." He had asked the owners to accept it and await the findings of an independent commission as to whether they might properly be entitled to some compensation for it. He now asked Congress to pass a law implementing this proposal while also giving the executive branch the power to take control of such railroads as might be necessary to national defense. Congress passed the bill just four days later, the first time that a federal law had regulated the hours of workers in interstate commerce, and, as it turned out, a fateful precedent. Earlier in that year the Congress, with Wilson's encouragement, had passed a law limiting interstate commerce in products made by child labor, another long-standing progressive demand, but Wilson never mentioned it in a public address and the Supreme Court struck it down in 1918.

Hughes appeared to have won on election night, as nearly the entire Northeast and Midwest returned to the Republican fold, but Wilson eked out a very narrow victory over the next few days thanks to the states of Ohio and California—the latter decided by fewer than 4,000 votes. With 277 electoral votes to Hughes's 254, Wilson remained a minority president with 49.2 percent of the popular vote to Hughes's 46.1 percent. The Republicans meanwhile gained in Congress again. They actually won 215 House seats to the Democrats' 214, but the Democrats kept control thanks to five minor party members. They also gained two Senate seats, but the Democrats kept a 54–42 edge there.

Wilson immediately attempted to bring the war to an end. On December 18 he addressed a note to both sides asking them to state their peace terms, and on January 22 he commented on their vague responses in perhaps his most remarkable address ever.

Both sides, he said, took for granted that peace would create "some definite concert of power which will make it virtually impossible that any such catastrophe should ever overwhelm us again. . . . It is inconceivable that the people of the United States should play no part in that great enterprise," an opportunity for which the nation had prepared itself since its founding—provided that the enterprise reflected certain principles that "the peoples of the New World" could accept. "The organized force of mankind" must secure the peace. . . . "There must be, not a balance of power, but a community of power; not organized rivalries, but an organized common peace." And it must be a "peace without victory." A peace "forced upon the loser . . . would be accepted in humiliation, under duress, at an intolerable sacrifice," and would rest "only as upon quicksand. Only a peace between equals can last." No president ever uttered more prophetic words. He then spoke specifically of the future of the many peoples subject to the German, Austro-Hungarian and Russian empires, specifically endorsing "a united, independent and autonomous Poland"—a nation that had been partitioned under foreign rule for more than a century—and "security of life, of worship, and of industrial and social development" to all peoples that had lived under "hostile governments." And the nations of the world must respect "freedom of the seas" and agree to the limitation of armaments.

The French ambassador in Washington—an astute observer—immediately wrote his Foreign Ministry that Wilson might have great difficulty securing the necessary Senate support for participation in an international organization.[5] Yet Wilson in this speech claimed the mantle not only of national but of world leadership, pointing the way to a new era in international politics. "Perhaps I am the only person in high authority amongst all the peoples of the world who is at liberty to speak and hold nothing back. . . . I am confident that I have said what the people of the United States would wish me to say." His stated principles, he said, were the principles and policies "of every modern nation, of every enlightened community. They are the principles of mankind and must prevail." The events of the next three years tested these claims.

---

5 Archives du ministère des affaires etrantgères, Guerre 1914–1918 États-unis 503, Jusserand à Briand, January 26, 1917.

Just nine days later, the German government responded by announcing that unrestricted submarine warfare would resume the next day. Addressing a joint session of Congress on February 2, Wilson announced the severance of diplomatic relations with Germany. Should the Germans carry out their threat, he said, he would return to ask for authority to protect American ships and citizens at sea. Calling a special session of the Congress that was about to expire on March 3, Wilson on February 26 asked for authority to arm American merchant ships. He was thinking, he said, not only of American rights, but of "those rights of humanity without which there is no civilization." A filibuster by Republican senators—several of them leading domestic progressives—killed the resolution giving him this authority, and he blasted them as "a little group of willful men." In his March 4 inaugural Wilson restated the principles of the Peace without Victory speech.

On April 2, Wilson appeared before a joint session again to ask for a declaration of war against Germany. Armed neutrality would not work against unrestricted submarine warfare, he said, and the country could not "choose the path of submission and suffer the most sacred rights of our Nation and our people to be ignored and violated." The country must exert all its power "to bring the government of the German Empire to terms and end the war." He now saw the war as a struggle by and for democracy. Neutrality was impossible against "autocratic governments backed by organized force which is controlled wholly by their will." Abandoning a previous neutrality regarding the responsibility for the war, Wilson said that the German government had acted without its people's knowledge or approval when it entered it—a highly questionable interpretation of the events of July and August 1914. "A steadfast concert for peace can never be maintained except by a partnership of democratic nations," he said, and he claimed that Russia, which had just overthrown the tsar in a democratic revolution, had always been democratic at heart—its autocracy "was not in fact Russian in origin, character or purpose." He also referred to the "Zimmerman note," a telegram in which the German foreign minister had sought an anti-US alliance with Mexico, offering to help the Mexicans to regain territory lost to the US seventy years earlier. He promised to fight for the liberation of the world and all its peoples, to "make the world safe for democracy." Congress approved war by large majorities.

During the remainder of 1917 the war remained largely stalemated on the western front, while the United States began the enormous task of raising an army of several million men, designed to tip the scales. In July 1917 the German Reichstag, or lower house, passed a Peace Resolution calling for a peace without annexations, but this resulted only in the fall of the government and more complete military control over policy. In November, the Communists overthrew the democratic Russian government, which had attempted a disastrous offensive against the Germans, and demanded an immediate peace without annexations or indemnities. They also published secret agreements between the imperial government and its French, British and Italian allies, parceling out territory in Europe and the Middle East, and opened peace talks with the Germans. Prime Minister David Lloyd George of Great Britain also delivered a speech on war aims. Wilson weighed in again before another joint session on January 8, 1918. He claimed, first, that the harsh German terms for the Russians—revealed in the negotiations—represented the German military leaders, not the Reichstag. He expressed some solidarity with the goals of the Russian leaders and declared that the US could help the Russian people make peace. Then he presented his Fourteen Points, a mixture of general principles (freedom of the seas and reduced armaments), specific territorial demands on behalf of France, Poland and Belgium, a demand for autonomy for the subjects of the Austro-Hungarian Empire, a reshuffling of colonial possessions designed to benefit the colonized peoples themselves, and, last of all, a "general association of nations." Germany and Austria-Hungary again replied vaguely, and Wilson in another address on February 11 accused them of wanting to return to the methods of the 1814–15 Congress of Vienna, which handed slices of territory to and fro. Governments now stood before "the court of mankind," he said, and could impose "no annexations, no contributions, no punitive damages." Only the "military and annexationist party" in Germany stood in the way. In March, the Brest-Litovsk peace treaty broke up the Russian Empire and ratified the German victory in the east.

Wilson never gave the American people any purely military reports. The Germans in early March 1918 launched a huge and initially successful offensive on the western front, one that was not really halted until July, just as large numbers of US troops were starting to take the field. In August a general Allied advance began, and in September, Wilson's great dream of mediation appeared to come true, when a new liberal government took over in Germany at the behest of a desperate military leadership and asked Wilson for an armistice based upon the Fourteen Points. While the Allied armies continued to advance, Wilson publicly negotiated with the new government, eventually demanding in effect that Emperor William II—if not his whole dynasty—give up his throne as a condition of peace. In the first days of November the German Navy mutinied and the Army began to follow suit. William did abdicate on November 9 and the Allies agreed on an armistice two days later. The Allied military leaders had worked out the terms, which would make it completely impossible for Germany to resume the war and leave Germany at the Allies' mercy. The French and British governments had also guardedly accepted the Fourteen Points as a basis for peace. Meanwhile, the Austro-Hungarian and Ottoman Empires also collapsed completely. Wilson triumphantly announced on November 11 that the Allies had achieved the war's objective: "The arbitrary power of the military caste of Germany which once could secretly and of its own single choice disturb the peace of the world is discredited and destroyed." Communist revolutionaries were rising up in various parts of Eastern Europe and in Germany itself, and Wilson warned that the new political situation would take a lot of time to sort out. "The present and all that it holds," he said, "belongs to the nations and the peoples who preserve their self-control and the orderly processes of their governments; the future to those who prove themselves the true friends of mankind."

Wilson had converted a broad spectrum of Americans to his vision and his cause. In July 1918, the NAACP leader W. E. B. DuBois, a bitter critic of Wilson's segregation policies, echoed the president that the war would lead either to submission "to military despotism and an endless armed peace," or to putting down "the menace of German militarism" and inaugurating "the United States of the World." A German victory, he told his fellow black Americans, would spell "death to the aspirations of Negroes and all darker races for equality, freedom and democracy," and he asked them to "forget our special grievances, and close ranks shoulder to shoulder with our white fellow citizens and the allied nations that are fighting for democracy."[6] Yet as Wilson looked forward to the realization of his dreams, he had lost other critical ground at home. On October 25, in the midst of a heated midterm election campaign, he had issued an unprecedented statement to the nation. "My fellow countrymen," he said, "if you have approved of my leadership and wish me to continue to be your unembarrassed spokesman in affairs at home and abroad, I earnestly beg that you will express yourself unmistakably to that effect by returning a Democratic majority to both the Senate and the House of Representatives. . . . the difficulties and delicacies of our present task are of a sort that makes it imperatively necessary that the nation should give its undivided support to the Government under a unified leadership, and that a Republican Congress would divide the leadership." Once again the nation disappointed him. Gaining 24 seats in the House and 6 in the Senate, the Republicans effectively reestablished themselves as the nation's majority party and emerged with a 240–192 majority in the House and a 49–47 edge in the Senate. Any peace treaty would need 64 Senate votes.

Wilson did not refer to the election in his annual address on December 2. He reviewed the success of the war effort, which had sent nearly two million soldiers to Europe with the loss en route of only 758, praised the troops, and included special thanks to the women in America—"their instant intelligence, quickening every task that they touched; their capacity for organization and cooperation, which gave their action discipline and enhanced the effectiveness of everything they attempted; their aptitude at tasks to which they had never before set their hands; their utter self-sacrifice alike in what they did and in what they gave." He added his second plea for the ratification of the Nineteenth Amendment to grant them the vote. He also announced his unprecedented decision to travel to Europe to discuss with other leaders "the main features of peace," and asked for Congress's united support. Having accepted his principles, those European leaders "very reasonably desire my personal counsel in their interpretation and application." That annual address also confirmed Wilson's ability to ignore unpleasant subjects. Previous presidents had referred to epidemics sweeping

---

6 https://www.blackpast.org/african-american-history/w-e-b-du-bois-close-ranks-editorial-from-the-crisis-july-1918/.

parts of the country, and McKinley in 1897 had called for national quarantine restrictions and a commission to investigate the cause of yellow fever. In December 1918 the worst epidemic in the history of the modern world, the so-called Spanish flu, had been raging in the US for months, killing thousands of young adults, but Wilson did not mention it either then or at any other time.

Arriving in France on December 13, Wilson spent several weeks touring France, Great Britain, and Italy, sharing his hopes for the peace with enormous crowds who applauded his vision of the future. The peace conference opened in January, and he remained in Paris for six months, with one two-week break for a quick return to the US. Opening the conference discussion of the League of Nations on January 25, 1919, he insisted that he and his fellow leaders represented not governments but peoples, and must "satisfy the opinion of mankind. . . . We are here to see, in short, that the very foundations of this war are swept away"— the secret choices of civil and military rulers, the designs of great powers on the small, "the holding together of empires of unwilling subjects by the duress of arms." On February 14, presenting the draft Covenant of the League to the conference, he stressed the new mandate system, which had given former German colonies and liberated areas from the Ottoman Empire to various victorious powers as "mandates." "It shall be the duty of the league to see that the nations who are assigned as the tutors and advisers and directors of those peoples shall look to their interest and to their development before they look to the interests and material desires of the mandatory nation itself." The Germans, he said, had disregarded these principles. Their interest "was rather their extermination than their development."

The eventual treaty disappointed several different constituencies.[7] Many Republicans argued that the League Covenant surrendered too much American sovereignty and would needlessly involve the nation in quarrels all over the world. Many progressives, meanwhile, felt that the Treaty of Versailles's favoritism toward the Allies, including large reparations payments and accretions to their empires, and unequal treatment of Germany—now trying

---

7 See Selig Adler, *The Isolationist Impulse: Its Twentieth Century Reaction* (New York, 1957), pp. 55–111.

to put together a republican government—betrayed everything Wilson claimed to have stood for. Wilson addressed the Senate on the treaty on July 18. Admitting that the negotiations had been long and difficult and had to overcome many earlier entanglements and promises, he insisted that the League was "a practical necessity" to make many parts of the treaty work. "Every true heart in the world, and every enlightened judgment," he said, "demanded that, at whatever cost of independent action, every government that took thought for its people or for justice or for ordered freedom should lend itself to a new purpose and utterly destroy the old order of international politics. . . . The League of Nations was not merely an instrument to adjust and remedy old wrongs under a new treaty of peace; it was the only hope for mankind. . . . Shall we or any other free people hesitate to accept this great duty? Dare we reject it and break the heart of the world?" The war and the treaty, he said, meant that America had just reached "her majority as a world power," twenty-one years after the war with Spain had acquired distant lands. "It was of this that we dreamed at our birth. America shall in truth show the way. The light streams upon the path ahead, and nowhere else."

The Senate vote was clearly very doubtful. Henry Cabot Lodge, the Republican chairman of the Senate Foreign Relations Committee, refused to accept the treaty without some explicit changes and reservations affirming ultimate US sovereignty, which Wilson refused to consider, and other senators for various reasons would not vote for it in any case. In early September, with the vote still pending, Wilson embarked upon a tour of the Midwest and the West, giving lengthy addresses restating his arguments at every stop. On the night of September 25, 1919, Wilson suffered a serious stroke and had to return to Washington. He never recovered his health during his last seventeen months in office, and his second wife, Edith Bolling Wilson, became his gatekeeper, isolating him from his cabinet and closest associates and claiming when necessary to speak for him. On November 19, 1919, the Senate rejected the treaty with Lodge's reservations by a vote of 55–39, eight votes short of the necessary two-thirds majority, and voted down the original treaty 53–38. A further vote on March 19, 1920, rejected the treaty with the Lodge reservations by a 49–35 vote. The nays in that vote—as in the parallel vote four months earlier—included twenty-three Democrats who followed Wilson's orders to reject all reservations.

Wilson took some very progressive positions on domestic issues during the war, and presided over an unprecedented expansion of the government's economic role and of its tax base. No other president had ever referred by name to the American Federation of Labor, the umbrella organization of trade unions, but he gave a friendly address to its annual convention on November 12, 1917. His December 1919 annual message—written, to be sure, by various cabinet members during his illness—noted that the League of Nations Covenant recognized the rights of labor, and endorsed workers' desire "to make the conditions of his life and the lives of those dear to him tolerable and easy to bear. . . . Governments must recognize the right of men collectively to bargain for humane objects that have at their base the mutual protection and welfare of those engaged in all industries. Labor must not be longer treated as a commodity. It must be regarded as the activity of human beings, possessed of deep yearnings and desires." On September 30, 1918, he addressed the Senate asking it to pass the Nineteenth Amendment decreeing nationwide women's suffrage, a step "vitally essential to the successful prosecution of the great war of humanity in which we are engaged." He called for (and enforced) strong measures against opponents of the war, of which his Justice Department successfully prosecuted several, and on July 6, 1918, he made a strong attack on lynching, likening it to the international outlawry of the German government, which had made "lynchers of her armies."

The financing of the war led to perhaps the most significant innovations of his presidency, even though he chose never to discuss it at length and left policy mainly to his secretary of the treasury (and son-in-law) William Gibbs McAdoo.[8] In his war message of April 1917 Wilson rejected huge loans that would produce inflation, and proposed that wartime appropriations draw as far as possible on "well-conceived taxation." In a special message on Mary 27 he called for higher taxes on "war profits, luxuries, and

---

8 In an offhand remark to one of his own cabinet members in June 1940, Franklin Roosevelt—a member of Wilson's subcabinet for the whole of his administration—remarked that Wilson had essentially let his cabinet members run everything. See *The Secret Diary of Harold Ickes*, vol. III (New York, 1953), pp. 228–36.

incomes." As it turned out, loans played a greater role and inflation followed, but taxes, with the help of the Sixteenth Amendment, reached utterly unprecedented heights. Federal income and profits tax receipts increased from $125 million in fiscal 1916 to $387 million in fiscal 1917, $2.852 billion in fiscal 1918, $2.601 billion in fiscal 1919, and $3.957 billion in fiscal 1920 (driven partly by significant inflation). Total revenues including loans increased from $1.153 billion in fiscal 1916 to $3.882 billion in 1917, $21.5 billion in fiscal 1918, $34.095 billion in fiscal 1919, and $22.994 billion in fiscal 1920. Total expenditures rose from $1.073 billion in fiscal 1916 to $3.083 billion in 1917, $21.824 billion in 1918, and $35.152 billion in 1919, falling to $23.597 billion in 1920.[9] Borrowing still financed most of the war, but the income tax was extraordinarily progressive, with a top rate of 67 percent on incomes over $2 million a year, and the wealthy paid a very large part of the total. The idea that they should pay significant portions of their incomes in times of crisis had taken hold, with huge consequences in the next half century. The government expanded its powers in other ways. On January 4, 1918, Wilson announced that the government was exercising authority recently granted by Congress to take over the operation of the nation's railroads and water transport to ensure making maximum usage of them for the war effort. He pledged to maintain railroad property and to pay salaries to employees based on the average over the last three years.

The defeat of the Versailles Treaty, Wilson's disappearance from public view for his last eighteen months in office, and postwar economic turmoil paved the way for a crushing Republican victory in the 1920 elections. The collapse of wartime demand for farm products and industrial goods alike also led to a severe deflation and depression with which the leaderless administration could not cope. Senator Warren G. Harding of Ohio, a genial compromise Republican candidate, and Governor Calvin Coolidge of Massachusetts swamped James M. Cox of Ohio and young Franklin D. Roosevelt, with 404 electoral votes to 127 and 60 percent of the popular vote to 34 percent. They also gained 63 seats and margins of 303–131 in the House and 59–37 in the Senate. Despite

---

9 *Statistical Abstract of the United States 1922,* pp. 563, 594, 601.

Cleveland's and Wilson's two terms each, the Democratic Party had failed to win a majority of the popular vote since 1852. For the moment the nation had entirely repudiated Wilson and all his works. Yet he had defined the modern presidency, riding herd on Congress to pass his program in his first term and establishing the role of the United States as the guardian of universal values in the world in his second. Doomed to failure by hubris and illness, he nonetheless bequeathed a legacy that shaped both the nation and the world during the last two-thirds of the twentieth century.

# XIV

# Warren G. Harding, Calvin Coolidge, and Herbert Hoover

1921–3 • 1923–9 • 1929–33

Senator Warren G. Harding of Ohio had won the 1920 Republican nomination as a compromise candidate after better-known Republicans deadlocked in the initial balloting. He won a huge victory amidst the controversy over the Versailles Treaty and a disastrous economic mixture of unemployment, inflation, agricultural depression, and the biggest wave of strikes in the nation's history. As he took office, the new 1920 census reported that the nation now numbered 106 million people, a 15 percent increase since 1910. Harding struck the eastern intellectuals who had found Wilson inspirational as a Midwestern boob, and corruption in his administration's Navy Department, Justice Department, Interior Department and Bureau of Veterans Affairs has permanently stained his reputation. Yet his short tenure in office included a remarkable achievement in foreign affairs—the naval disarmament treaties negotiated in Washington in 1922—and he tried to address the problems of a modern industrial state that Roosevelt and Wilson had first defined. His inaugural showed his love for alliteration and long words. Amidst a world of passion run wild, he said—referring to civil wars and revolutions in Russia, China, Eastern Europe and the Middle East—"we contemplate our Republic unshaken, and hold our civilization secure." Rejecting the League of Nations and affirming the voters' verdict, he rejected any "permanent military alliance" or "world supergovernment." During the war, he said, "we have riveted the gaze of all civilization to the unselfishness and the righteousness of representative democracy, where our freedom never has made offensive warfare, never has sought territorial aggrandizement through force, never has turned to the arbitrament of arms until reason has been exhausted." Peace would come, he said, when other nations emulated the United States.

At home, he continued, "Our supreme task is the resumption of our onward, normal way. Reconstruction, readjustment, restoration, all these must follow." The government must reduce abnormal expenditures and war taxation, and while it would be impossible to restore prewar wages and prices, it must seek stability and "normalcy"—the word Harding had given to the language during the 1920 campaign. "With the nationwide induction of womanhood into our political life," he continued, "we may count upon her intuitions, her refinements, her intelligence, and her influence to exalt the social order. We count upon her exercise of the full privileges and the performance of the duties of citizenship to speed the attainment of the highest state." The nation must reject revolution and strive for industrial peace, and "ought to find a way to guard against the perils and penalties of unemployment"—a word that Wilson had used a few times in 1919. Harding immediately called the new, heavily Republican Congress into special session and laid out an agenda before it on April 12, 1921.

The prophet of normalcy never claimed to have achieved it. The most pressing problem, he told the special session, was to match expenditures and revenue while lifting the burden of war taxation. Expenditures had fallen from $5 billion in fiscal 1920 to $4.5 billion in the current fiscal year, and they must fall to $4 billion in each of the next two. Meanwhile the Congress should repeal the wartime excess profits tax and abolish "iniquities and unjustifiable exasperations." Higher tariffs might provide some new revenue. "I believe in the protection of American industry," Harding said, announcing a return to Republican orthodoxy, "and it is our purpose to prosper America first." Congress immediately passed an emergency tariff bill with higher rates on some key agricultural commodities, and began a very lengthy debate over a general tariff increase. In his first annual message the following December Harding praised the special session for a $1 billion tax reduction. This was the beginning of a decade-long series of reductions orchestrated by Secretary of the Treasury Andrew Mellon, an industrialist and banker who held that key position under Harding, Coolidge, and Hoover, and who cut the top personal income tax rate from 77 percent to 24 percent.[1] He also thanked Congress for creating a key new federal institution, the Bureau of the Budget.

The 1921 law that created the Bureau provided for an annual presidential budget message, and on December 4, 1922, Harding delivered the first one four days before his second annual address. Not only had expenditures fallen even further than anticipated during fiscal 1922, to $3.795 billion, but receipts had also risen to $4.109 billion, leaving a surplus of $314 million. Of the $3.7 billion expenditures forecast for fiscal 1923, $1.43 billion would go for principal and interest on the public debt and $442 million for the Veterans Bureau—most of that for disabled veterans of the world war.[2] Congress in 1922 had passed the new Fordney-McComber Tariff, raising rates on many commodities. In each of his two annual messages Harding also protested a key provision of the relatively new income tax laws that exempted interest on state and local government bonds from taxation. This, he claimed, was allowing many governments to borrow irresponsibly, and he called for a constitutional amendment to ban this exemption. Earlier in 1922, in the midst of the congressional election campaign on September 9, Harding had vetoed a bill to provide a bonus for all world war veterans, not merely the disabled. The bill, he claimed, would have cost the government $4–5 billion for bonds redeemable in 1942, and Congress had turned down the national sales tax he proposed to pay for it. Thus began a long controversy that bedeviled his two successors as well.

While trying to restore fiscal orthodoxy, Harding did not abandon the idea of a government role in the economy. He noted continuing distress among many farmers in his 1921 annual address, but could only propose better "cooperative marketing arrangements" to stabilize prices as a solution. He spent more time talking about labor disputes. Strikes had increased dramatically during the war, from about 1,200 in 1914 to a peak of 4,450 in 1917, and remained at 2,385 in 1921. On August 30, 1921, Harding threatened to send in the military to put down "domestic violence" in West Virginia, where miners were

---

1 Steven R. Weisman, *The Great Tax Wars* (New York, 2002), pp. 350–51.
2 This budget message is not in the UC Santa Barbara archive and may be found in the *New York Times*, December 5, 1922, p. 1.

striking, and the miners put down their arms. In his December 1921 annual message Harding said that unions, like corporations, needed "regulation and supervision," and asked for unspecified procedures for mediation and conciliation. On August 8, 1922, long and sometimes violent strikes in the critical coal industry and against the railroads led Harding to address Congress. The miners' strike had begun with the expiration of a 1920 agreement on April 1, and Harding on July 1 had convened a conference of miners and operators that had failed to reach agreement. They had also refused Harding's request to return to work pending an agreement, and Harding asked Congress for emergency measures to deal with a potential coal shortage in the fall and winter. More recently, 400,000 railway workers had struck against a recommendation for lower wages from the Railway Labor Board. While Harding tried to be evenhanded in discussing the dispute, he now focused on violent and sometimes lethal efforts by strikers to keep other men from returning to work. "Strikers have armed themselves and gathered in mobs about railroad shops to offer armed violence to any man attempting to go to work. There is a state of lawlessness shocking to every conception of American law and order and violating the cherished guaranties of American freedom," he said. "If free men cannot toil according to their own lawful choosing, all our constitutional guaranties born of democracy are surrendered to mobocracy and the freedom of a hundred millions is surrendered to the small minority which would have no law." He did not propose emergency legislation, and the address simply prepared the way for Attorney General Harry Daugherty—who was already accused of wrongdoing in one scandal and would eventually go to trial twice on another—to secure a federal injunction to force the workers back to work. The coal strike subsequently came to an end as well. By 1922, total strikes had fallen below prewar levels.[3]

Agricultural distress, the first signs of major scandal, and the inevitable ebb and flow of American politics led in November 1922 to a significant Republican defeat in the congressional elections. The Democrats gained 76 seats in the House and 6 in the Senate, cutting the Republican majorities to 225–207 and 53–42. Undaunted,

---

3 On strikes see Florence Peterson, *Strikes in the United States, 1880–1936* (Washington, 1938), pp. 38–40. See also Robert K. Murray, *The Politics of Normalcy* (New York, 1973), pp. 80–81.

Harding called a special session of the lame duck Congress for November 20—about two weeks before it would normally have met—and asked it to pass a subsidy bill that would allow some of the new large merchant fleet that the government had built during the war to operate at a profit. A filibuster killed the bill.

Harding took moderate positions on several social issues. He called in his March 1921 special session message for Congress "to wipe the stain of barbaric lynching from the banners of a free and orderly representative democracy," and suggested a commission that might develop "at least a national attitude of mind calculated to bring about the most satisfactory possible adjustment of relations between the races, and of each race to national life"—this in the midst of a series of racial clashes in midwestern cities. The prohibition amendment to the Constitution had now gone into effect, and in December 1922 Harding complained that it had highlighted the issue rather than removing it from the national life, and was now determining people's votes. Its scandalous non-enforcement was demoralizing, and he suggested a governors' conference to make enforcement responsibilities clear. In the same message he called for a constitutional amendment to outlaw child labor, now that the Supreme Court had thrown out legislation to that effect. Such an amendment passed Congress in 1924, but only twenty-eight of forty-eight states ever ratified it. Echoing Theodore Roosevelt, Harding also complained in that message that US immigration laws were allowing too many "advocates of revolution" onto our shores, and that "hyphenated Americanism" was once again on the rise. He did not, however, call for severe general restrictions on immigration.

Although Harding in his inaugural stated that the nation had definitively rejected the League of Nations, he hardly pursued an isolationist course. In his first inaugural he referred to the separate peace treaty the US had now concluded with Germany, and said that although the United States had refused to recognize Russia's new Communist government, it did not "forget the traditions of Russian friendship," and should supply food to ease the famine there. Later that year, Secretary of State and former and future Supreme Court justice Charles Evans Hughes opened the Washington Naval Conference of all the great maritime powers. It concluded treaties limiting the future battleship construction of the British, the US and the Japanese, fixing their battle fleets at a ratio 5-5-3; pledging the US and Britain not to fortify Singapore or the Philippines; and pledging nine different nations to respect the territorial integrity of China. Harding asked for the ratification of these treaties in his December 1922 address, and the Senate concurred. And in a special address to the Senate on February 2, 1923, Harding became the first of three successive presidents to recommend that the United States accept the jurisdiction of the new World Court at The Hague. Five days later, he announced agreement with London on a payments schedule for the $4 billion war debt that the British owed the US, a "covenant of peace" that should lead to similar settlements with other nations.

Aides to the head of the Veterans Bureau and the attorney general committed suicide in the spring of 1923, a harbinger of greater scandals to come. Harding that summer decided to make a trip to the west coast, including Alaska. He apparently had a heart attack on a train to San Francisco on July 27, and died in that city three days later. Once again the vagaries of American politics anointed an almost random successor. At the 1920 Republican convention, the party leadership had initially offered the vice presidency to Senator Hiram Johnson of California, a dedicated progressive who had also led the opposition to the League of Nations. After he declined, the convention had nominated Governor Calvin Coolidge of Massachusetts, who had become nationally known when he broke a Boston police strike. Coolidge's political luck continued in 1924. In the first half of that year the new Congress exposed huge scandals at the Veterans Bureau, in the Justice Department, and above all in the Interior Department, where Secretary Albert B. Fall had accepted $100,000 to award an oil lease to the Teapot Dome reservation. Things looked good for the Democrats, but a sectional split doomed them at their convention. Their urban bloc, led by Governor Alfred E. Smith of New York, favored prohibition repeal and a condemnation of the Ku Klux Klan, which had emerged as a political power in much of the Midwest as well as the South. The South and West, supporting Wilson's son-in-law William Gibbs McAdoo, favored prohibition and refused to denounce the Klan. With a two-thirds majority required for nomination, it took the convention 103 ballots to agree on a compromise candidate, the corporate attorney John W. Davis. In the general election Davis won only the states of the old Confederacy plus Oklahoma, while Coolidge took 54 percent of the popular vote compared to 29 percent for Davis and 17 percent for Senator Robert

M. LaFollette of Wisconsin, who revived the Progressive Party and carried his home state. The Republicans increased their congressional majorities as well, and Coolidge became the last successful representative of the conservative Republican principles that had largely ruled the nation since the Civil War.

From his first annual message in December 1923 onward, Coolidge displayed a moral certainty about all the great issues of the day characteristic of the small-town New Englander that he was. In foreign affairs, he confirmed a definite rejection of the League of Nations and foreign alliances, but endorsed entry into the World Court. While reaffirming traditional Russian–American friendship, he ruled out relations "with another regime which refuses to recognize the sanctity of international obligations"—a reference to the regime's huge repudiated debts—and added, "I do not propose to make merchandise of any American principles." Other nations had a "moral obligation" to follow the British example and pay their war debts. Germany had paid the US $255 million for the costs of the post-armistice occupation, but owed $500 million more, and that gave the US an interest in the economic recovery of Germany, now wracked by inflation. Three days later, on December 11, Coolidge announced that the US was appointing representatives to committees designed to arrange for German reparations payments to the Allies. Turning to the government's finances, he said that the new budget system had cut expenditures to $3 billion, and called for lower income taxes and the repeal of the excess profits tax. "High taxes," he said, "reach everywhere and burden everybody. They bear most heavily upon the poor." He pledged if necessary to use existing authority to raise tariffs to equalize production costs. Four months later, on March 11, 1924, he called for a 25 percent reduction in income taxes.

Coolidge promised to continue to operate the government's merchant fleet until it could be advantageously sold. He proposed three big water projects: flood control on the Mississippi and Colorado Rivers, improved navigation from the Great Lakes to the Gulf, and a St. Lawrence Seaway to link those lakes to the Atlantic for merchant shipping. He also called for $5 million worth of new government buildings in Washington. Despite "an inescapable personal responsibility for the development of character, of industry, of thrift and of self-control," the government could do more for the public welfare. The Congress, he said, "ought to exercise all its powers of prevention and punishment against the hideous crime of lynching, of which the Negroes are by no means the sole sufferers, but for which they furnish a majority of the victims."

Together with Andrew Mellon, Coolidge remained focused on the issue of lowering taxes for the whole of his tenure. In his December 1924 annual message he bluntly attacked "the fallacy of the claim that the costs of government are borne by the rich and those who make a direct contribution to the National Treasury," and called for more cuts. "I am convinced," he said paradoxically, "that the larger incomes of the country would actually yield more revenue . . . if the basis of taxation were scientifically revised downward." Such reductions would "encourage and stimulate investment" and give the country "the economic leadership of the world." In his budget message of December 12, 1925 he reported a surplus of $251 million for fiscal 1925, estimated a $262 million surplus for the current year, and credited tax reductions for increased revenue. The next day in his annual message he declared that wealth belonged to the people, not the government; opposed "all proposals for assuming new obligations" unless absolutely necessary to pay off the debt; cited (somewhat misleadingly) the nation's success in paying off the Revolutionary and Civil War debt; and proposed paying off the current debt in much less than the estimated sixty-two years.[4] The House was already working on new tax reductions. A year later in December 1926 he proposed dividing a $383 million surplus between tax reduction and debt reduction. On December 5, 1927, his 1929 budget message reported that three major tax reductions in 1921, 1924 and 1926 had reduced annual taxes by $1.604 billion, while the national debt fell by $8.2 billion. He proposed a further $225 million tax cut, and Congress acted. Projected surpluses were falling somewhat by the time of his last 1928 budget message on December 3, but he bragged again in the annual message the next day that the government had now cut taxes four times yet steadily increased revenue.

Coolidge's other views of the federal government's role never changed. He annually proposed the same improvements for the Mississippi basin, which Congress eventually authorized, and called upon the states of the Southwest to make an agreement on water

---

4 Coolidge claimed that the nation had paid off the Civil War debt in twenty-three years, but the nation's debt had been nowhere near zero in 1888.

that would allow for a great dam on the Colorado River at Boulder Canyon in Nevada. In December 1927, however—after huge floods had devastated the lower Mississippi Valley—he insisted that states must pay for new dikes, and that "the government is not an insurer of its citizens against the hazard of the elements." And while acknowledging that agricultural distress continued in some sectors, including cotton, he vetoed the McNary-Haugen bill twice, in 1927 and 1928. That bill would have established a federal board to fix higher prices on cotton, grains, and a few other products, while selling surplus harvests overseas at a loss. This, he claimed on February 25, 1927, would increase acreage and force prices down. "We must be careful in trying to help the farmer not to jeopardize the whole agricultural industry by subjecting it to the tyranny of bureaucratic regulation and control," he said. By December 1927 he was advocating the sale of the government-owned merchant marine, and also of the dam and nitrate plant on the Tennessee River at Muscle Shoals, Alabama, which the Wilson administration had built during the war. Labor relations remained relatively peaceful during his term. Coolidge routinely called for better enforcement of prohibition in annual messages, but without offering any specifics.

Coolidge's optimism extended to all Americans. On June 6, 1924, he delivered the commencement address at Howard University in Washington, DC, then as now perhaps the leading black college in the US. "Here has been established a great university, a sort of educational laboratory for the production of intellectual and spiritual leadership among a people whose history, if you will examine it as it deserves, is one of the striking evidences of a soundness of our civilization," he said. "The accomplishments of the colored people in the United States, in the brief historic period since they were brought here from the restrictions of their native continent, cannot but make us realize that there is something essential in our civilization which gives it a special power. . . . The progress of the colored people on this continent is one of the marvels of modern history," far more rapid than "the slow and painful upward movement of humanity as a whole." Indeed, he claimed, the "ordeal of slavery" on the American continent and the developments since emancipation showed that Africa, too, would eventually adopt modern civilization. He cited impressive statistics: while only 32,000 "Negroes" had owned homes or farms at the time of emancipation, Negroes now owned 50,000 businesses and their aggregate wealth had grown from $20 million to $1.1 billion. The future of "the Negro Community" was now in its own hands. "Racial hostility, ancient tradition, and social prejudice are not to be eliminated immediately or easily. But they will be lessened as the colored people by their own efforts and under their own leaders shall prove worthy of the fullest measure of opportunity." He praised the selfless service of Negro soldiers in the war and Negro workers at home. Coolidge spoke similarly in nearly every one of his annual addresses, and called for legislation to prevent the crime of lynching. The legal segregation that prevailed all over the South and border states, however, remained as unmentionable as slavery had been before 1847, and on May 25, 1924, Coolidge spoke at the dedication of a memorial to Confederate soldiers at Arlington National Cemetery. In his 1927 message Coolidge claimed that the condition of the Indians, who had been granted full citizenship in 1924, was also improving, and recommended larger appropriations for their "medical care and industrial advancement." The idea of the superiority and destiny of western civilization—rather than of any particular race—prevailed over most of the world in the 1920s, and its adherents included foreign leaders like Kemal Ataturk of Turkey and American black leaders such as Booker T. Washington, by then dead, and W. E. B. DuBois.

On another key front, Congress in 1924 passed, and Coolidge signed, a new immigration law establishing strict quotas for immigrants from every country, based on their numbers within the US in 1890—a provision that disadvantaged Eastern and Southern Europeans relative to Irish and German ones. That law reduced annual immigration from about 528,000 in 1921–25 to 294,000 in 1926–30.[5] In his December 1924 message Coolidge praised the law for "shield[ing] our workers from the disastrous competition of a great influx of foreign peoples," although he added that it should be amended to make it easier to allow immigrants' family members to join them. Congress, however, rejected his moral absolutism on another key issue. On May 15, 1924, Coolidge, like Harding before him, vetoed a bill to appropriate $100 million a year for bonds for all world war veterans—bonds set to mature in 1944. "We have no

---

5 US Department of Commerce, *Statistical Abstract of the United States 1950* (Washington, 1950), p. 97.

money to bestow upon a class of people that is not taken from the whole people," he said. "Our first concern must be the nation as a whole. This outweighs in its importance the consideration of a class, and the latter must yield to the former. The one compelling desire and demand of the people today, irrespective of party or class, is for tax relief. . . . Considering this bill from the standpoint of its intrinsic merit, I see no justification for its enactment into law. We owe no bonus to able-bodied veterans of the World War." They had fought, he said, out of duty, not greed. Congress overrode the veto.

Coolidge showed a similar consistency in foreign affairs. The American participants in reparations negotiations that he had authorized in 1923 included banker Charles Dawes, and the 1924 reparations plan upon which the European powers agreed bore his name. The US government, Coolidge said in that year, had contributed to the settlement by its attitude that this was "not a political problem but a business problem." To resume their productivity and support the advance of civilization, the Europeans, too, must practice "hard work and self-denial." The next year he took some credit for the Locarno agreement that recognized the frontier between Germany and France, a step he had encouraged in a long address in Cambridge, Massachusetts, on July 3. The United States, he reported several times, was taking part in preliminary general disarmament negotiations. In December 1926 he reported that the US had reached agreements with nearly all its foreign debtor nations. Year after year he recommended participation in the World Court, which isolationists continued to oppose. In January 1926 the Senate finally passed a resolution in favor of joining after breaking a filibuster, but only with reservations that every single previous adherent to the court would have to approve. This many refused to do, and Coolidge did not try to pass any further resolutions.[6] The president also expressed support for an agreement to ban aggressive war, and in his last annual message in December 1928 he noted that the Kellogg-Briand Pact, in which all the major nations of the world renounced it, was now before the Senate. It received almost unanimous ratification. He generally said very little about national defense, insisting in December 1924 that the nation would deal with other countries not "by terror and

---

6 Adler, *The Isolationist Impulse*, pp. 188–94.

force," but "through friendship and understanding." And on March 6, 1924, he emphatically vetoed a resolution passed by the Philippine legislature for an immediate up or down vote on independence, arguing that it would disenfranchise Filipinos who wanted eventual independence but understood that they still needed US protection. Their progress toward self-government, he said, had depended on American help; they would lose great economic advantages under independence; and the US would not agree to defend them without ultimate authority over the islands. The nation had the responsibility "both to the Philippine people and to civilization" to decide how much self-government they could handle.

With the economy growing and the stock market booming, Coolidge seemed assured of another full term in the summer of 1927. He shocked the nation and nearly his entire intimate circle by announcing on August 3, "I do not choose to run for president in 1928." Secretary of Commerce Herbert Hoover—who like Taft had never run for office in his life, but had originally made his name organizing food relief for Europe during and after the world war—emerged as the leading Republican, while the wet, urban Democrat Alfred E. Smith won the Democratic nomination—the first Roman Catholic seriously to contend for the presidency. Much of the Democratic base in the South and West would not accept an urban Catholic, and Hoover won in yet another Republican landslide with 58 percent of the popular vote. He carried every state outside the South but Massachusetts and Rhode Island—including Smith's New York—and Florida, Virginia, North Carolina, Tennessee and Texas as well. The Republicans gained 32 House seats for a 270–164 majority, and increased their margin in the Senate with 53 out of 96 seats. Coolidge painted a rosy picture in his last annual message a month later. "No Congress of the United States ever assembled, on surveying the state of the Union, has met with a more pleasing prospect than that which appears at the present time," he said. "In the domestic field there is tranquility and contentment, harmonious relations between management and wage earner, freedom from industrial strife, and the highest record of years of prosperity. . . . The requirements of existence have passed beyond the standard of necessity into the region of luxury." No one knew that an era of American history was nearly over.

The nation, Herbert Hoover announced on March 4, 1929, had reached "a higher degree of comfort and security than ever existed before in the history of the world. . . . We are steadily building a new race—a new civilization great in its own attainments." Referring to the illegal liquor trade, he cited "disregard and disobedience of law" and increasing crime as "most malign" dangers and suggested a national convention on prohibition enforcement. "The United States," he continued, "fully accepts the profound truth that our own progress, prosperity, and peace are interlocked with the progress, prosperity, and peace of all humanity." He supported new disarmament agreements, more conciliation and arbitration of international disputes, and adherence with reservations to the World Court. Yet he also announced a special session of the new Congress to consider farm relief and the tariff. Addressing it on April 16, he traced agricultural distress to worldwide overproduction beginning in the world war. He rejected active government intervention in agricultural markets in favor of a Farm Board that would help farmers' organizations build warehouses and improve marketing themselves, and called for higher tariffs in certain unspecified industries. Congress immediately passed a farm marketing act. When the new Smoot-Hawley Tariff passed in 1930, it raised tariffs on a wide variety of agricultural and industrial goods, the normal result under Republican administrations.[7]

Neither Coolidge nor Hoover ever seems to have referred publicly to the great credit expansion and stock market bubble that had raised the Dow Jones industrial average from an annual high of 121 in 1924 to 381 in 1929. The crash that October dropped it to 199 by the end of the year,[8] and the related issues of the crash, the subsequent collapse of economic activity, and the federal budget dominated the rest of Hoover's term. In his December 3 annual address, less than two months after the crash, Hoover explained that "overoptimism as to profits" had led to "a wave of uncontrolled speculation in securities," and "the inevitable crash." Some people had been "temporarily" forced out of work and farm prices had fallen. Precautionary measures by the Federal Reserve and "the strong position of the banks," he said, had "carried the whole credit system through the crisis without impairment." Businesses, unfortunately, had canceled plans for "continuation and extension" of their activities, and this might create a depression "with widespread unemployment and suffering."

---

7 Taussig, F. W., *Tariff History of the United States*, pp. 489–526.
8 https://www.macrotrends.net/1319/dow-jones-100-year-historical-chart.

Hoover had begun "systematic, voluntary measures of cooperation" with business, state and local authorities to try to make sure that business continued, wages held steady, and construction expanded. He recommended more money for public buildings. He was "convinced that through these measures we have reestablished confidence" and prevented unemployment. Meanwhile, he forecast a $225 million budget surplus for fiscal 1930 and $123 million for fiscal 1931, and recommended a new round of income tax cuts.

Increasing unemployment led Hoover to make a statement on the subject on March 7, 1930. He insisted that the nation had hit bottom around the turn of the year, that construction by public authorities, railroads and industry was up, and that unemployment was lower than at similar stages of the 1907–8 and 1920–22 crises. Addressing the convention of the A. F. of L. on October 6, Hoover argued that cooperation agreements at the White House the previous November, in which business had promised to maintain wages, distribute layoffs equally among workers, and avoid labor disputes, had "been carried out to an astonishing degree." Public works were up about $500 million, to $4.5 billion, from 1929, and labor disputes had fallen way down. The Depression was now a global phenomenon, and Hoover bragged that US unemployment was only half that of Britain or Germany. The country was not however buying his optimistic picture. GDP fell from $103.6 billion in 1929 to $91.2 billion in 1930, unemployment was up from 3.2 percent to 8.9 percent and rising fast, and farm prices were falling rapidly.[9] In the congressional elections of 1930—arguably one of two great political turning points in the American history of the twentieth century—the Democrats gained 52 seats, leaving the Republicans with a 218–216 majority that had evaporated by the time the new Congress finally met in December 1931. They also gained 8 seats in the Senate, leaving it tied at 48–48, with the Republicans in control thanks to the vote of Vice President Charles Curtis.

Hoover in his December annual message a month after the election blamed the Depression not primarily on speculation, but on the worldwide slump in commodity prices, the resulting fall in world purchasing power, and political turmoil in Europe, Asia, and South

---

9 https://www.shmoop.com/great-depression/statistics.html. On farm prices see https://voxeu.org/article/farm-product-prices-redistribution-and-early-great-depression-us.

America. While acknowledging a 15 to 20 percent drop in economic activity, he insisted that price levels were stabilizing and some industries were showing signs of greater demand—both "grounds for confidence." "Economic depression," he said, "cannot be cured by legislative action or executive pronouncement"; the people must depend on faith and self-reliance. He claimed that statistics exaggerated unemployment by incorporating "normal" temporary unemployment, and noted that the government was spending $520 million on waterways, harbors, public construction, highways, and military and naval improvements—spending he wanted to increase by another $100–150 million. These projects bore important fruit. The country had nearly completed the Mississippi and Ohio River improvements by the time he left office, and work had begun on what became first Boulder Dam, and later Hoover Dam. Such projects however had only local impact. Grasping at straws, Hoover in December 1931 argued that cotton and wheat, whose prices had fallen 40 percent, were to blame for the overall 20 percent drop in agricultural prices. He also had to acknowledge, however, that the forecasted $123 million surplus for fiscal 1931 had turned into an estimated $180 million deficit—yet bravely predicted a balanced budget for fiscal 1932. He also reported that the government had severely restricted immigration quotas—so tightly that net immigration, which averaged 235,000 a year from 1926 through 1930, fell to a net outflow of 48,000 a year during the next five years.[10] The 1930 census showed a slowing population increase of 14 percent over the last ten years, to 123 million.

As unemployment continued to increase, pressure grew for some direct government assistance to the growing destitute population. Hoover firmly opposed federal help. "It is a question as to whether the American people on one hand will maintain the spirit of charity and mutual self-help through voluntary giving and the responsibility of local government as distinguished on the other hand from appropriations out of the Federal Treasury for such purposes," he said in a statement on February 3, 1931. "My own conviction is strongly that if we break down this sense of responsibility

---

10 US Department of Commerce, *Statistical Abstract of the United States 1950* (Washington, 1950), p. 97. While the 1924 act had reduced immigration significantly, only Hoover's restrictions cut it down to negligible levels.

of individual generosity to individual and mutual self-help in the country in times of national difficulty and if we start appropriations of this character we have not only impaired something infinitely valuable in the life of the American people but have struck at the roots of self-government." Local charities, he claimed, were providing the necessary help. He declined to call the new Congress into session after the old one adjourned on March 4, 1931.

On June 21, 1931, Hoover took a major international step designed to ease financial and economic distress in Europe and promote global recovery. After first clearing his idea with leading senators and congressmen, he proposed a one-year moratorium on German reparations (none of which were going directly to the US) and Allied war debts. This step, he hoped, would contribute to the success of the general disarmament conference scheduled to meet in Geneva in the following year. The Depression in Germany had already led in 1930 to great gains by Adolf Hitler's National Socialist Party and the paralysis of the German government, which now had to govern by emergency decree. The major nations all accepted his proposal. Hoover insisted that he "did not approve in any sense of the cancellation of debts to us," but as it turned out, the moratorium led to the end of reparations in the summer of 1932, and the Allied nations subsequently refused to make any more war debt payments to the US.

Having refused to call the new Congress into session before December 1931, Hoover proposed three major new responses to the Depression in October and November. Bank failures were occurring all around the country because people were making unjustified withdrawals of funds, he said on October 7. He wanted the nation's banks to provide $500 million for a new institution that would rediscount questionable bank assets, and he wanted to create "a finance corporation similar in character and purpose to the War Finance Corporation, with available funds sufficient for any legitimate call in support of credit." This became the Reconstruction Finance Corporation. For two years, as we have seen, Hoover had boasted of increases in government spending on construction, but now he went all out for fiscal stringency. Trying to steal a march on the new Congress, he announced on November 6 that the new budget would reduce federal estimates by at least $350 million, and warned that "the many sectional interests throughout the country who are asking us to increase expenditures" would only "embarrass the earnest efforts of the administration and the Congress to maintain our governmental finance on a sound basis." On November 14 he proposed a new Home Loan Bank Discount system, which would play the Federal Reserve's role for the nation's troubled savings and loan institutions.

By the time of Hoover's December 1931 annual message unemployment had reached 16.3 percent and GDP had fallen from $103.6 billion in 1929 to $76.5 billion.[11] He responded by making fiscal austerity his top priority. The $180 million fiscal 1931 deficit that he had predicted a year earlier had instead reached $903 million, and he anticipated a $1.42 billion deficit for fiscal 1932. The nation, he said, had to raise taxes and cut expenditures sufficiently to limit the fiscal 1933 deficit to mandatory debt reduction, and he called for two-year emergency taxes to begin in mid-1932. To borrow any more money, he insisted, "will destroy confidence, denude commerce and industry of its resources, jeopardize the financial system, and actually extend unemployment and demoralize agriculture rather than relieve it." He praised the nation's response to the Depression. "In meeting the problems of this difficult period," he said, "we have witnessed a remarkable development of the sense of cooperation in the community. For the first time in the history of our major economic depressions there has been a notable absence of public disorders and industrial conflict. Above all there is an enlargement of social and spiritual responsibility among the people." Private charity was easing distress. "I am opposed to any direct or indirect Government dole," he continued. "The breakdown and increased unemployment in Europe is due in part to such practices"—a reference to unemployment insurance in Britain and Germany, which the US did not have. He also noted that executive action had vastly reduced immigration, which in turn, he said, had lowered unemployment by about 300,000 workers. "The Federal Government," he continued, "must not encroach upon nor permit local communities to abandon that precious possession of local initiative and responsibility. Again, just as the largest measure of responsibility in the government of the Nation rests upon local self-government, so does the largest measure of social responsibility in our country rest upon the individual. If the individual surrenders his

---

11  https://www.shmoop.com/great-depression/statistics.html.

own initiative and responsibilities, he is surrendering his own freedom and his own liberty."

Hoover also repeated his recent proposals for a new bank lending authority and a Reconstruction Finance Commission, called for measures to allow depositors to recover some money from closed banks, and asked Congress to investigate "the need for separation of different kinds of banking." That constituted an endorsement of proposals by Democratic senator Carter Glass of Virginia to bar commercial banks from carrying on investment banking as well, and Congress immediately passed the Glass Act forbidding them from doing so within five years. The new Congress also created the Reconstruction Finance Corporation and passed sweeping tax increases, including a dramatic and very significant rise in the top marginal income tax from 25 percent to 63 percent. All of these measures anticipated key aspects of Franklin Roosevelt's New Deal, but they did not prevent more bank failures and an additional 8 percent unemployment increase during 1932. The new Congress, in which the Democrats controlled the House, moved well to the left of Hoover. On July 1, 1932, Hoover vetoed a bill that would have required federal contractors to pay "prevailing wages," as determined by the Department of Labor. More than three months earlier, on March 23, he had signed the Norris-LaGuardia Act, which outlawed so-called "yellow dog" labor contracts forcing workers to forswear unions and placed severe limits on the power of the courts to issue injunctions against strikes—a long-standing demand of labor at least since the time of Theodore Roosevelt. He accompanied his signature with a memo from his attorney general suggesting that the courts would probably declare some of the act unconstitutional. On another front, Hoover on October 26 issued a Statement on Equality of Opportunity in Employment, declaring equal opportunity for all workers, including Negroes, official policy in government contracts.

Hoover's ideas of self-reliance became the foundation of his reelection campaign, during which he also praised the American people for not succumbing to revolution or dictatorship as many other nations had.[12] On March 6, 1932, however, he gave a radio address attacking the citizenry for withdrawing currency from banks

---

12 See his St. Paul address, November 5, 1932.

to hoard it. "I believe that the individual American has not realized the harm he has done when he hoards even a single dollar away from circulation," he said. "He has not realized that his dollar compels the bank to withdraw many times that amount of credit from the use of borrowers." That summer, thousands of world war veterans came to Washington to encourage Congress to pass a law paying the bonus now due them in 1945 immediately. The House passed it but the Senate refused. After a shooting incident involving veterans and the Washington police, Hoover on July 28 declared that the police could no longer maintain order and called upon the army, led by Chief of Staff Douglas MacArthur, to restore it. Troops broke up the marchers' encampment in Southeast Washington with tear gas and cavalry.[13] "We cannot tolerate the abuse of constitutional rights by those who would destroy all government, no matter who they may be," Hoover declared the next day. "Government cannot be coerced by mob rule."

On the foreign scene, Hoover involved the United States in efforts to create a more peaceful world while trying to conclude some imperial interventions. In his December 1929 address he welcomed the Kellogg-Briand Pact and mentioned a new naval disarmament conference that would soon meet in London. He also declared his intention to reduce the 1,600 American troops in Nicaragua—sent to help restore order and train police—the 700 remaining in Haiti for similar purposes, and the 2,605 in China. He again recommended adherence to the World Court, but isolationists kept the Senate from ever taking up this proposal.[14]

In December 1930 Hoover reported that the new London naval treaty had "abolished competition in the building of warships." A year later he reviewed the Depression's catastrophic effects abroad. The last two years had seen "revolutions or acute social disorders" in nineteen countries, ten countries had failed to meet international financial obligations, and fourteen of them—including Britain, although he did not mention it by name—had gone off the gold standard, reducing the international value of their currencies. He had proposed the debt moratorium to try to help, and the Federal Reserve had worked with European central banks to maintain credit. Meanwhile, the first

---

13 Arthur M. Schlesinger, Jr., *The Crisis of the Old Order 1919-33* (Cambridge, Ma.,1957), pp. 256–65.
14 Adler, *Isolationist Impulse*, p.p. 232–33.

military challenge to the postwar peace had arisen in the Far East, where the Japanese had taken full control of Manchuria. Hoover's secretary of state Henry M. Stimson believed devoutly in the need to enforce international law and favored some international steps to try to convince the Japanese to step back. Hoover feared war, and said only in December 1931 that "The difficulties between China and Japan have given us great concern, not alone for the maintenance of the spirit of the Kellogg-Briand Pact, but for the maintenance of the treaties to which we are a party assuring the territorial integrity of China." Just a month later, Stimson announced his doctrine of "nonrecognition," under which the US government would not recognize territorial changes brought about by force, but Hoover never referred to that doctrine and said nothing about Manchuria in his last annual message. In that message he mentioned the US ongoing participation in the general disarmament conference and attacked European plans to suspend war debt payments in another week or so—plans that they carried out. Meanwhile, Hoover probably said less about the state of the US Army and Navy than any previous president.

Hoover did reduce, although he did not totally withdraw, the US troop contingents in Nicaragua and Haiti, but he maintained Republican opposition to imminent independence for the Philippines. On January 13, 1933, in one of his last acts in office, he vetoed a bill that would have established a new Philippine government and abolished the governor generalship in two years. While the US would retain ultimate authority for another eleven years, full independence would follow in 1944. Claiming that the Philippines could not afford to lose their special trading status in the US and could not defend themselves against powerful neighbors, he suggested a plebiscite on independence in fifteen to twenty years. An anti-imperialist Congress passed the bill over his veto, but the Philippine legislature rejected its terms.

After a lively primary campaign and a spirited convention fight, the Democrats nominated Franklin D. Roosevelt, the 1920 vice presidential candidate and now governor of New York, over former governor and candidate Al Smith and Speaker of the House John Nance Garner. The economic news got worse than ever as 1932 wore on, with GDP falling from $76.5 billion to $58.7 billion and the average unemployment rate rising to 24.1 percent.[1] In his acceptance speech Roosevelt famously promised a "New Deal" for the American people. Having defeated Al Smith with 444 electoral votes to 87 and 58.2 percent of the vote in 1928, Hoover now lost to Roosevelt by 472 electoral votes to 59, receiving just 39.6 percent of the vote. He carried four of six New England states, Pennsylvania, and Delaware. The Democrats also gained an amazing 97 seats in the House, giving them a 313–117 edge over the Republicans, and 11 in the Senate for a 58–37 majority. A month later, Hoover's final annual address showed no second thoughts. "Our country is at peace," he said. "Our national defense has been maintained at a high state of effectiveness. . . . There has been a far larger degree of freedom from industrial conflict than hitherto known. Education and science have made further advances. The public health is today at its highest known level. While we have recently engaged in the aggressive contest of a national election, its very tranquility and the acceptance of its results furnish abundant proof of the strength of our institutions." "Legislation in response to national needs," he warned his successor, "will be effective only if every such act conforms to a complete philosophy of the people's purposes and destiny. . . . We have built a system of individualism peculiarly our own which must not be forgotten in any governmental acts, for from it have grown greater accomplishments than those of any other nation."

In March of 1932 Congress had passed the Twentieth Amendment to the Constitution, which shifted inauguration day from March 4 to January 20 and called upon newly elected Congresses to meet for the first time on the next January 3, rather than in early December of the following year. Although the states ratified it unanimously, it had not yet come into effect, and the country suffered through a dreadful winter that ended in a new banking crisis before Roosevelt took office. He made the most dramatic entry into the presidency since Lincoln.

---

1 https://www.shmoop.com/great-depression/statistics.html.

# XV

## Franklin D. Roosevelt

### 1933–45

Lincoln had taken office after seven states had seceded. Roosevelt delivered his first inaugural in the midst of a general financial and economic collapse. "The only thing we have to fear is fear itself," he famously declared, while detailing the disastrous economic state of the nation: shrunken values, higher taxes, low government revenue at all levels, dormant industry, agriculture without markets, wiped-out savings, and "a host" of unemployed. "Yet our distress," he continued, "comes from no failure of substance. We are stricken by no plague of locusts. . . . Plenty is at our doorstep, but a generous use of it languishes in the very sight of the supply. Primarily this is because rulers of the exchange of mankind's goods have failed through their own stubbornness and their own incompetence, have admitted their failure, and have abdicated. . . . The money changers have fled from their high seats in the temple of our civilization. We may now restore that temple to the ancient truths. The measure of the restoration lies in the extent to which we apply social values more noble than mere monetary profit." "Our greatest primary task," he continued, "is to put people to work. . . . in part by direct recruiting by the Government itself, treating the task as we would treat the emergency of a war." He called for higher agricultural prices, a stop to foreclosures on farms, lower costs of government, and "strict supervision of banking credits and investments," all to be put before a special session of Congress. The Constitution, he said, should prove equal to the task, and he would recommend suitable measures to Congress. If however they failed to act, "I shall not evade the clear course of duty that will then confront me. I shall ask the Congress for the one remaining instrument to meet the crisis—broad Executive power to wage a war against the emergency, as great as the power that would be given to me if we were in fact invaded by a foreign foe." He did not as it turned out find it necessary to carry out that threat.

Two days later, on March 6, Roosevelt used a 1917 emergency law to declare a four-day bank holiday closing all banks while Congress rushed new legislation through. A new act allowing federal takeovers of failing banks and making more cash available from the Federal Reserve passed in a single day. On March 12 Roosevelt introduced a vital new communications tool, the broadcast "fireside chat." He briefly explained the origins of the banking crisis—a loss of confidence leading to demands for cash which the banks lacked the currency to meet—thanked the country for its patience, and explained that the Federal Reserve would now be able to make all necessary cash available. "We have provided the machinery to restore our financial system; it is up to you to support and make it work," he said. Congress immediately went to work on many other fronts, and the president had much more to report when he gave a second fireside chat two months later on May 7.

Even before his inauguration, Roosevelt explained, he had concluded that further deflation—more bank and business failures and farm foreclosures—would have been "too much to ask the American people to bear." It would have meant "a loss of spiritual values—the loss of that sense of security for the present and the future so necessary to the peace and contentment of the individual and of his family." Instead, Congress had passed or was passing a dramatic new series of measures. First, the new Civilian Conservation Corps (CCC) would put 250,000 unemployed men to work in the nation's forests—twice as many as served in the regular army. Secondly, the government would build dams and produce electric power to develop the Tennessee Valley. Thirdly, new laws would provide mortgage relief to farmers and homeowners. The states would receive half a billion dollars for relief of the indigent. The new Agricultural Adjustment Act (AAA) would restrict farm production to raise prices, and he promised additional legislation to try "to give to the industrial workers of the country a more fair wage return, prevent cut-throat competition and unduly long hours for labor, and at the same time encourage each industry to prevent overproduction." This was not government control, but partnership. Ninety percent of cotton manufacturers, he claimed, would gladly eliminate starvation wages, excessive hours, and child labor, but they needed a legal framework to protect them against the ten percent who would not.

The second fireside chat established the pattern that made the Roosevelt presidency unlike any other for the whole of its twelve years. Rather than simply reporting annually on the state of the union and the budget, Roosevelt had laid out a sweeping program to change the government's relationship to the economy, and he reported regularly on its very rapid progress. With the Democrats' 313–117 majority in the House and 58–37 edge in the Senate—majorities that increased still further in the 1934 elections—he had enormous changes to discuss in each of his first four years in office, and a few more in 1937–40. Beginning in May 1940, he reported just as regularly on his response to a different kind of crisis, the threat of attack from Germany and Japan, and then, after December 1941, the course of the war that began with Pearl Harbor. By the time of his death in April 1945, Roosevelt had led the nation through the creation of a new economy at home and a new world role abroad, leaving behind a framework that endured for at least thirty-five years.

In a third fireside chat on July 24, Roosevelt distinguished between emergency measures on the one hand and long-term steps to create permanent, general prosperity on the other. The former included cuts in the normal expenditures of the federal government, the 300,000-strong CCC now supporting "the nearly one million people who constitute their families," $500 million for relief, and now, another $3 billion for public works, including highways, ships, flood prevention and inland navigation improvements, and state and municipal improvements, many of which, he said, might pay for themselves. The more general measures included the AAA and the more recent National Recovery Administration (NRA). Under its supervision, every industry was coming together to write codes regulating wages, hours, prices, and total production to promote a healthy recovery. Roosevelt on July 24 noted that the cotton textile code and other agreements had abolished child labor, making him "happier than any one thing with which I have been connected since I came to Washington." The National Industrial Recovery Act that had created it also guaranteed for the first time labor's right to organize and bargain collectively, but Roosevelt asked for cooperation between management and workers. He specifically rejected free-market orthodoxy: "I have no sympathy with the professional economists who insist that things must run their course and that human agencies can have no influence on economic ills." The NIRA also established the Public Works Administration (PWA), which immediately began large construction projects.

The Twentieth Amendment had been fully ratified by the end of 1933, and Roosevelt gave the first January annual address on January 3, 1934. Together with Congress, he hoped not only to restore "our national well-being," but also "to build on the ruins of the past a new structure designed better to meet the present problems of modern civilization. . . . It is our task to perfect, to improve, to alter when necessary, but in all cases to go forward" toward "progress through integrity, unselfishness, responsibility and justice." Several million unemployed were now back at work, he said, and the NRA had abolished child labor and established uniform wage and hour standards for nearly all of industry. New laws allowed for refinancing farms and homes, and the new agricultural policy was raising prices and increasing rural purchasing power. He referred quickly to his momentous decision to take the dollar off the gold standard—as Great Britain had done for the pound two years earlier—and to reduce its value in another attempt to raise prices. Then he listed new targets of government policy. "Groups who have been living off their neighbors" with "unethical or criminal" methods included tax evaders, predatory high officials of banks and corporations, speculators, bandits, common criminals, lynch mobs, and kidnappers. The Twenty-first Amendment repealing prohibition, he noted, was on its way to ratification, and that would reduce crimes involving liquor. The nation had to "reconstruct our life" in ways that left no room for over-expansion of industry, exploitation of labor, and the waste of natural resources. Much shorter than his predecessor's annual messages, this one stuck to sweeping principles and the impact of new measures.

On June 28, 1934, another fireside chat listed the achievements of the year's congressional session. They included new laws on corporate and municipal bankruptcy; the creation of the Securities and Exchange Commission to regulate the stock market; the creation of the Federal Communications Commission to regulate broadcasting; and more authority to the Reconstruction Finance Corporation to lend to troubled businesses. He could, he said, cite numerous statistics showing higher pay, greater employment, larger bank deposits, and tens of thousands of homes saved from foreclosure, but he preferred to let his listeners judge for themselves. "Are you better off than you were last year? And have you truly lost any individual liberty? . . . It is not the overwhelming majority of the farmers or manufacturers or workers who deny the substantial gains of the past year. The most vociferous of the Doubting Thomases may be divided roughly into two groups: First, those who seek special political privilege and, second, those who seek special financial privilege." With the congressional election looming, Roosevelt was drawing a line between the nation's economic elite, which was growing increasingly critical of him, and the people at large. While other unnamed nations—a clear reference to Germany and Italy—had sacrificed democracy for autocracy, "We are restoring confidence and well-being under the rule of the people themselves." He promised further new measures on land use, housing, and social insurance. Two months later, on September 30, he defended work relief measures and refused to follow Britain's example and accept "a permanent army of unemployed." Cases challenging the powers of some New Deal agencies were heading toward the Supreme Court, and Roosevelt optimistically quoted former Chief Justice White (1910–21), who had described the Constitution as "the broad highway through which alone true progress may be enjoyed."

Although unemployment had fallen only 3.2 percent to 21.7 percent by December 1934,[1] a large majority of Americans evidently shared Roosevelt's views. The Republicans lost another 14 seats in the House in the November elections, leaving the Democrats and two allied minor parties with 332 seats to 103 for the opposition. More remarkably, they gained 9 seats in the Senate, leaving the Republicans with just 25 out of 96. "We have undertaken a new order of things; yet we progress to it under the framework and in the spirit and intent of the American Constitution," Roosevelt began his annual address on January 4, 1934. While production

---

1 https://www.thebalancemoney.com/unemployment-rate-by-year-3305506.

increased, the "spirit of confidence and faith which marks the American character" renewed itself. Recovery could not be separated from reform, and the nation had not yet "weeded out the overprivileged" or "effectively lifted up the underprivileged." Some would always earn more than others, but "we do assert that the ambition of the individual to obtain for him and his a proper security, a reasonable leisure, and a decent living throughout life, is an ambition to be preferred to the appetite for great wealth and great power." His budget message on the previous day noted that the index of industrial production had risen 25 percent during fiscal 1934 and that unemployment had fallen by four million since March 1933, and that farm cash income was up 33 percent.

Roosevelt then promised several major new initiatives, including a broad measure to provide unemployment insurance, old age insurance, and benefits for needy mothers, children, and the handicapped, and a new agency to put more of the five million Americans on relief rolls back to work. "The work itself will cover a wide field including clearance of slums, which for adequate reasons cannot be undertaken by private capital; in rural housing of several kinds, where, again, private capital is unable to function; in rural electrification; in the reforestation of the great watersheds of the Nation; in an intensified program to prevent soil erosion and to reclaim blighted areas; in improving existing road systems and in constructing national highways designed to handle modern traffic; in the elimination of grade crossings; in the extension and enlargement of the successful work of the Civilian Conservation Corps; in non-Federal works, mostly self-liquidating and highly useful to local divisions of Government; and on many other projects which the Nation needs and cannot afford to neglect." A more specific message on social security, outlining the system that we have today, followed on January 17.[2]

In another fireside chat on April 28 Roosevelt promised a broad new public works agency to replace the Federal Emergency

---

[2] In one of the standard works on this period, Arthur M. Schlesinger Jr. stated that this annual address and the budget message that followed were "conciliatory in tone and unenterprising in content," and that only agitation in the country at large moved the New Deal forward. It is hard to square these statements with the actual record. See Schlesinger, *The Politics of Upheaval* (New York, 1960), p. 4.

Relief Authority and find additional work of many kinds for relief recipients, and a new law to eliminate holding companies that controlled power companies. On May 6 he created the Works Progress Administration that he had promised a week earlier. The National Youth Administration, which provided funds for education and employment, followed on June 26. On June 16, a long message to Congress asked for much higher inheritance taxes and income taxes on the highest earners and on corporations. "The transmission from generation to generation of vast fortunes by will, inheritance, or gift is not consistent with the ideals and sentiments of the American people," he said. "Such inherited economic power is as inconsistent with the ideals of this generation as inherited political power was inconsistent with the ideals of the generation which established our Government. . . . People know that vast personal incomes come not only through the effort or ability or luck of those who receive them, but also because of the opportunities for advantage which Government itself contributes. Therefore, the duty rests upon the Government to restrict such incomes by very high taxes." The corporation tax should also be graduated, he said. On July 5 Roosevelt announced his signing of the National Labor Relations Act or Wagner Act, which affirmed union rights and set up machinery to help resolve disputes over organization, and on August 14, he signed the Social Security Act. Meanwhile, however, in May, the Supreme Court had emerged as a mortal enemy of the New Deal.

For the whole of the Gilded Age and the Progressive Era, the Supreme Court had stood firmly against almost every measure of economic reform, including the income tax, state minimum wage laws, and laws against child labor.[3] It treated the constitutional obligation of contracts and the principle of freedom of contract as sacred cows, and in February 1935, Roosevelt had feared that the court would rule in favor of plaintiffs protesting that they were still entitled to the full gold value of bonds issued before he had reduced the gold value of the dollar. He had prepared a message explaining that only these measures had restored the purchasing power of the dollar after the extreme deflation of the Hoover years,

---

3 See the extraordinary survey by James MacGregor Burns, *Packing the Court* (New York, 2009), pp. 93–137. That book, a complete history of presidents and the Supreme Court, inspired me to write this one.

laying out the disastrous consequences for bond issuers, mortgage holders, and the federal government of a decision in favor of the plaintiffs, and announcing, in effect, that he would defy the decision and use proclamations, new laws, or both, to limit debts to their new reduced value.[4] As it turned out, however, the court ruled against the plaintiffs by a 5–4 vote, and he did not deliver the message. But three months later, on May 27, the court unanimously ruled two pieces of New Deal legislation unconstitutional: a farm bankruptcy bill designed to reduce foreclosures, and the act that had created the NRA, the centerpiece of the New Deal recovery program. The court specifically rejected the idea that the federal government could regulate wages, hours and prices in industries engaged in interstate commerce. The decision removed the ban on child labor that the NRA industry codes had included. On May 27, in a lengthy, detailed statement in a press conference, Roosevelt said that this decision threatened all the major work of the New Deal, and that the nation had to decide whether "we are going to turn over or restore to—whichever way you choose to put it—turn over or restore to the Federal Government the powers which exist in the national Governments of every other Nation in the world to enact and administer laws that have a bearing on, and general control over, national economic problems and national social problems." He declined to say what he would do. During its next term in 1935–36 the Supreme Court also declared the AAA and the Guffey-Snyder Coal Act, which had essentially tried to write the NRA's coal code into law, unconstitutional as well. It also threw out a New York state minimum wage law. Roosevelt evidently decided to delay any response until after the 1936 election.

Roosevelt's budgets during his first term matched his programs in their novelty and scope. Hoover's last budget, for fiscal 1933, had foreseen $2.8 billion in receipts and $4 billion in expenditures. In January 1934 Roosevelt reported that the fiscal 1934 budget would include $9.4 billion in expenditures—more than twice as much—and $3.3 billion in revenues. A deficit twice as large as revenues had no peacetime precedent, and was much larger in relation both

---

4 This message can be found at http://www.fdrlibrary.marist.edu/_resources/images/msf/msf00790.

to revenue and to GDP than the deficit for fiscal 2021.[5] Roosevelt specifically identified $6.4 billion as emergency expenditures, including $4 billion for the RFC to provide emergency assistance to business and $1.7 billion for the PWA. The RFC turned out to need much less money, and in January 1935 he could report that the emergency expenditures for fiscal 1934 had totaled only $4.3 billion, only slightly more than the total deficit of $4 billion. His new budget, he said, would balance if one omitted the emergency "expenditures to give work to the unemployed," and he anticipated another $4.6 billion in emergency expenditures for fiscal 1936.

"It is . . . a cause for congratulation within our own Nation," Roosevelt began his January 3, 1936 budget message, "to realize that a consistent, broad national policy, adopted nearly three years ago by the Congress and the President, has thus far moved steadily, effectively, and successfully toward its objective." The many measures undertaken to fight the Depression had vastly increased expenditures, and meant that government revenues would also increase and the need for unemployment relief would decline. That trend would continue, partly because of much higher estate and income taxes on the wealthy passed in 1936. Comparing present estimates for fiscal 1936—now half over—to those he had made a year earlier, he found estimated expenditures down $875 million, receipts up $419 million, and the estimated deficit down $1.3 billion to $3.2 billion, and he expected it to fall still further in fiscal 1937.

Roosevelt's January 1936 annual message struck a new note. During his first three years he had said astonishingly little about foreign affairs. His first inaugural had proclaimed a "good neighbor" policy toward the other countries of the western hemisphere, and he had withdrawn the last American troops from Nicaragua and abrogated the 1903 treaty with Cuba that gave the United States a right to intervene in Cuban internal affairs. Like his Republican predecessors, he had tried and failed to secure US adherence to the World Court, and on August 31, 1935 he signed a new Neutrality Act banning all sales of weaponry to belligerents in any foreign war—a result, in part, of a congressional investigation into the

---

5  2021 revenues are $4 trillion, expenditures $6.8 trillion, and GDP is $23.2 trillion.

role of munitions makers in the American decision to intervene in Europe in 1917. 1935 had begun with Adolf Hitler denouncing all the restrictions on German armaments imposed by the Versailles Treaty and announcing a new German air force, and had continued with Mussolini's war against Ethiopia in defiance of the League of Nations. Since the summer of 1933, Roosevelt now said, the "temper and the purposes of the rulers of many of the great populations in Europe and Asia have not pointed the way either to peace or to good will among men." We could not, he said, rely upon the peoples of unnamed, increasingly warlike nations to restrain their autocratic and aggressive rulers. Faced with these dangers, "We have sought by every legitimate means to exert our moral influence against repression, against intolerance, against autocracy and in favor of freedom of expression, equality before the law, religious tolerance and popular rule." A new era of great wars might be coming, and the United States and its neighbors must pursue neutrality, take adequate defensive measures against possible attack, and try to persuade other nations to seek peace and goodwill. Then he boldly linked foreign danger to domestic opposition.

Democratic nations, said Roosevelt, did not endanger peace, and for that very reason should pursue domestic policies that would prevent the rise of autocratic institutions "that beget slavery at home and aggression abroad. Within our borders, as in the world at large, popular opinion is at war with a power-seeking minority." Organized business opposition to the New Deal had become increasingly hysterical, and the president took it on directly as the election year began.[6] Comparing his opposition to that faced by Jefferson, Jackson, Theodore Roosevelt and Wilson, he referred to a "numerically small" group with "a large influence" in the economy which did not "speak the true sentiments of the less articulate but more important elements that constitute real American business." Since 1933 the nation had written "a new chapter in the history of popular government," creating "an economic constitutional order" based on "the adjustment of burdens, the help of the needy, the protection of the weak, the liberation of the exploited and the genuine protection of the people's property." Now, with danger passed,

---

6 See the remarkable book by George Wolfskill and John A. Hudson, *All But the People: Franklin D. Roosevelt and His Critics, 1933–39* (New York, 1969), pp. 143–171.

the money-changers who had "abdicated" at the time of his first inaugural "forget their damaging admissions and withdraw their abdication. They seek the restoration of their selfish power. . . . The principle that they would instill into government if they succeed in seizing power is well shown by the principles which many of them have instilled into their own affairs: autocracy toward labor, toward stockholders, toward consumers, toward public sentiment. Autocrats in smaller things, they seek autocracy in bigger things." He insisted that his policies were working and closed with a quote from the philosopher Josiah Royce: "What great crises teach all men whom the example and counsel of the brave inspire is the lesson: Fear not, view all the tasks of life as sacred, have faith in the triumph of the ideal, give daily all that you have to give, be loyal and rejoice whenever you find yourselves part of a great ideal enterprise. You, at this moment, have the honor to belong to a generation whose lips are touched by fire."

Three days later, on January 6, 1936, the Supreme Court declared the AAA unconstitutional. Within two months Congress passed a new Soil Conservation and Allotment Act continuing payments to farmers for taking some land out of production. Drought in the Midwestern "Dust Bowl" was also hurting farmers badly, and on September 6, 1936, as his reelection campaign began in earnest, Roosevelt reported on a tour of that region in a fireside chat. Once again he linked the fortunes of different sectors of the economy. "The very existence of the men and women working in the clothing factories of New York, making clothes worn by farmers and their families; of the workers in the steel mills in Pittsburgh, in the automobile factories of Detroit, and in the harvester factories of Illinois, depends upon the farmers' ability to purchase the commodities they produce," he said, and the farmers depended in turn on workers' purchasing power. "In this country," he continued, "we insist, as an essential of the American way of life that the employer-employee relationship should be one between free men and equals. . . . All American workers, brain workers and manual workers alike, and all the rest of us whose well-being depends on theirs, know that our needs are one in building an orderly economic democracy in which all can profit and in which all can be secure from the kind of faulty economic direction which brought us to the brink of common ruin seven years ago." He relied during the campaign on the image of a selfish minority attempting to control the nation that he had developed in his annual address—most famously in a Madison Square Garden address on October 31. During the past four years, he said, "We had to struggle with the old enemies of peace—business and financial monopoly, speculation, reckless banking, class antagonism, sectionalism, war profiteering. They had begun to consider the Government of the United States as a mere appendage to their own affairs. We know now that Government by organized money is just as dangerous as Government by organized mob. Never before in all our history have these forces been so united against one candidate as they stand today. They are unanimous in their hate for me—and I welcome their hatred."

Seventy-five percent of the nation's major newspapers opposed FDR's reelection, and as the vote drew near, leading Republicans and his opponent, Governor Alf Landon of Kansas, insisted that it would mean dictatorship and disaster.[7] Yet in the election on November 3 Roosevelt won 61 percent of the popular vote and carried every state but two, Maine and Vermont. In the House the Republicans lost another 15 seats, leaving the Democrats and their allies with a majority of 347–88, and the Democrats and their allies raised their working majority in the Senate to 79–17. For the first and only time in American history, one party had gained seats in both the House and Senate in four consecutive elections, from 1930 through 1936.

In his annual message on January 6, 1937, Roosevelt thanked the Congress for helping to prove, over that last four years, "that in the long run democracy would prove superior to more extreme forms of Government as a process of getting action when action was wisdom, without the spiritual sacrifices which those other forms of Government exact." The recovery, he said, "was not to be merely temporary. It was to be a recovery protected from the causes of previous disasters," and they had therefore established "sound currency, guaranteed bank deposits, protections for investors, the removal of agricultural surpluses, guarantees for collective bargaining, and social security." "The deeper purpose of democratic government," he continued, "is to assist as many of its citizens as

---

7 Schlesinger, *Politics of Upheaval*, p. 633.

possible, especially those who need it most, to improve their conditions of life, to retain all personal liberty which does not adversely affect their neighbors, and to pursue the happiness which comes with security and an opportunity for recreation and culture." He promised a plan to reorganize the executive branch, and turned back to economic problems such as overproduction, underproduction, and too much speculation. He praised the NRA's objectives and said the problems they aimed at continued and that the states could not solve them. Cases challenging the National Labor Relations Act and the Social Security Act had come before the Supreme Court, and he proclaimed a "growing belief" that the real problem was not the Constitution itself but the court's interpretation of it. "Means must be found," he said, "to adapt our legal forms and our judicial interpretation to the actual present national needs of the largest progressive democracy in the modern world." His reorganization plan, sent to Congress on January 12, called for a larger White House staff, new cabinet departments of Public Works and Social Welfare, and a tighter chain of command that would bring all independent agencies under the control of a cabinet officer.

He elaborated on these themes two weeks later in his second inaugural. "Nearly all of us," he said, "recognize that as intricacies of human relationships increase, so power to govern them also must increase power to stop evil; power to do good. The essential democracy of our Nation and the safety of our people depend not upon the absence of power, but upon lodging it with those whom the people can change or continue at stated intervals through an honest and free system of elections. The Constitution of 1787 did not make our democracy impotent." The nation had changed "the moral climate of America," rejecting "heedless self-interest" as "bad morals" and "bad economics." Prosperity was returning, but much remained to be done: "I see one-third of a nation ill-housed, ill-clad, ill-nourished." "Today we reconsecrate our country to long-cherished ideals in a suddenly changed civilization. In every land there are always at work forces that drive men apart and forces that draw men together. In our personal ambitions we are individualists. But in our seeking for economic and political progress as a nation, we all go up, or else we all go down, as one people."

The invalidation of the NRA had led to a new effort to ratify the constitutional amendment outlawing child labor that had passed under Coolidge, and Roosevelt endorsed this in a letter to the governor of New York on February 4. On the next day he dropped the biggest bombshell of his tenure in a message to Congress on "the Reorganization of the Judicial Branch." Without mentioning his ideological struggle with the Supreme Court, he claimed that the federal judiciary was overwhelmed with work and raised "the question of aged or infirm judges—a subject of delicacy and yet one which requires frank discussion." Sixty of 237 federal judges were over seventy—including, although he did not mention it, six members of the Supreme Court. None of its justices in fact was under sixty, and columnists Drew Pearson and Robert Allen had christened them "the nine old men." Roosevelt proposed legislation to allow him to appoint one new judge to any federal court for every sitting judge who had declined to retire at seventy—raising the size of the Supreme Court to fifteen at one blow. He said more frankly in a fireside chat on March 9 that "the courts . . . have cast doubts on the ability of the elected Congress to protect us against catastrophe by meeting squarely our modern social and economic conditions." Two of the three great "horses" provided by the Constitution were pulling together, and the American people expected "the third horse to pull in unison with the other two." The courts, he said, had expanded their power to veto laws "since the rise of the modern movement for social and economic progress through legislation," and the Supreme Court had become a "super-legislature," as one dissenting judge had put it. "We have, therefore, reached the point as a nation where we must take action to save the Constitution from the Court and the Court from itself." He invited the six justices over seventy to resign and defended himself against the charge—already loudly heard—of "packing the court."

Three weeks later, on March 29, Chief Justice Charles Evans Hughes and some of his brethren yielded to Roosevelt's threat. Reversing two previous decisions, they narrowly upheld another state minimum wage law—reversing their long-standing views on freedom of contract—and a national anti-foreclosure measure very similar to the one they had thrown out in 1935. After another few weeks, they upheld the Wagner Act guaranteeing labor's right to organize, and they later turned down an effort to void the Social Security Act. One aged conservative also decided to take Roosevelt's advice and retire, giving him a chance to make the first appointment of his own, the southern liberal senator Hugo Black.

Whether intentionally or not, Roosevelt accompanied his attack on the court with a sharp turn toward fiscal conservatism. The Revenue Act of 1936, which had raised estate and income taxes on higher brackets, he said in his January 7 budget message, would increase income tax revenues by nearly $1 billion to $2.4 billion total, and he forecast a fiscal 1937 deficit of about $2.2 billion, down from $4.4 billion in fiscal 1936. Counting on further recovery, he predicted that recovery and relief expenditures for 1938 would fall to $1.5 billion, that total federal expenditures would fall from $8.4 billion to $6.2 billion, and that the government would run a $1.5 billion surplus. On April 20 he had to revise these optimistic estimates because of disappointing revenues, forecasting deficits of $2.6 billion for the current year and $418 million for 1938, and appealing to Congress "to join with me in a determined effort" to balance the budget for that year with further cuts. "It is a matter of common knowledge," he said, "that the principal danger to modern civilization lies in those nations which largely because of an armament race are headed directly toward bankruptcy. In proportion to national budgets the United States is spending a far smaller proportion of Government income for armaments than the nations to which I refer. It behooves us, therefore, to continue our efforts to make both ends of our economy meet." He called for closing tax loopholes and limiting other expenditures.

Roosevelt submitted two additional major pieces of legislation during that session. On May 25, he asked Congress to fill the void left by the death of the NRA by passing nationwide legislation specifying minimum wages and maximum hours for all workers in enterprises involved in any way in interstate commerce, and once again outlawing child labor. "All but the hopelessly reactionary will agree," he said, "that to conserve our primary resources of man power, government must have some control over maximum hours, minimum wages, the evil of child labor and the exploitation of unorganized labor." In a further effort to nudge the Supreme Court along, he quoted at length from Justice Oliver Wendell Holmes's dissent from the 1918 5–4 decision that had declared a previous federal law against child labor unconstitutional. And on June 3 he submitted a plan for seven new "regional authorities or agencies" similar to the Tennessee Valley Authority, which was building several dams to control floods and generate electric power, covering all the major watersheds in the country.

Unfortunately for Roosevelt, the court packing plan had become a lightning rod both for all the pent-up resentment against him among the wealthy and for fears of what he might do with his unprecedented powers. The fearful included many white southern Democrats. The party had dropped its two-thirds requirement for nomination in 1936, taking away their veto in the Democratic convention. After the 1936 election they were no longer essential to the Democratic congressional majorities. Some of them hated Roosevelt for what he had done for Negroes, and feared that Roosevelt might try to secure black southerners the right to vote.[8] When the court packing bill finally came to a Senate procedural vote in July, only eighteen Democrats voted against sending it back to the Judiciary Committee, with fifty-three of them voting to kill it. Roosevelt's proposal had successfully removed the Supreme Court's roadblock against further economic legislation, but it had cost him the control over Congress that he had exercised throughout his first term. Congress adjourned in August without taking any action on his proposals for reform of the executive branch, for wages and hours legislation, or for new regional water authorities.

In an October 12 fireside chat Roosevelt announced that he was calling the Congress back into special session the next month in response to clear signs of a new business recession. On November 22 he declared in effect that Congress had to repair the damage the Supreme Court had done to the New Deal in 1935–36 by passing a new agricultural bill to control production and his proposed wages, hours and child labor legislation. Congress had not acted by the time of his annual message on January 3, and he added an attack on business practices such as collusion among producers and manipulation of securities. His Justice Department was about to undertake an antitrust offensive in the courts, and he declared, "The work undertaken by Andrew Jackson and Woodrow Wilson is not finished yet." Roosevelt laid new stress on another statistic, national income—later called GNP or GDP—in this address. It had risen

---

8 Harvard Sitkoff, *A New Deal for Blacks* (New York, 1978), pp. 106–11.

from $38 billion in 1932 to about $68 billion in 1937, and he looked forward to its reaching $90–100 billion. Recognizing three roughly equal sectors of the economy—agriculture, industry, and services, including distribution—he asked rural representatives to help industry by supporting the wages and hours law while industrial representatives supported the new AAA. On February 16, he signed the new AAA law. The reorganization bill that would have created two new cabinet departments passed the Senate by a single vote in late March, and Roosevelt published on March 29 a long letter denying any intention to become a dictator, as opponents of the bill claimed. The bill failed in the House nonetheless.

The January 3 budget message presented impressive figures on the effect of the new 1936 income tax law, which had increased its yield from $1.4 billion in that year to $2.2 billion in 1936 and an estimated $2.7 billion in 1938. The recession, however, would create a deficit of about $1 billion for fiscal 1938. On April 14, however, Roosevelt reversed course in a message to Congress and a fireside chat. Purchasing power had not kept pace with a new round of overproduction of cotton, cars, and steel in early 1937, he said, and layoffs had begun in the fall. The Congress had passed only one of four recommended new economic measures, the new AAA. Now the government must once again act. National income was projected to fall from $68 billion in 1937 to $56 billion this year, and he set an $80 billion target for "the next year or two." He now called for substantially increased appropriations for fiscal 1939 for the WPA, the CCC, and the National Youth Administration (NYA), and $750 million for new housing projects and for public works. The foreign scene, as we shall see, was becoming far more menacing, and he asked Congress to show that democracy could work. He elaborated on that theme in the fireside chat. "Democracy has disappeared in several other great nations—not because the people of those nations disliked democracy, but because they had grown tired of unemployment and insecurity, of seeing their children hungry while they sat helpless in the face of government confusion and government weakness through lack of leadership in government. . . . If by democratic methods people get a government strong enough to protect them from fear and starvation, their democracy succeeds; but if they do not, they grow impatient." "I believe we have been right in the course we have charted," he concluded.

And just two weeks later on April 29, Roosevelt gave Congress the longest and most detailed analysis of economic inequality and its consequences ever presented by a president. His written "Message to Congress on Curbing Monopolies" reported that one-tenth of 1 percent of all corporations owned 50 percent of corporate assets and earned 50 percent of corporate net income, and that 4–5 percent of them owned more than 87 percent of total assets and earned 84 percent of total income. While 47 percent of American families and single individuals earned less than $1,000 per year, about 1.5 percent of families had incomes that equaled *the entire income* of that 47 percent. Financial institutions' control over industrial enterprise made the problem of concentrated power even worse. "The liberty of a democracy was not safe," he declared, "if the people tolerate the growth of private power to a point where it becomes stronger than their democratic state itself," or "if its business system does not provide employment and produce and distribute goods in such a way as to sustain an acceptable standard of living." Roosevelt blamed the recession on the failure of large corporations to lower their prices in response to falling demand. He asked for significant new appropriations to expand the antitrust division of the Justice Department and to create a commission to study the problem of concentrated economic power, and for various changes in the antitrust laws. Those changes did not pass, but the appropriations did, inaugurating a new era of antitrust enforcement that culminated in 1945 with the judicial breakup of the great ALCOA aluminum company on the grounds that its market share was simply too large to allow for real competition in its industry.

Two months later on June 24, in another fireside chat in the wake of the adjournment of Congress, Roosevelt praised the adoption of the Fair Labor Standards Act—the wages and hours law—which after many amendments and ups and downs of enforcement remains a key piece of legislation to this day. The long struggle to eliminate child labor was over. Congress had also appropriated the additional money for New Deal agencies that he had asked for. Referring to recent court decisions that had left new legislation intact, he bluntly said that the court packing plan "had lost a battle which won a war. . . . The attitude of the Supreme Court toward constitutional questions is entirely changed. Its recent decisions are eloquent testimony of a willingness to collaborate with the two other branches of Government to make democracy work." He compared the die-hard opponents of reform to the pro-southern Copperheads during the Civil War who tried "to make Lincoln and his Congress give up the fight." On other fronts, Roosevelt had had to accept a much scaled-down reorganization plan that did not create any new cabinet departments, and Congress had never created the new watershed authorities like the TVA that he had asked for. It also refused repeated calls to provide the money for the St. Lawrence Seaway, a system of new dams and locks on the St. Lawrence that would allow oceangoing vessels to sail all the way to the Great Lakes, which northeastern shipping interests opposed.

Organized labor had been militantly expanding since the formation of the Congress of Industrial Organizations (CIO) in late 1935, and Roosevelt—who had never directly addressed the sit-down strikes against the auto industry in early 1937—blamed labor as well as business (for over-expansion) and government (for over-caution) for the slump in the June 24 broadcast. Unions had gone too far, "using methods which frightened many well-wishing people" and adding jurisdictional disputes between rival unions to bargaining requests. Once again he identified "a very articulate group of people in this country, with plenty of ability to procure publicity for their views, who have consistently refused to cooperate with the mass of the people" until measures were taken to restore their "confidence." Roosevelt then distinguished between liberals and conservatives and announced his intention to speak against some conservative Democratic incumbents in forthcoming Democratic primaries.

The president had maintained the momentum of reform and taken new work relief measures to fight a new recession, but much of the public had for the moment turned away from him. All but one of his five campaigns against incumbent Democrats failed to unseat them.[9] Then, in the congressional election, the Republicans gained 81 seats in the House, cutting the Democrats' and their progressive allies' majority to 266–169, and 8 seats in the Senate,

---

9 See the excellent study by Susan Dunn, *Roosevelt's Purge: How FDR Fought to Change the Democratic Party* (Cambridge, Mass., 2010).

leaving them on the short end of a 73–23 count.[10] The southern Democrats now had split between a minority of New Dealers and a larger group of dedicated conservatives. In his annual message on January 4, 1939, FDR rejected immediate attempts to balance the budget, suggesting instead that the country could reach that goal by raising national income from about $60 billion to $80 billion. The budget message the next day forecast a $4 billion deficit for fiscal 1939 and $3.3 billion for 1940. The combination of tight immigration quotas introduced by Hoover and low Depression-era birth rates had slowed US population growth to an all-time low, and the 1940 census showed an increase of just 7.6 percent in ten years, to 123 million.

Domestic affairs began to become an adjunct to foreign affairs beginning with his January 1939 annual address. The outbreak of the Spanish Civil War in 1936—in which both Fascist Italy and Nazi Germany gave important support to the Spanish Fascists led by General Francisco Franco—and the outbreak of the undeclared Sino-Japanese War in the summer of 1937 had led Roosevelt to sound a first, loud alarm in an October 5, 1937 speech in Chicago. "The present reign of terror and international lawlessness," he said, seriously threatened "the very foundations of civilization." "Let no one imagine that America will escape," he said, effectively repudiating isolationism. "There can be no stability or peace either within nations or between nations except under laws and moral standards adhered to by all. International anarchy destroys every foundation for peace." As usual, he named no specific aggressor nations but mentioned that some of them were spending 30–50 percent of their national income on arms, compared to about 12 percent in the United States. "War is a contagion, whether it be declared or undeclared," he said, and the US had to "quarantine" it to keep it out of its hemisphere. Asked by the press a few days later to elaborate, Roosevelt refused to do so. He evidently had in mind a distant Anglo-American blockade of Japan designed to force it to give up the war with China, but the British government was not

---

10 The minor parties included the Progressive of Wisconsin, the Farmer-Labor Party in Minnesota, and the American Labor Party, a Communist front that sent one congressman to Washington from New York.

interested.[11] He returned to some of these themes in his January 1938 annual address, arguing that only democratic nations seemed willing to keep world peace through international agreements.

Roosevelt's January 1939 annual message began with the world situation, which teetered on the brink of another world war in September 1938, when only the Munich agreement had seemed to avert a new struggle between Germany on one side and Britain and France on the other. He did not tell his countrymen that he had expected the US to join that war had it broken out,[12] but he repeated that "world peace is not assured." Storms from abroad, he continued, threatened religion, democracy and good faith—"three institutions indispensable to Americans." A world without those values would have "no place within it for the ideals of the Prince of Peace," and the United States had to reject it. "There comes a time in the affairs of men," he continued, "when they must prepare to defend, not their homes alone, but the tenets of faith and humanity on which their churches, their governments and their very civilization are founded"—a warning, surely of an imminent war for American principles. Only a "united democracy" could meet these threats, and "Our nation's program of social and economic reform is therefore a part of defense, as basic as armaments themselves." "Once I prophesied that this generation of Americans had a rendezvous with destiny," he concluded, referring to his 1936 convention acceptance speech. "That prophecy comes true. To us much is given; more is expected." This generation, he said in an echo of Lincoln, would "nobly save or meanly lose the last best hope of earth. . . . The way is plain, peaceful, generous, just—a way which if followed the world will forever applaud and God must forever bless." While reaffirming the principles of the New Deal before a much more conservative Congress, Roosevelt was also stating even broader principles that hardly any Republican or conservative southern Democrat could dare to oppose.

In March 1939 new moves by Hitler into the remainder of Czechoslovakia and Lithuania and his threats against Poland started the crisis that led to the Second World War six months later. On

---

11 David Kaiser, *No End Save Victory: How FDR Led the Nation into War* (New York, 2014), pp. 30–39.
12 *Ibid.*, pp. 40–41

July 14, Roosevelt asked Congress to amend the 1935 Neutrality Act to allow warring nations to buy munitions from the US for cash, provided that they carried them on their own ships. "Those of us who support the recommendations formulated for the elimination of the embargo," he said, were convinced that the arms embargo played into the hands of those nations which had taken the lead in "building up their fighting power. It works directly against the interests of the peace-loving nations, especially those which do not possess their own munitions plants." Congress refused to act. Germany attacked Poland on September 1, and France and Britain declared war on Germany two days later. Roosevelt gave a fireside chat that evening. "When peace has been broken anywhere," he said, "the peace of all countries is everywhere in danger." Once again he took sides based upon principles, not upon assessments of different belligerents. "Most of us in the United States believe in spiritual values. Most of us, regardless of what church we belong to, believe in the spirit of the New Testament—a great teaching which opposes itself to the use of force, of armed force, of marching armies and falling bombs. The overwhelming masses of our people seek peace—peace at home, and the kind of peace in other lands which will not jeopardize our peace at home. We have certain ideas and certain ideals of national safety, and we must act to preserve that safety today, and to preserve the safety of our children in future years. . . . We seek to keep war from our own firesides by keeping war from coming to the Americas." He then called Congress back into session and on September 21, asked them again to amend the 1935 Neutrality Act, which he now regretted having signed. While asking again to allow belligerents—which in practice meant Britain and France—to buy arms, he promised to keep American ships out of declared war zones. This time Congress agreed.

More than any other president save Lincoln—who, let it be remembered, served for only four critical years, not twelve—Roosevelt kept a few fundamental principles in the foreground, citing them as the basis for nearly all his policies. Thus by the time of his 1940 annual address he had repeatedly insisted that American values could not survive in a world ruled by force; that the United States and its neighbors must take defensive measures to keep war out of their hemisphere; and that the whole New Deal program for a fairer, more equal America with a productive economy crucially served the national defense. In that address, he acknowledged the right of other peoples "to choose their own form of government" but added that "we in this nation still believe that such choice should be predicated on certain freedoms which we think are essential everywhere. We know that we ourselves shall never be wholly safe at home unless other governments recognize such freedoms." He added that the nations of the Americas, "a peaceful community of free peoples" with increasingly free trade, could provide the necessary example for the whole world. Beginning in the spring of 1940, when Germany rapidly conquered Denmark, Norway, the Low Countries and France, and clearly threatened Britain, Roosevelt's many major addresses focused on the specific measures the nation had to take to defend itself, and, after December 1941, on how exactly it would win the war. We shall now look successively at his presentation of the four critical issues that dominated his last five years in office: the strategic planning for the Second World War and its course after December 1941; the domestic mobilization that the war required; the creation of a new postwar economy and society; and the planning for a new international order. To an astonishing extent, his response to all of these huge problems drew on the same principles that he had laid down from the time he came into office, and shaped the postwar world.

In a message to Congress on May 16, 1940—while German troops were sweeping through northern France—Roosevelt insisted that new weaponry, especially in the air, had drastically increased the vulnerability of the United States and the Americas. "From the fiords of Greenland it is four hours by air to Newfoundland; five hours to Nova Scotia, New Brunswick and to the Province of Quebec; and only six hours to New England. The Azores are only 2,000 miles from parts of our eastern seaboard and if Bermuda fell into hostile hands it would be a matter of less than three hours for modern bombers to reach our shores. From a base in the outer West Indies, the coast of Florida could be reached in two hundred minutes." The United States had to defend against potential aggressors before they reached our vital interests. To do so, he asked for about $1 billion of new defense spending, including the capability to increase annual aircraft production from about 9,000 to 50,000 planes. On May 26, with the battle of France pretty clearly lost, he warned against panic. Congress was meeting his requests, he said, but more might soon be necessary. The government would advance the money needed to increase capacity. Because the country needed more than arms, however, "we must make sure, in all that we do, that there be no breakdown or cancellation of any of the great social gains we have made in these past years." He warned both against irresponsible elements who might organize strikes to stop production—a reference to Communists, who had become allies of Germany since the Nazi-Soviet Pact of August 1939—and against creating new "war millionaires" or causing inflation. "For more than three centuries we Americans have been building on this continent a free society, a society in which the promise of the human spirit may find fulfillment. . . . This is the promise of America. It is this that we must continue to build—this that we must continue to defend," for future generations and "for all mankind." And about seven weeks later, on July 10, he asked for $4.8 billion more—to fund a near-doubling of the navy which the Congress had just passed almost without debate; to increase the army to 1.2 million men, with equipment for 800,000 more; and to increase aircraft production and industrial capacity. "We will not send our men to take part in European wars," he said, but the nation would "repel aggression. . . . This nation through sacrifice and work and unity proposes to remain free."

On July 7, 1940—after many months of speculation about his plans—Roosevelt accepted the Democratic nomination for a third term as president. Since other Americans were willing to serve, he said, he must serve as well in the fight against a "revolution which proposes not to set men free to but reduce them to slavery." On September 3, he reported to Congress on a deal with Britain, whereby the United States acquired a chain of bases from Newfoundland through Bermuda to the Caribbean in return for fifty older destroyers—"an epochal and far-reaching act of preparations for continental defense in the face of grave danger." The president and the military were taking the danger very seriously, doubting whether Britain would survive, and work on the new bases began immediately. On September 16 he noted the passage of the first peacetime draft in the nation's history, affecting men from twenty-one to thirty-five. The Republican Party, meanwhile, had rejected isolationist candidates and nominated a corporate lawyer, Wendell Willkie. Willkie supported Roosevelt's defense and foreign policies but insisted that a third term would mean dictatorship for America. Once again the nation's leading newspapers generally endorsed Roosevelt's opponent, but once again the people reelected him, with 55 percent of the popular vote and 449 electoral votes to 82. The Democrats also gained 5 seats in the House for a working majority of 272–162, although the Republicans gained 4 in the Senate, cutting the Democrats and their allies' margin to 68–28.

On December 29, 1940, Roosevelt broke new ground in another fireside chat, specifically naming the country's enemies for the first time. The United States was now in grave danger, he said, because of the September 27 Tripartite Pact among Germany, Italy and Japan. The "Nazi masters of Germany," he said, in his first direct reference to them, wanted to dominate Europe and the world, and "the Axis not merely admits but proclaims that there can be no ultimate peace between their philosophy of government and our philosophy of government." The US must therefore keep "European and Asiatic war-makers" from gaining control of the oceans leading to the western hemisphere, by doing what it could to save Britain. He proposed to provide the British and their allies with any arms they needed via "lend-lease"—without charging them for them, or forcing them to incur new war debts. "We must be the great arsenal of democracy," he said. His January annual message repeated all these themes and asked for a world "founded upon four essential human freedoms:" freedom of speech, freedom of religion, freedom from want, and freedom from fear, by which he meant reduced armaments. "That is no vision of a distant millennium," he said. "It is a definite basis for a kind of world attainable in our own time and generation." The budget message foresaw $17.5 billion in expenditures for fiscal 1942, more than 60 percent of it for defense. He asked for progressive tax increases but estimated a $9.2 billion deficit for that year, even while recommending domestic cuts for work relief and new flood control projects. His third inaugural on January 20 specifically compared the present crisis to those of the American Revolution and the Civil War, which had created and then preserved democracy. "Democracy alone," he said, "has constructed an unlimited civilization capable of infinite progress in the improvement of human life. . . . As Americans, we go forward, in the service of our country, by the will of God."

It took about three months to pass the Lend-Lease Act, which provided a reason to increase defense production further. An expected German invasion of Britain never took place, and on May 27, Roosevelt announced an "Unlimited National Emergency" in a radio address. The Nazis, he said, now controlled much of Europe and the Middle East, threatened Egypt and the Suez Canal, and could at any moment move into the Iberian Peninsula, French North Africa, Dakar, and the Azores and Cape Verde Islands. They would then threaten the western hemisphere, and could gain influence in South America and prepare "to strangle the United States and the Dominion of Canada." The US must now help Britain defend the freedom of the seas, and he announced somewhat vaguely that the navy had "extended our patrol in North and South Atlantic waters." The army and navy were in fact preparing to occupy some key Atlantic positions, and on June 20 Roosevelt informed Congress that American troops had landed in Iceland, Trinidad, and British Guiana.

Two days later Hitler transformed the world situation yet again by attacking the Soviet Union. Roosevelt immediately recognized this as a great turning point that offered the opportunity to seek the complete defeat of the Axis alliance of Germany, Italy and Japan, and on July 9 he asked Secretary of War Henry M. Stimson to prepare estimates of the military and naval forces needed to achieve that goal.[13] The Japanese government also regarded the new war as a turning point, and decided in the near future to attack both British and American possessions in the Far East to create their new empire. They immediately completed their occupation of French Indochina. In response, Roosevelt on July 26 announced that the US had frozen Japanese assets, making it impossible for Japan to buy more American oil. About three weeks later, Roosevelt met with British prime minister Winston Churchill for the first time on warships off Newfoundland, and on August 14 they issued a joint declaration known as the Atlantic Charter. It laid out general principles for peace "after the final destruction of the Nazi tyranny," paraphrasing much of the language of Roosevelt's recent speeches, including a call for "assurance

---

13 Kaiser, *No End Save Victory*, p. 243.

that all the men in all the lands may live out their lives in freedom from fear and want."

American ships were now patrolling the western Atlantic and cooperating with British ones, and that led to a German submarine firing on the US destroyer *Greer* on September 4. In a fireside chat on September 11 Roosevelt linked this incident to three other cases of German attacks on US vessels. "This attack on the *Greer*, he said, "was one determined step toward creating a permanent world system based on force, on terror, and on murder.... When you see a rattlesnake poised to strike, you do not wait until he has struck before you crush him." More specifically, he announced that the US Navy would now protect British ships between the mid-Atlantic and the US and fire on any German or Italian ships west of a defined line. The Germans sank more American ships in September and October, including the destroyer *Kearny*, and on October 27 Roosevelt in a broadcast address declared, "America has been attacked." He spoke of documents in his position laying out Nazi plans to rule South and Central America and eliminate religion all over the world.[14] "All of us Americans, of all opinions, in the last analysis are faced with the choice between the kind of world we want to live in and the kind of world which Hitler and his hordes would impose upon us.... We are pledged to pull our own oar in the destruction of Nazism." He also noted that Congress was amending the Neutrality Act to allow merchant ships to arm themselves and to sail all the way to belligerent nations such as Great Britain. Clearly the president was ready to enter the war at any moment.

The war nearly broke out in the Atlantic on November 5, when American warships were preparing to do battle with the German battleship *Scheer* in the North Atlantic before the *Scheer* developed engine trouble and returned home.[15] Instead, it came a month later when the Japanese government executed its war plan, attacking not only Malaya, the Dutch East Indies and the Philippines, but the US fleet at Pearl Harbor as well. Roosevelt never had any intention of fighting only the Japanese, and he knew from diplomatic intercepts that the Germans had promised to carry out their obligations under

---

14 This is one of Roosevelt's claims that historians have not been able to verify.
15 *Ibid.*, p. 309.

the Tripartite Pact and enter the war if Japan attacked the US. He did not mention Germany on December 8 when he asked Congress to declare war on Japan, but in a fireside chat on December 9 he insisted that Germany had been encouraging Japan "in accordance with a joint plan," and that "Germany and Italy, regardless of any formal declaration of war, consider themselves at war with the United States at this time." Those two nations formally declared war on the US the next day.

From then until April 1945, every fireside chat and annual message put recent military events into a long-term strategic perspective. The annual message of January 1942 reviewed the history of Japanese, Italian and German expansion. Promising "powerful and offensive operations" in due time, he proclaimed, "The militarists of Berlin and Tokyo started this war. But the massed, angered forces of common humanity will finish it." "There never has been—there never can be—successful compromise between good and evil," he concluded. "Only total victory can reward the champions of tolerance, and decency, and freedom, and faith." In his second wartime fireside chat on February 23, 1942, Roosevelt asked his listeners "to open up their atlases" to understand the scope of the war. The United States would have to secure supply lines to and establish bases in distant regions across the Pacific as well as in Europe, requiring hundreds of new ships. He gave the figure of 2,340 men killed at Pearl Harbor, and insisted, truthfully, that only three ships had been permanently put out of action. "We Americans have been compelled to yield ground, but we will regain it," he said. "We and the other United Nations are committed to the destruction of the militarism of Japan and Germany." He concluded with a quote from Tom Paine's *Common Sense.*

In his next fireside chat on April 28 Roosevelt cited the Russians' "crushing counteroffensive," which had driven the Germans back from Moscow, as the most important recent development. He spoke directly to the people of half-occupied France, promising not to allow the Axis to make military use of French territory anywhere in the world. He acknowledged "serious losses" in the Far East, where the Japanese had seized much of the Philippines, Malaya, Singapore, and the Dutch East Indies, but added that the Japanese were taking losses as well. On September 7 in another broadcast he ran down four major theaters of the war. Hitler had failed to destroy the Russian Army despite large new advances in southern Russia. In the Far East, "We have stopped one major Japanese offensive and we have inflicted heavy losses on their fleet," he said, referring to the Battle of Midway in June, where the Japanese had lost four carriers. He cautiously urged listeners not to "overrate the importance of our successes in the Solomon islands"—that is, on Guadalcanal—where he evidently doubted whether the US would be able to hold on. The British and Dominion troops were fighting hard in North Africa, and in Europe the nation was preparing to "launch" attacks against the Germans at various points. "This is the toughest war of all time," he concluded. "We need not leave it to historians of the future to answer the question whether we are tough enough to meet this unprecedented challenge." Two months later, in the congressional elections, the Republicans won another big victory, reducing the administration majorities to 226–209 in the House and 58–38 in the Senate, but Roosevelt did not allow this setback to divert attention from the course of the war.

In his annual message in early January 1943 Roosevelt listed four key military events: the great Russian offensive since the end of the Battle of Stalingrad in November, which was continuing; the halt to the Japanese advance in the Pacific thanks to the Battle of Midway; the British counterattack in North Africa that had driven the Germans out of Egypt and Libya; and lastly, the November Anglo-American landings in French North Africa, which had forced the Germans to divert forces, "removed the danger" of an attack through North and West Africa on South America, and brought French troops there into action on the Allied side. On July 18, a fireside chat reported that the US was on its way to winning the war, as he had promised eighteen months before. The British and Americans had landed in Sicily and Mussolini's regime had fallen after Hitler, Roosevelt claimed, declined to send him enough help. He explained that the Allies had planned the North African invasion a year ago and the Sicilian campaign six months ago. The US was now building twenty million tons of new shipping a year, and the war at sea, where the Allies had suffered heavily during 1942, was going much better. "The heaviest and most decisive fighting today is going on in Russia," he said, paying tribute to the unprecedented "devotion, determination and self-sacrifice" of the Russian people and their armies under Stalin's leadership. On September 9, after the Allies and then the Germans had invaded Italy from the south and north, he announced the armistice reached with the post-Mussolini Italian government, and listed Berlin and Tokyo as the ultimate war objectives. In a special message to Congress on September 17 he reported that a recent conference with Churchill at Quebec had planned "further blows of equal or greater importance against Germany and Japan with definite times and places for other landings." He talked at length about the strategic bombing campaign against Germany, acknowledging heavy losses, but claiming "devastating blows at carefully selected, clearly identified strategic objectives—factories, shipyards, munition dumps, transportation facilities, which make it possible for the Nazis to wage war."[16]

On Christmas Eve 1943, another fireside chat reported on the first meeting of Churchill, Roosevelt and Stalin at Teheran. "We agreed on every point concerned with the launching of a gigantic attack upon Germany," he said, and named General Dwight D. Eisenhower as its commander—a clear announcement of an all-out invasion of France, now planned for May 1944. In the last year American forces overseas had grown from 1.7 million to 3.8 million, and they would reach 5 million by next July. "The war is now reaching the stage where we shall all have to look forward to large casualty lists—dead, wounded, and missing," he added. 1944 saw the Normandy landing on June 6, and Roosevelt surveyed the extraordinary progress of the last two years in a fireside chat on June 12 that also called for the purchase of war bonds. The climactic offensives in the Pacific began in the Mariana Islands in the same month and moved to the Philippines in October.

That summer, Roosevelt, whose health was failing, accepted the nomination for a fourth term as president and waged a brief new campaign against Governor Thomas Dewey of New York. His popular majority fell to a solid 53 percent, but he won 432 electoral votes to Dewey's 99. The Democrats gained 22 House seats for a 246–189 majority and lost 1 Senate seat, leaving them at 58–38. In his last annual message in January, he tried to reassure the nation after the nasty scare of the Battle of the Bulge in December. "The high tide

---

16 This claim was certainly exaggerated. Postwar studies showed that the bombing was not very effective until much later.

of this German effort was reached two days after Christmas. Since then we have reassumed the offensive, rescued the isolated garrison at Bastogne, and forced a German withdrawal along the whole line of the salient. . . . General Eisenhower has faced this period of trial with admirable calm and resolution and with steadily increasing success. He has my complete confidence." He defended the original decision to concentrate forces against Germany first, and also called the Pacific advance "the fastest-moving offensive in the history of modern warfare," covering 3,000 miles. He specifically anticipated the end of the war against Germany in 1945, but spoke only of "the closing in of the forces or retribution" around Japan. By now his focus had shifted to the planning for the postwar world.

Although Roosevelt made the major strategic decisions of the war himself, he allowed his military leaders to plan and execute all these huge operations almost unhindered. He directed the other requirement for victory—the mobilization of the nation's resources needed to put overwhelming military forces in the field—much more actively, continually setting production targets in public, discussing the financing of the war effort, and asking for measures to allow the economy to function smoothly. "The superiority of the United Nations in munitions and ships," he said in his January 1942 annual message, "must be overwhelming—so overwhelming that the Axis Nations can never hope to catch up with it." Aircraft production should reach 60,000 planes in 1942 and double in 1943; tanks should more than triple to 75,000 in 1943; and the country should build six million tons of shipping in 1942 and ten million the next year. His January 5 budget message projected $24 billion in war expenditures for fiscal 1942—compared to a total federal expenditure of $9.5 billion in fiscal 1939—and $53 billion in 1943. With war industry needing every worker, the WPA, the CCC and the NYA could finally be cut. Current taxes, he said, would bring in $18 billion in fiscal 1943 compared to $6 billion in fiscal 1940, but he called for higher progressive taxes as well. He also wanted to expand Social Security to cover new categories of workers. He estimated necessary borrowing at $19 billion for fiscal 1942 and $34 billion for fiscal 1943, and called for steps to control inflation. It took the better part of the year, and two special messages to Congress on April 27 and September 7, to get the authority to impose price ceilings on all the goods that he wanted, but Congress granted it after the second message. The first of these messages also proposed a 100 percent tax on all personal income over $25,000 a year, but Congress refused to go along. The September 7 message noted that wages and salaries had risen from $43.7 billion in 1939 to $75 billion in 1942—purchasing power that had to be soaked up to avoid inflation.

The 1943 annual message noted that some military production figures had fallen short of his targets while others had exceeded them, showing what a free society could do. The simultaneous budget message predicted total expenditures of $77 billion for fiscal 1943 and $100 billion for fiscal 1944. The nation had added ten million workers since the summer of 1940 and would need six million more during 1943, many of them "women and young people." Civilian consumption must fall 25 percent from 1941 levels, and the country must fill out lots of paperwork to allocate resources and control prices. Tax receipts had grown sixfold to $35 billion for fiscal 1944, and he wanted an additional $16 billion so as to fund 50 percent of expenditures with taxes.

Thanks in large part to the NRA and the Wagner Act, organized labor had made its most rapid gains ever during Roosevelt's presidency, but he had said relatively little about them in major addresses, other than to bemoan jurisdictional disputes between the A. F. of L. and the CIO and the strikes they led to. On May 2, 1943, he gave a fireside chat about a coal strike called by John L. Lewis of the United Mine Workers, who had opposed entry into the war and never accepted ultimate government authority. After Pearl Harbor, Roosevelt noted, Lewis and other major labor leaders had agreed to forego strikes, and the administration had set up a new War Labor Board to handle disputes. Now Lewis had defied it. "I want to make it clear that every American coal miner who has stopped mining coal—no matter how sincere his motives, no matter how legitimate he may believe his grievances to be, every idle miner directly and individually is obstructing our war effort. We have not yet won this war." The government, he announced, was seizing control of the mines, and Secretary of the Interior Harold Ickes would administer them. Lewis ordered his men back to work the next day, although disputes continued. Roosevelt wanted to make all men under sixty-five subject to the draft to allow the government to force them to continue working, but Congress never approved this either. Walking a tightrope, on June 25 he vetoed a bill that would have forbade wartime strikes and prohibited union contributions to political campaigns during the war. Another dispute broke out during the fall, and on November 1 he announced that Ickes was in charge of the mines once again.

The January 1944 budget message reported slightly lower war expenditures than anticipated for fiscal 1944—about $92 billion—and estimated a little less for fiscal 1945. Roosevelt boasted that the cost of living had been quite stable since the previous April but complained that Congress had not passed all his tax proposals. On June 12, 1944, he gave a fireside chat to kick off a fifth War Loan drive. Eighty-one million Americans, he said, had already bought $32 billion in war bonds, and the current drive called for $60 billion more. The nation subscribed the loan within two months. In January 1945, with the defeat of Germany clearly in sight, he tentatively predicted about $70 billion in war expenditure for fiscal 1946, and warned Congress not to underestimate the cost of defeating Japan, which had occupied a much larger territory than Germany and required supply lines two or three times longer for the US. By early 1944, however, the Roosevelt's domestic focus had shifted from war production to the preparation for a new postwar economic order at home.

As early as a fireside chat on July 18, 1943—a year, as he well knew, before decisive offensives could begin—Roosevelt proposed a sweeping program for veterans' welfare, to include a large separation bonus, unemployment insurance, opportunities for further education and job training, and health care and pensions for disabled veterans. Three months later, on October 27, he passed on the recommendation of an experts' committee on the education of war veterans. "For many, what they desire most in the way of employment will require special training and further education. As a part of a general program for the benefit of the members of our armed services, I believe that the Nation is morally obligated to provide this training and education and the necessary financial assistance by which they can be secured. It is an obligation which should be recognized now; and legislation to that end should be enacted as soon as possible." He initially recommended one year of schooling for every veteran and up to three years for selected individuals, including funds for living expenses as well as tuition.

On June 22, 1944, he signed the GI Bill of Rights, which went considerably further than his original proposal. Six months earlier, in his December 24, 1943 fireside chat, he had called for a new "economic bill of rights," including the right to a job and income to pay for food, clothing, and recreation; adequate farm income; businesses free from monopolies' domination; a decent home for every family; "the right to adequate medical care"; protection against old age, sickness, accidents and unemployment; and the right to a good education. America's place in the world, he said, depended on carrying these rights into practice. His budget message on January 10, 1944 discussed the difficulties of converting war production to civilian production, the need to find jobs for veterans, and a plan to revive public works.

On November 2, 1944, in a radio address, he promised to avoid mass unemployment and a "false boom" like that of the 1920s after the war. "I look forward," he said prophetically, "to millions of new homes, fit for decent living; to new, low-priced automobiles; new highways; new airplanes and airports; to television; and other miraculous new inventions and discoveries, made during this war, which will be adapted to the peacetime uses of a peace-loving people. . . . Our postwar job will be to work, to build—for a better America than we have ever known." His last budget message on January 3, 1945 noted that with fifty-two million men and women in war-related production and twelve million men in the armed forces, the nation would have to find employment for sixty million workers after the war. "Manifestly, full employment in peacetime can be assured only when the reduction in war demand is approximately offset by additional peacetime demand from the millions of consumers, businesses, and farmers, and by Federal, State, and local Governments. And that means that consumers' expenditures and business investments must increase by about 50 percent, measured in constant prices, above the level of the year 1939 if full employment is to be provided by private enterprise." The government would need to maintain the wartime price control machinery to contain pent-up demand. "Our productive achievements during the war have demonstrated once and for all the progress which this Nation can support, the progress which will be required if all our resources are to be put to adequate peacetime use. The war, however, will also leave us deep distortions in our economic life which must be overcome. We owe it to those who give everything that we set our sights as high for peace as we set them for war." He called for expanding Social Security to cover agricultural and domestic workers. He repeated these proposals in his annual message on January 6.

And meanwhile, the war mobilization and the war itself led Roosevelt to take specific steps and more forthright stands on behalf of black Americans. Months before the war broke out, on June 12, 1941, he issued a Memorandum Condemning Discrimination in Defense Work in response to pressure from civil rights organizations. The Office of Production Management—the agency supervising war production—had already urged contractors to "make ample provision for the full utilization of available and competent Negro workers." "No Nation combating the increasing threat of totalitarianism," he said, "can afford arbitrarily to exclude large segments of its population from its defense industries. Even more important is it for us to strengthen our unity and morale by refuting at home the very theories which we are fighting abroad." He now formed a Fair Employment Practices Commission to hear any complaints of discrimination in war industries. The armed forces remained segregated, but the administration agreed to have black soldiers serve in every military specialty. And on October 5, 1944, in a radio address calling upon all Americans to vote, he referred to obstacles to voting in some states. "The right to vote must be open to our citizens irrespective of race, color, or creed—without tax or artificial restriction of any kind. The sooner we get to that basis of political equality, the better it will be for the country as a whole."

And at the same time, beginning with the Atlantic Charter in August 1941, Roosevelt laid down the foundations of the postwar international order. That document, signed by Roosevelt and Churchill, had opposed territorial changes opposed to the wishes of the peoples concerned; recognized the right of all nations to govern themselves as they wished, and called for the restoration of self-government to those forcibly deprived of it; called for equal access to raw materials and trade, and international cooperation to secure labor standards and economic advancement; endorsed disarmament of aggressor nations; and foresaw "the establishment of a wider and permanent system of general security," a possible new world organization. For the first eighteen months of the war he confined himself to very general statements about the future. "We are fighting today for security, for progress, and for peace, not only for ourselves but for all men, not only for one generation but for all generations," he said in his January 1942 annual message. "We are fighting to cleanse the world of ancient evils, ancient ills. . . . We are inspired by a faith that goes back through all the years to the first chapter of the Book of Genesis: 'God created man in His own image.'" He got marginally more specific in a special New Year's Day address on war and peace on January 1, 1943, promising "to organize relations among Nations that forces of barbarism can never again break loose." In his fireside chat of July 28, 1943 after the invasion of Sicily, he referred to "our determination to restore these conquered peoples to the dignity of human beings, masters of their own fate, entitled to freedom of speech, freedom of religion, freedom from want, and freedom from fear." Five months later, reporting on the Teheran conference on December 24, he assured the nation that he and Churchill and Stalin agreed on the need to wipe out "Nazism and Prussian militarism," and that they would not, as after the First World War, depend on disarmament to keep peace after the war. In the annual message on January 11, 1944 he promised that "we shall not repeat the tragic errors of ostrich isolationism." The Big Four—himself, Churchill, Stalin and Chiang Kai-shek of China—had made no secret commitments, but had discussed economic, social, physical and moral security. "The best interests of each Nation, large and small, demand that all freedom-loving Nations shall join together in a just and durable system of peace." Determined not to repeat Wilson's disastrous clash with Congress over the League of Nations, Roosevelt allowed Democratic senators to take the lead in securing congressional approval of two resolutions "which pledged this nation to cooperate in a world organization for peace," as he noted in a radio address on November 2, 1944.

Four days later, in another address from Hyde Park, he guardedly prepared the American people for the revelation of the greatest secret of the war. There was another reason, he said, why the victors must "create a world peace organization which will prevent this disaster—or one like it—from ever coming upon us again." "When we think of the speed and long-distance possibilities of air travel of all kinds to the remotest corners of the earth, we must consider the devastation wrought on the people of England, for example, by the new long-range bombs"—a reference to the German V-2 rocket, the first ballistic missile. "Another war would be bound to bring *even more devilish and powerful instruments of destruction* to wipe out civilian populations. No coastal defenses, however strong, could prevent these silent missiles of death, fired perhaps from planes or ships at sea, from crashing deep within the United States itself." The late McGeorge Bundy identified this passage—added to the speech in Roosevelt's own hand—as a reference to the atomic bomb, now in the last stage of its development. Drawing once again on his extraordinary capacity for long-range thinking, he had foreseen the strategic dilemma of the postwar world.[17]

In late 1944, Americans watched in shock as the British in Italy and Greece and the Soviets in Rumania and Poland used their occupation forces to install governments of their own choosing in apparent violation of the Atlantic Charter. "We have seen already, in areas liberated from the Nazi and the Fascist tyranny, what problems peace will bring," Roosevelt commented in his last annual address. "And we delude ourselves if we attempt to believe wishfully that all these problems can be solved overnight. . . . The nearer we come to vanquishing our enemies the more we inevitably become conscious of differences among the victors." The Atlantic Charter might not provide "rules of easy application" for every situation, but remained a statement of principles "toward which we can aim." Admitting concern over events in Greece and Poland, he rejected exploiting or exaggerating differences with allies. They all must in any case move forward to build "permanent machinery for the maintenance of peace. . . . The aroused conscience of humanity will not permit failure in this supreme endeavor."

On March 1, 1945, Roosevelt made his last major address, a report to Congress on the recent Yalta meeting with Churchill and Stalin. In failing health, he addressed them sitting down and referred for the first time in public to the steel braces he had had to wear to stand since his polio attack in the early 1920s. The Big Three, he announced, had made plans both to defeat Germany completely and to "build the foundation for an international accord" that would restore peace and "give some assurance of a lasting peace."

---

17 McGeorge Bundy, *Danger and Survival: Choices About the Bomb in the First Fifty Years* (New York, 1988), p. 90.

The conference to create the new United Nations Organization was now set to meet in San Francisco in April. The Senate would have to approve its charter and he had kept them informed about it. He discussed the plans for the four-power occupation of Germany (which would include France as well) in great detail, and promised, not for the first time, that "Nazi war criminals" would face punishment. He claimed that the three powers would "join together, during the temporary period of instability—after hostilities—to help the people of any liberated area, or of any former satellite state, to solve their own problems through firmly established democratic processes." The foreign ministers of the leading nations would meet every few months. "Twenty-five years ago," he said, "American fighting men looked to the statesmen of the world to finish the work of peace for which they fought and suffered. We failed them then. We cannot fail them again, and expect the world again to survive." Six weeks later, on April 12, 1945—almost exactly eighty years to the day after Lincoln's assassination—Roosevelt died at his vacation home in Warm Springs, Georgia of a cerebral hemorrhage. Former Missouri senator Harry Truman, who had become his third vice president on January 20, succeeded him.

Franklin Roosevelt's twelve years in office represented the climax of the American experiment that had begun in 1789. Faced with a domestic crisis, he used large congressional majorities, progressive ideas that had been gaining strength for several decades, a remarkable band of collaborators, and the idealism of the American people to transform and enormously expand the role of the federal government and provide a whole new level of security to the American people. Then, in a worldwide ideological struggle, the genius of American industry, the dedication of the workforce, and superb military leadership allowed him and the United States to defend and extend its values from the middle of Germany around the globe to the western shore of the Pacific. We shall find that future presidents of both parties continued the application of his principles for at least another thirty-five years, until new ideas and conflicts began to undermine the extraordinary consensus of postwar America. He left behind both a rhetorical legacy and a record of accomplishment unique in their scope and impact in the modern history of the western world.

# XVI

## Harry S. Truman and Dwight Eisenhower

### 1945–53 • 1953–61

Although Harry Truman was the last president not to attend college, he had read very extensively in US history. After a career in county government around Independence, Missouri, he had served in the Senate as a staunch New Dealer from 1934 until 1944, when Roosevelt eased him into the vice presidency in place of the more controversial Henry A. Wallace. Not long before the convention, Dr. Frank Lahey, one of the nation's foremost physicians, had examined Roosevelt and told him that his heart disease was so advanced that he would not serve another term, and must choose his running mate accordingly.[1] According to one perceptive witness to the 1944 Democratic Convention, the party leaders and delegates knew how ill Roosevelt was, and that they were probably selecting the next president.[2]

The last phases of the war and the dawn of the postwar world, of course, dominated Truman's first few months. In an address to Congress on April 16—four days after Roosevelt's death—he promised to fight to total victory, punish war criminals, and found security on law and justice. Appealing for support of the new United Nations, he promised that the nation would "lead the world to peace and prosperity." On May 3 he announced Germany's unconditional surrender, and on June 1, in another message to

---

1 See the remarkable book of Harry S. Goldsmith, *A Conspiracy of Silence, The Health and Death of Franklin D Roosevelt*(New York, 2007), pp. 171–2.
2 *A Man Called White, The Autobiography of Walter White* (New York, 1948), pp. 265–66. White was the executive secretary of the NAACP.

Congress, he reviewed the whole course of the Pacific War, boasted of the effects of the strategic bombing of Japan—which had burned one city after another almost to the ground—and warned of a huge effort to defeat the Japanese over the next year, requiring more than 3.5 million men, and involving very heavy casualties. On June 26, he congratulated the delegates at San Francisco for creating the UN Charter, and on July 2 he asked the Senate to ratify it.

In July Truman traveled to Europe to meet with Stalin and Churchill at Potsdam—only to see Churchill give way to a new Labour Party prime minister, Clement Attlee, in the middle of the conference. At sea on his way home on August 6, he announced somewhat euphemistically that the first atomic bomb, "harnessing the basic power of the universe," with the power of 20,000 tons of TNT, had dropped on "Hiroshima, an important Japanese Army base." The Germans, he said, had been "working feverishly" to develop such a weapon, but the US had won "the battle of the laboratories" with British help. Atomic power might eventually supplement other sources of energy, he said. On August 9, the day after the second bomb hit Nagasaki, he gave a radio address on the Potsdam conference, laying out plans for reparations in kind from Germany and mentioning that millions of Germans had been moved out of territory now awarded to Poland. He spoke again of the atomic bomb, repeating that the "military base" of Hiroshima had been chosen "to avoid, insofar as possible, the killing of civilians," and promised plans "for the future control of this bomb." The United States, he said, was now the most powerful nation on earth, because "a society of self-governing men is more powerful, more enduring, more creative than any other kind of society, however disciplined, however centralized." On September 1 he announced Japan's formal surrender. "The evil done by the Japanese war lords can never be repaired or forgotten," he said. "But their power to destroy and kill has been taken from them."

Domestic affairs, for the most part, dominated the first of the two parts of Truman's presidency—divided not by his election in his own right in November 1948, but rather by the North Korean attack on South Korea in the middle of 1950. The whole nation had dreaded a new depression after the war ended, and Truman in his first annual message in January 1946 declared, "It is the responsibility of Government to gear its total program to the achievement of full production and full employment." Demobilization proceeded rapidly, and the armed forces fell from more than twelve million to less than two million by January 1947. Two million veterans, Truman reported in that month, were now students supported by the GI Bill. Civilian production revived very rapidly, and unemployment averaged just 1.9 percent in 1945, 3.9 percent in 1946, 3.6 percent in 1947 and 4 percent in 1948. Responding to Truman, Congress passed the Full Employment Act in 1946, committing the government in principle to that objective without prescribing specific steps to reach it. An endless wave of strikes had broken out when the war ended, and Truman in that first message endorsed wage increases but also proposed "fact-finding boards" to investigate labor disputes and head off strikes when collective bargaining failed.

Inflation became a huge and politically explosive problem. Truman warned in January 1946 that many wartime controls had to remain in force to keep prices in check, but that summer Congress bowed to business pressure and passed a much-weakened version of the law reauthorizing the Office of Price Administration, and initially failed to act again after Truman vetoed it as too weak on June 29. Sudden, huge price increases induced Truman to sign virtually the same bill later in the summer, but inflation reached 18 percent for the year 1946, with meat prices leading the way.[3] The November congressional elections showed a full-scale reaction against Democratic rule. Republicans gained 55 seats in the House and 12 in the Senate, emerging with majorities of 246–188 and 51–45 for the first time since 1928. The new members included a number of youthful war veterans, including Congressmen Richard Nixon of California and John F. Kennedy of Massachusetts and Senator Joseph McCarthy of Wisconsin.

"It looks like a good many of you have moved over to the left since I was here last!" Truman declared in his next annual message on January 6, 1947, quickly adding that nineteen other presidents had also faced Congresses dominated by the opposing party. Within five months Congress had passed the Taft-Hartley Act, a sweeping new labor law requiring union officials to declare

---

[3] For these inflation and previous unemployment figures see https://www.thebalance.com/unemployment-rate-by-year-3305506.

under oath that they were not Communists, banning unions from managing pension funds, allowing states to pass "right-to-work" laws banning union shops, and giving the president the power to stop strikes. Truman vetoed it—as he had vetoed a similar bill a year earlier—but the House and Senate overrode the veto 331–83 and 68–25. Truman called for its repeal or amendment in every subsequent annual message, without success. Meanwhile, the Republican Congress also took aim at the high tax rates of the New Deal and the Second World War.

In his budget messages of January 1946 and 1947, Truman reported that expenditures were falling from $100 billion in fiscal 1945 to $67 billion in fiscal 1946, $42.5 billion in fiscal 1947, and an estimated $37.5 billion for fiscal 1948. Tax receipts meanwhile had fallen from $45.7 billion in fiscal 1945 to $43 billion in fiscal 1946, $40 billion in fiscal 1947, and $37.7 billion estimated for fiscal 1948, bringing the budget into balance for the first time since fiscal 1929. The new Republican Congress regarded this as an invitation to cut taxes, but Truman vetoed their first attempt to do so on July 18, 1947, arguing that the nation still needed the revenue to control inflation and that the cuts focused too much on the higher brackets. The House overrode his veto easily, but the Senate failed to do so, as 37 voted to sustain him against 57 against. He vetoed a similar bill on April 2, 1948, but this time, with the presidential election looming, both houses overrode. Before the cut, married couples with incomes of $50,000 or more had been paying an effective tax rate of 50 percent. After it, only those with incomes of $125,000 or more had to pay that much.[4]

In foreign affairs, the slow, difficult work of occupation and peacemaking began in 1947 to make way for a new era of ideological conflict. "It is the hope of all Americans," Truman told Congress in January 1946, "that in time future historians will speak not of World War I and World War II, but of the first and last world wars." Four-power control of Germany, he said, was moving ahead slowly, the US had taken responsibility for Japan's future, and General Marshall was in China trying to mediate between the Nationalist government and the Communists to create "a strong, independent,

---

4 *Chicago Tribune*, April 2, 1948, p. 3.

united and democratic China." Truman announced, fatefully, that the US would not recognize new governments imposed by force. Working in the UN, he hoped to establish "effective international control of atomic energy" and "prohibit, outlaw and prevent the use of atomic energy for destructive purposes." The USSR rejected the US plan to do this at the end of the year. A year later he acknowledged "the difficulty of reaching agreements with the Soviet Union" on peace terms for the defeated nations, but added that both nations had an interest in peace, and that the US took the same attitude toward the Soviets as toward other nations.

Truman struck a very different note on March 12, 1947, when he addressed the new Republican Congress again on threats to Greece and Turkey. The British government had occupied Greece and supported a conservative government in late 1944—arousing almost unanimous criticism in the US—but they were now withdrawing in the midst of civil war. "The very existence of the Greek state is today threatened by the terrorist activities of several thousand armed men, led by Communists," Truman said. "One of the primary objectives of the foreign policy of the United States is the creation of conditions in which we and other nations will be able to work out a way of life free from coercion. This was a fundamental issue in the war with Germany and Japan. . . . We shall not realize our objectives, however, unless we are willing to help free peoples to maintain their free institutions and their national integrity against aggressive movements that seek to impose upon them totalitarian regimes," as had already happened in Poland, Rumania, Bulgaria and elsewhere. "I believe that it must be the policy of the United States to support free peoples who are resisting attempted subjugation by armed minorities or by outside pressures," he concluded. He also asked for military aid for Turkey, which had remained neutral throughout the Second World War. These principles became known as the Truman Doctrine.

Truman in his recent annual message had specifically denied that partisanship divided the two parties on questions of foreign affairs. The Republican Congress agreed that Communism was a threat, although many of them feared it more at home than abroad. They rapidly agreed to meet Truman's relatively small request of about $400 million for fiscal 1948. Later that spring, they also responded to his request in his annual message to create the Defense Department and the National Security Council and put the US Air Force on an equal footing with the Army and Navy. On November 17, 1947, Truman opened a special session of Congress that he had called to consider two issues: the needs of Western Europe, and new anti-inflation measures. Austria, Italy and France, he said, needed almost $600 million of emergency aid to buy sufficient fuel and food to last them through the winter. He delivered another special message on European recovery on December 19, presenting what was already known as the Marshall Plan after George Marshall, who had become secretary of state earlier in the year. The United States, he declared, wanted to create "conditions of enduring peace" throughout the world. The US had already supported the UN, sought the limitation and control of atomic weapons, worked toward peace treaties with defeated nations, and provided more than $15 billion since the Axis surrender to help victims of the war and rebuild economies. He now asked for more help for European recovery, both for the sake of the American economy, and to maintain "the civilization in which the American way of life is rooted." "The next few years can determine whether the free countries of Europe will be able to preserve their heritage of freedom. If Europe fails to recover, the peoples of these countries might be driven to the philosophy of despair—the philosophy which contends that their basic wants can be met only by the surrender of their basic rights to totalitarian control." Last summer, he said, responding to Marshall's original suggestion in June, the European states, including the western zones of Germany, had met to plan their recovery jointly. The Communists had decided to oppose the program. Truman asked for an authorization of $17 billon through June 30, 1952, with $6.8 billion by June 30, 1949—an additional 20 percent of total federal outlays. He emphasized that western Germany would receive some of the aid to promote its recovery, while insisting that the US would never allow Germany to threaten Europe again.

On March 17, while Congress debated the proposal, the president broadcast another much more militant address, specifically blaming the failure to establish peace on the Soviet Union, which with its agents had "destroyed the independence and democratic character of a whole series of nations in Europe," including, most recently, Czechoslovakia, where Communists had just taken over in a bloodless coup, and Finland, where they seemed to have acquired a dominant influence in the government.[5] The Soviets and their satellites, he noted, had refused to take part in the European Recovery Program and were trying to sabotage it. Meanwhile, five major European nations had just signed a mutual defense pact. Congress then approved the European Recovery Program. In late June the Soviet Union responded to new steps to create a West German state by blockading Berlin. Truman left it to Secretary Marshall to explain that the US would supply West Berlin by air.

Meanwhile, despite the increasingly conservative Congress, Truman in 1945–48 presented a new domestic agenda. Two major proposals went well beyond the New Deal. In his very first annual message in January 1946, he asked for an increase in the minimum wage from 40 cents to 75 cents an hour over two years, and an expansion of Social Security to cover more workers, including farm laborers and domestics. He also called for federal measures to encourage housing construction and money "to rebuild slums and blighted areas," and to provide low-income housing in both cities and rural areas. He wanted more federal money for public works, including school construction, and more progress on rural electrification, much of which remained to be done. He favored continued agricultural price supports, and called for statehood for Alaska and Hawaii and more self-government for the District of Columbia, now ruled by appointed commissioners. And he repeated a proposal that he had first made on November 19, 1945. The nation's health, he said then, was inadequate, citing the total of five million men whom selective service had rejected on medical grounds during the war. Noting that only 3–4 percent of Americans had health insurance, he proposed a comprehensive national health program, including health insurance paid for by worker contributions. This proposal alone has never been fully implemented.

Equally significantly, Truman became the first president explicitly to call for national civil rights legislation. In his January 1947 annual message he deplored "numerous attacks upon the constitutional rights of individual citizens as a result of racial and religious bigotry," including restrictions on the right to vote and

---

5 That influence turned out to be only temporary, and Finland remained an independent and democratic neutral for the whole of the Cold War.

to "engage in lawful callings," and created the President's Commission on Civil Rights. He also wanted to make the wartime Fair Employment Practices Commission permanent. He repeated these statements a year later. Then, on February 2, 1948, he drew upon his commission's report to advocate a long series of measures: a permanent Civil Rights Commission, a federal anti-lynching measure, a voting rights law that would eliminate the poll tax in the seven states that still had it, and an end to segregation in interstate travel (the first reference to segregation in a presidential address). He also called for an end to all racial barriers to immigration and naturalization, and a law—which Congress promptly passed—to allow Japanese Americans to pursue claims against the government growing out of their internment during the war. On July 26, he issued an executive order desegregating the armed forces. The program split the Democratic Party. When the Democratic convention that nominated Truman for reelection adopted it as part of its platform, delegates from the Deep South walked out, formed their own Dixiecrat Party, and nominated Governor J. Strom Thurmond of South Carolina for president. Southerners managed to block any new legislation, but Truman continued repeating these demands for the rest of his time in office.

As soon as he was nominated, Truman called the Congress back into session yet again and submitted new anti-inflation and housing measures, which the Republicans refused to pass. He now faced not only Republican New York governor Thomas Dewey and Thurmond in the general election, but also former cabinet member and vice president Henry Wallace, running for the Communist-dominated Progressive Party, and expected to win substantial numbers of votes in major states such as New York. Emphasizing New Deal themes and civil rights, Truman campaigned from one end of the nation to the other attacking "the do-nothing 80th Congress" while every pundit predicted a big Republican victory. On November 2, Truman defeated Dewey with 49.6 percent of the popular vote to 45.1 percent, and 303 electoral votes to Dewey's 189 and Thurmond's 39. A significant Wallace vote cost Truman New York and he lost most of New England and the Mid-Atlantic states, but he carried more than half of the South, most of the farm belt, and Ohio, Illinois, and California. In other extraordinary results, the Democrats more than reversed the congressional verdict of 1946, gaining 75 seats in the House for a 264–171 majority, and 9 seats in the Senate for a 54–42 edge.

"During the last 16 years," Truman began a triumphant 1949 annual message, "our people have been creating a society which offers new opportunities for every man to enjoy his share of the good things of life. . . . The recent election shows that the people of the United States are in favor of this kind of society and want to go on improving it. . . . Every segment of our population and every individual has a right to expect from our Government a fair deal."[6] Since 1929, he noted, US population had increased 20 percent, agricultural production 45 percent, and industrial production 75 percent. He repeated his proposals on civil rights, expanded Social Security, national health insurance, a higher minimum wage, the repeal of Taft-Hartley, tax increases, appropriations to build the St. Lawrence Seaway together with Canada, and anti-inflation measures. Congress passed the requested minimum wage increase and a slum clearance bill during 1949, and expanded Social Security to cover full-time farm laborers and domestics and increase benefits in the next year. It failed either to repeal Taft-Hartley or to pass any civil rights legislation, and the American Medical Association lobbied hard and successfully to keep national health insurance even from coming to a vote. The nation went into its first economic recession in twelve years during 1949, with unemployment rising from 4 to 6.6 percent. In a televised address on July 13, Truman blamed the recession on the inflationary spiral, swore off tax increases during the slump, and rejected Republican calls for new budget cuts. Of the $42 billion total federal expenditures in the last fiscal year, he noted, $32 billion was "due to international events," including $14 billion for national defense, $7 billion for peaceful international programs, and $11 billion in payments on government bonds and veterans' benefits. Recovery began by the end of the year.

Truman also continued on the same course in foreign affairs. In his inaugural address, he reaffirmed the US's and its allies' belief in peace, equal justice, and equal opportunity, now "directly opposed by a regime of contrary aims and a totally different concept of life,"

---

6 "Fair Deal" became the Truman-era equivalent of "New Deal," but the words were not capitalized in the official text.

adhering to the "false philosophy" of Communism. Reaffirming his commitment to the UN, the European Recovery Program, and new alliances with European and other American nations, he added a new proposal known as Point 4: "a bold new program for making the benefits of our scientific advances and industrial progress available for the improvement and growth of underdeveloped areas." On January 5, 1949, he sent the Rio Treaty creating the Organization of American States to the Senate for ratification, and on May 5, 1949, he signed the North Atlantic Treaty, creating the NATO alliance. On September 26, 1949, he announced briefly and calmly that the Soviet Union had exploded its first atomic bomb, noting that he had predicted that other nations might follow the US lead four years earlier, and on January 31, 1950, he declared that he had asked the new Atomic Energy Commission to work on "all forms of atomic weapons, including the so-called hydrogen or superbomb." No great military buildup, however, accompanied these moves. His 1950 budget message showed that the defense budget had increased from $11.9 billion in fiscal 1949 to $13.1 billion in fiscal 1950 and projected just $13.5 billion in fiscal 1951, and Truman hoped to cut it to $11.4 billion in fiscal 1952. And at no time in any major address did Truman ever refer to the other great international event of 1949, the victory of the Chinese Communists in the Chinese Civil War. Truman's policies in early 1950 still reflected the view of George F. Kennan, until recently the head of the Policy Planning Council in the State Department, that the contest with the Soviet Union was mainly political and economic and that the United States did not have to prepare for all-out war. Elements within his administration were already pushing for increased military spending, however, when war broke out in the Far East.[7]

Japan had ruled Korea from the time of the Russo-Japanese War in 1905 until 1945, and the United States and the USSR had jointly occupied it when Japan surrendered, dividing the country into northern and southern zones at the 38th parallel. The Soviets, as in Germany, had refused to create a new government for the whole country, and the USSR and the US had respectively established a Communist North Korean state and a non-Communist South Korean

---

7  Melvin P. Leffler, *A Preponderance of Power* (Stanford, 1992), pp. 345–60.

one, each one, as in Germany, claiming to be the country's sole legitimate government. On June 25, 1950, the North Korean dictator Kim Il-Sung launched an invasion of South Korea, strengthened by tanks and other weapons that Stalin and the USSR had provided. Truman's response began a new era in American diplomacy and world history, one that lasted through nine presidencies and thirty-nine years, until 1989, and which in some respects continues to this day.

On June 26, Truman announced that the United Nations Security Council—which Russia was boycotting because of the United States' refusal to seat Communist Chinese representatives—had demanded that North Korea withdraw its invading forces. On the very next day, he announced that since the North Koreans had refused that demand, "I have ordered United States air and sea forces to give the Korean Government troops cover and support." Critically, Truman did not justify this move on narrow legal grounds—that since the US had assumed responsibility for South Korea when Japan surrendered, it remained the sovereign power there until a peace treaty with Japan had been signed, even though it had withdrawn its occupation forces in 1949.[8] "The attack upon Korea makes it plain beyond all doubt," he said instead, "that communism has passed beyond the use of subversion to conquer independent nations and will now use armed invasion and war. It has defied the orders of the Security Council of the United Nations issued to preserve international peace and security." As a result, Truman continued, the United States 7th Fleet would now defend the island of Formosa (now Taiwan), where the Chinese Nationalist government had taken refuge, and the United States would accelerate "the furnishing of military assistance to the forces of France and the Associated States in Indochina and the dispatch of a military mission to provide close working relations with those forces." France had been fighting a Communist insurgency in Indochina for four years. The Korean attack had become, in its first few days, the trigger for a whole new response to the Communist threat. Its consequences rivaled those of the fall of France ten years earlier.

On July 19 Truman broadcast an address on Korea and its worldwide implications. The attack on South Korea, he said, was

---

8 See George F. Kennan, *Memoirs, 1925–1950* (Boston, 1967), p. 490.

"a direct challenge to the efforts of the free nations to build the kind of world in which men can live in freedom and peace." The UN Security Council had now passed a new resolution calling upon member states to assist South Korea in resisting the attack, and a unified command under General Douglas MacArthur—who had been commanding occupation forces in Japan—had begun to do so. "The free nations," he said, "have now made it clear that lawless aggression will be met with force. The free nations have learned the fateful lesson of the 1930s. That lesson is that aggression must be met firmly. Appeasement leads only to further aggression and ultimately to war." This, Truman warned, might be the first of several attacks—a clear warning of danger in Europe—and the US must not only reinforce MacArthur but "build up our own Amy, Navy and Air Force over and above what is needed in Korea" and work "with other countries in strengthening our common defenses." He had already authorized an additional $10 billion in military spending and sent a message to Congress asking for new measures to control inflation while enlarging defense production "for the next several years." "We know that the cost of freedom is high. But we are determined to preserve our freedom—no matter what the cost. . . . Our country stands before the world as an example of how free men, under God, can build a community of neighbors, working together for the good of all. That is the goal we seek not only for ourselves, but for all people." Truman built on these themes in two more broadcast addresses on September 1 and September 9. The United Nations forces had by then been pushed into the Pusan perimeter in the southeast corner of South Korea, but Truman looked ahead to a broader struggle. The defense budget, he said, would increase from $15 billion to $30 billion in the current fiscal year, and perhaps more in the next. This would demand longer hours, harder work, "additional jobs for women and older people," higher taxes, anti-inflation measures, and cutbacks in civilian production in favor of military equipment. Americans could easily believe that they were living through a replay of 1940–41 and preparing for a new world war.

On September 10, MacArthur's forces successfully landed at Inchon, hundreds of miles behind the North Korean lines, and rapidly liberated South Korea. The administration decided to try to unify the whole country, and Truman on October 10 announced that he was about to meet with MacArthur in the Pacific to discuss "the final phase of United Nations Action" in Korea, designed to establish "a unified, independent and democratic Korea." The UN General Assembly had now adopted that goal, authorizing an advance all the way to the Chinese and Soviet borders.[9] On October 15 Truman reported briefly and optimistically on his talk with MacArthur. United Nations forces—mostly United States and South Korean troops, but including some European and Asian allies as well—now advanced deep into North Korea, widening their front by hundreds of miles. In November they encountered Communist Chinese troops. The Chinese eventually surrounded some American units, forcing a desperate retreat. Truman did not address the nation in the midst of this disaster, but stated in a November 30 press conference, "Because of the historic friendship between the people of the United States and China, it is particularly shocking to us to think that Chinese are being forced into battle against our troops in the United Nations command." He also suggested that MacArthur might be authorized to use atomic weapons in his defense, but quickly backed away from that statement. In the November 7 congressional elections the Republicans gained 28 seats in the House, leaving the Democrats with a 235–199 majority, and 5 in the Senate, cutting the Democratic majority to 49–47.

The UN troops were still in full retreat and were about to abandon the capital of Seoul once again when Truman gave his annual message on January 8, 1951. He stuck to the big picture. "Our men are fighting, alongside their United Nations allies," he said, "because they know, as we do, that the aggression in Korea is part of the attempt of the Russian Communist dictatorship to take over the world, step by step. . . . The present rulers of the Soviet Union have shown that they are willing to use [their] power to destroy the free nations and win domination over the whole world." "If Western Europe were to fall to Soviet Russia," he warned, "it would double the Soviet supply of coal and triple the Soviet supply of steel. If the free countries of Asia and Africa should fall to Soviet Russia, we would lose the sources of many of our most vital raw

---

9 When the Soviet delegate with his veto power had returned to the Security Council, it had become impossible for the US to get Security Council resolutions to support the war, and the US had turned to the General Assembly for support instead.

materials, including uranium, which is the basis of our atomic power. And Soviet command of the manpower of the free nations of Europe and Asia would confront us with military forces which we could never hope to equal." The free nations were standing up in Korea, he said, as they had failed to do in Manchuria in 1931, Ethiopia in 1935, and Austria in 1938. The United States was now expanding its military to 3.5 million men and women and its manufacturing capacity to 50,000 planes a year (an echo of Roosevelt in 1940) and 35,000 tanks. His budget message of January 15 reflected these priorities. Total spending for fiscal 1952 would increase from $47.2 billion to $71.6 billion. The fiscal 1951 defense budget was four times the 1950 figure. Despite an excess profits tax, the deficit would reach $16.5 billion. Foreign assistance, most of it military, would increase from $2.7 billion to $7.5 billion under a new Mutual Security Act. By April 11, a new commander in the field, General Matthew Ridgway, had stabilized the front and begun a new advance to the 38th parallel. Truman had abandoned the goal of uniting Korea, but MacArthur had continued to make public statements calling for complete victory. Truman announced that he was relieving him of command because the general "could not give his wholehearted support" to government policy. Republicans hailed MacArthur as a hero, and he addressed a joint session of Congress.

Although armistice talks began in July 1951 after the military front had stabilized around the 38th parallel, nothing fundamental had changed when Truman gave his next annual message in January 1952. Partisan conflict had become as bitter as in the Reconstruction era, and Truman asked his listeners to differ "without destroying our free institutions and without abandoning our bipartisan foreign policy for peace." Greece and Turkey, he reported, had joined NATO, and NATO was looking for a way to allow West Germany to contribute to its own defense. The US had new mutual assistance treaties with Japan, Australia, New Zealand and the Philippines. The United States, France and Britain had presented disarmament proposals to the UN, but the Soviet delegate had laughed at them. Truman complained that the massive defense buildup did not include enough money for civil defense. Trying to find a middle course, he said that the US had avoided "world war on the one hand, and appeasement on the other." It faced a long and difficult task, and the threat of world war remained real. His budget message contemplated even larger military forces, including twenty-four army and marine divisions and sixteen carrier groups. The country, apparently, faced many years of full-scale preparedness for world war, if not war itself, and Truman said that it would be at least two years before the defense budget could be cut. The Twenty-second Amendment limiting presidents to two terms was now law, but it had exempted Truman, the incumbent when it was ratified. On March 29, Truman announced that he would not be a candidate.

Less than two weeks later, Truman invoked emergency powers to stop nationwide strikes in order to make sure that defense production continued. On April 8, 1952, he announced that the government was taking over the steel industry to prevent a strike. His target was not the strikers but the steel companies, who were insisting on raising prices to make up for wage increases. The Supreme Court ruled the seizure unconstitutional on June 2, but the two sides rapidly reached agreement. The government's anti-inflation measures had proven effective, keeping inflation down to less than 1 percent in 1952, after two previous years at 6 percent.

Although the Korean armistice talks had reached agreement on nearly every issue by the end of 1951, the war continued through 1952 because Truman absolutely refused to return North Korean or Chinese prisoners who did not want to return to Communist rule. To do so, he told the country on May 7, 1952, would be "repugnant to the fundamental moral and humanitarian principles which underlie our action in Korea," resulting in "misery and bloodshed to the eternal dishonor of the United States and the United Nations." The Republicans now nominated Dwight D. Eisenhower, whom Truman had made the NATO Supreme Commander, for president, and the Democrats countered with Illinois governor Adlai Stevenson. Truman in the fall campaigned almost as hard for Stevenson as he had for himself in 1948, but to no avail. Promising an end to the fighting in Korea, Eisenhower won a landslide victory with 55 percent of the popular vote and 442 electoral votes to 89, including those of Virginia, Tennessee, Texas and Florida. Gaining 22 seats in the House, the Republicans regained control, 221–213, and 2 new Senate seats gave them a 49–47 edge. Republicans would control the government for the first time since 1929.

Domestic anti-Communism had become another big issue in Truman's second term. Ever since 1948, Republicans such as Congressman Richard Nixon—elected senator in 1950 vice president in 1952—and Senator Joseph McCarthy of Wisconsin had railed against Communists within the government. Soviet agents had indeed penetrated the government, and Truman himself had established a Loyalty Program for federal employees in early 1947. The attorney general had compiled a list of Communist-influenced organizations as part of the program, and many employees had been driven out of the government because they were members. The Justice Department had uncovered an atomic spy ring, convicting Julius and Ethel Rosenberg of giving atomic secrets to the Soviets. Former State Department official Alger Hiss had been convicted of perjury for denying that he had been a Communist spy. Truman, however, had told various federal agencies to resist congressional investigators' demands for the full records of their employees. On September 9, 1950, he had vetoed the McCarran Act, an omnibus anti-Communist measure that would require Communist and "Communist front" organizations to register with the government, calling these provisions "the greatest danger to freedom of speech, press and assembly, since the Alien and Sedition Laws of 1798." Although the Democrats controlled Congress, the measure passed over his veto.

Truman foreswore any new legislative proposals in his last annual message in January 1953, instead delivering a detailed review of his nearly eight years in office. At home, the government had doubled social security benefits, increased the minimum wage, helped build three million private homes and 155,000 housing units, and seen payrolls increase by ten million workers. Eight million veterans had received educational benefits, 90 percent of farmers now had electricity, and the nation had spent $5 billion on the development of various river basins, following up on Roosevelt's 1937 proposal to mimic the TVA. Once more he called for national health insurance and civil rights legislation. He could not, he said, forecast what would happen abroad, but the administration had done what it could for peace, security, freedom and justice "for us and for all mankind." It had avoided total war and "may have already succeeded" in establishing conditions that would prevent one. The world war, he said, had left behind two dominant powers with "diametrically opposite principles and policies." "The 'cold war' between the communists and the free world," he said, "is nothing more or less than the Soviet attempt to checkmate and defeat our peaceful purposes, in furtherance of their own dread objective"—worldwide tyranny. He reviewed all the steps the US had taken to resist Communist expansion, and he acknowledged, as he had not at the time, that the Soviet atomic explosion of 1949, *not* the Korean War, had triggered the nation's massive defense buildup. "When the Soviets produced an atomic explosion—as they were bound to do in time—we had to broaden the whole basis of our strength. We had to endeavor to keep our lead in atomic weapons. We had to strengthen our armed forces generally and to enlarge our productive capacity—our mobilization base. Historically, it was the Soviet atomic explosion in the fall of 1949, nine months before the aggression in Korea, which stimulated the planning for our program of defense mobilization. What we needed was not just a central force that could strike back against aggression. We also needed strength along the outer edges of the free world, defenses for our allies as well as for ourselves, strength to hold the line against attack as well as to retaliate."

Harry Truman left two enormous legacies to the postwar world. On the one hand, his administration's vision of the Soviet threat and the necessary means to counter it—alliances, foreign aid, and a massive military buildup—remained orthodoxy for four decades. On the other, he laid out the post–New Deal agenda for the Democratic Party, led by civil rights legislation, a federal role in education, and some kind of national health plan. Defeated in his administration by southern filibusters and coalitions of Republicans and conservative Democrats, most of those measures eventually passed under presidents who entered Congress in 1946 and the Senate in 1948. Truman's ironclad commitment to his beliefs, in good times and bad, remains a remarkable model of presidential leadership.

For the third time in its history, the nation had turned to the victorious general in a critical war to lead it in the postwar period. This time, Eisenhower's victory also marked the Republican Party's return to power for the first time in twenty years. At home, Eisenhower left the reforms of the New Deal in place, but backed away from some of Truman's biggest initiatives and put a new priority on balanced budgets. In foreign affairs, he managed to end one war and avoid any new ones, but also led the nation through eight years of defense buildups based upon new technology, a more aggressive stance in many areas of the developing world, and continual warnings that only heightened vigilance could prevent the spread of Communism all over the world.

Eisenhower and his running mate Richard Nixon had made the Communist penetration of the federal government a centerpiece of their 1952 campaign. During the first two years of their administration they came into conflict with the anti-Communist demagogue Senator Joseph McCarthy, ending in 1954 with McCarthy's censure by the Senate and his complete loss of influence. Yet during the same period Eisenhower himself repeatedly stressed the gravity of the internal Communist threat and the need for new measures to combat it. The government, he told Congress in his first annual address on February 2, 1953, needed "reliable" and "loyal" employees, and the FBI was investigating all his choices carefully. "I know that the primary responsibility for keeping out the disloyal and the dangerous rests squarely upon the executive branch," he said, and the executive departments were putting new policies in place based on the principle that public employment "is not a right but a privilege." Twice, on February 11 and June 3, he issued statements explaining his refusal to commute the death sentences of Julius and Ethel Rosenberg for atomic spying. "The nature of the crime for which they have been found guilty and sentenced far exceeds that of the taking of the life of another citizen; it involves the deliberate betrayal of the entire nation and could very well result in the death of many, many thousands of innocent citizens," he said in the first statement. He went further in the second on the eve of their execution: "by immeasurably increasing the chances of atomic war the Rosenbergs may have condemned to death tens of millions of innocent people all over the world." In his next annual message in January 1954 he reported that the government had fired more than 2,200 federal employees on internal security grounds, and asked for a new law to deprive anyone convicted of "conspiring to advocate the overthrow of the government by force or violence" of their US citizenship. That was the charge upon which the government had convicted leaders of the American Communist Party in 1949 under the Smith Act of 1940.

In a broadcast address on the state of the nation on April 5, 1954, when the McCarthy controversy was nearing its height, Eisenhower referred again to the threat of domestic Communism, which "it would be completely false to minimize." 25,000 "doctrinal Communists" remained in the US today, he said, and the FBI was our best defense against "those people." A related fear, he continued, held "that we will use intemperate investigative methods, particularly through congressional committees, to combat communistic penetration." He did not mention McCarthy's name, but promised that the country remained committed to "fair play and decency and justice." And on August 24, 1954, he proudly announced that he had signed "an act to make illegal the Communist Party and to prohibit members of Communist organizations from serving in certain representative capacities." Having convicted forty-one top Communist leaders of "conspiracy to advocate," he said, the government had indicted thirty-one more in the last nineteen months. The Congress had also passed new laws depriving those convicted of the charge of their citizenship and forcing "Communist front organizations" to register with the government. The Communist Control Act also provided for the arrest and detention of persons deemed subversive in time of national emergency—a provision that the FBI was preparing to implement in October 1962, when war threatened over Soviet missiles in Cuba.[10] Frequently contrasting godless Communism with American religious belief, Eisenhower broke precedent on January 20, 1953 by beginning his inaugural address with a prayer, and on June 14, 1954—Flag Day—he announced that his administration had added the words "under God" to the Pledge of Allegiance.

A year into his presidency, in January 1954, Eisenhower sent Congress a series of messages making his attitude toward the domestic legacies of Roosevelt and Truman clear. A January 11 message on agriculture accepted the need for price supports to guarantee farmers a certain income level. On the same day, a message on

---

10 See Carl Bernstein, *Loyalties, A Son's Memoir* (New York, 1989), pp. 224–26. Retired FBI agent James Hosty also confirmed this for me when I interviewed him for my book *The Road to Dallas*.

labor–management relations noted that while legislation in this field had a "long, contentious history," "we have now achieved a measure of practical experience and emotional maturity in this field which, I do not doubt, is responsible for the relatively peaceful character of recent industrial relations," and no more legislation was needed now. On January 14 he called for expanding Social Security to include more categories of workers, including self-employed professionals and state and local government workers. But on January 18, in a message on the nation's health, he put Truman's national insurance proposals aside and flatly rejected the "socialization" of medicine. A year later, on February 22, 1955, Eisenhower unveiled his biggest domestic initiative, a proposed interstate highway system. It took a year to pass the program, financed entirely by a new Highway Trust Fund fed by increased gas taxes, and the president made remarkably few references to this enormous legacy during the rest of his term. Eisenhower also persuaded the Congress finally to approve the St. Lawrence Seaway—the new system of locks that allowed oceangoing ships to reach the Great Lakes—and in 1953 to create the Department of Health, Education and Welfare, which it had refused to do for Truman. In all these ways, the legacy of the New Deal lived on. The administration did not however manage to make Republican domestic stewardship more popular, and the Democrats in 1954 regained control of the House and the Senate by narrow majorities of 232–203 (a 19-seat gain) and 49–47 (a 2-seat swing).[11]

For the whole of his two terms, balancing the federal budget remained Eisenhower's greatest domestic priority. Helped by the termination of hostilities in Korea in July 1953, he managed to reduce total federal spending from $74 billion in fiscal 1954 to $70.9 billion in fiscal 1954 and $63.5 billion in 1955. It then began to rise slowly, from $65.6 billion in fiscal 1956 all the way up to an estimated $79 billion in his last budget for fiscal 1961. Meanwhile, the Congress passed only one significant tax cut in 1954, and receipts increased pretty steadily until fiscal 1958. As a result, the deficit fell from $9.4 billion in fiscal 1953 to $4.5 billion in 1955, and the government showed a surplus of $1.6 billion

---

11 The Senate majority included Wayne Morse of Oregon, formerly a Republican, who had declared himself an independent and moved to the Democratic Party shortly thereafter.

for fiscal 1956 in time for the presidential election. It was almost perfectly balanced in 1957, but the severe recession that began late that year cut revenues drastically. Unemployment rose from 4.2 percent in 1956 to 6.2 percent in 1958. Eisenhower asked for and secured an extension of unemployment benefits, but he never made a broadcast address about the recession, which had a devastating effect on the Republicans at the polls in November 1958. The Democrats gained an astonishing 49 seats in the House and 15 in the Senate, giving them majorities of 283–153 and 64–34.

Speaking to the new Congress in January 1959, Eisenhower had to note a "recession-induced deficit of $12.9 billion" for fiscal 1958, a peacetime record upon which he did not dwell. The deficit remained at $4 billion in fiscal 1959, but the budget balanced again, thanks largely to severe domestic spending cuts, in 1960, when another severe recession struck. The balanced budget, Eisenhower insisted, provided the best safeguard against inflation, which he regarded as the most serious economic threat. Since as we shall see defense expenditures continued to rise, he achieved this record only with very tight restrictions on domestic spending.

Throughout his term Eisenhower argued that current farm programs were piling up agricultural services without providing many farmers enough income, but Congress would never agree with him on what should be done. New domestic issues emerged during his second term. A Senate committee investigation of labor racketeering and corruption in 1957–58 led to congressional debates on new labor laws during 1959. On August 6, Eisenhower broadcast an address arguing that legislation had to deal with unfair picketing and secondary boycotts, as well as criminal diversion of funds. Despite the big new Democratic majorities, a coalition of Republicans and southern Democrats passed the Landrum-Griffin Act embodying these restrictions—an attempt, largely successful, to prevent unions from organizing in the South. The Boom generation was now overcrowding the nation's schools, but Congress rejected Eisenhower's proposals for money for school construction, partly because liberals wanted to do more and partly because Catholics wanted some of the aid to go to parochial schools. Twice, in 1958 and 1960, he vetoed bills designed to "redevelop" "depressed areas" such as Appalachia because they would create a new federal agency and cost too much.

Civil rights—the great issue that Truman had brought to the forefront of national debate for the first time since Reconstruction—played a far more equivocal role in Eisenhower's presidency, especially after the Supreme Court unanimously ruled school segregation unconstitutional in the spring of 1954. "A cardinal ideal in this heritage we cherish is the equality of rights of all citizens of every race and color and creed," he declared in his first annual message, and he recognized that discrimination persisted all around the nation. But he pledged only to eliminate it in two areas of clear federal authority: in the armed forces, where Truman had already begun the process, and within the District of Columbia. On May 19, 1954, in his first press conference after the school segregation decision, Eisenhower pointedly declined to offer the South any advice on how to respond to it while adding that he himself was sworn to uphold the law. He ignored the ultimately successful boycott of the segregated Montgomery, Alabama bus system that lasted through most of 1955. In his January 1956 annual message he declared most optimistically that "voluntary cooperation" was ending segregation in public accommodations in DC, but also called for Congress to create a commission to examine "allegations" that some citizens were deprived of their right to vote. On November 5, in a televised election eve address, he endorsed "cooperation" and "conscience," not "force" or "writing a hard and fast dictum of law," as the best means of achieving civil rights.

Taking a stronger stand in his January 1957 annual message, Eisenhower called for the creation of a Civil Rights Division in the Justice Department and a new law to help enforce voting rights, partly by allowing federal authorities to sue to enforce them. Congress passed a law embodying most of these provisions in August of that year. Eisenhower on August 2 protested bitterly that the Senate had amended the bill to provide for jury trials for contempt charges against individuals denying voting rights. He made no statement when he signed the amended bill, which Senate Majority Leader Lyndon Johnson of Texas had shepherded through the Senate without a filibuster in exchange for the amendment.

A few weeks later, the first and last major civil rights crisis of the Eisenhower years broke out when Governor Orville Faubus of Arkansas, who had promised in a September 4 meeting with the president to abide by a court order desegregating Central High

School in Little Rock, double-crossed him and sent the National Guard home, allowing an angry white mob to prevent black students from entering. On September 23 Eisenhower called upon Arkansans to halt all "unlawful assemblages, combinations and conspiracies" against the court order, and the next evening, in a national broadcast address, he announced that he had had to send in federal troops to enforce it. Refusing once again actually to advocate school integration in principle, he declared, "Our personal opinions about the decision have no bearing on the matter of enforcement; the responsibility and authority of the Supreme Court to interpret the Constitution are very clear." "The overwhelming majority of the people in the South," he claimed, were "united in their efforts to preserve and respect the law even when they disagree with it." This remained his only address to the nation on civil rights. Speaking to Negro leaders on May 12, 1958, he called for "patience and forbearance," dependence on "better and more profound education than simply on the letter of the law," and ensuring "that enforcement will not in itself create injustice." In his January 1959 annual message he complained that "the image of America abroad is not improved" when localities (such as a Virginia county) closed schools rather than integrated them. On February 5 he submitted his first special message on civil rights, calling for strengthening the 1957 law and creating a Commission on Equal Job Opportunity—but only to oversee government contractors. Congress eventually passed a slightly stronger law over a year later. In 1958 and 1959 Congress also approved Truman's and Eisenhower's request to make Alaska and Hawaii the forty-ninth and fiftieth states.

From 1953 through 1960, however, all these domestic issues paled before the single, ever-present, nearly all-consuming focus of the Eisenhower administration: the perceived Communist threat to take over the world. "Freedom is pitted against slavery; lightness against the dark," he said in his first inaugural. "There has been, to this moment, no reason to believe that Soviet policy has changed its frequently announced hope and purpose—the destruction of freedom everywhere," he said in a May 19, 1953 radio address two months after Stalin's death. A televised address to the nation on April 5, 1954—the first of many on foreign policy—declared that all the nation's dangers stemmed from "the threat that we have from without, the great threat imposed upon us by aggressive communism, the atheistic doctrine that believes in statism as against our conception of the dignity of man, his equality before the law—that is the struggle of the ages." "The existence of a strongly armed imperialistic dictatorship poses a continuing threat to the free world's and thus to our own Nation's security and peace," he said in his January 1957 annual message. A year later he warned of "the massive economic offensive that has been mounted by the communist imperialists against free nations," and cited "economic penetration, particularly of newly-developing countries, as a preliminary to political domination." A March 13, 1959 message to Congress calling for more aid to US allies referred to "a fanatic conspiracy, International Communism, whose leaders have in two score years seized control of all or parts of 17 countries, with nearly one billion people, over a third of the total population of the earth." The Chinese Communist leaders showed "the same ruthless drive for power" as the Soviets. "We face a hostile ideology—global in scope, atheistic in character, ruthless in purpose, and insidious in method," he said in his famous Farewell Address of January 17, 1961. "Unhappily the danger it poses promises to be of indefinite duration." Picking up where Truman had left off, Eisenhower painted an indelible picture of a continuous, worldwide life-and-death struggle comparable to the Second World War.

Eisenhower spent most of his time and energy on three kinds of responses to these perceived threats: the remodeling of the American military establishment; the building and strengthening of the largest possible coalition against Communism; and local military and political moves to stop Communist advances in Iran, Guatemala, Lebanon, the Taiwan Strait, Berlin and elsewhere. Two high-level contacts with Soviet leaders, meanwhile, failed to produce any serious results.

Thanks in large part to the death of Joseph Stalin, which led to a change in the Chinese position on the repatriation of prisoners of war, Eisenhower managed to reach an armistice in Korea within six months that left that nation divided, as it remains to this day. "We have won an armistice on a single battleground—not peace in the world," he said in his brief announcement on June 26, 1953. "We may not now relax our guard nor cease our quest." About five weeks earlier, on May 19, he had laid out his military strategic concept to the nation in a radio address. The military plans inherited from the Truman administration, he said, were too expensive and must lead to more deficits and more disastrous inflation. The nation could not afford total mobilization all the time. To secure "a defense strong enough both to discourage aggression and beyond this to protect the nation—in the event of any aggression—as it moves swiftly to full mobilization . . . we are putting major emphasis on air power, which daily becomes a more important factor in war." With the air force receiving 40 percent of the fiscal 1954 military budget and half the navy's budget also going for air power, air power soaked up 60 percent of the defense budget. His budget message next January 1 reported that from fiscal 1953 to fiscal 1955, the army's budget was dropping from $16.2 billion to $10.2 billion while the air force's increased from $15.1 billion to $16.2 billion and the navy's dropped slightly. And the annual message of January 1955 added that the budget emphasized air power and new weapons, "especially those of rapid and destructive striking power"—that is, nuclear weapons. The new Atomic Energy Commission was also essentially a defense agency since it produced nuclear warheads, and its budget had reached $2 billion by fiscal 1956. Combined with $34.2 billion for the Defense Department, that meant that 58 percent of total federal expenditures for that year went for defense.

In October 1957, the USSR's successful launch of the first Sputnik satellite sent the nation into a panic over its scientific prowess in general and a new competition in intercontinental missiles in particular. Eisenhower addressed these concerns in a November 13 broadcast address a month later, assuring the nation that we already had thirty-eight types of operational missiles and that one of the new B-52 bombers could "carry as much destructive capacity as was delivered by all the bombers in all the years of World War II combined." He assured the nation that the US was developing intercontinental missiles, but conceded—wrongly as we now know—Soviet advantages in "some missile and other special areas." To stay ahead, he said, the nation had to give a higher priority to scientific education, and he appointed a new presidential science adviser, the president of the Massachusetts Institute of Technology. In his January 1958 budget message he announced a $2.8 billion increase in spending on missiles, paid for in part with $1.5 billion in cuts in other military programs and in civilian expenditures.

Two years later in his January 1960 budget message he boasted of new Atlas and submarine-based Polaris missiles and promised that while "our country might sustain great losses" if attacked, the attacker would "promptly suffer a terrible destruction." The country was also developing solid-fuel Minuteman missiles. Eisenhower in these last three years resisted pressure from both Democrats and Republicans to spend substantially more on defense, but he certainly took the threat to the nation as seriously as anyone. And only in his farewell address did he warn of the growing influence of the "military-industrial complex" or of the domination of a "scientific-technological elite."[12]

Meanwhile Eisenhower and Secretary of State John Foster Dulles built a worldwide alliance system with treaties on the one hand and military and economic assistance on the other. In January 1955 Eisenhower told Congress that West Germany would soon join NATO and that the Organization of American States was another anti-Communist bulwark. France had given up Indochina and left Communism in control of North Vietnam in the previous year, and Eisenhower now proclaimed that the new SEATO Treaty among the US, Britain, France, the Philippines, Australia and New Zealand promised that "future military aggression and subversion against the free nations of Asia will meet united response."[13] Later that same month he endorsed the Formosa Resolution, committing the US to defend the Nationalist Chinese on Formosa and various other offshore islands against a Chinese Communist attack. Congress passed it. In his next annual message he lauded another similar anti-Communist alliance, the Baghdad Pact of the US, Britain, Turkey, Iraq, Iran, and Pakistan. That pact fell apart two years later when Arab nationalists overthrew the Iraqi government. In 1960 the US concluded a new security treaty with Japan.

Eisenhower also campaigned annually for billions of dollars of assistance to foreign nations, mostly for military purposes, but also for economic development. On May 21, 1957, he broadcast an address to the nation on the subject defending a proposed $4 billion appropriation. Such funds, he said, helped "friendly nations

---

12 January 17, 1961.
13 SEATO was in fact a much less binding agreement than NATO and did not commit its signatories to military action.

equip and support armed forces for their own and our defense" and helped "less advanced countries grow in the strength that can sustain freedom as their way of life." If we did not help one billion people in newly independent countries grow economically, Communists would "expand their brand of despotic imperialism." The address kicked off a summer-long battle against the Congress, where many wanted to cut these requests, and Eisenhower signed the eventual reduced bill on September 3 under protest. Messages to Congress on February 19, 1958 and March 3, 1959 struck a similar note, and the president had to fight the same legislative battles in both of those years as well. The latter message introduced a new element—nuclear sharing—into the issue of help for US allies. "As we move into the age of missile weapons, this plan of collective security will grow in importance. Already intermediate range ballistic missiles are being deployed abroad [in Europe]. Our friends on whose territory these weapons are located must have the continued assurance of our help to their own forces and defense in order that they may continue to have the confidence and high morale essential to vigorous participation in the common defense effort." On May 26, in a message to Congress, he became more explicit. "It is our conviction and the conviction of our NATO allies that the introduction into NATO defenses of the most modern weapons available is essential in maintaining the strength necessary to the Alliance." In fact, European allies now had their own aircraft loaded with nuclear weapons, ready to go at a moment's notice without any real US control over them. Meanwhile, on December 8, 1953, Eisenhower proposed to the UN General Assembly the establishment of an International Atomic Energy Agency that could stockpile fissionable material and make it widely available for peaceful uses. That proposal came to fruition in 1957.

Between December 1959 and June 1960, Eisenhower made three extended goodwill trips overseas. The first took him to eleven different countries from India to Morocco; the second, in February 1960, to four nations in the southern tier of South America; and the last, to four American allies in the Far East. These trips, he told the nation in a broadcast address on June 27, 1960—as well as the many visits foreign leaders had made to Washington—were designed to learn more about our friends' problems and show our willingness to work for peace. "Let me stress, however," he added, "that all the profit gained by past and any possible future trips will be quickly dissipated should we Americans abandon our present course in foreign relations or slacken our efforts in cooperative programs with our friends."

Meanwhile, Eisenhower reported on periodic crises over the fate of individual nations in the Cold War. Asked at a press conference on April 7, 1954 about the Communist threat to Indochina, he famously replied, "Finally, you have broader considerations that might follow what you would call the 'falling domino' principle. You have a row of dominoes set up, you knock over the first one, and what will happen to the last one is the certainty that it will go over very quickly. So you could have a beginning of a disintegration that would have the most profound influences." He did not explicitly take credit for the CIA-directed overthrow of leftist governments in Iran in 1953 and Guatemala in 1954, but in a broadcast address on August 24, 1954, he argued that Iran's "huge reserve of oil" might have fallen into Communist hands in Iran and spoke of a "beachhead of international communism starting in Guatemala." On October 31, 1956—just days before the country would choose once again between him and Adlai Stevenson—he broadcast an address on crises in Eastern Europe and the Middle East. The USSR had invaded Hungary to overthrow a new, more liberal Communist government, and Eisenhower demanded that they withdraw "to permit the Hungarian people to enjoy and exercise the human rights and fundamental freedoms affirmed for all peoples in the United Nations Charter." Meanwhile, Britain, France and Israel had attacked Egypt, the British and French because President Nasser had seized the Suez Canal some months earlier, and the Israelis because of border clashes and their desire to extend their territory into the Sinai Peninsula. "We do not accept the use of force" to settle disputes, he said, attacking the actions of all three powers, and demanding that the Israelis withdraw from the Sinai. Pulling behind the president at a moment of crisis, the nation reelected him with an even larger electoral majority of 457–73, but the Democrats retained their razor-thin congressional majorities. Eisenhower continued to insist that Israel withdraw unconditionally from the territory it had occupied, broadcasting a long address on the subject on February 20, 1957. On March 3 he thanked the Israeli government for giving in.

More crises erupted in the summer of 1958. On July 15 the president reported on the overthrow of the Iraqi monarchy by anti-western army officers, and parallel threats to the governments of Jordan and Lebanon. The US had landed a battalion of troops in Lebanon to head off Communist "indirect aggression" such as the Communists had tried in Greece, Czechoslovakia, mainland China, Korea and Indochina. The threat turned out to be exaggerated and the troops withdrew in October. On September 11, Eisenhower made a long broadcast address on a new crisis in the Taiwan Strait, where the Chinese were bombarding the offshore islands of Quemoy and Matsu and threatening to invade them. To allow them to do so, he said, would revive the disastrous appeasement of the 1930s over Manchuria, Ethiopia, the Rhineland, Austria and Czechoslovakia, which had cost the democracies their chance to avoid world war. The 1955 Formosa Resolution gave him the authority to defend the offshore islands if an attack on them was the beginning of an attack on Taiwan, and he now insisted that it would be. He did not think there would be war, and there was not. On March 16, 1959, another broadcast address responded to Soviet leader Khrushchev's threats to sign a peace treaty with East Germany that would take way western rights in West Berlin. The Soviets, he claimed, had rejected "a free and unified Germany," and their demands were part of their effort to secure "world domination . . . by gaining political power successively in each of the many areas which had been afflicted by the war." The US could not give up its commitments or accept the division of Germany or the loss of West Berlin. "We have lived and will continue to live in a period where emergencies manufactured by the Soviets, follow one another like beads on a string," he said, and the nation must remain ready to repel aggression of all kinds.

On January 26, 1960, Eisenhower denied accusations that the US was trying to overthrow the year-old government of Fidel Castro in Cuba, and accused Cuba of mounting invasions of other Latin American countries itself. A year later, after secretly approving assassination plots against Castro, the Eisenhower administration broke diplomatic relations with Cuba in its last days in office after Castro demanded that the US embassy drastically reduce its staff. And although Eisenhower never really shared this with the American people, at the turn of the year 1960–61 his administration was preparing to intervene militarily in Laos, where pro-US forces were losing a civil war.[14]

Meanwhile, from the death of Stalin in March 1953 through the collapse of a Paris summit conference in May 1960, Eisenhower expressed interest in agreements with the Soviet Union but complained that Soviet attitudes made them impossible. On April 16, 1953 he suggested that Stalin's recent death could lead to a new era of peace—if the USSR agreed to an armistice in Korea followed by free elections to create a unified Korea; ended the Communist insurgencies in Malaya and Indochina; concluded an Austrian peace treaty; agreed to a reunified Germany with a government chosen by "free and secret elections"; and gave the Eastern European nations full independence. Then the world could disarm. On July 25, 1955, he reported on the first summit with the Soviet leaders—Nicolai Bulganin and Nikita Khrushchev—since Truman met Stalin at Potsdam. He had presented the same proposals for Germany, and also put forth his "Open Skies" plan for aerial reconnaissance of the USSR and the US, to allow both nations to guard against surprise attack. In his next annual message in January 1956 he had to report that a subsequent foreign ministers meeting had failed to reach agreement on either of these issues, but said that "the conflict between international communism and freedom has taken on a new complexion." Mistrustful exchanges of letters between Eisenhower and Soviet leaders continued for several years. In the fall of 1958, after lengthy preliminary discussions, the US, the USSR and Great Britain agreed to a voluntary one-year moratorium on nuclear tests. The moratorium was extended twice more, into 1961.

Encouraged by this step, the US invited Premier Khrushchev to visit in September 1959, but when Eisenhower reported on the well-publicized trip on September 27 he assured the nation that the two leaders had simply exchanged views, rather than negotiated on outstanding issues. They scheduled a summit in Paris in May 1960 and a return visit to the USSR the following fall. The Soviet Union shot down an American U-2 spy plane and captured its pilot on the eve of the summit. After Eisenhower strongly defended the

---

14 See David Kaiser, *American Tragedy: Kennedy, Johnson, and the Origins of the Vietnam War* (Cambridge, Mass., 2000), pp. 23–33.

U-2 program as essential to American security at a press conference, Khrushchev at the summit demanded a public apology and punishment of those responsible for the mission before the talks could proceed, and Eisenhower refused. In his broadcast message on the Paris trip on May 25 he made a new and interesting statement: "In a nuclear war there can be no victors—only losers. Even despots understand this." That idea remained controversial for three more decades.

In this turbulent year of 1960, marred also by another serious recession, Senator John F. Kennedy of Massachusetts won the Democratic nomination for president. Richard M. Nixon became the first sitting vice president since Martin Van Buren to win his party's presidential nomination. Twenty-seven and twenty-three years younger than Eisenhower, respectively, these candidates made the most dramatic generational break in American history. Proclaiming that the administration had fallen behind the Soviet Union in space, missiles, and education, Kennedy won the presidency with a comfortable 303–219 electoral margin[15] despite very thin popular vote pluralities nationwide and in several key states. The Republican Party rebounded from its 1958 debacle and gained 22 House seats and 2 in the Senate, but the Democrats retained majorities of 262–175 and 64–36.

During the Eisenhower years, the strong unions, the heavily progressive tax structure the New Deal left behind, and high defense spending had kept the country growing and low- and middle-incomes rising. The postwar baby boom, now in its fifteenth year, had increased US population by 14.5 percent from 1940 to 1950, to 151 million, and by another 19 percent by 1960, to 179 million. Now the generation that had lived through the New Deal as young adults wanted to revive some of its spirit. Meanwhile, Truman and Eisenhower bequeathed a legacy of a large peacetime defense establishment and a worldwide anti-Communist posture. Attempts under their successors to combine domestic progress on several fronts with a new anti-Communist war led to a newly turbulent period in American history.

---

15 Eight Mississippi and six Alabama Democratic electors refused to vote for Kennedy and voted for Senator Harry Byrd of Virginia.

# XVII

# JOHN F. KENNEDY AND LYNDON JOHNSON

## 1961–3 • 1963–9

John F. Kennedy took office at forty-three years of age and remains the youngest man ever elected. Kennedy drew almost his entire cabinet from his own generation, and most of his White House staff was even younger. He combined a commitment to a Roosevelt-Truman kind of agenda at home with sweeping ambitions in foreign affairs. His famous inaugural address focused entirely on the US role in a turbulent world, poised as he saw it between progress and destruction. The presidential oath had not changed, he remarked, but now "man holds in his mortal hands the power to abolish all forms of human poverty and all forms of human life. And yet the same revolutionary beliefs for which our forebears fought are still at issue around the globe—the belief that the rights of man come not from the generosity of the state but from the hand of God." His own generation—"born in this century, tempered by war, disciplined by a hard and bitter peace, proud of our ancient heritage"—would "pay any price, bear any burden . . . to assure the survival and the success of liberty." Kennedy then spoke, one by one, to various regions of the world. He pledged "the loyalty of faithful friends" to old allies "whose spiritual values we share." He pledged to new nations that they would not fall under a new tyranny, and specifically offered an "Alliance for Progress" to Latin America, while reaffirming the Monroe Doctrine—a clear warning to communist Cuba. And he asked America's adversaries to "renew the quest for peace" before encountering "accidental or planned self-destruction," and hoped for agreements on arms control and for cooperation in space. He famously called on Americans to "ask not what your country can do for you, but what you can do for country," and on "fellow citizens of the world" to ask "what together we can do for the freedom of man." The originally clear distinction between domestic and foreign politics had now broken down almost completely.

Kennedy began his first State of the Union address just ten days later with a long discussion of domestic problems, but then spoke more specifically about a number of Cold War crises. The Chinese Communists, he said, threatened Laos and South Vietnam; the newly independent Congo, one of the largest black African nations, was torn by civil strife; and though Communism was trying to expand from its new base in Cuba into Latin America, "Communist domination in this Hemisphere can never be negotiated." The United States, he urged, had to persuade the USSR and Communist China to turn to "open and peaceful competition" rather than war. To do so, he continued, the nation had to strengthen its defenses—a major theme of his presidential campaign. He had asked Secretary of Defense Robert McNamara, he explained, for a full reappraisal of our defense posture, with particular emphasis on our capacity to airlift troops, the Polaris submarine program with its sea-launched intercontinental ballistic missiles, and an expanded land-based missile program. Only an invulnerable missile force could keep the peace. He then turned back to peaceful initiatives: the Alliance for Progress with Latin American states, an expanded Food for Peace program, Soviet-American cooperation in space, and stronger support for the UN. Lastly, he declared arms control to be a central goal, and specifically called for an agreement to ban nuclear tests, which as we have seen had been suspended in the atmosphere by an informal agreement for two years.

1961 disappointed nearly all of the hopes that Kennedy articulated, and the president had to report on one crisis after another. At a March 23 press conference he read a long statement on Laos, citing Soviet and North Vietnamese intervention in its civil war, declaring that the SEATO alliance was considering a response, but also supporting a new neutral government in Laos as a solution. In April, the Bay of Pigs invasion of Cuba by CIA-supported exiles, which he had inherited from the Eisenhower administration, failed disastrously. On May 25 he delivered an additional State of the

Union message to Congress—citing "extraordinary times"—calling for a larger army to allow for non-nuclear responses to crises and new missions for "special forces and unconventional warfare units." "The great battleground for the defense and expansion of freedom today," he echoed Eisenhower, "is the whole southern half of the globe—Asia, Latin America, Africa and the Middle East—the lands of the rising peoples. Their revolution is the greatest in human history." They were threatened by "adversaries of freedom" who wanted to "exploit, to control, and finally to destroy the hopes of the world's newest nations." The USSR had just sent the first man into orbit around the earth, and Kennedy took up the challenge. "I believe that this nation should commit itself to achieving the goal, before this decade is out, of landing a man on the moon and returning him safely to the earth," he said. "No single space project in this period will be more impressive to mankind, or more important for the long-range exploration of space; and none will be so difficult or expensive to accomplish." He also announced that he would meet Khrushchev in Vienna the next month.

Reporting on that trip in a broadcast address on June 6, Kennedy summarized his exchanges with Khrushchev. "We have wholly different views of right and wrong," he said, "of what is an internal affair and what is aggression, and, above all, we have wholly different concepts of where the world is and where it is going." "However difficult" it might seem, the two nations must try to find a way for their systems to live together in peace. He rejected Khrushchev's threat to sign a separate peace treaty with East Germany and asserted the West's rights in West Berlin. He also mentioned that they had agreed on a neutral Laos. On July 25 he gave a long broadcast address on the Berlin crisis. West Berlin, he said, was now "the great testing place of Western courage and will. . . . We shall not be driven out." He called for $3.2 billion in additional defense funds to enlarge the army—making a total increase of $6 billion since January—a reserve call-up that eventually totaled 135,000 men, and more non-nuclear munitions, all to make a non-nuclear response possible. But he also abandoned Eisenhower's rigid position on German unification and opened the door to some different kind of agreement on Germany with the USSR. On August 30 Kennedy told the nation that the Soviets had resumed nuclear tests in the atmosphere—a decision that "will be met with deepest concern and resentment throughout the world." The Soviet tests climaxed with the explosion of a 50-megaton bomb, and on March 2, 1962, Kennedy broadcast that the US would conduct both underground and atmospheric tests of its own.

Kennedy's second annual message in January 1962 echoed most of the objectives of his first. He called for "a peaceful world community of free and independent states—free to choose their own future and their own system, so long as it does not threaten the freedom of others." Congress had agreed to his nuclear strategic goals, and he reported that the pace of the Polaris and Minuteman missile programs had doubled, and more intercontinental bombers were now on standby alert against a surprise attack. But he also conveyed his determination to resist a non-nuclear attack. The nation had increased its strength in Europe, built up the marines, and "expanded our anti-guerilla forces" to whom Kennedy had given green berets. He hoped to bring some of the mobilized reserve troops home soon. He also noted progress on several diplomatic fronts. Prospects for peace had improved in the Congo, and the US and the USSR were working at Geneva on an agreement for an independent and neutral Laos that was concluded later in the year. That in turn he said, would help the situation in South Vietnam, "where the local government has initiated new programs and reforms to broaden the base of resistance"—a statement more of hope than fact—and where Kennedy had just approved, without any announcement, significant increases in the US military advisory role. He did not mention, and the country did not know, that he had repeatedly rejected the unanimous recommendations of his senior advisers to begin full-scale war in Laos, South Vietnam, or both, nearly from the beginning of 1961 until the end.[1]

Kennedy also praised the work of the renamed Agency for International Development (AID), the Food for Peace program, and his own new Peace Corps, which had sent thousands of young Americans into the developing world. Meanwhile, the nation had undertaken "a great new effort in outer space," with the goal of reaching the moon, where it should be at least "among the first." He also reiterated his hope of a breakthrough on disarmament and

---

1 See David Kaiser, *American Tragedy: Kennedy, Johnson, and the Origins of the Vietnam War* (Cambridge, Mass., 2000), pp. 36–121.

nuclear tests, as well as a diplomatic solution to the Berlin crisis. He did not mention Cuba, where his government had undertaken a covert effort to bring down the Castro regime. The space program moved ahead, and on February 20, Kennedy congratulated Col. John Glenn on the first American orbital flight around the earth. On March 18, however, he publicly proposed to Khrushchev that their two nations undertake a joint exploration of space, and five days later, receiving an honorary degree at the University of California at Berkeley, he hailed Khrushchev's acceptance of the proposal as a step toward peace. "Beyond the drumfire of daily crisis, therefore," he said, "there is arising the outlines of a robust and vital world community, founded on nations secure in their own independence, and united by allegiance to world peace."

1962 was a much quieter year abroad than 1961—until October, when CIA surveillance found that the Soviet Union was installing two types of nuclear missiles in Cuba, both capable of hitting targets in large parts of the United States. After lengthy, detailed conversations among the leaders of the foreign policy, defense and intelligence agencies, Kennedy on October 22 informed the nation of these new installations and announced that the US Navy was establishing a "quarantine"—a carefully chosen word to distinguish it from a blockade, an act of war—around the island, and demanding that the missiles be withdrawn. "These actions," he continued, "may only be the beginning. We will not prematurely or unnecessarily risk the costs of worldwide nuclear war in which even the fruits of victory would be ashes in our mouth—but neither will we shrink from that risk at any time it must be faced." In fact, the US military was preparing for a full-scale air strike and invasion of Cuba in the event that Khrushchev refused to withdraw the missiles. On October 28 he agreed to do so, after the Kennedy administration had privately assured the Soviet ambassador that corresponding US nuclear missiles in Turkey and Italy would shortly be withdrawn as well. Not for seven more years did that promise become known.

"I welcome Chairman Khrushchev's statesmanlike decision to stop building bases in Cuba, dismantling offensive weapons and returning them to the Soviet Union under United Nations verification," Kennedy declared on October 28. "It is my earnest hope that the governments of the world can, with a solution of the Cuban crisis, turn their urgent attention to the compelling necessity for ending the arms race and reducing world tensions." The missile crisis and its outcome undoubtedly helped the Democrats a week later, when they lost only 4 House seats, retaining a 258–176 majority, and gained 5 Senate seats for a 68–32 margin in the midterm elections. Kennedy said almost nothing about the missile crisis in his State of the Union message in January 1963. Instead, he boasted that the American position was stronger in space, where the US had sent several men into orbit and returned them in 1962 and intended to be first to the moon. Turning to Europe, he welcomed the movement toward a real European Union—which French president Charles de Gaulle was about to halt—and said that a recent agreement to supply Polaris nuclear submarines to the British might pave the way for a broader agreement on a multilateral nuclear force within NATO. The developing world, he said, had been shocked by the Soviets' behavior in Cuba and reassured by the help the US had given India in a brief border war with Communist China, as well as by advances within the US on civil rights. Then, in a fascinating portent of things to come, he referred to the increasingly bitter ideological conflict between the USSR and Communist China. "It is the closed Communist societies," he said, "not the free and open societies which carry within themselves the seeds of internal disintegration." And once again, he offered to take any further possible steps to ease tensions with the USSR. As it turned out, he managed to realize some of those hopes later in the fateful year of 1963.

Meanwhile, these three State of the Union addresses recorded a largely successful response to the recession that was in progress when Kennedy came into office, much slower progress on other proposals, and an increasing importance of civil rights, brought to the forefront by numerous campaigns of civil disobedience that had begun in the late 1950s. "The present state of our economy is disturbing," Kennedy began his January 1961 address. The recession was now seven months old, bankruptcies had reached a post-Depression peak, unemployment was just below the 1958 peak, and 150,000 workers were losing their unemployment benefits every month. While production fell, prices rose. "In short, the American economy is in trouble," he concluded, and had failed to validate Eisenhower's prediction of a year before that 1960 would be "the most prosperous year in our history." He promised proposals for additional unemployment compensation, help for depressed areas, and a higher and broader minimum wage. Meanwhile, the balance of payments deficit was worsening, now totaling $11 billion over the last three years, leading to $5 billion in lost gold. While he rejected panic—$22 billion in gold remained—or exchange controls, he promised measures to improve the situation. He acknowledged that the budget would run a deficit. Then, following in FDR's and Truman's footsteps, he announced an ambitious domestic agenda. Twenty-five million Americans, he said, lived in substandard housing twelve years after Congress had promised a decent home to every family, and he promised new housing programs. The nation had to build two million new classrooms for the schoolchildren of the Boom generation, and the colleges had to prepare for a doubling of their student bodies. Kennedy called for "measures to provide health care for the aged under Social Security"—the program already referred to as Medicare, which had replaced Truman's national health insurance proposal in the Democratic platform. "Organized and juvenile crimes" were costing taxpayers too much money, and the nation needed new measures to fight them—a priority of the new attorney general, the president's brother Robert. Lastly, he declared, "The denial of constitutional rights to some of our fellow Americans on account of race—at the ballot box and elsewhere—disturbs the national conscience, and subjects us to the charge of world opinion that our democracy is not equal to the high promise of our heritage."

The economy did rebound, and Kennedy reported a year later that the nation had completed 1961 "on the high road of recovery and growth," with one million new jobs. He promised to submit a balanced budget for fiscal 1963. Prices, meanwhile, had been stable. In his January 1962 address, Kennedy also detailed many efforts to help US cities—"America's glory, and sometimes America's shame." The nation had increased funds for "urban renewal"—too often, the bulldozing of poorer residential neighborhoods to build new downtowns—attacked water pollution, and asked for more money both for highways and for mass transit systems. He again called for Medicare. He also praised the Congress for enacting new laws against "organized crime and racketeering" and reported that various agencies were making a coordinated attack on it.[2] He regretted

---

2 As I have shown in another book, *The Road to Dallas* (Cambridge, Mass., 2008), this offensive against organized crime—led by Robert Kennedy—cost John Kennedy his life.

in January 1962 that the Congress had failed to pass aid for school construction and teachers' salaries, blocked in the House of Representatives by advocates of aid to parochial schools. He added that the administration had used law enforcement and other action to assure the right of integrated interstate transportation (steps forced upon it by Freedom Rides), and to try to extend the right to vote and integrate schools. A special message on February 22 called once again for health insurance for the elderly under Social Security, but in July the Senate failed to approve it by two votes. Kennedy responded with a July 17 statement turning the bill into a major issue in the November elections. In April 1962, White House pressure persuaded the steel industry to roll back a potentially inflationary price increase.

On August 13, 1962, Kennedy broadcast a long report on the nation's economy and a new proposal on taxes. During the last eighteen months, the national income had grown 10 percent, industrial production had increased by 16 percent, and the international balance of payments had improved dramatically. Because of two recessions since 1957, however, the nation had been "more or less standing still economically, at least in comparison to the countries of Western Europe and Japan," and unemployment—now 5.5 percent—was still too high. Proposing additional public works measures and an investment tax credit, he credited "similar actions . . . taken under President Roosevelt and others" for making it possible "for us to move ahead in the period since the war," and called out "those who oppose all these moves as they opposed moves in other days much as they opposed Social Security, much as they opposed minimum wage, much as they opposed a ban on child labor and, more recently in the Senate, medical care for the elderly." And he announced plans for a tax cut aimed at reducing revenues to what would be necessary to balance the budget at full employment.

Kennedy spelled out the proposal in his January 1963 annual message. "Our obsolete tax system," he said, "exerts too heavy a drag on private purchasing power, profits and employment. Designed to check inflation in earlier years, it now checks growth instead," lowering output, restricting revenues, and causing chronic budget deficits. He suggested cutting individual income tax rates, now running from 20 percent to 91 percent on the highest incomes, to 14 percent to 65 percent, and cutting corporate rates from 52 percent to 47 percent. A net reduction of $10 billion in taxes—the biggest share for low-income consumers—would increase purchasing power for all Americans. While initially the deficit would rise somewhat, in the long run it would disappear thanks to greater employment and income. Congress did not act on this proposal in 1963, but it was the first step toward dismantling the very high top rates the nation had adopted during two world wars, a process to continue into the next century. In the same message he introduced a new issue. "I believe that the abandonment of the mentally ill and the mentally retarded to the grim mercy of custodial institutions"—a group then numbering about one million Americans, and including his own sister Rosemary—"too often inflicts on them and on their families a needless cruelty which this Nation should not endure."

The civil rights issue, meanwhile, grew in importance. In September 1962 the federal government had to use troops to integrate a school for the first time since 1957, when the state of Mississippi defied court orders to admit James Meredith, its first black student. Announcing the mobilization of National Guard troops to keep the peace, if necessary, on September 30, Kennedy took a line parallel to Eisenhower in 1957, emphasizing the need to obey the law as laid down by the courts. "Even among law-abiding men few laws are universally loved, but they are uniformly respected and not resisted." He also thanked "those southerners" who had begun integrating state universities at every other southern state except South Carolina and Alabama. But in a special message to Congress asking for civil rights legislation on February 28, 1963, he went much further. "The harmful, wasteful and wrongful results of racial discrimination and segregation," he said, "still appear in virtually every aspect of national life, in virtually every part of the Nation. The Negro baby born in America today-regardless of the section or state in which he is born—has about one-half as much chance of completing high school as a white baby born in the same place on the same day—one-third as much chance of completing college—one-third as much chance of becoming a professional man—twice as much chance of becoming unemployed—about one-seventh as much chance of earning $10,000 per year—a life expectancy which is seven years less—and the prospects of earning only half as much." "Above all," he continued, racial discrimination "is wrong. . . . let it be clear, in our own hearts and minds, that it is not merely because of the Cold War, and not merely because of the economic waste of discrimination, that we are committed to achieving true equality of opportunity. The basic reason is because it is right."

Continuing, Kennedy noted that the Justice Department had been making slow progress on voting rights in the Deep South, where "thousands of Negro citizens are registering and voting for the first time—many of them in counties where no Negro had ever voted before." But he now wanted federal officials appointed who could register voters *while suits to secure voting rights went forward*, and the recognition of a sixth-grade education as proof of literacy. Turning to schools, he used language Eisenhower had never used regarding their integration. The 1954 Supreme Court decision "represented both good law and good judgment—it was both legally and morally right." The federal government should help communities carry it out. Kennedy had created a Committee on Equal Employment Opportunity which, he said, had opened up new opportunities, but he wanted it to become a permanent legal body. Then he turned to the issue that had been the target of sit-ins since 1960, and that no president had previously addressed. "No act is more contrary to the spirit of our democracy and Constitution—or more rightfully resented by a Negro citizen who seeks only equal treatment—than the barring of that citizen from restaurants, hotels, theaters, recreational areas and other public accommodations and facilities," he said. The administration had moved against segregation in railway stations, bus depots and airports, and would continue to encourage local progress—but he did not call for a new law banning discrimination in privately owned hotels and restaurants.

"You and I," Kennedy had told the Congress in January 1963, "are privileged to serve the great Republic in what could be the most decisive decade in its long history. The choices we make, for good or ill, may well shape the state of the union for generations to come." Six months later, a single week in early June 1963 changed the course of history on two critical fronts and led the nation into a new era.

On June 10, 1963, in a commencement address at American University in Washington, DC Kennedy boldly moved to make peace in the Cold War. "What kind of peace do I mean?" he asked. "What kind of peace do we seek? Not a *Pax Americana* enforced on the world by American weapons of war. Not the peace of the grave or the security of the slave. I am talking about genuine peace, the kind of peace that makes life on earth worth living, the kind that enables men and nations to grow and to hope and to build a better life for their children—not merely peace for Americans but peace for all men and women—not merely peace in our time but peace for all time." Since nuclear war made no sense, "I speak of peace, therefore, as the necessary rational end of rational men"—echoing the very generation of presidents. He did not offer universal and eternal peace, but rather "a more practical, more attainable peace—based not on a sudden revolution in human nature but on a gradual evolution in human institutions," a series of definite agreements. "Let us re-examine our attitude toward the Soviet Union. . . . No government or social system is so evil that its people must be considered as lacking in virtue." The USSR and the United States had never been at war, and shared a mutual abhorrence of war—in the Soviet case, because of its unprecedented suffering in the Second World War. Kennedy called specifically for a comprehensive test ban treaty and promised not to resume atmospheric testing if no other country did so. "Confident and unafraid," he continued, "we labor on—not toward a strategy of annihilation but toward a strategy of peace."

Within less than six weeks, US, Soviet and British negotiators concluded a Test Ban Treaty ending atmospheric testing in Moscow, and Kennedy addressed the American people on July 26. "I speak to you tonight in a spirit of hope," he began. While the treaty would allow underground testing to continue, it would end the "atmospheric tests which have so alarmed mankind" because of their fallout. The treaty was "not a victory for one side—it is a victory for mankind." Open to any nation willing to sign, it might presage further important agreements on other issues. Three times in his presidency, he said, he had had to tell the American people that the US and the USSR "stood on the verge of direct military confrontation—in Laos, in Berlin, and in Cuba." A full-scale nuclear exchange, he continued, would be utterly disastrous for all—an argument that some of his successors would echo in future years, while at least one would dispute it. Already, nuclear fallout had given some young people bone cancer, leukemia, and lung disease. That now might stop. The treaty might also help prevent the spread of nuclear weapons to new nations who in turn might unleash atomic war. Knowing that plenty of opposition to the treaty remained in the US Senate, he assured the nation at length that it would require and allow the US to remain both strong and vigilant, and that it could withdraw from it at any time if necessary. On September 24, after lengthy hearings and debate, the Senate ratified the treaty by a vote of 80–14.

At home, meanwhile, the civil rights crisis entered a new phase in the spring of 1963, when Dr. Martin Luther King led a civil disobedience campaign designed to integrate public accommodations in the segregationist stronghold of Birmingham, Alabama. Shortly thereafter, in early June, the federal government had to use National Guard troops to secure the peaceful admission of two black students to the University of Alabama over the objections of Governor George Wallace. Kennedy now decided to act in sweeping fashion.

On the evening of June 11, the very day after the American University speech, Kennedy addressed the nation on civil rights. The Guardsmen, he said, had assured the admission in Alabama of "two clearly qualified young Alabama residents who happened to have been born Negro." "I hope that every American, regardless of where he lives, will stop and examine his conscience about this and other related incidents. This Nation was founded by men of many nations and backgrounds. It was founded on the principle that all men are created equal, and that the rights of every man are diminished when the rights of one man are threatened." Americans of any color, he said clearly and calmly, should be able freely to attend any public educational institution they selected; "to receive equal service in places of public accommodation;" and to register and vote in elections. The public accommodations proposal broke new ground. "This is not a sectional issue," he continued, prophetically, and noted discontent within northern cities. A moral crisis now demanded congressional action. A few days later, Congress took up legislation covering all these aspects of civil rights, including free access to public accommodations, and the Civil Rights Bill took its place alongside the tax bill as the administration's major legislative priorities as it moved toward a new election year.

Southern Democrats, still determined to preserve the racial status quo in their states, used timeworn techniques to keep either bill from coming to a vote in order to try to prevent action on civil rights at least until the next session. Neither bill had been voted on before Kennedy was assassinated on November 22, 1963. Yet they remained at the top of the legislative agenda when Vice President Lyndon Johnson succeeded to the presidency on that day, and became the basis, along with the Test Ban Treaty, for a truly new era in American life.

On November 27, 1963, Lyndon Johnson, a Texan who had served in the House from 1937 to 1948 and in the Senate from 1949 until 1961, addressed Congress as president for the first time. "The greatest leader of our time has been struck down by the foulest deed of our time," he said. "Today John Fitzgerald Kennedy lives on in the immortal words and works that he left behind. He lives on in the mind and memories of mankind. He lives on in the hearts of his countrymen. . . . The dream of conquering the vastness of space—the dream of partnership across the Atlantic—and across the Pacific as well—the dream of a Peace Corps in less developed nations—the dream of education for all of our children—the dream of jobs for all who seek them and need them—the dream of care for our elderly—the dream of an all-out attack on mental illness—and above all, the dream of equal rights for all Americans, whatever their race or color—these and other American dreams have been vitalized by his drive and by his dedication. And now the ideas and the ideals which he so nobly represented must and will be translated into effective action." Congress and the president, he said, must show that the terrible shock of Kennedy's death would spur them to greater action. "No memorial oration or eulogy," he continued, "could more eloquently honor President Kennedy's memory than the earliest possible passage of the civil rights bill for which he fought so long. We have talked long enough in this country about equal rights. We have talked for one hundred years or more. It is time now to write the next chapter, and to write it in the books of law. . . . And second, no act of ours could more fittingly continue the work of President Kennedy than the early passage of the tax bill for which he fought all this long year. This is a bill designed to increase our national income and Federal revenues, and to provide insurance against recession." Kennedy in 1960 had chosen Johnson as his vice presidential candidate to help carry much of the South, and without much thought about the possibility that he might succeed, but now the choice proved fortuitous. Johnson now combined the country's feeling for Kennedy and what he had stood for—stronger, inevitably, in death than in life—with consummate legislative skill.

Six weeks later, on January 8, 1964, Johnson amplified his call to action in his first annual address, and laid down the goal of surpassing even his mentor Franklin Roosevelt. "Let this session of Congress be known as the session which did more for civil rights than the last hundred sessions combined; as the session which enacted the most far-reaching tax cut of our time; as the session which declared all-out war on human poverty and unemployment in these United States; as the session which finally recognized the health needs of all our older citizens; as the session which reformed our tangled transportation and transit policies; as the session which achieved the most effective, efficient foreign aid program ever; and as the session which helped to build more homes, more schools, more libraries, and more hospitals than any single session of Congress in the history of our Republic." The address also revealed his strategy. Knowing that he would have to overcome widespread conservative opposition to a tax cut, Johnson promised to *reduce* expenditures in the fiscal 1965 budget from $98.4 billion to $97.9 billion, to cut federal employment, and to close down "obsolete institutions" and curtail "less urgent programs."

Turning to his economic plans, he unveiled his own signature phrase. "This administration today, here and now, declares unconditional war on poverty in America," a struggle designed to help the one-fifth of Americans "with incomes too small to meet their basic needs." He called specifically for help for poverty-stricken Appalachia and other depressed areas, for a youth unemployment program such as he had worked on during the New Deal, for "food stamps," a domestic National Service Corps, an expanded minimum wage, aid to education, more libraries, and more hospitals, and for Medicare—all this, along with an $11 billion tax cut. And all these new benefits and opportunities, he continued, would be open to all Americans. "As far as the writ of Federal law will run, we must abolish not some, but all racial discrimination. For this is not merely an economic issue, or a social, political, or international issue. It is a moral issue, and it must be met by the passage this session of the bill now pending in the House." He said relatively little about foreign policy, promising to maintain military superiority and to resist both outright aggression and "the infiltration practiced by those in Hanoi and Havana, who ship arms and men across international borders to foment insurrection," and paraphrasing his predecessor on arms control, NATO, the alliance for progress, foreign aid, and unspecified agreements with the Soviet bloc. He did announce another important move: a substantial reduction in the production of both fissionable uranium and plutonium, the key ingredients of nuclear weapons.

The legislative output of the next two years rivaled 1935–36 in its breadth and significance. The tax cut, the great Civil Rights Act, and the War on Poverty all passed during the 1964 session. Speaking around the nation in the spring of 1964, Johnson put himself squarely in the domestic policy tradition of Wilson, FDR and Truman, and announced his own intention to build a "Great Society."[3] Meanwhile, the Republican Party, for the first time since 1932, nominated a candidate fundamentally opposed not only to those measures, but to all the domestic achievements of the New Deal, including TVA and Social Security, Senator Barry Goldwater of Arizona. In the November election Johnson won 60 percent of the popular vote and carried every state but Arizona and five Deep South States, a contiguous belt from South Carolina to Louisiana—and the Democrats increased their majorities by 37 seats in the House, to 295–140, and by 2 in the Senate, to 68–32. That paved the way for phase II of Johnson's domestic offensive, which he laid out in his January 1965 annual address.

Attempting somewhat awkwardly to find a new rhythm in American history, Johnson began by referring to 1765 as the year that the colonies had first come together in a continental congress, and 1865 as the year that reestablished national unity. Having now "achieved a unity of interest among our people that is unmatched in the history of freedom," he continued, "tonight, now, in 1965, we begin a new quest for union. We seek the unity of man with the world that he has built . . . we seek to establish a harmony between man and society which will allow each of us to enlarge the meaning of his life and all of us to elevate the quality of our civilization." His

---

3 He began using that phrase in April 1964.

language remained vague and elliptical when he returned to this theme later in the speech—"Ahead now is a summit where freedom from the wants of the body can help fulfill the needs of the spirit"—but much stronger when he listed specifics. He proposed help for education at every level, with $1.5 billion in the first year; passage of the Medicare program at last; metropolitan planning and crime control for the cities; more beautiful highways and better pollution control, starting in the Potomac River; a national "foundation" for the arts; amendments to the Taft-Hartley Law to outlaw "right-to-work" laws; new cuts in federal excise taxes; and "an immigration law based on the work a man can do and not where he was born or how he spells his name," which would loosen the strict quotas established forty-one years earlier.

Nor was this all. As Johnson spoke, Dr. Martin Luther King was beginning a new campaign of civil disobedience to register voters in Selma, Alabama, and the administration was already thinking about new voting rights measures, since the voting provisions of the 1964 act had had essentially no impact in the recent election. Like the Birmingham demonstrations nearly two years earlier, this campaign provoked appalling violence from state and local authorities, and Johnson on March 15 met the Congress again with a new message on the right to vote. His new legislation—hearkening back to congressional Reconstruction in 1867—called specifically for federal registrars to register voters in designated districts in the Deep South, the only solution, now as then, to the unshakeable resistance of white officials. Restating his limitless goals in education, feeding the hungry, helping the poor to find their way, protecting the right to vote, and helping "to end hatred among his fellow men" and promoting "love among the people of regions and all races and all parties," he concluded, in the words of a civil rights anthem, "We shall overcome."

And Congress during this session passed not only the Education Bill and Medicare, but also the Voting Rights Act, the new National Endowments for the Arts and for the Humanities, a repeal of some excise taxes, a new, more welcoming immigration law that eventually changed the face of the United States once again, and more. Medicare also included Medicaid, a new program to provide health care for the poor. The economy meanwhile continued to thrive. Yet in that very same year of 1965, Johnson in foreign affairs set himself and the nation on a disastrous course—a perfect example of an Aristotelian tragic hero, whom fate and error doom to catastrophe at the very moment of his greatest triumph.

Neither Eisenhower nor Kennedy, as we have seen, had ever made any but the briefest references to Vietnam in annual addresses, and neither had ever devoted a single major speech to it. Johnson had taken office in the same month that South Vietnamese President Ngo Dinh Diem had been overthrown—a development he had opposed—and he had immediately identified the war there as his gravest foreign danger and highest priority. We have seen that he referred only briefly to "infiltration" from North Vietnam in January 1964, but by March of that year he and the Pentagon were preparing for full-scale American intervention after he had been elected in his own right. And in early August 1964, Johnson had secured almost unanimous congressional support for armed action to resist aggression in Southeast Asia by reporting—in part, falsely—that American destroyers in the Tonkin Gulf had twice been attacked by North Vietnamese patrol boats, while concealing that they had been cruising there while South Vietnamese forces staged attacks from the sea. "The determination of all Americans to carry out our full commitment to the people and to the government of South Viet-Nam will be redoubled by this outrage," he said. In November 1964, after the election, an interagency committee prepared detailed plans for war in Vietnam, and Johnson approved them in early December, while postponing their execution.

The January State of the Union address struck just as visionary a note in foreign affairs as in domestic. "Our Nation was created to help strike away the chains of ignorance and misery and tyranny wherever they keep man less than God means him to be," he said—going further than any previous president—and was now "moving toward that destiny." "Our goal is peace in Southeast Asia," he added—which helped convince quite a few people that he was not going to war there at all. In early February, however, with South Vietnam in turmoil, he approved the execution of the war plan surreptitiously, beginning with a sustained bombing campaign against North Vietnam and the deployment of marines at Da Nang. He refused for months to announce any fundamental change in policy so as not to alarm the public or check the momentum of all his pending legislation. On April 7, 1965, he defined the stakes of the conflict publicly as he saw them in a nationally televised address. "The central lesson of our time is that the appetite of aggression is never satisfied. To withdraw from one battlefield means only to prepare for the next." In the same speech, he offered both North and South Vietnam assistance in developing the Mekong River. Three weeks later, on April 28 and April 30, he also announced that marines were landing in the Dominican Republic to protect American citizens in the midst of a civil war—the first such armed US intervention in Latin America since before Franklin Roosevelt's administration.[4]

Nearly three months later, in a press conference on July 28, Johnson confirmed that 135,000 troops were now going to Vietnam and that more would be sent as needed. He also recited the list of his domestic goals for equal opportunity, decent housing, healing for the sick and dignity for the old. "Without the courage to resist . . . men who hate and destroy," he said, "all that we have built, all that we hope to build, all of our dreams for freedom—all, *all* will be swept away on the flood of conquest."[5]

As the numbers of American troops and casualties rose during the next three years, reaching nearly half a million men and 20,000 killed in action by January 1968, Johnson repeatedly defined the stakes of the conflict in ways that ruled out giving it up short of victory. We were, he said in January 1966, defending national independence in South Vietnam, just as we had in Berlin and in Korea. He had made many offers of peace and he hoped to bring America's sons home soon. "Yet as long as others will challenge America's security and test the clearness of our beliefs with fire and steel, then we must stand or see the promise of two centuries tremble." His terms for peace included a full withdrawal of North Vietnamese troops from South Vietnam and agreement by the Viet Cong—the South Vietnamese Communists—to give up their arms and recognize the South Vietnamese government. Hanoi on the other hand demanded a coalition government in Saigon and eventual reunification of the country. A year later he began with a general statement of his foreign policy goals—"Our objective is not to continue the cold war,

---

4 The troops remained for most of the year.
5 Kaiser, *American Tragedy*, pp. 284–483.

but to end it"—but insisted that the nation was in Vietnam because of the SEATO agreement, the 1962 agreement on Laos, the rights of the people of South Vietnam, and the goals set by the Tonkin Gulf resolution. He could not report that the war was nearly over: "We face more cost, more loss and more agony."

In his January 1968 annual message he insisted that the nation still had the strength to meet its foreign and domestic challenges, and then turned immediately to Vietnam. He boasted that the South Vietnamese had carried out several elections during 1967 and that the enemy had lost battle after battle, but added that North Vietnam continued to pour troops into the South. He repeated his formula for peace talks, enunciated in San Antonio the previous September, that we would accept any offer of "prompt" and "productive" negotiations—a formula designed to avoid the two-year frustration of the Korean peace talks by insisting that the enemy must accept American terms almost at once.[6] Two weeks later, the Tet Offensive struck every major city in South Vietnam, and kicked off the worst year of fighting in the war. After a lengthy debate, Johnson decided not to add yet another 200,000 troops to the half million already there, and on March 31 announced that the United States was halting the bombing of most of North Vietnam in an attempt to get peace talks going. He also stunned the nation by withdrawing from the race for the Democratic presidential nomination. Preliminary talks began in Paris some weeks later, and in the last week of October, on the eve of a new election, the American and North Vietnamese negotiators agreed to start formal talks after a full bombing halt. The talks failed to get going, however, as the South Vietnamese government objected to them.

With Vietnam and new domestic conflict taking up most of Johnson's time, it is not surprising that he could not report many other diplomatic achievements. And in sharp contrast to his two immediate predecessors, he made almost no broadcast reports to the nation on international crises, including the Six Day War between Israel, Egypt, Jordan and Syria in June 1967. On June 25, 1967, he made a very brief and vague statement at the White House about two days of informal talks with Soviet premier Alexei

---

6 Dean Rusk, the secretary of state from 1961 through 1968, had been deeply involved in the Korean talks as well.

Kosygin in Glassboro, New Jersey. On August 21, 1968, he made a short statement condemning the invasion of Czechoslovakia by the Soviet Union and its Warsaw Pact allies to remove a reforming Communist government, and futilely asked them to withdraw. And he declined to address the nation about his administration's greatest diplomatic achievement, the conclusion of the Nuclear Non-Proliferation Treaty with Great Britain and the USSR in mid-1968. When on July 9 he submitted the treaty to the Senate for ratification, he praised it as an outgrowth of the policies of preceding administrations. He did not mention that it included an obligation of the signatories to work toward the elimination of their own nuclear weapons. The Senate did not ratify it until the next year. And in December 1968, Johnson issued only the briefest of statements when the Apollo 8 mission embarked to orbit (but not land on) the moon for the first time, and made no formal announcement when it returned at all.

The Vietnam War also had dramatic impacts on the federal budget and the economy. Johnson in January 1966 promised a deficit of only $1.8 billion for the current year, but suggested that it might be necessary to raise taxes. A year later he had to report expenditures of $126.7 billion and a coming deficit of $9.7 billion—the highest since fiscal 1959—and proposed a two-year, 6 percent surcharge on both personal and corporate income taxes, which Congress eventually agreed to grant. In January 1968 he announced that the Social Security and highway trust funds were now being listed within the overall federal budget, not separately as in the past, raising estimated expenditures for fiscal 1969 to $186 billion with revenues of $178 billion. Inflation, which had been less than 2 percent a year from 1958 through 1965, reached 3.5 percent in 1966 and 4.7 percent in 1968.[7] Interest rates had hit a new high, and Johnson hoped to reduce foreign travel to cut down on the revived balance of payments deficit. And meanwhile, back home, the related issues of civil rights and urban problems took an entirely new turn, marked by big outbreaks of urban violence, the emergence of a new generation of black activists, and rapidly increasing crime rates.

---

7  https://www.thebalance.com/unemployment-rate-by-year-3305506.

On August 15, 1965, Johnson commented on riots in the Watts section of Los Angeles, which eventually left thirty-five people dead, 900 injured, and millions of dollars of property burnt. These disorders, he said, "flow from a violent breach of rooted American principles. . . . There is no greater wrong, in our democracy, than violent, willful disregard of law. . . . To resort to terror and violence . . . strikes from the hand of the Negro the very weapons with which he is achieving his own emancipation. Those who strike at the fabric of ordered liberty also erode the foundation on which the house of justice stands." In January 1966 he called for money to rebuild the "central and slum areas" of American cities and for a fair housing law, but also for more help for law enforcement to "meet the growing menace of crime in the streets." In January 1967, after the Republicans had won a big victory in the off-year elections, gaining 47 seats in the House and 3 in the Senate, Johnson acknowledged that many of the "new instruments of social progress" were going through a process of "trial and error," and that some poverty programs hadn't used their money wisely. He also called in more strident terms for "an all-out effort to combat crime. . . . I will support—with all the constitutional powers the President possesses—our Nation's law enforcement officials in their attempt to control the crime and the violence that tear the fabric of our communities." Riots comparable in scope and impact to the Watts one struck Newark, New Jersey, and Detroit that summer, and on July 24, 1967, Johnson had to issue a proclamation reminiscent of so many others in the past, noting that "conditions of domestic violence and disorder exist in the City of Detroit," that the governor needed federal forces to restore order, and "command[ing] all persons engaged in such acts of violence to cease and desist therefrom." Three days later, on July 27, he devoted one of his very rare broadcast addresses to the nation to civil disorders. Announcing the appointment of a commission to investigate their causes and make recommendations, he noted that the commission would draw on investigations of conspiracy by the FBI. "Let there be no mistake about it," he continued, "the looting, arson, plunder and pillage which have occurred are not part of the civil rights protest"—they were crimes that public authorities must stop. Yet "The only genuine, long-range solution for what has happened lies in an attack—mounted at every level—upon the conditions that breed despair and violence."

In his last annual message six months later, he reaffirmed his commitments both to do more for the inner cities and to escalate the war on crime, including 30 percent more drug control officers and one hundred new FBI agents. When the Commission on Civil Disorders issued its report in March, blaming the disorders principally on the impact of "white racism," Johnson made no public statement about it. A few weeks later, on April 4, James Earl Ray assassinated Martin Luther King, Jr. in Memphis, and new riots struck dozens of American cities. "I know that every American of good will joins me in mourning the death of this outstanding leader and in praying for peace and understanding throughout this land," Johnson said in a brief statement that evening. One week later, on April 11, Johnson signed the Fair Housing Act outlawing racial discrimination in the sale or rental of housing, which Congress had passed in the wake of King's death. It was his last domestic triumph.

Johnson in his last few annual messages made several other proposals: for new measures to provide for presidential disability, as the Twenty-fifth Amendment eventually did; for a 20 percent increase in Social Security benefits; to merge the Departments of Commerce and Labor into a single Department of Business and Labor; and to outlaw most wiretapping and bugging, which did produce a new law. He also proposed a constitutional amendment to increase the term of congressmen to four years and to elect them along with the president. The combination of urban riots, street crime, inflation, and an apparently endless war had soured some of the nation on the Democratic Party and the domestic liberalism that most of it stood for. Before deciding to drop out of the presidential race, Johnson had faced primary challenges first from Senator Eugene McCarthy of Minnesota, and then from Robert Kennedy, now a senator from New York. Vice President Hubert Humphrey entered the race after Johnson dropped out. Primaries in 1968 still selected delegates in only a small minority of states, and Humphrey seemed likely to be nominated even before the June assassination of Robert Kennedy. On the night of Kennedy's shooting on June 5, Johnson addressed the country, stating that the nation "faces once again the consequences of lawlessness, hatred, and unreason in its midst," asking Congress to "pass laws to bring the insane traffic in guns to a halt," and announcing the appointment of another commission to investigate the causes of violence.

Richard Nixon, meanwhile, reemerged as the leader of the Republicans, while George Wallace of Alabama mounted one of the more successful third-party campaigns in US history. Although Nixon won only a narrow electoral victory in November, the Democratic vote fell from 60 percent in 1964 to about 43 percent in 1968, with Nixon and Wallace winning every southern state but Texas. The Republicans gained 5 seats in the House and 5 in the Senate, leaving the Democrats with majorities of 243–192 and 57–43. In a final annual message on January 14, 1969, Johnson focused on domestic issues, arguing that the nation's biggest problems had originated much earlier and must also command the attention of the new administration. He called for increased Social Security benefits, more money for job training, a renewal of the Voting Rights Act (scheduled to expire in 1970), and a renewed commitment to an amended poverty program. Because of full employment and increased revenues, he proudly announced the fiscal 1969 budget would show a surplus of $3.4 billion. "In meeting some [new] challenges," he said frankly, "the Nation has found a new confidence. In meeting others, it knew turbulence and doubt, and fear and hate."

Together the inspiring Kennedy and the legislative master Johnson had enacted a sweeping new agenda at home, including Medicare and critical civil rights legislation. Kennedy's handling of the missile crisis and the subsequent Test Ban Treaty had substantially reduced the tension and danger of the Cold War for the first time. But the emergence of new forms of civil rights activism, urban violence, and above all Johnson's decision to fight and persist in the Vietnam War, had also transformed American politics and destroyed forever the postwar consensus that they had inherited and attempted to expand. The Democratic Party in 1969 had occupied the White House for twenty-eight out of thirty-six years. The Republican Party would now replace them for twenty of the next twenty-four.

# XVIII

## RICHARD NIXON, GERALD FORD, AND JIMMY CARTER

### 1969–74 • 1974–77 • 1977–81

The long, dramatic series of events that forced Richard Nixon from office in 1974 has obscured the remarkable story of his presidency. Like Lyndon Johnson, Nixon had served a long apprenticeship in national politics before winning the office in his second attempt, and like Kennedy and Johnson, he planned to leave a great and lasting impact on the nation and the world. Few other presidents have laid out their agenda so clearly or stuck to it so doggedly during their time in office, and the American people in 1972 rewarded him with a reelection victory comparable to Franklin Roosevelt's in 1936. While he focused above all on attempts to secure world peace, he also had a substantial domestic agenda and tried to reverse some of the policy trends of the previous thirty-six years. It seemed in early 1973 that he might do so, but cascading revelations about the Watergate break-in and cover-up added a whole new dimension to the presidency and brought him down in just nineteen more months.

Misquoting Roosevelt's 1933 inaugural, Nixon on January 20, 1969 argued that now, in contrast to 1933, the nation faced not a material crisis but a spiritual one. Praising America's youth—"better educated, more committed, more passionately driven by conscience than any generation in our history"—he asked all Americans to lower their voices and seek "the decent order that makes progress possible and our lives secure." Then he revealed his true focus. "The greatest honor history can bestow is the title of peacemaker. This honor now beckons America—the chance to help lead the world at last out of the valley of turmoil and onto that high ground of peace that man has dreamed of since the dawn of civilization. . . . Where peace is unknown, make it welcome; where peace is fragile, make it strong; where peace is temporary, make it permanent. After a period of confrontation, we are entering an era of negotiation." No people, he said, should "live in angry isolation"—and the nation eventually learned that he was thinking of Communist China, which four administrations had shunned since 1949. Then, turning to domestic affairs, he cited the unprecedented expansion of government "in this past third of a century," and added that "we are approaching the limits of what government alone can do. Our greatest need now is to reach beyond government, to enlist the legions of the concerned and the committed." Forswearing either "uninspiring ease" or "grim sacrifice," he invited the nation to "join in a high adventure—one as rich as humanity itself, and exciting as the times we live in."

Nixon did not immediately reveal his specific plans for new relations with the Communist powers. Inevitably, he had first to address the ongoing war in Vietnam—the subject of twelve major broadcast addresses in his first four years in office. The peace agreement his national security adviser Henry Kissinger reached with North Vietnam in January 1973 did not prevent the fall of South Vietnam in the spring of 1975, and his military moves kept US casualties high for more than another year and inflicted tremendous damage on Vietnam and Cambodia. Still, Nixon in those first four years sold most of the American people on his strategy of troop withdrawals, occasional escalation of the war, and apparently reasonable peace offers. No other president has communicated so thoroughly with the American people about the progress of a war.

In the first of these addresses on May 14, 1969, Nixon ruled out either an imposed military solution or a precipitate withdrawal that would encourage Communist aggression elsewhere. "If we are to move successfully from an era of confrontation to an era of negotiation," he said, "then we have to demonstrate—at the point at which confrontation is being tested—that confrontation with the United States is costly and unrewarding." The South Vietnamese, he said, had to choose their form of government and their policy themselves, within the framework of their existing government. He insisted on withdrawal of all North Vietnamese forces from South Vietnam,

Laos, and Cambodia, and offered to withdraw all US forces within twelve months in return. On June 10, after meeting with South Vietnamese president Thieu on Midway Island, he announced a withdrawal of 25,000 men. Five months later on November 4—halfway between two enormous student demonstrations against the war in Washington—he elaborated on the same positions in another broadcast address. A quick withdrawal would lead to massacres by the North Vietnamese, he said, but the US had now taken out 60,000 men, the South Vietnamese were assuming more of the burden of the fight under a new "Vietnamization" policy, and US casualties had fallen. This reflected his new "Nixon doctrine": the United States "shall look to the nation directly threatened to assume the primary responsibility of providing the manpower for its defense." Insisting that he could not allow a demonstrating minority to dictate policy, he concluded, "And so tonight—to you, the great silent majority of my fellow Americans—I ask for your support." On December 15 he gave another broadcast address promising 50,000 more troop withdrawals by next April 15, and thanking the country for its support.

A few days after that target date, on April 20, 1970, Nixon said that the training of the South Vietnamese forces had gone so well that he planned to withdraw another 150,000 troops over the next twelve months. Unfortunately, he said, the enemy still insisted on a coalition government in South Vietnam that would lead to a Communist takeover, and the North Vietnamese were increasing their presence in Cambodia and Laos. He insisted that the enemy could not win on the battlefield, or politically either in South Vietnam or in the US. Just ten days later on April 30, he dropped a political bombshell in a new televised address. "Increased enemy activity" in Cambodia and Laos threatened the remaining US troops, he said, and American forces were crossing into Cambodia to attack enemy "sanctuaries." Campus turmoil was continuing and Nixon linked the war to conflict at home. "My fellow Americans," he said, "we live in an age of anarchy, both abroad and at home. We see mindless attacks on all the great institutions which have been created by free civilizations in the last 500 years. Even here in the United States, great universities are being systematically destroyed. Small nations all over the world find themselves under attack from within and from without. If, when the chips are down, the world's most powerful nation, the United States of America, acts like a pitiful, helpless giant, the forces of totalitarianism and anarchy will threaten free nations and free institutions throughout the world." The decision set off new campus demonstrations nationwide, and at Kent State University in Ohio, National Guardsmen called to the campus to keep order shot and killed four students during a demonstration. "This should remind us all once again that when dissent turns to violence, it invites tragedy," Nixon said in a prepared statement. Broadcasting again on June 3, he called the invasion "the most successful operation of this long and very difficult war," listing huge quantities of captured supplies, and promised 50,000 of the scheduled 150,000-man withdrawal by October 15.

On October 7 he addressed the nation again, and abandoned a key peace demand. Instead of insisting on mutual withdrawal of US and North Vietnamese troops, he called for a supervised cease-fire in place and an international conference on peace throughout Indochina. He also asked the enemy immediately to release its American prisoners, whose plight was figuring more and more in his rhetoric. Five days later a new statement promised total withdrawals of 205,000 by Christmas. By the time of the fall elections Nixon had apparently weathered the shock of the Cambodian invasion, and the Democrats gained a modest 12 seats in the House for a 255–180 majority while losing 1 in the Senate,

The Congress meanwhile had banned any US ground action across the borders of South Vietnam, and in March 1971, South Vietnamese troops, with American air support, attacked North Vietnamese bases along the Ho Chi Minh trail in Laos. Although they had to withdraw within a few days, Nixon in another broadcast on April 7 painted the operation as a success that proved that Vietnamization had succeeded, and promised an additional 100,000 troops to be withdrawn by December 1, 1971, for a total of 365,000 taken out since his entry into office. Dramatic developments domestically and elsewhere in the world filled up the news for the rest of 1971, and Nixon did not make his next broadcast address on Vietnam until January 25, 1972. Angered by North Vietnamese claims that he had failed to respond to enemy peace proposals, he revealed that national security adviser Henry Kissinger had visited Paris twelve times for secret talks since August of 1969. His last offer, he explained, called for an American withdrawal within six months of an agreement, a prisoner exchange, a cease-fire all over Indochina, and a new presidential election in South Vietnam. "The only thing this plan does not do," he said, "is to join our enemy to overthrow our ally, which the United States of America will never do." Nixon in these years also frequently referred to cutbacks in draft calls and plans to end the draft altogether, which the Congress did in 1973.

The military situation had improved enormously in South Vietnam because the North Vietnamese Army, after taking huge casualties in 1968–69 offensives, had largely withdrawn from the South in 1970–71. It had however been preparing for by far its biggest offensive yet, which stormed across the borders from North Vietnam, Laos and Cambodia in April 1972. Broadcasting to the nation on April 26, Nixon pointed to "a clear case of naked and unprovoked aggression across an international border," but reported that General Creighton Abrams—the US troop commander since 1968—had assured him that the South Vietnamese would successfully resist it. He defended the newly increased bombing of the North in response and announced that US troop strength would fall to 49,000 by July 1. North Vietnamese advances continued, however, and Nixon took to the airwaves again on May 8. "We now have a clear, hard choice among three courses of action," he said: "immediate withdrawal of all American forces, continued attempts at negotiation, or decisive military action to end the war. . . . There is only one way to stop the killing. That is to keep the weapons of war out of the hands of the international outlaws of North Vietnam." US air power would mine all North Vietnamese harbors to stop supplies coming from the USSR by sea, and bombing would cut rail communications with China to the maximum extent possible. He offered "generous terms": American withdrawal in response to a cease-fire and the return of US prisoners. These new steps, and continued very heavy bombing, managed first to halt, and then in some areas to reverse, the North Vietnamese gains.

Nixon was now campaigning for reelection and his likely Democratic opponent, Senator George McGovern, was demanding an immediate withdrawal from South Vietnam and an end to aid to its government. By the time of the fall campaign Nixon was clearly going to win. On October 27, the American people learned that Henry Kissinger had negotiated an agreement with Hanoi—not from

Nixon or Kissinger, but from the North Vietnamese, who released the text to put pressure on the US and the South Vietnamese to sign it. Later that day Kissinger gave a press conference and announced that "peace is at hand."[1] The agreement left Thieu in power in Saigon, but required no North Vietnamese withdrawal from South Vietnam and pledged Thieu and the Communist National Liberation Front to negotiate South Vietnam's future on a footing of equality. Evidently ambivalent about the agreement, Nixon did not address the nation on Vietnam for the rest of the year, even after his tremendous victory over McGovern. South Vietnamese intransigence delayed progress and induced Kissinger to ask the North for more concessions, which they refused. In the last week of December, Nixon ordered all-out bombing of Hanoi and the port of Haiphong with B-52 aircraft, triggering a firestorm of criticism at least equal to that of the Cambodian invasion. After it was over, Kissinger and the North Vietnamese agreed on almost exactly the same text they had put together in October. On January 23, just days after the deaths of former presidents Truman and Johnson, Nixon told the nation that the new agreement met the conditions that he had laid down in his previous addresses and that the US would still stand by the South Vietnamese government. "To all of you who are listening, the American people," he said, "your steadfastness in supporting our insistence on peace with honor has made peace with honor possible." The agreement did not end the war in Indochina, and US bombing of Communist forces in Cambodia continued, but it marked one critical milestone in Nixon's quest for world peace. During the last eighteen months he had taken two even more dramatic steps in that direction, revolutionizing US relations with Russia and China.

Shortly after taking office, on February 5, Nixon submitted the Nuclear Non-proliferation Agreement to the Senate for ratification. A month later on March 14 he asked for $6–7 billion for an anti-ballistic missile system designed to protect US land-based missiles. Meanwhile, Strategic Arms Limitation talks (SALT) with the USSR began. In a presidential innovation, he began submitting a long, written "State of the World" message to Congress at

---

1 This was the first time in Nixon's first term that Kissinger had spoken publicly at any length.

the beginning of every session, but until the middle of 1971 Nixon had said relatively little to the American people about foreign policy issues other than Vietnam. He dropped the biggest bombshell of his tenure on July 15, 1971, announcing that Kissinger had spent July 9–11 in Beijing[2] and that he himself would visit China early in the next year, "seeking a new relationship with the People's Republic of China." Seven months later, in a "State of the World" radio address on February 9—just weeks before his visit to Beijing—he announced that the nation had a new relationship with China and could have one with the USSR. The administration had concluded a new agreement on access to West Berlin with the Soviets and the SALT talks were nearing agreement in advance of a Moscow summit in May. The China trip was a media spectacular, but Nixon made only a brief statement when he returned, saying that the demonstration that nations with deep differences could discuss them "calmly, rationally and frankly" was "the basis of a structure for peace." The joint communiqué at the end of the visit had confirmed that Taiwan was part of a single China, without resolving its status. The May summit in Moscow seemed threatened after Nixon announced the mining of North Vietnamese harbors on May 8, but it too went ahead, with far-reaching results. In a triumphant address to a joint session of Congress on June 1, he hailed "the treaty and the related executive agreement which will limit, for the first time, both offensive and defensive strategic nuclear weapons in the arsenals of the United States and the Soviet Union." An ABM treaty limited each side to just two ABM sites and the SALT agreement capped land- and sea-based missiles at approximately equal levels. "In the brief space of four months," he said, "these journeys to Peking and to Moscow have begun to free us from perpetual confrontation. We have moved toward better understanding, mutual respect, point-by-point settlement of differences with both the major Communist powers." If this trend continued, "the historians of some future age will write of the year 1972, not that this was the year America went up to the summit and then down to the depths of the valley again, but that this was the year when America helped to lead the world up out of the lowlands of constant war,

---

2  Beijing was spelled Peking in English at that time.

and onto the high plateau of lasting peace." Like Johnson, Nixon never managed to express his enormous hopes gracefully.

By the time of his reelection campaign Nixon had evidently convinced the American people that he was fulfilling his pledge to move to a much more peaceful world. Meanwhile he had pursued an ambitious, multifaceted domestic agenda as well. He gave no State of the Union address in early 1969, but on April 14 of that year he told Congress that while "peace has been the first priority," his administration had many other plans. They included Social Security increases to cover inflation; new measures to fight organized crime, urban crime, narcotics, and pornography; a program to share federal revenues with states and localities; an anti-inflation program; and a reform of the now-controversial welfare system to replace programs "which have aggravated the troubles they were meant to cure, perpetuating a dismal cycle of dependency from one generation to the next." Not only did he follow up on all of these promises, but he also weighed in repeatedly on issues of school integration and had in his last years in office to face the nation's first serious energy crisis.

Nixon's own generation had begun to retire when he took office, and he proposed and signed a series of increases in Social Security benefits designed to more than keep pace with inflation, the major economic issue of his presidency and of the whole of the 1970s. The last of these, in the election year of 1972, finally included his longstanding proposal to index benefits to the rate of inflation, although this provision did not take effect until 1975. Criticizing the growth of centralized power in Washington since 1933, Nixon in October 1969 proposed to share $1 billion to $5 billion in federal revenues with states and localities from 1970 through 1976, and he finally signed this program into law on October 20, 1972. Nixon had made the nationwide crime wave a big issue in the 1968 campaign, and in his first official annual message in January 1970 he declared a "war on crime," calling for federal assistance to local authorities and a federal attack on "organized crime, narcotics and pornography." He signed an omnibus crime bill in January 1971, and two years later, in a radio address on March 10, 1973, he "totally disagreed" with the 1960s philosophy, as he saw it, that society, not criminals, was responsible for crime. "Society is guilty of crime only when we fail to bring the criminal to justice," he said. Nixon also spoke of ending poverty in America—although he also parceled out Johnson's Office of Economic Opportunity among other agencies—and in a televised address on August 8, 1969, he presented the biggest domestic initiative of his presidency, a sweeping welfare reform called the Family Assistance Plan.

The original Social Security Act had established the Aid to Dependent Children program, designed mostly for widows' children. With hardly any discussion by any president, that program had begun to grow precipitously during the 1960s despite the achievement of nearly full employment during that decade, and it had become a political issue. Nixon now seized upon it to try to beat the Democrats at their own anti-poverty game. Having already proposed to exempt two million low-income families from federal taxes, he called for replacing the "colossal failure" of AFDC—which mothers could collect for their children only if the fathers left them—with a set federal benefits for all poor people, combined with work requirements, job training, and even expanded child care. It would provide benefits to the working poor and eliminate the incentive for family breakdown. "Abolishing poverty, putting an end to dependency—like reaching the moon a generation ago—may seem to be impossible," he said. "But in the spirit of Apollo"—referring to the first moon landing in the previous month—"we can lift our sights and marshal our best efforts." The House eventually passed a version of the plan twice, but the Senate refused to do so. It became however the model for much later changes.

In his first annual message in January 1970 and a detailed message on February 10, Nixon also made the new cause of a cleaner environment his own. "The great question of the seventies is, shall we surrender to our surroundings, or shall we make our peace with nature and begin to make reparations for the damage we have done to our air, to our land, and to our water?" he said. This cause was "of particular concern to young Americans. . . . Clean air, clean water, open spaces—these should once again be the birthright of every American. If we act now, they can be." He proposed $10 billion for municipal water treatment plans over five years, and more efficient automobiles for cleaner air. The Congress responded with legislation. Nixon on October 17, 1972 vetoed the Clean Water Act on the grounds that Congress had quadrupled his proposed price tag, but it passed over his veto.

Nixon on the other hand bluntly opposed some new social trends gaining ground in the country. On October 24, 1970, he violently attacked the report of his own National Commission on Obscenity and Pornography, which had concluded that pornography did not increase crime. "Pornography can corrupt a society and a civilization," he said. "The people's elected representatives have the right and obligation to prevent that corruption." And on December 9, 1971, he vetoed a measure that would have established a nationwide system of day care centers for small children. His own welfare reform program, he argued, would already provide child care for welfare recipients going back to work, and the nation needed a broader national debate before taking such a sweeping step. "Good public policy," he said, "requires that we enhance rather than diminish both parental authority and parental involvement with children—particularly in those decisive early years when social attitudes and a conscience are formed, and religious and moral principles are first inculcated."

Mainstream America now accepted the basic principles of the civil rights movement, and Nixon himself declared *Brown vs. Board of Education* to be "right in both constitutional and human terms" and signed the first extension of the Voting Rights Act in 1970. At the same time, he tried to solidify his appeal to white southern voters who might well hold the key to his reelection by nominating two white southerners to fill a Supreme Court vacancy in 1969 and 1970—both of whom the Senate narrowly failed to approve. He also repeatedly and fervently expressed opposition to a new issue that was making its way through the federal courts: the use of crosstown busing to integrate school systems. On March 24, 1970 he attacked it at length. "Several recent decisions by lower courts," he said, "have raised widespread fears that the Nation might face a massive disruption of public education: that wholesale compulsory busing may be ordered and the neighborhood school virtually doomed. . . . I have consistently expressed my opposition to any compulsory busing of pupils beyond normal geographic school zones for the purpose of achieving racial balance. . . . An open society does not have to be homogeneous, or even fully integrated. There is room within it for many communities. Especially in a nation like America, it is natural that people with a common heritage retain special ties;

it is natural and right that we have Italian or Irish or Negro or Norwegian neighborhoods; it is natural and right that members of those communities feel a sense of group identity and group pride." In the same address he cited aid to minority business enterprises and his administration's Philadelphia plan—essentially affirmative action in the construction industry—as effective measures to promote equality. In April 1971, however, the Supreme Court unanimously upheld a busing plan in the Charlotte-Mecklenburg school district of North Carolina to achieve integration.

Nixon's Justice Department had brought more school desegregation suits in Mississippi and Georgia, and he boasted in his 1972 annual address that "Since 1969, we have virtually eliminated the dual school system in the South." In March of that year Governor George Wallace of Alabama won a big victory in the Florida Democratic presidential primary and seemed poised to repeat his third-party bid in 1968 and take more electoral votes away from Nixon. On the very next night, March 16, Nixon demanded action to stop school busing in a broadcast address to the nation. Lower court decisions ordering busing, he said, "have left in their wake confusion and contradiction in the law; anger, fear, and turmoil in local communities; and, worst of all, agonized concern among hundreds of thousands of parents for the education and the safety of their children who have been forced by court order to be bused miles away from their neighborhood schools. . . . Many have invested their life's savings in a home in a neighborhood they chose because it had good schools. They do not want their children bused across the city to an inferior school just to meet some social planner's concept of what is considered to be the correct racial balance or what is called 'progressive' social policy." Since a constitutional amendment would take too long, he asked Congress for immediate legislation to stop busing, but when Congress did address the subject in June he complained when signing the bill on June 23 that its measures were "inadequate, misleading, and entirely unsatisfactory."

Economic policy in general and inflation in particular became serious issues for the Nixon administration. Defense cutbacks were slowing the economy in his first two years. Unemployment rose from 3.4 percent in December 1968 to 6.1 percent in December 1970, but Nixon refused ever to admit that the country was in recession. Inflation meanwhile rose from 4.7 percent in 1968 to 6.2

percent in 1969, and Nixon broadcast an address on the subject on October 17 of that year. Blaming inflation "fundamentally on the past policies of your Government"—deficit spending—he rejected a purposeful economic slowdown and a severe recession, wage and price controls, or government guidelines, relying instead on miscellaneous measures and budget cuts. He stuck to his guns eight months later on June 17, 1970, admitting "some slowdown," but restating his goal of "avoid[ing] a recession while we bring a major inflation to an end." Inflation remained at 5.6 percent and unemployment rose to 6.1 percent in 1971, however. With the election looming, Nixon dramatically reduced course in a new broadcast address on August 15, 1971, combining some stimulus measures with a ninety-day freeze of all wages and prices. The trade balance had also worsened, and he imposed a 10 percent tax on exports and suspended—permanently as it turned out—the convertibility of the dollar into gold. On October 7 he reported to the nation again that the program was working and appointed two new bodies to hold down wages and prices when the freeze expired. And on December 18, after lengthy negotiations with other industrial powers, he announced "the most significant monetary agreement in the history of the world," one which effectively devalued the dollar by about 10 percent against other currencies. Inflation did fall to 3.3 percent in 1971 and held steady in 1972, and unemployment dropped to 5.2 percent as economic growth rose. Despite all his budget rhetoric and occasional vetoes of appropriations bills, Nixon allowed Johnson's income tax surtax to lapse after one more year, and the government ran deficits of $3 billion in fiscal 1970, $23 billion each in the next two fiscal years, and $15 billion in fiscal 1973. Johnson's 1969 budget ran the last federal surplus until 1998. Nixon adopted the idea of the full employment surplus—first put forward by Roosevelt in the late 1930s, and then by Kennedy during his term—to argue that the deficit was in some sense illusory. And in early 1973, the advanced nations abandoned fixed exchange rates altogether, and the dollar began floating freely against other currencies. The trade balance ceased to be an issue as a result.

Nixon had evidently won most of the country over with his foreign policy successes, and had successfully taken the lead on a number of important domestic issues despite the handicap of a Democratic Congress. No president since Franklin Roosevelt had used broadcasts to stay in such continual touch with the American people, both on Vietnam and on several important domestic issues. The Democratic Party, meanwhile, had rewritten its rules after its 1968 defeat to reduce the influence of party bosses. Senator George McGovern of South Dakota, a leading opponent of the Vietnam War and a favorite of young voters, won a series of primary victories against establishment candidates Hubert Humphrey and Senator Edmund Muskie of Maine, and eventually won the nomination at a bitter Democratic convention. Meanwhile, an assassination attempt paralyzed George Wallace from the waist down, making a second third-party run impossible. In November, only days after Kissinger had announced that peace was at hand in Vietnam, Nixon won the most overwhelming Republican victory in history to date, with 60.7 percent of the popular vote and every electoral vote except those of Massachusetts and the District of Columbia. The Republicans reversed the 1970 outcome in the House, winning 12 new seats to cut the Democratic majority to 243–192, but the Democrats increased their Senate majority by 2, to 56–42.

"When we met here 4 years ago," Nixon began his second inaugural, "America was bleak in spirit, depressed by the prospect of seemingly endless war abroad and of destructive conflict at home. As we meet here today, we stand on the threshold of a new era of peace in the world. . . . Just as building a structure of peace abroad has required turning away from old policies that have failed, so building a new era of progress at home requires turning away from old policies that have failed. . . . In our own lives, let each of us ask—not just what will government do for me, but what can I do for myself?[3] . . . Above all else, the time has come for us to renew our faith in ourselves and in America. In recent years, that faith has been challenged. Our children have been taught to be ashamed of their country, ashamed of their parents, ashamed of America's record at home and its role in the world. At every turn we have been beset by those who find everything wrong with America and little that is right. But I am confident that this will not be the judgment of history on these remarkable times in which we are privileged to live. . . . Let us pledge together to make these next 4 years the best

---

3 The paraphrase of his great rival Kennedy in 1961 was unmistakable.

4 years in America's history, so that on its 200th birthday America will be as young and as vital as when it began, and as bright a beacon of hope for all the world."

It was not to be. Seven months earlier, on June 17, 1972, five burglars hired by officials of Nixon's reelection committee and his White House staff had been arrested burglarizing the Democratic National Committee in the Watergate building in Washington. Despite a good deal of press reporting, the White House had kept the story under control until after the election, but the Senate had now created a select committee to investigate the break-in and the possible responsibility of higher officials. By the end of April 1973 the Watergate scandal had replaced Vietnam as the continuing story of the Nixon administration, and just sixteen months later it forced Nixon to become the first and only president to resign his office.

On March 12, 1973, Nixon issued a long statement on the concept of executive privilege, claiming that it would exempt any White House aides from testifying before the Senate committee. On April 17, in a brief broadcast statement, he claimed to have begun new inquiries of his own after hearing new information about the scandal on March 21, and said that "real progress has been made in finding the truth." On April 30, he claimed to have learned "new information" about the cover-up of responsibility for the Watergate break-in since then, and accepted the resignations of his two top aides, Chief of Staff H. R. Haldeman and chief domestic aide John Ehrlichman, and of Attorney General Richard Kleindienst. He rejected any implication that they were guilty of anything. He also denied having supervised the 1972 campaign—in contrast to every earlier campaign—but accepted responsibility for any wrongdoing the campaign had carried out. He also announced the resignation of Counsel to the President John Dean, who was about to accuse Nixon himself of participating in the cover-up, partly by authorizing payments to the accused Watergate burglars. Responding to new revelations on May 22, he denied any prior knowledge of the burglary and any participation in the cover-up, including discussions of executive clemency for the burglars or fund-raising for them. He defended wiretaps of newsmen and staffers in 1969 designed to trace the leak of secret bombing of Cambodia, and the creation of the so-called Plumbers Squad in the White House, composed of former intelligence operatives, who had broken into the office of the psychiatrist of Daniel Ellsberg, who had leaked the *Pentagon Papers*, a secret history of the Vietnam War, to the press in 1971. Nixon had meanwhile agreed to appoint a special prosecutor, Archibald Cox, to investigate the burglary and cover-up. Testimony in the Senate committee over the next few months revealed that Nixon had been recording all his conversations in the Oval Office, and both the committee and the special prosecutor immediately subpoenaed some of them.

On August 15 Nixon gave another broadcast address on Watergate. "As the weeks have gone by," he said, "it has become clear that both the hearings themselves and some of the commentaries on them have become increasingly absorbed in an effort to implicate the President personally in the illegal activities that took place." He insisted once again that he had not known of any cover-up until March 21, and explained that he could not turn over any recordings of conversations because it would weaken the presidency. In a separate scandal, Vice President Spiro Agnew resigned his office on October 9 and pleaded nolo contendere to having taken bribes as governor of Maryland. "I respect your decision," Nixon wrote him on October 10, "and I also respect the concern for the national interest that led you to conclude that a resolution of the matter in this way, rather than through an extended battle in the Courts and the Congress, was advisable in order to prevent a protracted period of national division and uncertainty." Nixon chose House Republican leader Gerald Ford to replace Agnew, and Congress confirmed him under the new Twenty-fifth Amendment.

The Watergate crisis escalated on Saturday, October 20. After trying and failing to get Special Prosecutor Cox to drop his request to hear tapes, Nixon asked his attorney general, Elliot Richardson, to fire Cox. When both Richardson and his deputy William Ruckelshaus refused to do so, Nixon fired them both, and Solicitor General Robert Bork, fired Cox. Nixon made no public statement at this time, but such was the outburst of criticism that he reversed course on two fronts almost immediately, agreeing to release some tapes and appointing a new special prosecutor, Leon Jaworski. The House Judiciary Committee meanwhile began a formal impeachment inquiry.

The emerging scandal changed Nixon's relationship with Congress and cut into his power in foreign affairs. On June 27,

1973, he vetoed an appropriations bill that included an immediate ban on any further bombing of Cambodia. The House sustained that veto, but on August 3 he had to acknowledge that Congress had now passed such a ban. He still warned that "the American people" would respond to any renewed North Vietnamese aggression against South Vietnam. He also vetoed a War Powers Resolution that curtailed the president's power to deploy troops without a declaration of war on October 24, calling it unconstitutional, but the Congress passed it over his veto as well.

An unprecedented energy crisis struck the country in the fall of 1973. Egypt and Syria attacked Israel to try to regain territory lost in 1967 in October, and the Arab nations imposed an oil embargo on western countries. This, Nixon explained in a November 7 broadcast address, had exacerbated an already looming energy shortage, and the country would be 10–17 percent short of its normal energy requirements during the winter. In the short term he demanded that home and office temperatures drop to 68°, that speed limits drop to 50 mph nationwide, and that daylight saving time be extended year-round. Meanwhile he asked for a long-term program like the Manhattan or Apollo project to make the nation self-sufficient once again by increasing coal use and nuclear power, partly with the help of new breeder reactors. The Congress immediately passed legislation freezing the price of "old" domestic oil to prevent profiteering by the oil companies. On March 6, 1974 Nixon vetoed Congress's new emergency energy act because it tried too hard to hold costs down, included a new program to fight unemployment, and promised too much in consumer loans to insulate houses. Congress amended it to his specifications.

In his January 1974 annual message Nixon promised to cooperate with the House impeachment investigation, but also called for bringing all the Watergate investigations to an end. "One year of Watergate is enough," he said, and he had "no intention whatever of ever walking away from the job that the people elected me to do." The message struck a triumphal note, referring once again to the state of the nation in early 1969—confrontation with the USSR, isolation from China, war in Southeast Asia, "burning and besieged" cities, the "battleground" of college campuses, terrifying increases in crime and drug addiction, and no action on the environment.

He listed all the measures taken to solve those problems. Despite "prophets of doom," he added, "There will be no recession in the United States of America." Discussions to end the oil embargo were proceeding. His last budget for fiscal 1975 forecast receipts of $295 billion and spending of $304.4 billion.

On April 29, 1974, Nixon made another preemptive Watergate strike, releasing many hundreds of pages of transcripts of his conversations which, he claimed, proved his innocence. In June he toured the Middle East, reporting on his return on June 19 that millions of people had shown their friendship for the United States in the streets of Damascus and Cairo—capitals of nations with whom the US was improving relations after the 1973 war. He visited Russia for the second time later that month, and reported to the American people on the trip on July 3 "Our generation, which has known so much war and destruction—four wars in this century—now has an opportunity to build for the next generation a structure of peace in which we hope war will have no part whatever," he said. Moves toward peace in the Middle East, a new spirit in NATO, and a new relationship with the USSR, he said, promised "a continuing, irreversible process that will build its own momentum and will develop into a permanent peace."

In late July, the Supreme Court unanimously ordered Nixon to turn over additional tape recordings of key Watergate-related conversations, and he agreed to comply. On July 25 he gave another broadcast address to the nation on inflation, once again rejecting wage and price controls and relying on the Federal Reserve and the public spirit of the American people to fight it, and declining even to mention the possibility of recession. Late that month the House Judiciary Committee voted articles of impeachment. On August 5 Nixon released transcripts of three conversations between him and H. R. Haldeman on June 23, 1972—just six days after the Watergate break-in. They showed him authorizing Haldeman to tell the director and assistant director of the CIA to ask the FBI to curtail the Watergate investigation so as not to expose CIA operations—which in fact did not exist. "I am firmly convinced that the record, in its entirety, does not justify the extreme step of impeachment and removal of a President," he said. "I trust that as the constitutional process goes forward, this perspective will prevail." Instead, his support collapsed completely even within the

Republican Party, and on August 8, he announced his resignation. "Throughout the long and difficult period of Watergate," he said, "I have felt it was my duty to persevere, to make every possible effort to complete the term of office to which you elected me. In the past few days, however, it has become evident to me that I no longer have a strong enough political base in the Congress to justify continuing that effort.... To continue to fight through the months ahead for my personal vindication would almost totally absorb the time and attention of both the President and the Congress in a period when our entire focus should be on the great issues of peace abroad and prosperity without inflation at home." He concluded with a reference to the original hopes for peace he had expressed on January 20, 1969.

Nixon had followed the model of the powerful, activist president that the two Roosevelts, Wilson, Truman, Eisenhower, Kennedy and Johnson had established. In foreign affairs, one might argue, he had picked up where Kennedy had left off, and they remain the two great peacemakers of the Cold War era. Domestically he had accepted and in some ways added to Johnson's vision of the Great Society in the same way that Eisenhower had accepted the New Deal, while trying to cut back the role of the federal government somewhat and to find a new equilibrium on civil rights. Yet he had also created the climate within his administration that led to the Watergate break-in, and later revelations confirmed that he had directed the cover-up from the beginning.[4] The unfolding of that scandal created a new model of presidential relations with Congress and a new role for the press that changed American politics for the rest of the century and beyond. His presidency fit the mold of a classical tragedy every bit as much as those of his two predecessors, and marked the beginning of the end of the era of heroic leadership in the United States.

Gerald Ford was to some extent a throwback to the vice presidents of earlier eras, a loyal party politician who had never shown any presidential ambitions himself. His twenty-five years in the House set a new presidential record for previous national service.

---

4 Stanley Kutler, *Abuse of Power, The New Nixon Tapes* (New York, 1997).

"My fellow Americans," he declared on his first day in office on August 9, 1974, "our long national nightmare is over. . . . As we bind up the internal wounds of Watergate, more painful and more poisonous than those of foreign wars, let us restore the golden rule to our political process, and let brotherly love purge our hearts of suspicion and of hate." Three days later, addressing a joint session of Congress, he stated his "motto" toward the Congress: "communication, conciliation, compromise, and cooperation." Although he found the state of the union "excellent," "the state of our economy is not so good. . . . the unanimous concern of America is inflation," and the people blamed the government. He pledged to balance the budget by fiscal 1976. He also promised to continue "the outstanding foreign policy of President Nixon. . . . A strong defense is the surest way to peace. Strength makes détente attainable." The nation rallied around the genial, unpretentious Midwesterner, but Ford dropped a bombshell on September 8. "The tranquility to which this nation has been restored by the events of recent weeks," he declared, "could be irreparably lost by the prospects of bringing to trial a former President of the United States." He therefore granted Nixon an unprecedented pardon for any crimes that he "has committed or may have committed or taken part in" during the whole of his presidency—the only such blanket pardon ever issued by a president of the United States. Ford's popularity never recovered from that step. The anti-Watergate backlash and the domestic economic crisis led in November to a midterm landslide. The Democrats gained 49 House seats, their biggest win since 1958, and 4 Senate seats, leaving them with majorities of 291–144 and 61–39.

Inflation, energy and unemployment dominated Ford's presidency at home. In his first annual message in January 1975 he contrasted himself with Truman in 1949: "I must say to you that the state of the Union is not good: Millions of Americans are out of work. Recession and inflation are eroding the money of millions more." He proposed a one-year, $16 billon tax cut to fight the recession, a 5 percent cap on federal pay and Social Security increases, and new spending restraints. The price of energy had now quadrupled in a single year, and he promised a new tax on imported oil, plans to decontrol the price of domestic crude oil, and initiatives to increase the mining and use of coal. The Democratic Congress quickly passed the tax cut but refused to lift controls on domestic crude. On October 6, 1975, Ford broadcast a major address on the economy. Conservative Ronald Reagan, who had just finished two terms as governor of California, was clearly planning to challenge him for the Republican nomination, and Ford asked the nation to reverse the budgetary trends of the last four decades. "We must decide," he said, "whether we shall continue in the direction of recent years—the path toward bigger government, higher taxes, and higher inflation—or whether we shall now take a new direction" by cutting both taxes and spending at once. He asked for a permanent $28 billion tax cut in place of the soon-to-expire temporary one and a balancing reduction of spending, which had doubled in the eight years after 1962 and would double again in the next year without cuts. The nation must cut "the swollen federal bureaucracy." "America's greatness was not built by taxing people to their limits, but by letting our people exercise their freedom and their ingenuity to their limits . . . only by getting the Government off your back and out of your pocket will we achieve our goals of stable prices and more jobs."

Ford returned to the same themes in his January 1976 annual address, which looked forward to the coming bicentennial celebration. He called specifically for the deregulation of key industries—"the airlines, trucking, railroads, and financial institutions"—higher production of coal and nuclear energy, and cuts in estate taxes. He also proposed block grants to the states to consolidate programs for education, health care, and poverty. In June he sent Congress a message on school busing, arguing, like Nixon, that court decisions had gone too far, and suggesting a five-year limit on all busing orders, which should also be limited to remedies for proven discrimination. Commenting on the work of the Congress on October 5, however, he had to acknowledge that Congress had failed to act on most of his major proposals, including his tax cut and most of his energy legislation. Unemployment fell only from 7.2 percent in 1974 and 8.2 percent in 1975 to 7.8 percent in 1976, while inflation in the same three years registered 12.3 percent, 6.9 percent, and 4.9 percent. Prices had now risen 83 percent in the last eleven years.[5]

---

5 https://www.thebalance.com/unemployment-rate-by-year-3305506.

Attempting with the help of Secretary of State Henry Kissinger to continue Nixon's foreign policies,[6] Ford had to contend with criticisms of détente from Republicans like Reagan and with a newly assertive Congress. The Watergate scandal had led to a series of revelations of wrongdoing in the FBI and the Central Intelligence Agency, which two congressional committees began investigating in 1975. Ford complained in his January 1975 annual message that Congress had passed too many legislative restrictions on foreign policy recently "under the stress of the Vietnam war." In February he strongly protested a congressional ban on aid to Turkey, which was involved in a serious conflict with Greece over the future of Cyprus. And by the time he addressed a joint session of Congress on foreign policy on April 10, he faced the most serious setback to US policy in the Cold War, the impending military collapse of South Vietnam.

Ford began by boasting once again of "a more stable, if still competitive relationship" with the USSR, the beginning of strategic arms control, and "an historic opening" with China. Peace in Southeast Asia after the American withdrawal two years earlier, he said, depended on "publicly stated premises": that the US would help "sustain the terms" of the Paris accords and that it would continue to assist the South Vietnamese. Congress, however, had reduced aid requests in 1974, and the North Vietnamese had begun another major invasion of the South early in the year. While conceding that the US might have to evacuate all personnel from South Vietnam, he asked for $722 million in additional military assistance. While reevaluating American commitments abroad, he said, "We cannot, in the meantime, abandon our friends while our adversaries support and encourage theirs. We cannot dismantle our defenses, our diplomacy, or our intelligence capability while others increase and strengthen theirs." Turning to the USSR, he insisted that he would not allow détente "to become a license to fish in troubled waters," but complained that Congress had blocked the extension of most-favored-nation trade status to Moscow by insisting that the Soviets liberalize their immigration policies for Soviet Jews. And while intelligence agencies needed congressional

---

6 Kissinger had become secretary of state in 1973.

oversight, he said, "a sensationalized public debate over legitimate intelligence activities is a disservice to this Nation and a threat to our intelligence system. . . . We cannot afford indecision, disunity, or disarray in the conduct of our foreign affairs."

Ford's aid request for South Vietnam had come much too late to affect the course of events. He had to announce the evacuation of Phnom Penh, the Cambodian capital that was falling to Khmer Rouge guerrillas, just two days later, and by the last week of April the fall of Saigon was clearly imminent. Speaking in New Orleans on April 26—away from Kissinger's watchful eye—Ford had his finest hour. "Today," he said, "America can regain the sense of pride that existed before Vietnam. But it cannot be achieved by refighting a war that is finished as far as America is concerned. As I see it, the time has come to look forward to an agenda for the future, to unify, to bind up the Nation's wounds, and to restore its health and its optimistic self-confidence." Kissinger immediately began blaming the Congress, as well as the USSR, for the debacle, but Ford never did.

About three months later, on October 8, 1975, Ford spoke at the Helsinki European security conference, whose Final Act recognized the altered borders of Europe after 1945 and pledged all its signatories to respect basic human rights. "The era of confrontation that has divided Europe since the end of the Second World War may now be ending," he said cautiously. "There is a new perception and a shared perception of a change for the better, away from confrontation and toward new possibilities for secure and mutually beneficial cooperation. . . . Participation in the work of détente and participation in the benefits of détente must be everybody's business—in Europe and elsewhere. But détente can succeed only if everybody understands what détente actually is." Hostility toward the Soviets was growing, however, partly because they and Cuba had intervened in a civil war in newly independent Angola, where Congress had prevented Ford from subsidizing a rival revolutionary faction in return. The SALT II treaty was now complete, but Ford never submitted it to Congress. And on March 1, 1976, shortly after winning a narrow victory in the New Hampshire primary over Reagan, Ford in a television interview announced that he would no longer characterize US policy as "détente," but rather as "peace through strength."

Governor Jimmy Carter of Georgia was meanwhile winning the Democratic presidential nomination against a wide range of Democrats. Ford faced one of the strongest intraparty challenges ever mounted against an incumbent from Reagan, but won a narrow first ballot victory at the Republican convention. Promising to restore trust in government and adopt a national energy policy, Carter began the campaign with a big lead, but eventually emerged with only a narrow victory. Splitting the Northeast and the Midwest with Ford and losing all the mountain states and the Far West, Carter won with 297 electoral votes to 240 by carrying every southern and border state but Virginia, and winning the popular vote by 2 percentage points. The Democrats meanwhile retained their large congressional majorities, gaining 1seat in the House while losing 1 in the Senate. In his final annual message in January Ford boasted of lowering inflation and unemployment, defended executive authority in international affairs again, and called for stronger military forces to meet a Soviet buildup. In no way did his policies differ significantly either from his predecessor's or his successor's—and none of them managed to find solutions to continuing high inflation, higher unemployment, and energy shortages.

Jimmy Carter, as he always preferred to be called, gave one of the most general inaugural addresses in history on January 20, 1977. A devout Southern Baptist who probably referred more frequently to his faith than any predecessor, he opened with a quotation from Micah, and called for a new spirit in the land: "Let us learn together and laugh together and work together and pray together, confident that in the end we will triumph together in the right." He had campaigned against the lies and criminal acts of previous administrations, and he continued in that vein as well: "Let our recent mistakes bring a resurgent commitment to the basic principles of our Nation, for we know that if we despise our own government, we have no future." And he added his signature foreign policy issue: "Because we are free, we can never be indifferent to the fate of freedom elsewhere. Our moral sense dictates a clear-cut preference for those societies which share with us an abiding respect for individual human rights. We do not seek to intimidate, but it is clear that a world which others can dominate with impunity would be inhospitable to decency and a threat to the well-being of all people." On the very next day, he kept another campaign promise, issuing a blanket pardon for Vietnam-era draft resisters and deserters, except those charged with force and violence. Then, following in Nixon's and Ford's footsteps, he turned to his most important domestic priority, a new energy policy.

"Tonight," Carter began a broadcast address to the nation on April 18, 1977, "I want to have an unpleasant talk with you about a problem that is unprecedented in our history. With the exception of preventing war, this is the greatest challenge that our country will face during our lifetime. . . . The energy crisis has not yet overwhelmed us, but it will if we do not act quickly." "National catastrophe," he said, could be the only alternative to his "unpopular proposals." Since 1973 domestic production had fallen and imports had doubled, and the world might not have enough available oil by the early 1980s and use up its whole supply by the end of that decade. The nation had to shift from reliance on oil and natural gas "to strict conservation and to the renewed use of coal and to permanent renewable energy sources like solar power." The United States was "the most wasteful nation on earth" in its energy use. Oil imports now totaled $36 billion a year and could reach $550 billion by 1985.[7] The nation needed more coal production, smaller cars, and better public transportation—or else more nuclear power plants, which had become highly controversial politically. "This difficult effort will be the 'moral equivalent of war,'" he said, "except that we will be uniting our efforts to build and not to destroy." In a progress report to the nation on November 8, he lauded the Congress for creating the Department of Energy, but had to repeat and expand upon the same themes. The United States had not only to reduce energy consumption but also to let oil and gas prices rise to encourage production. "This will not be the last time that I, as President, present difficult and controversial choices to you and ask for your help," he said. "I believe that the duties of this office permit me to do no less." He made the same proposals in his January 1978 annual message, noting that Congress had passed the Surface Mining Control and Reclamation Act and approved a new Alaska pipeline. In the 1978 midterm elections the Democrats lost

---

7 This turned out to be an extraordinary overestimate. The US spent $32 billion on crude oil imports in 1985. See https://www.census.gov/foreign-trade/statistics/historical/petr.pdf.

3 Senate seats and 15 house seats in the midterm elections, leaving them with majorities of 58–41 and 277–157.

Carter mixed the themes of discipline and sacrifice with movement toward the free market in another broadcast address to the nation on energy on April 5, 1979. The US must increase oil, gas and coal production at home, and the recent accident at the Three Mile Island nuclear plant in Pennsylvania, he said, "has demonstrated dramatically that we have other energy problems." He announced plans to begin lifting price controls on domestic oil on June 1. That would raise prices still further, and he proposed a windfall profits tax on oil companies, the proceeds to provide an "energy security fund" for low-income families, to pay for mass transit, and "to put American genius to work solving our long-range energy problems." "This is a painful step," he said typically, "and I'll give it to you straight: Each of us will have to use less oil and pay more for it. But this is a necessary step, and I want you to understand it fully."

On July 15, 1979, after a long series of meetings with political, business, labor and opinion leaders at Camp David, Carter broadcast the most controversial address of his presidency. He explained that he had originally planned to talk once more about energy, but that his meetings had convinced him that legislation alone could not fix that great problem. The "fundamental threat to American democracy," he said, was "a crisis of confidence . . . that strikes at the very heart and soul and spirit of our national will . . . the growing doubt about the meaning of our own lives and in the loss of a unity of purpose for our nation." Nor was this all. "In a nation that was proud of hard work, strong families, close-knit communities, and our faith in God, too many of us now tend to worship self-indulgence and consumption. . . . As you know, there is a growing disrespect for government and for churches and for schools, the news media, and other institutions." He blamed these changes on the assassinations of John and Robert Kennedy and Martin Luther King, Jr., "the agony of Vietnam," "the shock of Watergate," ten years of inflation, and the oil embargo. The country now had to choose between "the path that leads to fragmentation and self-interest" and "a mistaken idea of freedom" on the one hand, and "the path of common purpose and the restoration of American values" that "leads to true freedom for our Nation and ourselves" on the other. Solving our energy problems by adopting his long-standing proposals would be a first step.

Carter had identified real problems and real changes. He did not mention that the widespread availability of birth control, the legalization of abortion in 1973, and the entrance of far more women into the workforce had also slowed population growth from 19 percent in the 1950s to 13.4 percent during the 1960s and just 11.4 percent in the 1970s, reaching a total of 203 million in 1980. His claim that the nation was failing to live up to his own high moral standards, however, fell flat. The address immediately became known as his "malaise" speech, although that word did not appear in it.[8] Carter's policies did change the energy picture somewhat. Congress passed a windfall profits tax on crude oil in April 1980, and conservation did cut oil and natural gas use and oil imports into the early 1980s, while coal consumption rose. Other events however made the energy situation worse.

Meanwhile Carter had followed centrist economic policies. In his first major message to Congress on January 31, 1977, he did ask for a two-year, $31.2 billion economic recovery program to fight the recession, including a public works program, some tax breaks, and 415,000 public service jobs. He repeated that proposal in an address to the nation two days later, but also promised significantly to reduce the size of the federal government, beginning with one-third of the White House staff; to cut down on regulations; and to reform the welfare system. In his first annual message on January 19, 1978, however, he noted that Congress had not passed his plan to consolidate several welfare programs into one, or to expand the earned income tax credit, which Congress had passed in 1975 to help low earners. He also presented a budget that increased federal spending by just 2 percent, the lowest figure in many years. Inflation remained a serious problem, and Carter addressed the nation about it on October 24, 1978. Admitting that he had not controlled it, he promised that "fighting inflation will be a central preoccupation of mine during the months ahead" and asked the nation to join in. Rejecting either wage and price controls or a severe recession to control it, he noted that the federal deficit was

---

8 On July 9, Clark Clifford, the longtime Washington lawyer and sometime public servant, had told the *Washington Post* that Carter was concerned by the "national malaise" that he had noticed on travels around the country. "Camp David Talks Cover Wide Range," *Washington Post*, July 10, 1979, p. A1.

coming down, that a single federal agency had eliminated "nearly 1000 unnecessary regulations," and that the Congress had deregulated air travel—as Ford had originally suggested—in the previous year. He hoped to do the same for railroads and trucking. In his January 1979 annual message he called for "first steps to develop a national health plan" to control hospital costs, but he rejected Senator Edward Kennedy's call for national health insurance. His January 1979 budget message presented a "lean and austere" fiscal 1980 budget, with the deficit falling from the current $37 billion to $29 billion. Unemployment—7.8 percent when he took office—stubbornly refused to fall below 6 percent in 1978 and 1979. While Carter did not say a great deal about civil rights, he broadened that issue to include women in his 1978 annual message: "A major priority for our Nation is the final elimination of the barriers that restrict the opportunities available to women and also to black people and Hispanics and other minorities."

Foreign affairs became the arena of Carter's biggest successes and most serious setbacks. His first annual message in January 1978 restated his commitment to worldwide human rights, "the heart of our identity as a nation." He did not mention that his new SALT proposal the previous year for more drastic arms cuts had been immediately rejected by the Soviets, but held out hope for a new agreement in the coming year. On February 1, 1978, Carter addressed the nation about the pending Panama Canal Treaty, which would return sovereignty over the Canal Zone, and later over the canal itself, to Panama. The terms of the original treaty dissatisfied the Panamanian people, he said, and President Johnson had begun renegotiating it with the support of ex-presidents Truman and Eisenhower. Former president Ford and former secretaries of state Rusk and Kissinger and the Joint Chiefs now endorsed the new pact, and the Joint Chiefs also approved of it. The treaty, he said, "will strengthen our position in the world" and lead to a new era in relations with Latin America. Theodore Roosevelt, he proclaimed boldly, would have approved of it. The Senate subsequently ratified it by a narrow margin. A few months later, on September 18, 1978, Carter spoke to a joint session of Congress about the successful conclusion of many days of negotiations at Camp David with President Anwar Sadat of Egypt and Prime Minister Menachem Begin of Israel for peace in the Middle East. The agreements, he said, would provide a real peace, including full diplomatic relations, between Israel and Egypt, nations who had fought four wars from 1948 to 1973; reached agreement "on secure and recognized boundaries, the end of military occupation, and the granting of self-government or else the return to other nations of territories which have been occupied by Israel since the 1967 conflict"; and give the Palestinian people a role "in the resolution of the Palestinian problem in all its aspects." The agreement called for further agreement "on the final status of [occupied] West Bank and Gaza" within five years. He repeatedly paid tribute to Sadat and Begin, who eventually received the Nobel Peace Prize for the accord. "Let me say," he concluded, "that for many years the Middle East has been a textbook for pessimism, a demonstration that diplomatic ingenuity was no match for intractable human conflicts. Today we are privileged to see the chance for one of the sometimes rare, bright moments in human history—a chance that may offer the way to peace." Although many of these goals remain unfulfilled decades later, those accords rank with Theodore Roosevelt's mediation of the Russo-Japanese War as the most remarkable episodes of personal diplomacy by any president. And three months later, on December 15, Carter broadcast his announcement of the establishment of full diplomatic relations with the People's Republic of China, while maintaining "nongovernmental" relations with Taiwan. This step, he said, "will be of great long-term benefit to the peoples of both our country and China—and, I believe, to all the peoples of the world."

In his January 1979 annual message Carter looked forward to a "sound, verifiable" SALT II agreement. Carter had revived the use of "détente" to describe the goal of Soviet-American relations, but now, a series of shocking events ushered in a new, heightened phase of the Cold War instead.

In March 1979, a popular revolution forced the Shah of Iran—a close American ally since US and British intelligence had placed him in power in 1953—to flee his country, and a theocratic regime soon took power. Carter made only fleeting references to these events for months, usually in connection with their impact on oil supplies. On October 1, he broadcast an alarming report to the nation on "persuasive evidence" of a new Soviet combat brigade in Cuba. The brigade, he said, "raises the level of responsibility that the Soviet Union must take for escalating Cuban military actions abroad," a reference to the intervention of Cuban troops in the civil war in newly independent Angola. He announced more maneuvers in the Caribbean and a new joint task force headquarters in Key West. At the same time, he called again for the Senate to ratify the SALT II agreement. "SALT II is crucial to American leadership and to the further strengthening of the Western Alliance," he said. "The purpose of the SALT II treaty and the purpose of my actions in dealing with Soviet and Cuban military relationship are exactly the same—to keep our Nation secure and to maintain a world at peace." The government meanwhile had decided to let the deposed Shah of Iran come to the United States for cancer treatment, and in early November, Iranian revolutionaries retaliated by entering the US Embassy in Teheran and seizing more than sixty Americans as hostages. The White House press office on November 9 simply issued a statement affirming that the president shared the nation's outrage, frustration, and anger over these events, but that also called on all Americans "to exercise restraint" for the sake of the safety of the hostages.

In the last days of 1979, the Soviet Union invaded neighboring Afghanistan to restore a pro-Soviet government that had lost power. Addressing the nation once more on January 4, 1980, Carter announced a new, more serious phase of the Cold War, and linked it to the global energy situation. The invasion, he said, "is an extremely serious threat to peace because of the threat of further Soviet expansion into neighboring countries in Southwest Asia and also because such an aggressive military policy is unsettling to other peoples throughout the world." The new move threatened Iran and Pakistan and was a "stepping stone to possible control over much of the world's oil supplies." Reviving the domino theory, he said that the Soviets would go even further if encouraged by success, and "threaten the security of all nations." Under the circumstances, no nation "can continue to do business as usual with the Soviet Union." Carter announced the withdrawal of the American ambassador from Moscow, a partial embargo on grain exports to the USSR, and a pause in any further action on the SALT treaty. His annual message on January 23 specifically linked the Iranian hostage crisis, the free world's dependence on Middle Eastern oil, and the new act of Soviet aggression. After reviewing major episodes in the containment of the USSR from the 1940s through the 1970s, he proclaimed what immediately became known as the Carter doctrine: "An attempt by any outside force to gain control of the Persian Gulf region will be regarded as an assault on the vital interests of the United States of America, and such an assault will be repelled by any means necessary, including military force." He also announced a greater US naval presence in the Indian Ocean, stronger ties with Middle Eastern nations and Pakistan, and an American boycott of the coming Summer Olympics in Moscow. He repeated his energy proposals, focusing on conservation. Last, but hardly least, he asked Congress to approve a new "Five year Defense Program" which would raise defense spending authorizations by 5 percent a year. It included the deployment of new intermediate-range nuclear missiles in Europe in response to similar Soviet deployments. The era of détente was over.

Thanks largely to his very centrist economic policies, Carter now faced a primary challenge from Senator Edward Kennedy of Massachusetts, while ex-California governor Ronald Reagan pretty quickly wrapped up the Republican nomination that he had nearly won four years earlier. Inflation and unemployment were surging again thanks in part to the disruption of Iranian oil supplies, with price increases of 13.3 percent and 12.5 percent in 1979 and 1980, and unemployment rising from 6 percent to 7.2 percent in the same year. And on April 25, 1980, Carter reported to the nation that he had had to abort an armed mission to rescue the hostages in Teheran because of helicopter failures at a desert staging area. Eight American soldiers had also died when two aircraft collided on the ground. "The mission on which they were embarked was a humanitarian mission," he said. "It was not directed against Iran; it was not directed against the people of Iran." Secretary of State Cyrus Vance, who had opposed the rescue mission, resigned in protest.

Carter faced down Kennedy's challenge and won renomination, but like Ford four years earlier, he could not overcome the political effects of unemployment, inflation, energy shortages, the collapse of détente, and divisions within his own party. Although his popular vote percentage of 41 percent was slightly higher than Hoover's in 1932, he suffered the worst defeat of any incumbent except Taft in the Electoral College, 489–49, and carried just six states and the District of Columbia. Having swept the South in 1976, he now carried only his home state of Georgia there. Nor was this all. The

Republican Party gained 12 seats in the Senate, the biggest swing since 1958, and emerged with a 52–46 majority, their first since 1953. They also gained 34 seats in the House, but still trailed the Democrats there, 244–191. This was the biggest watershed election since 1932. Nixon, Ford and Carter had all criticized the growth of the federal government and promised to cut back its reach. Ronald Reagan now planned to go much further, and to take the drastic steps they had all resisted to control the inflation that had nearly tripled prices from 1965 through 1980.

# XIX

# Ronald Reagan and George H. W. Bush

## 1981–89 • 1989–93

Ronald Reagan opened his inaugural with a picture of "an economic affliction of great proportions . . . one of the longest and one of the worst sustained inflations in our national history. . . . Idle industries have cast workers into unemployment, human misery, and personal indignity. Those who do work are denied a fair return for their labor by a tax system which penalizes successful achievement and keeps us from maintaining full productivity. . . . For decades we have piled deficit upon deficit, mortgaging our future and our children's future for the temporary convenience of the present. . . . In this present crisis government is not the solution to our problem; government is the problem. From time to time we've been tempted to believe that society has become too complex to be managed by self-rule, that government by an elite group is superior to government for, by, and of the people. Well, if no one among us is capable of governing himself, then who among us has the capacity to govern someone else?" While peace remained the aspiration of the American people, "we will not surrender for it, now or ever. . . . We will maintain sufficient strength to prevail if need be, knowing that if we do so we have the best chance of never having to use that strength." Not since Franklin Roosevelt had a new president entered office with such a clear and novel vision of the path he wanted to take. On that very same day, after protracted negotiations, the Iranian government released the US hostages it had been holding in Teheran. Reagan stuck to those themes for the next eight years.

On February 18 Reagan presented his program for economic recovery in a televised address to a joint session of Congress. He listed the nation's ills: two years of double-digit inflation, mortgage interest rates at 15 percent, eight million unemployed and a $1 trillion debt. "Adding to our troubles is a mass of regulations imposed on the shopkeeper, the farmer, the craftsman, professionals, and major industry that is estimated to add $100 billion to the price of the things we buy, and it reduces our ability to produce." He proposed to cut a projected increase of about $80 billion in federal spending for fiscal 1982 in half, while cutting income taxes 10 percent a year for three years in a row. Many federal programs would be consolidated into block grants to the states and the government would tighten eligibility for food stamps and welfare, cut spending on school lunches, and cap Medicaid spending. Defense spending, meanwhile, would increase sharply to make up, he said, for years of neglect. He promised big rollbacks of regulations and suggested that the government could save $25 billion a year in "waste and fraud." He also endorsed "a consistent monetary policy aimed at maintaining the value of the currency"—a euphemism for Fed chairman Paul Volcker's determination to keep interest rates at 15 percent or more until inflation fell. "I've had advice that in 1985 our real production in goods and services will grow by 20 percent and be $300 billion higher than it is today," he said, and that worker purchasing power would rise 8 percent in real terms. Those predictions came from "supply-side economics," a new theory that large tax cuts would unleash investment and unprecedented economic growth that would provide the government with even higher revenue.

Reagan addressed another joint session plugging this program on April 28—just a few weeks after he narrowly survived an assassination attempt—and addressed the whole nation on July 27, after Congress had passed his budget proposals. "Your voices have been heard—millions of you, Democrats, Republicans, and Independents, from every profession, trade and line of work, and from every part of this land," he said—demanding a change from "control by government" to "control of government." "Because of what you did, Republicans and Democrats in the Congress came together and passed the most sweeping cutbacks in the history of the Federal budget. . . .¹ And starting next year, the deficits will get smaller until in just a few years the budget can be balanced." He asked his viewers to urge the House of Representatives to pass his three-year, 25 percent tax cut rather than a Democratic alternative. He also tried to reassure voters who had reacted angrily to a Social Security reform proposal that would have made it much harder to retire at sixty-two on reduced benefits. On August 8 he thanked congressional leaders for passing both the budget and the tax bills.

By the time of his first annual message on January 26, 1982, Reagan had to admit that some things were not going according to plan. The prime interest rate had fallen but remained at 15.75 percent—and the economy was clearly in recession. "The economy will face difficult moments in the months ahead. But the program for economic recovery that is in place will pull the economy out of its slump and put us on the road to prosperity and stable growth by the latter half of this year," he said. Unemployment had in fact risen from 7.2 percent in 1980 to 8.5 percent in 1981 and reached 10.8 percent—a post-Depression record—in 1982. This message introduced what became a new tradition in annual messages, references to individual Americans whom the president had invited to the address because their life experiences somehow embodied points that he wanted to make. In his budget message on February 8 he had to announce that the deficit would rise from $57.9 billion in fiscal 1981 to $98.6 billion in fiscal 1982, but predicted that it would fall to $71.9 billion by 1985. Yet he rejected any tax increases to close the gap and boasted of personal and business tax cuts, planned indexing of tax brackets to inflation beginning in 1985, $41 billion in planned entitlement cuts over three years, and the elimination of several programs. He addressed the nation twice more on the budget during 1982, on April 29 and on August 16. In the first he detailed his attempts to reduce the deficit in talks with congressional leaders, and also called for a constitutional amendment to require a balanced federal budget. In the second, after talks had produced an agreement, he denied that he had abandoned his original program but had to admit that he had agreed to $99 billion in "revenue increases" over the next three years, as

---

1 This was an exaggeration: cuts after the Civil War and each of the two world wars were much larger.

well as $280 billion in spending cuts. The increases, he explained, came mostly from more efficient tax collection and closing some loopholes, although they also included higher taxes on telephone calls and cigarettes. The budget agreement, he claimed, would also reduce spending by $280 billion over three years.[2]

The public, however, remained focused on increased unemployment, and the Democrats gained 26 House seats for a 269–165 majority in November 1982, while the Republicans maintained a 54–46 margin in the Senate. In his January 1983 annual message Reagan acknowledged that "we have a long way to go" on the economy, but praised a bipartisan commission that had proposed significant payroll tax increases to keep Social Security solvent. He also promised to "revitalize American education," and to "eliminate, once and for all, all traces of unjust discrimination against women from the United States Code." His January 31 budget message spelled out his plans for education—tuition tax credits for private and religious schools, and voucher programs to pay for such schools in states and localities—and called for a less generous federal pension system. He also announced drastically revised targets for the budget deficit, now hoping to cut it from $208 billion to $148 billion in fiscal 1986. While focusing on the economy, Reagan also took unprecedented positions on at least two social issues that the Republican Party was now adopting as platform planks. The Supreme Court had outlawed public school prayer in 1961 and legalized abortion in 1973, and during his first term Reagan endorsed or proposed constitutional amendments to ban abortion and to legalize school prayer. He also struck an important blow against organized labor on August 3, 1981, when he announced that the nation's air traffic controllers, who had just begun a strike for higher wages, would be terminated if they did not return to work, and carried out that threat.

Meanwhile, Reagan repudiated the détente policies that had begun with Kennedy and flowered under Nixon and waged a revived

---

2 In April 1982 Reagan introduced a new form of presidential communication, a very brief weekly radio address, broadcast on Saturdays, to keep his concerns in the public eye. Presidents Clinton and George W. Bush continued this practice, but President Obama dropped it. Because these addresses never broke new ground, they have not been used in this study.

Cold War against Communism on three fronts. Regarding strategic weapons—where the USSR had made very big gains during the 1970s—he had promised in his inaugural to "maintain sufficient strength to prevail if need be, knowing that if we do so we have the best chance of never having to use that strength." "During the last several years," he added on October 2, 1981, "a weakening in our security posture has been particularly noticeable in our strategic nuclear forces—the very foundation of our strategy for deterring foreign attacks. A window of vulnerability is opening, one that would jeopardize not just our hopes for serious productive arms negotiations, but our hopes for peace and freedom." He asked for one hundred supersonic B-1 bombers—a plane that every other president since Kennedy had refused to authorize—a new Stealth bomber, more Trident missile submarines, and a new land-based MX missile. Already on September 12 he had announced planned defense budget increases from $182 billion in fiscal 1982 to $243 billion in fiscal 1984. In another broadcast address on November 18, he announced that NATO would deploy hundreds of Pershing intermediate-range ballistic missiles and cruise missiles in Western Europe in response to the Soviet deployment of similar missiles—unless the Soviets would agree to remove their new missiles.

"In the last decade," Reagan said in his 1982 annual message, "while we sought the moderation of Soviet power through a process of restraint and accommodation, the Soviets engaged in an unrelenting buildup of their military forces. The protection of our national security has required that we undertake a substantial program to enhance our military forces." The United States, he explained repeatedly, was now pushing for very large reductions in strategic arms in renewed arms control talks with the Soviets, and he believed they would eventually accept them. And in a broadcast address on March 23, 1983, Reagan dropped a bombshell, repudiating the doctrine of deterrence by mutual assured destruction in favor of new attempts to design an effective anti-missile defense. "What if free people could live secure in the knowledge that their security did not rest upon the threat of instant U.S. retaliation to deter a Soviet attack, that we could intercept and destroy strategic ballistic missiles before they reached our own soil or that of our allies? . . . I call upon the scientific community in our country, those who gave us nuclear weapons, to turn their great talents now to the cause of mankind and world peace, to give us the means of rendering these nuclear weapons impotent and obsolete." This controversial proposal, quickly christened Star Wars, now became his key plan for the future.

The second front involved areas in the third world where the Soviets or their allies or clients were trying to expand their control, led by, but not limited to, the Caribbean region and the Middle East. On April 27, 1983, he addressed a joint session on conflict in the Caribbean, highlighting the dangers posed by Communist Cuba and the leftist regime that had taken power on the tiny island of Grenada. Referring specifically to Truman's March 1947 message on Greece and Turkey, he detailed how a newly elected democratic government in El Salvador now faced threats from Communist guerrillas. The leftist government that had taken power in Nicaragua in 1979, he added, had spurned US help and had begun encouraging revolution elsewhere, and the US wanted to stop its arms exports. He soon appointed a commission to recommend Central American policies.

In late September 1983 Reagan ordered hundreds of marines into Lebanon, where a civil war had been complicated by an Israeli invasion to expel the Palestine Liberation Organization from the country, to help establish a stable government. A few weeks later, he ordered a quick invasion of Grenada to overthrow the leftist government there. At almost exactly the same moment, a truck bomb struck and destroyed the marine barracks in Lebanon, killing 241 US servicemen. Regan discussed Lebanon and Grenada in a lengthy broadcast address to the nation on October 27. The troops in Lebanon, he said, might help establish peace in the Middle East, which "is of vital concern to our nation and, indeed, to our allies in Western Europe and Japan." Since 1948, he added, the nation had recognized "a moral obligation to assure the continued existence of Israel as a nation." Withdrawing the marines would deal "a devastating blow" to the peace process. Turning to Grenada, he noted that leftist leader Maurice Bishop had been overthrown just before the invasion, but that the US had had to intervene to protect hundreds of Americans and forestall another hostage crisis. "Grenada, we were told," he said, "was a friendly island paradise for tourism. Well, it wasn't. It was a Soviet-Cuban colony, being readied as a major military bastion to export terror and undermine democracy.

We got there just in time. . . . The events in Lebanon and Grenada, though oceans apart, are closely related. Not only has Moscow assisted and encouraged the violence in both countries, but it provides direct support through a network of surrogates and terrorists."

Four months later, on February 7, 1984, Reagan announced that the remaining marines in Lebanon had redeployed offshore in troop ships. Three more months later, however, on May 9, he escalated his rhetoric and his goals again in another broadcast address on Central America. Soviet leaders, he said, "are presently challenging us with a different kind of weapon: subversion and the use of surrogate forces, Cubans, for example. We've seen it intensifying during the last ten years, as the Soviet Union and its surrogates move to establish control over Vietnam, Laos, Cambodia, Angola, Ethiopia, South Yemen, Afghanistan, and recently, closer to home, in Nicaragua and now El Salvador." El Salvador, he said, was now slowly bleeding to death, and needed far more help to survive. More significantly, he now accused Fidel Castro of fomenting the Sandinista revolution, which he claimed was now persecuting Jews and Catholics. Thousands of Nicaraguans, he said, had taken up arms against the Sandinistas—they were known as Contras—and the United States should assist these "freedom fighters." Congress eventually approved very limited aid to what was actually a CIA-sponsored operation.

And meanwhile, throughout his first term—during which death replaced Leonid Brezhnev with Yuri Andropov, and Andropov with Konstantin Chernenko—Reagan reopened an all-out propaganda offensive against the USSR such as had not been heard since the time of Eisenhower. "In the face of a climate of falsehood and misinformation," he said in his January 1982 annual address, "we've promised the world a season of truth—the truth of our great civilized ideas: individual liberty, representative government, the rule of law under God. We've never needed walls or minefields or barbed wire to keep our people in." And on March 8, 1983, addressing the convention of the National Association of Evangelicals, he asked them, while considering current proposals for a freeze in nuclear arms, "to beware the temptation of pride—the temptation of blithely declaring yourselves above it all and label both sides equally at fault, to ignore the facts of history and the aggressive impulses of an evil empire, to simply call the arms race a giant misunderstanding and thereby remove yourself from the struggle between right and wrong and good and evil. . . . Yes, let us pray for the salvation of all of those who live in that totalitarian darkness—pray they will discover the joy of knowing God. But until they do, let us be aware that while they preach the supremacy of the state, declare its omnipotence over individual man, and predict its eventual domination of all peoples on the Earth, they are the focus of evil in the modern world." And six months later, after the USSR had shot down a Korean airliner that had strayed into its territory, killing all aboard, he went even further. "Despite the savagery of their crime," he said, "the universal reaction against it, and the evidence of their complicity, the Soviets still refuse to tell the truth. They have persistently refused to admit that their pilot fired on the Korean aircraft. . . . And make no mistake about it, this attack was not just against ourselves or the Republic of Korea. This was the Soviet Union against the world and the moral precepts which guide human relations among people everywhere. It was an act of barbarism, born of a society which wantonly disregards individual rights and the value of human life and seeks constantly to expand and dominate other nations."

In that fall of 1983, the combination of Reagan's buildup of US strategic forces, his rhetoric, and a NATO exercise codenamed Able-Archer seriously frightened the Soviet leadership that he might be about to unleash a first strike against them. Informed of this by US intelligence, Reagan became seriously concerned himself.[3] Substantial elements of US opinion were also frightened by the hostile climate, and Reagan struck a different note in yet another broadcast address on January 6, 1984. "I believe that 1984 finds the United States in the strongest position in years to establish a constructive and realistic working relationship with the Soviet Union. We've come a long way since the decade of the seventies, years when the United States seemed filled with self-doubt and neglected its defenses, while the Soviet Union increased its military might and sought to expand its influence by armed forces and threat." With our own forces restored, he said, we might now pursue "credible deterrence and peaceful competition"—an unacknowledged echo of Kennedy, Nixon, and détente. He called for "a better working

---

3 See the remarkable book by James Mann, *The Rebellion of Ronald Reagan* (New York, 2009), pp. 77–79.

relationship with each other, one marked by greater cooperation and understanding," and added, "Living in this nuclear age makes it imperative that we do talk." He referred to his own dream "to see the day when nuclear weapons will be banished from the face of the earth." He called for the resumption of arms control negotiations, which the Soviets had abandoned when NATO had gone through the deployment of Pershing and cruise missiles in the fall.

Reagan's campaign for reelection against Carter's vice president Walter Mondale was now beginning. Like Roosevelt in 1936, who had significantly eased, but hardly ended, the Depression, Reagan had hardly managed to achieve all his economic goals. Inflation had now fallen from 12.5 percent in 1980 to just 3.8 percent in 1983, and interest rates had fallen to more reasonable levels—but unemployment was still 8.3 percent at the end of 1983, compared to 7.2 percent when he had taken office. Supply-side economics had proven a budgetary disaster, and the federal deficit had grown from $79 billion in fiscal 1981 to a new peacetime record of $208 billion in fiscal 1983 and $185 billion in fiscal 1984. Yet like Roosevelt, Reagan had evidently sold the bulk of the nation on his view of what was wrong with the United States and how to fix it. "This election offers us the clearest choice in many years: whether we go forward together with courage, confidence, and common sense, making America strong again; or turn back to policies that weakened our economy, diminished our leadership in the world, and reversed America's long-revered tradition of progress," he said in his last preelection broadcast address. Days later, the voters apparently joined in his repudiation of Roosevelt's domestic legacy in the November election. His margins of victory over Mondale—58.8 percent to 40.6 percent in the popular vote, and 525–13 in the Electoral College, where Mondale carried only Minnesota and the District of Columbia—were only very slightly smaller that Roosevelt's margins over Landon in 1936. The Republicans gained back 16 House seats, cutting the Democratic majority to 254–181, but lost 2 Senate seats to cut their lead to 53–47.

Reagan's second inaugural promised four more years of travel down the same path. "We are creating a nation once again vibrant, robust, and alive. But there are many mountains yet to climb. We will not rest until every American enjoys the fullness of freedom, dignity, and opportunity as our birthright. . . . And if we meet this challenge, these will be years when Americans have restored their confidence and tradition of progress; when our values of faith, family, work, and neighborhood were restated for a modern age; when our economy was finally freed from government's grip; when we made sincere efforts at meaningful arms reductions and by rebuilding our defenses, our economy, and developing new technologies, helped preserve peace in a troubled world; when America courageously supported the struggle for individual liberty, self-government, and free enterprise throughout the world and turned the tide of history away from totalitarian darkness and into the warm sunlight of human freedom." He promised more tax cuts, more spending cuts, and a balanced budget. The last goal proved increasingly elusive over the next four years, but developments on the foreign scene began to vindicate his hopes. Meanwhile, his policies in the third world led him into the biggest scandal since Watergate.

In his budget message of February 4, 1985, Reagan asked for cuts in Medicare, the federal payroll (which had already been reduced by 78,000 workers), and agriculture payments. The deficit for fiscal 1985 now stood at $222 billion—not the $72 billion he had predicted early in 1982—and he assured Congress that his cuts would reduce it to $144 billion by fiscal 1988. Appealing to the American people on April 24, he complained once again that government had taken over far too many functions "in the name of the Great Society," and called for the elimination of Amtrak, the Export-Import Bank, and the Small Business Administration, and a complete overhaul of the tax code. The national debt, he reported, had now reached $1.7 trillion—not mentioning that he had bewailed its $1 trillion level just four years earlier. A month later on May 28 he addressed the nation again, calling for a new round of tax cuts. His new proposals established just three income tax rates of 15, 25 and 35 percent, and cut the top corporate rate from 46 to 33 percent. Before acting on this proposal, Congress passed and Reagan signed the Gramm-Rudman-Hollings law in late 1985, setting deficit reduction targets for five years that would lead to a balanced budget in 1991, and mandating across-the-board spending cuts if Congress failed to meet those targets on its own. Reagan's budget message of February 5, 1986 forecast deficits falling to $144 billion in fiscal 1987, $68 billion in fiscal

1989 and a $1.3 billion surplus in 1991, as called for by the law. Meanwhile, Reagan focused on good economic news. "Tonight," he said in the February 4, 1986 annual message, "the American people deserve our thanks for 37 straight months of economic growth, for sunrise firms and modernized industries creating 9 million new jobs in 3 years, interest rates cut in half, inflation falling from over 12 percent in 1980 to under 4 today, and a mighty river of good works—a record $74 billion in voluntary giving just last year alone. And despite the pressures of our modern world, family and community remain the moral core of our society, guardians of our values and hopes for the future."

The Tax Reform Act that passed in the fall of 1986 lowered the top rate even further, from 50 percent to 28 percent, while raising the bottom bracket to 15 percent. The January 5, 1987 budget message had to admit that the previous year's targets had been far too optimistic—the fiscal 1987 deficit was now projected at $173 billion, not $144 billion—largely, he claimed, because Congress had refused to make many of his proposed spending cuts. He called in every annual message for a constitutional amendment requiring a balanced budget and a law creating line-item veto power, neither one of which Congress was inclined to grant. As it turned out, his last three budgets ran deficits for in the $150 billion range, significantly higher as a percentage of GDP than any of Carter's deficits. The unemployment rate, as Reagan frequently boasted, had fallen from 10.8 percent in 1982 to 5.7 percent in 1987, but it fell only to 5.3 percent in the remainder of his term. Inflation, which had fallen below 4 percent from 1982 through 1986, rose to about 4.5 percent annually during the second term.[4]

Reagan also made new proposals to revive the US space program, and during 1985, NASA staged a competition to select a teacher to join the crew of a forthcoming space shuttle mission. That mission was scheduled for the day of the 1986 State of the Union address—January 28—but instead of giving the address, Reagan had to make a brief, sad broadcast address on the explosion of the shuttle and the deaths of all aboard. "I hope that we are now ready to do what they would want us to do," he said in

---

4 https://www.thebalance.com/unemployment-rate-by-year-3305506.

the rescheduled February 4 address: "Go forward, America, and reach for the stars." On another front, Reagan in his February 5 budget message had just referred for the very first time to the AIDS epidemic, promising to fund a search for a cure. AIDS had been identified by the CDC four years earlier and had now taken tens of thousands lives. He also continued to call for legislation to protect "the unborn," but Congress did not act on any.

Meanwhile, Reagan continued fighting the Cold War on all fronts. His 1985 annual address called for "fair and verifiable arms agreements"—along with deployments of the MX missile, renamed the Peacekeeper, and more work on SDI—and called again for assistance to the Nicaraguan Contras. "Support for freedom fighters is self-defense and totally consistent with the OAS and U.N. Charters," he said boldly. "It is essential that the Congress continue all facets of our assistance to Central America." Mikhail Gorbachev took power in the USSR only weeks later after the death of Konstantin Chernenko, and Reagan evidently decided that he might turn out to be a different kind of Soviet leader. He arranged to meet with him in Geneva in November 1985—the first such summit since the days of Ford and Brezhnev—and addressed the nation optimistically before the meeting on November 14. "My mission, stated simply, is a mission for peace," he said . . . "to sit down across from Mr. Gorbachev and try to map out, together, a basis for peaceful discourse even though our disagreements on fundamentals will not change." He was "pleased . . . with the interest expressed in reducing offensive weapons by the new Soviet leadership." "I've said before, I will say again: A nuclear war cannot be won and must never be fought."[5] Reporting on the trip in a broadcast address to Congress a week later, he announced "a fresh start. . . . I can't claim that we had a meeting of the minds on such fundamentals as ideology or national purpose, but we understand each other better, and that's a key to peace." The two sides, he said, had agreed to the objective of reducing "nuclear arms by 50 percent in appropriate categories," and he had spoken frankly about human rights issues and local wars. They would exchange visits to their capitals in the next two years.

---

5 Although Reagan and other administration officials such as Secretary of Defense Caspar Weinberger had frequently spoken of "prevailing" in a nuclear war, Reagan had also made this contradictory statement many times since 1982.

Third-world conflicts once again took center stage. Rejecting Reagan's views about Nicaragua, Congress in late 1984 had forbade any federal government assistance to the Contra rebels. Undeterred, Reagan in a message to Congress on March 14, 1986 linked the Nicaraguan conflict to a number of other civil wars in the third world against Communist or Soviet client regimes. A democratic revolution was in progress around the world, he said, citing recent events in the Philippines, Haiti, and South Africa, and the US must help. "Growing resistance movements now challenge Communist regimes installed or maintained by the military power of the Soviet Union and its colonial agents—in Afghanistan, Angola, Cambodia, Ethiopia, and Nicaragua. We did not create this historical phenomenon, but we must not fail to respond to it. . . . Our goal, in short—indeed our necessity—is to convince the Soviet Union that the policies on which it embarked in the 70's cannot work." In many cases, he said, covert aid would work best. The strategy of aiding (or standing up) resistance movements in Soviet client states became known as the Reagan Doctrine. Two days later he addressed the whole nation about Nicaragua, asking Congress to approve $100 million "for the more than 20,000 freedom fighters struggling to bring democracy to their country and eliminate this Communist menace at its source. . . . Will we give the Nicaraguan democratic resistance the means to recapture their betrayed revolution, or will we turn our backs and ignore the malignancy in Managua until it spreads and becomes a mortal threat to the entire New World?" Just a month after the Nicaragua address, on April 14, Reagan told the nation that American air and naval forces had struck targets in Libya in retaliation for a terrorist attack on a Berlin nightclub that had killed American soldiers. Claiming proof of Libyan responsibility, Reagan called Libyan leader Muammar Qadhafi "an enemy of the United States" and cited his "subversion and aggression against the neighboring states in Africa." "Despite our repeated warnings," he continued, Qadhafi "continued his reckless policy of intimidation, his relentless pursuit of terror. He counted on America to be passive. He counted wrong. I warned that there should be no place on Earth where terrorists can rest and train and practice their deadly skills. I meant it." This was the first use of American military power to punish a single violent act.

Congress eventually approved $100 million in Contra aid in October. In the November 4 congressional elections the Democrats gained 5 seats in the House, increasing their majority to 258–177, and 8 seats in the Senate, reversing many of the 1980 results and regaining control by 55–47. Two days later, the *Washington Post* revealed that three American hostages held in Lebanon had been released over the preceding year in return for shipments of American weapons to the government of Iran, with which the US had had no diplomatic relations since the Islamic revolution of 1979. Within days the nation learned that Reagan's National Security Council staff had been organizing assistance to the Nicaraguan Contras for more than two years in violation of the congressional prohibition, and then, that some of the proceeds of the Iranian arms sales had gone to help the Contras. National Security Adviser John Poindexter and staffer Marine Lt. Col. Oliver North resigned, and Congress immediately announced plans to investigate. Forced onto the defensive and potentially threatened with impeachment, Reagan addressed the nation on the scandal three times over the next four months. On November 13, just a week after the story had broken, he claimed that contacts with Iran had aimed at ending the five-year Iran-Iraq War. They had, he said, led to the release of three hostages, and he acknowledged shipments of "small amounts of defensive weapons and spare parts for defensive systems to Iran," but he insisted, "We did not—repeat—did not trade weapons or anything else for hostages, nor will we. Those who think that we have gone soft on terrorism should take up the question with Colonel Qadhafi." He said nothing about Nicaragua at all. On December 2 he told the nation that he had agreed to his attorney general's decision to appoint an independent counsel to investigate the whole matter, but said nothing at all about the facts of the case. He also appointed a friendly commission of inquiry under Senator John Tower, a Republican, and after it reported he addressed the nation again on March 4, 1987. "A few months ago I told the American people I did not trade arms for hostages," he said. "My heart and my best intentions still tell me that's true, but the facts and the evidence tell me it is not." He claimed not to have known about any diversion of funds to the Contras. He repeated these claims in another broadcast address on August 12, after televised congressional hearings had concluded. Adding that he had changed personnel and procedures at the White

House and reviewed all covert operations to avoid any similar mistakes, he then moved on to other foreign policy issues and called again for a balanced budget amendment. The Iran-Contra scandal now moved into the courts.

Reagan's relations with Gorbachev and the Soviet Union had meanwhile entered a dramatic new phase. On October 13, 1986, he addressed the nation about a sensational meeting they had conducted in Reykjavik, Iceland. He had, he assured his listeners, discussed human rights within the USSR and regional conflicts, and he insisted that any improvement in relations depended on internal changes there. "A government that will break faith with its own people," he said, "cannot be trusted to keep faith with foreign powers." He also accused the Soviets of violating the existing ABM treaty by working on a nationwide missile defense. Yet he had also proposed eliminating *all* strategic nuclear weapons within ten years, while continuing to develop SDI. Unfortunately, he explained, the talks had failed. "The General Secretary wanted wording that, in effect, would have kept us from developing the SDI for the entire 10 years. In effect, he was killing SDI. And unless I agreed, all that work toward eliminating nuclear weapons would go down the drain—canceled. I told him I had pledged to the American people that I would not trade away SDI, there was no way I could tell our people their government would not protect them against nuclear destruction. . . . SDI is America's insurance policy that the Soviet Union would keep the commitments made at Reykjavik. SDI is America's security guarantee if the Soviets should—as they have done too often in the past—fail to comply with their solemn commitments. SDI is what brought the Soviets back to arms control talks at Geneva and Iceland. SDI is the key to a world without nuclear weapons." He did not mention that his proposal to eliminate all strategic nuclear weapons had deeply unsettled the rest of NATO, which had relied on them to deter Soviet aggression for almost forty years. Meanwhile, keeping up political pressure, Reagan in West Berlin on June 12, 1987, famously called upon Gorbachev, "Mr. Gorbachev, tear down this wall!"

Reagan and Gorbachev never resolved the SDI impasse, but a year later, on December 10, 1987, Reagan proudly announced that they had formally agreed in Washington to eliminate their intermediate-range nuclear missiles in Europe and elsewhere—the first agreement, he boasted, to eliminate an entire class of weapons with provision for on-site inspection. "Your support over these last 7 years," he told the American people, "has laid the basis for these negotiations. Your support made it possible for us to rebuild our military strength, to liberate Grenada, to strike hard against terrorism in Libya, and more recently to protect our strategic interests and bolster our friends in the Persian Gulf. Your support made possible our policy of helping freedom fighters like those in Afghanistan, Nicaragua, Angola, Cambodia, and other places around the globe. And when last year at Reykjavik I refused Soviet demands that we trade away SDI, our Strategic Defense Initiative that could erect a space shield against ballistic missiles, your overwhelming support made it clear to the Soviet leaders that the American people prefer no deal to a bad deal and will back their President on matters of national security. In short, your support for our foreign policy goals—building a safer peace as we advance the cause of world freedom—has helped bring the Soviets to the bargaining table. It makes it possible now to hope for a real, fundamental improvement in our relations." Like Wilson, Franklin Roosevelt, and Nixon, Reagan had proved that he had his own particular view of international affairs and was willing to implement it. He had pushed ahead with the INF treaty despite the public opposition of Nixon, Henry Kissinger, and much of the Republican foreign policy establishment.[6]

Six weeks later, in his last annual message on January 25, he went even further: "In international relations, too, there's only one description for what, together, we have achieved: a complete turnabout, a revolution. Seven years ago, America was weak, and freedom everywhere was under siege. Today America is strong, and democracy is everywhere on the move." He referred specifically to changes in Latin America, where 90 percent of the population, he said, now lived under democracy. He asked again for more Contra aid. He also mentioned a new free trade agreement with Canada which he was "determined to expand" to Mexico, and looked forward to a day when all the borders in the western hemisphere would be as open as the US-Canada one.

---

6 This is the theme of Mann, *The Rebellion of Ronald Reagan*.

The election of 1988 pitted Reagan's loyal vice president, George W. Bush—the sixth immediately preceding vice president to secure his party's nomination since 1960—against Governor Michael Dukakis of Massachusetts. Initially trailing in polls, Bush gained ground rapidly during the summer and fall and won overwhelmingly, with 53 percent of the popular vote and 426 electoral votes to Dukakis's 111. Reagan gave a farewell address to the nation on January 11, 1989, the first president to do so after two terms since Eisenhower. "The way I see it," he said, "there were two great triumphs, two things that I'm proudest of. One is the economic recovery, in which the people of America created—and filled—19 million new jobs. The other is the recovery of our morale. America is respected again in the world and looked to for leadership. . . . They called it the Reagan revolution. Well, I'll accept that, but for me it always seemed more like the great rediscovery, a rediscovery of our values and our common sense." The tax cuts, he said, had produced the longest peacetime economic expansion in history. He briefly expressed regrets about the budget deficit, but then turned to the emerging American culture war. "Younger parents aren't sure that an unambivalent appreciation of America is the right thing to teach modern children. And as for those who create the popular culture, well-grounded patriotism is no longer the style. . . . we've got to teach history based not on what's in fashion but what's important—why the Pilgrims came here, who Jimmy Doolittle was, and what those 30 seconds over Tokyo meant. . . . I'm warning of an eradication of the American memory that could result, ultimately, in an erosion of the American spirit. Let's start with some basics: more attention to American history and a greater emphasis on civic ritual." "My friends," he concluded, "we did it. We weren't just marking time. We made a difference. We made the city [John Winthrop's "city on a hill"] stronger, we made the city freer, and we left her in good hands. All in all, not bad, not bad at all."

Americans inevitably remain divided over the long-term impact of Reagan's economic policies—which halted rampant inflation but also reversed the decades-long movement toward greater economic equality—and historians differ on the question of how much his foreign policy really contributed to changes within the Soviet Union and the collapse of Communism that followed almost immediately. Yet he undoubtedly ranks with Franklin Roosevelt as one of the two most influential presidents of the twentieth century. Both of them changed, in opposite ways, the federal government's relationship to the national economy not merely during their own term, but for decades afterwards, regardless of which party was in power. They did so partly because of their skill as communicators. In addition to his annual messages, Reagan gave twenty-eight broadcast addresses to the American people in eight years, compared to Roosevelt's twenty-seven fireside chats in twelve years. Both put the events of the day into clear patterns, and both spoke powerfully to different parts of the American psyche.

The son of a US senator from Connecticut, George H. W. Bush had moved to Texas as a young adult and gone into the oil business. Running for federal office four times from 1964 to 1980, he lost two races for the US Senate and won two for Congress, eventually making him one of the few elected presidents who had not previously won more elections than he had lost.[7] He had served in the Nixon and Ford administrations as ambassador to the UN, the first informal diplomatic representative to the People's Republic of China, and head of the CIA, and Reagan had chosen him as vice president. The dramatic changes in the world scene that had begun under Reagan dominated his term of office, and his memoirs completely omitted any discussion of domestic issues.

After thanking President Reagan for "the wonderful things that you have done for America," Bush, who had carefully courted the Republican Party's religious factions, became the second president to offer an inaugural prayer. Then he echoed Reagan's rhetoric and promised more of the same. "We live in a peaceful, prosperous time," he said, "but we can make it better. . . . For in man's heart, if not in fact, the day of the dictator is over. The totalitarian era is passing, its old ideas blown away like leaves from an ancient, lifeless tree. A new breeze is blowing, and a nation refreshed by freedom stands ready to push on. . . . We know how to secure a more just and prosperous life for man on Earth: through free markets, free speech, free elections, and the exercise of free will unhampered by the state." America's purpose today, he said, "is to make kinder the

---

7 It is only fair to note that Abraham Lincoln in 1860 had lost *more* elections than he had won.

face of the nation and gentler the face of the world," for example by helping young mothers who chose not to abort their pregnancies. The budget, he said, must be balanced, and he chided congressmen for increasingly questioning one another's motives since the Vietnam War. "That war cleaves us still," he continued. "But, friends, that war began in earnest a quarter of a century ago, and surely the statute of limitation has been reached. This is a fact: The final lesson of Vietnam is that no great nation can long afford to be sundered by a memory." He cautiously promised to "continue the new closeness with the Soviet Union, consistent both with our security and with progress."

Gorbachev had loosened the bonds between Moscow and the satellite countries of Eastern Europe, and by the fall of 1989 they were becoming increasingly restive. The government of Hungary suddenly opened its border with neutral Austria, allowing East Germans, in particular, to move freely into the West, as they had not been able to do since 1961. That in turn triggered a new popular revolt in East Berlin, and the Berlin Wall came down on November 9. Bush met with Gorbachev in Malta on December 3, but he did not speak directly to the American people either about the fall of the wall or that meeting. At a NATO meeting the very next day he endorsed the reunification of Germany within NATO, reiterated "our support for the principles of the [1975] Helsinki Final Act"—which had confirmed the postwar borders of the European states—and argued that NATO should encourage the spread of democracy in Eastern Europe.

Bush's first address to the nation on foreign affairs dealt with a new war closer to home. The United States under Reagan had fallen out with Panamanian dictator Manuel Noriega, and Noriega in May 1989 had voided the results of a presidential election in a coup. The Bush administration pressured him to resign, and on December 15, the Panamanian government declared that a state of war existed between Panama and the United States. Security forces set upon off-duty American soldiers and killed several of them. "35,000 Americans in Panama" were in imminent danger, Bush explained to the nation on December 20. "As President, I have no higher obligation than to safeguard the lives of American citizens. And that is why I directed our Armed Forces to protect the lives of American citizens in Panama and to bring General

Noriega"—now publicly accused of drug trafficking—"to justice in the United States. . . . The Panamanian people want democracy, peace, and the chance for a better life in dignity and freedom." A brief military operation did just that—the first example of how the end of the Cold War had opened up new opportunities for US military action abroad.

Bush's first annual message on January 31, 1990, announced the coming of a new, US-centered world, marked by the global triumph of American ideals. For forty-four years, he said, "Nineteen forty-five provided the common frame of reference, the compass points of the postwar era we've relied upon to understand ourselves. And that was our world, until now. The events of the year just ended, the Revolution of '89, have been a chain reaction, changes so striking that it marks the beginning of a new era in the world's affairs." Referring to Noriega's overthrow and the fall of Communism throughout Eastern Europe, he called "Remarkable events—events that fulfill the long-held hopes of the American people; events that validate the longstanding goals of American policy, a policy based on a single, shining principle: the cause of freedom. America, not just the nation but an idea, alive in the minds of people everywhere. As this new world takes shape, America stands at the center of a widening circle of freedom—today, tomorrow, and into the next century. . . . I say it is time to acclaim a new consensus at home and abroad, a common vision of the peaceful world we want to see."

Six months later, on August 2, 1990, Iraqi leader Saddam Hussein occupied neighboring Kuwait and opened up another new, fateful chapter in American foreign policy. Just six days later Bush announced the deployment of American troops to Saudi Arabia to protect that critical oil producer against any possible Iraqi threats, and laid down sweeping new US goals. "There is no justification whatsoever for this outrageous and brutal act of aggression. A puppet regime imposed from the outside is unacceptable. The acquisition of territory by force is unacceptable. No one, friend or foe, should doubt our desire for peace; and no one should underestimate our determination to confront aggression. . . . We succeeded in the struggle for freedom in Europe because we and our allies remain stalwart. Keeping the peace in the Middle East will require no less. . . . If history teaches us anything, it is that we must resist aggression or it will destroy our freedoms. Appeasement does not work. As was the case in the 1930s, we see in Saddam Hussein an aggressive dictator threatening his neighbors." Now sixty-six, Bush, the last of six Second World War veterans to occupy the White House, was reliving the great dramas of his youth. He did not yet specifically threaten offensive action, but reported that various world leaders agreed that "Iraq cannot be allowed to benefit from its invasion of Kuwait."

In an address to a joint session on September 11, he noted Gorbachev's agreement that "Iraq's aggression must not be tolerated," and laid out a vision of a new world. "We stand today at a unique and extraordinary moment. The crisis in the Persian Gulf, as grave as it is, also offers a rare opportunity to move toward an historic period of cooperation. Out of these troubled times, our fifth objective—a new world order—can emerge: a new era—freer from the threat of terror, stronger in the pursuit of justice, and more secure in the quest for peace. . . . A hundred generations have searched for this elusive path to peace, while a thousand wars raged across the span of human endeavor. Today that new world is struggling to be born, a world quite different from the one we've known. A world where the rule of law supplants the rule of the jungle. . . . We're now in sight of a United Nations that performs as envisioned by its founders."

The UN Security Council in late November authorized the use of force by member states if Iraq did not withdraw from Kuwait by January 15, and the United States deployed half a million troops on the Iraqi and Kuwaiti border, with active support from many other nations. On January 16, Bush announced the beginning of offensive military action—initially from the air—in a broadcast address to the nation. "Saddam Hussein systematically raped, pillaged, and plundered a tiny nation, no threat to his own," he said. "This is an historic moment. We have in this past year made great progress in ending the long era of conflict and cold war. We have before us the opportunity to forge for ourselves and for future generations a new world order—world where the rule of law, not the law of the jungle, governs the conduct of nations." He continued in the same vein in his annual message on January 29. "The triumph of democratic ideas in Eastern Europe and Latin America and the continuing struggle for freedom elsewhere all around the world all confirm the wisdom of our nation's founders," he said. "Tonight, we work to achieve another victory, a victory over tyranny and savage aggression." "Yes," he continued, "the United States bears a major share of leadership in this effort. Among the nations of the world, only the United States of America has both the moral standing and the means to back it up. We're the only nation on this Earth that could assemble the forces of peace." On February 23 he briefly announced to the nation that a ground war had begun, and just four days later he announced that a cease-fire had been declared after one hundred hours of fighting. "Kuwait is liberated. Iraq's army is defeated," he said. "Our military objectives are met. Kuwait is once more in the hands of Kuwaitis, in control of their own destiny. We share in their joy, a joy tempered only by our compassion for their ordeal." He expressed "pride in our nation and the people whose strength and resolve made victory quick, decisive, and just." In an address to a joint session on March 6 he reported "as Commander in Chief . . . our armed forces fought with honor and valor," and again hailed the coming of a new world "in which freedom and respect for human rights find a home among all nations."

Bush's mood had not changed by the time he gave his next annual message in January 1992. "We gather tonight at a dramatic and deeply promising time in our history and in the history of man on Earth. For in the past 12 months, the world has known changes of almost Biblical proportions. . . . Communism died this year. . . . The biggest thing that has happened in the world in my life, in our lives, is this: By the grace of God, America won the cold war. . . . A world once divided into two armed camps now recognizes one sole and preeminent power, the United States of America. And they regard this with no dread. . . . We are still and ever the freest nation on Earth, the kindest nation on Earth, the strongest nation on Earth." In the same message, however, Bush had to acknowledge serious economic problems at home. Inflation and interest rates, he said, remained low. "But unemployment is too high, some industries are in trouble, and growth is not what it should be. Let me tell you right from the start and right from the heart, I know we're in hard times. But I know something else: This will not stand." The search for similarly decisive measures at home had proven elusive, and the nation entered a recession again.

Bush had promised during the 1988 campaign never to raise federal taxes, and his first address to Congress on February 9, 1989 stuck to the Reagan program. Government, he said, "should not be the provider of first resort for things that the private sector can reward better . . . I believe that family and faith represent the moral compass of the nation." He wanted $500 million to reward the US's best public schools, but he also wanted to encourage school choice. "Over 23 million Americans used illegal drugs last year, at a staggering cost to our nation's well-being," he continued. "Let this be recorded as the time when America rose up and said no to drugs." His very first broadcast address to the nation on September 5, 1989 presented his National Drug Control Strategy. Although he claimed that regular drug users had fallen from twenty-three million in 1985 to fourteen million, he said that the social costs of drugs were "mounting," especially "cocaine, and in particular, crack"—a new, cheaper form that was taking over in urban areas. He asked for $1.5 billion in federal money for state and local law enforcement to fund "more prisons, more jails, more courts, more prosecutors," and "stiffer bail, probation, parole and sentencing." This was, he said, "the toughest domestic challenge we've faced in decades." Congress did not respond, however, and three years later, in his annual message of January 1992, he was still calling for the passage of his "comprehensive crime bill." During that same first summer of his presidency, Bush and the Congress had to deal with the biggest national financial crisis since the Depression: the failure of more than one thousand Savings and Loan institutions, due to a combination of higher interest rates and disastrous deregulation that had begun in 1980. The rescue plan that Congress approved ultimately cost the government $124 billion over the next six years. Bush only referred to the crisis briefly and informally, and never mentioned it in an annual address.

The budget rapidly became the great domestic issue of the Bush administration. Bush initially promised to reach the targets of Ronald Reagan's fiscal 1990 budget—submitted on January 9, 1989. It had forecast a deficit of $162 billion that year, falling to $92.5 billion in fiscal 1991 and reaching a small surplus by fiscal 1993. In his January 29, 1990 budget message Bush raised the projected fiscal 1991 deficit to just $94 billion and promised again not to raise taxes. Economic growth halted during 1990, however, and on June 26 Bush issued a bombshell statement on the need to reduce the deficit: "It is clear to me that both the size of the deficit problem and the need for a package that can be enacted require all of the following: entitlement and mandatory program reform, *tax revenue increases*, growth incentives, discretionary spending reductions, orderly reductions in defense expenditures, and budget process reform to assure that any bipartisan agreement is enforceable and that the deficit problem is brought under responsible control [emphasis added]." The reference to tax increases, in total contradiction to his campaign pledges, started a firestorm among Republicans. On September 11 Bush had to combine his address to Congress on the situation in the Gulf with a drastically revised deficit estimate of $232 billion for fiscal 1991. To meet that threat, he had proposed a five-year, $500 billion deficit reduction program. "To the extent that the deficit reduction program includes new revenue measures, it must avoid any measure that would threaten economic growth or turn us back toward the days of punishing income tax rates. That is one path we should not head down again," he said. He also repeated Reagan's ritual requests for a balanced budget amendment and a line-item veto.

The debate over the "$500 billion" program was the first time that public discussion of a budget revolved around a figure for more than one year. Thirty years later another president was announcing ten-year spending programs. A few weeks later on October 10 Bush told the nation that he had concluded a bipartisan agreement along those lines, that $300 billion of the $500 billion would come from spending cuts, many of them in defense, and that the deal would not raise personal or corporate income taxes. In fact, it raised the top income tax rate from 28 percent to 31 percent, and raised the Alternative Minimum Tax as well. But with unemployment reaching 7.3 percent in 1991 and 7.4 percent in 1992, the deficit increased from $221 billion in fiscal 1990 to $269 billion in fiscal 1991 and $290 billion in fiscal 1992. The Reagan revolution had given the nation a permanent and increasing deficit, and Bush's five-year plan had not solved the problem. In the congressional elections of November 1990—held in the midst of the buildup for the invasion of Iraq—the Democrats gained 7 seats in the House and 1 in the Senate, giving them margins of 267–167 and 56–44.

On May 1, 1992, Bush made his first broadcast address to the American people since the Gulf War about a breakdown in public order. Fourteen months earlier, a Los Angeles resident had photographed a confrontation between a black motorist, Rodney King, and four Los Angeles police officers, who had brutally beaten him after a high-speed chase through the city. A judge had agreed to move the officers' trial to a neighboring county after they were indicted for the beating, and on April 29, 1992 a jury acquitted them on all counts. The riot that followed in Los Angeles was bigger in some respects than any of the urban riots of the 1960s, killing more than sixty people, injuring almost 2000, and burning more than 3000 buildings. Bush on May 1 reported that 3000 National Guardsmen were on duty, that he had sent in 1000 federal riot control personnel, and that 5000 federal troops were on alert. "What we saw last night and the night before in Los Angeles," he said, "is not about civil rights. It's not about the great cause of equality that all Americans must uphold. It's not a message of protest. It's been the brutality of a mob, pure and simple. And let me assure you: I will use whatever force is necessary to restore order." Mentioning Rodney King's name for the first time ever, he said that the video of his beating had given him "anger and pain," and noted that civil rights leaders felt betrayed by the verdict. The federal government had opened its own investigation of the beating. However, "The wanton destruction of life and property is not a legitimate expression of outrage with injustice. It is itself injustice. . . . We must keep on working to create a climate of understanding and tolerance, a climate that refuses to accept racism, bigotry, anti-Semitism, and hate of any kind, anytime, anywhere."

Bush's reelection campaign was now underway, complicated by ongoing negotiations with Mexico to join the US and Canada in NAFTA, the North American Free Trade Agreement, which Bush had called for repeatedly in annual messages. Opposition to NAFTA lay behind the third-party candidacy of a well-known software magnate, H. Ross Perot, who claimed that it would send US industrial jobs to Mexico. The Democrats meanwhile nominated the first candidate from the Boom generation, forty-six-year-old Governor Bill Clinton of Arkansas. Despite all his triumphs on the world stage—including the first brief and successful war that the nation had fought since 1898—Bush could not overcome national anger over the recession. Clinton won only 43 percent of the popular vote, but Bush received just 37.5 percent and Perot a remarkable 18.9 percent, the highest third-party vote since 1912. In the Electoral College Clinton swept the Northeast and the West

Coast and made inroads in the West and the Upper South, piling up 370 electoral votes to Bush's 168.

Bush made three major moves as a lame duck in December. First, on December 4, he addressed the nation on the situation in the East African nation of Somalia. Famine, he explained, had already taken the lives of 250,000 people and might kill 1.5 million more, and the United States had already sent food and pilots to deliver it. Now he had ordered in contingents of marines and army troops to make sure that the food reached its destination amidst general anarchy in a failed state. He assured the Somali people that the US "did not plan to dictate political outcomes" and "respect[ed] your sovereignty and independence." Secondly, he completed the NAFTA negotiations, leaving ratification of the agreement up to Clinton. Then, on December 24, he announced that he was pardoning Reagan's secretary of defense Caspar Weinberger—who was under investigation for concealing evidence in the Iran-Contra investigation—and four other men convicted for their role in the scandal. These men, he said, had acted from patriotic motives, and had not benefited personally from anything that they had done.

Bush had served as president in truly historic times. The collapse of Communism and the Gulf War had left the United States in an unprecedented position of world leadership. Meanwhile, however, the budget crisis and the new recession had laid bare the contradictions in Reagan's policies, which had lost their popularity in much of the nation, and Bush had failed to convince the American people that he was really on their side. The full effects of the new economic policies did not become clear for more than a decade.

# XX

# BILL CLINTON AND GEORGE W. BUSH

### 1993–2001 • 2001–2009

Nominated and elected as a centrist Democrat, Bill Clinton[1] in his first inaugural combined faint echoes of New Deal liberalism with paraphrases of recent Republican presidents. "When most people are working harder for less; when others cannot work at all; when the cost of health care devastates families and threatens to bankrupt our enterprises, great and small; when the fear of crime robs law-abiding citizens of their freedom; and when millions of poor children cannot even imagine the lives we are calling them to lead," he said, "we have not made change our friend.... We must do what America does best: offer more opportunity to all and demand more responsibility from all. It is time to break the bad habit of expecting something for nothing from our Government or from each other. Let us all take more responsibility not only for ourselves and our families but for our communities and our country.... Let us resolve to reform our politics so that power and privilege no longer shout down the voice of the people." Focusing on domestic affairs for nearly his entire tenure, Clinton eventually developed a politically effective and financially successful set of policies within the new framework established by Reagan.

Neither Bush nor Clinton gave a State of the Union address in January 1993, but Clinton presented his economic program to the nation on February 15 and a statement of his goals to a joint session

---

1 Clinton, like Carter, avoided his formal first name.

of Congress two days later. In the first he bluntly attacked the philosophy of the last twelve years: "It declared that Government is the problem, that fairness to the middle class is less important than keeping taxes low on the wealthy, that Government can do nothing about our deepest problems: lost jobs, declining wages, increasing inequality, inadequate educational opportunity, and a health care system that costs a fortune but does too little." While living standards had at one point been doubling every twenty-five years, he noted, at current rates they would not double for one hundred years. He boasted of having cut the White House staff by 25 percent and planning to trim 100,000 federal jobs through attrition, while adding that "the wealthiest must pay their share." He began his speech to Congress with proposals for a stimulus package to fight the recession, and then promised a drastic health care reform proposal later in the year, then in preparation by a team led by First Lady Hillary Rodham Clinton, an attorney. The nation now spent 14 percent of its national income on health care, much more than any other advanced nation, and without changes, he warned, by 2000, that figure might reach 20 percent.[2] Turning to the nation's youth, he asked for an expanded pre-school Head Start program and a large national service program, linked to college loans, that could do for the next generation of members of Congress what the land grant college act and the GI Bill had done for previous generations. He proposed taxing energy by the British thermal unit (BTU) to raise more revenue and encourage energy conservation. Warning that current trends would raise the federal deficit to $635 billion by the end of the decade—80 percent of GDP—he proposed raising the top income tax rate from 31 to 39.6 percent for incomes over $250,000, and increasing corporate taxes from 34 to 36 percent. These measures, he said, would cut the federal deficit from the current $347 billion for 1993 to $207 billion in fiscal 1997. Yet at the same time, echoing Nixon, Reagan, and Bush, he promised a plan "to end welfare as a way of life and make it a path to independence and dignity" and called for "a tough crime bill," including Bush's proposal to add 100,000 police officers. "I believe

---

2 In fact health care spending reached 18.3 percent of GDP by 2021. See https://www.cms.gov/Research-Statistics-Data-and-Systems/Statistics-Trends-and-Reports/NationalHealthExpendData/NationalHealthAccountsHistorical.

we will find our new direction in the basic old values that brought us here over the last two centuries: a commitment to opportunity, to individual responsibility, to community, to work, to family, and to faith," he added in a paraphrase of Reagan.

The plan proved a tough sell, and Clinton, copying Reagan, broadcast an address to the nation on it on August 3. 80 percent of the new tax burden, he insisted, would fall on those making $200,000 or more, and ordinary people would only pay a slightly increased gas tax. Meanwhile the earned income tax credit would increase the income of twenty million low-income families. "Our opponents," he continued, "want to bring the plan down. The guardians of gridlock will do anything to preserve the status quo, to serve special interests, and to drag this thing out." The plan made it through the Congress, passing both the House of Representatives and the Senate by a single vote as Republicans unanimously opposed it and Vice President Gore had to break a Senate tie. Attempting to follow up on this narrow victory, Clinton on October 27, 1993, presented his Health Security Act to Congress in a broadcast address—"an important building block in trying to restore the kind of self-confidence that our country needs to face the future, to embrace the changes of the global economy, and to turn our Nation around." Rather than build upon Medicare or Medicaid, which had now provided insurance to the elderly and the poor for about twenty-five years, the plan proposed requiring all employers to offer health care packages to their employees. Republicans immediately mounted a sweeping attack upon it.

Clinton renewed the call for health care reform in his first annual message in January 1994. Once again he complained that wages had been stagnant or declining for twenty years. "For too many families," he said, "even when both parents were working, the American dream has been slipping away." He lauded the Congress for passing his budget plan, approving the NAFTA free trade agreement with Canada and Mexico—which he had not supported until becoming president—and passing the Brady Bill, a gun control measure named after Reagan's press secretary who had been seriously wounded in the assassination attempt on Reagan in 1981, and a separate ban on semiautomatic assault weapons. The deficit for the current fiscal year, he reported, would be less than $180 billion, 40 percent lower than previously predicted. Once again he pushed for a welfare reform that would force recipients off the rolls after two years of job training and force "deadbeat dads" to pay their child support. He also asked for a pending crime bill to add 100,000 police for "community policing," increase prison capacity, and institute a "three strikes and you're out" law to imprison three-time offenders for life. He pleaded again for renewed values. "We cannot renew our country when within a decade more than half of the children will be born into families where there has been no marriage. We cannot renew this country when 13-year-old boys get semiautomatic weapons to shoot 9-year-olds for kicks. We can't renew our country when children are having children and the fathers walk away as if the kids don't amount to anything." The Clinton administration continued to submit annual budgets to Congress every February as required by the Budget and Accounting Act of 1921, but Clinton replaced the practice of providing a detailed budget message signed by himself with a brief statement of his administration's priorities—a practice maintained by his successor.

A bipartisan majority passed the crime bill during 1994, but opposition forced Clinton to abandon his health care reform without a vote. His energy tax also went nowhere. Then, in November, the Democratic Party suffered its worst defeat in a congressional election since 1946. The Republicans gained 54 seats in the House of Representatives, many of them in the South, and emerged with a 230–205 majority led by young Speaker Newt Gingrich. They also gained 8 Senate seats, turning a 52–44 deficit into 52–48 control of the upper body. Not since 1953 had they controlled both chambers, and the future seemed to belong to them.

Harry Truman also failed to get Congress to vote on his 1945 national health insurance proposal, but he stuck to it even after the Republican congressional victory in 1946. Clinton's January 1995 annual message, on the other hand, set a new tone that lasted for the rest of his presidency. Marking a break with the past, he announced a "New Covenant" and effectively repudiated the whole New Deal tradition. "I think we all agree that we have to change the way the Government works. Let's make it smaller, less costly, and smarter; leaner, not meaner. The old way of governing around here protected organized interests. We should look out for the interests of ordinary people. The old way divided us by interest, constituency, or class. The New Covenant way should unite us behind a common vision of what's best for our country. The old way dispensed services through large, top-down, inflexible bureaucracies. The New Covenant way should shift these resources and decision-making from bureaucrats to citizens, injecting choice and competition and individual responsibility into national policy. . . . Our job here is to expand opportunity, not bureaucracy." He boasted of $250 billion in spending cuts over two years, announced plans to cut another $130 billion more, and renewed the call for a line-item veto. Raising a new issue, he said that "all Americans . . . are rightly disturbed by the large numbers of illegal aliens entering our country," most of them from Mexico. "The jobs they hold might otherwise be held by citizens or legal immigrants. The public service they use impose burdens on our taxpayers. That's why our administration has moved aggressively to secure our borders more by hiring a record number of new border guards, by deporting twice as many criminal aliens as ever before, by cracking down on illegal hiring, by barring welfare benefits to illegal aliens."[3]

The new Republican majorities, elected on Gingrich's Contract with America platform, tried for the whole of the 1995 congressional session to reshape budget priorities, proposing tax cuts and severe cuts in Medicare, Medicaid, and many other programs. On June 13, 1995, Clinton addressed the nation on the budget. Committing himself to balancing it, he rejected proposed Republican cuts in Medicare and education and their proposed tax cut for the highest earners, while agreeing to cut discretionary spending other than defense and education by 20 percent. On December 6 Clinton vetoed their budget and its plan to balance the budget within seven years. The Republican plan, he repeated, "would cut deeply into Medicare, Medicaid, student loans, and nutrition programs; hurt the environment; raise taxes on millions of working men and women and their families by slashing the Earned Income Tax Credit (EITC); and provide a huge tax cut whose benefits would flow disproportionately to those who are already the most well-off." Detailed analysis supported each one of those points.

---

3 This was not at the time merely a conservative position. Clinton followed the recommendations of a bipartisan commission headed by liberal Democratic congresswoman Barbara Jordan.

Despite a brief government shutdown in December after the Republican Congress failed to raise the national debt ceiling, the two parties had not agreed on a budget by the time Clinton gave his next annual message on January 23, 1996. He had however definitely established his new voice and laid the groundwork for his reelection campaign. He reported "the lowest combined rates of unemployment and inflation in 27 years," nearly eight million new jobs, and lower crime rates, welfare and food stamp rolls, and poverty and teen pregnancy rates. "We know big Government does not have all the answers," he said. "We know there's not a program for every problem. . . . The era of big Government is over. . . . I believe our new, smaller Government must work in an old-fashioned American way, together with all of our citizens through State and local governments, in the workplace, in religious, charitable, and civic associations." His 1993 budget plan had now cut the deficit nearly in half, reducing interest rates, and he estimated that the budget could be balanced within seven years, even with a modest tax cut. The president's reelection campaign had begun, and the Republicans, whom polls showed the nation blamed for the government shutdown, gave up their hopes of large cuts in entitlement programs that year. Congress yielded to the entreaties of the last three presidents and passed an act authorizing line-item presidential vetoes, but the Supreme Court immediately ruled it unconstitutional. And on August 22, 1996, Clinton signed a welfare reform measure—the "Personal Responsibility and Work Opportunity Reconciliation Act of 1996"—after vetoing several Republican versions. It eliminated the Aid to Families with Dependent Children program that originated with Social Security in 1936, turned the program largely over to the states, and required most recipients to find work within two years. During the same summer of 1996 Clinton signed the Defense of Marriage Act, affirming that marriage must be defined as the union of a man and a woman and denying the right of any state to authorize gay marriages that other states would have to recognize.

The Republicans had by then nominated Second World War veteran Bob Dole for president, and Ross Perot renewed his third-party candidacy. Clinton's centrist strategy paid dividends. He improved his share of the popular vote from 43 percent to 49.2 percent, while Dole got 40.7 percent and Perot fell to 8.4 percent.

The Democrats however gained just 2 seats in the House, leaving the Republicans with a 226–207 majority, and the Republicans increased their Senate margin by 2 to 55–45. Since Clinton had shown his willingness to use the veto power to stop a new conservative revolution, his second term figured to be largely a repeat of the first.

Clinton's inaugural restated his moderate position. "In these 4 years," he said, "we have been touched by tragedy, exhilarated by challenge, strengthened by achievement. America stands alone as the world's indispensable nation. Once again, our economy is the strongest on Earth. . . . And once again, we have resolved for our time a great debate over the role of Government. Today we can declare: Government is not the problem, and Government is not the solution. We—the American people—we are the solution." In his subsequent annual message he called for passage of the bipartisan McCain-Feingold campaign finance reform act, and proclaimed new education goals: "Every 8-year-old must be able to read; every 12-year-old must be able to log on to the Internet; every 18-year-old must be able to go to college; and every adult American must be able to keep on learning for a lifetime. . . . Tonight I issue a challenge to the Nation: Every State should adopt high national standards, and by 1999, every State should test every fourth grader in reading and every eighth grader in math to make sure these standards are met." He called for $5 billion annually for new school construction, public school choice for parents, and the establishment of 3,000 charter schools around the country. Serious crime, he reported, had fallen, but he asked for 100,000 more community police to fight a larger war on gangs. Lastly, Clinton presented extraordinary news about the federal budget. The deficit had now fallen from $255 billion in fiscal 1993 to $107 billion in fiscal 1996, and would total just $22 billion for fiscal 1997. Clinton predicted, correctly as it turned out, that the government would run a surplus for fiscal 1998. The combination of sustained economic growth and the 1990 and 1993 tax increases had more than closed the fiscal gap that Reagan's tax cuts had opened up.

These themes dominated Clinton's whole second term. In his last three annual messages he praised a series of measures to increase access to college and declared in January 1999 that the nation had opened the door to college for all Americans. He now identified more education as the key to further economic progress. He repeatedly called with less success for more school construction funds, and asked for an end to social promotions in primary and secondary schools. On health care he asked unsuccessfully for a patients' bill of rights to make health insurance more secure, and various measures to discourage smoking. Congress in 1997 passed a new Children's Health Insurance Program that immediately enrolled two million children, but he wanted more. It also passed the McCain-Feingold campaign finance law. In January 1998 he raised a new issue. "Our overriding environmental challenge tonight is the worldwide problem of climate change, global warming, the gathering crisis that requires worldwide action. The vast majority of scientists have concluded unequivocally that if we don't reduce the emission of greenhouse gases, at some point in the next century, we'll disrupt our climate and put our children and grandchildren at risk. This past December, America led the world to reach a historic agreement committing our Nation to reduce greenhouse gas emissions through market forces, new technologies, energy efficiency. . . . I propose $6 billion in tax cuts and research and development to encourage innovation, renewable energy, fuel-efficient cars, energy-efficient homes." And having adopted NAFTA, he repeatedly called in annual addresses for the authority to conclude further new trade agreements to increase commerce.

This record of fairly steady achievement, especially in the fiscal realm, took place against a background of minor scandals and investigations. Allegations of impropriety in an Arkansas land deal known as Whitewater had led to the appointment of two special prosecutors in 1994. The second one, Kenneth Starr, broadened the investigation to include allegations relating to Clinton's possible sexual harassment while governor of Arkansas and his possibly perjured testimony about it in a civil suit. In January 1998, allegations of a Clinton affair with a White House intern, Monica Lewinsky, broke into the open. Clinton initially denied any sexual relationship with her but eventually had to admit to sexual encounters.[4]

---

4 It emerged, however, that Clinton and Lewinsky had never had intercourse.

Clinton addressed the nation about the matter on August 17, 1998. "As you know," he said, "in a deposition in January I was asked questions about my relationship with Monica Lewinsky. While my answers were legally accurate, I did not volunteer information. Indeed, I did have a relationship with Ms. Lewinsky that was not appropriate." He apologized profusely, but also complained that independent counsel Kenneth Starr's investigation had "gone on too long, cost too much, and hurt too many innocent people." While the media excoriated Clinton, the American people did not seem to care very much. In the November midterm elections the Democrats gained 5 seats in the House, reducing the Republican majority to 223–211, and the balance in the Senate remained unchanged with 55 Republicans and 45 Democrats. The House of Representatives however impeached Clinton for lying about the Lewinsky matter and obstruction of justice, 228–206 and 221–212, but the Senate acquitted him by votes of 55–45 for acquittal and 50–50.

A year later, on November 12, 1999, Clinton signed the fateful Gramm-Leach-Billey Act, making "the most important legislative changes to the structure of the U.S. financial system since the 1930s." It specifically repealed the provisions of the 1933 Glass-Steagall Act that had required that commercial and investment banks be completely separate institutions so as to insulate depositors from investment risks, and parts of the Bank Holding Company Act, which had limited relationships between banks and insurance companies. "Removal of barriers to competition will enhance the stability of our financial services system. Financial services firms will be able to diversify their product offerings and thus their sources of revenue. They will also be better equipped to compete in global financial markets," Clinton said. He never referred to this law again, but it revolutionized American economic life, and set the stage for the events that led to the nation's first big financial crisis since the Depression in 2008. Meanwhile, Clinton stopped pointing out that most working Americans were no longer sharing in economic growth, whose rewards were concentrated at the top of the economic pyramid, after the Republican congressional sweep of 1994.

"The state of our Union is the strongest it has ever been," Clinton declared in his last annual message on January 27, 2000. "We restored the vital center, replacing outmoded ideologies with a new vision anchored in basic, enduring values: opportunity for all, responsibility from all, a community of all Americans." Education, he insisted once again, would allow Americans to compete in the new global economy. Crime was down 20 percent, teen births had fallen, and the welfare rolls had been cut in half. The fiscal 1999 surplus had reached $126 billion and would almost double in fiscal 2000, and Clinton discussed what to do with it. While proposing to retain some of it to shore up Social Security and Medicare, he also promised to pay off the whole national debt for the first time since 1835. He proposed new gun control measures, one of which the House had already refused to pass, in the wake of the Columbine high school massacre in Colorado, and called again for action on global warming. The government ran an all-time record surplus of $236 billion in fiscal 2000, and unemployment for 2000 fell below 4 percent for the first time since 1969.

Domestically, Clinton had closed the fiscal gap that Reagan had opened up with one substantial top-bracket tax increase, while preserving the Great Society safety net against Republican attacks. And while he probably devoted less time to foreign policy than any president since the 1920s, he, like Bush, repeatedly took advantage of the United States' freedom to act abroad in the wake of the collapse of the USSR and the end of the Cold War. On June 26, 1993, in his first broadcast address devoted to foreign policy, he told the nation that the Kuwaiti government had uncovered an Iraqi plot to assassinate former president Bush while he visited that country. "We should not be surprised by such deeds," he said, "coming as they do from a regime like Saddam Hussein's, which is ruled by atrocity, slaughtered its own people, invaded two neighbors, attacked others, and engaged in chemical and environmental warfare." Sixteen months later, on October 10, 1994, he reported deploying ships, troops and aircraft to the Persian Gulf in response to new Iraqi troop movements threatening Kuwait. Under the terms of the 1991 cease-fire Iraq remained subject to UN weapons inspections and significant economic sanctions, and on December 16, 1998, at the height of the Lewinsky scandal, Clinton announced that the United States had taken military action to enforce these terms and declared a new goal of overthrowing Saddam's regime. Saddam, he reported, now refused to allow United Nations inspectors into the country, and might resume the production of weapons of mass destruction (WMDs). Joined by Prime Minister Tony Blair of Great Britain, Clinton had ordered "a strong, sustained series of airstrikes against Iraq" to "degrade" Saddam's WMD capability. Saddam remained a danger to the region and the world. "We should not be surprised by such deeds," he continued, "coming as they do from a regime like Saddam Hussein's. . . . In a new century, we'll have a remarkable opportunity to shape a future more peaceful than the past but only if we stand strong against the enemies of peace. Tonight, the United States is doing just that." Saddam remained in power when Clinton left office.

Clinton also had to deal with two failed states elsewhere. After Bush had dispatched American troops into famine-ridden Somalia in East Africa, their goals had increased to include stabilizing the country politically. That led in October 1993 to a bloody battle in the capital of Mogadishu. "This past weekend," Clinton told the nation on October 10, "we all reacted with anger and horror as an armed Somali gang desecrated the bodies of our American soldiers and displayed a captured American pilot, all of them soldiers who were taking part in an international effort to end the starvation of the Somali people themselves." Only 5000 US troops now remained, and Clinton announced that he was sending a few thousand more to protect them and to prevent a return to anarchy throughout the country. Immediate withdrawal would undermine world leadership, he said, but he promised to remove the troops within six months, as indeed he did. A year later on September 15, 1994, he addressed the nation on foreign policy again. "My fellow Americans," he said, "tonight I want to speak with you about why the United States is leading the international effort to restore democratic government in Haiti." Military rulers led by General Raoul Cedras, he explained, had gone back on a promise to give up power to the newly elected Jean-Bertrand Aristide. The UN Security Council had authorized the use of force to overthrow them, and the US had to act to "protect our interests, to stop the brutal atrocities that threaten tens of thousands of Haitians, to secure our borders, and preserve stability and promote democracy in our hemisphere and to uphold the reliability of the commitments we make and the commitments others make to us." While agreeing that the US could and should not be "the world's policeman," he echoed McKinley nearly one hundred years earlier: "when brutality occurs close to our shores, it affects our national interests. And we have a responsibility to act. . . . Restoring Haiti's democratic government will help lead to more stability and prosperity in our region, just as our actions in Panama and Grenada did." Three days later he announced that the Haitian military leaders had agreed to step down.

The Clinton administration also worked to end two other conflicts. Beginning in 1990, the collapse of Communism had led to the breakup of Yugoslavia into several different states, accompanied by brutal wars between Serbs and Croats and Christians and Muslims. The Bosnian region had been the scene of particularly horrifying massacres. During 1995 American negotiators brokered a peace agreement among the parties calling for a multinational peacekeeping force in Dayton, Ohio, and on November 27, 1995, Clinton called upon Congress and the nation to support the agreement and provide some American troops to help implement it. The peace would bring "stability to Central Europe, a region of the world that is vital to our national interests." The US, he pointed out, had stepped back after the First World War and continued to lead after the Second. "As the cold war gives way to the global village," he said, "our leadership is needed more than ever because problems that start beyond our borders can quickly become problems within them. . . . My fellow Americans, in this new era there are still times when America and America alone can and should make the difference for peace. The terrible war in Bosnia is such a case." Clinton was in effect confirming a bipartisan consensus about the dominant US role in the post–Cold War world, and Congress approved the agreement. Earlier, in his January 1995 annual message, Clinton had referred to the historic meeting at the White House in which Prime Minister Yitzhak Rabin of Israel and Palestinian leader Yasir Arafat had shaken hands and agreed on a new path to peace that might lead to a Palestinian state. Despite Rabin's assassination by an Israeli opponent of peace later that year, their negotiations continued for the whole of Clinton's administration, but without reaching agreement.

The liquidation of the Cold War continued. In his 1995 annual message Clinton asked the Senate to approve a new START II treaty with Russia that would eliminate 5000 more nuclear warheads. The Senate did so a year later. He also promised to go forward with an agreement with North Korea to restrain its nuclear program. In his 1997 annual message he announced a new strategy in Europe. "When Europe is stable, prosperous, and at peace," he said, "America is more secure. To that end, we must expand NATO by 1999, so that countries that were once our adversaries can become our allies." Poland, Hungary and the Czech Republic joined NATO in 1999. More generally, Clinton in his 1994 annual address and later endorsed the idea that the spread of democracy would ensure peace. "Ultimately, the best strategy to ensure our security and to build a durable peace is to support the advance of democracy elsewhere," he said. "Democracies don't attack each other." In his last annual message in January 2000 he called upon the nation "to continue to encourage our former adversaries, Russia and China, to emerge as stable, prosperous, democratic nations," and advocated bringing China into the World Trade Organization.

On August 20, 1998, Clinton announced military action on a new front. "Today I ordered our Armed Forces to strike at terrorist-related facilities in Afghanistan and Sudan because of the imminent threat they presented to our national security," he said. "Our target was terror; our mission was clear: to strike at the network of radical groups affiliated with and funded by Usama bin Ladin [sic], perhaps the preeminent organizer and financier of international terrorism in the world today." In response to a series of actual or planned terrorist attacks—including attacks on the US embassies in Kenya and Tanzania—the US had "carried out simultaneous strikes against terrorist facilities and infrastructure in Afghanistan" and against a factory in Sudan "associated with the Bin Laden network" making materials for chemical weapons.[5] Bin Laden, Clinton said, had vowed to wage a terrorist war against Americans both military and civilian. The cruise missile attacks on his bases did not reach him personally.

In early 1999 Clinton, like Bush before him, embarked upon a distant war for American principles. In the wake of the breakup of Yugoslavia, Serbia, which had dominated Yugoslavia, had sent troops into the neighboring region of Kosovo to destroy its autonomy. "My fellow Americans," he told the nation on March 24, "today

---

5 The latter accusation remains very controversial. See the letter from John Ryle and the response from Gary Wills, *New York Review of Books*, October 21, 2004.

our Armed Forces joined our NATO Allies in airstrikes against Serbian forces responsible for the brutality in Kosovo." Echoing his predecessor's bloodcurdling rhetoric about Panama and Iraq, he continued that in Kosovo, "We've seen innocent people taken from their homes, forced to kneel in the dirt, and sprayed with bullets; Kosovar men dragged from their families, fathers and sons together, lined up and shot in cold blood. . . . Ending this tragedy is a moral imperative." NATO, he said, was "acting early" as nations had failed to do during the two world wars or in Bosnia, and it would have discredited NATO to allow massacres to continue, leading to a wider war. Clinton acted even though he could not, like Bush before him, secure a UN Security Council resolution in support of the use of force, because Russia and China would not agree to one. He promised that the United States would not send ground troops and that NATO would fight only from the air. On June 10 he announced that Serbia had agreed to withdraw its troops from Kosovo, and that "the one million men, women and children driven from their land are preparing to return home." The International Court of Justice had indicted Serbian leader Slobodan Milosevic for war crimes. Clinton thanked President Boris Yeltsin of Russia, who had opposed the war but helped bring about the cease-fire. He had reaffirmed US predominance in the post–Cold War era.

Vice President Al Gore, following in the footsteps of Hubert Humphrey and Walter Mondale, rapidly emerged as Clinton's presumed successor in 2000. The Republican nomination went to George W. Bush, the former president's oldest son, who had served six years as governor of Texas. A lackluster campaign led to the most controversial election since Hayes vs. Tilden in 1876. When the votes were counted on election night, Gore had won the popular vote 48.4 percent to 47.9 percent, and the electoral count depended on the state of Florida and its twenty-five electoral votes. The initial count gave Bush the victory by less than two thousand votes out of more than four million cast. Gore demanded a recount in four key heavily Democratic counties, and the Florida Supreme Court granted his request. In early December, however, the United States Supreme Court heard arguments in the case of *Bush vs. Gore* and by a 5–4 margin ordered that the recount stop because it denied Bush the equal protection of the laws. Gore immediately accepted that result. A subsequent study by a consortium of major newspapers showed that confusing instructions had led a much larger number of Gore voters than Bush voters to spoil their ballots, and that Gore might well have won a recount of the whole state, depending on the exact standards that were applied.[6] Meanwhile, the Republicans lost only 2 seats in the House, retaining a 221–214 majority, but lost 4 in the Senate, leaving it tied, 50–50.

"In all the work I have done as President—" Clinton said in a January 18, 2001 farewell address, "every decision I have made, every executive action I have taken, every bill I have proposed and signed—I've tried to give all Americans the tools and conditions to build the future of our dreams in a good society with a strong economy, a cleaner environment, and a freer, safer, more prosperous world." Once again he boasted of higher employment, smaller welfare rolls, lower crime rates, more tuition aid for college, more children with health insurance, and higher test scores and more effective schools. He concluded with three thoughts about the future. The nation "must maintain our record of fiscal responsibility"; "American's security and prosperity require us to continue to lead the world"; and "we here at home" must "weave the threads of our coat of many colors into the fabric of one America. As we become ever more diverse, we must work harder to unite around our common values and our common humanity." His successors have pursued those goals with extraordinarily mixed results.

George W. Bush's brief inaugural address focused mostly on domestic affairs, and included some unusually specifically religious elements. "The ambitions of some Americans," he said, "are limited by failing schools and hidden prejudice and the circumstances of their birth. . . . I will work to build a single nation of justice and opportunity. I know this is in our reach because we are guided by a power larger than ourselves, who creates us equal, in His image, and we are confident in principles that unite and lead us onward." He promised to "reclaim America's schools," "reform Social Security and Medicare," and "reduce taxes to recover the momentum of our economy and reward . . . enterprise." Abroad he promised to "confront weapons of mass destruction, so that a new century is spared

---

6 https://www.chicagotribune.com/news/sns-ballots-story.html.

new horrors." "Church and charity, synagogue and mosque lend our communities their humanity," he continued, "and they will have an honored place in our plans and in our laws." We shall eventually see that Bush's domestic policies followed this blueprint quite closely, but they were all thrust into the background by his sweeping response to the events of September 11, 2001. By the time of his first annual message on January 29, 2002, Bush, like Franklin Roosevelt in 1940–41 and Harry Truman in 1947–50, had developed a sweeping new worldview and announced new strategies to reach new objectives.

In a brief broadcast address that evening, after attacks on the World Trade Center and the Pentagon and the crash of United Flight 93 in Pennsylvania had taken nearly three thousand lives, Bush declared, "Today our fellow citizens, our way of life, our very freedom came under attack in a series of deliberate and deadly terrorist acts. . . . The search is underway for those who are behind these evil acts. . . . We will make no distinction between the terrorists who committed these acts and those who harbor them." A broadcast address to a joint session on September 20 went much further. He asked for the creation of a new Department of Homeland Security to prevent further attacks within the US. Identifying Osama Bin Laden and Al-Qaida as the perpetrators of the attacks, Bush identified Al-Qaida's goal as "remaking the world and imposing its radical beliefs on people everywhere. . . . The terrorists' directive commands them to kill Christians and Jews, to kill all Americans, and make no distinctions among military and civilians, including women and children. . . . The leadership of Al Qaida has great influence in Afghanistan and supports the Taliban regime in controlling most of that country." Bush now turned the Taliban, a radical Islamist group that had eventually taken power after the Soviet Union left Afghanistan in 1986, into a target as well. "We condemn the Taliban regime. It is not only repressing its own people; it is threatening people everywhere by sponsoring and sheltering and supplying terrorists. By aiding and abetting murder, the Taliban regime is committing murder." The Taliban, he said, must "hand over the terrorists, or they will share in their fate." Bush then addressed the world's Muslims. "We respect your faith. . . . Its teachings are good and peaceful, and those who commit evil in the name of Allah blaspheme the name of Allah. The terrorists are traitors to their own faith, trying, in effect, to hijack Islam itself." The terrorists, he said, "hate our freedoms. . . . They are the heirs of all the murderous ideologies of the 20th century. By sacrificing human life to serve their radical visions, by abandoning every value except the will to power, they follow in the path of fascism and Nazism and totalitarianism. And they will follow that path all the way, to where it ends, in history's unmarked grave of discarded lies. . . . Americans should not expect one battle but a lengthy campaign, unlike any other we have ever seen. . . . From this day forward, any nation that continues to harbor or support terrorism will be regarded by the United States as a hostile regime. . . . Our Nation—this generation—will lift a dark threat of violence from our people and our future. We will rally the world to this cause by our efforts, by our courage. We will not tire; we will not falter; and we will not fail."

Less than three weeks later on October 7 Bush announced that air strikes in Afghanistan had begun because the Taliban had rejected his demands. "Our military action is also designed to clear the way for sustained, comprehensive, and relentless operations to drive [the terrorists] out and bring them to justice," he warned. Speaking to the nation on homeland security from Atlanta on November 8, Bush insisted that the September 11 attacks had transformed America. "None of us would ever wish the evil that has been done to our country," he said, "yet we have learned that out of evil can come great good." He praised children for contributing more than $1 million for children in Afghanistan, the compassion of "Jewish and Christian Americans who have reached out to their Muslim neighbors," and "parents spending more time with their children and many people spending more time in prayer and in houses of worship. . . . We are a different country than we were on September the 10th, sadder and less innocent, stronger and more united, and in the face of ongoing threats, determined and courageous." He praised the passage of "a new antiterrorism law"—the Patriot Act— which would give law enforcement new tools "to track terrorists." Today's high school seniors, he said, "will graduate in the midst of a war in our own country." He also highlighted the dispatch of letters containing anthrax bacteria to news media outlets and senators, which had killed five people and were now under investigation.[7]

---

7 This crime was never solved.

Bush struck triumphant notes in his first annual message on January 29, 2002. Since the attacks, the nation had "captured, arrested, and rid the world of thousands of terrorists" and "freed a country [Afghanistan] from brutal oppression. America and Afghanistan are now allies against terror. We'll be partners in rebuilding that country." "Our discoveries in Afghanistan," he continued, "confirmed our worst fears and showed us the true scope of the task ahead. . . . We have found diagrams of American nuclear power plants and public water facilities, detailed instructions for making chemical weapons, surveillance maps of American cities, and thorough descriptions of landmarks in America and throughout the world." He defined "two great objectives." "First, we will shut down terrorist camps, disrupt terrorist plans, and bring terrorists to justice. And second, we must prevent the terrorists and regimes who seek chemical, biological, or nuclear weapons from threatening the United States and the world. . . . A terrorist underworld, including groups like Hamas, Hizballah [sic], Islamic Jihad, Jaish-e-Mohammed, operates in remote jungles and deserts and hides in the centers of large cities." Then he spoke his most fateful words.

"Our second goal is to prevent regimes that sponsor terror from threatening America or our friends and allies with weapons of mass destruction," he said. He referred specifically to North Korea, Iran, and Iraq—and while the first two states earned one sentence each, Iraq earned five. "States like these and their terrorist allies constitute an axis of evil, arming to threaten the peace of the world. By seeking weapons of mass destruction, these regimes pose a grave and growing danger. . . . I will not wait on events while dangers gather. I will not stand by as peril draws closer and closer. The United States of America will not permit the world's most dangerous regimes to threaten us with the world's most destructive weapons." "We have no intention of imposing our culture," he added. "But America will always stand firm for the nonnegotiable demands of human dignity: the rule of law; limits on the power of the state; respect for women; private property; free speech; equal justice; and religious tolerance." We will "take the side of brave men and women who advocate these values around the world." Bush was obviously echoing Wilson, Franklin Roosevelt, and many Cold War presidents, but none of them had used the first person singular pronoun so freely, and none of them had bluntly advocated *preemptive* war against potential enemies as he did. He was however elaborating an idea that both his father and Clinton had clearly stated: that with the Cold War over, nothing should stand in the way of whatever the United States wanted for the world. Once again he argued that 9/11 had forced America to see "our better selves." "For too long," he said, "our culture has said, 'If it feels good, do it.' Now America is embracing a new ethic and a new creed, 'Let's roll.'"

Bush broadcast three more major addresses on the new "War on Terror" during 2002. He claimed on June 2 that captured Al Qaida members had revealed "that thousands of trained killers are plotting to attack us, and this terrible knowledge requires us to act differently." He once again demanded the creation of the Department of Homeland Security, comparing it to the formation of the Defense Department and the National Security Council in 1947. Congress agreed within a few months. Speaking from Ellis Island, where millions of immigrants had landed in New York Harbor, Bush in a September 11 anniversary address proclaimed, "The attack on our Nation was also an attack on the ideals that make us a nation. Our deepest national conviction is that every life is precious, because every life is the gift of a Creator who intended us to live in liberty and equality. . . . I believe there is a reason that history has matched this Nation with this time. America strives to be tolerant and just." And in a broadcast address on October 7, he proclaimed "a grave threat to peace" and "America's determination to lead the world in confronting that threat." That threat, he said, came from Iraq, which "possesses and produces chemical and biological weapons," was "seeking nuclear weapons," and had "given shelter and support to terrorism and practices terror against its own people." "We know that Iraq and Al Qaida have had high-level contacts that go back a decade," he continued. He cited specific evidence that Saddam Hussein was once again trying to build nuclear weapons. "Facing clear evidence of peril, we cannot wait for the final proof, the smoking gun, that could come in the form of a mushroom cloud. . . . Saddam Hussein must disarm himself, or for the sake of peace, we will lead a coalition to disarm him." The Clinton administration had also stated that only Saddam's removal could remove a danger to our nation, and this would help the Iraqi people more than anyone. Congress responded by overwhelmingly approving a resolution for military action against Iraq if Saddam refused to disarm, and the American people responded by giving the Republican Party majorities of 51–48 in the Senate and 229–205 in the House in the November elections.[8] Bush repeated all the arguments of the October 7 speech in his annual message on January 28, adding more specific claims about Saddam's chemical weapons stocks and attempts to secure nuclear materials.

On March 17, 2003, Bush declared to the nation that Saddam Hussein had refused to disarm. He acknowledged that while the UN Security Council had agreed on the seriousness of the threat, various unnamed permanent members—who in fact included Russia, China, and France—would not vote for war against him. That gave him no pause. "The United Nations Security Council has not lived up to its responsibilities," he said, "so we will rise to ours." He gave Saddam Hussein and his two sons forty-eight hours to leave Iraq, or face "military conflict." Forty-eight hours later he announced that war had begun. American troops swiftly reached Baghdad, and on May 1, Bush staged another address to the nation wearing combat dress on the deck of the aircraft carrier USS Abraham Lincoln. "Major combat operations in Iraq have ended," he said. "In the battle of Iraq, the United States and our allies have prevailed. And now our coalition is engaged in securing and reconstructing that country."

The war in Iraq and the broader War on Terror—increasingly defined as a struggle for democracy all over the world, and especially in the Middle East—remained the centerpiece of each of Bush's five remaining annual messages from 2004 through 2008, and of five other broadcast addresses to the nation. The collapse of Saddam's regime did not lead to stability in Iraq, but rather to an uprising among the minority Sunni Muslims who had ruled the nation under him and a violent struggle for power among them and Shi'ite groups. Meanwhile, occupying forces discovered that Saddam had had no chemical or biological weapons at all and no active nuclear program. No war in US history had proven to be founded on such false assumptions. Bush never expressed any second thoughts. In his January 2004 annual message he blamed "a remnant of violent Saddam supporters" and foreign terrorists who had come to Iraq

---

8 The Republicans had lost control of the Senate in early 2001 when Republican Jim Jeffords of Vermont had become an independent caucusing with the Democrats.

for the continuing violence, but claimed, "we are making progress against them." He also praised Libyan dictator Qadhafi for abandoning his nuclear program and reported pressure against those of Iran and North Korea. "We also hear doubts that democracy is a realistic goal for the greater Middle East, where freedom is rare," he continued. "Yet it is mistaken and condescending to assume that whole cultures and great religions are incompatible with liberty and self-government. I believe that God has planted in every human heart the desire to live in freedom, and even when that desire is crushed by tyranny for decades, it will rise again." In his second inaugural after a close reelection victory, Bush went even further. "Across the generations," he said, "we have proclaimed the imperative of self-government, because no one is fit to be a master and no one deserves to be a slave. It is the policy of the United States to seek and support the growth of democratic movements and institutions in every nation and culture, with the ultimate goal of ending tyranny in our world. . . . We will persistently clarify the choice before every ruler and every nation, the moral choice between oppression, which is always wrong, and freedom, which is eternally right." Bush had meanwhile abandoned at least two other venerable US policies. On May 1, 2001, he had announced his intention to withdraw from the ABM treaty with Russia so as to allow the US to deploy missile defenses, a step he took later that year. And on April 14, 2004, in a statement on Israeli-Palestinian negotiations, he stated, "In light of new realities on the ground, including already existing major Israeli populations centers, it is unrealistic to expect that the outcome of final status negotiations will be a full and complete return to the armistice lines of 1949"—the lines hitherto described as Israel's "1967 borders," which the United States had previously regarded as the still-valid borders of Israel.

On June 28, 2005, in another address to the nation, Bush cited six cities around the world where terrorist attacks had taken place and called Iraq a front in the War on Terror. Many terrorists there, he said, followed the same ideology as the 9/11 attackers, and the nation had "to defeat them abroad before they attack us at home . . . . They know that as freedom takes root in Iraq, it will inspire millions across the Middle East to claim their liberty as well." The US was now suffering about nine hundred soldiers killed in action in Iraq every year. Six months later, on December 15, Bush told the American people that recent national elections in Iraq meant "that America has an ally of growing strength in the fight against terror." In fact, those elections, in which Sunnis, Shi'ites and Kurds all voted almost entirely along ethnic lines, foreshadowed the violent political conflict and civil war that has continued in Iraq to this day. He repeated that the terrorists wanted to drive the US out of the Middle East and attack it at home. "Tonight," he said, "I ask all of you listening to carefully consider the stakes of this war, to realize how far we have come and the good we are doing, and to have patience in this difficult, noble, and necessary cause. . . . I know this war is controversial; yet being your President requires doing what I believe is right and accepting the consequences." In his January 2006 annual message he restated his "historic, long-term goal: We seek the end of tyranny in our world. Some dismiss that goal as misguided idealism. In reality, the future security of America depends on it." Terrorists, he said, wanted to seize Iraq to use it as a safe haven for attacks on the US and the world. He claimed that democracy was spreading. He repeated the same themes in a fifth-anniversary address on September 11, 2006, calling the conflict "the decisive ideological struggle of the twenty-first century and the calling of our generation." The torture of suspected terrorist prisoners at the new US prison in Guantanamo, in Cuba, and elsewhere, had become a fierce political issue, but Bush merely said that key suspects "have been questioned by the Central Intelligence Agency, and they provided valuable information that has helped stop attacks in America and across the world."[9] The administration, as we shall see, had run into major domestic difficulties as well, and the Republicans lost control of both houses of Congress for the first time since 1992 in the midterm elections, as the Democrats won a 233–202 House majority with 31 new seats and an effective 51–49 majority in the Senate thanks to a gain of 6 seats.

Bush promptly accepted the resignation of Secretary of Defense Donald Rumsfeld and announced a new Iraq strategy to the nation on January 10, 2007. After the election, he said, "Al Qaida terrorists and Sunni insurgents recognized the mortal danger that Iraq's

---

9 Bush never referred to the abuse of Iraqi prisoners by US soldiers at Abu Ghraib prison in Baghdad.

elections posed for their cause, and they responded with outrageous acts of murder aimed at innocent Iraqis," creating "a vicious cycle of sectarian violence." In response the United States would now add 20,000 new troops to its contingent in Baghdad, the center of the violence, to assist Iraqi troops. Led by General David Petraeus, the Surge, as it was called, eventually reduced the violence substantially. In his last annual message on January 28, 2008, Bush announced that 20,000 troops would now be withdrawn—while 3,200 new troops went to Afghanistan, where the Taliban was enjoying something of a resurgence. He also promised a new effort to secure peace between Israel and the Palestinians, and demanded that Iran suspend the enrichment of uranium—a possible step toward a nuclear weapon—and cease oppression at home and support for terror abroad. During the rest of his last year foreign affairs retreated into the background as the nation's worst economic crisis since 1929 broke out.

Domestically, Bush built on the Clinton legacy in education and health care, and returned to the Reagan era with respect to fiscal policy. Addressing a joint session of Congress on February 27, 2001, he proposed an additional $1 billion a year "to help every child in America learn to read" and to triple funding for "character education" to teach "right and wrong." Children, he said, needed testing on reading and math every year from third to eighth grade, and children in failing schools needed access to private tutoring and charter schools. A year later he praised Congress for passing the No Child Left Behind Act, embodying some of these proposals, and he claimed in every subsequent annual message that the act was raising test scores and closing racial gaps. Average fourth-grade reading scores did rise from 213 in 2000 to 221 in 2009, but they peaked at 223 in 2014 and have never reached the Proficient level of 238.[10] On health care Bush proposed that Medicare add prescription drug coverage, and praised Congress for passing this proposal in January 2004. Like Clinton, he called unsuccessfully for a patients' bill of rights. On energy, Bush told the Congress on February 27, 2001 that Vice President Cheney was heading a committee to develop a national energy policy. That task force

---

10  https://www.nationsreportcard.gov/reading/nation/scores/?grade=4.

eventually recommended that hydraulic fracturing or "fracking," a new technique for extracting underground oil and natural gas, be exempted from regulation by the EPA. Although Bush never discussed this openly, it was probably the key step toward dramatically higher domestic energy production, which eventually made the US self-sufficient in fossil fuels.[11]

In that same February 2001 address to a joint session, Bush gave out contradictory signals about the budget. One the one hand, he promised to use the large surpluses he had inherited from Clinton to pay off $2 trillion of the national debt over the next ten years—but on the other, he appealed to the examples of Kennedy and Reagan and proposed new tax cuts. Citing an economic slowdown apparently provoked by the bursting of a technology stock bubble, he proposed cutting the bottom income tax rate from 15 percent to 10 percent and the top rate from 39 percent to 33 percent. Congress did not go as far as that, gradually cutting the top rate only to 35 percent in 2006, but it also reduced the long-term capital gains rate from 10 percent to 8 percent and raised the exclusions from the estate tax from $675,000 in stages to $3.5 million in 2009, with the tax to be entirely repealed in 2010. To hold out the promise of continuing surpluses, the income tax changes were scheduled to last only through 2010. After the midterm elections of 2002 increased Republican majorities, Bush proposed and Congress passed a second round of tax cuts, making the 2001 cuts take effect immediately. New laws also doubled the Earned Income Tax Credit, essentially an income subsidy for the working poor that Clinton had pioneered and that Nixon had originally anticipated in his Family Assistance Plan. In subsequent years Bush asked Congress unsuccessfully to make all these cuts permanent. These tax cuts, combined with vast new expenditures for defense and the wars in Afghanistan and Iraq, totally reversed the short- and long-term balance sheet of the federal government. The Clinton budget surplus of $236 billion for fiscal 2000 fell to $128 billion in fiscal 2001, and gave way to deficits of $158 billion, $378 billion, $413 billion, and $318 billion in 2002–5. Bush never discussed the state of the budget in any detail in annual messages, and the administration

---

11 https://earthworks.org/issues/inadequate_regulation_of_hydraulic_fracturing/.

tried to hide the extent of the deficit by leaving the costs of the two wars out of its budget. His budgets began forecasting 50 percent cuts in the deficit by 2009 in 2004, but these plans, unlike Clinton's never came true. The national debt, which had increased from $4.4 trillion to just $5.7 trillion under Clinton, doubled to $11.9 trillion under George W. Bush.

No president has ever spoken more publicly about his own religious faith than Bush, a born-again Christian who credited his faith for his recovery from alcoholism, and he linked it to aggressive positions on certain social issues. Bush's annual message of January 2004 introduced these issues into his reelection campaign. Claiming that 400,000 fewer young people were using illegal drugs than in 2001, he called for more drug testing in schools and asked professional sports leagues to crack down on steroid use. Sexually transmitted diseases were increasing, he said, and he asked Congress to "double Federal funding for abstinence programs . . . the only certain way to avoid" STDs. He asked Congress to embody a recent executive order granting "faith-based charities" equal access to government grants in a new law. And last but hardly least, he reacted sharply to a recent Massachusetts court decision striking down the state's law against gay marriage. In spite of the 1996 Defense of Marriage Act, he said, "Activist judges . . . have begun redefining marriage by court order, without regard for the will of the people and their elected representatives. On an issue of such great consequence, the people's voice must be heard. If judges insist on forcing their arbitrary will upon the people, the only alternative left to the people would be the constitutional process. Our Nation must defend the sanctity of marriage."

Bush in his 2004 reelection campaign faced Democratic senator and Vietnam veteran John Kerry of Massachusetts. Helped by scurrilous and unfounded attacks on Kerry's war record, the wartime spirit that still pervaded the country, and targeted campaigning on gay marriage and other social issues, he managed to eke out a narrow victory—the first president ever to win reelection after losing the popular vote four years earlier. This time he won a narrow popular majority, 50.7 percent to 48.3 percent, but his electoral majority was only slightly larger than in 2000, 286–251, with the state of Ohio making the difference. The Republicans gained 4 Senate seats, raising their majority to 55–45, and three House seats, for a 233–202 edge.

After once again promising a worldwide crusade for democracy in his second inaugural, Bush in his February 2, 2005 annual message proposed a fundamental reform of Social Security. Claiming that the system would be paying out more than it took in by 2018 and would reach bankruptcy by 2042, he suggested that younger workers be offered the chance to put a large portion of their payroll taxes into individual retirement accounts. He also endorsed a constitutional amendment to ban gay marriage again, but with respect to abortion, said only that "We must strive to build a culture of life." He continued to make these proposals for the rest of his term, but his Social Security reform never went anywhere in Congress. In September 2005 Bush's prestige suffered a major blow when the Federal Emergency Management Agency failed to respond adequately to the devastation of Hurricane Katrina in New Orleans and on the Mississippi Gulf Coast. Addressing the nation from New Orleans on September 15, he recognized "the kind of desperation no citizen of this great and generous Nation should ever have to know, fellow Americans calling out for food and water, vulnerable people left at the mercy of criminals who had no mercy, and the bodies of the dead lying uncovered and untended in the street." He praised the heroism of many first responders, as he had so often with respect to the War on Terror, and added that the victims "need to know that our whole Nation cares about you, and in the journey ahead, you're not alone." No one knew that a much worse crisis awaited the country on the economic front.

In 2005–6 Bush also took up the issue of illegal immigrants, whose numbers had risen from 3.5 million people in 1990 to about 8.6 million in 2000 and 11.1 million in 2005.[12] US population growth had fallen to a new low of 10 percent during the 1980s, reaching 249 million people in 1990, and immigration had helped it increase by 13.2 percent in the 1990s, reaching 281 million by 2000. In an address to the nation on May 15, 2006, Bush tried to take a middle position on immigration. While agreeing that illegal immigrants put pressure on public services, strained budgets, and brought "crime to our communities," he added that the vast major-

---

12 https://www.pewresearch.org/fact-tank/2019/06/12/5-facts-about-illegal-immigration-in-the-u-s/ft_19-06-12_5factsillegalimmigration_us-unauthorized-immigrant-total/.

ity of immigrants were "decent people who work hard, support their families, practice their faith, and lead responsible lives." He proposed tightening the border and making it easier to deport illegal immigrants at once, a strictly enforced temporary worker program, and new identification cards for foreign workers. While rejecting "an automatic path to citizenship" for illegal immigrants already in the country as "amnesty," he endorsed citizenship for them provided that they paid some penalty for breaking the law; paid taxes; learned English; and had worked at a job for several years. "The success of our country," he added, "depends upon helping newcomers assimilate into our society and embrace our common identity as Americans." The Republican leadership in Congress refused to act.

In his last annual message in January 2008, Bush noted that "our economy is undergoing a period of uncertainty. America has added jobs for a record 52 straight months, but jobs are now growing at a slower pace," and "the housing market has declined." In fact, since the financial deregulation of the Clinton years, new, larger and more powerful financial institutions had offered trillions of dollars' worth of new mortgages that lenders would never be able to service, and bundled those mortgages into securities backed by new financial instruments called credit default swaps. Just six weeks after Bush spoke, the venerable Bear Stearns investment bank faced bankruptcy thanks to billions of dollars of worthless mortgage assets, and managed to sell itself at a rock-bottom price only with the help of a Federal Reserve guarantee of those assets. The stock market began falling. On September 15, in the midst of the presidential campaign, Lehman Brothers, one of the oldest investment banks on Wall Street, went into bankruptcy when the Federal Reserve refused to guarantee its bad assets in the same way. That triggered a huge drop in the stock market and a global financial panic. Now a lame duck, Bush addressed the nation on the financial crisis for the first time on September 24. "This is an extraordinary period for America's economy," he said. "Over the past few weeks, many Americans have felt anxiety about their finances and their future. I understand their worry and their frustration. We've seen triple-digit swings in the stock market. Major financial institutions have teetered on the edge of collapse, and some have failed. As uncertainty has grown, many banks have restricted lending. Credit markets have frozen, and families and businesses have found it harder to borrow money." After reviewing the history of the housing boom and bust and its consequences, he advocated drastic action to avoid economic collapse. A proposed rescue plan would earmark $700 billion in federal funds to "remove the risk posed by the troubled assets, including mortgage-backed securities, now clogging the financial system. This would free banks to resume the flow of credit to American families and businesses." "In the long run," he said, "Americans have good reason to be confident in our economic strength. Despite corrections in the marketplace and instances of abuse, democratic capitalism is the best system ever devised." By solving the crisis, he said, "we will show the world once again what kind of country America is."

Republican legislators bridled at this unprecedented government bailout, and the House of Representatives rejected it on September 29. Bush made a brief further appeal for passage the next day, and the House passed the bill on October 3. That did not stop the crisis, which spread rapidly around the world, paralleling the events of the fall of 1929. US unemployment doubled from January 2008 to mid-2009, and the Dow Jones average fell from about 19,000 in November 2007 to 10,600 in March 2009. Two of the three major US automakers had to ask for federal help to avoid bankruptcy. Not since Roosevelt's inauguration had a new president faced a comparable crisis.

The 2008 presidential campaign had taken a surprising turn when forty-seven-year old Barack Obama, a senator from Illinois, had outpolled former first lady and now New York senator Hillary Clinton in key primaries and secured the Democratic nomination, becoming the first black major party candidate in American history. The Republican Party had nominated John McCain, a longtime senator who had spent years as a prisoner during the Vietnam War. Obama's youth, obvious intelligence, and novelty captured the imagination of the American people in Kennedy-like fashion, and he won the biggest Democratic victory since Lyndon Johnson in 1964 with 52.9 percent of the popular vote to McCain's 45.7 percent and a 365–173 margin in the Electoral College. He swept the Northeast, the Midwest, and the West Coast, and picked up Virginia, North Carolina and Florida in the South. The Democrats also won 8 new Senate seats for a 60–40 margin and 21 new House seats, increasing their majority to

257–178. The media began comparing Obama's potential impact to Franklin Roosevelt's. In a brief farewell address on January 15, 2009, Bush paid tribute to Obama, "a man whose history reflects the enduring promise of our land" and "a moment of hope and pride for our whole nation." "As the years [after 9/11] passed," he said, most Americans could return to life much as it had been before 9/11. "But I never did," he added typically. "Every morning, I received a briefing on the threats to our Nation. I vowed to do everything in my power to keep us safe. . . . America has gone more than 7 years without another terrorist attack on our soil." Once again he spoke of a great struggle between freedom and terror. "When challenges to our prosperity emerged," he added, "we rose to meet them. Facing the prospect of a financial collapse, we took decisive measures to safeguard our economy. . . . America must maintain our moral clarity. I've often spoken to you about good and evil, and this has made some uncomfortable. But good and evil are present in this world, and between the two there can be no compromise."

Like Lincoln in his first year and Roosevelt in his and again after 1939, Bush had seized upon 9/11 to unite the American people behind a great vision of the future. But while each of them had brought their great plans to fruition and left the American people a legacy of pride in success and a new consensus, Bush bequeathed an expensive, indecisive fight for democracy in distant lands and a landscape of economic chaos. While 2001 might have been 1861 or 1933 all over again, 2009 was not 1865 or 1945. The great international and economic issues of Bush's tenure in office remained to be resolved.

# XXI

## Barack Obama, Donald Trump, and Joseph Biden

2009–17 • 2017–21 • 2021–23

Barack Obama's first inaugural certainly echoed Franklin Roosevelt's seventy-seven years earlier, while foreshadowing the broad lines of his two terms to a remarkable extent. "That we are in the midst of crisis is now well understood. Our Nation is at war against a far-reaching network of violence and hatred. Our economy is badly weakened, a consequence of greed and irresponsibility on the part of some, but also our collective failure to make hard choices and prepare the Nation for a new age. Homes have been lost, jobs shed, businesses shuttered. Our health care is too costly. Our schools fail too many. And each day brings further evidence that the ways we use energy strengthen our adversaries and threaten our planet." Yet these challenges, he promised, "will be met. . . . On this day, we come to proclaim an end to the petty grievances and false promises, the recriminations and worn-out dogmas that for far too long have strangled our politics." Yet he also echoed Ronald Reagan. "For as much as Government can do and must do, it is ultimately the faith and determination of the American people upon which this Nation relies. . . . What is required of us now is a new era of responsibility, a recognition on the part of every American that we have duties to ourselves, our Nation, and the world." As it turned out, his first two years in office resembled Bill Clinton's far more closely than Franklin Roosevelt's.

With 60 Senate votes—the total required to stop the filibusters that had now become a routine tactic to block any piece of legislation—the Democrats effectively controlled the Senate as well as the House, and a $787 billion stimulus package, the American Recovery and Reinvestment Act, passed Congress on February 11. Obama addressed a joint session of Congress for the first time on February 24. The nation's economic problems, he said, had not begun with the housing market's collapse and the stock market crash. "We have known for decades that our survival depends on finding new sources of energy, yet we import more oil today than ever before. The cost of health care eats up more and more of our savings each year, yet we keep delaying reform. Our children will compete for jobs in a global economy that too many of our schools do not prepare them for. And though all these challenges went unsolved, we still managed to spend more money and pile up more debt, both as individuals and through our Government, than ever before." Then he described the stimulus plan, promising to "*save or create* 3.5 million jobs [emphasis added]" over the next two years. In fact unemployment kept rising for another year and had not fallen by the time of the midterm elections in 2010. He listed the major provisions of the recently passed bill: a tax cut for most Americans, a $2,500 annual tax credit for college tuition, massive aid to states and localities to prevent layoffs, and extended unemployment benefits—but no public works program such as Roosevelt had inaugurated. He saw the financial markets as critical, and promised "a new lending fund" to provide "auto loans, college loans and small-business loans," and a housing plan to allow "families facing foreclosure" to "lower their monthly payments and refinance their mortgages." He shared the nation's anger over the previous year's bank bailout, he said, and promised, "This time, CEOs won't be able to use taxpayer money to pad their paychecks or buy fancy drapes or disappear on a private jet. Those days are over." The task of saving financial institutions and keeping credit flowing fell mainly to the Federal Reserve, which made extraordinary sums of credit available, with Obama's evident approval.

Rather than wait for these measures to work or propose more radical moves to stop foreclosures or put people to work, Obama on September 9, 2009, asked another joint session for a sweeping health care reform. "Thanks to the bold and decisive action we've taken since January," he said, "I can stand here with confidence and say that we have pulled this economy back from the brink."

Thirty million Americans, he said, lacked health insurance, and desperately sick people lost theirs every day. The nation spent 1.5 times per person as much as any other advanced nation on health care. Crucially, he rejected both liberal Democratic proposals for a single-payer system and Republican calls to end employer-sponsored insurance as radical shifts "that would disrupt the health care most people currently have." He denied Republican claims that his plans would "set up panels of bureaucrats with the power to kill off senior citizens" or "insure illegal immigrants."[1] The plan—very similar to the 1993 Clinton plan—would provide a new health care exchange where people without coverage could purchase affordable, subsidized insurance; forbid companies from denying coverage to applicants with preexisting conditions; and impose a penalty on those refusing to buy coverage. It would also allow states to extend Medicaid coverage to millions more people. And Obama cautiously advocated "a not-for-profit public option available in the insurance exchange," which might have been the beginning of single-payer coverage.

Senator Edward Kennedy, the leading health care reform advocate in Congress for decades, had died of cancer in the previous month. The House and Senate passed different versions of the Affordable Care Act late in 2009 on party lines, but needed to reconcile their versions. When Obama gave his first annual message on January 27, 2010, Republican Scott Brown had just won the special election for Kennedy's seat, reducing the Democratic majority to 59-41. Obama repeated that his most urgent task a year earlier had been "to shore up the same banks that helped cause this crisis." Unemployment was higher than it had been a year earlier, but he insisted that "because of the steps we took, there are about 2 million Americans working right now who would otherwise be unemployed," and that figure could increase by another 1.5 million by the end of the year. He called for financial reforms and new steps in energy. Those would include new nuclear plants, more oil and gas exploration, and incentives for "clean energy"—the cap-and-trade bill to discourage the use of carbon fuels that the House had passed the previous year. The country, he said, had to double

---

[1] In response to the latter claim, Congressman Joseph Wilson, Republican of South Carolina, loudly exclaimed, "You lie!"

its exports in five years—a target it failed to meet—and continue improving its schools and community colleges, while increasing tax credits for college and forgiving debt for graduates who entered public service. He acknowledged skepticism about his health care plan and took "my share of the blame for not explaining it more clearly to the American people," but pleaded with the Congress not to "walk away from reform." "Neither party should delay or obstruct every single bill just because they can," he said. "I will not give up on trying to change the tone of our politics." In this he would be disappointed.

The budget reconciliation process enabled Congress to pass the Affordable Care Act with simple majorities in both houses. It had no public option because a few Democratic senators opposed it, however, and most of it would not go into effect until late 2013, another three years later. The Congress also passed the Dodd-Frank Bill to reform financial practices, although it also took years to implement. The cap-and-trade bill died in the Senate. Unemployment rose from 7.3 percent in December 2008 to 9.9 percent in December 2009 and remained at 9.3 percent in December 2010.[2] Home foreclosures increased from 1.3 million in 2008 to 1.5 million in 2009 and 1.7 million in 2010.[3] Unlike Franklin Roosevelt, Obama had failed to provide immediate help to the American people in his first two years, and much of the nation's anger turned against him and his party. In the midterm elections the Republicans gained 63 seats in the House, good for a 242–193 majority, and 6 seats in the Senate, cutting the effective Democratic majority to 53–47. Like Bill Clinton, Obama now faced at least partial Republican control of Congress for the rest of his term. Taking the hint, Obama and the outgoing Democratic Congress in December extended all the Bush tax cuts for another two years, until 2013, and added an unprecedented one-year 2 percent reduction in Social Security payroll taxes.[4]

Like Clinton in 1995, Obama in January 2011 used his State of the Union address to define the goals of the rest of his presidency.

---

2 https://www.thebalancemoney.com/unemployment-rate-by-year-3305506.
3 https://www.attomdata.com/news/market-trends/foreclosures/attom-midyear-2022-u-s-foreclosure-market-report/.
4 *New York Times*, December 17, 2010, p. A1.

Could the administration and the new Congress work together? "I believe we can, and I believe we must." Global economic competition, he said, would dominate the future. "We need to outinnovate, outeducate, and outbuild the rest of the world. . . . We need to take responsibility for our deficit and reform our Government," he said. The government must follow Eisenhower's example and support basic research: "This is our Sputnik moment." He called again for increased energy production of all kinds and vastly improved infrastructure, including high-speed rail. Promoting globalization, he asked Congress to approve new trade deals with India, China, and South Korea, which would "support" 320,000 American jobs. Yet he also promised new rounds of budget cuts. "The final critical step in winning the future," he continued, "is to make sure that we aren't buried under a mountain of debt." He did not mention that the deficit had gone from $459 billion in fiscal 2008 to $1.412 trillion in fiscal 2009 and $1.294.4 trillion in fiscal 2010, but he proposed freezing annual domestic spending for the next five years, and thereby cutting "discretionary spending" to the lowest level as a percentage of the budget since the Eisenhower administration. He had already frozen federal salaries and planned tens of billions of defense cuts, but reductions in Medicare and Medicaid, he said, would also be necessary. Echoing both Clinton and Reagan, he declared, "We can't win the future with a government of the past." He joked that the Interior Department was responsible for salmon in fresh water while the Commerce Department took over in salt water, adding, "I hear it gets even more complicated once they're smoked."

Like Clinton in 1995, Obama by July 25, 2011, faced a government crisis because House Republicans were insisting on more drastic budget cuts than he. Addressing the nation on that day, he contrasted his own "balanced approach" that would eliminate some tax breaks for "the wealthiest Americans and biggest corporations" while cutting domestic spending and making "some adjustments" in Medicare, with a "cuts-only approach" favored by "a significant number of Republicans in Congress" that would ask nothing of "those at the top" and close the deficit with "more severe cuts to programs we all care about, cuts that place a greater burden on working families." Those Republicans were once again threatening not to raise the debt ceiling and shut down the government if they did not get their way. The Republicans successfully insisted on a two-stage process. Passing initial cuts totaling $21 billion—but optimistically projected to save $917 billion over the next decade—Congress pledged to try to reach agreement on additional cuts of $1.2 trillion over that same decade by the following January. If they could not, the budget agreement mandated a "sequester," automatic across-the-board cuts in both domestic and defense spending, to reach the target. Obama endorsed this deal in a September 8, 2011 address to a joint session on job growth. "We continue to face an economic crisis that has left millions of our neighbors jobless and a political crisis that's made things worse," he said. "These men and women grew up with faith in an America where hard work and responsibility paid off. For decades now, Americans have watched that compact erode." He called again for a big infrastructure program and tax incentives for businesses to hire unemployed workers (unemployment remained at more than 8.5 percent), extending the payroll tax cut, and closing loopholes for the wealthy. Senate filibusters killed bills to fund infrastructure and keep state and local government workers employed, and the Republican House voted down the payroll tax cut extension late in the year.

In foreign policy, meanwhile, Obama tried to handle the War on Terror the way that Nixon had handled Vietnam—endorsing its ends, while scaling back its means. In his first address to Congress on February 24, 2009, he promised an early end to the war in Iraq and "a new and comprehensive strategy for Afghanistan and Pakistan to defeat Al Qaida and combat extremism, because I will not allow terrorists to plot against the American people from safe havens halfway around the world." He had "ordered," he said, the closure of the Guantanamo detention center where American jailers had tortured suspected terrorists, and he unequivocally declared "that the United States of America does not torture." Three months later on June 4, in Cairo, Egypt, he proclaimed "a new beginning between the United States and Muslims around the world, one based on mutual interest and mutual respect and one based upon the truth that America and Islam are not exclusive and need not be in competition." Then he gave a kinder, gentler version of Bush's plans to spread democracy. "America does not presume to know what is best for everyone, just as we would not presume to pick the outcome of a peaceful election. But I do have an unyielding belief that all people yearn for certain things: the ability to speak your mind and have a say in how you are governed, confidence in the rule of law and the equal administration of justice, government that is transparent and doesn't steal from the people, the freedom to live as you choose."

Turning in a more warlike direction, Obama on December 1, 2009 announced at West Point that he would send an additional 30,000 troops to Afghanistan for eighteen months. Afghanistan and Pakistan were "the epicenter of violent extremism practiced by Al-Qaida. It is from here that we were attacked on 9/11, and it is from here that new attacks are being plotted as I speak." Working in "partnership with Pakistan," the US would deny Al-Qaida a safe haven and keep a growing Taliban from overthrowing the Afghan government. This was not, he insisted, "another Vietnam," because we were leading a large coalition and did not face "a broad-based popular insurgency." The global War on Terror simply continued our six-decade support for global security. Nine months later, on August 31, 2010, he told the nation in a broadcast address that 100,000 US troops had left Iraq, and "Operation Iraqi Freedom is over." Iraqi forces had taken over security and the Iraqis had held "credible elections." "A proud people," they "have rejected sectarian war, and they have no interest in endless destruction." The US could now leave its divisions over the war behind. "American influence around the world is not a function of military force alone," he said. "We must use all elements of our power, including our diplomacy, our economic strength, and the power of America's example, to secure our interests and stand by our allies."

Yet seven months later on March 28, 2011, Obama announced to the nation that the United States had deployed its military to help change the government of Libya, where "our interests and values" were at stake. In recent months popular uprisings had overthrown dictatorships in nearby Tunisia and Egypt, and the Syrian and Libyan people had risen up as well. The longtime dictator Muammar Qadhafi "began attacking his people," Obama said, and the United States had imposed sanctions. "I made it clear that Qadhafi had lost the confidence of his people and the legitimacy to lead, and I said that he needed to step down from power," Obama said. Supported by the Arab League and European allies, the United States had imposed a no-fly zone and undertaken action to stop a massacre in the city of Benghazi. "To brush aside America's responsibility as a leader, and more profoundly, our responsibilities to our fellow human beings under such circumstances would have been a betrayal of who we are. . . . I refused to wait for the images of slaughter and mass graves before taking action." He rejected "broadening our mission to include regime change" in favor of giving the Libyan people "time and space" to determine their future. "Born, as we are, out of a revolution by those who longed to be free, we welcome the fact that history is on the move in the Middle East and North Africa, and that young people are leading the way." It took about six months for rebel forces to capture and execute Qadhafi. Meanwhile, on May 1, 2011, Obama announced the killing of Usama Bin Laden by American troops at his hideout in Pakistan. "Tonight," he said, "let us think back to the sense of unity that prevailed on 9/11. I know that it has, at times, frayed. Yet today's achievement is a testament to the greatness of our country and the determination of the American people." On June 22 he addressed the American people again, announcing the beginning of the withdrawal of the troops he had sent to Afghanistan eighteen months earlier. Afghan security forces, he said, had become stronger while the Taliban became weaker.

In his election year annual message on January 24, 2012, Obama began with a long encomium to the nation's troops and their achievements. "Imagine what we could accomplish if we followed their example," he continued. "Think about the America within our reach: a country that leads the world in educating its people; an America that attracts a new generation of high-tech manufacturing and high-paying jobs; a future where we're in control of our own energy and our security and prosperity aren't so tied to unstable parts of the world; an economy built to last, where hard work pays off and responsibility is rewarded." While acknowledging that the country had lost eight million jobs in 2008–9, he noted that it had regained three million since then, and that "we've agreed to cut the deficit by more than $2 trillion" over some unspecified period of years. (In fact the deficit remained at $1.077 trillion, compared to $459 billion in fiscal 2008.) He called again for better education, cheaper college, and increased energy production on all fronts, while offering a new joke about the inefficiency of much-despised federal regulations. He endorsed "comprehensive immigration reform" without offering specifics while focusing on the plight of so-called

Dreamers, young people brought to the United States illegally as children who had no path to citizenship. Despite immigration, the 2010 census had shown that population growth had slowed to 9.7 percent in the last decade, reaching a total of 309 million. Obama never discussed the social issues of abortion, race, and gay rights at any length in any major address during his first term, except to praise Congress for repealing the ban on openly gay Americans serving in the military in his January 2011 annual address. Turning to the foreign scene, he echoed his predecessor regarding the spread of democracy in the Middle East. "As the tide of war recedes, a wave of change has washed across the Middle East and North Africa, from Tunis to Cairo, from Sana'a to Tripoli. A year ago, Qadhafi was one of the world's longest serving dictators, a murderer with American blood on his hands. Today, he is gone. And in Syria, I have no doubt that the Assad regime will soon discover that the forces of change cannot be reversed and that human dignity cannot be denied. . . . tyranny is no match for liberty."

The Congress did not act on any of his major proposals, but Obama won a secure reelection victory in November over former Massachusetts Republican governor Mitt Romney, with 51.1 percent of the popular vote to Romney's 47.2 percent, and a 332–206 Electoral College majority that included every midwestern state except Indiana, and Florida and Virginia in the South. Aggressive Republican redistricting in a number of states allowed the Republicans to retain a reduced 234–201 majority in the House despite losing the national House popular vote by 1 percentage point, while the Democrats increased their effective Senate majority by 2 to 55–45—well shy of the 60 needed to overcome a filibuster. In the lame duck session Obama refused finally to make the Bush income tax cuts permanent unless the top rate for the highest earners was restored to 39.6 percent, and the Republicans gave in.

"This generation of Americans has been tested by crises that steeled our resolve and proved our resilience," Obama declared in his second inaugural. "A decade of war is now ending. An economic recovery has begun." He struck the same note in his annual message on February 12. "Tonight, thanks to the grit and determination of the American people, there is much progress to report. After a decade of grinding war, our brave men and women in uniform are coming home. . . . So together, we have cleared away the rubble of crisis, and we can say with renewed confidence that the state of our Union is stronger." He turned again to the problem of soaring corporate profits and stagnant wages and incomes, and added a reference to group identities. "It is our unfinished task to restore the basic bargain that built this country: the idea that if you work hard and meet your responsibilities, you can get ahead, no matter where you come from, no matter what you look like or who you love," but made no new proposals beyond an increase in the minimum wage to $9.00 per hour and the creation of new "manufacturing hubs" in older cities. Obama frequently appealed to unions on the campaign trail but never talked about their decline in a major address. Citing increased wildfires in the West and the recent, devastating Hurricane Sandy in the Northeast, he called more strongly for action on climate change and proposed a public–private partnership to rebuild infrastructure. On immigration he insisted that "leaders from the business, labor, law enforcement, faith communities, they all agree that the time has come to pass comprehensive immigration reform." That would include stronger border security and "a responsible pathway to earned citizenship . . . .passing a background check, paying taxes and a meaningful penalty, learning English, and going to the back of the line behind the folks trying to come here legally."

Citing the recent slaughter of twenty-six students and teachers at a Newtown, Connecticut elementary school, he demanded that Congress bring stronger gun control legislation to a vote. He renewed that call six weeks later in the White House on March 28 in the presence of some of the victims' parents, asking for universal background checks and the reinstatement of the Clinton-era ban on assault rifles, which Bush had allowed to lapse. "The notion that 2 months or 3 months after something as horrific as what happened in Newtown happens and we've moved on to other things, that's not who we are . . . .we can make a difference if not just the activists here on this stage, but the general public—including responsible gun owners—say, you know what, we can do better than this." None of those proposed measures secured the sixty votes in the Senate necessary to stop a filibuster when they came up the next month, and the assault weapons ban fell ten votes short even of a majority.[5]

---

5 *New York Times*, April 18, 2013, p. A1.

The automatic cuts mandated by the sequester had gone into effect during fiscal 2013, and after long negotiations with the Republican congressional leadership Obama reached agreement to halt them in December of that year. The Republicans however refused to act on his proposals for immigration, infrastructure, and gun control for the remainder of his second term. The economic news improved. Unemployment fell from 7.9 percent in December 2016 to 4.7 percent in 2018, and the deficit fell from $680 billion in fiscal 2013 to $442 billion in fiscal 2015, before rising again to $585 billion in fiscal 2016. Meanwhile, the Affordable Care Act—commonly known as Obamacare—went into full effect late in 2013, providing new insurance for thirty-one million Americans by 2021, including new Medicaid recipients.[6] The act's major provisions narrowly survived by a 5–4 vote in the Supreme Court in 2012, while the Republican House of Representatives passed numerous bills to repeal it. Obama continued to advocate steps to improve education to enable Americans to compete in a global economy, while also proposing new trade deals with East Asian nations and with Europe. On November 20, 2014 he addressed the nation on immigration reform, boasting that his administration had cut illegal border crossings by more than half and increased deportations of criminal illegal immigrants by 80 percent, while explicitly adopting suggestions of George W. Bush to give millions of others legal status without an explicit path to citizenship—"a commonsense, middle-ground approach." The debate, he said, was about "who we are as a country and who we want to be for future generations." Congress failed to act again.

Racial controversies became louder during Obama's second term. They included the shooting of Florida teenager Trayvon Martin by George Zimmerman, whom a jury acquitted, and sustained violence in Ferguson, Missouri, after a police officer killed another young black man, Michael Brown. Obama never discussed these incidents at any length during a major address. He did make a moving appeal for interracial understanding in his Chicago farewell address to the nation on January 10, 2017. "For Blacks and other minority groups," he said, "that means tying our own very

---

6 "The Affordable Care Act: A Brief History," *Wall Street Journal*, June 17, 2021.

real struggles for justice to the challenges that a lot of people in this country face, not only the refugee or the immigrant or the rural poor or the transgender American, but also the middle-aged White guy who, from the outside, may seem like he's got advantages, but has seen his world upended by economic and cultural and technological change. . . . For White Americans, it means acknowledging that the effects of slavery and Jim Crow didn't suddenly vanish in the sixties, that when minority groups voice discontent, they're not just engaging in reverse racism or practicing political correctness." Regarding another social issue, Obama on June 26, 2015 praised the Supreme Court's 5–4 decision holding that the Constitution protected the right of gay Americans to marry one another. "This morning the Supreme Court recognized that the Constitution guarantees marriage equality. In doing so, they've reaffirmed that all Americans are entitled to the equal protection of the law; that all people should be treated equally, regardless of who they are or who they love." In July 2016 the Defense Department announced that transgender Americans could now serve openly in the US military.

Meanwhile, Obama's Secretary of state John Kerry, who had replaced Hillary Clinton, reached important agreements with two longtime American adversaries, while Obama's optimistic Middle Eastern narrative fell apart. On December 17, 2014 Obama reviewed fifty-five years of American estrangement from Cuba. Our policy of supporting democracy and human rights by isolating Cuba, he said, had failed. Kerry was discussing reestablishing diplomatic relations and reviewing the US's designation of the regime as a state sponsor of terrorism. Obama asked Congress to debate the trade embargo on Cuba, which had been enshrined in law. He expressed respect for the "passion" and "commitment to liberty and democracy" of those who opposed this step—mostly conservative Cuban Americans in Florida—but insisted that it was "the right thing to do." On July 1, 2014, Obama announced that the two nations had indeed resumed diplomatic relations, referred to steps to increase contacts between them, and once again asked Congress to end the embargo and rely on "American engagement . . . to advance our interests and support for democracy and human rights." The embargo remains in effect to this day.

Throughout his tenure Obama had repeatedly promised to prevent Iran from developing a nuclear weapon. His January 2015 annual message referred to attempts to reach a new agreement with Iran, and on April 2 of that year he announced that the US, "together with our allies and partners, has reached a historic understanding with Iran, which, if fully implemented, will prevent it from obtaining a nuclear weapon." Sanctions, he said, had brought Iran to the negotiating table with the US along with Britain, France, Germany, Russia, China and the European Union, and they had now tentatively agreed that Iran would stop producing fissionable material in response to the lifting of sanctions. On July 15 he announced that the deal was complete. "Meanwhile, we will maintain our own sanctions related to Iran's support for terrorism, its ballistic missile program, and its human rights violations."

Unfortunately, the situation around the Middle East took several turns for the worse. The Assad regime stubbornly held onto power in Syria, and on September 10, 2013, Obama addressed the nation on the civil war there. Over two years, he reported, peaceful protests had turned into a civil war, killing an estimated 100,000 people. While providing humanitarian help, he said, "I have resisted calls for military action because we cannot resolve someone else's civil war through force, particularly after a decade of war in Iraq and Afghanistan." The situation had worsened on August 21, when Assad's military had gassed more than 1,000 people. In response Obama had asked Congress to authorize a strike against Assad "to deter Assad from using chemical weapons, to degrade his regime's ability to use them, and to make clear to the world that we will not tolerate their use." Assad, however, had now offered to negotiate the elimination of his chemical weapons arsenal and Obama was therefore asking Congress to postpone the vote. He reported that Syria was eliminating these weapons in his annual message the following January. Another setback for democracy took place in Egypt. After the fall of Hosni Mubarak's dictatorship in 2011, a 2012 presidential election chose Mohammed Morsi of the Islamist Muslim Brotherhood as the new president. After a bitter political struggle over a new constitution, protests calling for Morsi's resignation began in June 2013, and the Egyptian military overthrew him in a coup without any protest from the United States. Obama did not refer to these events in his next annual message.

Dramatic new developments in Syria and Iraq, however, led Obama to address the nation on the situation there on September

10, 2014. Al-Qaida in Iraq—which had not even existed before the 2003 invasion of that country under Bush—had transformed itself into ISIL or ISIS, the Islamic State of Iraq and the Levant. Helped by tanks and other weapons captured from the Iraqi Army, it had seized large parts of the Sunni area in Iraq—eventually including the city of Mosul—and parts of Syria, and proclaimed an Islamic state in the regions that it controlled. The much-touted reconciliation of Shi'ites and Sunnis in Iraq had evidently never taken place. This "brutal terrorist organization," Obama said, "poses a threat to the people of Iraq and Syria and the broader Middle East, including American citizens, personnel, and facilities. If left unchecked, these terrorists could pose a growing threat beyond that region, including to the United States." Thousands of foreigners, including some Americans, had joined ISIL. Obama announced "that America will lead a broad coalition to roll back this terrorist threat. . . . We will degrade and ultimately destroy ISIL through a comprehensive and sustained counterterrorism strategy," including advisory teams for local forces fighting ISIL and air strikes. "My fellow Americans," he concluded, "we live in a time of great change. Tomorrow marks 13 years since our country was attacked. Next week marks 6 years since our economy suffered its worst setback since the Great Depression. Yet, despite these shocks, through the pain we've felt and the grueling work required to bounce back, America is better positioned today to seize the future than any other nation on Earth." Earlier in the year Russian leader Vladimir Putin had reacted to the fall of a pro-Russian government in Ukraine by annexing Crimea, which had been part of Ukraine since the 1950s, and the United States had imposed some sanctions on Russia in response. "It is America that has rallied the world against Russian aggression and in support of the Ukrainian peoples' right to determine their own destiny," Obama said. Yet the November congressional elections saw another serious setback, as the Republicans gained 9 Senate seats in the South, Midwest and mountain states for a 54–46 majority, and 13 House seats, running their majority to 245–188 as they carried the national House popular vote by 51–46 percent. The loss of the Senate became critical in early 2016 when conservative Supreme Court justice Antonin Scalia died suddenly, and Republican Senate leader Mitch McConnell refused even to hold hearings on Obama's nomination for a successor, arguing that the next president should fill the seat.

In one of his last addresses to the nation on December 6, 2015, Obama linked the counterterrorism campaign in the Middle East to a mass shooting in San Bernardino, California, where a radicalized Muslim couple had killed fourteen of the husband's fellow government workers at a holiday party. The killers, Obama said, had embraced "a perverted interpretation of Islam." "Since the day I took this office," he said, "I've authorized U.S. forces to take out terrorists abroad precisely because I know how real the danger is." These words referred guardedly to US drone strikes against suspected terrorists *outside of* the war zones in Afghanistan, Iraq and Syria, which US intelligence estimated to have killed about 2,500 enemy combatants and perhaps 100 non-combatants under Obama.[7] That campaign would continue, he said, and the United States was pursuing a cease-fire and a political settlement in Syria as part of the fight against ISIL, which still held parts of Sunni Iraq, including Mosul, when Obama left office.

Throughout his tenure, Obama said relatively little about relations among the world's great powers. He went very lightly over Russia's annexation of Ukraine in 2014 and he said almost nothing about relations with China. And after the nations of the world reached the Paris accords to combat climate change in late 2015, he did not even bother to mention them in his next annual message, and made only a brief mention of them in one of his short weekly radio addresses.

Despite their many differences, Clinton, George W. Bush and Obama had pursued remarkably similar policies on many important issues. These included international trade agreements to promote globalization; attempts to improve American education to make the nation more competitive within that framework, and to expand opportunities for ordinary Americans; support for the new financial system that had emerged after deregulation under Clinton; increased domestic energy production; and some kind of immigration reform to give legal status to millions of undocumented aliens. All three had embraced American supremacy in the wake of the collapse of Communism, and the similarities in Bush's and Obama's approaches to the War on Terror far outweighed the

---

7   https://www.dni.gov/files/documents/Newsroom/Presspercent20Releases/DNI+Release+on+CT+Strikes+Outside+Areas+of+Active+Hostilities.PDF.

differences. Although Obama repeatedly announced plans to close the Guantanamo detention center, the Congress managed to block him from doing so. Not surprisingly, the trend toward greater economic inequality and the stagnation of wages that had begun under Reagan had continued. The War on Terror had failed to spread democracy in the Middle East, and war continued in Syria, Iraq, and Afghanistan. Congress had refused to act on immigration reform.

In the Democratic primary campaign of 2016, another establishment candidate, former first lady, New York senator and secretary of state Hillary Clinton, staved off a surprisingly strong challenge from Senator Bernie Sanders of Vermont, an avowed socialist. Establishment Republican candidates such as former Florida governor Jeb Bush—George W.'s brother—and Senators Marco Rubio of Florida and Ted Cruz of Texas did much worse. Donald Trump, a celebrity real estate developer and reality television star who had survived six corporate bankruptcies, easily defeated them all by attacking the establishment's approaches to trade and foreign policy while defying customary norms of political debate and personal behavior. Then, in a general election marked by low turnout and a surprisingly high third-party vote, Trump lost the popular vote to Clinton, 46.1 percent to 48.2 percent, but won with a 304–227 margin in the Electoral College thanks to victories in Florida, Ohio, Pennsylvania, Michigan and Wisconsin—all states that Obama had carried twice. The Republicans also maintained 52–48 and 241–194 majorities in the Senate and the House. Trump became the first president never to have held any government office of any kind. In his last annual message in January 2016, Obama cited "one of the few regrets of my Presidency: that the rancor and suspicion between the parties had gotten worse instead of better." Trump's election raised that problem to an entirely new level.

In 1861–65 and 1933–45, the United States government had renewed its bond with the American people by successfully completing enormous enterprises under the leadership of Lincoln and Franklin Roosevelt.[8] The United States was chronologically due for another great crisis as the new century began, and we have seen that both Bush and Obama had used the language of crisis after 9/11

---

8 Strauss and Howe, *The Fourth Turning, passim.*

and the financial panic and economic collapse of 2008. Obama had repeatedly praised his countrymen for coping with both of those cataclysmic events. Yet Bush had cut taxes instead of raising them, bequeathing a new permanent deficit to his successors, while Obama, unlike Roosevelt, had not concluded that the American financial system needed fundamental change. Neither of them had brought about any political realignment or created any new consensus on the critical question of where the United States was going and what kind of country it was going to be. And that failure had led to an unprecedented collapse of American politics—the failure of either party to find a candidate who could defeat Donald J. Trump.

Donald Trump found new ways to communicate with the American people. He vented his feelings in a uniquely unrestrained style on the social media platform Twitter more than 25,000 times in four years, an average of eighteen times a day.[9] During the first three years of his presidency—that is, before his actual reelection campaign began—he held sixty-nine "Make America Great Again" or "Keep America Great" rallies, nearly all of them in states that he had carried in 2016. Meanwhile, he faced investigations such as had bedeviled Nixon and Clinton literally from the moment that he took office until he left it, starting with a two-year investigation into Russian interference in the 2016 election. No *elected* president ever spent nearly so much time defending his legitimacy.[10] Yet despite all his, his major addresses marked out clear ideas and policies in the same way as his predecessors'.

Trump's inaugural began with a bitter attack on the political establishment but also included echoes of Reagan and Kennedy. "For too long," he said, "a small group in our Nation's Capital has reaped the rewards of Government while the people have borne the cost. Washington flourished, but the people did not share in its wealth. Politicians prospered, but the jobs left, and the factories closed. The establishment protected itself, but not the citizens of

---

9 https://www.cnn.com/2020/12/18/politics/trump-presidency-by-the-numbers/index.html. Earlier presidents including Richard Nixon and Lyndon Johnson had expressed themselves similarly in private, we now know, but also took care to show a different side of themselves in public. Trump did not.

10 Both John Tyler and Andrew Johnson encountered similar hostility but both of them were succeeding vice presidents.

our country. . . . while they celebrated in our Nation's Capital, there was little to celebrate for struggling families all across our land. That all changes, starting right here and right now." Americans wanted "great schools, "safe neighborhoods," and "good jobs," but faced "a different reality": "Mothers and children trapped in poverty in our inner cities; rusted-out factories scattered like tombstones across the landscape of our Nation; an education system, flush with cash, but which leaves our young and beautiful students deprived of all knowledge; and the crime and the gangs and the drugs that have stolen too many lives and robbed our country of so much unrealized potential. This American carnage stops right here and stops right now." He announced a new relationship with the rest of the world, economically and politically. "The wealth of our middle class has been ripped from their homes and then redistributed all across the world. . . . From this day forward, it's going to be only America first. . . . We must protect our borders from the ravages of other countries making our products, stealing our companies, and destroying our jobs. Protection will lead to great prosperity and strength. . . . We've defended other nations' borders while refusing to defend our own and spent trillions and trillions of dollars overseas while America's infrastructure has fallen into disrepair and decay. We've made other countries rich while the wealth, strength, and confidence of our country has dissipated over the horizon. . . . We stand at the birth of a new millennium, ready to unlock the mysteries of space, to free the Earth from the miseries of disease, and to harness the energies, industries, and technologies of tomorrow," he concluded. "A new national pride will stir our souls, lift our sights, and heal our divisions."

Trump's administration immediately tried to implement sweeping immigration restrictions through executive order, and parts of his first address to Congress on February 28, 2017, read more like a progress report than a wish list. "My administration has answered the pleas of the American people for immigration enforcement and border security," he said. "By finally enforcing our immigration laws, we will raise wages, help the unemployed, save billions and billions of dollars, and make our communities safer for everyone. We will soon begin the construction of a great, great wall along our southern border. As we speak tonight, we are removing gang members, drug dealers, and criminals that threaten our communities and prey on our very innocent citizens," he said. "We are also taking strong measures to protect our Nation from radical Islamic terrorism." Two executive orders had sharply reduced quotas for refugees and totally banned immigration from six Muslim countries. Federal district courts initially blocked the implementation of those orders, but the Supreme Court eventually approved them in June 2018 by a 5–4 majority. He then turned to his other signature issue, international trade. "We've lost more than one-fourth of our manufacturing jobs since NAFTA was approved, and we've lost 60,000 factories since China joined the World Trade Organization in 2001," he said. The trade deficit—which previous presidents had stopped mentioning—had reached $800 billion, and the nation had to "equalize tariffs." He listed nine major corporations which, he said, had announced that they were investing billions in the US to crate "tens of thousands of new American jobs."

Trump then followed in the footsteps of Reagan and George W. Bush: "My economic team is developing historic tax reform that will reduce the tax rate on our companies so they can compete and thrive anywhere and with anyone. . . . At the same time, we will provide massive tax relief for the middle class." He announced that the US had withdrawn from "the job-killing Trans-Pacific Partnership," a pending multilateral trade deal with Asian countries. Echoing Obama, he proposed a massive $1 trillion infrastructure program combining public and private funding. On the other hand, he asked Congress to "repeal and replace Obamacare with reforms that expand choice, increase access, lower costs, and at the same time, provide better health care. . . . Obamacare is collapsing." His budget would include "one of the largest increases in national defense spending in American history," and more funding for veterans.

In his first annual message on January 30, 2018, Trump detailed the provisions of tax cuts that Congress had now passed: a near-doubling of the standard deduction for all taxpayers, the doubling of the child tax credit to $2,000 per child, and a corporate tax cut from 35 percent to 21 percent. He did not mention the cut in the top income tax rate from 39.6 percent to 37 percent. Congress had refused to repeal Obamacare, but Trump boasted that the new tax law had eliminated the tax on those who refused to buy insurance. He took credit for ending "the war on American energy, and . . . the war on beautiful, clean coal." He talked in detail about the opioid epidemic that prescription opioids had unleashed, which in 2016 had killed 64,000 Americans by overdoses. "We must get much tougher on drug dealers and pushers if we are going to succeed in stopping this scourge." Five weeks later on March 8 he announced that he was using national security authority to impose a 25 percent tariff on foreign steel and a 10 percent tariff on foreign aluminum. His administration had also begun renegotiating and renaming the NAFTA agreement with Canada and Mexico. And on August 25, 2017, he issued a memorandum restoring the ban on transgender service in the US military.

Unemployment did fall from 5 percent at the end of 2015 and 4.7 percent a year later to 4.1 percent in December 2017 and 3.9 percent in 2018. Yet thanks to Trump's tax cuts and his increased spending on defense, the federal deficit rose from $585 billion in fiscal 2016 to $665 billion in fiscal 2017, $779 billion in 2018, and $984 billion in 2019. Trump never even mentioned the federal deficit in any major address, and after submitting a one-page cover letter about the fiscal 2018 budget on March 16, 2017 that gave no figure for a deficit, he never released even such a brief personal message along with the administration's detailed budget again. And despite the strong economy, the unpopular and unsuccessful attempt to repeal Obamacare, the angry tone of so many of his tweets, and the ongoing Russia investigations allowed the Democrats to gain 41 seats in the House of Representatives in November 2018 and regain a 235–200 majority. The Republicans however picked up 2 more Senate seats for a 53–47 majority.

The Democrats had opposed Trump's anti-immigration measures, and refused in particular to appropriate money for his border wall. Trump in December 2018 refused to agree to combine the money for the wall with some legal status for so-called Dreamers. In late December he refused to sign any funding bill for the Department of Homeland Security that did not include money for the wall, and that agency and various others shut down on December 23. Trump addressed the nation on border security on January 8, proclaiming "a growing humanitarian and security crisis at our southern border. Every day, Customs and Border Patrol agents encounter thousands of illegal immigrants trying to enter our country." In the past two years, he claimed, ICE—the Immigration Customs and Enforcement agency— had arrested 266,000 "aliens with criminal records," and "thousands of Americans" had been killed by illegal immigrants. He insisted again that Congress approve "$5.7 billion for a physical barrier"—a steel barrier rather than a concrete wall. In return he offered to extend the Dreamers' protected status for three years. The shutdown dragged on and he repeated these demands in another address on January 19. On January 25 he announced that he would sign a bill ending the shutdown until February 15, and if Congress still refused money for the wall he would "use the powers afforded to me under the laws and the Constitution of the United States to address this emergency." He declared that emergency on February 19 and diverted several billion dollars of the Pentagon budget and funds from other agencies to fund the wall. That emergency remained in effect for the rest of his term. On May 16, 2019, he restated his immigration proposals. "Democrats are proposing open borders, lower wages, and frankly, lawless chaos," he said. "We are proposing an immigration plan that puts the jobs, wages, and safety of American workers first."

Trump had given his second annual message on February 5, 2019, and began with words almost indistinguishable from his predecessor's on similar occasions. "Millions of our fellow citizens are watching us now, gathered in this great Chamber, hoping that we will govern not as two parties, but as one Nation. . . . we must reject the politics of revenge, resistance, and retribution, and embrace the boundless potential of cooperation, compromise, and the common good." Once again listing statistical evidence of "an economic miracle," he warned that it might be stopped by "foolish wars, politics, or ridiculous, partisan investigations." He claimed that wages were now rising the fastest for "low-income workers" and that the net worth of the lower half of wage earners had increased 47 percent in two years. He praised Congress for passing a criminal justice reform bill lowering sentencing guidelines and for nearly eliminating the estate tax. Promising "to lower the cost of health care and prescription drugs and to protect patients with preexisting conditions"—which Obamacare already did—he claimed that drug prices had seen "their single largest decline in 46 years."[11] "Tonight," he added unnecessarily, "we renew our resolve

---

11 This was a random effect over the last year—drug prices overall continued to rise during the Trump years. https://www.cnn.com/2019/02/05/politics/fact-check-trump-state-of-the-union/index.html.

that America will never be a socialist country." Six weeks later, on March 24, he boasted that the final report of the Mueller investigation of Russian involvement in the 2016 campaign had been a "complete exoneration. No collusion. No obstruction." Trump eventually pardoned five associates for offenses uncovered in the course of the Mueller investigation—four of them on the eve of his departure from the White House.

In foreign affairs, Trump first departed from previous policy on June 1, 2017, when he announced that the United States was withdrawing from the recently concluded Paris climate accords that had committed the country to major greenhouse gas reductions and to contributions to a Green Climate Fund. "This agreement is less about the climate and more about other countries gaining a financial advantage over the United States," he said. In the Middle East he began his tenure with a visit to Saudi Arabia for a regional summit. On May 21 he announced "a $110 billion Saudi-funded defense purchase, and we will be sure to help our Saudi friends to get a good deal from our great American defense companies, the greatest anywhere in the world." Echoing Bush and Obama, he insisted that terrorists did not represent Islam. He identified his main enemy in the region. "From Lebanon to Iraq to Yemen, Iran funds, arms, and trains terrorists, militias, and other extremist groups that spread destruction and chaos across the region. . . . It is a Government that speaks openly of mass murder, vowing the destruction of Israel, death to America, and ruin for many leaders and nations in this very room." In an address at Fort Meyer in Northern Virginia on August 21, 2017, he announced that he had changed his mind about leaving Afghanistan. After justifying the war in terms identical to his predecessors, he announced, "I have already lifted restrictions the previous administration placed on our warfighters that prevented the Secretary of Defense and our commanders in the field from fully and swiftly waging battle against the enemy. . . . we are already seeing dramatic results in the campaign to defeat ISIS, including the liberation of Mosul in Iraq." In his January 30, 2018 annual message he announced that "close to 100 percent" of ISIS-held territory had been liberated. Trump eventually pardoned several Americans who had been convicted of serious war crimes during the War on Terror.

Addressing the United Nations on September 19, 2017, Trump revived the language of Bush in January 2002 and specifically repudiated Obama's attempts to improve relations with former enemies. "The scourge of our planet today is a small group of rogue regimes that violate every principle on which the United Nations is based. They respect neither their own citizens nor the sovereign rights of their [sic] countries." They included "the depraved regime in North Korea." "The United States has great strength and patience," Trump said, "but if it is forced to defend itself or its allies, we will have no choice but to totally destroy North Korea." He insisted that President Kim Jong-Un give up nuclear weapons. He added Iran to this list, another reckless nation "that speaks openly of mass murder, vowing death to America, destruction to Israel, and ruin for many leaders and nations in this room." He attacked the nuclear agreement with Iran, "one of the worst and most one-sided transactions the United States has ever entered into." And reversing the Obama administration's attempt to improve relations with Cuba, he referred to its "corrupt, destabilizing regime" and announced that the US would not lift sanctions until the Cuban government made "fundamental reforms." He also committed the US to the overthrow of the socialist Maduro government in Venezuela. On December 6 he reversed another fifty-year-old US policy. Congress, he noted, had urged the nation to recognize Jerusalem as Israel's capital thirty years earlier. Because the refusal to do so had failed to bring about peace with the Palestinians, he said, "I have determined that it is time to officially recognize Jerusalem as the capital of Israel. . . . Israel is a sovereign nation with the right like every other sovereign nation to determine its own capital."

Trump in his 2018 annual message added "rivals like China and Russia that challenge our interests, our economy and our values" to his list of worldwide threats, and on April 13 he issued a challenge to Russia in connection with the ongoing conflict in Syria, which Moscow had joined as an ally of Syria and Iran. Trump announced new Anglo-French-US air strikes against Syrian chemical weapons capabilities "to establish a strong deterrent against the production, spread, and use of chemical weapons. . . . To Iran and to Russia, I ask: What kind of a nation wants to be associated with the mass murder of innocent men, women, and children? . . . Russia must decide if it will continue down this dark path or if it will join with civilized nations as a force for stability and peace." And on May 8 Trump carried out his threat to withdraw from the nuclear agreement with Iran and reimpose economic sanctions. "As we exit the Iran deal, we will be working with our allies to find a real, comprehensive, and lasting solution to the Iranian nuclear threat," including "efforts to eliminate the threat of Iran's ballistic missile program, to stop its terrorist activities worldwide, and to block its menacing activity across the Middle East."

Trump had continued his threats of destruction against North Korea, but after an unprecedented meeting with Kim Jong-Un in Singapore on June 15, 2018, he reversed course even more dramatically than Nixon in the days of détente. "The summit also made a clean break from the failed approaches of past administrations. . . . Our conversation was open, honest, direct, and very, very productive. We produced something that is beautiful. . . . a joint statement in which Chairman Kim, quote, 'reaffirmed his firm and unwavering commitment to complete denuclearization of the Korean Peninsula.' This is the beginning of the process toward the denuclearization of North Korea." In his February 2019 annual message he reported that North Korea had stopped conducting underground nuclear tests. Had he not been president, he said, war with North Korea would have broken out. He also noted that the United States had recognized a rival government in Venezuela led by "its new President, Juan Guaidó," but that government never took power. He announced that the US had withdrawn from the Intermediate-range Nuclear Forces treaty with Russia—concluded by Reagan—on the grounds that Russia had violated its terms.

In September 2019 the House of Representatives opened an impeachment inquiry against Trump after the leak of a phone conversation he had had on July 25 with new Ukrainian president Volodymyr Zelensky. Trump had asked Zelensky both to announce an investigation of former vice president Joseph Biden—the front-runner for the 2020 Democratic presidential nomination—and his son Hunter, who had been hired by a Ukrainian energy firm, and also to endorse the idea that Ukraine, not Russia, had interfered in the 2016 election. He had then withheld promised military aid from Ukraine after Zelensky failed to comply. While the inquiry proceeded, Trump escalated the War on Terror. On October 27 he announced that an American raid had killed the leader of ISIS, Abu Bakr al-Baghdadi, in Syria. And on January 3, 2020, he announced an unprecedented drone strike that had killed Qasem Soleimani, a senior Iranian military officer, while he was visiting Iraq. "Soleimani was plotting imminent and sinister attacks on American diplomats and military personnel," he said, "but we caught him in the act and terminated him." Never before had an American president openly taken responsibility for the intentional killing of an official of a country with whom the United States was not at war. Later that month, as his impeachment trial in the Senate proceeded, he met with Prime Minister Benjamin Netanyahu of Israel at the White House and on January 28 announced—but did not attempt to explain—a new peace proposal that once again repudiated decades-long US positions. It proposed a noncontiguous Palestinian state on the West Bank that would not include any land now settled by Israelis. The Palestinians immediately rejected it. Months later, on September 15, Trump announced the conclusion of the Abraham Accords between Israel and the Arab states of Bahrain and the United Arab Emirates, establishing diplomatic relations among them and making it easier for Arabs to visit Jerusalem.

On February 6 Trump addressed the nation after the Senate had voted 52–48 for acquittal, with just one Republican voting for conviction. "A tremendous thing was done over the last number of months, but really, if you go back to it, over the last number of years," he said. "We had the witch hunt. It started from the day we came down the elevator[12]. . . . And it never really stopped. We've been going through this now for over 3 years. It was evil. It was corrupt. It was dirty cops. It was leakers and liars. And this should never, ever happen to another President—ever." He called two leading Democratic House members, Adam Schiff and Speaker Nancy Pelosi, "a vicious, horrible person" and "a horrible person."

By the end of February Trump faced an entirely new crisis: the COVID epidemic, which had started in China and spread to Europe and thence to the United States. Americans began dying of the disease during February. Keenly aware that the epidemic might severely hurt the US economy and his chances for reelection, Trump quickly banned travel from China but downplayed the seriousness of the disease. Addressing the nation on the situation for the first and last time on March 11, he announced that the government

---

12 This referred to the day in 2015 that he had announced his presidential candidacy.

was making "the most aggressive and comprehensive effort to confront a foreign virus in modern history." He boasted of his quick ban on travel from China and announced that he was extending it to all of Europe, which now had higher infection rates, except the United Kingdom. Congress, he reported, had already appropriated $8.3 billion to fight the virus, support the rapid development of vaccines, and distribute medical supplies. He insisted that "the risk is very, very low" for "the vast majority of Americans," and promised "emergency action, which is unprecedented, to provide financial relief" to workers who had to stay home. He left the issue of specific quarantine measures or masks (which he did not mention) to local officials. By the end of March a White House task force headed by Vice President Mike Pence was giving daily briefings on the epidemic, encouraging masks, social distancing, and other safety measures. Trump at the March 24 briefing set a goal of easing "the guidelines and open[ing] things up to very large sections of our country" by Easter, which was only two weeks away. That goal proved overoptimistic, and on April 24 he signed the Paycheck Protection Program and Health Care Enhancement Act, authorizing $320 billion worth of relief to businesses and the unemployed. The unemployment rate rose from 3.5 percent in February to 14.7 percent in May.[13] The nation's schools and most workplaces shut down, with workers and children using Zoom for classes and work for the next year. And the almost instantaneous, deep recession slashed federal revenues and created a record peacetime deficit of $3.132 trillion in fiscal 2020.

In late May the country fell into its worst racial crisis in decades, after a bystander videotaped the killing of George Floyd, a black man, by a police officer kneeling on his neck in Minneapolis, Minnesota. Large nightly protests began not only in Minneapolis, where the governor called out the National Guard, but in Portland, Los Angeles, Memphis, New York, Washington, DC, and elsewhere. Led by the loosely organized Black Lives Matter movement, they often called for "defunding the police." Some protests led to clashes with police and outbursts of arson and looting. Trump spoke to the nation from the Rose Garden on June 1. "All Americans were

---

13 https://www.bls.gov/charts/employment-situation/civilian-unemployment-rate.htm.

rightly sickened and revolted by the brutal death of George Floyd," he began. "My administration is fully committed that, for George and his family, justice will be served. . . . But we cannot allow the righteous cries and peaceful protesters to be drowned out by an angry mob. . . . In recent days, our Nation has been gripped by professional anarchists, violent mobs, arsonists, looters, criminals, rioters, Antifa, and others. A number of State and local governments have failed to take necessary action to safeguard their residents." He recited a long list of beaten innocent bystanders, attacks on police, burned businesses and vandalized monuments. "These are acts of domestic terror. The destruction of innocent life and the spilling of innocent blood is an offense to humanity and a crime against God. . . . I am mobilizing all available Federal resources—civilian and military—to stop the rioting and looting, to end the destruction and arson, and to protect the rights of law-abiding Americans, including your Second Amendment rights." If state governors failed to deploy enough National Guardsmen to "dominate the streets . . . I will deploy the United States military and quickly solve the problem for them." "I want the organizers of this terror to be on notice that you will face severe criminal penalties and lengthy sentences in jail," he said. On September 22, Trump issued an executive order banning workplace diversity training based on certain principles in the federal government or in government contractors. It specifically targeted "a different vision of America that is grounded in hierarchies based on collective social and political identities rather than in the inherent and equal dignity of every person as an individual. This ideology is rooted in the pernicious and false belief that America is an irredeemably racist and sexist country; that some people, simply on account of their race or sex, are oppressors; and that racial and sexual identities are more important than our common status as human beings and Americans."

The election turned out to be as novel as the Trump presidency itself. Former vice president Joseph Biden, now seventy-seven, overcame a slow start to become the Democratic nominee. Many states passed new voting laws encouraging early voting from home because of the pandemic, and Trump immediately began arguing that they opened the way to large-scale fraud. Polls showed Biden with a big lead. On election night, Trump and the Republicans outperformed expectations, and because Democrats had cast far more mail-in ballots than Republicans, Trump by the next morning still led in the key states of Michigan, Wisconsin, Pennsylvania, Arizona and Georgia. By the evening of Thursday, November 5, it was becoming clear that Biden would carry most or all of those states and win comfortable popular and electoral majorities. Trump addressed the nation from the White House that evening, providing "an update on our efforts to protect the integrity of our very important 2020 election. If you count the legal votes, I easily win. If you count the illegal votes, they can try to steal the election from us—if you count the votes that came in late—we're looking at them very strongly." By the following week Biden had clearly won the election with 51.3 percent of the popular vote to Trump's 46.8 percent—a plurality of seven million votes—and 306 electoral votes to 232. The Democrats also secured a 50–50 tie in the Senate after runoffs in two Georgia contests, giving them a majority with the help of Vice President Kamala Harris, but the Republicans gained 14 seats in the House and cut the Democratic majority to 222–213. Nearly a month later, on December 2, Trump videotaped and posted on Facebook another long speech claiming that fraud had decided the election. "Today I will detail some of the shocking irregularities, abuses, and fraud that have been revealed in recent weeks. . . . I want to explain the corrupt mail-in balloting scheme that Democrats systematically put into place that allowed voting to be altered, especially in swing states, which they had to win." Lawyers for his campaign had been pushing these accusations in court in many states, but to no effect. "When those votes are corrupt, when they're irregular, when they get caught, they're terminated," he continued. "And I very easily win, in all states, I very easily win these swing states, just like I won them at 10 o'clock in the evening, the evening of the election." All the contested states certified Biden victories.

Using social media, Trump encouraged his supporters to congregate in Washington on January 6, the day that Congress in joint session would certify the vice president's official count of the electoral votes. That morning at a rally of his supporters he called on Vice President Pence to alter the election result. "All Vice President Pence has to do is send it back to the states to recertify," he said, "and we become president, and you are the happiest people. . . . So we are going to—we are going to walk down Pennsylvania Avenue . . . and we are going to the Capitol, and we are going to try and give . . . our Republicans, the weak ones because the strong ones don't need any of our help, we're try—going to try and give them the kind of pride and boldness that they need to take back our country." Trump returned to the White House, but some supporters broke through police lines, entered the Capitol building, forced Congress into hiding and interrupted the certification. After several hours Trump issued a video repeating that the election had been stolen but telling the protesters to go home. After they left the Capitol Congress certified Biden's victory by votes of 93–6 in the Senate and 303–121 in the House.[14] The next day Trump issued a new statement. "I would like to begin by addressing the heinous attack on the United States Capitol," he said. "Like all Americans, I am outraged by the violence, lawlessness, and mayhem. I immediately deployed the National Guard and Federal law enforcement to secure the building and expel the intruders. America is and must always be a nation of law and order. The demonstrators who infiltrated the Capitol have defiled the seat of American democracy. . . . Now Congress has certified the results. A new administration will be inaugurated on January 20th."

Moving swiftly, the House of Representatives leaders first asked Vice President Pence to depose Trump under the Twenty-Fifth Amendment on January 12, and when he refused, impeached Trump for inciting the insurrection at the Capitol on January 13 by a vote of 232–197. The Senate trial did not take place until after he left office. On January 19 he gave a long farewell address, listing once again his signature accomplishments on the domestic and foreign fronts. "Together, we put the American people back in charge of our country. We restored self-government." On February 13 the Senate voted to convict Trump and bar him from holding federal office again by a 57–43 margin that included 7 Republicans—10 short of the two-thirds majority necessary for conviction, which would have disqualified Trump from ever holding federal office again.

Despite his grandiose rhetoric, Trump in 2017–19—that is, before the pandemic struck—had no more success in reaching his

---

14 "Congress Affirms Biden's Presidential Win Following Riot at U.S. Capitol," *Washington Post*, January 7, 2021.

goals than his predecessors. The trade deficit grew from $506 billion in 2016 to $596 billion in 2019.[15] Unemployment continued to fall at the same rate as it had since 2010, and manufacturing did not employ a higher percentage of the workforce than before. Confirmed illegal border crossings over the southwest border rose from 106,080 in 2016 to 155,994 in 2020. The 2020 census recorded a ten-year population increase of just 7.4 percent, the second lowest in history, to a total of 331 million. Trump's tax cuts ballooned the federal deficit once again. His administration had completed the campaign against ISIS, but the Afghan government, it would develop, was near collapse. And he had substituted bitter opposition to states like Cuba and Iran and closer alliances than ever with Israel and Saudi Arabia for more evenhanded diplomacy. Trump above all had changed the nature of presidential rhetoric. The United States had lived through intensely partisan periods in the 1790s, the 1860s and 1870s, and the 1940s and early 1950s, but presidents in those periods had usually tried to keep themselves above the rhetorical fray. Trump did not, referring to enemies in the opposition party and his own and unfriendly media outlets with bitter contempt. He bequeathed a deeply divided nation to his successor, and he had not abandoned his political career.

Joseph Biden took office in January 2021 after thirty-six years in the Senate and eight years as vice president—by far the longest tenure in elected federal office of any chief executive.[16] His two runs for president as a senator had gone nowhere, but the name recognition and party stature of a vice president allowed him—like Humphrey, Mondale, and Gore—to become the consensus candidate in 2020. Claiming a victory "for the cause of democracy" to open his inaugural address, he continued, "We've learned again that democracy is precious, democracy is fragile. And at this hour, my friends, democracy has prevailed." The nation's enormous challenges included the pandemic that had killed more Americans than

---

15 https://www.macrotrends.net/countries/USA/united-states/trade-balance-deficit#:~:text=U.S.percent20tradepercent20balancepercent20forpercent202020,apercent206.65percent25percent20increasepercent20frompercent202016.
16 Second place belongs to Gerald Ford, who had served twenty-five years in Congress and one year as vice president when he took office.

had died in the Second World War, the loss of millions of jobs, "a cry for racial justice some 400 years in the making," and "a cry of survival . . . from the planet itself. . . . And now, a rise of political extremism, White [sic] supremacy, domestic terrorism that we must confront and we will defeat." With "unity," he said, "we can do great things, important things. We can right wrongs. We can put people to work in good jobs. We can teach our children in safe schools. We can overcome the deadly virus. We can reward work and rebuild the middle class and make health care secure for all. We can deliver racial justice, and we can make America, once again, the leading force for good in the world. . . . Our history has been a constant struggle between the American ideal that we all are created equal and the harsh, ugly reality that racism, nativism, fear, demonization have long torn us apart." Abroad he promised to "repair our alliances and engage with the world once again."

Biden's staff had carefully prepared his accession, and on inauguration day he issued eight executive actions and a proclamation laying down a range of policies—"Advancing Racial Equity and Support for Underserved Communities though the Federal Government," "restoring science to tackle the climate crisis," fighting "Discrimination on the Basis of Gender Identity or Sexual Orientation"—and revoking some of Trump's executive orders on federal regulation and immigration policies. The next day he personally announced new policies against COVID. The United States had suffered nearly 20 percent of the world's COVID deaths, he said, and it "has disproportionately impacted on Blacks, Latinos, and Native Americans, who are about four times as likely to be hospitalized and nearly three times more likely to die from the COVID-19 pandemic than White Americans." The use of masks had become political under Trump—who had conspicuously refused to wear one—and Biden asked Americans to use them for his first one hundred days, while the administration started "a full-scale wartime effort" to vaccinate one hundred million mostly older Americans. Much of this early rhetoric, including the capitalizations of "Black" and "White," "underserved communities," "equity," and the reference to disproportionate impact, reflected a new view of American society and history whose roots dated back to the late 1960s but which previous presidents, Republican and Democratic, had generally avoided until late in the Obama administration.

On March 11 Biden marked the first anniversary of the pandemic with an emotional broadcast address to the nation. Children had lost learning by missing a year of school, the virus had kept extended family members apart, and the nation had gone without customary activities. He spoke of "vicious hate crimes against Asian Americans, who have been attacked, harassed, blamed, and scapegoated." "I'm using every power I have as President of the United States to put us on a war footing to get the job done," he said. "It sounds like hyperbole, but I mean it: a war footing. . . . It's truly a national effort, just like we saw during World War II." The vaccine rate had risen from 8 percent to 65 percent in fifty days, and he promised to beat the goal of 100 million shots in one hundred days. And on that day, he reported, he had signed the American Rescue Plan, a massive new infusion of cash into businesses, state and local governments, and households, which would provide most Americans with a $1,400 payment, extend unemployment benefits, cut child poverty in half, and bring 800,000 more people under the Affordable Care Act. He did not mention that the plan cost $1.8 trillion. "My fervent prayer for our country," he said, "is that, after all we have been through, we'll come together as one people, one Nation, one America."

Biden gave his first address to a joint session of Congress on April 28, his ninety-ninth day in office. He had, he said, inherited a nation in crisis: "the worst pandemic in a century, the worst economic crisis since the Great Depression, the worst attack on our democracy since the Civil War. Now, after just 100 days, I can report to the Nation: America is on the move again, turning peril into possibility, crisis to opportunity, setbacks into strength." He referred to 1.3 million "new jobs created in 100 days." Then he turned to two new proposed pieces of legislation. The American Jobs Plan would be "the largest jobs plan since World War II." It "creates jobs to upgrade our transportation infrastructure; jobs modernizing our roads, bridges, highways; jobs building ports and airports, rail corridors, transit lines." It would also modernize the power grid, provide more home health care, and attack climate change by building "more energy efficient buildings and homes, installing charging stations, and planting cover crops to reduce greenhouse gas emissions." Biden dropped Obama's and Trump's idea of a private–public infrastructure partnership. He asked for a new "Advanced Research Projects Agency for Health" to find cures or preventive strategies for diabetes, Alzheimer's disease, and cancer. "And all the investments in the American Jobs Plan will be guided by one principle: buy American," he added in an unacknowledged bow to his predecessor. Nearly 90 percent of the infrastructure jobs in this "8-year program," he said, would not require a college degree—it "is a blue-collar blueprint to build America." He also asked for a minimum wage increase to $15/hour, and for the passage of a new Protect the Right to Organize Act to support unions, making him the first president of either party since Lyndon Johnson to ask to extend union rights.

Next came an "American Families Plan," starting with ideas to improve education by guaranteeing every American sixteen years of education, including two years of preschool and two years of community college. He asked for increased student loans and investments in "Historical [sic] Black Colleges and Universities, Tribal Colleges, Minority-Serving Institutions," because "they don't have the endowments." Families should be able to secure child care for a maximum of 7 percent of their income and enjoy twelve weeks of paid family leave and medical leave, and he asked to make the new temporary $3,000–$3,600 child tax credit, which was substantially reducing child poverty, effective through 2025. Turning to familiar topics, he called for a new gun control measure to ban assault weapons with high-capacity magazines and make background checks for gun purchases universal. He also mentioned a bill to create a path to citizenship for eleven million undocumented immigrants and protection for "Dreamers," and touted assistance to Central American countries to reduce the incentives for their people to migrate northward. And to pay for all this—without, he claimed, increasing the deficit—he proposed new taxes to make Americans earning more than $400,000 annually pay "their fair share." The tax on the highest brackets would go back up to 39.6 percent from Trump's 37 percent, a law would eliminate loopholes that allowed CEOs to pay a lower rate "on their capital gains than Americans who receive a paycheck"—presumably a reference to the "carried interest" loophole that benefited hedge funds—and corporations, many of which now avoided taxes entirely, would pay a minimum rate. Within months, the American Families Plan, the tax proposals and the clean energy proposals had a new name, the Build Back Better plan, and the infrastructure bill proceeded separately.

Succeeding where Obama and Trump had failed, Biden secured Senate approval for the Infrastructure Investment and Jobs Act by a bipartisan 69–30 vote in August, and the House passed it on party lines in November. The bill increased authorized infrastructure spending from about $700 billion to $1.2 trillion over an unspecified period of years. The Democratic congressional leadership then tried to pass the Build Back Better bill through the reconciliation process, requiring only a one-vote majority in the 50–50 Senate, but in December 2021 Senator Joe Manchin of West Virginia, a Democrat, announced that he could not vote for it.

On January 11, 2022, Biden gave a speech in Atlanta, Georgia linking the insurrection of a year earlier to more recent Republican attempts to change election laws in various states, both by limiting the use of mail-in voting and drop boxes and by putting more partisan officials in charge of vote counts. Referring in particular to a Georgia provision that barred anyone from providing food or water to voters waiting in line, he said, "That's not America. That's what it looks like when they suppress the right to vote." Nineteen states had passed thirty-four laws "attacking voting rights." "Jim Crow 2.0 is about two insidious things: voter suppression and election subversion. . . . The goal of the former President and his allies is to disenfranchise anyone who votes against them." He asked Congress once again to pass two new laws that would overrule many of the new Republican voting rules and restore provisions of the 1965 Voting Rights Act that the Supreme Court had invalidated in 2013. He asked every elected official in America, "How do you want to be remembered? At consequential moments in history, they present a choice: Do you want to be the side—on the side of Dr. King or George Wallace? Do you want to be on the side of John Lewis or Bull Connor? Do you want to be on the side of Abraham Lincoln or Jefferson Davis?" Republicans blocked action on these bills in the Senate.

In his first annual message on March 2, 2022, Biden reported more progress on COVID. He fulsomely praised the infrastructure bill and reiterated all the major proposals of the now-stalled Build Back Better plan. He also addressed two new issues. Major crimes had increased sharply in the nearly two years since George Floyd's death, and Biden noted that the $350 billion in state and local aid in the American Rescue Plan could be used "to hire more police, invest in more proven strategies like community violence interruption.... We should all agree the answer is not to defund the police." Secondly, while unemployment had now fallen all the way back to 3.9 percent from 6.7 percent when he took office, inflation, fueled by problems in the supply chain and severe disruption of world energy and food supplies, had leapt all the way to an annual rate of 7 percent, the highest since 1981. Biden called getting prices under control "my top priority." To do so he planned "to lower your costs and lower the deficit" by passing some earlier suggestions: letting Medicare negotiate the cost of prescription drugs such as insulin, increasing energy efficiency, and limiting the cost of child care. He said nothing about the Federal Reserve's sudden, significant increase in interest rates, which aimed at slowing down the economy—perhaps even into recession—until inflation eased, just as it had under Reagan in 1981–82. Repeating his proposals on immigration, gun control, and taxes on the wealthy, he added a four-point "unity agenda" that Republicans could support: action against the opioid epidemic that was now killing tens of thousands a year; attempts to improve mental health, perhaps by putting some limits on social media platforms; better care for veterans; and an end to "cancer as we know it." He also boasted that he was "the first president to cut the deficit by more than $1 trillion in a single year." Here he was anticipating: it fell from $2.775 trillion in fiscal 2021 to $1.375 trillion in fiscal 2022, still $400 billion higher than in fiscal 2019.

Two foreign policy issues dominated Biden's first eighteen months in office. On April 11, 2021, he had announced his intention to carry out Trump's plans to withdraw from Afghanistan. "With the terror threat now in many places, keeping thousands of troops grounded and concentrated in just one country at a cost of billions each year makes little sense to me and to our leaders [sic]," he said. "We cannot continue the cycle of extending or expanding our military presence in Afghanistan, hoping to create ideal conditions for the withdrawal, and expecting a different result." He promised to withdraw "responsibly, deliberately, safely" by August 31. On August 14, he announced the deployment of 5,000 new troops to protect the evacuation of all US citizens and Afghans "at special risk from the Taliban advance," which was taking control of large parts of the country. On August 20 he reported significant progress in the evacuation, but on August 26, he had to note that an ISIS terrorist attack had killed thirteen Americans and more than one hundred Afghans at Kabul airport. On August 31, reporting on the end of the evacuation, he acknowledged, "The assumption . . . that more than 300,000 Afghan National Security Forces that we had trained over the past two decades and equipped would be a strong adversary in their civil wars with the Taliban" had turned out "not to be accurate." The Afghan forces had declined to fight without direct American support, and the Taliban now controlled the whole country, as in 2001.

The world situation changed dramatically when Russia invaded Ukraine on February 23, 2022. A day later Biden announced new economic sanctions on Russia and new US deployments to NATO allies Poland, Romania, and the Baltic States. In the State of the Union message on March 1 he declared that Putin had "miscalculated" that he could "shake the very foundations of the Free World." All our European allies had joined in sanctions, and the US was finding ways to punish "Russian oligarchs." The US was also providing military, economic and humanitarian assistance to Ukraine, but "Our forces are not engaged and will not engage in the conflict with Russian forces in Ukraine." Helped by US and other aid, the Ukrainian Army managed to halt Russia's advance and inflict heavy casualties, and was regaining some territory by the end of 2022. On August 9, Biden confirmed that formerly neutral Sweden and Finland were joining NATO to protect themselves against Russian aggression. NATO also attempted to embargo Russian oil and natural gas, and the war drove up energy prices dramatically, fueling the inflation in the United States.

By the middle of 2022 inflation loomed as one of the most important issues in the upcoming midterm elections, and the Democrats renamed the Build Back Better bill the Inflation Reduction Act. Senator Manchin at length agreed to a scaled-back version of it, which Biden described on July 28. Medicare would begin negotiating prescription drug prices—he did not mention that this would apply initially to a list of only ten drugs, yet to be determined—and Medicare annual drug costs would be capped at $2,000. The bill included $349 billion in spending and tax credits for cleaner energy, but it also allowed for increased domestic production of fossil fuels. It established a 15 percent corporate tax minimum and added numerous enforcement personnel to the IRS but left individual rates unchanged, and Biden had to give up his plans for affordable child care, expanded preschool, and wider Medicaid eligibility in the states that so far had refused to grant it.

On June 24, 2022, the Supreme Court overruled the 1973 decision *Roe v. Wade* by a 6–3 vote and returned the issue of abortion to the states or to Congress. Biden reacted instantly. "Today the Supreme Court of the United States expressly took away a constitutional right from the American people that it had already recognized. . . . It's a sad day for the Court and for the country. . . . The health and life of women in this Nation are now at risk. . . . The only way we can secure a woman's right to choose and the balance that existed is for Congress to restore the protections of Roe v. Wade as Federal law." Abortion rights ranked with inflation as the biggest issues in the congressional campaign, and Republican candidates also campaigned hard on crime and the introduction of new ideologies of race and gender into school curriculums. Although on November 8, 2022 the Democrats did better than anticipated, Biden became the third consecutive Democratic president, after Clinton and Obama, to lose control of the House of Representatives after just two years in office. Winning 9 new seats in the House, the Republicans emerged with a 222–213 majority, and won the national House popular vote by nearly 3 percentage points. The Democrats did gain 1 Senate seat for a 51–49 majority, and in Georgia, Democrat Rafael Warnock narrowly won reelection despite the new voting laws that Biden had attacked so bitterly. A week after the election Donald J. Trump announced his presidential candidacy for 2024.

In his second annual message on February 2, 2023, Biden praised Congress for passing bipartisan measures on infrastructure, increased domestic production of computer chips, new procedures for certifying presidential elections, and help for veterans who had been exposed to toxic burn pits. He boasted of low unemployment and declining inflation and insisted that manufacturing jobs would continue to increase. The new infrastructure projects, he said, would use only US-made materials. He pointed to new measures to encourage clean energy *and* to continue oil and gas production, and impose higher minimum taxes on large corporations. He repeated calls for expanded union rights, paid family leave, the higher child care credit that had now lapsed, and a ban on assault weapons—none of which the Republican House was remotely likely to pass. He called for more action against violent crime while highlighting another recent police killing of a black man in Memphis, Tennessee, and introducing the victim's parents, sitting in the audience. He lauded NATO's united assistance to Ukraine against Russia and argued that allies were coming together to resist both Russia and China. And he referred again to the danger to democracy and called for a new spirit. "We have to see each other not as enemies, but as fellow Americans. We're good people. The only nation in the world built on an idea—the only one. Other nations are defined by geography, ethnicity, but we're the only nation based on an idea that all of us, every one of us, is created equal in the image of God. A nation that stands as a beacon to the world. A nation in a new age of possibilities."

While Biden had presided over the end of the pandemic and the rapid recovery of the economy, he had not created a new consensus among the American people. In two years he had given only two nationally televised addresses, and he had not, unlike Trump, found any other way to keep himself and his message front and center in a new media environment. Indeed, Trump's legal problems in several states attracted at least as much media attention as Biden's actions did in the first few months of 2023, while the nation waited to hear whether the eighty-year old president would run for reelection. The state of the union remained uncertain.

# XXII

## THE AMERICAN EXPERIMENT, 1789–2023

This book has explored how successive presidents defined the issues and problems facing the United States, how they proposed to solve them, what steps they took with or without the cooperation of the Congress, and how successfully they managed to achieve their stated aims. It lays out *what happened*, not what twenty-first century people think *should have happened*, or how twenty-first century politicians or activists might have tried to change US history had they been there to do so. That required the use of the presidents' own words. Modern language cannot convey how they and their contemporaries saw their nation and its needs or what they wanted to do about them. For the last 234 years one federal government, led by one president, has had an enormous impact upon every aspect of American life and on more and more of the rest of the world. And like every great human story, this one alternates between the heroic and the tragic, giving us an ever-changing mix of inspiration, pity, and terror to which we naturally return in calmer times. History has many uses, but none is more reliable or more important than what Samuel Johnson described as the function of literature: better to enjoy life, and better to endure it.

From George Washington onwards, American presidents have spoken of their nation as a new experiment whose success or failure would resonate powerfully around the world. "The situation in which I now stand for the last time, in the midst of the representatives of the people of the United States," Washington declared in

December 1796 in his last annual message, "naturally recalls the period when the administration of the present form of government commenced, and I cannot omit the occasion to congratulate you and my country on the success of the experiment, nor to repeat my fervent supplications to the Supreme Ruler of the Universe and Sovereign Arbiter of Nations that His providential care may still be extended to the United States, that the virtue and happiness of the people may be preserved, and that the Government which they have instituted for the protection of their liberties may be perpetual." The United States was indeed the first nation founded on the principles of equality before the law and governments chosen by the governed, however long it took to extend those principles to the whole population. From Washington through Jackson, Lincoln, Wilson, Franklin Roosevelt, Kennedy, Reagan, George W. Bush and Joseph Biden, the survival of that experiment within a broader world and the role of the United States in spreading its ideals have remained central preoccupations of presidents and the whole nation. A second critical issue—the government's relation to the economic life of the United States, with particular reference to the distribution of wealth and income through the population—first emerged in its modern form under Jackson, faded from view in the late nineteenth century, arose once again under Theodore Roosevelt and Woodrow Wilson, and then became the central question of American politics from Franklin Roosevelt through Lyndon Johnson. Ronald Reagan definitely reversed the trend of the previous half century, and set the pattern for the next forty years. Both those issues remain controversial in 2023, and both remain unsettled. Where do they stand in the era of Presidents Trump and Biden?

We have seen that presidents beginning with Monroe expressed satisfaction whenever democratic institutions made progress around the globe. Lincoln explicitly linked the Civil War to world history when he argued that the conflict would decide the future of the democratic experiment. McKinley and Theodore Roosevelt avowedly ranged the United States within the ranks of the imperial powers, and Woodrow Wilson declared a crusade to protect and spread democracy. And even before the US entered the Second World War, Franklin Roosevelt defined it as a struggle between different systems and different philosophies in which American ideals must prevail for the sake of civilization. During the Cold War, presidents from Truman through Reagan took on the mission of defending all non-Communist territory from Communism. And since Communism collapsed in 1989, every president has declared that the United States must exercise unrivaled power and influence in the world and deal freely with threats as it sees fit. That tendency reached its apex under George W. Bush, who claimed the right to strike at terrorists anywhere in the world and overthrow *potentially* dangerous foreign regimes, and actively tried to spread democracy through the Middle East, sometimes by force. Barack Obama stuck to the broad lines of those policies. While Donald Trump often accused allies of profiteering at US expense, he did not really reverse those policies until he announced a withdrawal from Afghanistan late in his term. Joseph Biden carried out that withdrawal and explicitly gave up the project of turning Afghanistan into a democracy. The attempt to spread democracy through the Middle East has failed.

Biden now faces a new threat, the resurgence of international aggression by authoritarian great powers. Drawing on Cold War precedents, he has led a coalition to resist Russia's attack on Ukraine while ruling out direct US intervention in that conflict. Meanwhile, without ever discussing the situation in a major address to the American people, he has declared his intention to defend Taiwan against an increasingly possible Chinese attack. The outcome of these real and threatening conflicts will determine the future of a US-enforced world order among the great powers.

And what of the attempt to increase the share of national income enjoyed by common men and women, to restrain corporate power, and to finance public goods with heavy personal and corporate taxation that began under Franklin Roosevelt? That era coincided, of course, with the era of worldwide great power military conflict, which in the Second World War and the Cold War mobilized national resources for national defense. Top marginal tax rates of 91 percent helped finance those conflicts while they effectively created a ceiling on wealth and influence, and those top rates remained well over 50 percent until 1981. Ronald Reagan's combination of massive tax cuts for the wealthy with a new defense buildup established an unprecedented long-term peacetime federal deficit, and George W. Bush returned to that strategy after 2001. The results of lower income and corporate taxes and the erosion of unions have been striking. From 1979 to 2016, the bottom 20 percent of the nation's income distribution saw its average income increase by about 80 percent (including transfer payments), while the top 20 percent doubled its average income. The middle 60 percent of the distribution, however, saw an increase of only about 35 percent, less than 1 percent per year.[1] Meanwhile, from 1989 through 2019, the wealthiest 1 percent of US families have increased their share of national wealth from 25 percent to nearly 34 percent and the next-wealthiest 9 percent of families have increased their share from 37 percent to 39 percent. (We should note that those figures make the top 1 percent about eight times wealthier than the next-highest 9 percent.) Meanwhile, the wealth of the bottom 50 percent of families—who have never owned as much as 5 percent of the country's wealth—has fallen all the way to 2 percent.[2] While Presidents Clinton, Obama and Biden have referred to these trends, they have rarely even proposed any changes in tax policy that might reverse them. The concentration of income and wealth, combined with the increasing importance of money in political campaigns and the dependence of nearly all elected officials on wealthy contributors, has created a situation in which the views of majorities of Americans on key issues carry little or no weight.[3]

The 2022 Congressional elections marked the eighth time in nine national elections that the control of the White House or at least one House of Congress had changed hands. Democrats took control of the Congress in 2006 and the White House in 2008, only to lose the House in 2010 and the Senate in 2014. The Republicans regained the White House in 2016 and lost the House of Representatives in 2018, and the Democrats won the White House and the Senate back in 2020 but lost the House

---

[1] These figures are from the Congressional Budget Office: https://www.cbo.gov/publication/55413.

[2] https://www.federalreserve.gov/econres/notes/feds-notes/wealth-and-income-concentration-in-the-scf-20200928.html.

[3] Martin Gilens and Benjamin I. Page, "Testing Theories of American Politics: Elites, Interest Groups, and Average Citizens,"(2014) https://www.cambridge.org/core/journals/perspectives-on-politics/article/testing-theories-of-american-politics-elites-interest-groups-and-average-citizens/62327F513959D0A304D4893B382B992B.

again in 2022. American politics have no precedent for these rapidly repeated changes. They reflect a deeply divided electorate and a relatively small number of swing voters who express their discontent with the state of things every two years. The passion and prejudice of which Washington warned the nation in his Farewell Address once again threaten our national unity. These problems, as I have already discussed, reflect the failure of Presidents George W. Bush, Barack Obama, Donald Trump, and now Joe Biden successfully to mobilize the nation's energies and resources on behalf of a great enterprise, as Lincoln and Roosevelt did. While all of them have spoken of crisis, none have managed effectively to deal with it and leave a new consensus behind.

The nature of presidential communication has changed as well. Until Ronald Reagan the State of the Union address annually featured a simple accounting of current and expected receipts and expenditures. Reagan and his successors, as we have seen, have gradually abandoned frank statements of those figures in favor of vague promises, or, in Trump's case, no discussion at all. George H. W. Bush's "$500 billion deficit reduction plan" marked another unfortunate milestone, since the total figure covered five years, not one, and subsequent presidents have gone him one better, announcing ten-year estimates without even making clear that that is what they are doing. "Knowledge is in every country the surest basis of public happiness," George Washington said in his first annual address, and presidents in their speeches are now providing less definite information to allow citizens to understand where the nation is and where it is going. Meanwhile, presidents do not seem to have found a new medium of communication that can command the nation's sustained attention in the way that print media did in the eighteenth and nineteenth centuries and radio and network television did in the twentieth. They need to solve this problem if they are to bind the nation together once again, as they have in the past.

At least from Tocqueville onward, sensitive observers have linked the success of American democracy to the state of American society. "The establishment of our institutions," wrote James Monroe in 1822, "forms the most important epoch that history hath recorded. . . . To preserve and hand them down in their utmost purity to the remotest ages will require the existence and practice of virtues and talents equal to those which were displayed in acquiring them." The increasing fragmentation and discontent of the population of the United States and the declining effectiveness of its government today reflect broader social, economic and intellectual trends that have lessened the power of political institutions around the globe and lie far outside the scope of this book. I have written this political history of the United States both for its own sake and to inspire future readers—believing, with Tocqueville, that the choices between servitude or freedom, knowledge or barbarism, and prosperity or wretchedness depend upon ourselves.[4]

---

4 Alexis de Tocqueville, *Democracy in America*, translated by George Lawrence (New York, 1966), p. 680.

# INDEX

**A**

Abortion issue, 366, 375, 423, 435
Adams, Henry, 119n4
Adams, John, 15–17, 20, 61
Adams, John Quincy, 28, 32, 40–45, 47, 54, 58, 60
Adler, Selig, 223n7
Affordable Care Act, 429–430, 437, 458
Afghan government, 433, 456
Afghan National Security Forces, 462
Afghanistan, 369, 378, 413–415, 420–421, 432–434, 441–442, 467
Afghanistan War, 369, 410, 413–415, 420–421, 432–434, 441–442, 467
Agency for International Development (AID), 20, 291–292, 303, 331–332, 361–362, 378, 383–385, 462
Agnew, Spiro, 355
Agricultural Adjustment Association (AAA), 250–251, 256, 259, 265
Aguinaldo, Emiliano, 185

Aid to Families with Dependent Children, 349, 403
Air traffic controllers, 375
Al-Baghdadi, Abu Bakr, 450
Al-Qaida, 413, 433, 440
Alabama, 38, 44, 109, 133–134, 137, 140–141, 317n15, 340, 351
Alabama claims, 134, 140–141
Alaska, 102, 153, 185, 233, 293, 309, 364
Albertini, Luigi, 215n4
Alexander I, Tsar, 42
Alexandria, 27
Alien and Sedition Acts, 302
Allotment Act, 259
Alternative Minimum Tax, 395
American Jobs Plan, 458–459
American Recovery and Reinvestment Act, 428
American Rescue Plan, 458, 461
American Revolution, 94, 273
Amtrak, 381
Andropov, Yuri, 378
Anti-Jacksonians, 41, 48

Apollo program, 337, 349, 356
Arafat, Yasir, 409
Argentina, 171, 179
Aristide, Jean-Bertrand, 408
Arizona, 77, 91, 101, 104, 157, 205, 332, 454
Arkansas, 31, 47, 60, 111, 146, 308, 396, 405
Arkansas River, 31
Arthur, Chester A., 149, 155–158, 188–189, 198
Atomic Energy Commission, 296, 311
Attacks of 9/11, 6, 416, 418, 426, 433–434, 442
Attlee, Clement, 288
Australia, 300, 312
Austria-Hungary, 188, 215, 220
Azores Islands, 271, 274

**B**

Bank of England, 98
Bank Holding Company Act, 406
Bank of the United States, 3, 11, 28, 45, 48, 66, 68, 70, 84, 98
Barbary pirates, 19
Begin, Menachem, 367
Belgium, 220

471

Bell, John, 105
Benghazi, 434
Berlin, Germany, 276, 278, 315, 320, 322, 328, 384, 386, 390
Berlin Wall, 390
Bernstein, Carl, 305n10
Biden, Joseph, 6, 427, 450, 453, 456, 458, 460–463, 466–467
Bill of Rights, 8, 18, 107, 185, 282, 405, 420
Bin Laden, Osama, 410, 413
Birmingham, Alabama, 329, 333
Bishop, Maurice, 377
Black Americans, 116–117, 127, 188, 202, 221, 283 (*see also* Negroes)
Black Lives Matter movement, 452
Blaine, James G., 122n5, 149, 154, 158, 166, 189
Blair, Tony, 408
Bolivar, Simon, 68
Bonaparte, Louis Napoleon, 81
Bonus, *see* pensions
Bork, Robert, 355
Brazil, 42, 105, 140, 169, 179
Breckinridge, John, 105
Brezhnev, Leonid, 378
Britain, 2, 5, 8, 15, 38, 43, 61, 178–179, 215, 220, 269–275, 408, 439
British Guiana, 179, 274
British North America Act, 141
British West Indies, 32, 46
Brown, Michael, 437

Brown, Scott, 429
*Brown vs. Board of Education*, 350
Bryan, William Jennings, 181, 201, 214
Buchanan, James, 85, 96–107, 119–120
Budget, *see* Federal Budget
Budget and Accounting Act, 401
Buffalo, New York, 57, 158, 162, 188
Bulganin, Nicolai, 316
Bundy, McGeorge, 285
Burns, James MacGregor, 255n3
Burr, Aaron, 17, 20
Burr conspiracy, 28
Bush, George H. W., 6, 372, 388–399, 407–9, 410–411, 469
Bush, George W., 6, 375n,, 411–426, 430, 432, 435–437, 440–443, 445, 448, 466–467, 469
Bush, John Ellis (Jeb), 442
*Bush v. Gore*, 411

## C

Caesar, Julius, 68
Cairo, 357, 432, 435
Calhoun, John C., 87
California, 74, 78–80, 84–87, 97–98, 166, 180–181, 294, 322, 360, 370, 441
Cambodia, 342–346, 354, 384, 387
Canada, 9, 26, 46, 62, 68–69, 74–75, 387, 396, 400, 446
Cape Verde Islands, 274
Caribbean Sea, 88, 99–100, 139, 199–201, 377

Carlisle, Pennsylvania, 153
Carranza, Venustiano, 214
Carter Doctrine, 370
Carter, Jimmy, 245, 341, 363–371, 380, 382, 398n1
Castro, Fidel, 315, 378
Catholic Church, 142
Census:
   1790, 132
   1800, 16–18
   1810, 29
   1820, 37
   1830, 60
   1840, 84–85
   1850, 78, 93
   1860, 456
   1870, 456
   1880, 158–159
   1890, 194
   1900, 93
   1910, 203–204
   1920, 228–229
   1930, 242
   1940, 268
   1950, 366
   1960, 315–317
   1970, 61
   1980, 366–367
   1990, 423
   2000, 423
   2010, 435
   2020, 456
Charlotte-Mecklenburg School District, 351
Chase, Salmon P., 108
Chattanooga, 136
Chernenko, Konstantin, 378, 383
Cherokees, treaty with, 55, 57–58, 121
Chickasaw Indians, 44
Chihuahua, 101
Children's Health Insurance Program, 405

China, 5, 186–187, 246–
    247, 290–291, 342,
    345–347, 431, 439,
    449, 451–452, 464
Choctaw, 44, 55–56
Churchill, Winston, 274,
    278, 283–285, 288
Civil Rights, 5–6,
    293–295, 302–303,
    308–309, 329–333,
    337–338, 367, 396
    (*see also* Gay rights)
Civil Rights Act (1958),
    307–308
Civil Rights Act (1960),
    323–324
Civil Rights Act (1964),
    326, 329, 332
Civil rights movement,
    5, 350
Civil War, 33n2, 93–94,
    101–102, 118n2,
    131–133, 214–215,
    234–235, 267–268,
    369, 374n1, 439,
    462, 466
Civilian Conservation
    Corps (CCC), 250–
    251, 254, 265, 279
Clay, Henry, 40, 47–48,
    50, 68, 70, 72, 85, 87
Clayton Act, 212
Clayton-Bulwer treaty, 99
Clean Water Act, 349
Cleveland, Grover,
    158–158, 171–172,
    174–184, 195, 209,
    227
Clifford, Clark, 366n8
Clinton, Bill (William
    Jefferson), 6, 396,
    398, 401–412, 416,
    420–422, 424–425,
    427, 430
Clinton, DeWitt, 26

Clinton, Hillary, 399, 425,
    438, 442
Cold War, 5–6, 291–292,
    293n5, 296–301,
    303, 309–317,
    318–319, 336–337,
    340, 3460150347,
    368–369, 376–380,
    383–384, 391–393,
    415–416, 467
Colorado, 122, 129, 234,
    236, 407
Colorado River, 234, 236
Colombia, 100, 154–155,
    188, 199
Communism
    collapse of, 388, 397,
        409
    domestic, 268n10,
        272, 290, 294,
        302, 304–305
    foreign, *see* Cold War
Communist Control Act,
    305
Congress of Industrial
    Organizations (CIO),
    267, 280
Conkling, Roscoe, 155
Connor, Eugene "Bull",
    460
Constitution of the United
    States, 1, 8, 447
Constitutional Convention
    of 1787, 24
Constitutional Union
    Party, 105
Coolidge, Calvin, 4, 226,
    228, 230, 233–240,
    262
COVID epidemic, 451
Cox, James M., 226
Cozzens, Peter, 145n6
Crawford, William, 29, 40
Creek Indians, 27, 40
Crime, 348, 350, 356,

    394, 398–399, 401,
    403–404, 407,
    411–412, 423, 444,
    448, 453, 458, 460,
    463, 464
Crime Bill (1994), 401
Crimean War, 91–92
Cromwell, Oliver, 68
Cruz, Rafael Edward
    ("Ted"), 442
Cuba, 77, 99–100, 183–
    186, 188, 198–199,
    257, 322–323, 419,
    438, 449, 456
Czechoslovakia, 269, 292,
    315, 337
Czolgosz, Leon, 188

**D**

Dakar, Senegal, 274
Dakota Territory, 122
Damascus, 357
Daniels, Josephus, 213
Daugherty, Harry, 231
Davis, John W., 233
Dawes, Charles, 238
Dean, John, 354
Declaration of
    Independence, 15,
    43, 52
Defense of Marriage Act,
    403, 422
Del Norte River, 74n3
Delaware, 55, 113, 116,
    118, 123, 143, 248
Democratic Party, 65, 90,
    95–96, 116, 213,
    306n11, 339–340,
    353, 401
Democratic-Republicans,
    13, 17
Denmark, 25, 86, 134,
    271
Dewey, Thomas, 278, 294
Diaz, Porfirio, 206

Dickson, Peter R., 170n3
Diem, Ngo Dinh, 334
District of Columbia, 10, 59, 62, 87, 129, 142, 191, 353, 370, 380
Dodd-Frank Bill, 430
Dole, Robert, 403
Dominican Republic, 135, 139, 148, 169, 200, 215, 335
Doolittle, James, 388
Douglas, Stephen, 91, 93, 104, 108
*Dred Scott vs. Sanford*, 95, 102–104, 110
DuBois, W. E. B., 221, 237
Dukakis, Michael, 388
Dunn, Susan, 267n9

**E**

Earned Income Tax Credit (EITC), 366, 400, 402, 421
Egypt, 198, 274, 277, 314, 336, 367–368, 432–433, 439
Eighteenth Amendment, 232
Eisenhower, Dwight D., 5, 278–279, 301, 303–317, 319–320, 323, 326–327, 334, 358, 367, 378, 388, 431
El Salvador, 377–378
Ellis Island, 416
Ellsberg, Daniel, 355
Emancipation Proclamation, 116, 118–119, 122–123, 205
Embargo Act, 21
Ethiopia, 258, 300, 315, 378, 384
European Recovery Program, 293, 296

Export-Import Bank, 381

**F**

Fair Employment Practices Commission, 283, 294
Fair Housing Act, 339
Fair Labor Standards Act, 266
Fall, Albert B., 233
Family Assistance Plan, 349, 421
Fascism, 414
Faubus, Orville, 308
Federal budget, surpluses, deficits, and national debt:
  George Washington, 11–12
  Thomas Jefferson, 18–22
  James Madison, 27–28
  James Monroe, 35
  John Quincy Adams, 42–43, 47
  Andrew Jackson, 45, 51, 52, 131
  Martin Van Buren, 63–66
  John Tyler, 70–72
  James K. Polk, 81, 83, 84
  Zachary Taylor, 86, 87
  Millard Fillmore, 89, 92–93
  Franklin Pierce, 92
  James Buchanan, 97–99, 104
  Abraham Lincoln, 112, 119–120
  Andrew Johnson, 131–133
  Ulysses S. Grant, 131–132, 138, 142, 144–145

  Rutherford B. Hayes, 152, 156
  Chester A. Arthur, 156
  Grover Cleveland, 163–165, 168, 171–172, 175–177
  Benjamin Harrison, 171n4, 171, 272
  William McKinley, 182
  Theodore Roosevelt, 189, 196, 197, 200
  William Howard Taft, 202, 204–205
  Woodrow Wilson, 211, 226
  Warren Harding, 229–230
  Calvin Coolidge, 234–236
  Herbert Hoover, 240–242, 244
  Franklin D. Roosevelt, 249, 251, 256–257, 263, 265, 268, 273279–281
  Harry S. Truman, 290, 295, 311, 300
  Dwight Eisenhower, 306–307, 311
  John F. Kennedy, 323–324, 325, 326
  Lyndon Johnson, 330, 331, 337, 340, 352
  Richard Nixon, 340, 352, 348
  Gerald Ford, 367
  Jimmy Carter, 366–367
  Ronald Reagan, 372–374, 375, 380, 381, 382, 388, 469, 467
  George H.W. Bush, 394, 395

Bill Clinton, 399, 400, 403–405, 406, 407, 421
George W. Bush, 381–382, 421, 422
Barack Obama, 431, 434, 437
Donald Trump, 452, 445, 446, 456
Joseph Biden, 459, 461
Federal Communications Commission (FCC), 252
Federal Emergency Management Agency (FEMA), 423
Federal Government, 6, 12, 14, 51, 53–55, 65, 112, 116, 133, 191–192, 213, 453, 457, 465
Federal Reserve Act, 211
Fifteenth Amendment, 131, 137, 202
First World War, 4, 141, 215–225, 228, 284, 290, 409
Fillmore, Millard, 85, 87–92, 97, 103, 127, 189
Florida, 9, 21, 31–32, 40, 43, 64, 67, 76, 95, 105, 109, 425, 435, 437–438, 442
Floyd, George, 452–453, 460
Ford, Gerald, 355, 358–64, 383, 389, 456n16
Fordney-McComber Tariff, 230
Forest Grove, 153
Fort Donelson, 136
France, 2, 5, 8, 16, 20, 46, 59n3, 74, 223, 238, 269–271, 276, 312, 314, 417, 439
Franco-Prussian War, 141
Frankfurt, Kentucky, 86
French Revolution, 34, 46
Fugitive Slave Act, 90–91, 105, 109–110
Full Employment Act, 289

## G

Gadsden, William, 91
Garfield, James A., 122n5, 154–156
Garrison, William Lloyd, 60
Gaulle, Charles de, 323
Gay rights, 403, 422–423, 435, 438
Gaza strip, 368
George, David Lloyd, 220
Georgia, 10, 19, 37, 40, 55–58, 105, 286, 351, 363, 370, 454, 460, 463
Germany, 4–5, 80–81, 86, 141–142, 159, 174, 178, 200, 206, 215–216, 219–221, 223, 232, 234, 238, 241, 243–244, 251, 253, 268–274, 276, 278–279, 281, 285–288, 290–292, 296–297, 300, 312, 315–316, 320, 390, 439
Ghent, treaty of, 28, 31, 42
GI Bill, 282, 289, 399
Gilens, Martin, 468n3
Glass Act, 245
Glass-Steagall Act, 406
Glassboro, New Jersey, 337
Glenn, John, 322
Goldsmith, Harry S., 287n1
Gorbachev, Mikhail, 383, 386, 390, 392
Gore, Albert, 400, 411–412, 456
Gramm-Rudman-Hollings Act, 381
Gramm-Leach-Billey Act, 406
Grant, Ulysses S., 102, 124, 131, 135–149, 151–152, 154, 160, 172, 178, 187–188
Great Depression, 440, 458
Great Lakes, 36, 121, 141, 174, 234, 267, 306
Great Society, 332, 358, 381, 407
Greece, 32, 34, 42, 285, 291, 300, 315, 361, 377
Greeley, Horace, 116, 143
Green Climate Fund, 448
Greenbacks, *see* Legal Tender Notes
Grenada, 377–378, 387, 409
Guadalupe Hidalgo, Treaty of, 89
Guaidó, Juan, 450
Guatemala, 310, 314
Guffey-Snyder Coal Act, 256
Guiteau, Charles, 155
Gulf of Mexico, 31
Gulf War (1990–1), 395, 397

## H

Haiti, 117, 135, 215, 246–247, 384, 408–409
Haldeman, Harry R., 354, 357
Hamas, 415

Hamilton, Alexander, 11, 16–17, 28, 48, 139
Harding, Warren G., 4, 226, 228–233
Harris, Kamala, 454
Harrison, Benjamin, 160, 166, 168–174, 178, 202
Harrison, William Henry, 26–27, 66–68, 82, 85, 127
Hawaii, 91, 102, 184–185, 207, 215, 293, 309
Hayes, Rutherford B., 147, 149–159, 172, 411
Health Care Enhancement Act, 452
Health insurance, 293, 295, 324–325, 367, 401, 405, 412, 429
Health Security Act, 400
Helsinki Final Act, 390
Hepburn Act, 191, 203
Hiroshima, bombing of, 288
Hiss, Alger, 302
Hitler, Adolf, 5, 243, 258, 269, 274–277
Hizballah, 415
Hogeboom, Ari, 158n1
Holland, 11, 15
Holmes, Oliver Wendell, 263
Holy Alliance, 32
Homestead Act, 135
Hoover, Herbert, 4, 228–248, 255–256, 268, 370
House Judiciary Committee, 355, 357
Howe, Neil, 124n6
Hudson, John A., 258n6
Huerta, Victoriano, 214

Hughes, Charles Evans, 216, 232, 262
Humphrey, Hubert, 339, 353, 411, 456
Hussein, Saddam, 391–392, 407–408, 416–417
Hyde Park, New York, 284

I

Iceland, 274, 386
Illinois, 19, 38, 76, 91, 104, 259, 294, 301, 425
Immigration, 55, 93, 155–156, 173, 180, 194–195, 206, 232, 237, 242, 244, 268, 294, 333, 423, 434–437, 441–447, 457, 461
Immigration Customs and Enforcement Agency (ICE), 446
Income tax, 120, 176, 196, 203, 234, 352, 366, 373, 381, 395, 399–400, 402, 421, 435, 445
India, 198, 313, 323, 431
Indian Ocean, 370
Indian Territory, 45, 54–55, 58, 67, 121, 145
Indian tribes, relations with, 9–10, 19, 25–28, 31, 37–38. 40, 42–45, 47, 47, 54–58, 64, 66–67, 72, 80, 88–89, 91, 94, 101, 121, 135, 137, 145–146, 153, 155, 157, 160-162, 173, 185, 194, 206, 211, 237
Indochina, 274, 297, 312, 314–316, 344–346

Inflation, 89, 144, 225–226, 279–280, 294–295, 351–352, 357–360, 365–366, 370–374, 461–463
Inflation Reduction Act, 462
Infrastructure Investment and Jobs Act, 460
Internal improvements, 19, 30, 40–42, 47–48, 63, 84, 93, 139
Iran, 310, 312, 314, 368–370, 372, 385–386, 438–439, 448–450, 456
Iran-Contra scandal, 386
Iran-Iraq War, 385
Iranian government, 372
Iraq, 312, 385, 392–393, 415–419, 421, 432–433, 439–442, 448, 451
Islamic Jihad, 415
Islamic State of Iraq (ISIS), 440–441, 448, 450, 456, 462
Israel, 314, 336, 356, 367–368, 377, 409, 418, 420, 448–449, 451, 456
Israeli-Palestinian negotiations, 418
Italy, 5, 80, 142, 178, 180, 188, 268, 273–274, 276, 278, 285, 292, 322

J

Jackson, Andrew, 3, 27–28, 31, 40–41, 44–63, 67–68, 70, 72–73, 76, 103, 106, 108–109, 124, 136, 157, 165, 167,

174n5, 183, 211, 258, 264, 466
Jaish-e-Mohammed, 415
Japan, 5, 89, 99, 178, 195, 206, 273–279, 290–291, 296–298, 377
Jaworski, Leon, 355
Jefferson, Thomas, 3, 6, 13, 17–25, 27–29, 38, 52, 61, 66, 97, 108, 124, 208, 210, 258
Jeffords, Jim, 417n8
Jerusalem, 449, 451
Jews, 197, 361, 378, 413
Johnson, Andrew, 3, 5, 122n5, 127–137, 189
Johnson, Hiram, 233
Johnson, Lyndon, 308, 318, 330–341, 346, 348–349, 352, 358, 367, 425, 443, 459, 466
Jordan, 315, 336,
Jordan, Barbara, 402n3
Juan Island, 99, 141
Juarez, Benito, 101, 133
Judiciary Act, 10

## K

Kabul, 462
Kaiser, David, 269n11, 274n13, 316n14, 321n1, 335n5
Kansas, 93, 95–97, 101–105, 121, 260
Kansas-Nebraska Act, 104
Katz, Friedrich, 214n3
Kellogg-Briand Pact, 238, 246–247
Kennan, George F., 296, 297n8
Kennedy, Edward, 367, 370, 429
Kennedy, John F., 5, 289, 317–331, 334, 341, 352, 353n3, 358, 365, 367, 375, 379, 421, 443, 466
Kennedy, Robert, 324n2, 339, 365
Kent State University, 344
Kentucky, 16, 26, 40, 47–48, 105, 113, 116–117, 123, 137, 143, 146–147
Kenya, 410
Kerry, John, 422, 438
Khrushchev, Nikita, 316
Kim Il-Sung, 297
Kim Jong-Un, 449–450
King, Martin Luther, Jr., 329, 333, 339, 365
King, Rodney, 396
King, Rufus, 29
King's Speech, 1
Kinley, David, 83n5
Kissinger, Henry, 342, 344–347, 353, 361–362, 367, 387
Kleindienst, Richard, 354
Korean War, 288, 296–301, 303, 306
Kosovo War, 410–411
Kutler, Stanley, 358n4
Kuwait, 391–393, 407

## L

LaFollette, Robert M., 233–234
Lahey, Frank, 287
Lake Ontario, 27
Landrum-Griffin Act, 307
Laos, 316, 319–321, 328, 336, 343–345, 378
Latin America, 93, 99, 101, 140, 318–320, 335, 367, 387, 392
League of Nations, 223–225, 228, 232–234, 258, 284

Lebanon, 310, 315, 377–378, 385, 448
Lecompton Constitution, 102
Leffler, Melvin P., 296n7
Legal Tender Act, 119
Legal Tender Notes ("Greenbacks"), 120, 131–133, 138, 144, 177, 182
Lend-Lease Act, 274
Lewinsky, Monica, 405–407
Lewis, John, 460
Libya, 277, 384, 387, 433
Lincoln, Abraham, 3, 11, 13, 17, 104–105, 108–128, 142, 193, 209, 248, 267, 269–270, 286, 389n7, 417, 426, 442, 460, 466, 469
Livingston, Robert, 20
Lodge, Henry Cabot, 224
London, Great Britain, 21, 25, 38n3, 42, 65, 80, 92, 99, 166, 233, 246
London, Treaty of, 246
Los Angeles, 338, 395–396, 452
Louisiana Territory, 20, 22, 29, 76, 79, 95, 109, 146–151, 187, 332
*Lusitania*, 215–216
Lynching, 173, 187–188, 193–194, 197, 225, 232, 235, 237, 294

## M

MacArthur, Douglas, 246, 298
Madero, Francisco, 206
Madison, James, 22, 24–29, 33, 40, 48, 52, 83–84, 106, 108, 260

Mahan, Alfred Thayer, 198
Maine, 9, 26, 38, 46, 60,
    127, 149, 154, 260,
    353
*Maine* (battleship), 183
Malaya, 275–276, 316
Malta, 390
Manchin, Joseph, 460
Manchuria, 247, 300, 315
Marshall, George, 292
Marshall, John, 20, 57
Martin, Trayvon, 437
Maryland, 12, 31,
    112–113, 137, 143,
    146–147, 151, 355
Massachusetts, 8–9, 15,
    26n1, 38, 238–239,
    289, 311, 388, 422,
    435
Massachusetts Institute of
    Technology, 311
McAdoo, William Gibbs,
    212, 225, 233
McCain-Feingold Act, 404
McCain, John, 425
McCarran Act, 302
McCarthy, Eugene, 339
McCarthy, Joseph, 289,
    302, 304
McClellan, George, 113,
    123
McConnell, Mitch, 440
McCullough, David, 199n6
McGovern, George, 181,
    345, 353
McKenney, Thomas L., 44
McKinley Tariff, 171, 177
McKinley, William, 4,
    169, 171, 177, 181–
    201, 223, 408, 466*
McLean, John, 102n1
McLeod, Alexander, 68
McNamara, Robert, 319
Medicare, 324, 331, 333,
    335, 340, 381, 400,
    402, 407, 412, 420,
    431, 461–462
Medicaid, 333, 373, 400,
    402, 429, 431, 437,
    463
Mediterranean Sea, 31
Mekong River, 335
Mellon, Andrew, 229, 235
Memphis, Tennessee, 339,
    452, 464
Mexican War, 47, 75–78,
    85, 90, 108, 133, 167
Mexico, 21, 69–80,
    84–93, 133–134,
    205–206, 214, 446
Michigan, 26, 37, 60, 85,
    442, 454
Middle East, 6, 220, 228,
    357, 367–368, 377,
    391, 448, 450, 467
Milosevic, Slobodan, 411
Minimum wage, 5, 255–
    256, 262–263, 324–
    325, 331, 436, 459
Minneapolis, Minnesota,
    452
Minnesota, 121, 268n10,
    339, 380, 452
Mississippi, 19–22, 31,
    36–38, 44–45, 54–
    56, 109, 139, 147,
    242, 317n15, 326,
    351, 423
Mississippi Gulf Coast,
    423
Missouri, 38, 43, 60, 80,
    91, 113, 116, 181,
    286–287, 437
Missouri Compromise, 38,
    80, 91, 93, 95
Mogadishu, Somalia, 408
Mondale, Walter, 380, 411
Monroe Doctrine, 44, 75,
    91, 179, 200–201,
    318
Monroe, James, 3, 21,
    29–41, 43–44, 47,
    54, 75, 83, 91, 93,
    100, 179, 200–201,
    318, 466, 469
Montgomery, Alabama, 308
Morgan, J. Pierpont., 196
Mormons, 103, 163, 173,
Morocco, 313
Morrill Tariff, 120, 132
Morse, Wayne, 306n11
Morton, Oliver, 149
Moscow, Russia, 276, 328,
    347, 361, 369–370,
    378, 390, 449
Mosquito Coast, 88, 92
Mubarak, Hosni, 439
Murray, Robert K., 231n3
Muskie, Edmund, 353
Mutual Security Act, 300

**N**

Napoleon, 20, 25–26, 81,
    108
Napoleon III, Emperor,
    121, 133, 141
Napoleonic Wars, 42
National Association for
    the Advancement
    of Colored People
    (NAACP), 221,
    287n2
National Association of
    Evangelicals, 378
National Drug Control
    Strategy, 394
National Industrial
    Recovery Act, 251
National Labor Relations
    Act, 255, 261, 263,
    280
National Recovery
    Administration
    (NRA), 251–252,
    256, 261

National Security Council, 292, 385, 416
National Youth Administration (NYA), 255, 265, 279
Nazi-Soviet Pact, 272
Nazi war criminals, 286
Nebraska, 93, 95, 104, 122n5, 129, 181, 203
Negroes, 100, 102, 130, 194, 203, 221, 235–236, 245, 264
Netanyahu, Benjamin, 451
Neutrality Act, 270
Nevada, 122, 236
Nevins, Allen, 180n6
New Deal, 6, 245, 254n2, 255–256, 258, 264, 295n6, 331–332, 358, 398, 401
New England, 24, 26, 28–29, 54, 69, 248, 271, 294
New Freedom, 212
New Frontier, 9, 21, 25–26, 73, 121, 238
New Hampshire, 90, 197, 362
New Jersey, 12, 26, 105, 123, 149, 159, 207–208, 337–338
New Mexico, 77–80, 84–91, 93, 180, 205
New Orleans, Louisiana, 20, 28, 46, 79, 88, 362, 423
New York, 8, 26, 29, 65, 80, 83n5, 87, 108, 119n4, 285n17, 287, 436n5, 442, 452, 470n4
New Zealand, 300, 312
Niagara River, 27, 174
Nicaragua, 86, 88, 100, 206, 246–247, 377–378, 384–385, 387
Nineteenth Amendment, 222, 225
Nixon, Richard, 6, 289, 302, 304, 317, 340–359, 371, 379, 387, 389, 399, 421, 432, 443, 450
No Child Left Behind Act, 420
Nobel Peace Prize, 197, 368
Non-Proliferation treaty, 337
Norris-LaGuardia Act, 245
North Africa, 200, 274, 277, 434–435
North American Free Trade Agreement (NAFTA), 396–397, 400, 405, 445–446
North Atlantic Treaty, 296
North Atlantic Treaty Organization (NATO), 296, 300–301, 312–313, 376, 379–380, 410–411, 462, 464
North Carolina, 8, 111, 147, 193, 213, 239, 351, 425
North German Confederation, 134, 141
North Korea, 288, 296–298, 301
North, Oliver, 385
Nova Scotia, 271
Nuclear Non-Proliferation treaty, 337
Nueces River, 74

O

Obama, Barack, 6, 375n2, 425–443, 445, 448–449, 457–458, 460, 463, 467–469

Ohio, 9–10, 19, 26, 29, 36–37, 56–57, 95, 181, 201–202, 217, 242, 294, 344, 409, 422, 442
Ohio River, 9, 36, 202, 242
Oklahoma Territory, 45, 54–55, 58, 194, 233
Oregon territory, 69, 73–75, 79–80, 89, 153, 181, 306n11
Ottoman Empire, 42, 88, 221, 223

P

Paine, Thomas, 276
Pakistan, 312, 369–370, 432–434
Palestine Liberation Organization, 377
Palestinian people, 368, 420, 449, 451
Panama, 86, 92, 100, 140, 154–155, 204–205, 207, 367, 409, 411
Panama Canal, 188, 199, 202, 204–205, 207, 367
Panama Canal Treaty, 367
Panama City, 92
Paris, 9, 16, 20–21, 68, 92, 188, 223, 316–317, 441, 448
Paris, Treaty of, 68
Parker, Alton B., 201
Patriot Act, 414
Paycheck Protection Program, 452
Payne-Aldrich Tariff, 203
Pearl Harbor, 5, 207, 251, 275–276, 280
Peary, Oliver Hazard, 27
Peloponnesian War, 68
Pelosi, Nancy, 451

Pence, Michael, 452
Pendleton Act, 158
Pennsylvania, 8, 11–12, 16, 26, 151, 153, 248, 365, 413, 442, 454
Pensacola, Florida, 31
Pensions:
   Civil War, 132, 139, 152, 156, 163–164, 167–168, 170–172, 175–176, 180
   First World War (Bonus), 230, 238, 246
   Mexican War, 167
   War of 1812, 167
Perot, H. Ross, 396, 403
Pershing, John J., 215
Persian Gulf, 370, 387, 392, 407
Personal Responsibility and Work Opportunity Reconciliation Act, 403
Peterson, Florence, 231n3
Petraeus, David, 420
Philadelphia, 1, 12, 65, 216, 351
Philippine Islands, 4, 184–187, 197–198, 201, 205, 207, 215, 233, 239, 247, 275–276, 278, 300, 312, 384
Pickett, George, 99
Pierce, Franklin, 90–97, 104
Pinckney, Charles C., 17, 24
Pinckney, Thomas, 21
Pittsburgh, Pennsylvania, 259
Platt Amendment, 185, 198

Plattsburg, New York, 27
Poindexter, John, 385
Poland, 218, 220, 269–270, 285, 288, 291, 410, 462
Polk, James K., 70, 72, 74–85, 90, 93, 96–97, 165
Pornography, 348, 350
Portland, 452
Portsmouth, 197
Portugal, 32, 34, 46 Posse Comitatus Act, 157
Pribilof Island, 196
Prohibition, 94, 215, 232–233, 240, 252, 385
Prussia, 32, 69, 86, 134
Public Works Administration (PWA), 252, 257
Puerto Rico, 139–140, 169, 184, 199, 205, 215
Pure Food and Drug Act, 195
Public works, 98, 241, 251–252, 254, 261, 265, 282, 293, 325, 366, 428
Putin, Vladimir, 440

## Q

Qadhafi, Muammar, 384, 433
Quebec, 271, 278

## R

Rabin, Yitzhak, 409
Reagan Doctrine, 384
Reagan, Ronald, 6, 360–363, 370–390, 394–395, 397–400, 404, 407, 420–421, 427, 431, 442–443, 445, 450, 461, 466–467, 469

Reconciliation Act (1996), 403
Reconstruction, 127, 129–138, 229, 243, 308, 333
Reconstruction Finance Corporation (RFC), 243, 245, 253
Republic of Texas, 62
Republican Party, 23, 34, 40–41, 50, 127, 213, 216, 272, 375, 389, 417, 425
Revenue Act of 1936, 263
Revolutionary War, 15, 29, 42, 124
Reykjavik, Iceland, 386–387
Rhode Island, 8, 239
Richmond, Virginia, 124, 136
Ridgway, Matthew, 300
Rio Grande River, 74–78, 89
Rio De Janeiro, Treaty of, 296
Roman Republic, 68
Romania, 285, 291, 462
Roosevelt, Franklin D., 209, 225n, 226, 249–86, 331, 335, 341, 352, 358, 372, 379, 387–388, 413, 415, 425–427, 430, 443, 466
Roosevelt, Theodore, 4–6, 167, 184, 188–202, 206–212, 215–216, 228, 232, 245, 367
Rosenberg, Julius, 302, 304
Rosenberg, Ethel, 302, 304
Rubio, Marco, 442
Ruckelshaus, William, 355
Rusk, Dean, 336n6, 367

Russia, 25, 27, 105, 346, 357, 409–411, 439–441, 446, 449–450, 462, 467
Russian America (Alaska), 63, 73–74
Russo-Japanese War, 197, 296, 368

**S**

Sadat, Anwar, 367
SALT I Treaty, 347
SALT II treaty, 362, 369
San Bernardino, California, 441
Sandinista revolution, 378
Sandwich (Hawaiian) Islands, 86
Santa Anna, Antonio López de, 77
Saudi Arabia, 391, 448, 456
Scalia, Antonin, 440
Schlesinger, Arthur M., 246n13, 254n2
Schurz, Carl, 153
Scott, Winfield, 90, 99, 113, 154
SEATO treaty, 312
Second Amendment, 301, 453
Second Moroccan crisis, 206
Second World War, 269, 275–288, 290–291, 311, 392, 403, 457–458, 466–467
Serbia, 215, 410–411
Seventeenth Amendment, 16n2
Seward, William, 108, 133–134, 139
Seymour, Horatio, 135, 137
Sherman Anti-Trust Act, 170, 187, 204

Sherman Silver Purchase Act, 163, 168, 171–172, 175, 177
Sinai Peninsula, 314
Sino-Japanese War, 179, 268
Sitkoff, Harvard, 264n8
Six Day War, 336
Sixteenth Amendment, 210, 226
Slavery, 19, 84–87, 93–97, 104–110, 123–126, 438
Slidell, John, 75
Small Business Administration, 381
Smith Act, 305
Smith, Alfred E., 233, 239
Smoot-Hawley Tariff, 240
Social Security Act, 5, 255, 261–262
Social Security program, 279, 283, 293, 295, 302, 306, 324–325, 332, 337, 339–340, 348–349, 359, 374–375, 403, 407, 412, 423, 430
Soil Conservation and Allotment Act, 259
Soleimani, Qasem, 450
Solomon Islands, 277
Sonora, 101
South Africa, 384
South America, 32, 34, 41–42, 45, 116, 274, 277, 313
South Carolina, 48, 50–52, 91, 111–112, 294, 326, 332, 429n1
South Korea, 288, 297–298, 431
South Vietnam, 319, 334–336, 342–346, 361–362

South Yemen, 378
Soviet Union (USSR), 5–6, 291–293, 319–323, 345–347, 356–357, 368–369, 378–379, 388, 390, 407, 413
Spain, 9, 20–21, 31–32, 34, 99–100, 140, 153, 169, 183–185, 198, 224
Spanish-American War, 183–184
St. Lawrence River, 141, 174
Stalin, Joseph, 277–278, 284–285, 288, 297, 309–310, 316
Stanton, Edwin M., 135
Starr, Kenneth, 405–406
Stevenson, Adlai, 301, 314
Stigler, George J., 170n2
Stimson, Henry M., 247, 274
Strategic Arms Limitation talks (SALT), 103, 346–347, 362, 367–369, 431
Strategic Defense Initiative (SDI), 383, 386–387
Strauss, William, 124n6
Suez Canal, 274, 314
Sumner, Charles, 147
Supply-side economics, 373, 380
Supreme Court, 12, 36, 191–192, 255, 259, 261–264, 350–351, 437–438, 440, 445, 460, 463
Surface Mining Control and Reclamation Act, 364
Sweden, 25, 462
Syria, 336, 356, 435, 439–442, 449–450

## T

Taft-Hartley Act, 289
Taft, William Howard, 201–208, 210, 214–215, 239, 289, 295, 333, 370
Taiwan, 297, 310, 315, 347, 368, 467
Taiwan Strait, 310, 315
Taliban regime, Afghanistan, 413
Tanzania, 410
Tariffs, 35, 40, 43, 47–48, 52, 163–164, 166, 168–169, 170, 175–176, 203, 209–210, 229, 445
Taussig, Frank W., 212n2, 240n7
Tax Reform Act, 382
Taylor, Zachary, 75, 78, 85–87, 90, 97, 108
Teheran, Iran, 278, 284, 369–370, 372
Temin, Peter, 63n1
Tennessee, 19, 29, 40, 105, 111, 129, 137, 143, 239, 250, 264, 301, 464
Tennessee River, 236
Tennessee Valley Authority (TVA), 264, 267, 302, 332
Tenure of Office Act, 129, 132, 135, 142, 151
Test Ban treaty, 328, 330, 340
Texas, 21, 69–70, 73–77, 79–81, 89–90, 137, 143, 183, 308, 340, 389, 411, 442
Thirteenth Amendment, 123, 128
Thurmond, J. Strom, 294
Tilden, Samuel J., 147, 149

Tippecanoe, Battle of, 27
Tokyo, Japan, 195, 276, 278, 388
Tonkin Gulf, 334, 336
Tonkin Gulf Resolution, 334, 336
Tower, John, 385
Trans-Pacific Partnership, 445
Trinidad, 274
Tripoli, Libya, 19, 435
Truman Doctrine, 291
Truman, Harry S., 5, 286–306, 308–311, 316–318, 324, 332, 346, 358–359, 367, 377, 401, 413, 467
Trump, Donald, 442–461, 463–464, 466–467, 469
Tunis, Tunisia, 435
Turkey, 197, 207, 237, 291, 300, 312, 322, 361, 377
Twelfth Amendment, 26, 68
Twentieth Amendment, 248, 252
Twenty-fifth Amendment, 339, 355
Twenty-first Amendment, 252
Twenty-second Amendment, 301
Tyler, John, 68–74, 127, 189, 443n10

## U

Ukraine, 440–441, 450, 462, 464, 467
Underwood, Oscar W., 213
Underwood Tariff, 210, 212
Unemployment, 5, 253n1, 281–282, 337n7, 351–352, 363, 367, 370, 372, 374–375, 428–430, 452n13, 463
United Nations, 276, 279, 286–287, 297–299, 392, 407, 417, 448–449
United Nations Security Council, 297–298, 392, 408, 411, 417
Utah, 95, 103, 138, 152, 157, 163, 173, 180

## V

Van Buren, Martin, 61–67, 70, 72, 82, 160, 165, 317
Venezuela, 179, 188, 200, 449–450
Versailles, Treaty of, 223, 226, 228, 258
Vicksburg, 136
Vienna, 220, 320
Vietnam, 5, 181, 312, 316n14, 361–362, 422, 425, 432–433
Vietnam War, 5, 181, 316n14, 321n1, 334–337, 342–347, 353–356, 361–362, 390, 425
Virginia, 8, 12, 105, 111, 113, 116–117, 153, 230, 309, 317n15, 363, 425, 435, 448, 460
Volcker, Paul, 373
Voting Rights Act, 333, 340, 350, 460

## W

Wagner Act, 255, 262, 280
Wallace, George, 329, 340, 351, 353, 460

Wallace, Henry A., 287, 294
War of 1812, 25–28, 31, 42, 79, 83, 90, 97, 139, 167, 189
War on Terror, 416–418, 423, 432–433, 441–442, 448, 450
Warnock, Rafael, 463
Warsaw Pact, 337
Washington, Booker T., 153, 193, 203, 237
Washington, DC, 21, 25, 27, 31, 40, 44, 68, 80n4, 99, 112–113, 153, 155, 158, 166, 169, 205, 210, 218, 224, 228, 232, 234, 236, 246, 251, 313, 327, 343, 348, 366n8, 354, 386, 443, 452, 454, 469
Washington, George, 2, 7–15, 18–19, 28, 41, 45, 52, 61, 76, 84, 88, 103, 108, 113, 124, 168, 212, 465–466, 469

Washington (state), 80n4, 171
Washington Territory, 99
Weapons of mass destruction (WMDs), 6, 408, 412, 415
Weinberger, Caspar, 383n5, 397
Weisman, Steven R., 230n1
Welland Canal, 174
Wells, Philippa K., 170n3
West Virginia, 147, 151, 230, 460
Western Europe, 107, 292, 299, 325, 376–377
Whiskey Rebellion, 11, 28, 52
White House, 29, 61, 85, 120, 196, 208, 241, 261, 318, 325, 369, 392, 451–455, 468
Willkie, Wendell, 272
Wills, Gary, 410n5
Wilson, Edith Bolling, 224
Wilson, Joseph, 429n1
Wilson, Woodrow, 4, 21, 207–229, 236, 258, 264, 284, 332, 358, 387, 415, 466

Winthrop, John, 388
Wisconsin, 234, 268n10, 289, 302, 442, 454
Wolfskill, George, 258n6
*Worcester v. Georgia*, 57
World Court, 233–234, 238, 240, 246, 257
World Trade Center, 413
World Trade Organization, 410, 445
World War I, *see* First World War
World War II, *see* Second World War

**Y**

Yeltsin, Boris, 411
Yemen, 378, 448
Yosemite National Park, 195
Yugoslavia, 409–410

**Z**

Zelensky, Volodymyr, 450
Zimmerman, George, 437
Zollverein, 69

www.ingramcontent.com/pod-product-compliance
Lightning Source LLC
Chambersburg PA
CBHW060546080526
44585CB00013B/456